T0329646

Deep Learning

Deep Learning

A Practical Introduction

Manel Martínez-Ramón
Department of Electrical and Computer Engineering, The University of New Mexico,
Albuquerque, NM, USA

Meenu Ajith
Tri-Institutional Center for Translational Research in Neuroimaging and Data Science
(TReNDS), Georgia State University, Georgia Institute of Technology, and Emory
University, Atlanta, GA, USA

Aswathy Rajendra Kurup
Machine learning Engineer, Intel Corporation, Hillsboro, OR, USA

The right of Manel Martínez-Ramón, Meenu Ajith, and Aswathy Rajendra Kurup to be identified as the authors of this work has been asserted in accordance with law.

Registered Offices
John Wiley & Sons, Inc., 111 River Street, Hoboken, NJ 07030, USA
John Wiley & Sons Ltd, The Atrium, Southern Gate, Chichester, West Sussex, PO19 8SQ, UK

For details of our global editorial offices, customer services, and more information about Wiley products visit us at www.wiley.com.

Library of Congress Cataloging-in-Publication Data applied for:
Hardback ISBN: 9781119861867

Cover Design: Wiley
Cover Image: © Yuichiro Chino/Getty Images

Set in 9.5/12.5pt STIXTwoText by Straive, Chennai, India
Printed and bound by CPI Group (UK) Ltd, Croydon, CR0 4YY

C9781119861867_020724

To our families, who have been unwavering in their support and understanding throughout the long nights and weekends spent on this journey. Your love and encouragement have fueled our passion for the world of deep learning, and this book is dedicated to you with profound gratitude.

To all the dreamers, may this book inspire you to chase your passions and never give up. Keep reaching for the stars.

To our shared dreams, relentless passion, and enduring friendship – this book is a testament to our collective journey.

Contents

About the Authors

Dr. Manel Martínez-Ramón received his Telecommunication Engineering degree from Universitat Politècnica de Catalunya, Spain, in 1994 and his PhD in Telecommunication Engineering from Universidad Carlos III de Madrid, Spain, in 1999. He is currently a professor of Artificial Intelligence with the Department of Electrical and Computer Engineering of the University of New Mexico, NM, USA, where he holds the King Felipe VI Endowed Chair. His research interests are in the area of machine learning, where he has produced numerous contributions to kernel learning methods, Gaussian processes, and deep learning, with applications to electromagnetics and antenna array processing, smart grid, scientific particle accelerators, and others. As an instructor, he teaches graduate courses in statistical learning theory, Gaussian process learning, probabilistic machine learning, and deep learning both face-to-face and online.

Dr. Meenu Ajith earned her PhD in Electrical Engineering from the University of New Mexico, USA, in 2022. Presently, she serves as a postdoctoral research associate at the Tri-Institutional Center for Translational Research in Neuroimaging and Data Science (TReNDS), a collaborative research institute supported by Georgia State, the Georgia Institute of Technology, and Emory University in Atlanta, GA, USA. Her research focuses on deep learning, image processing, time-series analysis, and neuroimaging. She obtained her MS in Electrical Engineering from the University of New Mexico in 2017 and her bachelor's degree in Electronics and Communication Engineering from Amrita School of Engineering in 2015. In her current role as a postdoctoral researcher, Dr. Ajith concentrates on implementing and applying various deep-learning models and neuroinformatic tools that leverage advanced brain imaging data. Her objective is to translate these approaches into biomarkers, addressing pertinent aspects of brain health and diseases.

Dr. Aswathy Rajendra Kurup earned her PhD in Electrical Engineering from the University of New Mexico USA in the year 2022, where her research focused on designing CNN-based deep-learning models for applications such as smart grids, medical diagnosis, and computer vision. She completed her MS in Electrical Engineering from the University of New Mexico, USA, in 2017. Currently, she serves as a Machine Learning Engineer at Intel Corporation, a leading force in the semiconductor chip manufacturing landscape.

In her current role, she applies her extensive knowledge to address real-world challenges, utilizing her expertise in handling diverse data types, including images, videos, and time-series data. As a part of the role, she applies data mining and statistical modeling techniques along with developing Machine learning/Deep learning solutions for enabling factory decision-making, improved equipment performance, and higher product yields.

Foreword

Deep Learning: A Practical Introduction, authored by Manel Martínez-Ramón, Meenu Ajith, and Aswathy Rajendra Kurup, stands as a pragmatic guide, which prepares the engaged student to digest and understand advanced deep learning concepts. Designed primarily as an educational resource for graduate-level courses in deep learning, this book is enriched with a valuable collection of exercises and practical Python tutorials, making it an ideal educational tool.

Deep learning, a cornerstone of modern artificial intelligence, has seen a meteoric rise in usage, powering the creation of text, images, and videos, from simple prompts, and enhancing our predictive capabilities in a diverse array of applications. This book offers a thorough exploration of deep learning fundamentals, an essential component for students in engineering or computer science.

The authors begin by tracing the intriguing history of deep learning, setting the stage for a deeper dive into the subject. They skillfully introduce various methods for training and optimizing algorithms, alongside an overview of essential programming tools and libraries which are prevalent today, including Python, NumPy, TensorFlow, and Pytorch.

The book then covers a broad range of fundamental models including recurrent neural networks, transformers, unsupervised learning, and deep Bayesian networks. Within each of these chapters, there is an accessible introduction and detailed explanation of each modeling framework, which allows the reader who is new to deep learning to gain a foothold in this extraordinarily important space, while also providing practical examples including code and data as well as references for further learning. Additionally, it offers references for extended learning, bridging the gap between fundamental concepts and recent advancements in the field.

The author's provides a clear and comprehensive introduction to deep learning, making it an essential addition to the field's literature. Whether you are an instructor designing a course or a student embarking on self-directed learning, this book is an invaluable resource for navigating the complexities and applications of deep learning.

In essence, *Deep Learning: A Practical Introduction* is not just a textbook; it is a gateway to understanding and applying one of the most influential technologies in the field of artificial intelligence today. It is a useful tool for (i) instructors who want to teach core deep learning topics to their students, (ii) researchers in a variety of fields, including my own field of neuroimaging, who want to develop domain-specific methods, and (iii) students who are interested in self-learning on this important topic.

Overall, I strongly endorse *Deep Learning: A Practical Introduction* as a valuable resource for both educators aiming to impart core deep learning concepts to their students and for learners pursuing self-study in this vital area. The book's blend of theoretical insights and practical applications, including code and data examples, makes it a standout choice for anyone looking to delve into the world of deep learning.

Vince Calhoun

Preface

The present book is intended to be a comprehensive introduction to deep learning that covers all major areas in this discipline. This document is designed to cover a full semester graduate class in deep learning, and it contains all the materials necessary to build the class. We structured our work in a classical way, starting from the fundamentals of neural networks, which are then used to describe the different elements of deep learning used in artificial intelligence, from the classic convolutional neural network and recurrent neural networks (RNNs) to the transformers, plus unsupervised learning structures and algorithms. In every chapter, we follow a schema where first the structures are described, and then the criteria and algorithms to optimize them are developed. In most cases, full mathematical developments are included in the description of the structure optimization.

Chapter 1 is a first contact with deep learning, where we introduce the most basic type of feedforward neural network (FFNN), which is called the multilayer perception (MLP). Here, we first introduce the low-level basic elements of most neural networks and then the structure and learning criteria.

Chapter 2 is complementary to Chapter 1, but its contents are valid for the rest of the book since it provides details about the practical training of deep learning structures, which we have omitted from the first chapter in order to make it more concise and compact.

These readers who do not have a knowledge of basic Python will benefit from using Chapter 3 in order to start experimenting with learning machines in this programming language. In this chapter, authors assume that the reader has reviewed Chapter 1, which implies that they have been introduced to the concepts of structure, criteria, and algorithms. If so, readers already had the opportunity to see some basic Python codes containing at least a class with methods and an instantiation of it to be used in the examples and exercises, without needing to understand their Python structure. In this chapter, we introduce the basic elements of Python to be used throughout the book, and we will revisit the code previously introduced in Chapter 3, among other examples.

The concepts and structure of convolutional neural structures are described in Chapter 4. It starts with the concept of convolution in two dimensions and its justification for its use in deep learning, after which the structure of a convolutional neural network is described. The training of such a structure is not commonly found in the literature, assuming that the students and practitioners understand and can apply the backpropagation to them. We offer in this chapter a full development of the backpropagation for convolutional neural networks and we summarize the algorithms, so the practitioner can program it. Still, most importantly, they will understand exactly how it works.

Chapter 5 covers the basics of the RNN. The chapter starts off with the architecture of the RNN and then explains how these networks are used for modeling sequential information. Further into the chapter, the training criterion is introduced, which describes the feed-forward training, loss functions, and backpropagation through time. Next, the different types of RNN and their application are discussed. The following section explains the shortcomings of RNNs and highlights the details on different types of gradient problems and the solutions to these problems. Then, the shortcomings of RNNs and highlights the details on different types of gradient problems and the solutions to these problems are explained. After that, the details on other RNN-derived structures which were introduced to mitigate the short-term memory problem associated with the traditional RNNs are discussed.

Chapter 6 provides a structured and comprehensive overview of the developments in attention-based networks. The first section summarizes the different types of attention mechanisms based on sequence, levels, positions, and representations. Finally, we review the network architectures that widely use attention and also discuss a few applications in which attention-based networks have shown a significant impact.

Chapter 7 gives a comprehensive outline of deep unsupervised learning. The overview gives an introduction to the two main categories of deep unsupervised learning such as probabilistic and nonprobabilistic models. The chapter is mainly devoted to the autoencoder, which is one of the widely used nonprobabilistic deep unsupervised learning methods. First, the basic elements, training criteria, and the extensions of autoencoders are explained. Following this, an overview of the deep belief networks (DBNs) is given and it constitutes the basic blocks (restricted Boltzmann machines), training using contrastive divergence, and the variations of DBN. Finally, we also provide different applications of unsupervised deep learning.

Chapter 8 briefly covers the generative adversarial networks (GANs). Primarily, it introduces the two elements of GANs namely discriminator and generator. After this, the complete architecture of the GAN is illustrated to have a higher level of understanding of the network. Next, the training criteria are outlined which describes the alternate training process between the discriminator and the generator. The loss functions that model the probability distribution of the data is also added in this section. Finally, popular models derived from GAN are presented, and the chapter is concluded by summarizing the advantages and trade-offs of GAN.

Chapter 9 covers the main topics of deep Bayesian networks. Here, the authors do not intend to be exhaustive by covering the state of the art of deep Bayesian networks, Instead, we propose a chapter that gives the reader a general view of the characteristics and different philosophies of Bayesian networks with respect to previously introduced structures and algorithms. After introducing the general concepts of deep Bayesian networks, including structures and criteria (thus following the same format used in the rest of the book) we explain the main optimization algorithms used in the current literature, with several examples.

June, 2024
Albuquerque, New Mexico

Manel Martínez-Ramón
Meenu Ajith
Aswathy Rajendra Kurup

Acknowledgment

Manel Martínez-Ramón has been partially supported by the King Felipe VI Endowed Chair of the University of New Mexico, NM, USA.

About the Companion Website

A repository in GitHub with the URL

https://github.com/DeepLearning-book

contains all the additional materials of this book. In particular, readers will find:

- The Python code (in Jupyter Notebook format) of all the examples provided throughout the book, so that the student or the practitioner can run them immediately.
- A complete set of slides written in LaTex that summarize all chapters, intended to help instructors in the development of their lectures. The source files are also available so that instructors can modify the material and adapt it to each particular course design. All materials are available in the repository.

1

The Multilayer Perceptron

1.1 Introduction

The concept of artificial intelligence (AI) is relatively simple to explain, and it can be enunciated as a possible answer to the question of how to make a machine that is able to perform a given task without being explicitly programmed for it, but instead, extracting the necessary information from a set of data. Let us say, for example, that a machine is needed to classify green and red apples. The machine is provided with a camera, and all the mechanisms necessary to place one apple at a time in front of it and then throw it in one of two buckets. A machine wired to do this will relay in binary operators as "IF," "THEN." If the color is red, throw it in bucket A, otherwise, in bucket "B."

The limitations of this method are obvious. If a pear is mistakenly introduced in the process, it will be classified as a green apple. Also, how can we use the same or similar structure for a different or more complex task? As in the previous machine, an AI approach uses features found in the data in order to take the decision, but the algorithm is not explicitly programmed. Instead, the machine has a specific parametric structure capable of learning from data. The learning process involves the optimization of a certain measurable criterion with respect to the parameters. The deep learning (DL) structures for artificial intelligence are able to learn complex tasks from the available data, but they also have capabilities such as learning how to extract the useful features for the task at hand, provide probabilistic outputs (i.e. "the probability of apple is 97%"), and many others. The basic element of such a structure in DL is the so-called artificial neuron, a simple concept that provides the power and nonlinear properties.

This chapter is intended to be a first contact with DL, where we introduce the most basic type of feedforward neural network (FFNN), which is called the multilayer perceptron (MLP). Here, we first introduce the low-level basic elements of most neural network (NN)s, then the structure and learning criteria.

The elements introduced in this chapter will be used throughout the book. We start from the single perceptron, we construct a basic MLP, where the different activations are developed, and then the notation based on tensors is also justified as a generalized tool to be used throughout the book. After this, we present the maximum likelihood (ML) criterion as a general criterion, which is then particularized to the classic cases corresponding to the

Deep Learning: A Practical Introduction, First Edition.
Manel Martínez-Ramón, Meenu Ajith, and Aswathy Rajendra Kurup.
© 2024 John Wiley & Sons Ltd. Published 2024 by John Wiley & Sons Ltd.
Companion website: https://github.com/DeepLearning-book

different output activations. Finally, the backpropagation (BP) is detailed and then summarized so that can be translated into a computer program.

In this chapter, examples and exercises are presented in a way that assumes that the student does not necessarily know about programming in Python. Examples will be focused on the behavior of the MLP, without focusing on the programming, and the exercises intended to modify, at a high-level data, parameters, and structures in order to answer questions to different practical cases. Chapter 3 explains, in particular, how the different examples have been coded, thus they will be reviewed in that chapter from the point of view of practical programming.

1.2 The Concept of Neuron

The idea of the artificial neural network (ANN) is obviously inspired by the structure of the nervous system. The first attempt to understand how neural tissue works from a logical perspective was published in 1943 by Warren S. McCulloch and Walter Pitts (1943) (Fig. 1.1). They proposed the first mathematical model for a biological neuron in his paper. In this model, the neuron has two possible states, defined as 0 or 1 depending on whether the neuron is resting or it has been activated or *fired*. This represents the *axon* of the neuron. The input of this neuron model consists of a number of *dendrites* whose excitation is also binary. This elemental structure is completed with an inhibitory input. If this input

Figure 1.1 Warren S. McCulloch (left) and Walter Pitts in 1949. Source: R. Moreno-Díaz and A. Moreno-Díaz (2007)/with permission from Elsevier.

is activated, the neuron cannot fire. If the inhibitory input is deactivated, the neuron can be activated if the combination of inputs is larger than a given threshold. This model is fully binary and, since it includes mathematical functions that cannot be differentiated, it cannot be treated mathematically in an easy way. Certain modifications that will be seen further give rise to what is known as the artificial neuron in use today.

Section 1.2.1 contains an introduction to the concept of artificial perceptron from an algebraic point of view. A possible way to train a single perceptron is introduced in Sections 1.2.2 and 1.2.3, as well as the limitations of this structure as a linear classifier.

The concept of artificial NN was introduced by the psychologist Frank Rosenblatt (Fig. 1.2) in 1958 Rosenblatt (1957, 1958). In this paper, he proposed a structure of the visual cortex *perceptron* (Fig. 1.3). The structure presented in Rosenblatt (1958) contained the fundamental idea that is used in any artificial learning structure. In the first stage

Figure 1.2 Frank Rosenblatt. Source: https://news.cornell.edu/stories/2019/09/professors-perceptron-paved-way-ai-60-years-too-soon/ last accessed November 30, 2023.

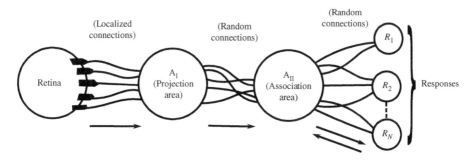

Figure 1.3 The perceptron as described in Rosenblatt (1958)/American Psychological Association.

(Retina), the device collects the available observation or input pattern intended to be processed in order to extract knowledge of it. The second stage (Projection area) is in charge of processing this observation to extract the information needed for the task at hand. This information is commonly called the set of features of the input pattern. The third stage (Association area) is intended to process these features to map them into a given response. For example, the response may be to recognize some given object classes present in the scene. Rosenblatt is the father of the artificial perceptron. He proved that by modifying the McCulloch–Pitts neuron model, the neuron could actually learn tasks from the data. In particular, his model had weights that multiplied each of the inputs to the neuron as well as the input bias or threshold that could be adjusted for the neuron to perform a given task. He developed the Mark 1 perceptron machine, which was the first implementation of his perceptron algorithm. This device was not a computer but an electromechanical *learning machine*. The machine consisted of a camera constructed with an array of 400 photocells, the output of each one connected randomly to the dendrites of a set of neurons. The weights, or attenuations applied to these inputs, were controlled with potentiometers whose axes were connected to electric motors. During the learning procedure, the motors adjusted the input weights. This machine was able to distinguish *linearly separable* patterns, or patterns that were at one or another side of a hyperplane in the space of 400 dimensions spanned by the camera inputs depending on its binary class. The invention was then limited in its capabilities until it was proven that a perceptron constructed with more than one layer of neurons MLP had nonlinear capabilities, that is, the ability to separate patterns that could not be separated by a hyperplane. Nevertheless, the MLP could not be trained using the techniques introduced by Rosenblatt for his perceptron. It was in 1971 that Paul Werbos, in his PhD thesis (P. J. Werbos 1974) introduced the BP algorithm, which made it possible to adjust the weights of a multilayer perceptron.

1.2.1 The Perceptron

From a conceptual point of view, a perceptron is a function made to perform a binary classification. In order to describe this function, let us first introduce the necessary notation and concepts associated with it. Assume a given observation that consists of a collection of D magnitudes observed from a physical phenomenon. These magnitudes are stored in a column vector, which will be called $\mathbf{x} \in \mathbb{R}^D$, which lies in a space of D dimensions. For illustrative purposes, let us construct a set of artificial data in a space of $D = 2$ dimensions as in Fig. 1.4.

The figure shows a set of points with coordinates $\mathbf{x} = (x_1, x_2)^\mathsf{T}$, where operator T denotes the transpose operation, meaning that the vector is a column one even if it is written as a row vector. In this toy example, the data belongs to one of two classes (black or white) that we will label arbitrarily with the labels 1, −1, though in some cases, labels 1, 0 are more convenient. It can be seen that the data is linearly separable, that is, both classes can be separated by placing a line between the black and white clusters of data. That is, roughly speaking, the idea of the perceptron. It must be trained to place a *separating hyperplane* between both classes. We define the hyperplane (particularized to a line in the two-dimensional example) as

$$\mathbf{w}^\mathsf{T}\mathbf{x} + b = 0 \tag{1.1}$$

Figure 1.4 A set of observations in a space of two dimensions.

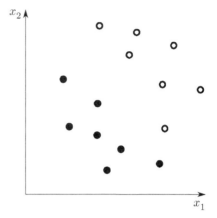

Figure 1.5 A point $\mathbf{x}_1$ lying in the semi-space opposite to the one pointed by vector $\mathbf{w}$.

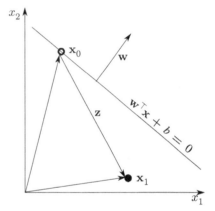

where $\mathbf{w} \in \mathbb{R}^D$ is a set of parameters, and thus operation $\mathbf{w}^\top\mathbf{x}$ defines an inner product or dot product between two vectors. Strictly speaking, Eq. (1.1) defines a space affine to hyperplane $\mathbf{w}^\top\mathbf{x} = 0$, which contains the origin.

The important point here is that all vectors $\mathbf{x}$ that belong to the hyperplane satisfy the above definition. Therefore, for all points outside the hyperplane, the result of operation (1.1) is different from zero. Moreover, all the points at one side of the plane have a positive response, and all the points at the opposite side have a negative response. In order to prove this, we have to notice that $\mathbf{w}$ is a vector normal to the hyperplane defined by Eq. (1.1). Indeed, that hyperplane is trivially parallel to the hyperplane defined by $\mathbf{w}^\top\mathbf{x} = 0$. Since the plane is defined as all vectors whose dot product with $\mathbf{w}$ is zero, all vectors in the plane are normal to $\mathbf{w}$ and, therefore, all vectors in the plane defined by Eq. (1.1) must be normal to $\mathbf{w}$. Now, let us assume arbitrarily that vector $\mathbf{w}$ has the direction depicted in Fig. 1.5. Assume a vector $\mathbf{x}_0$ that belongs to the plane, and another vector $\mathbf{x}_1$ that is placed in the semi-space opposite to the one pointed by the vector. For this vector, the response of the operation (1.1) is $\mathbf{w}^\top\mathbf{x} + b < 0$. Indeed, point $\mathbf{x}_1 = \mathbf{x}_0 + \mathbf{z}$ where $\mathbf{z}$ is the segment going from $\mathbf{x}_0$ to $\mathbf{x}_1$. Then,

$$\mathbf{w}^\top\mathbf{x}_1 + b = \mathbf{w}^\top(\mathbf{x}_0 + \mathbf{z}) + b = \mathbf{w}^\top\mathbf{x}_0 + b + \mathbf{w}^\top\mathbf{z} = \mathbf{w}^\top\mathbf{z} \tag{1.2}$$

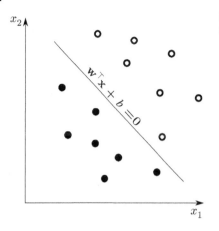

Figure 1.6 A separating hyperplane that classifies among the two classes of a set of data.

since by definition $\mathbf{w}^\mathsf{T}\mathbf{x}_0 + b = 0$ because $\mathbf{x}_0$ belongs to the plane. Then, notice that since $\mathbf{x}_1$ is opposite to $\mathbf{w}$, this vector forms an angle with $\mathbf{z}$ higher than 90°, and thus this dot product must be negative. If point $\mathbf{x}_1$ was in the semi-space pointed by $\mathbf{w}$, then the angle with $\mathbf{z}$ would be less than 90° and the dot product would be positive. This is the principle used in binary linear classification. In conclusion, to classify the points in Fig. 1.4, it is only necessary to place a hyperplane defined by parameters $\mathbf{w}, b$ between the two classes as seen in Fig. 1.6. The classification operation is then

$$f(\mathbf{x}) = \text{sign}\left(\mathbf{w}^\mathsf{T}\mathbf{x} + b\right) \tag{1.3}$$

where sign(z) is an activation function whose response is 1 if $z > 0$ and -1 otherwise. The dot product of this equation can be expanded as

$$f(\mathbf{x}) = \text{sign}\left(\sum_{i=1}^{D} w_i x_i + b\right) \tag{1.4}$$

and the operation can be expressed in a graphic form as the perceptron, depicted in Fig. 1.7. In this structure, an observation consisting of a vector $\mathbf{x}$ with components x_i, $1 \le i \le 3$ is element-wise multiplied by the elements w_i of parameter vector $\mathbf{w}$, and then a bias b is added. The corresponding operations are represented by the arrows incoming to the first node (an addition operator) that emulate the behavior of the dendrites in a neuron. All the products are added together and then passed to a sign detector. This is equivalent to applying a threshold to dot product $\mathbf{w}^\mathsf{T}\mathbf{x}$ to obtain an output equal to 1 if the dot product is higher than $-b$ and -1 otherwise. The sum and comparison operations emulate the behavior of the *soma* of a neuron. The output arrow represents the axon.

1.2.2 The Perceptron (Training) Rule

The training of the perceptron described by Rosenblatt, usually called the Perceptron Rule, is very easy to implement. The training procedure needs to use a *training dataset* composed by a set of samples $\mathbf{x}_i$, $1 \le i \le N$ for which the corresponding labels $y_i \in \{0, 1\}$ are known. Usually, we will define the labeled datasets as $D = \{\mathbf{x}_i, y_i\}$, $1 \le i \le N$.

Figure 1.7 Structure of a perceptron where the input **x** has three dimensions.

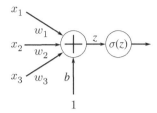

The goal of the perceptron rule is to reduce the classification error over the training dataset. We define the error of the response to input sample $\mathbf{x}_i$ as

$$e_i = \frac{1}{2}\left(y_i - \text{sign}(\mathbf{w}^\top \mathbf{x}_i + b)\right) \tag{1.5}$$

This error is zero if the sample has been classified correctly. If the sample is labeled with $y = -1$ and the classification is 1, the error is $e_i = -1$, and if the sample is labeled with 1 and the classification is 0, then the error is $e_i = 1$. That is, when a misclassification is observed, the error is equal to the true label.

The algorithm has to be initialized with some arbitrary values for $\mathbf{w}, b$, for example, all coefficients can be initialized at zero. Then, all samples are classified using the perceptron until an error, say for sample $\mathbf{x}_k$, is reported. At this moment, the algorithm updates the weights using the following rule:

$$\begin{aligned} \mathbf{w}(k+1) &= \mathbf{w}(k) + y_k \mathbf{x}_k \\ b(k+1) &= b(k) + y_i \end{aligned} \tag{1.6}$$

where $\mathbf{w}(k), b(k)$ denote the values of the parameters at iteration k. It is relatively easy to prove that this algorithm converges to a solution if the data set is linearly separable, but convergence is not guaranteed when the data is not linearly separable. We must assume that the norm of the data vectors is bounded by some value, i.e. $\forall i, 1 \leq i \leq N, \|\mathbf{x}_i\| < R$. Assume further that, since the data is linearly separable, some optimal parameters $\mathbf{w}^*, b^*$ must exist that define a separating hyperplane able to classify the data with no errors. These parameters are thus normalized such that $\|\mathbf{w}^*\|^2 + |b^*|^2 = 1$. For this classification hyperplane, and for some $\eta > 0$, it must be the case that

$$y_i\left(\mathbf{w}^{*\top}\mathbf{x}_i + b^*\right) > \eta, \quad \forall i \in [1, N] \tag{1.7}$$

This is true for an optimal classifier since the sign of $\mathbf{w}^{*\top}\mathbf{x}_i + b^*$ will be the same as the one of the labels for all samples.

Theorem 1.2.1 If the training dataset is linearly separable, then the perceptron rule converges in a finite number of iterations (Novikoff 1963).

Proof: The following inequality holds:

$$\begin{aligned} \mathbf{w}^{*\top}&\mathbf{w}(k+1) + b^* b(k+1) \\ &= \mathbf{w}^{*\top}\left(\mathbf{w}(k) + y_k \mathbf{x}_k\right) + b^*\left(b(k) + y_i\right) \\ &= \mathbf{w}^{*\top}\mathbf{w}(k) + y_k \mathbf{w}^{*\top}\mathbf{x}_k + b^* b(k) + b^* y_i > \mathbf{w}^{*\top}\mathbf{w}(k) + b^* b(k) + \eta \end{aligned} \tag{1.8}$$

where we have used, in the first line, the perceptron rule of Eq. (1.6), and in the second line, inequality (1.7). By induction, then, it can be seen that

$$\mathbf{w}^{*\top}\mathbf{w}(k+1) + b^* b(k+1) > k\eta \tag{1.9}$$

On the other side, we know that the optimal parameters have been normalized to $\|\mathbf{w}^*\|^2 + |b^*|^2 = 1$, and then using the Schwartz inequality $k^2\eta^2 < \left(\mathbf{w}^{*\top}\mathbf{w}(k+1) + b^*b(k+1)\right)^2 \leq \|\mathbf{w}(k+1)\|^2 + (b(k+1))^2$. Thus,

$$\|\mathbf{w}(k+1)\|^2 + (b(k+1))^2 > k^2\eta^2 \tag{1.10}$$

On the other side, by applying again the perceptron rule, it can be said that

$$
\begin{aligned}
\|\mathbf{w}(k+1)\|^2 + (b(k+1))^2 &= \|\mathbf{w}(k) + y_k\mathbf{x}_k\|^2 + \left(b(k) + y_k\right)^2 \\
&= \|\mathbf{w}(k)\|^2 + \|\mathbf{x}_k\|^2 + 2y_k\mathbf{w}(k)^\top\mathbf{x}_k + (b(k))^2 + 2b(k)y_k + 1 \\
&\leq \|\mathbf{w}(k)\|^2 + \|\mathbf{x}_k\|^2 + (b(k))^2 + 1 \leq \|\mathbf{w}(k)\|^2 + R^2 + (b(k))^2 + 1
\end{aligned}
\tag{1.11}
$$

then by induction

$$\|\mathbf{w}(k) + 1\|^2 + (b(k+1))^2 \leq k\left(R^2 + 1\right) \tag{1.12}$$

Using both inequalities (1.10) and (1.12) together

$$k^2\eta^2 < k\left(R^2 + 1\right) \tag{1.13}$$

and then $k < \dfrac{\left(R^2 + 1\right)}{\eta}$.

Example 1.2.1 **(Perceptron rule)**
In the following example, a set of data is generated in a space of two dimensions that is linearly separable. The data is classified with a function (1.4), whose parameters $\mathbf{w}, b$ are updated following the perceptron rule. The result of the iteration is shown in Fig. 1.8. The first pane shows the initial position of the classifier, which has been initialized randomly. The classifier is given all the samples in an arbitrary sequence, and it is found that the first sample is misclassified (black dot). This sample is used to update the classifier, which goes to the position shown in the right upper pane. The samples are classified again and, this time, sample number 8 is misclassified. This sample is used to update the classifier function. The process is repeated 16 times. Since after this iteration, there are no misclassified samples, the algorithm stops. For this particular set of data, the data separability is $\eta = 0.2$ (see the corresponding script) and, by computing the radius of the sphere containing the data, the bound of the number of iterations is $\dfrac{R^2 + 1}{\eta} = 228$, which is clearly very conservative taking into account that the actual number of iterations was 16. This upper bound is not meant to be a practical estimate of the number of iterations, but merely the result of the proof that the convergence is achieved in a finite number of iterations if the data is linearly separable.

The example is expanded in Exercise 1.1, where the reader is asked to modify the parameters of the example, code in the corresponding Jupyter notebook, in particular, to make the data nonseparable.

1.2.3 The Minimum Mean Square Error Training Criterion

The limitations of the above-presented perceptron are two, the first one being that it can only synthesize linear functions. The second one is that it will not converge if the data is not linearly separable.

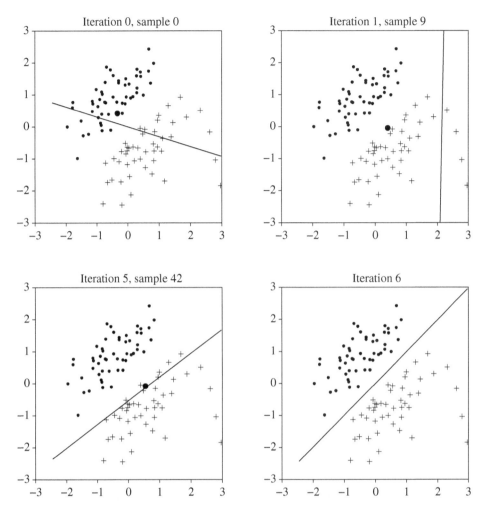

Figure 1.8 Example of the application of the perceptron rule in a set of separable data in dimension 2. Before the first iteration (upper left pane), the classifier is set with random parameters. The first sample in the dataset gives a misclassification, so the classifier parameters are updated in iteration 1, after which sample number nine is found to be misclassified. The algorithm goes through six iterations until it classifies all samples with no errors. In this particular example, the bound on the number of iterations is $\dfrac{R^2+1}{\eta} = 228$.

The first limitation is to be corrected by the introduction of the MLP, which will provide nonlinear properties to the classifier, but then the perceptron rule cannot be applied as it has been presented. The second limitation comes from the fact that the error measure applied to the perceptron is binary rather than continuous. The first modification applied to the structure in order to obtain a continuous measure of the error is to change the sign operator by a continuous *activation* function that tends to 1 when the machine classifies the sample as +1 and to 0 or −1 when the sample is classified as −1. Such activations are often called sigmoids because they have a shape that reminds of a stylized *s*. For this example,

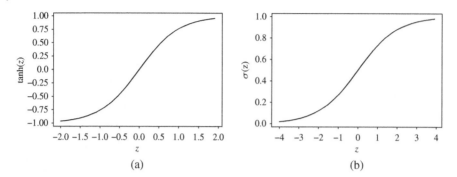

Figure 1.9 Hyperbolic tangent function (a) and logistic function (b).

we use the hyperbolic tangent function, and the classification function will have the following form:

$$f(\mathbf{x}) = \tanh\left(\mathbf{w}^\mathsf{T}\mathbf{x} + b\right) \tag{1.14}$$

where the expression of the hyperbolic tangent is

$$\tanh(z) = \frac{e^z - e^{-z}}{e^z + e^{-z}} \tag{1.15}$$

where $z = \mathbf{w}^\mathsf{T}\mathbf{x} + b$. It is straightforward to see that when argument z tends to ∞, the function approaches 1, and if z tends to $-\infty$, then the function tends to -1. The function is represented in Fig 1.9a.

Its derivative will be needed in the construction of the algorithm, and it has the expression

$$\frac{d\tanh(z)}{dz} = 1 - \tanh^2(z) \tag{1.16}$$

Instead of using a hyperbolic tangent, one may prefer to use a function that goes from 0 to 1 in order to give the activation properties of a probability measure. The logistic function $\sigma(z)$ can be obtained by adding a bias to the tangent to raise it so it tends to 0 instead of tending to -1 when $z \to \infty$ and rescaling it so it tends to -1

$$\frac{1}{2}\left(1 + \tanh(z)\right) = \frac{1}{2}\left(1 + \frac{e^z - e^{-z}}{e^z + e^{-z}}\right) = \frac{e^z}{e^z + e^{-z}} = \frac{1}{1 + e^{-2z}} \tag{1.17}$$

Since the constant multiplying the argument is arbitrary, it is often removed, and the logistic function has the expression

$$\sigma(z) = \frac{1}{1 + e^{-z}} \tag{1.18}$$

The logistic function is represented in Fig. 1.9b. Its derivative has the expression

$$\frac{d\sigma(z)}{dz} = \sigma(z)\left(1 - \sigma(z)\right) \tag{1.19}$$

The differentiation of both sigmoid functions is left to the reader in Exercise 1.2.

The optimization criterion for the classifier (1.14) or its equivalent with the logistic function consists of minimizing the expectation of the mean square error (MSE) over the training dataset. This criterion, usually called minimum mean square error (MMSE), will provide a solution since it is a convex function of the error, thus having a single minimum. The criterion for the optimal set of parameters is

$$\min_{\mathbf{w},b} \mathbb{E}\left[e_i^2\right] = \min \mathbb{E}\left[\left(\tanh\left(\mathbf{w}^\top \mathbf{x}_i + b\right) - y_i\right)^2\right] \tag{1.20}$$

The expectation cannot be computed, but, by virtue of the weak law of large numbers (WLLN), a sample average of the training errors tends in probability to the actual mean when the number of samples tends to infinity. Then, an adequate approximation to the previous criterion is

$$\min_{\mathbf{w},b} \sum_{i=1}^{N}\left(\tanh\left(\mathbf{w}^\top \mathbf{x}_i + b\right) - y_i\right)^2 \tag{1.21}$$

This expression, to be minimized with respect to the parameters, is a particular example of what is often referred to as a *cost function*. In order to derive the optimization, it is sufficient to compute the gradient of this cost function with respect to parameters $\mathbf{w}$

$$\nabla_{\mathbf{w}} \sum_{i=1}^{N}\left(\tanh\left(\mathbf{w}^\top \mathbf{x}_i + b\right) - y_i\right)^2 = \sum_{i=1}^{N} 2e_i\left(1 - \tanh^2\left(\mathbf{w}^\top \mathbf{x}_i + b\right)\right) \mathbf{x}_i \tag{1.22}$$

and the derivative of the cost function with respect to parameter b.

$$\frac{d}{db} \sum_{i=1}^{N}\left(\tanh\left(\mathbf{w}^\top \mathbf{x}_i + b - y_i\right)\right)^2 = \sum_{i=1}^{N} e_i\left(1 - \tanh^2\left(\mathbf{w}^\top \mathbf{x}_i + b\right)\right) \tag{1.23}$$

In this derivation, we made use of the definition (1.14) and the derivative of the hyperbolic tangent in Eq. (1.16). This is a way to solve the classification problem at hand. Nevertheless, there is a problem with this approach, as pointed out above. This problem is related to the fact that when the argument of the tangent has a high absolute value, the tangent tends to 1. When this happens, gradient (1.23) tends to zero, thus stalling the training. In Section 1.5, we will revisit this problem, and we will propose a more justified solution that, among other properties, overcomes this issue.

An optimization algorithm consists of initially choosing arbitrary values for the parameters of the classifier and then iteratively modifying them in a direction opposite to the direction of the squared error gradient, with the purpose of approaching the values of the parameters to the point of minimum squared error. For this reason, the algorithms based on this strategy are called *gradient descent* algorithms (see e.g. (S. S. Haykin 2005)). The procedure is illustrated in Fig. 1.10, and the update rule can be applied in batch mode

$$\mathbf{w}(k+1) = \mathbf{w}(k) - \mu \sum_{i=1}^{N} e_i\left(1 - f^2(\mathbf{x}_i)\right) \mathbf{x}_i \tag{1.24}$$

$$b(k+1) = b(k) - \mu \sum_{i=1}^{N} e_i\left(1 - f^2(\mathbf{x}_i)\right) \tag{1.25}$$

where $f(\mathbf{x}) = \tanh\left(\mathbf{w}^\top \mathbf{x}_i + b\right)$. Once the update has been applied, it must be repeated until a criterion has been reached. Similarly, the update can be applied one sample at a time

$$\mathbf{w}(k+1) = \mathbf{w}(k) - \mu e_k\left(1 - f^2(\mathbf{x}_k)\right) \mathbf{x}_k \tag{1.26}$$

$$b(k+1) = b(k) - \mu e_k\left(1 - f^2(\mathbf{x}_k)\right) \tag{1.27}$$

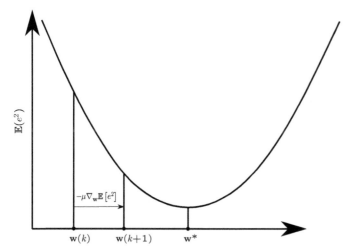

Figure 1.10 Illustration of the gradient descent procedure. The graph represents a cost function consisting of the expectation of a square error as a function of a parameter **w**. The optimum value **w**** of the parameters is achieved when the cost function is the minimum. At this point, the gradient is zero. At iteration k, the value of the parameter is $\mathbf{w}^k$. The gradient $\nabla_{\mathbf{w}}\mathbb{E}\left[e^2\right]$ of the cost function is computed, and then the parameter is modified in the direction opposite to the gradient, multiplied by a small constant μ. The operation must be repeated until the gradient is zero.

where μ is a small scalar usually called *learning rate*, and it determines the length of the movement toward the minimum of the cost function relative to the gradient. Notice the similarity of these two expressions with the perceptron rule of Eqs. (1.6). The difference consists of that now the error is a continuous function, that can be differentiated, and that a new term relative to the activation function appears in these equations. This new term is precisely the reason why such an update rule is still not a good algorithm. Indeed, when the machine classifies the samples almost correctly, term $\left(1 - f^2(\mathbf{x}_k)\right)$ tends to zero, which may seem a good sign, but since the activation is squared, if a sample is misclassified and the corresponding activation saturates to 1 or −1, this term tends to zero, which may stall the learning. Therefore, this criterion must be further modified in order to obtain an adequate criterion that does not suffer from this effect. A different approach to optimization and its relationship with the activation functions will be explained in Sections 1.5.1 and 1.5.2.

An equivalent expression of the update rule can be obtained with the use of a logistic activation. Note that if a logistic function is used, then the labels should be changed to $y \in \{1, 0\}$. A stronger justification for the use of these activations is provided in this chapter. The derivation of such rules is left to the reader as exercise 1.3.

Example 1.2.2 *(MMSE update rule for a perceptron.)*
The graphics of Fig. 1.11 correspond to the application of the MMSE criterion to the perceptron whose activation has been set as a hyperbolic tangent. The learning rate μ has been set at 0.1. The upper row corresponds to the initial and final positions of the classifier for a separable case, whereas the lower row corresponds to a nonseparable case. A noticeable difference between the perceptron rule and the MMSE is that the number of iterations increases

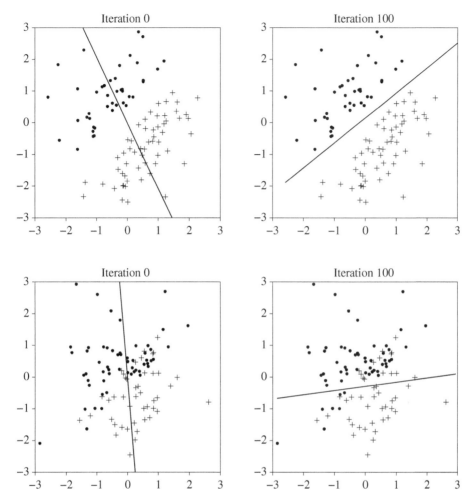

Figure 1.11 Example of the application of the MMSE criterion to a perceptron with hyperbolic tangent activation. The first row corresponds to a separable case and the second one to a nonseparable one.

significantly since the update is applied for all samples and not for the misclassified ones. The other difference is that the MMSE achieves a stable solution after a number of iterations even in the nonseparable problem.

1.2.4 The Least Mean Squares Algorithm

Notice that when the activation tends to 1, the gradient will stall. If a linear activation is used, that is, $f(\mathbf{x}) = \mathbf{w}^{\mathsf{T}}\mathbf{x} + b$, then the gradient becomes

$$\mathbf{w}(k+1) = \mathbf{w}(k) - \mu e_k \mathbf{x}_k \tag{1.28}$$

$$b(k+1) = b(k) - \mu e_k \tag{1.29}$$

This algorithm is known as the least mean squares (LMS) algorithm, and it was first derived in Widrow and Hoff (1960).

1.3 Structure of a Neural Network

The perceptron unit in the structure presented before has a linear nature, that is, it can only classify problems that are linearly separable for data distributed in other ways, it would be impossible for such a structure to do a good job. The exclusive OR (XOR) problem in Fig. 1.12, is a classic example that a linear perceptron cannot solve. In this example, the data has a label that is an XOR function of its coordinates. Therefore, the black dots are labeled as +1, and the white dots are labeled as 0.

It is clear that a linear function cannot classify the data. Nevertheless, it is possible to construct a nonlinear function with several perceptrons in two layers. The proposed structure to solve this problem is shown in Fig. 1.13.

The input data represented by column vector $\mathbf{x} = [x_1, x_2]^\top$ is applied the linear affine transformation

$$\mathbf{z} = \begin{bmatrix} z_1 \\ z_2 \end{bmatrix} = \mathbf{W}^\top \mathbf{x} + \mathbf{b} = \begin{bmatrix} w_{11} & w_{21} \\ w_{12} & w_{22} \end{bmatrix} \begin{bmatrix} x_1 \\ x_2 \end{bmatrix} + \begin{bmatrix} b_1 \\ b_2 \end{bmatrix} \tag{1.30}$$

where $\mathbf{W}$ is a 2×2 matrix, and $\mathbf{b} = [b_1, b_2]^\top$ is a column vector containing bias terms, as shown in Eq. (1.30). The output of this linear transformation is then passed by a nonlinear

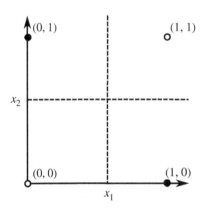

Figure 1.12 The XOR problem. The black dots are labeled as 1, and the white dots are labeled hyperplane as −1. This corresponds to the XOR function between the coordinates of the points, i.e. $f(x_1, x_2) = x_1 \oplus x_2$. Clearly, a linear algorithm cannot classify the points of this problem. A possible solution is the boundary represented with dashed lines.

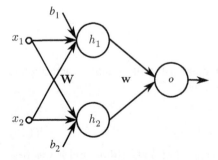

Figure 1.13 A two-layer perceptron. The data input is fed into a layer of two neurons through the linear transformation represented by matrix $\mathbf{W}$ and bias vector $\mathbf{b} = [b_1, b_2]^\top$. The neurons apply a nonlinear activation and pass the outputs h_j to the next layer, which applies another transformation with vector $\mathbf{w}$.

monotonic function as, for example, the logistic function (1.18) to produce output $\mathbf{h} = [h_1, h_2]^{\mathsf{T}}$:

$$\mathbf{h} = \sigma(\mathbf{z}) = \begin{bmatrix} \sigma(z_1) \\ \sigma(z_2) \end{bmatrix} \tag{1.31}$$

where we use the notation $\sigma(\cdot)$ to represent a vector of functions $\sigma(\cdot)$ each one applied to the elements of a vector.

The layer of two neurons is often called a hidden layer, and its corresponding output is vector $\mathbf{h}$, which is a nonlinear transformation of the input. The vector is then linearly transformed using vector $\mathbf{w}$, and then the result is passed through another monotonically increasing activation function $\phi(\cdot)$

$$o = \phi(\mathbf{w}^{\mathsf{T}} \mathbf{h}) \tag{1.32}$$

This is the simplest possible example of an NN, which applies a nonlinear transformation to the input in order to produce a nonlinear classification. But let us take a close look at how this simple NN with three neurons is able to solve the XOR problem in Fig. 1.12. This is explained in Example 1.3.1.

Example 1.3.1 *(The XOR problem)*
Let us assume the XOR problem above and the structure of Fig. 1.13 (see also I. Goodfellow et al. 2016). A possible hand-made solution for this problem can be constructed by drawing a line that separates points $(0, 0)$ from the rest of the points in Fig. 1.12, and another line that discriminates between point $(1, 1)$ and the rest. Both lines are defined for $z_i = 0$ (see Fig. 1.14) where

$$z_1 = x_1 + x_2 - \frac{1}{2} = 0$$
$$z_2 = x_1 + x_2 - \frac{3}{2} = 0 \tag{1.33}$$

Notice that the above equations can be expressed as

$$\mathbf{z} = \mathbf{W}^{\mathsf{T}} \mathbf{x} + \mathbf{b} = \mathbf{0} \tag{1.34}$$

where $\mathbf{W} = \begin{bmatrix} a & a \\ a & a \end{bmatrix}$ and $\mathbf{b} = \left[-\frac{a}{2}, -\frac{3a}{2} \right]^{\mathsf{T}}$, and where $a > 0$ is an arbitrary constant. The expression of z_1 classifies point $(0, 0)$ as "negative," and the rest are classified as "positive." Indeed $z_1(0, 0) = 0 + 0 - \frac{a}{2} < 0$, and for the other three points the response is positive. z_2 classifies as positive point $(1, 1)$ and the rest are classified as negative. Let us now construct an input data matrix $\mathbf{X}$ with the points of the XOR problem:

$$\mathbf{X} = \begin{bmatrix} 0 & 1 & 0 & 1 \\ 0 & 1 & 1 & 0 \end{bmatrix} \tag{1.35}$$

and the corresponding linear transformation is

$$\begin{aligned} \mathbf{z} &= \begin{bmatrix} a & a \\ a & a \end{bmatrix} \begin{bmatrix} 0 & 1 & 0 & 1 \\ 0 & 1 & 1 & 0 \end{bmatrix} - \frac{1}{2} \begin{bmatrix} a & a & a & a \\ 3a & 3a & 3a & 3a \end{bmatrix} \\ &= \frac{a}{2} \begin{bmatrix} -1 & 3 & 1 & 1 \\ -3 & 1 & -1 & -1 \end{bmatrix} \end{aligned} \tag{1.36}$$

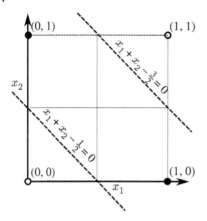

Figure 1.14 The two neurons of the example apply a linear function over the sample, which can be seen as a linear classifier. The lower line corresponds to the points that satisfy $x_1 + x_2 - \frac{1}{2} = 0$. The points under the line are classified as negative. The same effect is given by the upper line.

It can be seen that the first row of the last matrix in Eq. (1.36) has negative outputs, corresponding to input $(0, 0)$ in matrix (1.35), and the second row of last matrix in (1.36) has positive outputs, corresponding to input $(1, 1)$. But most importantly, the transformation has collapsed both $(0, 1)$ and $(1, 0)$ into point $\left(\frac{a}{2}, \frac{-a}{2}\right)$.

Now, in order to proceed to the classification, we need to apply a nonlinear activation $\sigma(z)$ to each one of the neurons. The idea in this example is to apply an activation whose output tends to be 1 if z is positive and zero otherwise. To make this more evident, we choose a large number for a, for example, $a = 10$. If we apply a logistic function, then the result of the operation is

$$
\mathbf{h} = \sigma \left(10 \begin{bmatrix} -\frac{1}{2} & \frac{3}{2} & \frac{1}{2} & \frac{1}{2} \\ -\frac{3}{2} & \frac{1}{2} & -\frac{1}{2} & -\frac{1}{2} \end{bmatrix} \right) = \begin{bmatrix} 0.01 & 1.00 & 0.99 & 0.99 \\ 0.00 & 0.99 & 0.01 & 0.01 \end{bmatrix} \tag{1.37}
$$

and finally, we apply a linear transformation with $\mathbf{w} = [1, -1]^{\mathsf{T}}$:

$$
o = \mathbf{w}^{\mathsf{T}}\mathbf{h} = [1, -1] \begin{bmatrix} 0.01 & 1.00 & 0.99 & 0.99 \\ 0.00 & 0.99 & 0.01 & 0.01 \end{bmatrix} \tag{1.38}
$$
$$
= [0.01, 0.01, 0.98, 0.98]
$$

This output is clearly close to the values of the labels, which are $[0, 0, 1, 1]$.

The previous example shows the bare minimum structure of an NN able to solve a non-linear problem. As it can be seen, the parameters of the NN have been found painfully and after some heuristic considerations that cannot constitute a criterion to construct a learning algorithm similar to the perceptron rule or the MMSE introduced in Sections 1.2.2 and 1.2.2.

Nevertheless, it is possible to have a much better solution to this problem. A better solution will provide a classification with a lower probability of error in an extended version of this problem, and the parameters should be obtained automatically by a learning algorithm from data. In order to achieve such a solution, we first need to introduce more about activation functions and a generalized algorithm to train an MLP, known as the BP algorithm, which will be introduced respectively in Sections 1.3.1 and 1.5.3.

1.3.1 The Multilayer Perceptron

In the previous example, a two-layer perceptron has been presented to demonstrate its capability to solve a nonlinear problem. The expressive capacity of an NN relies primarily on the use of nonlinear activations, and on the complexity of this network, or, in other words, in the number of layers and neurons or *nodes* in its layers. A generalized NN or MLP is then a structure with $L + 1$ layers, where layer $l = 0$ is the input $\mathbf{x}$ and, therefore, its number of nodes $D_0 = D$ is equal to the dimension of input space. The network has $L - 1$ *hidden* layers with D_l nodes that produce the column vector of outputs $\mathbf{h}^{(l)} = \left[h_1^{(l)}, \ldots, h_{D_l}^{(l)} \right]^{\mathsf{T}}$. The last layer is the output $\mathbf{o} = \left[o_1, \ldots, o_{D_L} \right]^{\mathsf{T}}$ of the MLP.

The layers are interconnected by edges. Each edge contains a weight $w_{i,j}^{(l)}$ that connects the output of node i of layer $l - 1$ to the input of node j in layer l. Also, each node has a bias input $b_j^{(l)}$. In summary, each node contains an affine transformation of the output of the previous layer as

$$z_j^{(l)} = \sum_{i=1}^{D_{l-1}} w_{i,j}^{(l)} h_i^{(l-1)} + b_j^{(l)} = \mathbf{w}_j^{(l)^{\mathsf{T}}} \mathbf{h}^{(l-1)} + b_j^{(l)} \tag{1.39}$$

where $\mathbf{w}_j^{(l)} = \left[w_{1,j}^{(l)}, \ldots, w_{D_{l-1},j}^{(l)} \right]^{\mathsf{T}}$ is the column weight vector of node j in layer l. Each hidden node applies a nonlinear activation function $\phi(\cdot)$ to the affine transformation of the input. Therefore, the output of each hidden node $h_i^{(l)}$ is

$$h_j^{(l)} = \phi \left(z_j^{(l)} \right) = \phi \left(\mathbf{w}_j^{(l)^{\mathsf{T}}} \mathbf{h}^{(l-1)} + b_j^{(l)} \right) \tag{1.40}$$

The corresponding graphical representation of the operation is in Fig. 1.15. At each layer l, the corresponding parameters are matrix $\mathbf{W}^{(l)}$ that can be constructed with the concatenation of the weight vectors of the layer as

$$\mathbf{W}^{(l)} = \left[\mathbf{w}_1^{(l)} \cdots \mathbf{w}_{D_l}^{(l)} \right] \in \mathbb{R}^{D_{l-1} \times D_l} \tag{1.41}$$

and a column bias vector $\mathbf{b}^{(l)}$ as

$$\mathbf{b}^{(l)} = \left[b_1^{(l)} \cdots b_{D_l}^{(l)} \right]^{\mathsf{T}} \tag{1.42}$$

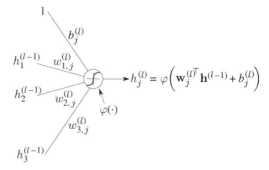

Figure 1.15 Graphical representation of a neuron or node l in an MLP, where the input is the vector of outputs $\mathbf{h}^{(l-1)}$ of the previous layer with dimension $D_{l-1} = 3$. The node performs affine transformation $z_j^{(l)} = \mathbf{w}_j^{(l)^{\mathsf{T}}} \mathbf{h}^{(l-1)} + b_j^{(l)}$ over this vector, and then a nonlinear activation $\phi(\cdot)$ is applied to compute the node output $h_j^{(l)}$.

With this, the expression of the vector of outputs $\mathbf{h}^{(l)}$ of layer l can be written with the following pair of equations

$$
\begin{aligned}
\mathbf{z}^{(l)} &= \mathbf{W}^{(l)\mathsf{T}}\mathbf{h}^{(l-1)} + \mathbf{b}^{(l)} \\
\mathbf{h}^{(l)} &= \boldsymbol{\phi}\left(\mathbf{z}^{(l)}\right)
\end{aligned}
\tag{1.43}
$$

This operation is often referred to as a *forward step* in an MLP since the operation transforms the output of one layer into the output of the next layer. Function $\boldsymbol{\phi}(\cdot)$, written in bold font, represents a vector of operations $\phi(\cdot)$ applied elementwise over each one of the elements of $\mathbf{z}^{(l)} = \left[z_1^{(l)}, \ldots, z_{D_l}^{(l)}\right]^{\mathsf{T}}$.

The output of the last layer is applied to a nonlinear transformation that can be different from $\phi(\cdot)$, which will be called $\mathbf{o}(\cdot)$ hereinafter. The expression of the MLP output is therefore

$$
\mathbf{o}\left(\mathbf{z}^{(L)}\right) = \mathbf{o}\left(\mathbf{W}^{(L)\mathsf{T}}\mathbf{h}^{(L-1)} + \mathbf{b}^L\right)
\tag{1.44}
$$

The graphical representation of the MLP is shown in Fig. 1.16, where biases $b_j^{(l)}$ are not shown for simplicity.

Usually, the graphical representation of a multilayer perceptron is purely illustrative, and the information about its structure is given in the number of layers and the number of nodes in each layer. Nevertheless, sometimes one wants to represent a very dense MLP, in whose case, instead of drawing all nodes and connections or edges between nodes, a more compact drawing is used, as the one shown in Fig. 1.17. The upper pane of the figure shows a traditional way of representing the MLP, while the lower one shows a more compact representation where the nodes are symbolized by boxes.

It is common to think of an MLP as a structure to process inputs in the form of vectors, but as a general matter of fact, an MLP can be used to process information organized as multidimensional arrays, particularly 2D or 3D arrays or matrices when the input data is an image. In these cases, the weight matrices become 3D or 4D arrays, and then it is also common to call them tensors. We do not use any of the properties of tensors in machine learning, and the use of this name for a multidimensional array of an NN is controversial;

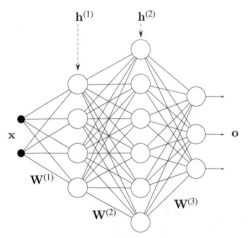

Figure 1.16 Graphical structure of a multilayer perceptron with $L = 3$, where the biases $b_i^{(l)}$ connected to each one of the nodes are not shown.

Figure 1.17 An MLP with three hidden layers and a compact representation of the same structure.

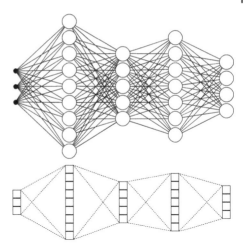

therefore, we will avoid the use of this term except when it is needed in order to be consistent with nomenclature in other scholarship or software.

1.3.2 Multidimensional Array Multiplications

So far, matrix-vector multiplications have been used as a basic operation to express the MLP operation, which, among other issues, constrains the MLP input to a vector of components. But, in general, it is possible to use different configurations as inputs. For example, an input may be a matrix representing an image, or a 3D matrix representing information in the space, as a 3D image. In order to construct an MLP with data organized in these structures, it is sufficient to vectorize or *flatten* the inputs, that is, reorganize the data in a vector with arbitrary order. Nevertheless, if the spatial information is important, this limits or heavily difficulties the types of operations to apply to the inputs, such as the convolution operation, as is seen in Chapter 4. In general, it is more convenient not to flatten the input (though sometimes it will be done) and, instead of using matrices and vectors, use the more general concept of multidimensional arrays. Let us define, as an example, an array $\mathbf{A} \in \mathbb{R}^{P \times Q \times R}$ in three dimensions. It has entries i, j, k defined as

$$[\mathbf{A}]_{i,j,k} = a_{i,j,k} \tag{1.45}$$

where $1 \le i \le P, 1 \le j \le Q, 1 \le k \le R$.

Assume two multidimensional arrays A, B with different dimensions and number of elements, but with a dimension with a common number P of elements. For example, take $\mathbf{A} \in \mathbb{R}^{P \times Q}$ and $\mathbf{B} \in \mathbb{R}^{R \times P \times S}$. The first one has two dimensions (a matrix) whose first dimension has P components and the second one is an array of three dimensions with P elements in its second dimension. The product between both arrays along the first dimension of $\mathbf{A}$ and second dimension of $\mathbf{B}$ is possible, which produces an array $\mathbf{C}$ whose dimensions with components $c_{j,k,l}$

$$c_{j,k,l} = [\mathbf{A} \cdot \mathbf{B}]_{j,k,l} = \sum_{i=1}^{P} a_{i,j} b_{k,i,l} \tag{1.46}$$

As a result, the common dimension disappears, and the new array has as many dimensions as the sum of the remaining ones. In this case, the first dimension of array $\mathbf{A}$ and the second dimension of tensor $\mathbf{B}$ disappear, so the remaining dimensions are $Q \times R \times S$. In general, the dimension across which the product is performed must be specified, but on occasions, there is only one common dimension, in which case the operation will not need such specification.

Example 1.3.2 *(Vector-matrix product)*
Assume vector $\mathbf{a} \in \mathbb{R}^P$ and matrix $\mathbf{B} \in \mathbb{R}^{Q \times P}$. The vector-matrix product assumes that the vector is a row or a column, and then it needs a particular disposition of the operands. For example, if the vector is a row, then the operation must be written as

$$\mathbf{c} = \mathbf{B}\mathbf{a}^\top \tag{1.47}$$

and the result is a column vector of Q components. The orientation of the vector and the matrix is irrelevant if the operation is defined in Eq. (1.46). Indeed

$$\mathbf{c} = \mathbf{B} \cdot \mathbf{a} \tag{1.48}$$

whose elements are[1]

$$c_i = \sum_{j=1}^{P} a_j b_{i,j} \tag{1.49}$$

and the orientation of the resulting array (particularized in this case as a vector) is also irrelevant.

Example 1.3.3 *(Forward step in an MLP multidimensional layer)*
The MLP in Fig. 1.18 is organized in layers represented by 2D arrays. Each node of a layer receives inputs from all the elements of the array of the previous layer. Each node of a given 2D layer can be denoted as $h_{i,j}^{(l)}$, so it is entry i, j of an order 2 array $\mathbf{H}^{(l)}$. The transformation

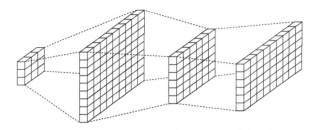

Figure 1.18 A compact representation of an MLP structured to process data presented in the form of 2D arrays. In this structure, the input is a 2D array with 3×3 components. The second layer is an array of 9×9 elements. Therefore, the set of weights that transform from the first layer to the second layer is array $\mathbf{W} \in \mathbb{R}^{3 \times 3 \times 9 \times 9}$, that is, it must be a 4D array with dimensions $3 \times 3 \times 9 \times 9$.

---

1 A very widely used convention in tensor calculus is the use of the Einstein notation, which omits the sum symbol, and it assumes that the element to accumulate is the one that is repeated in the product. Therefore, using Einstein's notation, the product is simply written as $c_i = a_j b_{i,j}$.

from the previous layer to a node of the next layer is

$$z_{i,j}^{(l)} = \sum_m \sum_n h_{m,n}^{(l-1)} w_{m,n,i,j}^{(l)} + b_{i,j}^{(l)}$$

$$h_{i,j}^{(l)} = \phi\left(z_{i,j}^{(l)}\right)$$

(1.50)

In this expression, we find:

- Element $w_{m,n,i,j}^{(l)}$, which is the weight that connects node m, n of layer $l-1$ with node i,j of layer l. This is therefore an entry of a four-dimensional array $\mathbf{W}$ whose first two dimensions are equal to the dimensions of layer $l-1$, and the third and fourth dimensions are equal to the dimensions of layer l. That is, if $\mathbf{H}^{(l-1)} \in \mathbb{R}^{D_{l-1,1} \times D_{l-1,2}}$ and $\mathbf{H}^{(l)} \in \mathbb{R}^{D_{l,1} \times D_{l,2}}$, then

$$\mathbf{W} \in \mathbb{R}^{D_{l-1,1} \times D_{l-1,2} \times D_{l,1} \times D_{l,2}}$$

(1.51)

  The transformation between the first layer and the second one in Fig. 1.18 is then an array of order 4 with dimensions $3 \times 3 \times 9 \times 9$, that is, $\mathbf{W} \in \mathbb{R}^{3 \times 3 \times 3 \times 9 \times 9}$.
- The set of bias elements is in this case a 2D array with the same dimensions as layer l.

Equation (1.50) simply describes a product along two of the dimensions of both arrays $\mathbf{H}^{(l-1)}$ and $\mathbf{W}^{(l)}$. As a result, these dimensions disappear from the resulting array $\mathbf{H}^{(l)}$. In Chapter 4, it is shown that the 2D convolutions used in convolutional NNs are nothing but a particular case of this expression.

1.4 Activations

As seen before, activations play an important role in the MLP. The activations that are applied in the hidden nodes are necessary in order to endow the structure with nonlinear properties. But it also makes sense to use nonlinear activations in the output layer for a different purpose. The activations here play the role of probability estimation. The simplest example consists of using logistic activations at the output of a binary classifier, so the output approaches zero when the input sample is classified as belonging to class "0" and to one when the sample is classified as belonging to class "1." With this, the intention is to use this output as an approximation of the probability that the class is 1 given the observation, i.e. $p(y = 1|\mathbf{x})$. The usual activations for hidden and output layers are presented here, where the use of output activations as a probabilistic estimation is treated in Section 1.5.

So far, we have presented the hyperbolic tangent and the logistic activation in Eqs. (1.15) and (1.18) that we reproduce here. If $z = \mathbf{w}^\top \mathbf{x} + b$ is the affine operation performed into any arbitrary neuron, the hyperbolic tangent is defined as

$$\tanh(z) = \frac{e^z - e^{-z}}{e^z + e^{-z}}$$

$$\sigma(z) = \frac{1}{1 + e^{-z}}$$

Among them, the most used is the logistic activation, since it has an interpretation in terms of probability, which is important in some kinds of NNs as restricted Boltzmann machines, that are treated in Chapter 7. Nevertheless, these activations are not widely used in other

NNs because they may produce training stalling (see Subsection 1.2.3). A more suitable activation for the hidden nodes of an MLP is a surprisingly simple one (Jarrett et al. 2009), called rectified linear unit (ReLU). The expression of the ReLU is

$$\phi_{ReLU}(z) = \max(0, z) \tag{1.52}$$

This activation is hardly nonlinear, but it has proven to be very powerful (Nair and Hinton 2010) even in structures such as the above-mentioned restricted Boltzmann machines. One can argue that this activation can also stop an algorithm since its derivative is always zero for negative inputs. An easy modification of this unit is the following:

$$\phi_{MaxOut}(z) = \max(0, z) + a \min 0, z \tag{1.53}$$

In this activation, the derivatives are 1 when $z > 0$ and a when $z < 0$, which fixes the issue. The value of a is supposed to be smaller than 1. This is usually referred to as a leaky ReLU.

Another activation, called maximum output (MaxOut), was presented in Ian Goodfellow et al. (2013a). In a traditional activation, each neuron is assigned a weight vector $\mathbf{w}$ and a bias b. In a MaxOut, each neuron is assigned K vectors $\mathbf{w}_k$ and weights b_k. The dot products between the input and all the vectors are computed, and the biases are added to each dot product. The MaxOut chooses the result with the maximum value as

$$\phi(z) = \max\left(\mathbf{w}_1^\top \mathbf{x} + b_1, \ldots, \mathbf{w}_K^\top \mathbf{x} + b_K\right) \tag{1.54}$$

The MaxOut activation can be seen as a generalization of the ReLU activation, which comes with the advantage that each neural network learns multiple functions of the same feature through the training of multiple weight vectors. Nevertheless, this has the disadvantage of an increased computational burden and the need to cross validate the number K of weight vectors.

1.5 Training a Multilayer Perceptron

The simple MMSE criterion has been applied to the solution of a linear problem in Section 1.2.3, in order to solve a problem that is not purely linearly separable. Then, the multilayer perceptron has been defined in Subsection 1.3.1, where a two-layer structure has been applied to solve the classical XOR problem using the bare minimum structure with two nodes in the hidden layer. Nevertheless, this solution is purely ad hoc for this problem, and this cannot be generalized to a higher dimensional arbitrary problem. Nevertheless, a strategy similar to the algorithm applied to the linear perceptron can be generalized to the MLP. Also, we have seen different forms of activation for hidden nodes and activations adequate to binary and multiclass problems. In this section, we put everything together to construct a generalized set of training algorithms depending on the nature of the classification problem at hand. These algorithms fall under the umbrella of the so-called BP algorithm. The general criterion to apply is called ML.

1.5.1 Maximum Likelihood Criterion

Assume a dataset $\{\mathbf{x}_i, y_i\}$, $1 \leq i \leq N$ consisting of N labeled patterns to be used for training purposes, where the labels are binary, that is, $y_i \in \{0, 1\}$. In order to develop the training criterion, we assume further that a conditional probability of the labels over the samples $p(\mathbf{y}|\mathbf{X})$ exists, where we defined $\mathbf{y} = (y_1, \dots, y_n)^\top$ as the sequence of labels corresponding to the training input patterns $\mathbf{X} = (\mathbf{x}_1, \dots, \mathbf{x}_N)$. An adequate way to perform a classification would be to know this probability. In this case, we just need to find the sequence $\mathbf{y}$ of labels that maximizes this probability. Besides, it is reasonable to assume that the labels are conditionally independent, that is, for any pair $\mathbf{x}_i, y_i$, we assume

$$p(y_i|\mathbf{x}_i, \mathbf{x}_j) = p(y_i|\mathbf{x}_i), \ \forall j \tag{1.55}$$

The second probability $p(y_i|\mathbf{x}_i)$ is the probability of y_i conditional to $\mathbf{x}_i$. If we had this probability, then we can easily make a decision: if the probability $p(y_i = 1|\mathbf{x}_i)$ is higher than 0.5, then we decide that $y_i = 1$, or zero otherwise. The first probability is the probability of y_i conditional to observations $\mathbf{x}_i, \mathbf{x}_j$. In principle, adding more observations may add more information to a better decision. While this may be true in specific scenarios, we will assume that all the information needed to make a decision on y_i is contained in $\mathbf{x}_i$, and that adding a new observation does not change the probability, and this is what Eq. (1.55) means. Now, assume that we have two samples $\mathbf{x}_1$ and $\mathbf{x}_2$ and we want to compute the probability $p(y_1, y_2|\mathbf{x}_1, \mathbf{x}_2)$ of the sequence y_1, y_2. By using Bayes' rule, we get

$$\begin{aligned} p(y_1, y_2|\mathbf{x}_1, \mathbf{x}_2) &= p(y_1|y_2, \mathbf{x}_1, \mathbf{x}_2)p(y_2|\mathbf{x}_1, \mathbf{x}_2) \\ &= p(y_1|\mathbf{x}_1)p(y_2|\mathbf{x}_2) \end{aligned} \tag{1.56}$$

We have used here the assumption that y_1 is independent of $\mathbf{x}_2$ and y_2 given the knowledge of $\mathbf{x}_1$ and that y_2 is independent of $\mathbf{x}_1$ given the knowledge of $\mathbf{x}_2$. It is worth noting that this does not mean that y_1 and y_2 are independent, they are independent only if their respective patterns $\mathbf{x}_1, \mathbf{x}_2$ are known. This can be easily generalizable as

$$p(\mathbf{y}|\mathbf{X}) = p(y_1, \dots, y_n|\mathbf{x}_1, \dots, \mathbf{x}_N) = \prod_{i=1}^{N} p(y_i|\mathbf{x}_i) \tag{1.57}$$

If these patterns and their labels are known, that is, they are a set of training data, the above expression (1.57) is called a *likelihood*, and it has the property of being *factorizable* in elements $p(y_i, \mathbf{x}_i)$.

Provided that likelihood is constructed by a parametric function with a set of parameters θ containing all weights and biases $w_{i,j}^{(l)}, b_j^{(l)}$ of a learning machine, for example, an MLP, the training criterion for this MLP is to maximize this likelihood with respect to its parameters. Since the logarithm is a monotonically increasing function, maximizing the logarithm of the likelihood, or *log-likelihood* is equivalent to maximizing Eq. (1.57). This is the ML criterion.

$$J_{ML}(\theta, \mathbf{X}, \mathbf{y}) = \log p(\mathbf{y}|\mathbf{X}) \tag{1.58}$$

In many situations, an information-theoretic interpretation of this cost function is used. For this purpose, we change the sign, and divide the equation by the number N of training data to obtain the so-called negative log-likelihood (NLL)

$$J_{ML}(\theta, \mathbf{X}, \mathbf{y}) = -\frac{1}{N} \log p(\mathbf{y}|\mathbf{X}) = -\frac{1}{N} \sum_{i=1}^{N} \log p(y_i|\mathbf{x}_i) \approx -\mathbb{E}_{\mathbf{x}, \mathbf{y}} \log p(\mathbf{y}|\mathbf{x}) \tag{1.59}$$

where θ represents the set of parameters of an MLP that needs to be optimized by maximizing this cost function. The purpose of dividing the expression by N is to obtain the sample average of log probabilities $-\frac{1}{N}\sum_i \log p(\mathbf{y}_i|\mathbf{x}_i)$, which is, by virtue of the WLLN (Bertsekas and Tsitsiklis 2000), an approximation to the expectation of these logarithms. Assuming that the actual probabilities of $\mathbf{y}_i$ are known, one can change this measure by $-\mathbb{E}_{\mathbf{x},\mathbf{y}}\left[p(\mathbf{y})\log p(\mathbf{y}|\mathbf{x})\right]$, which is, by definition, the cross-entropy measure between the actual and the estimated probabilities (Cover and Thomas 2006).

1.5.2 Activations and Likelihood Functions

Apart from the above interpretation in terms of Information Theory, the logarithm has a practical purpose, which will become apparent next, when we formulate the probabilities in terms of the output of an MLP, which is related to the chosen form for the output activations. Assume an MLP with a number of hidden layers and some activation functions for the hidden nodes. We take care here of the justification and interpretation of the choice of the activation function for the output layer. The first activation to be presented is the logistic one, which must be adequately constructed, and it is useful when the MLP is used for binary classification, so the output gives an estimation of the probability $p(y = 1|\mathbf{x})$, that is, the probability that the label corresponding to input $\mathbf{x}$ is one, which is a Bernoulli distribution. Then we generalize this activation for the case where the classification neuron is multiclass, where the probability is a Multinoulli distribution. Finally, we present the activation used when the output is assumed to have a Gaussian distribution.

1.5.2.1 Logistic Activation for Binary Classification

Here we assume that an MLP is used for binary classification (Fig. 1.19). Then, as mentioned before, the output is modeled as the probability of that $y = 1$, that is, the probability function is a Bernoulli mass function. We start by constructing an *unnormalized* log probability function as

$$\log \tilde{p}(y|\mathbf{x}) = yz \longrightarrow \tilde{p}(y|\mathbf{x}) = e^{yz} \tag{1.60}$$

The probability is unnormalized because $\tilde{p}(y = 0|\mathbf{x}) + \tilde{p}(y = 1|\mathbf{x}) \neq 1$, so this output does not have probability mass function properties. The way it works is the following: for $y = 1$, if the linear output z produced by the last layer of the MLP is positive, the product will be positive, producing a high value for the unnormalized probability, implying that the probability of 1 is high, but if z is negative, this implies that the probability of 1 is low since the unnormalized probability will be close to zero. In order to provide this function with probability mass function properties, we must construct a function for which

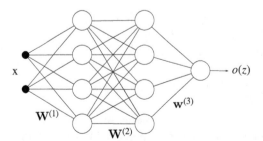

Figure 1.19 An MLP for binary classification, where the output $o(z)$ is a scalar. The set of parameters of the last layer (layer 3) is organized in a vector, and $z = \mathbf{w}^{(3)\top}\mathbf{h}^{(2)} + b^{(3)}$. The biases are not shown.

$p(y = 0|\mathbf{x}) + p(y = 1|\mathbf{x}) = 1$ as

$$o(z) = p(y|\mathbf{x}) = \frac{\tilde{p}(y|\mathbf{x})}{\tilde{p}(y = 0|\mathbf{x}) + \tilde{p}(y = 1|\mathbf{x})} = \frac{e^{yz}}{1 + e^z} = \frac{1}{e^{-yz} + e^{-(y-1)z}} \tag{1.61}$$

Since y can only be 1 or 0, the following expression is equivalent to the previous one

$$o(z) = p(y|\mathbf{x}) = \frac{1}{1 + e^{-(2y-1)z}} = \sigma((2y - 1)z) \tag{1.62}$$

This is then the log-likelihood expression for the Bernoulli model, and it is often called *logistic* activation. According to Eq. (1.59), the cost function to be optimized in the case of binary classification is

$$J_{ML}(\theta, \mathbf{X}, \mathbf{y}) = -\sum_{i=1}^{N} \left[\log \sigma((2y_i - 1)z_i)\right] = \sum_{i=1}^{N} \left[\log \left(1 + e^{(1-2y_i)z_i}\right)\right] \tag{1.63}$$

Any cost function $J(\theta, \mathbf{X}, \mathbf{y})$ uses a loss function between the estimator output (in our case a classifier output) and the actual label of the sample. In subsection 1.2.3, the used similarity measure was the squared error $e_i = o(z_i) - y_i$, where the output $o(z_i)$ was a logistic function. Here, the loss function ℓ_i is

$$\ell_i = \log \left(1 + e^{(1-2y_i)z_i}\right) \tag{1.64}$$

that compares the sign of the output z with $(2y - 1)$, which is a signed version of the labels.

In order to later make the derivation of the training of an MLP, it is worth computing the derivative of this loss with respect to input z_i, which is

$$\frac{d\ell_i}{dz_i} = \frac{(1 - 2y_i)e^{(1-2y_i)z_i}}{1 + e^{(1-2y_i)z_i}} \tag{1.65}$$

Now we particularize to the possible values of label $y_i \in \{0, 1\}$ in order to find a more compact expression. If $y_i = 0$, then

$$\frac{d\ell_i(y_i = 0)}{dz_i} = \frac{e^{z_i}}{1 + e^{z_i}} = \frac{1}{1 + e^{-z_i}} = \sigma(z_i) \tag{1.66}$$

and for the case $y_i = 1$ the corresponding expression is

$$\frac{d\ell_i(y_i = 1)}{dz_i} = \frac{-e^{-z_i}}{1 + e^{-z_i}} = \frac{1}{1 + e^{-z_i}} - 1 = \sigma(z_i) - 1 \tag{1.67}$$

and thus both cases the expression of the derivative can be written as

$$\frac{d\ell_i}{dz_i} = \sigma(z_i) - y_i = \delta_i^{(L)} \tag{1.68}$$

where $\delta_i^{(L)}$ is the classification error measured at the output (layer L) of the. This expression will be used later for the derivation of the MLP training.

The following example shows a fundamental difference between the use of the ML loss and the application of the MMSE loss.

Example 1.5.1   *ML versus MMSE in binary classification*
An MMSE criterion to optimize a linear classifier with logistic activation is explained in Section 1.2.3. The loss function between the label and the output of the classifier used in

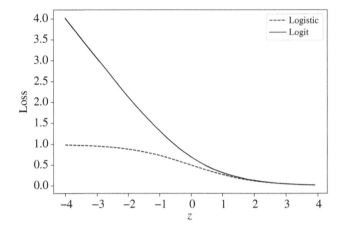

Figure 1.20 Cross-entropy loss function and square error loss function for a single sample with $y = 1$. The cross-entropy loss function has a derivative that increases when the value of the function increases. The squared error loss function has a very small derivative when the function tends to its maximum.

MMSE is the square error. In a classifier with logistic activation and labels $y \in \{0, 1\}$ used with the MMSE criterion (see Problem 1.2). This loss is computed as $e_i^2 = (\sigma(z_i) - y_i)^2$, whereas the loss in ML is $\ell_i = \log\left(1 + e^{(1-2y_i)z_i}\right)$ as stated in Eq. (1.64).

Assume without loss of generality that the label corresponding to sample i is $y_i = 1$. If z is positive, then in both cases the similarity measures tend to zero, and the derivatives of these functions tend to zero, as it can be seen in Fig. 1.20 (see (Y. A. LeCun et al. 2012) for a general study of this effect). So, using a gradient descent algorithm should converge to situations where for $y = 1$, output z is positive. Nevertheless, when z_i is negative and y_i is positive, there is an important difference between both similarity functions. In this case, the logistic function $\sigma(z)$ tends to zero and hence the squared error tends to one, while the ML similarity $\log\left(1 + e^{(1-2y_i)z_i}\right)$ tends to infinity. We can see in the figure that while using the square error, the derivative tends to zero, thus stopping the gradient descent. The ML similarity gradient is positive, actually tending to -1, which prevents a gradient descent algorithm from stopping in case z takes large negative values.

1.5.2.2 Softmax Activation for Multiclass Classification

In multiclass classification, it is common to construct structures whose output is vectorial, that is, the NN has an output consisting of a node per each one of the possible classes of the input patterns. These outputs are interpreted as the posterior probability of each one of the classes given the input. That is, if the number of possible classes is K, then one can denote a predictive posterior as $p(y = k|\mathbf{x})$, $0 \le k \le K - 1$. The linear component of the output is then written as

$$\mathbf{z} = \mathbf{W}^{(L)\mathsf{T}} \mathbf{h}^{(L-1)} \tag{1.69}$$

Then, each element z_k in $\mathbf{z}$ is modeled through an unnormalized probability, and it has the form

$$z_k = \log \tilde{p}(y = k|\mathbf{x}) \tag{1.70}$$

with

$$\tilde{p}(y = k|\mathbf{x}) = \exp(z_k) \tag{1.71}$$

The *softmax* function is an activation consisting of the normalization of the above probability

$$p(y = k|\mathbf{x}) = o_k(\mathbf{h}^{(L-1)}) = \text{softmax}(z_k) = \frac{\exp(z_k)}{\sum_{j=1}^{K} \exp(z_j)} \tag{1.72}$$

This output has probability mass function properties, as the sum of outputs adds to 1. In order to construct a loss function, the common approach is to maximize the cross entropy between the outputs and the labels, which is equivalent to maximizing the likelihood. Since the output is a vector with K elements, we transform the scalar label $y_i = k$ corresponding to training input $\mathbf{x}_i$ into a binary vector $\mathbf{y}_i = [y_{0,i}, \ldots, y_{K-1,i}]^{\top}$ where only element $y_{k,i} = 1$ and the rest are zeros, which denotes that the class of the input pattern is k. This is often called one-hot encoding.

We denote the real probability of that $y_i = k$ as

$$q\left(y_{k,i} = 1\right) = q_i(k) = \begin{cases} 1, \ y_i = k \\ 0, \ y_i \neq k \end{cases} \tag{1.73}$$

and then the cross-entropy loss function can be written as

$$\ell_i = -\sum_{k=0}^{K-1} q_i(k) \log p(y_i = k|\mathbf{x}) \tag{1.74}$$

Then, by identifying terms with Eq. (1.72) and by assuming that $q_i(k) = y_{k,i}$, we obtain the following expression for the cross entropy:

$$\begin{aligned} \ell_i &= -\sum_{k=0}^{K-1} y_{k,i} \log \text{softmax}\left(z_{k,i}\right) \\ &= -\sum_{k=0}^{K-1} y_{k,i} \log \frac{\exp(z_{k,i})}{\sum_{j=0}^{K-1} \exp(z_{j,i})} \\ &= -\sum_{k=0}^{K-1} y_{k,i} z_{k,i} + \sum_{k=0}^{K-1} y_{k,i} \log \sum_{j=0}^{K-1} \exp(z_{j,i}) \end{aligned} \tag{1.75}$$

where $z_{i,k}$ is the kth output for input sample $\mathbf{x}_i$. Since only one of the elements of vector $\mathbf{y}_i$ is one, then we can simplify the second summation of Eq. (1.75) to obtain the expression of the loss function:

$$\ell_i = -\sum_{k=0}^{K-1} y_{k,i} z_{k,i} + \log \sum_{k=0}^{K-1} \exp(z_{k,i}) \tag{1.76}$$

The cost function is obtained by adding all the losses corresponding to all samples:

$$J_{ML}(\theta, \mathbf{X}, \mathbf{Y}) = -\sum_{i=1}^{N} \left(\sum_{k=0}^{K-1} y_{k,i} z_{k,i} - \log \sum_{k=0}^{K-1} \exp(z_{k,i}) \right) \tag{1.77}$$

where $\mathbf{Y} = (\mathbf{y}_1, \ldots, \mathbf{y}_N)$ is a matrix containing all the multiclass labels corresponding to the training dataset. The derivative of the loss function with respect to $z_{k,i}$ has the expression

$$\frac{d\ell_i}{dz_{k,i}} = -y_{k,i} + \frac{\exp(z_{k,i})}{\sum\limits_{j=0}^{K-1} \exp(z_{j,i})} = \text{softmax}(z_{k,i}) - y_{k,i} = \delta_{k,i}^{(L)} \tag{1.78}$$

which tends to zero when the norm of $z_{k,i}$ increases if it has the same sign as the label, and otherwise, it tends to ± 1. That is, again the classification error of output k of the multiclass classifier.

The loss function obtained in Eq. (1.64) for binary classification can be also obtained by applying the cross entropy reasoning above. The corresponding proof is given in the following example.

Example 1.5.2 The application of the cross entropy to a binary classifier leads to the loss function of Eq. (1.64). The binary classifier is modeled with a single output whose activation is a logistic function. Nevertheless, in order to proceed with the derivation, we can model an NN with two redundant outputs modeling probabilities $p(y_i = 1|\mathbf{x}) = \frac{1}{1+e^{-z_i}}$ and $p(y_i = 0|\mathbf{x}) = 1 - p(y_i = 1|\mathbf{x}) = \frac{e^{-z_i}}{1+e^{-z_i}}$. The corresponding labels are straightforwardly $y_i^{(0)} = 1 - y_i$ and $y_i^{(1)} = y_i$ since the logistic activation is used to model the first probability, then the cross entropy of Eq. (1.75) is particularized here as

$$\ell_i = -(1 - y_i) \log \frac{e^{-z_i}}{1 + e^{-z_i}} - y_i \log \frac{1}{1 + e^{-z_i}}$$
$$= -y_i \log e^{z_i} - \log \frac{e^{-z_i}}{1 + e^{-z_i}} = -\log \frac{e^{-z_i}(e^{z_i})^{y_i}}{1 + e^{-z_i}} \tag{1.79}$$

If $y_i = 1$, then $l_i = \log(1 + e^{-z_i})$ and otherwise $l_i = \log(1 + e^{z_i})$. Then, we can write this loss function by using the equivalent expression

$$\ell_i = \log\left(1 + e^{(1-2y_i)z_i}\right) \tag{1.80}$$

which matches the loss function in Eq. (1.64).

1.5.2.3 Gaussian Activation in Regression

A multitask regression can be considered in problems where a vector $\mathbf{y} \in \mathbb{R}^K$ is the desired output for a given pattern $\mathbf{x}$. A simple model assumes that the estimation error components are conditionally independent and Gaussian. Therefore, the error distribution given sample $\mathbf{x}$ is

$$p(\mathbf{y}|\mathbf{x}) = \frac{1}{(2\pi\sigma^2)^{K/2}} \exp\left(-\frac{1}{2\sigma^2}\|\mathbf{y} - \mathbf{z}\|^2\right) \tag{1.81}$$

The cost function in Eq. (1.59) to this model is

$$J_{ML}(\theta) = -\mathbb{E}_{\mathbf{x},\mathbf{y}} \log p(\mathbf{y}|\mathbf{x}) = \mathbb{E}_{\mathbf{x},\mathbf{y}} \left(\frac{1}{2\sigma^2}\|\mathbf{z} - \mathbf{y}\|^2 + \frac{K}{2}2\pi\sigma^2\right)$$
$$= \frac{1}{2\sigma^2}\mathbb{E}_{\mathbf{x},\mathbf{y}} \left(\|\mathbf{z} - \mathbf{y}\|^2\right) + \text{constant} \tag{1.82}$$
$$\propto \sum_{i=1}^{N} \|\mathbf{W}^{(L)\top}\mathbf{h}^{(L-1)} + \mathbf{b}^{(L)} - \mathbf{y}_i\|^2$$

In other words, the ML criterion applied in regression is simply the MMSE. The output of the NN in this case is the linear expression

$$\mathbf{z}\left(\mathbf{h}^{L-1}\right) = \mathbf{W}^{(L)\mathsf{T}}\mathbf{h}^{(L-1)} + \mathbf{b}^{(L)} \tag{1.83}$$

The loss function of a single input sample is then

$$\ell_i = \|\mathbf{z}_i - \mathbf{y}_i\|^2 \tag{1.84}$$

and its derivative with respect to the output $z_{i,k}$ is the regression error, with an expression identical to the ones obtained for binary and multiclass classification. In particular,

$$\frac{d\ell_i}{dz_{k,i}} = z_{i,k} - y_{i,k} = \delta_{i,k}^{(L)} \tag{1.85}$$

1.5.3 The Backpropagation Algorithm

The BP algorithm seeks to optimize the parameters of the NN according to the ML criterion or a regularized criterion as summarized in Section 2.3. The BP algorithm uses a gradient descent procedure, where the derivative of the cost function corresponding to each training sample is computed with respect to each one of the weights of the network, and then these weights are updated in the direction opposite to this gradient.

A gradient procedure applied to an NN is in principle cumbersome since the weights of each layer are connected to the next layer through nonlinear functions; however, the use of the chain rule of derivatives, extended to gradients, is applied to solve the problem in a generalized way that is simple and efficient to program.

The optimization of the NN, then, takes two steps. In the first one, the estimation cost function evaluated for a training sample is computed. This step is often called the forward step. Once the cost is computed, the backward step is applied to recursively compute the derivative of the error with respect to each weight, from the output layer to the input layer, and finally update the weights. The backward step optimizes the structure with respect to all parameters $\theta : \{w_{j,k}^{(l)}, b_k^{(l)}\}$ by

$$\frac{\partial J(\theta)}{\partial w_{j,k}^{(l)}} = 0, \quad \frac{\partial J(\theta)}{\partial b_k^{(l)}} = 0 \tag{1.86}$$

The chain rule is used to compute this derivative as follows.

1.5.3.1 Gradient with Respect to the Output Weights

Let us first express the function implemented by the NN as a composition of functions

$$\begin{aligned}
\mathbf{f}(\mathbf{x}) &= \mathbf{o}\left(\mathbf{z}^{(L)}\right) = \mathbf{o}\left(\mathbf{W}^{(L)\mathsf{T}}\mathbf{h}^{(L-1)} + \mathbf{b}^{(L)}\right) \\
&= \mathbf{o}\left(\mathbf{W}^{(L)\mathsf{T}}\boldsymbol{\phi}\left(\mathbf{W}^{(L-1)\mathsf{T}}\mathbf{h}^{(L-2)} + \mathbf{b}^{(L-1)}\right) + \mathbf{b}^{(L)}\right) = \cdots
\end{aligned} \tag{1.87}$$

The objective now is to compute a general expression of the derivative of the cost function with respect to a weight of layer L. In order to express this derivative, we first write the derivative as a function of the weights $\mathbf{W}^{(L)}$ of this layer

$$\frac{d}{dw_{i,j}^{(L)}} J_{ML}(\mathbf{y}, \mathbf{f}(\mathbf{x})) = \frac{d}{dw_{i,j}^{(L)}} J_{ML}\left(\mathbf{y}, \mathbf{o}\left(\mathbf{z}^{(L)}\right)\right)$$
$$= \frac{d}{dw_{i,j}^{(L)}} J_{ML}\left(\mathbf{y}, \mathbf{o}\left(\mathbf{W}^{(L)\top}\mathbf{h}^{(L-1)} + \mathbf{b}^{(L)}\right)\right) \tag{1.88}$$

The derivative is then a function of three elements, namely, the output activation $\mathbf{o}$ with components o_j and the outputs $\mathbf{z}^{(L)} = \mathbf{W}^{(L)\top}\mathbf{h}^{(L-1)} + \mathbf{b}^{(L)}$ as a function of the previous layer, with components $h_i^{(L-1)}$. We need to apply the chain rule to these three elements, first computing the derivative of the cost function with respect to o_j, then the derivative of o_j with respect to $z_j^{(L)}$, and then the derivative of $z_j^{(L)}$ with respect to a weight $w_{i,j}^{(L)}$.

$$\frac{dJ_{ML}}{dw_{i,j}^{(L)}} = \frac{dJ_{ML}}{do_j} \frac{do_j}{dz_j^{(L)}} \frac{dz_j^{(L)}}{dw_{i,j}^{(L)}} \tag{1.89}$$

The first derivative of the chain can be computed directly for any differentiable cost function. The second one can be also computed directly for any differentiable output function, and it is defined hereinafter as $\frac{do_j(z^{(L)})}{dz_j^{(L)}} = o_j'$. Finally, the third one is the derivative of a linear function of, that is, $\frac{dz_j^{(L)}}{dw_{i,j}^{(L)}} = h_i^{(L-1)}$. Therefore,

$$\frac{dJ_{ML}}{dw_{i,j}^{(L)}} = \frac{dJ_{ML}}{do_j} o_j' h_i^{(L)} = \delta_j^{(L)} h_i^{(L-1)} \tag{1.90}$$

In the above expression, we use the definition

$$\delta_j^{(L)} = \frac{dJ_{ML}}{dz_j^{(L)}} = \frac{dJ_{ML}}{do_j} \frac{o_j\left(\mathbf{z}^{(L)}\right)}{dz_j^{(L)}} = \frac{dJ_{ML}}{do_j} o_j' \tag{1.91}$$

from which we can define the output error term vector $\delta^{(L)} = \left[\delta_0^{(L)}, \dots, \delta_{K-1}^{(L)}\right]^\top$ of a single input sample as the elementwise product of the cost function gradient with respect to $\mathbf{o}$ and the vector of output derivatives $\mathbf{o}'$, this is

$$\delta^{(L)} = \nabla_{\mathbf{z}^{(L)}} J_{ML} = \nabla_{\mathbf{o}} J_{ML}(\mathbf{y}, \mathbf{o}) \odot \mathbf{o}' \tag{1.92}$$

The expression of this vector will depend on the nature of the classification or regression task at hand. In Section 1.5.2 we have seen the derivation of the error term for the case of binary classification in Eq. (1.68), for multiclass classification in Eq. (1.78), and for multitask regression in Eq. (1.85). In all cases, the elements of the error vector are expressed as the actual output minus the desired output, that is, as a general matter of fact

$$\delta^{(L)} = \mathbf{o} - \mathbf{y} \tag{1.93}$$

This vector will be propagated backward during the BP operation. Derivative in Eq. (1.90) is the element i,j of a matrix computed as the product of column vector $\mathbf{h}^{(L-1)}$, with $D^{(L-1)}$

elements, and row vector $\delta^{(L)\mathsf{T}}$, with $D^{(L)}$ elements. The gradient with respect to the last weight matrix evaluated for an input sample can be written as

$$\nabla_{\mathbf{W}^{(L)}} J_{ML} = \mathbf{h}^{(L-1)} \delta^{(L)\mathsf{T}} \tag{1.94}$$

In order to update the output weights, we use the above cost function gradient together with expression (1.92). The single input sample update rule is then

$$\mathbf{W}^{(L)} \leftarrow \mathbf{W}^{(L)} - \mu \mathbf{h}^{(L-1)} \delta^{(L)\mathsf{T}} \tag{1.95}$$

where μ is a small scalar usually called the learning rate.

In order to compute the update of the bias vector $\mathbf{b}^{(L)}$, we must repeat the derivation particularized to these parameters, and the result is

$$\mathbf{b}^{(L)} \leftarrow \mathbf{b}^{(L)} - \mu \delta^{(L)} \tag{1.96}$$

1.5.3.2 Gradient with Respect to Hidden Layer Weights

Using the same reasoning as before, let us now compute the gradient, evaluated for a sample pair $(\mathbf{x},\ \mathbf{y})$, of the cost function with respect to weight $w_{i,j}^{(L-1)}$, that is,

$$\frac{d}{dw_{i,j}^{(L-1)}} J_{ML}(\mathbf{y}, \mathbf{f}(\mathbf{x})) = \frac{d}{dw_{i,j}^{(L-1)}} J_{ML}\left(\mathbf{y}, \mathbf{o}\left(\mathbf{W}^{(L)\mathsf{T}} \phi\left(\mathbf{W}^{(L-1)\mathsf{T}} \mathbf{h}^{(L-2)}\right)\right)\right) \tag{1.97}$$

Figure 1.21 depicts the situation. First, notice that $w_{i,j}^{(L-1)}$ is inside of each output o_k, so in order to apply the chain rule, we need to compute the derivative of the cost function with respect to all of them. Second, the derivative to be computed is with respect to $w_{i,j}^{(L-1)}$, which connects $h_i^{(L-2)}$ with $h_j^{(L-1)}$.

Specifically, the elements of the chain are

$$\begin{aligned}
o_k &= o(z_k^{(L)}), \ \forall k \\
z_k^{(L)} &= \mathbf{w}_k^{(L)} \mathbf{h}^{(L-1)}, \ \forall k \\
h_j^{(L-1)} &= \phi\left(z_j^{(L-1)}\right) \\
z_j^{(L-1)} &= \mathbf{w}_j^{(L-1)} \mathbf{h}^{(L-2)}
\end{aligned} \tag{1.98}$$

Figure 1.21 Elements involved in the computation of the derivative of the cost function J_{ML} with respect to $w_{i,j}^{(L-1)}$.

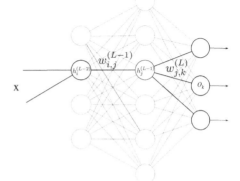

where vector $\mathbf{w}_j^{(L-1)}$ in the last equation contains the element of interest $w_{i,j}^{(L-1)}$. With this in mind, we can compute the derivative of the cost function with respect to $w_{i,j}^{(L-1)}$ as follows

$$\frac{d}{dw_{i,j}^{(L-1)}} J_{ML}(\mathbf{y}, \mathbf{f}(\mathbf{x})) = \sum_k \frac{\delta J_{ML}}{do_k} \frac{do_k}{dz_k^{(L)}} \frac{dz_k^{(L)}}{dh_j^{(L-1)}} \frac{dh_j^{(L-1)}}{dz_j^{L-1}} \frac{dz_j^{(L-1)}}{dw_{i,j}^{(L-1)}} \qquad (1.99)$$

which, taking into account the expressions in Eq. (1.98), turns into equation

$$\frac{d}{dw_{i,j}^{(L-1)}} J_{ML}(\mathbf{y}, \mathbf{f}(\mathbf{x})) = \sum_k \delta_k^{(L)} w_{k,j}^{(L)} \phi' \left(z_j^{(L-1)} \right) h_i^{L-2} = h_i^{(L-2)} \delta_j^{(L-1)} \qquad (1.100)$$

where element $\delta_k^{(L)} = \frac{dJ_{ML}}{do_k} \frac{do_k}{dz_k^{(L)}}$ is defined in Eq. (1.91). We can write now the derivatives with respect to all parameters in matrix $\mathbf{W}^{(L-1)}$ in matrix form. To this purpose, notice that expression $\sum_k \delta_k^{(L)} w_{k,j}^{(L)}$ is an element of vector $\mathbf{W}^{(L)} \delta^{(L)}$, which is then elementwise multiplied with the elements of $\phi' \left(\mathbf{z}^{(L-1)} \right)$. Therefore, we can define the error term of layer $L-1$ from Eq. (1.100) as

$$\delta^{(L-1)} = \mathbf{W}^{(L)} \delta^{(L)} \odot \phi' \left(\mathbf{z}^{(L-1)} \right) \qquad (1.101)$$

The update rule of the previous layer for a single input sample is in matrix form,

$$\mathbf{W}^{(L-1)} \leftarrow \mathbf{W}^{(L-1)} - \mu \mathbf{h}^{(L-2)} \delta^{(L-1)\top} \qquad (1.102)$$

The process can be iterated down to the input layer, with the same result and therefore the update of weight matrix $\mathbf{W}^{l-1}$ is

$$\mathbf{W}^{(l-1)} \leftarrow \mathbf{W}^{(l-1)} - \mu \mathbf{h}^{(l-2)} \delta^{(l-1)\top} \qquad (1.103)$$

with the definition

$$\delta^{(l-1)} = \mathbf{W}^{(l)} \delta^{(l)} \odot \phi' \left(\mathbf{z}^{(l-1)} \right) \qquad (1.104)$$

Again, the process can be repeated for bias vector $\mathbf{b}^{(l-1)}$, which leads to the update rule

$$\mathbf{b}^{(l-1)} \leftarrow \mathbf{b}^{(l-1)} - \mu \delta^{(l-1)} \qquad (1.105)$$

Example 1.5.3 *(A single BP step)*
Consider the NN of Fig. 1.22. This is a structure with a single hidden layer, with ReLU activations in this layer, of three nodes, and whose output has a single node and sigmoid activation for binary classification. The hidden weights have the values

$$\mathbf{W}^{(1)} = \begin{pmatrix} 1 & 1 & -1 \\ 1 & 1 & -1 \end{pmatrix}$$

and the output layer has weights $\mathbf{w}^{(2)} = (1, -1, -2)^\top$. The biases are all zeros. Assume an input vector whose values are all ones, i.e. $\mathbf{x} = (1, 1)$. The desired output is $y = 1$.

In the forward step, for the present input, and assuming that the biases are zero, the linear values of the hidden layer are

$$\mathbf{z}^{(1)} = \mathbf{W}^{(1)\top} \mathbf{x} = \begin{pmatrix} 1 & 1 \\ 1 & 1 \\ -1 & -1 \end{pmatrix} \begin{pmatrix} 1 \\ 1 \end{pmatrix} = \begin{pmatrix} 2 \\ 2 \\ -2 \end{pmatrix}$$

Figure 1.22 Structure of the NN of Example 1.5.3.

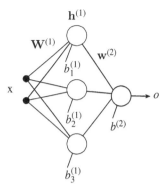

This vector has to be processed through the nonlinear activation to produce $\mathbf{h}^{(1)}$. The activation is the ReLU, therefore,

$$\mathbf{h}^{(1)} = \mathbf{ReLU}\begin{pmatrix} 2 \\ 2 \\ -2 \end{pmatrix} = \begin{pmatrix} 2 \\ 2 \\ 0 \end{pmatrix}$$

The output of the second layer is then

$$z^{(2)} = \mathbf{w}^{(2)\mathsf{T}}\mathbf{h}^{(1)} = (1, -1, -2)\begin{pmatrix} 2 \\ 2 \\ 0 \end{pmatrix} = 0$$

Then, the output of the NN is $o = \sigma(0) = 0.5$.

The corresponding error is $\delta^{(2)} = o - y = -0.5$. The BP applied to this error gives an error for the previous layer as

$$\delta^{(1)} = \mathbf{w}^{(2)}\delta^{(L)} \odot \mathrm{sign}(\mathbf{h}^{(1)}) = \begin{pmatrix} 1 \\ -1 \\ -2 \end{pmatrix} \cdot 0.5 \odot \begin{pmatrix} 1 \\ 1 \\ 0 \end{pmatrix} = \begin{pmatrix} -0.5 \\ 0.5 \\ 0 \end{pmatrix}$$

since $\mathrm{sign}(\cdot)$ is the derivative of the ReLU function. With these errors, we can apply the weight updates. If we assume, for example, that is, $\mu = 1$

$$\mathbf{w}^{(2)} = \begin{pmatrix} 1 \\ -1 \\ -2 \end{pmatrix} - \mu\delta^{(2)}\mathbf{h}^{(1)} = \begin{pmatrix} 2 \\ 0 \\ -2 \end{pmatrix} \tag{1.106}$$

and for the bias of the output layer, the update is

$$b^{(2)} = 0 - \mu\delta^{(2)} = 0.5 \tag{1.107}$$

The hidden layer weight matrix and biases have an update given by

$$\mathbf{W}^{(1)} = \begin{pmatrix} 1 & 1 & -1 \\ 1 & 1 & -1 \end{pmatrix} - \mu\mathbf{x}\delta^{(1)\mathsf{T}} = \begin{pmatrix} 1.5 & 0.5 & -1 \\ 1.5 & 0.5 & -1 \end{pmatrix} \tag{1.108}$$

and

$$\mathbf{b}^{(1)} = \begin{pmatrix} 0 \\ 0 \\ 0 \end{pmatrix} - \mu \delta^{(1)} = \begin{pmatrix} 0.5 \\ -0.5 \\ 0 \end{pmatrix} \tag{1.109}$$

Finally, if we repeat the forward pass with the new parameters, the resulting output is $o \approx 0.9999$ which reduces the error to $\delta^{(L)} = -10^{-4}$.

1.5.4 Summary of the BP Algorithm

The BP algorithm derived above is formulated for a single input sample. The BP of a single error is depicted in Fig. 1.23. In the figure, a training sample is applied to the input, and then the error δ is computed. With it, the BP starts by updating the weights of the output layer with the product between the input to this layer and the error. The process continues with the error BP, which consists of transforming the error with the previous weight matrix and the derivatives of the activations, after which the update of the weights of this layer is applied.

Nevertheless, the gradient with respect to all weights must be computed and averaged for all samples in the batch of training data and then used to update the weights. A general BP algorithm can be summarized as follows. Assume a training set of data $\{\mathbf{x}_1, \dots, \mathbf{x}_N\}$ with corresponding labels $\{\mathbf{y}_1, \dots, \mathbf{y}_N\}$. The machine learning task can be a multiclass classification or a multitask regression. Here, without loss of generality, all data is used in a BP step, but later the concept of minibatch is discussed where the dataset is broken into training subsets, which generally improves the training results.

The first step will be the forward step, where all training data is applied to the NN, and all outputs are computed. In particular, we compute vectors $\mathbf{z}_i^{(l)}, \mathbf{h}_i^{(l)}$ for al layers and input samples $\mathbf{x}_i$, output $\mathbf{o}_i$, and output errors $\delta^{(L)}(\mathbf{x}_i, \mathbf{y}_i) = \mathbf{o}_i(\mathbf{x}_i) - \mathbf{y}_i = \delta_i^{(L)}$ corresponding to all input samples.

This error can be backpropagated with Eq. (1.104), that is, we compute $\delta_i^{(l-1)} = \mathbf{W}^{(l)}\delta_i^{(l)} \odot \varphi'\left(\mathbf{z}_i^{(l-1)}\right)$ for all samples. Once the error is backpropagated to layer l, one can apply an

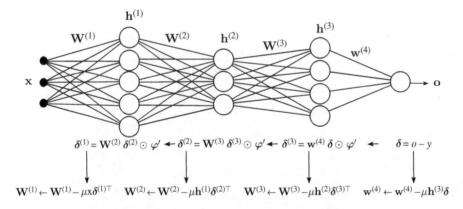

Figure 1.23 Illustration of the BP procedure in a binary multilayer perceptron with three hidden layers and an input of three dimensions. The biases are not depicted in the figure.

update to this layer as

$$\mathbf{W}^{(l)} \leftarrow \mathbf{W}^{(l)} - \mu \sum_{i=1}^{N} \mathbf{h}_i^{(l-1)} \boldsymbol{\delta}_i^{(l)^\top}$$
$$\mathbf{b}^{(l)} \leftarrow \mathbf{b}^{(l)} - \mu \sum_{i=1}^{N} \boldsymbol{\delta}_i^{(l)} \qquad\qquad (1.110)$$

where the update term is always equal to the input to this layer (or the output of the previous one) times the error. The bias term has the same treatment, where it can be assumed that the input that goes through this parameter is a constant equal to 1. For the first layer, with $l = 1$, the input is $\mathbf{h}_i^{(0)} = \mathbf{x}_i$.

This is the basic procedure for the training of an MLP. This procedure is nevertheless applied to optimize the NN using the ML criterion with any suitable likelihood function of the output. This procedure is illustrative of the strategy applied to the optimization of other structures, in particular, the convolutional NNs introduced in Chapter 4 or the recurrent NNs introduced in Chapter 5.

Example 1.5.4 Two common toy examples to play with NNs are the *XOR* and the *CIRCLE* binary problems depicted in Fig. 1.24. The output corresponds to a Bernoulli likelihood. In the experiments, we train and test two NNs, both with an input layer of two nodes, corresponding to the dimensions of the input data, and two hidden layers, with 40 and 10 nodes, respectively. One NN uses logistic activations in all the nodes, while the other one uses ReLU activations in the hidden nodes. The results and training parameters are depicted in Figs. 1.25 and 1.26. For the XOR problem, with 200 samples per class, the ReLU activations seem to solve the problem in a more accurate way, with a slightly lower validation error. The convergence of this NN is also much faster than the one with logistic activations in the hidden nodes. The same effect in the convergence can be seen in the CIRCLE problem, with 250 samples per class, where again the ReLU activations achieve a slightly lower error in the validation dataset.

Further experiments are proposed with this NN and its corresponding notebook in the problems section.

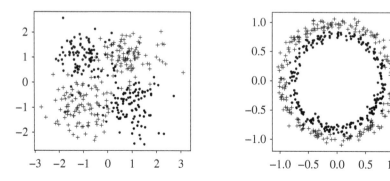

Figure 1.24 The *XOR* and the *circles* toy problems.

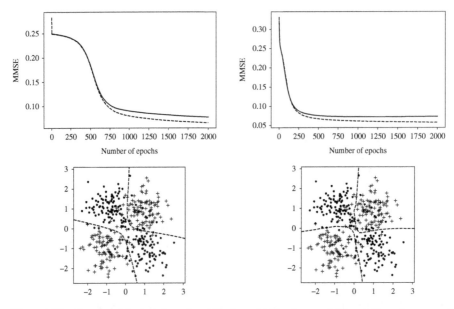

Figure 1.25 Results of the training of an NN of two hidden layers of 40 and 10 nodes, respectively, with the XOR example. The upper left pane corresponds to the training (dashed line) and validation MMSE for an NN with logistic activations in all layers and $\mu = 0.8$. The upper right pane shows the results for ReLU activations in the hidden layers and logistic activations at the output, and $\mu = 0.1$. The lower panes show the validation data and the constructed classification boundaries

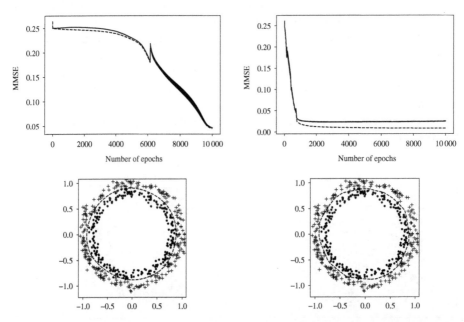

Figure 1.26 Results of the training of an NN of two hidden layers of 40 and 10 nodes, respectively, with the CIRCLE example. The upper left column corresponds to the training (dashed line) and validation MMSE for an NN with logistic activations in all layers and $\mu = 0.5$. The upper right pane shows the results for ReLU activations in the hidden layers and logistic activations at the output, and $\mu = 0.5$. The lower panes show the validation data and the resulting classification boundaries.

1.6 Conclusion

The multilayer perceptron is the earliest form of deep learning that ever appeared, but it establishes the basics of the training procedures applied to any deep learning structure.

The concept of neuron is an idea that roughly reproduces the structure of a biological neuron, though the dynamics of an artificial neuron are very simplistic compared to the dynamics of a biological neuron. Nevertheless, this simple idea is able to implement powerful machine learning structures, as the multilayer perceptron summarized in this chapter. The first activation ever to be applied to a neuron is the sigmoid, but later it has been seen that simpler mathematical operations produce good results in an MLP. Namely, in present days, the most used nonlinear operation is the ReLU and its generalizations. The output layers usually contain activations that provide a probabilistic interpretation. While the first criterion to optimize an MLP is the MSE, we have seen that, when the output activation is a sigmoid, this criterion has points with vanishing gradient, which may make a gradient descent algorithm to stall.

In particular, we choose sigmoidal activations to represent the conditional probability of a training output given the corresponding input patterns, that is, its likelihood. We have seen likelihoods for binary outputs (Bernoulli) or multiclass outputs (Multinoulli) that lead to optimization criteria that do not show the risk of stalling in a point of vanishing gradient. Besides, in regression, we may use linear activations. The interpretation of these activations is given by the modeling of the regression error as a Gaussian distribution, which leads to a log-likelihood that is estimated via these linear outputs.

The BP algorithm summarized here is a powerful way to implement the ML criterion in an MLP. The chain rule of calculus is used to derive a general procedure to implement a gradient descent algorithm to the weights of the MLP that computes an error term from the derivative of the cost function that is later transformed back through the MLP weights. This transformed error term is used to iteratively update the NN.

Problems

1.1 *Change the parameters of Example 1.2.1 in order to*
1. *Decrease and increase the separability of the data.*
2. *Increase or decrease the radius of the sphere R containing the data.*
3. *Produce nonseparable data.*
What is the effect of the number of iterations in each case?

1.2 *Obtain the derivatives of sigmoid functions in Eqs. (1.15) and (1.18) provided in Eqs. (1.16) and (1.19)*

1.3 *Obtain the derivations of the MMSE algorithm for the perceptron when the activation is the logistic function in Eq. (1.18) and when the activation is linear, that is, $f(\mathbf{x}) = \mathbf{w}^{\mathsf{T}}\mathbf{x} + b$.*

1.4 *Modify the code of Example 1.2.2 in order to use the logistic and the linear activations whose corresponding algorithms are derived in Exercise 1.3.*

1.5 *Modify the code of Example 1.2.2 to run in batch mode, that is, by using the update rules described in Eqs. (1.24) and (1.25). Plot a graph with the evolution of the errors of the batch algorithm and the algorithm that updates the weights one sample at a time. What are the conclusions that can be extracted from the differences between both errors?*

1.6 *Reproduce Example 1.3.1 but using ReLU activations, where the parameters are (I. Goodfellow et al. 2016).*

$$\mathbf{W} = \begin{bmatrix} 1 & 1 \\ 1 & 1 \end{bmatrix}, \quad \mathbf{w} = \begin{bmatrix} 1 \\ -2 \end{bmatrix}, \quad \mathbf{b} = \begin{bmatrix} 0 \\ -1 \end{bmatrix} \tag{1.111}$$

What is the effect of multiplying $\mathbf{W}$ and $\mathbf{b}$ by a large scalar (e.g. $a = 10$ as in the example)?

1.7 *Equation (1.82) gives the maximum likelihood cost function for regression where the error is assumed to be Gaussian and independent across elements of the output.*

1. *Derive a general expression for this likelihood that does not assume that the error components are independent.*
2. *Assume that a prior distribution exists for the weight matrices. Using this expression, write a posterior distribution for these weights. By applying a log-posterior maximization criterion rather than the ML, prove that the cost function takes the form*

$$\sum_{i=1}^{N} \left\| \mathbf{y_i} - \mathbf{W}^{(L)\top} \mathbf{h}^{(L-1)} \right\|^2 + \sigma^2 \|\mathbf{W}\|_F^2 \tag{1.112}$$

if the prior is a Gaussian distribution over all weights that assumes independence across terms.

1.8 *Derive expressions for the binary MLP activation like the ones in Eqs. (1.62) and (1.63) but for the case where the label takes values -1 and 1.*

1.9 *(Cross entropy in binary classification) The loss function for multiclass classification is shown in Eq. (1.76). By particularizing the multiclass classification to two classes and using the cross-entropy criterion, find a binary loss function equivalent to the one in Eq. (1.64) by using unnormalized probability functions as activations.*

1.10 *By applying the procedure in Eq. (1.100), prove the general BP step in Eq. (1.104).*

1.11 *In example 1.5.4 we present an NN with two hidden layers and its test with two different problems and activations. Modify that example to see the result of changing the number of layers and hidden nodes. In particular, by changing parameter D in the notebook, test the NN with only a hidden layer of 10 nodes and 100 nodes. Comment on the aspect of the classification boundary and error. Try then an NN with three layers. What are the differences in convergence time and validation error with respect to the NN of 10 nodes?*

1.12 **(Cross validation of the number of epochs)** *Use the notebook of example 1.5.4 to write a script able to validate the number of epochs. To this end, save the set of parameters of the NN at each epoch. Keep the set of parameters that minimize the validation error. Check the error rate in a separate test set and check whether this is the best choice. Repeat this for a training set of only 100 samples and a validation set of 10 samples. Compare the results.*

1.13 **(Cross validation of the number of layers and nodes)** *Work out a script to validate the number of nodes and layers for both the XOR and the CIRCLE problems when the number of training data is 400 samples and for a validation set of 100 samples. Try the test error in a separate set of 1000 samples.*

2

Training Practicalities

2.1 Introduction

In this chapter, it is assumed that the reader is familiar with the fundamental, classic concepts of DL. Namely, Chapter 1 reviews the concept of neuron, the structure of a NN and associated functions like the ReLU, the softmax, the criteria used for the optimization of a NN, and the backpropagation algorithm, which should be connected with the concepts of gradient descent (GD) and overfitting, which is discussed below. Therefore, the reader is able to construct a basic learning machine and train it. Nevertheless, the training of a machine has certain particularities, among them, overfitting or local minima problems, low training speed, or others. These difficulties can be properly addressed by the use of additional training techniques that help to ease the learning process of a machine.

Under the above prerequisites, the present chapter is intended to introduce the reader to these techniques. First, the concept of generalization and overfitting is introduced, as overfitting is a phenomenon that is inherent to any learning machine, and it is particularly important in DL when the models to be trained have a large number of parameters. The overfitting is usually controlled by controlling the expressive capacity of the machine, which is achieved by the use of the so-called regularization techniques.

First, it must be noticed that the gradient descent is initiated from an arbitrary point, that is, from arbitrary values of the parameters. It is obvious that not all initial values are adequate. This chapter presents the two main methods to properly initialize the NN parameters.

A common element in DL is the use of normalization techniques. They are necessary to have a set of features that are scaled in the same range of values. This makes the parameter optimization more efficient since normalization eases the machine from the burden of adapting its parameters to features of different scales. This would force the parameters associated with different features to converge to different scales associated with different dynamic ranges and average values, which, in turn, can lead to convergence difficulties.

Finally, it is common to modify the gradient descent procedure in order to speed it up through the use of features that modify the speed and direction of the parameter update vector with respect to the one produced by the gradient only.

Deep Learning: A Practical Introduction, First Edition.
Manel Martínez-Ramón, Meenu Ajith, and Aswathy Rajendra Kurup.
© 2024 John Wiley & Sons Ltd. Published 2024 by John Wiley & Sons Ltd.
Companion website: https://github.com/DeepLearning-book

2.2 Generalization and Overfitting

The whole purpose of training a learning machine is to achieve the best possible accuracy in a test sample, not previously seen by the training algorithm. If the training procedure is designed so it just minimizes a loss function over the training data, this may compromise the test performance. It is desired that the training dataset contains enough information about its structure, and this information is what one wants to transmit to the NN. Nevertheless, the information about the structure of the data is always limited, and this limitation becomes more important as the number of samples decreases. When the data does not contain enough information to represent its distribution, the difference between the performance of the NN during training and test may be significant. For a training dataset with a low number of data, the training error may be arbitrarily low if the complexity or the number of layers and nodes of the NN is sufficiently high. However, the test error rate will be high, as the NN will not be able to learn the distribution of the data. The difference between the training and test errors in an NN with sufficient complexity is called *overfitting*. The ability to obtain a sufficiently low error both in training and test is called *generalization* ability. Let us illustrate this in the following example.

Example 2.2.1 *(Overfitting of a linear classifier)*
Figure 2.1 shows a set of data in two dimensions generated with two Gaussian distributions with equal covariances $\Sigma = \sigma^2 I$ with $\sigma = 0.5$. The Gaussian distributions are centered at points $(-1, 1)$ and $(1, -1)$. Therefore, the optimal classification boundary is a line normal to the line defined by these two points, thus being a line of slope 1 crossing the origin of coordinates. The figure shows the optimal boundary as a dashed line.

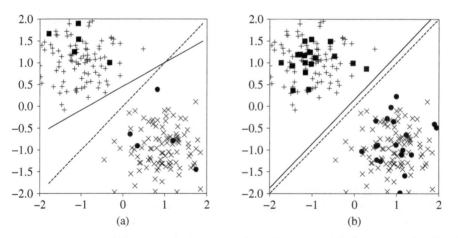

Figure 2.1 A set of two class data is generated where each class is drawn from one of two circularly symmetric Gaussian distributions with $\sigma = 0.5$ centered at $(-1, 1)$ and $(1, -1)$. The optimal classification boundary is represented with a dashed line. A classifier is trained with only the 10 samples highlighted as squares and dots. The resulting classifier is depicted as a solid line that is clearly biased with respect to the optimum. As the number of training data increases, the classifier gets closer to the optimum (b).

A linear classifier $y = \mathbf{w}^\top \mathbf{x} + b$ is trained with the 10 samples highlighted in the figure, where the training criterion is the MMSE. Since the 10 data do not represent sufficiently the structure of the data, the classifier shows a significant bias with respect to the optimal one (Fig. 2.1a). Nevertheless, if the number of training data increases, the classifier gets closer to the optimal one, as can be seen in Fig. 2.1b.

The classifier is trained with an increasing number of data from 2 samples to 100 samples and then tested with 100 new samples not used during the training. Figure 2.2 shows, in logarithmic units, the error rate or fraction of misclassified data e for the training data (dashed line) and test data (continuous line) averaged for 10^4 realizations of the experiment. When the number of training data is low, then the training error is low. Indeed, when the number of samples is 2, the error is of the order $10^{-3.5}$. Conversely, the test error rate for the test is over 0.1. The difference between both errors is the overfitting. If the training data increases, the difference between both errors decreases, and then the classifier is able to generalize.

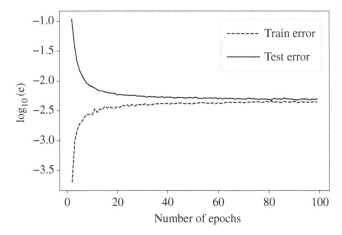

Figure 2.2 Test error rate (continuous line) and train error rate (dashed line) as a function of the number of training samples, for example, Example 2.2.1.

Generalization bounds in NNs are treated in the works by Cao and Gu (2019), Hole (1996) among others. The last work provides, with a given probability, the bounds on the performance of NNs as a function of the NN complexity and the number of training samples. This number has a high impact in the generalization ability of an NN, and authors show that for an NN that is overly complex, the generalization bounds are good as long as the number of training samples is high enough.

2.2.1 Basic Weight Initializations

With the use of the BP algorithm, it is straightforward to code a procedure to train an MLP given a set of input data. The easiest way to program it consists of computing the gradient of the cost function with respect to the weight matrices for each one of the samples. The very first step of training consists of assigning initial values to the weights of the MLP. The techniques may slightly vary depending on the kind of activations used, but all of them assume implicitly that the optimal weights are distributed with a given probability that is centered around the origin.

If one initializes all weights to zero, the inputs to all activation functions will be zero. If the output layer contains sigmoidal activations modeling a Bernoulli or Multinoulli probability mass function, then the outputs will be uniform. For the case of a Bernoulli, the activation will show an output of 0.5, and for the case of a Multinoulli, the activations will be $1/K$. The entropy of the output is then maximized, which can be interpreted as that initially the uncertainty of the NN is maximized. This may not work properly in the BP. Indeed, once the error term of the first layer is computed, it is back-propagated to the previous layers. As a result, as the last layer has weights initialized to zero, the transformed error term will be simply zero and during the first update, only the last layer is updated, and all values of the weight matrix will be low. In the second iteration, only error terms of layer L and $L-1$ will be different from zero, but the one for $L-1$ will be low, thus producing a low update speed and possibly a local minimum solution.

In order to improve the results, it is advisable to start with random values in the weights. This may also pose problems to the training. If the values are too small, we may encounter the same difficulties as above, while if the values are too high, in these cases where the hidden activations are sigmoidal, all of them will be showing values close to 1 or to zero, and with derivatives close to zero, which will stall the training as well. While the problem is partially solved with the use of ReLU units, a more effective initialization can be applied that depends on the type of activation and the size of each layer (Mishkin and Matas 2015). These are the activation aware initializations, namely the Xavier (Glorot and Yoshua Bengio 2010) and He initializations (He et al. 2015) described below.

2.2.2 Activation Aware Initializations

Xavier Glorot and Yoshua Bengio proposed in Glorot and Yoshua Bengio (2010) an optimal initialization for sigmoidal activations. This initialization consists of applying random values to the weights of layer l distributed using a Gaussian distribution with standard deviation $\sigma = \frac{1}{\sqrt{D_{l-1}}}$, that is, the variance of the distribution is set as the number of nodes of the previous layer. This is commonly known as the Xavier initialization. They experimentally show that this simple initialization produces good results in NNs with logistic and hyperbolic tangent activations. Authors provide reasoning about the adequacy of their initialization, but they agree that many effects remain not understood. Nevertheless, He et al. (2015) show that this initialization does not produce adequate results when the used activations for the hidden layers are ReLU, since they are not symmetric. They proposed a modified initialization (known as He initialization) with standard deviation $\sigma = \sqrt{\frac{2}{D_{l-1}}}$. In their work, they test a NN with 30 layers and ReLU activations where their initialization results in convergence, but where the results with the Xavier initialization show a poor convergence. The reasons for this are not fully understood (Kumar 2017).

2.2.3 MiniBatch Gradient Descent

The standard gradient descent (GD) method, also called batch descent method and defined as the one that uses the whole data to compute the gradient, is quantitatively discussed against the stochastic gradient descent (SGD) (that uses one sample at a time) in Y. A. LeCun et al. (2012). The GD method has several advantages. First, under some assumptions, the convergence of the algorithm is properly understood. Also, the conjugate gradient approach (Shewchuk 1994) can be used to accelerate the convergence.

Nevertheless, the cost function landscape does not usually present a single minimum, but it may have many local minima. A batch gradient descent will converge to the minimum, which is closer to the initial position of the weights, which precludes finding the optimal solution. On the contrary, the use of SGD translates into a poor (often called noisy) estimation of the gradient, so at every iteration, the gradient will point to a different direction that, on average, would be the same as the one computed by the batch method. This turns out to be advantageous because it tends to avoid local minima, and it has been shown to converge to better solutions.

Also, in some structures, if the convergence rate is high enough, the algorithm can be adaptive, this is, if the distribution of the data changes with time (i.e. it is nonstationary), an SGD may track these changes. The disadvantage of the SGD is also inherent to this noisy convergence. Due to this, the convergence is not consistent in variance, that is, while the expected solution of the SGD is the same as the one of the gradient descent if they converge to the same minimum, the SGD will have a variance in the solution that depends on the learning rate.

A natural solution that takes advantage of both methods is the use of mini batches (Møller 1993; Orr 1996). This consists of computing the gradient with a fraction or minibatch of the data, then making an update, choosing another fraction, and repeating the process until convergence. This reduces the noise, which provides a better convergence, and it reduces the risk of local minima. Besides, conjugate descent or second-order methods can be applied when using mini-batches. The methods described below usually take advantage of mini-batch training.

2.3 Regularization Techniques

Any model's overall performance depends on its ability to generalize any new input data from the problem domain. In the case of convolutional neural network (CNN) and other deep learning models, bias error, and variance significantly influence the model's quantitative performance. The bias error is an error from incorrect assumptions in the learning algorithm and performs poorly on a training dataset. The algorithm fails to capture the relevant relations between features and target outputs and causes underfitting due to high bias. On the other hand, variance is an error from sensitivity to small fluctuations in the training set. A high variance may result in modeling the training data's random noise and overfitting. In both these cases, the model does not perform well with new unseen test data. A proper bias-variance trade-off is necessary to develop an optimal model that achieves better generalization. Regularization is an essential technique in machine learning that can prevent the model from overfitting and underfitting by minimizing these two sources of error. We can address underfitting by changing the structure of the model so that it can fit more types of functions for mapping inputs to outputs. It is more common to have an overfit model since it is easier to identify and resolve an underfit model. An overfit model can be diagnosed by either training the network on more samples or changing the model's complexity. The structure and parameters of a model define its complexity. The complexity reduces when there is either a change in the number or the value of weights. The regularization techniques penalize the coefficients of the features so that it will result in a simpler network. For example, in some instances, the regularization coefficient is so high that some weight matrices are nearly equal to zero. Thus, it reduces the significance of each feature by keeping the same number of features.

2.3.1 L_1 and L_2 Regularization

The most popular ways of regularization are L_2 and L_1. The concept underlying regularization is that smaller weights result in simpler models, which helps to minimize overfitting. So, to produce a smaller weight matrix, these methods incorporate a regularization term and add it to the loss function. The L_2 regularization works by adding a norm penalty $\|\mathbf{W}^{(l)}\|_F^2$ to the parameters of each layer (Hoerl and Kennard 1970). This corresponds to the sum of squares of all feature weights to the loss function. The regularization rate λ is the hyperparameter (defined as non-trainable parameter) that weighs the regularization term. The L_2 approach pushes the weight to decrease but never to zero. This strategy works best when all input attributes impact the output and all the weights are the same size (A. Y. Ng 2004).

In the case of L_2 regularization, when our training algorithm tries to minimize the new loss function $J(\theta)$, it will lower both the original loss function $J_{ML}(\theta)$ and the regularization term as

$$J(\theta) = J_{ML}(\theta) + \frac{\lambda}{2} \sum_l \|\mathbf{W}^{(l)}\|_F^2 \tag{2.1}$$

In linear estimators, this is known as also known as ridge regression (Shawe-Taylor and Cristianini 2004; Hastie 2020), and it is a form of Tikhonov regularization (see Tikhonov and Arsenin 1977).

We can calculate the gradient of the new loss function and incorporate it into the update algorithm for the weights in the next step:

$$\nabla_{\mathbf{W}^{(l)}} J(\theta) = \nabla_{\mathbf{W}^{(l)}} J_{ML}(\theta) + \lambda \sum_l \mathbf{W}^{(l)} \tag{2.2}$$

The L_1 regularization, also known as least absolute shrinkage and selector operator (Lasso) regression (Tibshirani 1996), uses another regularization term $\|\mathbf{W}^{(l)}\|_1$, which is the sum of the absolute values of the weight parameters in a weight matrix. Unlike L_2 regularization, this approach assigns zero weight to irrelevant input features and nonzero weight to important input features.

$$J(\theta) = J_{ML}(\theta) + \lambda \sum_l \|\mathbf{W}^{(l)}\|_1 \tag{2.3}$$

The following expression is the result of the derivative of the new loss function obtained by adding the gradient of the previous loss function and the sign of the weight value times λ.

$$\nabla_{\mathbf{W}^{(l)}} J(\theta) = \nabla_{\mathbf{W}^{(l)}} J_{ML}(\theta) + \lambda \sum_l \text{sign}(\mathbf{W}^{(l)}) \tag{2.4}$$

Choosing an appropriate value for λ is necessary to achieve the right balance between low complexity and high accuracy. If a high value of λ is chosen, the solution will be simple, but it will not contain sufficient information from the training data to produce efficient predictions. When the value of λ is too low, the solution becomes increasingly complicated. It retains too much information about the data specificities, and it will not make accurate predictions on new data.

2.3.2 Dropout

Dropout regularization is a method in which specific neurons are deactivated randomly with probability p during training (N. Srivastava et al. 2014). These randomly picked neurons are dropped out and temporarily removed from the network for the current forward pass, and no weight updates are made on the backward pass. During dropout, the remaining neurons will search for alternative paths to pass the information and provide predictions for the missing neurons. As a result, the network learns separate internal representations, making it less sensitive to the specific weight of the neurons. A network of this type is more generic and helps to minimize overfitting. For example, in Fig. 2.3a, the NN is fully connected; hence, all the neurons are active. While using this model for training, some neurons tend to memorize the patterns within the training data. Hence, without dropout, the model does not generalize well to the test data. In Fig. 2.3b, dropout enhances the sparsity of the network. This drives neurons to extract robust features from training data and also aids in eliminating co-adaptations across neurons, allowing each neuron to function more independently.

In this section, the dropout is formulated for the dense NNs presented in Chapter 1, but the formulation can be straightforwardly adapted for any structure, in particular for the convolutional models presented in Chapter 4.

The training of a NN with dropout is performed the following way. At each layer, a vector $\mathbf{r}^{(l)}$ with binary components $r_j^{(l)} \sim Bernoulli(p)$ is drawn at random from a Bernoulli distribution. This vector acts as an inhibitor for the nodes such that the forward operation of this

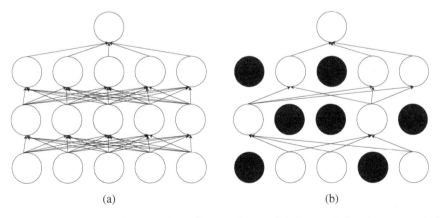

(a)   (b)

Figure 2.3 The network connections of a neural network before and after dropout regularization. (a) Before dropout and (b) after dropout.

layer becomes

$$\tilde{\mathbf{h}}^{(l)} = \mathbf{r}^{(l)} \odot \mathbf{h}^{(l)}$$
$$\mathbf{z}^{(l+1)} = \mathbf{W}^{(l+1)\mathsf{T}}\tilde{\mathbf{h}}^{(l)} = \mathbf{b}^{(l+1)}$$
$$\mathbf{h}^{(l+1)} = \phi\left(\mathbf{z}^{(l+1)}\right) \tag{2.5}$$

This iteration is repeated in all layers. The values of $\mathbf{r}^{(l)}$ are drawn once and kept constant for all elements of a given mini-batch of data. Then the backpropagation is applied to the network by using hidden outputs $\tilde{\mathbf{h}}^{(l)}$ instead of the originals. This prevents nonselected nodes from having their weights updated. New vectors $\mathbf{r}^{(l)}$ are then generated and the operation is repeated for all data mini-batches until the end of the training.

A NN trained like that is equivalent to training 2^n different NNs, where n is the total number of nodes of the original NN. Therefore, the test should be performed by averaging the outputs of these NNs. However, this is not feasible because 2^n is usually a very large number. An approximation to this ensemble training consists of scaling the weights of every node by factor p. The interpretation of this is that if a node is retained during training with probability p, the *expected* output of this node is the same as the actual output at test time.

The dropout is usually combined with max-norm regularization, which is a form of regularization that imposes that the maximum norm of the weight vector associated with each node must be lower than a given constant. This constant must be cross-validated during the training. This strategy usually improves the results over the generalization achieved by dropout only.

2.3.3 Early Stopping

It is a regularization strategy in which one part of the training set is utilized as a validation set, this is, the model's performance is measured using it (Bishop 2006). The network fits the training data for each iteration and tests the model on the unseen validation data. If the validation error worsens or remains the same for a particular number of iterations, the model's training immediately stops. Early stopping refers to this technique of stopping the model's training before it reaches the lowest training error (Prechelt 1998). Overfitting during training causes the training error to decrease steadily, while the validation error also reduces until a point and rises hereafter. Even if training continues after this moment, early stopping effectively returns the set of parameters used at this stage and is thus comparable to terminating training at that point. So, the final model will have the lowest variance and better generalization. In contrast to L_1 and L_2 regularization, early stopping takes less training time. It is usually integrated into the experiment using the callbacks offered by popular frameworks such as Pytorch, Keras, and TensorFlow.

2.3.4 Data Augmentation

Data augmentation refers to generating new training data samples and increasing the diversity of the original dataset. In the case of images, primary data augmentation is done by performing geometric transformations on data. Cropping, flipping, zooming, translations, and blurring specific pixels in the original image generate the new image instances as shown in Fig. 2.5. Though geometric transformations can fix the positional biases in training data, the lighting biases can only be fixed using color space transformations. Another quick color space manipulation is to decrease or increase the pixel values by a constant value to change highly bright or dark images. Another modification is to limit pixel values to a specific minimum or maximum value. Deep learning-based data augmentation employs GAN (Ian Goodfellow et al. 2020) and feature space augmentations. Generative modeling is the process of constructing fake instances from a dataset that preserves comparable features to the original set. GANs can create new training data, resulting in more robust classification models. Feature space augmentation is commonly done using autoencoders and CNNs. Autoencoders extract latent representations and add noise to them so that it results in the transformation of the data. In the case of CNN, feature space augmentation can be accomplished by separating the vector representations. Consequently, adding more data will make it more difficult for the network to drive the training error to zero. The resultant model has reduced variance and more generalization capability on test data (Taylor and Nitschke 2018).

Example 2.3.1 *(Image data augmentation)*

In this example, the CIFAR10 database (Krizhevsky 2009) is used to perform data augmentation to artificially increase the size of the training data. The CIFAR-10 dataset contains 60,000 images at low resolution as shown in Fig. 2.4, and they are in color, so each image has three channels corresponding to the R, G, and B colors. The images are labeled in 10 different classes or categorical values, corresponding to the objects that they contain, which are airplane, automobile, bird, cat, deer, dog, frog, horse, ship, and truck. They are divided

Figure 2.4 Some images from the CIFAR10 dataset in their original resolution of 32 × 32 pixels.

in 50,000 images for training and another 10,000 for test. Here additional training images are created by using geometric operations with rotation range of 359°, horizontal flip, width shift range of 0.1, height shift range of 0.1, and zoom range equal to 0.1. A few sample images after this data augmentation are shown in Fig. 2.5.

Figure 2.5 Data augmentation on the CIFAR10 dataset.

2.4 Normalization Techniques

The main aim of normalization is to create a set of features that are on the same scale as each other. When the data is not normalized, it makes the network drastically harder to train and decreases its learning speed.

Hence, normalizing inputs to the model aids in improving model performance. However, normalizing the inputs to intermediate layers is more challenging than normalizing the model's inputs since the activations are dynamic. It is also computationally expensive to repeatedly calculate statistics over the entire training data.

Batch normalization (Ioffe and Szegedy 2015) is a technique for training deep NNs that standardizes the inputs to a layer for each mini-batch. This technique helps to reduce the internal covariate shift (Shimodaira 2000), which refers to the phenomenon where the distribution of network activations changes across layers due to the change in network parameters during training. Generally, batch normalization layers are inserted after a convolutional or fully connected layer. Since it is done along mini-batches instead of the entire data set, it serves to speed up training and has the effect of stabilizing the learning process (Santurkar et al. 2018).

While performing batch normalization, we first calculate the mean and variance of the mini-batch for the forward pass. The normalization of the data using these mini-batch statistics is performed by subtracting the mean from the data and dividing it by the standard deviation. Finally, two learnable parameters are used to scale and shift this data.

In a CNN (see Chapter 4), at layer l, the linear output $\mathbf{Z}^{(l)}$ is a multidimensional instead of a vector. Let us assume that the batch normalization is performed over a mini-batch of size M. First, the mean for each component of the array is computed as

$$\mathbf{M} = \frac{1}{M} \sum_{i=0}^{M} \mathbf{Z}_i^{(l)} \tag{2.6}$$

Then, for every component $z_{ik}^{(l)}$ of the arrays $\mathbf{Z}_i^{(l)}$, the variance is computed as

$$\sigma_k^2 = \frac{1}{M} \sum_{i=0}^{M} (z_{ik}^{(l)} - m_k)^2 \tag{2.7}$$

and the component is normalized with the mean and the variance

$$\hat{z}_{ik}^{(l)} = \frac{(z_{ik}^{(l)} - m_k)}{\sigma_k^2 + \epsilon} \tag{2.8}$$

where ϵ is a small number added for stability.

The primary drawback of batch normalization is that it requires bigger batch sizes during training to successfully estimate the population mean and variance from the mini-batch since it calculates the batch statistics in every training iteration. It is computationally expensive to operate with high input resolution and train with bigger batch sizes for tasks like object recognition, segmentation, and 3D medical image processing. Second, despite reducing the total number of iterations needed for convergence, the per-iteration time has increased while using batch normalization. Additionally, it is also unsuitable for online learning since the data may arrive individually or in batches during test time. Due to this, there is a change in batch size at every iteration. It leads to poor scale and shift parameter generalization, which eventually reduces the performance. Furthermore, with recurrent NNs (Rumelhart et al. 1986) (see Chapter 5), batch normalization does not perform well. The issue is that these networks would require distinct parameters β and γ for each timestep in the batch normalization layer. Since they have a recurrent relationship to earlier timestamps adding a batch normalization layer increases complexity during training. Later, in the following years, several alternatives such as layer normalization (J. L. Ba et al. 2016), instance normalization (Ulyanov et al. 2016), group normalization (Y. Wu and He 2018), and many others were introduced to mitigate the drawbacks of batch normalization.

During batch normalization, statistical parameters are calculated for both the batch and the spatial dimensions (height and width of the image). In contrast, the mean and variance are calculated for all channels and spatial dimensions during layer normalization. Hence, eliminating reliance on batches improves the drawbacks of batch normalization and makes it easier to use with recurrent structures.

Instance normalization, also known as contrast normalization, was used instead of batch normalization for real-time image generation for style transfer (Jing et al. 2020). The normalization method allows the elimination of instance-specific contrast information from an image while performing style transfer. It normalizes over the width and height of a single sample's feature map. As a result, this minor modification to the stylization structure results in a large qualitative improvement in the generated images. Furthermore, unlike batch normalization, instance normalization can be implemented at test time as it is not dependent on mini-batch.

Group normalization divides the channels into groups, computes mean and variance along spatial dimensions, and a group of channels. The number of groups G is a hyperparameter that is normally necessary to partition channels C. When $G = C$, indicating that each group has just one channel, group normalization becomes instance normalization; when $G = 1$, it becomes layer normalization. Hence, group normalization interpolates between layer and instance normalizations. Layer normalization assumes that all channels in a layer contribute equally. Group normalization, on the other hand, is more adaptable since it enables different distributions to be learned for each group of channels. It is also superior to instance normalization, which fails to utilize channel dependency and only normalizes across each sample for each channel.

2.5 Optimizers

The optimization of convolutional structures (Chapter 4), as well as the MLP in Chapter 1, has been described above as a simple gradient descent where the optimizer computes an approximation to the gradient of the cost function and then updates the weights in the direction opposite to this gradient with the purpose of moving it to a position closer to a cost function minimum. This method was first described in Robbins and Monro (1951), and it has been used in a myriad of different learning machines. The scholarship about the topic tends to distinguish between GD, where the gradient is estimated with the whole batch of data, and SGD where the gradient is estimated based on the use of one sample at a time (Y. A. LeCun et al. 2012).

Probably, the first learning machine to use an SGD approach was the Adaline, introduced in 1960 by Widrow and Hoff (1960). The device (Fig. 2.6) had essentially the structure of a neuron with a sign detector as nonlinear activation, and it was similar to the perceptron, except that this device used a gradient descent in its training. The LMS algorithm, summarized in Section 1.2.4, became universally used in linear adaptive filtering structures (S. Haykin 1996). While that form of gradient descent was very simplistic, the more complex form of gradient descent method called backpropagation, introduced in Sections 1.5.3 and 4.3.2, has been used with great success in many NN approaches and structures (see, for example, Y. LeCun et al. (1989), Geoffrey E. Hinton and R. R. Salakhutdinov (2006) or Graves et al. (2013) as examples of highly successful contributions).

Although gradient descent methods have been widely used in the DL literature, there is a need for speeding up the learning processes, mainly when the structures are highly complex and when a large number of data is used for the training. Also, these methods tend to have decreased performance when the input data is noisy. Gradient descent is essentially based on a first-order approximation of the cost function around the parameter vector. Second-order methods, or methods that, roughly speaking, use a second-order approximation of the cost function surface through the computation of the Hessian matrix of the cost function (D. C. Liu and Nocedal 1989; Byrd et al. 2011; Bollapragada et al. 2018) were introduced in

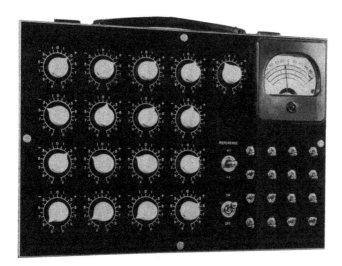

Figure 2.6 Photograph of the Adaline developed at the Stanford Electronics Laboratory at the University of Stanford in 1960. This is possibly the first electronic learning device to use a gradient descent approach. Source: Widrow and Hoff (1960).

machine learning to speed up the process, although they may be ill-posed in situations with many data or parameters and, in general, they require a higher computational power. Therefore, in the last decade, some first-order approximations have been proposed that became very popular among DL practitioners. The methods are summarized later.

2.5.1 Momentum Optimization

The momentum optimization (B. T. Polyak 1964) can be understood if one thinks of the gradient descent as a particle that moves over the surface of the error in the direction of the steepest descent. If we ignore the aspects related to the position, velocity, and acceleration units, the gradient can be thought of as an instantaneous change in the velocity of the particle. If the gradient is zero, the particle will not move.

This mechanical analogy is useful for interpreting momentum optimization. Assume that the particle has a certain mass and that at every update, the optimizer gives an impulse to the particle, thus increasing its speed. Assume that the particle has an initial velocity vector $\mathbf{v}_0$, and assume without loss of generality that the set of weights to update are arranged in a vector $\mathbf{w}$. If a gradient $\nabla_{\mathbf{w}} J(\mathbf{w})$ is computed with respect to a mini-batch of training samples, the particle velocity at optimization iteration k can be written as

$$\mathbf{v}_k = \mathbf{v}_{k-1} - \mu \nabla_{\mathbf{w}} J(\mathbf{w}_k) = \mathbf{v}_0 - \sum_{k'=0}^{k} \mu \nabla_{\mathbf{w}} J(\mathbf{w}_{k'}) \tag{2.9}$$

The gradient plays the role of acceleration, and the integral of this quantity determines the relative position from a given initial one. Notice that, in this situation, if the gradient has always the same sign, the particle accelerates. Therefore, we need to model a viscous friction component proportional to the speed, so that when no impulses are applied to the particle, its velocity will asymptotically vanish. The model of this particle decreases its velocity in a quantity proportional to itself at every iteration. This is

$$\mathbf{v}_k = \gamma \mathbf{v}_{k-1} - \mu \nabla_{\mathbf{w}} J(\mathbf{w}_k) \tag{2.10}$$

The position of the particle at iteration k is the integral of the above velocity, this is

$$\mathbf{w}_{k+1} = \mathbf{w}_0 + \sum_{k'=0}^{k} \mathbf{v}_{k'} = \mathbf{w}_k + \mathbf{v}_k \tag{2.11}$$

This produces a convergence that is more stable than the original SGD optimization because the particle tends to keep a direction similar to the one of the previous step, and the changes are parsimonious.

2.5.2 Nesterov-Accelerated Gradient

When using the momentum optimization, if the particle arrives at the minimum, it will not stop until the gradient changes its direction. At this point, it will go back, and it will keep moving with a vanishing oscillatory movement. It is desirable to modify this algorithm so that when the oscillation appears, it vanishes faster. The Nesterov-accelerated gradient descent tackles this problem by looking at the gradient one step ahead. Assume that at a given point, the velocity vector is $\mathbf{v}_k$. With this velocity, the update of the weight vector would be

$$\tilde{\mathbf{w}}_{k+1} = \mathbf{w}_k + \mathbf{v}_k \tag{2.12}$$

The strategy consists of updating the velocity vector with the gradient computed at that position, rather than computing it at the present position. The updating equations are

$$\mathbf{v}_k = \gamma \mathbf{v}_{k-1} - \mu \nabla_{\mathbf{w}} J(\tilde{\mathbf{w}}_k)$$
$$\mathbf{w}_{k+1} = \mathbf{w}_k + \mathbf{v}_k \tag{2.13}$$

Essentially, the algorithm updates the velocity with the gradient ahead of its actual position, which decreases the velocity if this gradient is smaller, thus stopping at the minimum faster than with the momentum gradient. The name of the algorithm is due to Yuri Nesterov, who introduced the algorithm in 1983 (Nesterov 1983), but it was first used and analyzed in deep learning in article by Sutskever et al. (2013).

2.5.3 AdaGrad

The adaptive gradient (AdaGrad) is the basic implementation of a family of subgradient methods presented in algorithm (Duchi et al. 2011) that take into account the geometry of the cost function of previous iterations in order to incorporate them into the optimization. The underlying idea comes from the fact that in gradient descent, when the algorithm encounters features that are dense (i.e. that appear frequently), the update as a response to these features will be faster than for those features that are sparse (i.e. that appear more rarely).

The AdaGrad algorithm adapts the learning rate to each one of the parameters as a function of the norm of the gradient at each one of these parameters. Specifically, the algorithm first computes the gradient with respect to all parameters, and then it computes the accumulated square value of each component of the gradient as follows:

$$\mathbf{g}_k = \mathbf{g}_{k-1} + \nabla_{\mathbf{w}} J(\mathbf{w}_k) \odot \nabla_{\mathbf{w}} J(\mathbf{w}_k) \tag{2.14}$$

Since operator $\odot$ performs an elementwise product of the gradient, the result is a vector containing the square values of the elements of this gradient. Then, this vector is used elementwise to update each one of the parameters $w_{i,k}$ in $\mathbf{w}_k$ as

$$w_{i,k+1} = w_{i,k} - \frac{\mu}{\sqrt{g_{i,k}} + \varepsilon} \left[\nabla_{\mathbf{w}} J(\mathbf{w}_k) \right]_i \tag{2.15}$$

where $\left[\nabla_{\mathbf{w}} J(\mathbf{w}_k) \right]_i = \frac{d}{dw_i} J(\mathbf{w}_k)$ is the ith element of the gradient vector, and ε is a small number that is used for numerical stability.

The Adadelta algorithm (Matthew D. Zeiler 2012) is similar to the AdaGrad one, where the learning rate μ is changed by an average of the squared gradient of the weight. This way, when the gradient is high, this produces a fast convergence, and when the weights are close to the optimum, the convergence gradually slows down, leading to a faster convergence and better stability than SDG.

2.5.4 RMSProp

As pointed out in (I. Goodfellow et al. 2016), however, using a learning rate that accumulates squared gradients from the beginning of the training can produce a very slow learning speed, and then it may be inadequate for deep learning algorithms. Indeed, the AdaGrad algorithm has a learning rate that decreases monotonically with time, which will end up in a learning rate that tends to zero, thus stalling the learning if the number of training epochs is sufficiently large. A variant more suitable for deep learning, where the number of epochs may be considerable, is the root mean square propagation (RMSProp) algorithm, introduced in 2012 by Geoffrey Hinton in a series of deep learning lectures (Geoffrey E. Hinton et al. 2012a). The idea in RMSProp is to allow the algorithm to forget about the squared gradients of remote time instants, which is done through a forgetting factor $\gamma < 1$. The modification of the algorithm is thus very simple, and it consists of computing the accumulated squared gradient through an exponential decay window. This is

$$\mathbf{g}_k = \beta \mathbf{g}_{k-1} + (1 - \beta) \nabla_{\mathbf{w}} J(\mathbf{w}_k) \odot \nabla_{\mathbf{w}} J(\mathbf{w}_k) \tag{2.16}$$

where if $\beta = 1$, the algorithm only takes into account the square value of the last gradient, thus forgetting everything about the past gradients. If $\gamma = 0$, the algorithm is identical to the AdaGrad one.

2.5.5 Adam

The adaptive moment estimation (Adam) algorithm (Kingma and J. Ba 2014) can be seen as a combination of the momentum and the RMSProp algorithms. Specifically, the first algorithm computes the update of the algorithm in a similar way as in (2.10)

$$\mathbf{v}_k = \beta_1 \mathbf{v}_{k-1} + (1 - \beta_1) \nabla_{\mathbf{w}} J(\mathbf{w}_k) \tag{2.17}$$

where $\beta_1 < 1$ plays the role of a forgetting factor or exponentially decaying window. Then, the accumulated squared gradient is computed as in Eq. (2.16) of the RMSProp algorithm.

$$\mathbf{g}_k = \beta_2 \mathbf{g}_{k-1} + (1 - \beta_2) \nabla_{\mathbf{w}} J(\mathbf{w}_k) \odot \nabla_{\mathbf{w}} J(\mathbf{w}_k) \tag{2.18}$$

Then, these two magnitudes are biased

$$\tilde{\mathbf{v}}_k = \frac{\mathbf{v}_k}{1 - \beta_1^k}$$

$$\tilde{\mathbf{g}}_k = \frac{\mathbf{g}_k}{1 - \beta_2^k} \tag{2.19}$$

The justification for this bias is related to its initialization. Assume, for example, that the gradient has a constant value $\mathbf{v}$ in Eq. (2.18). In this case, we want that $\mathbf{v}_k = \mathbf{v}$ at all iterations k, but, by iterating Eq. (2.18), it is straightforward to see that if $\nabla_{\mathbf{w}} J(\mathbf{w}_k) = \mathbf{v}, \forall k$, then $\mathbf{v}_k = \left(1 - \beta_1^k\right)\mathbf{v}$, which asymptotically converges to $\mathbf{v}$ and therefore, it is sufficient by dividing $\mathbf{v}_k$ by $1 - \beta_1^k$ to make it constant.

Finally, each element of the weight vector $\mathbf{w}_k$ is updated as

$$w_{i,k+1} = w_{i,k} - \mu \frac{\hat{v}_{i,k}}{\sqrt{\hat{g}_{i,k} + \varepsilon}} \tag{2.20}$$

The authors of the algorithm suggest in Kingma and J. Ba (2014) to set the parameters at values $\beta_1 = 0.9$, $\beta_2 = 0.999$, and $\varepsilon = 10^{-8}$. The robustness of this choice is shown in a variety of experiments. However, in some circumstances, these values may need to be cross-validated.

A variant of this algorithm is the Nesterov-accelerated adaptive momentum estimation (Nadam) algorithm (Dozat and Adam 2016). It is a modification of the Adam optimizer that includes the Nesterov method.

2.5.6 Adamax

In the Adam algorithm, the term $\mathbf{g}_k$ accumulates the history of the squared elements of the gradient, whose square root is later used to inversely proportionally weight the gradient of the parameters. A generalization of the algorithm could be to use an L_p norm, which is the pth power of the components of the gradient. Nevertheless, this method will lead to instability if p is too large, except if p tends to infinity. First, we redefine components $g_{i,k}$ of $\mathbf{g}_k$ by changing power 2 by power p and rewrite it in a convenient way.

$$g_{i,k} = \beta_2^p g_{i,k-1}^p - (1 - \beta_2^p) \left| \frac{dJ(\mathbf{w}_k)}{dw_{i,k}} \right|^p$$

$$= (1 - \beta_2^p) \sum_{j=1}^{k} \beta_2^{p(k-j)} \left| \frac{dJ(\mathbf{w}_j)}{dw_{i,j}} \right|^p \tag{2.21}$$

Then we define update $u_{i,k}$ as the limit when p tends to infinity of the update of its inverse.

$$u_{i,k} = \lim_{p \to \infty} \left((1 - \beta_2^p) \sum_{j=1}^{k} \beta_2^{p(k-j)} \left| \frac{dJ(\mathbf{w}_j)}{dw_{i,j}} \right|^p \right)^{1/p}$$

$$= \max\left(\beta_2^{t-1}\left|\frac{dJ(\mathbf{w}_1)}{dw_{i,1}}\right|, \ldots, \beta_2\left|\frac{dJ(\mathbf{w}_{k-1})}{dw_{i,k-1}}\right|, \left|\frac{dJ(\mathbf{w}_k)}{dw_{i,k}}\right|\right) \qquad (2.22)$$

which leads to the simpler expression

$$u_{i,k} = \max\left(u_{i,k-1}, \left|\frac{dJ(\mathbf{w}_k)}{dw_{i,k}}\right|\right) \qquad (2.23)$$

with what we can construct the Adamax update as

$$w_{i,k+1} = w_{i,k} - \mu\frac{\hat{v}_{i,k}}{u_{i,k} + \varepsilon} \qquad (2.24)$$

The justification of these two equations is left as an exercise for the reader.

Example 2.5.1 (Comparison between SGD and Adam)
In order to compare the standard SGD to the Adam methods, a toy example is constructed where the Beale function is used to simulate a cost function. This bivariate function was introduced by Beale (1955) in order to experiment with different optimization algorithms.

The function is defined as

$$L(w_1, w_2) = (a - w_1 + w_1 w_2)^2 + (b - w_1 + w_1 w_2^2)^2 + (c - w_1 + w_1 w_2^3)^2 \qquad (2.25)$$

with $a = 1.5, b = 2.25, c = 2.2625$. The shape of this function is shown in Fig. 2.7

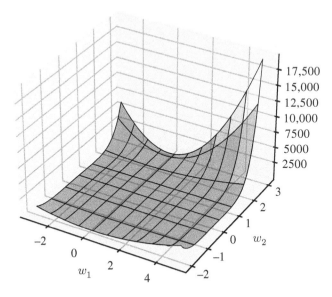

Figure 2.7 Representation of the Beale function.

The function has a minimum around the point $(2.5, 1.5)$ invisible in this figure. Figure 2.8 shows a contour plot of the surface, where the minimum can be seen. The continuous line shows the evolution of the gradient descent during 100 iterations with a value of the learning parameter $\mu = 0.1$. The Adam algorithm (dotted line) has been tested on this surface

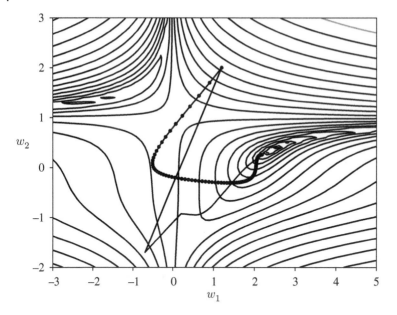

Figure 2.8 Evolution of the gradient descent (continuous line) and Adam (dotted line) algorithms.

with $\mu = 0.3$, $\beta_1 = 0.9$, $\beta_2 = 0.999$, $\varepsilon = 10^{-8}$. It can be seen that the Adam algorithm is more parsimonious in this example, which makes it less prone to instability.

2.6 Conclusion

The idea of gradient descent introduced in Chapter 1 is the key to training most of the DL models presented in this book, and it is widely used as a training procedure in artificial intelligence (AI). Nevertheless, this technique is not sufficient to produce satisfactory test results. First of all, the practitioner has to deal with the overfitting phenomenon that is present in all learning machines and it increases when the complexity of the data increases and when the number of training samples is low in relationship with the number of parameters of a machine (see e.g. (Vapnik 1998)). Also, the likelihood cost function that is used as a criterion to optimize is almost always guaranteed to have multiple local minima and finding one that produces test results sufficiently accurate for the problem at hand is not straightforward. This chapter has presented the main technologies that are in use in order to overcome these difficulties, which are usually applied in the order for this chapter, namely, parameter initialization, data normalization, regularization, and optimization.

Problems

2.1 *In order to experiment with overfitting, construct a binary classification problem. The training data of each class consists of a pair of $N/2$ points drawn from two Gaussian distributions with dimension D with means m_1 and m_2 and covariances $\sigma^2 \mathbf{I}$, where $\sigma^2 = 0.5 \| m_1 - m_2 \|^2$.*

Measure the overfitting of a binary classifier trained as in Example 2.2.1 for various values of N and D between 2 and 1000. The overfitting can be measured as the difference between the training error and the test error.

2.2 *Use the code corresponding to Example 1.5.4 to implement the Xavier initialization of Section 2.2.2. Compare the results to other initializations as a Gaussian random initialization with unitary variance. What other initialization may be used and how do they compare to the Xavier initialization?*

2.3 *Repeat Problem 2.1 but with the use of L_1 and L_2 regularization for various values of λ and comment on the differences.*

2.4 *Justify Eqs. (2.22) and (2.24). For the first one, use the fact that*

$$\lim_{p \to \infty} \left(\sum_{j=1}^{k} |x_i|^p \right)^{1/p} = \max \left(|x_1|, \ldots, |x_k| \right)$$

which is, by definition, the L_∞ norm of vector $\mathbf{x}$ with components $x_1, \ldots, x_k$. The second equation can be justified by analyzing its recursion.

2.5 *Use the code corresponding to Example 2.5.1 to implement and test the rest of the optimizers in Section 2.5.1.*

2.6 *Use the code corresponding to Example 1.5.4 to apply the optimizers implemented in Problem 2.5 in a simple neural network with the data provided in the example.*

3

Deep Learning Tools

3.1 Python: An Overview

Python is a high-level object-oriented dynamic programming language developed by Guido van Rossum and first released on February 20, 1991. It provides a well-defined syntax designed to give emphasis on code readability and to demonstrate concepts in fewer lines of code. Python programming can be done in both interactive mode and script mode. The interactive mode is suitable for testing and debugging a few lines of code. It runs in the Python shell that is accessible from the terminal of the operating system. The script mode is used for larger applications, and it requires you to create a file with a.py extension to run the code.

Python is an extendable language. This property allows interfacing Python with libraries written in other languages such as C/C++. It converts the program into byte code, and any platform can add or modify this code to improve efficiency. Python also allows easy error checking compared to other languages such as C/C++. The datatypes used in Python are dictionaries and arrays, which are more flexible and higher level. The main advantage of Python is that it offers a wide spectrum of libraries that are compatible with multiple platforms such as UNIX (as MAC OS), Windows, and Linux. It provides a vast range of libraries for various fields such as Web Development, Data Science, Machine Learning, Mathematics, and Statistical Programming. Python also supports graphical user interface (GUI) programming across different cross-platform frameworks. The available toolkits for developing GUIs are PyQT5, Tkinter, and WxPython. Python is an open-source programming language that is freely usable and distributable from its official website www.python.org.

The installation of Python is the basic step if you are a Python programmer. There are several methods that can be used for the installation of the Python package. The installation process varies depending on the type of operating system you are working on. Based on whether you have Windows, Mac OS, or Linux/UNIX OS, the step for installation varies. This section gives an overview of the installation of Python on different platforms. The official Python distributions and the different versions can be downloaded from ***python.org***. There are multitudes of specialized packages or distributions depending on the area of interest. For example, there are specific distributions that can be used for applications on

Deep Learning: A Practical Introduction, First Edition.
Manel Martínez-Ramón, Meenu Ajith, and Aswathy Rajendra Kurup.
© 2024 John Wiley & Sons Ltd. Published 2024 by John Wiley & Sons Ltd.
Companion website: https://github.com/DeepLearning-book

embedded systems, machine learning, and the Internet of Things. However, official distributions are preferable if you are starting to learn Python.

In this section, the programming fundamentals of Python are discussed. Here, we cover the understanding of the data types, the complex data structures used, conditionals, loops, functions, and object-oriented programming basics. In further sections of the chapter, we introduce the basic libraries, packages, and functions that are useful for data analysis, data processing, data visualization, and the implementation of machine learning algorithms. Later we move on to advanced libraries for deep learning such as Tensorflow, Keras, and PyTorch. Throughout the chapter, these tools are used to familiarize with the structural framework and working of a basic neural network.

3.1.1 Variables

They are used to store data values in reserved memory locations. The variables are assigned using an equal sign (=) to a data type. Since Python is a dynamically typed programming language, it is not required to declare the variable type before using it. Python's basic variables comprise numbers, lists, tuples, strings, and dictionaries. The variables supported by Python are as follows:

Numbers: The commonly used numbers consist of integers, floating point numbers, and complex numbers.

```
mynum = 1          #assigning an integer.
myfloat = 1.0      #assigning a floating point.
mycomplex = 2+5j   #assigning a complex number.
```

Lists: It is a collection of ordered elements separated by commas, enclosed in square brackets [].

```
a_list = [5, 6, 7, 8] #defining a list.
```

The items in a list can belong to different data types. Hence, the list can also include another list as an element, thereby forming a nested list.

```
b_list = ['hai', 3.5, 10] #a list with different data types
c_list = [5.8, [4,5,9], 15] #a nested list
```

The elements in a list can be extracted by using square brackets. Since Python facilitates negative indexing, the last element of the list can be extracted by using the index [−1] and the second last using [−2] and so on. Further, multiple list elements can be extracted using the slicing operator : (colon).

```
d_list = [1,3,5,7]
print(d_list[2]) #outputs the value 5
print(d_list[-1]) #outputs the value 7
print(d_list[1:3]) #output values [3, 5, 7]
e_list = [1,4,[8,12]]
print(e_list[2][1]) #outputs the value 12 from the nested list
```

Output:

```
5
7
[3, 5]
12
```

The elements of the list can be modified, the order of the values can be changed and each individual value can be replaced even after creating the list. Hence, lists belong to the category of mutable data types. However, due to its mutable nature, Python allocates an extra memory block to allow the extension of its size.

```
f_list = [2, 4, 6, 8, 10]
f_list[0] = 'hai'
print(f_list) #outputs the list ['hai', 4, 6, 8, 10]
```

Output:

```
['hai', 4, 6, 8, 10]
```

Finally, the list also allows the user to add and remove elements easily.

```
g_list = [10, 20, 30, 'first', 'second']
del g_list[4]
print(g_list) # outputs the list [10, 20, 30, 'first']
g_list.remove(20) # removes 20
print(g_list)
h_list = [1, 2, 3]
h_list.extend([4,5]) # add each element to the list and extend it
print(h_list)
h_list.append([4,5]) # adds one element to the end of the list
print(h_list)
```

Output:

```
[10, 20, 30, 'first']
[10, 30, 'first']
[1, 2, 3, 4, 5]
[1, 2, 3, 4, 5, [4, 5]]
```

Tuples: It is an immutable data type that cannot be modified after it is created, unlike lists. Hence, it can be used for memory-efficient programming. All the elements of a tuple are placed inside parentheses () separated by commas. A tuple consists of ordered elements, and it also allows different data types as its elements. The below code shows how to define a tuple and its memory efficiency over a list.

```
import sys
tuple_one = (3,6,7,1.9, 'hai', [3,4], (8,10,12)) # defining a tuple.
list_one = [3,6,7,1.9, 'hai', [3,4], (8,10,12)] # defining a list
print(sys.getsizeof(tuple_one)) #outputs the size of tuple in bytes
print(sys.getsizeof(list_one)) #outputs the size of list in bytes
```

Output:

```
96
112
```

A tuple can also be created without using parenthesis, and each element can be accessed using square tuple elements.

```
tuple_two = 4, 3
u,v = tuple_two
print(u) #outputs 4
print(v) #outputs 3
tuple_three = (5,6,7, 8, 9,10, 11)
print(tuple_three[0]) #outputs 5
print(tuple_three[3:5]) #outputs (8, 9, 10)
tuple_three[0] = 2
#It causes an error.
#The elements in a tuple cannot be changed once it is created.
```

Output:

```
4
3
5
(8, 9)
TypeError: 'tuple' object does not support item assignment
```

Strings: These are sequences of characters enclosed using single or double quotes. The character at each index position can be extracted by using square brackets []. Strings are also immutable and hence cannot be changed after it is created.

```
a = 'hai' #defining a string
b = "hai"
str_one = 'welcome'
str_two = 'all'
str_three = str_two[0] #extracts the character 'a' from position 0
str_four = str_one + str_two
print(str_four) #outputs the concatenation of two strings
```

Output:

```
welcomeall
```

Sets: It represents a group of unordered elements separated by commas inside curly braces {} without any duplicates. A set can have any number of elements belonging to different immutable data types (integer, float, string, tuple, and boolean), whereas mutable data types (lists, dictionaries, and sets) generate an error. Further, it does not allow slicing and indexing since there is no order associated with the elements.

```
set_item = {3,66,87,5,448} #defining a set.
set_item1 = {5, 4.2, 'hai', True, (1, 2, 3)} #set with immutable data
                                   types.
set_item2 = {1, 4, [7, 9]}
#Here [7,9] is a list that is a mutable data type.
#Hence it will cause an error.
```

Output:

```
TypeError: unhashable type: 'list'
```

Dictionaries: It is a collection of elements represented as key-value pairs separated using the colon operator and placed inside curly braces {}. Each element is separated by commas and has a key and a corresponding value associated with it. Here the keys are immutable data types whereas values can belong to any data type. The curly braces without any elements correspond to an empty dictionary. To access each element of a dictionary, the keys are used along with the square brackets. Since dictionaries are mutable, we can easily add and remove element values to it.

```
diction = {'number':23, 'name':'Tom','age': 16} #define a dictionary
the_diction = {} #empty dictionary
print(diction['age']) #outputs the value corresponding to the key 'age'
diction['name'] = 'Harry'
print(diction) #outputs the new dictionary
del diction['age']
print(diction) #outputs the new dictionary
print(diction.pop('name')) #removes the value corresponding to key 'name
                           ' from the dictionary
```

Output:

```
16
{'number': 23, 'name': 'Harry', 'age': 16}
{'number': 23, 'name': 'Harry'}
Harry
```

Example 3.1.1 *(Manipulating lists and dictionaries)*
Create a list, t1= ['Germany', 'George', 'Sam', 'Italy', 30, 90].

1. Extract the zeroth, second, and fifth elements from the given list and print them.
2. Add these elements to the keys in the dictionary, diction1 = 'Country': [], 'Name': [], 'Age': []and print the dictionary.

3.1.2   Statements, Indentation, and Comments

Statements are the executable instructions written in the Python source code. The different types of statements include print statements, assignment statements, conditional statements, etc. In the case of print statements, when Python executes the statement in the command line it outputs a value, whereas an assignment statement does not display the result. Multiline statements represent the line continuation using parentheses (), braces {}, square brackets [], semi-colon (;), and continuation character slash (\).

```
print('Welcome') #print statement
a = 10 #assignment statement
b = 1 + 2 + 3 + \
5 + 6 + 7 + \
8 + 4 #multiline statement
elements=['air', 'water', 'earth',
'wind', 'fire']
```

Output:

```
Welcome
```

A block consists of a group of statements used for a defined task. Python uses indentation to indicate this block of code. Generally in C, C++, and Java curly braces are used to highlight a particular block of code, whereas Python uses whitespaces to indent the statements. The indentation moves the statements to the right using the same number of whitespaces for the same block of code.

```
if a < 0:
    print('Negative number')
elif a == 0:
    print('Neither positive nor negative')
else:
    print('Positive number')
```

Output:

```
Positive number
```

```
if 10
    print('10 is divisible by 2')
        print('10 is a multiple of 2') #Indentation error
```

Output:

```
IndentationError: unexpected indent
```

In Python, single-line comments are denoted using the hash symbol #, whereas, for multiline comments, the # is used before each line. A multiline string enclosed in triple quotes either " or """ is yet another way to represent multiline comments.

```
#The hash symbol is used for single-line comments.
print('Welcome to Python Coding')
"""
The triple quotes denote a multiline comment.
It is commonly used when we need to give a brief description of the code.
"""
print('Welcome to Python Coding')
```

Output:

```
Welcome to Python Coding
Welcome to Python Coding
```

3.1.3 Conditional Statements

In Python, decision-making is done after evaluating certain conditions while executing a program. The 'if' statement is used to evaluate whether the boolean expression is True or False. When the statement is false, the else or the elif statement is executed.

```
a = 1
if a == 2:
    print('Even prime number')
elif a == 3:
    print('Odd prime number')
else:
    print('Neither prime nor composite number')
```

Output:

```
Neither prime nor composite number
```

3.1.4 Loops

They are used to iterate over the same block of code multiple times. The commonly used iterators are for loop and while loop. The for loop iterates over a sequence of numbers until the last element of the sequence is reached. The range function can be called in several ways, while it is used in the for loop. In the first example, it is *range (stop number)*.

```
for i in range(2):
    print(i)
```

Output:

```
0
1
```

Here the format of the range function is *range (start number, stop number)*.

```
for j in range(6,10):
    print(j)
```

Output:

```
6
7
8
```

Finally, in the below example, the range function used in the for loop has the start number, stop number, and increment value.

```
for k in range(2,10,3):
    print(k)
```

Output:

```
2
5
8
```

On the other hand, the while loop executes and iterates over the code, only if the conditional statement is true.

```
a = 1
while a <= 5:
    print(a)
    a = a+1
```

Output:

```
1
2
3
4
5
```

The loop also has control statements such as break, continue, and pass. As shown below, a loop can be terminated using a break statement.

```
num = [2,4,6,8,10]
for i in num:
    if i == 6:
        break
    print(i)
```

Output:

```
2
4
```

The continue statement skips the rest of the loop during the current iteration and proceeds to execute the next iteration.

```
for k in range(5):
    if k == 3:
        continue
    print(k)
```

Output:

```
0
1
2
4
```

A pass statement on the other hand is a null operation used as a placeholder for future functionality.

```
seq = ['h','e','l','l','o']
for j in seq:
    pass
#Acts as a placeholder for code that will be implemented in the future.
#An empty for loop can generate an error.
```

Example 3.1.2   (For loop example for creating patterns)
Use a nested 'for' loop to create a full diamond of stars '*'. Initialize n = 5 to create a diamond that looks like the pattern shown below:

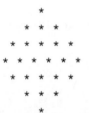

The first step is to use 1 outer loop and 2 nested loops to print the upper triangle. In this case, the outer loop is used to iterate the rows and the first nested loop handles the number of spaces, whereas the second nested loop is used for printing the star patterns. These steps need to be repeated to print the lower triangle. Later, change the n values to see how the diamond grows bigger for larger values of n.

3.1.5 Functions

It is a reusable block of code that is used to perform a specific task. Functions make the code more structured and help to eliminate repetitions. Every function starts with the keyword 'def' followed by a function name. Next, we can either pass the parameters to the function or avoid this step. Following this, the body of the function is defined with an optional return value toward the end.

```python
def addition(a,b): #function name and parameters.
    out = a+b #function body.
    return out #return value of the function.
#Here the function definition ends.
#Note the indentation change from the next line.
a = 10
b = 40
out = addition(a,b)
print(out)
```

Output:

```
50
```

A variable can be defined inside as well as outside the function, which further defines the scope of the variable. When it is defined inside a function, it has a local scope whereas when it is outside the function it has a global scope.

```python
global_name = 'Harrison' #variable with global scope.
def new_func():
    local_name = 'Harry'#variable with local scope.
    print(local_name)
new_func()
print(global_name)
```

Output:

```
Harry
Harrison
```

3.1.6 Objects and Classes

Python uses an object-oriented programming model to design and represent a program using objects and classes. A class is a user-defined design of the object whereas an object is a group of variables and functions that form an instance of the class. This process of declaring an object is called instantiation.

The body of a class consists of two main elements named attributes and methods. Attributes correspond to the properties of an object and methods are the functions that represent the behaviors of an object. For example, we can define class as a prototype of a smartphone that has different attributes such as brand, color, camera, and storage. The methods would be the activities carried out using a smartphone such as making phone calls, sending text messages, playing games, and the object corresponds to the smartphone.

```
class Smartphone: #Defining the object.
    def _ _init_ _(self, brand,storage):
        self.brand=brand #Attribute defining the property of the object.
        self.storage=storage #Attribute defining the property of the
                                                               object.

    def capacity(self): #Method defining the behavior of the object.
        if self.storage >= 512:
            return 'Large Storage'
        elif (self.storage < 512) & (self.storage > 128):
            return 'Average Storage'
        else:
            return 'Low Storage'
phone1 = Smartphone('EyePhone',256)
space = phone1.capacity()

print(phone1.brand)
print(phone1.storage)
print(phone1.brand, ":",space)
```

Output:

```
EyePhone
256
EyePhone: Average Storage
```

In the above example, we have created a class to denote smartphones. Unlike functions that use the 'def' keyword, a class definition is created using the keyword 'class'. This is followed by the name of the class beginning with a capital letter. Next, we have the _init_() method that is used while creating a new instance of this class. This method passes different variables to initialize the state of the object. The first attribute of the _init_() method will always be the variable named self, which is the object calling itself. Meanwhile, in this example, the other two attributes are brand and storage which denote the company and space capacity of the smartphone. The second method is *capacity()*, which returns the extent of storage available depending on the type of smartphone. Next, we create an object named phone1 with the parameters "EyePhone" and 256. Further, the storage capacity of phone1 is checked using the *capacity()* method, and the results are displayed.

Example 3.1.3 *(Defining datasets using classes)*
Let us now look into Example 1.5.4 from Chapter 1 where we use toy datasets to work with a basic neural network using functions. Similarly, in the below code, we use numpy arrays and classes to define these datasets. We first define a class named *data* that generates toy datasets. Our datasets are the xor problem and the circle problem. We define them here using two methods namely *data_xor* and *data_circle*. The two main attributes for both the functions are *self.N* and *self.sigma* corresponding to the number of data per cluster and the standard deviation of the clusters. Additionally, the *data_xor* method has an instance attribute named *classes* that corresponds to the labels of the cluster.

```python
import numpy as np

class Data:
    def _ _init_ _(self, N, sigma):
        self.N=N #Number of data per cluster.
        self.sigma=sigma #standard deviation of the clusters.

    def data_xor(self, classes):
    # Generate 4*N random vectors (gaussian) centered around zero.
        X=self.sigma*np.random.randn(2,4*self.N)
        mean=np.array([[-1,-1, 1, 1],[-1,1,-1,1]]) # define four means
        M=np.ones((self.N,2))*mean[:,0] # Means of the first cluster
        y=np.ones((1,self.N))*classes[0] # Labels of the first cluster
        for i in range(1,4):
            m=np.ones((self.N,2))*mean[:,i] # Means of cluster i
            M=np.concatenate((M,m))      #Concatenate all means
            y=np.concatenate((y,np.ones((1,self.N))*classes[i]),axis=1) #
                                            concatenate labels
        M=M.T
        X=X+M # Add means to the data.
        return X,y

    def data_circle(self):
        theta=np.random.rand(1,self.N)*np.pi*2
        rho=np.random.randn(1,self.N)*self.sigma+1
        X1=rho*np.block([[np.cos(theta)],[np.sin(theta)]]) #circular data
                                          corresponding to class 1

        theta=np.random.rand(1,self.N)*2*np.pi
        rho=np.random.randn(1,self.N)*self.sigma+0.8
        X2=rho*np.block([[np.cos(theta)],[np.sin(theta)]])

        y=np.concatenate((0*np.ones((1,self.N)),np.ones((1,self.N))),
                                        axis=1) # labels
        X=np.concatenate((X1,X2),axis=1)
        return X,y
#The class definition ends here.

np.random.seed(30) # allows to reproduce the same results
N=100; sigma=0.6 #attributes for xor.
N1=250; sigma1=0.05 #attributes for circle.
classes=[0,1,1,0] #attribute for xor.
T=Data(N,sigma) #define the object corresponding to xor data.
T1=Data(N1,sigma1) #define the object corresponding to circle data.
X,y=T.data_xor(classes) #method with instance variable classes.
X1,y1=T1.data_circle() #method without any instance variable.
print(X.shape,y.shape,X1.shape,y1.shape)
```

Output:

```
(2, 400) (1, 400) (2, 500) (1, 500)
```

3.2 NumPy

NumPy is a standard package used in Python for scientific computing. NumPy basically stands for numerical Python and is useful in facilitating advanced mathematical computations and operations using multidimensional arrays and matrices. The operations that are generally dealt with include mathematical, logical, statistical, algebra, selection, sorting, shape-changing operations, and transforms such as Fourier transform, and much more. The base of NumPy packages constitutes *ndarray*. It allows to work around with multidimensional arrays. It can be used to get the shape information and other properties associated with the array. This section explores how we can initialize an array using NumPy, the types of operations that can be performed on an array using the package, and extracting the shape, and axis properties of an array using the package. The main advantage of using NumPy for array operations is that it reduces the need for the usage of loops and is faster as it is based on C.

3.2.1 Installation and Importing NumPy Package

NumPy package can be installed using *pip* or *conda install command* depending on the environment you are working on.

Using the *pip* command, the installation can be done using the following command:

pip install numpy

In Anaconda prompt, the installation of the package can be done using the following command:

conda install numpy

Once the NumPy package is installed, the basic step is to import the package in Python as shown below. You can also check the version of the NumPy package using .__version__ command.

```
import numpy as np
print(np.__version__)
```

Output:

```
1.21.6
```

3.2.2 NumPy Array

Arrays can be initialized in Python using *np.array* command.

There are several attributes associated with NumPy arrays. The size, shape, data type, and number of dimensions of the array can be checked using the package.

array.shape: This gives the shape of the array
array.size: This gives the total number of elements in an array
array.ndim: Number of axes in an array
array.dtype: Gives the datatype of elements in the array

Example 3.2.1 *(NumPy array)*

In the following code, we start with initializing different types of arrays.

A one-dimensional array can be initialized as

```
arr1 = np.array([1,2,3,4]) #intializing a simple array
print(arr1) # printing the 1-d array
```

Output:

```
[1 2 3 4]
```

Next, we define a two-dimensional array as follows:

```
arr2 = np.array([[1,2],[3,4]]) #initializing a 2 dimensional array
print(arr2) # printing the 2-d array
```

Output:

```
[[1 2]
 [3 4]]
```

Using np.array we can also define arrays with different data types as shown below:

```
arr3 = np.array([[1.5, 3.2, 4.5, 3.8],
                 [1.3, 3.2, 5.6, 4.2]]) #initializing a different data
                                                         type array
print(arr3)
```

Output:

```
[[1.5 3.2 4.5 3.8]
 [1.3 3.2 5.6 4.2]]
```

Additionally, NumPy package can also be used to check the shape, size, dimension, and data type of the initialized arrays as shown below:

```
print(arr1.shape, arr2.shape, arr3.shape) #shape of the array
```

Output:

```
(4,) (2, 2) (2, 4)
```

Output:

```
print(arr1.size, arr2.size, arr3.size) # size of different arrays
```

Output:

```
4 4 8
```

```
print(arr1.ndim, arr2.ndim, arr3.ndim) #number of dimensions of the arrays
```

Output:

```
1 2 2
```

```
print(arr1.dtype, arr2.dtype, arr3.dtype) # the data type of array
                              elements
```

Output:

```
int64 int64 float64
```

3.2.3 Creating Different Types of Arrays

NumPy package can be used to define different types of arrays such as arrays with zeros and ones using *np.zeros* and *np.ones* commands. *np.eye* is used for creating an identity matrix, and *np.full* can generate a matrix containing one constant value. You can also define an empty array using *np.empty*. *np.arange* can be used to create arrays containing sequences of numbers. *np.linspace* function work similar to that of *np.arange* but is generally used for creating graphs. This function can create lots of data points within a specified range. *np.arange* command uses a step to generate the sequence, whereas for *np.linspace* the number of data points or elements needed within a range can be specified.

```
mat1 = np.zeros((5,4)) #using the function to create a zero matrix
print(mat1)
```

Output:

```
[[0. 0. 0. 0.]
 [0. 0. 0. 0.]
 [0. 0. 0. 0.]
 [0. 0. 0. 0.]
 [0. 0. 0. 0.]]
```

```
mat2 = np.ones((3,2))   #using the function to create a ones matrix
print(mat2)
```

Output:

```
[[1. 1.]
 [1. 1.]
 [1. 1.]]
```

```
mat3 = np.empty((2,2)) #using the function to create a random empty matrix
print(mat3)
```

Output:

```
[[ 2.04114407e-316  0.00000000e+000]
 [-3.50519043e-210  6.90618343e-310]]
```

```
mat4 = np.eye(3)        #defining an 3x3 identity matrix
print(mat4)
```

Output:

```
[[1. 0. 0.]
 [0. 1. 0.]
 [0. 0. 1.]]
```

```
mat5 = np.full((3,3),2) #creating a matrix containing a constant value
print(mat5)
```

Output:

```
[[2 2 2]
 [2 2 2]
 [2 2 2]]
```

```
mat6 = np.arange(1,50,3) #generating a sequence of data
print(mat6)
```

Output:

```
[ 1  4  7 10 13 16 19 22 25 28 31 34 37 40 43 46 49]
```

```
mat7 = np.linspace(1,50,3) #another way to generate sequence data
print(mat7)
```

Output:

```
[ 1.  25.5 50.]
```

3.2.4 Manipulating Array Shape

The shape of the array can be changed using a few commands. *.ravel* is used to flatten a matrix to array. *.reshape* can modify the shape of the array or matrix as shown in the code example. The transpose of a matrix can be obtained using the *.T* command. Similar to *.reshape*, *.resize* can also be used to modify the shape of the array or matrix. The main difference between the two is that *.reshape* gives a modified array and does not change the original array, whereas *.resize* modifies the original array.

```
ar = np.array([[1,3,4,6,7],[1,5,6,5,4], #initializing an array
           [1,6,2,1,1],[2,4,5,8,3]])
print(ar)
print(ar.shape) #checking the shape of the array
ar1 = ar.reshape((5,4)) #modifying the shape of the array
print(ar1)
print(ar1.shape) #checking the shape of the modified array
```

Output:

```
[[1 3 4 6 7]
 [1 5 6 5 4]
 [1 6 2 1 1]
 [2 4 5 8 3]]
(4, 5)
[[1 3 4 6]
 [7 1 5 6]
 [5 4 1 6]
 [2 1 1 2]
 [4 5 8 3]]
(5, 4)
```

```
ar2 = ar.ravel() #flattening a 2d array to 1d
print(ar2)
print(ar2.shape) #checking the shape of the modified array
```

Output:

```
[1 3 4 6 7 1 5 6 5 4 1 6 2 1 1 2 4 5 8 3]
(20,)
```

```
ar3 = ar.T #taking the transpose of the array
print(ar3)
print(ar3.shape) #checking the shape of the transposed array
```

Output:

```
[[1 1 1 2]
 [3 5 6 4]
 [4 6 2 5]
 [6 5 1 8]
 [7 4 1 3]]
(5, 4)
```

```
ar.resize((2,10)) #using resize to modify the original array
print(ar)
print(ar.shape) #checking the shape of the original array
```

Output:

```
[[1 3 4 6 7 1 5 6 5 4]
 [1 6 2 1 1 2 4 5 8 3]]
(2, 10)
```

3.2.5 Stacking and Splitting NumPy Arrays

NumPy package is useful in doing concatenation and splitting operations. *.hstack* and *.vstack* are the most commonly used stacking methods. Stacking along the rows, that is, along the first axes is done using *.vstack*. *.hstack* can be used to stack along the second axes. *.column_stack* and *.row_stack* are similar commands when stacking 1D arrays to 2D arrays. However, *.column_stack* might work slightly different compared to *.hstack* as shown below. *.r_* and *.c_* can be used for some complex cases where you need to include sequences or ranges.

```
import numpy as np
array1 = np.array([1,2,3,4])
array2 = np.array([5,6,3,1])

ar_horizontal = np.hstack((array1,array2))     # using hstack
print(" Using hstack")
print(ar_horizontal, np.shape(ar_horizontal))
ar_vertical = np.vstack((array1,array2))       # using vstack
print( "using vstack")
print(ar_vertical, np.shape(ar_vertical))
```

```
ar_column = np.column_stack((array1,array2))   # using column_stack
print("Using column_stack: ")
print(ar_column, np.shape(ar_column))

ar_row = np.row_stack((array1, array2))        # using row_stack
print("Using row_stack:")
print(ar_row, np.shape(ar_row))

ar_r = np.r_[4:10,5:16, 0,1,2]                 # using r_
print(ar_r)
ar_c = np.c_[4:10,5:11]                         # using c_
print(ar_c)
```

Output:

```
Using hstack
[1 2 3 4 5 6 3 1] (8,)
using vstack
[[1 2 3 4]
 [5 6 3 1]] (2, 4)
Using column_stack:
[[1 5]
 [2 6]
 [3 3]
 [4 1]] (4, 2)
Using row_stack:
[[1 2 3 4]
 [5 6 3 1]] (2, 4)
[ 4  5  6  7  8  9  5  6  7  8  9 10 11 12 13 14 15  0  1  2]
[[ 4  5]
 [ 5  6]
 [ 6  7]
 [ 7  8]
 [ 8  9]
 [ 9 10]]
```

Similar to stacking the splitting can also be done using NumPy. The two most common commands used for this are the *.hsplit* and *.vsplit* to do splitting along the horizontal axis and vertical axis, respectively. Alternatively, *.array_split* can be used for doing the splitting similarly by specifying the axis.

```
import numpy as np
print("\n using hsplit")
print(np.hsplit(ar_row,2))                      # using hsplit for splitting
                                                along the columns
print("\n using vsplit")
print(np.vsplit(ar_row,2))                      # using vsplit for splitting
                                                along the rows

print("\n using array_split")

print("\n along column similar to hsplit")
print(np.array_split(ar_row,2, axis = 1))       # using array_split command
print("\n along row similar to vsplit")
print(np.array_split(ar_row,2, axis = 0))
```

Output:

```
using hsplit
[array([[1, 2],
        [5, 6]]), array([[3, 4],
        [3, 1]])]

 using vsplit
[array([[1, 2, 3, 4]]), array([[5, 6, 3, 1]])]

 using array_split

 along column similar to hsplit
[array([[1, 2],
        [5, 6]]), array([[3, 4],
        [3, 1]])]

 along row similar to vsplit
[array([[1, 2, 3, 4]]), array([[5, 6, 3, 1]])]
```

3.2.6 Indexing and Slicing

Indexing is used for accessing an array element. In the case of a 1D array, the nth element can be accessed using ar[n] and the rest can be accessed by changing the index value. For a 2D array, the row elements can be accessed by changing the row index and the column elements can be accessed using column index, i.e. ar[i,j] accesses the element located at the ith row and jth column. For higher dimensions, a similar pattern applies.

Slicing allows us to access certain portions of the array. Slicing works similarly to indexing, however, we can use the colon operation to select a range of data.

Example 3.2.2 *(Slicing and indexing)*
In this example, we will be using NumPy arrays to demonstrate different slicing and indexing operations.

Let us initialize a one-dimensional array (array1) as follows:

```
[1 2 3 4]
```

Next, display the elements at different locations. Note that the first element of the array corresponds to index 0 in Python.

```
printing first and fourth elements:
 1 4
```

Compute the sum of the displayed elements, for example:

```
sum of the 2nd and 3rd element:
 5
```

Next, we create another 1D array (array2):

```
[2 3 4 6]
```

Using any stacking operation let us create a two-dimensional array from array1 and array2, for example, using *np.vstack* we can obtain a 2D array (array3) as follows:

```
[[1 2 3 4]
 [2 3 4 6]]
```

Now, use the indexing method to display the individual elements of the resulting 2D array (array3). You can explore different types of indexing such as row, column, and negative indexing to familiarize yourself with these operations.

```
2nd row, 4th element:   6
1st row, 3rd element:   3
last element of 1st row:   4
```

Similarly create another 2D array (array4) as follows:

```
[[1 2]
 [2 3]
 [3 4]
 [4 6]]
```

Let us examine how we can perform a slicing operation on this array. Note that we can do the slicing across individual dimensions to get certain regions of the matrix. Also, the slicing can be simultaneously performed across both dimensions. An example output would be:

```
Slicing a 2D array along a row:
 [[2 3]
 [3 4]
 [4 6]]
Slicing a 2D array along a column:
 [[1]
 [2]
 [3]
 [4]]
Negative slicing 2D:
 [[1 2]
 [2 3]
 [3 4]]
Slicing along both row and column:
 [[1]
 [2]]
```

3.2.7 Arithmetic Operations and Mathematical Functions

NumPy library can be used to perform basic arithmetic and mathematical operations. This helps the user to perform complex functions on a multidimensional array without complications. The different kinds of operations and functions are discussed below:

Arithmetic operations: You can use the package to perform basic arithmetic operations such as addition, subtraction, multiplication, division, remainder, and reciprocal.

```
import numpy as np

a = np.array([1,2,3,4])     # creating two arrays a and b
b = np.array([4,5,1,2])
print(a,b)
add_ab = np.add(a,b)        # using the NumPy addition operation
print("after addition")
print(add_ab)
```

Output:

```
[1 2 3 4] [4 5 1 2]
after addition
[5 7 4 6]
```

While using the np.*reciprocal* function in case of elements larger than 1, the return value is always 0 as this operation comes under integer division.

```
c = b*0.1                       # creating another array by multiplying "b"
                                              with 0.1

rec_b = np.reciprocal(b)    # computing the reciprocal of array b
rec_c = np.reciprocal(c)    # computing the reciprocal of new array c
print("using reciprocal on b and b*0.1")
print(rec_b, rec_c)
```

Output:

```
using reciprocal on b and b*0.1
[0 0 1 0] [ 2.5   2.    10.    5.]
```

You can use *np.pow(a,b)* to compute the power of *a* to *b*. There are other functions such as *np.sqrt* to compute the square root of the array.

```
pow_ab = np.power(a,b)     # computing the power of a to b
print("taking the power of a & b")
print(pow_ab)

sqrt_a = np.sqrt(a)         # computing the square root of a
print("taking the square root of a")
print(sqrt_a)
```

Output:

```
taking the power of a & b
[ 1 32   3 16]
taking the square root of a
[1.          1.41421356 1.73205081 2.
```

When working with complex arrays, the package can be used for getting the real, imaginary, conjugate, absolute, and angle of the elements of the array.

```
zip_obj = zip(a, b)         # lets zip the two arrays to get a complex data
comp = []                    # create an empty list

for a,b in zip_obj:          # use for loop to obtain the elements of arrays
                                            a & b
    c = np.complex(a,b)     # compute a+jb using np.complex function
    comp.append(c)           # append these to the empty list
print("complex array:")
print(comp)

print("real part of the array")
print(np.real(comp))        # getting real part of the complex array
```

Output:

```
complex array:
[(1+4j), (2+5j), (3+1j), (4+2j)]
the real part of the array
[1. 2. 3. 4.]
```

Mathematical functions: The main advantage of this package is the use of trigonometric functions. We can use NumPy commands to do trigonometric operations such as computing the sine, cosine, and tan of different angles arranged in an array. You can also take values of angles in radians, and convert them to degrees or vice versa.

```
import numpy as np
a = np.array([30,45,60,90])     # creating an array of degrees
print(a)
print("\n sin(a) = ")
print(np.sin(np.radians(a))) # convert to radians and print the sine of
                                 it
print("\n tanh(a) = ")
print(np.tanh(np.radians(a))) # convert to radians and print the tanh of
                                 it
```

Output:

```
[30 45 60 90]

 sin(a) =
[0.5          0.70710678 0.8660254  1.         ]

 tanh(a) =
[0.48047278 0.6557942   0.78071444 0.91715234]
[0.3506607 2.6782232]
```

NumPy also provides functions to work around with decimals. *np.around* is used to round the decimal numbers to the desired number of decimal places (the default is 0).

```
b = np.array([0.35066070245,2.67822320434]) # creating an array of
                                       decimal numbers
print(b)

print("\n round of decimal to fourth decimal place:")
print(np.around(b, 4)) #print the round of decimal values to the 4th
                               decimal place
```

Output:

```
round of decimal to fourth decimal place:
[0.3507 2.6782]
```

Similarly, other commands such as *np.floor* and *np.ceil* can be used to specify the type of rounding that can be done based on whether we need to round to the lower value or the upper value.

```
print("\n using floor")
print(np.floor(b))     # use floor command
print("\n using ceil")
print(np.ceil(b))      # use ceil command
```

Output:

```
using floor
[0. 2.]

 using ceil
[1. 3.]
```

NumPy is a basic tool used for handling arrays of different dimensions. It can be used to simplify larger loops, and it helps in several mathematical operations. Here we looked into a few basic commands that can be used as building blocks for creating datasets and models for various machine-learning applications. The extensive information on the wide range of commands can be found in https://NumPy.org/.

Example 3.2.3 *(Neural network with NumPy and classes)*
Again we are going to revisit Example 1.5.4 from Chapter 1. In Example 3.1.3, we define the two datasets as a class. Similarly, we are going to construct a class named *'NeuralNetwork'* for defining the structure of the multilayer perceptron. In both these cases, we are using basic NumPy to construct the code. Through these examples, you can learn various functionalities associated with the NumPy package.

```python
import numpy as np

class NeuralNetwork:
    def __init__(self,D,activation,output):
        # Puts the neural network as a dictionary
        self.NN={"weights":[],"bias":[],"dimensions":[],"activation":[]}
        # D: np. array with the number of nodes in each layer, including
        #                                         input and output
        self.D=D
        # activations: Hidden node activations--'ReLU', 'logistic', '
        #                                     maxOut'
        self.activation=activation
        # output: Output layer activations--'linear', 'logistic', 'softMax
        self.output=output

    def layer(self,Di,Do):
        # Create some structures for the weights and the biases
        # Here we assume that the input is a vector, so the weights are a
        #                                     2D array
        W=np.random.randn(Di,Do)/np.sqrt(Di) #This is simply the Xavier
        #                                     initialization
        b=np.random.randn(1,Do)/np.sqrt(Di)
        return W,b

    def network_structure(self):
        for i in range(self.D.size-1):
            W,b= self.layer(self.D[i],self.D[i+1])
            self.NN["weights"].append(W)
            self.NN["bias"].append(b)
            self.NN["dimensions"]=self.D
            if i<self.D.size-2:
                self.NN["activation"].append(self.activation)
            else:
                self.NN["activation"].append(self.output)
        MLP=self.NN
        return MLP
output_activation="logistic" #define the activation.
hidden_activation="relu" #define the activation.
D=np.array([2,100,1]) #define the number of nodes in each layer.
#define the object and the instance variables.
NN1=NeuralNetwork(D,hidden_activation,output_activation)
#define the method corresponding to the network structure.
neural_net=NN1.network_structure()
```

3.3   Matplotlib

Matplotlib is a powerful Python package created by John. D. Hunter in 2003 for the task of data visualization. It is an open-source and cross-platform plotting library for implementing 2D graphics across Python and various interactive environments such as IPython, and Jupyter Notebooks.

The Matplotlib package can be installed in the Anaconda prompt using either of the following commands:

pip install matplotlib
conda install matplotlib

After installation, Matplotlib is imported as follows.

```
import matplotlib
print(matplotlib._ _version_ _) #outputs the version of Matplotlib.
```

Output:

```
3.2.2
```

The most commonly used module of Matplotlib is pyplot, which has a set of functions that is modeled similarly to MATLAB. Despite its analogy to the MATLAB commands, all the plotting commands in pyplot are written in Python and NumPy. Pyplot can be imported under *plt* alias using the following command.

```
import matplotlib.pyplot as plt
```

3.3.1   Plotting

After importing pyplot under the alias of *plt*, we can use this command to do various types of plotting. The pyplot module adds text, images, color, and lines while plotting a figure. A few of the plotting functions supported by pyplot are bar plot, histogram, pie plot, scatter plot, quiver plot, etc. Further, it can also be used to read, save, and display images. We can use two different methods for plotting.

3.3.1.1   Functional Method

The first method is to directly use plt.plot command as shown below. Note that while using this method we need to add the *plt.show()* command to display the plots. The plt.plot has several additional attributes such as color, and markers, and *plt.plot(x,y)* can be used directly for plotting the data. Further, additional commands such as *plt.title*, *plt.legend*, *plt.xlabel*, and *plt.ylabel* can also be added to label the figure and the axes. Simple plotting using the functional method can be done using the following code snippet. The data generated for implementing the xor dataset in Example 3.1.3 can be visualized using Matplotlib in Fig. 3.1.

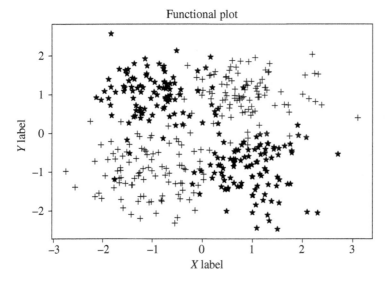

Figure 3.1 Visualization of toy dataset using functional plot.

```
import matplotlib.pyplot as plt
import numpy as np
indexn=np.where(y==0) #get the index corresponding to class 0
indexp=np.where(y==1) #get index corresponding to class 1
plt.plot(X[0,indexp], X[1,indexp], 'k*') #plot the data of class 0
plt.plot(X[0,indexn], X[1,indexn], 'k+') #plot the data of class 1
csfont = {'fontname':'serif'} #define the font family
plt.xlabel("X label",fontsize=12,**csfont) #Set the x-axis label of the
                                  current axes
plt.ylabel("Y label",fontsize=12,**csfont) #Set the y-axis label of the
                                  current axes
plt.title("Functional plot",fontsize=12,**csfont) #Set a title of the
                                  current axes
plt.show() #Display a figure
```

3.3.1.2 Object Oriented Method
The second method is to indirectly use the plt command by first specifying the figure method and then adding axes using the figure method *.add_axes*. We can then use these axes to get the desired plots. Further, we can use the *set_* commands to set the xlabel, ylabel, and title of the plot. The below code snippet uses the object-oriented method for implementing the toy dataset.

```
fig = plt.figure() #create a new figure.
#add_axes contains a list [x0, y0, width, height]
# The list denotes the lower left point of the new axes in figure
                                  coordinates (x0,y0) and its width and
                                  height
axes = fig.add_axes([0.1,0.1,0.8,0.8])
indexn=np.where(y==0) #get the index corresponding to class 0
indexp=np.where(y==1) #get index corresponding to class 1
axes.plot(X[0,indexp], X[1,indexp], 'k*') #plot the data of class 0
```

```
axes.plot(X[0,indexn], X[1,indexn], 'k+') #plot the data of class 1
csfont = {'fontname':'serif'} #define the font family
axes.set_xlabel("X Label",fontsize=12,**csfont) #Set the x-axis label of
                                 the current axes
axes.set_ylabel("Y Label",fontsize=12,**csfont) #Set the y-axis label of
                                 the current axes
axes.set_title("Object Oriented Plot",fontsize=12,**csfont) #Set the title
                                 of the current axes
```

3.3.2 Customized Plotting

The plots can be customized by specifying the size of the figure, changing the axes limits, and adding an *x-y* grid. In an object-oriented plot, the properties of the line plot are specified using various arguments such as *color*, *marker*, *markersize*, *markerfacecolor*, *linestyle*, and *linewidth*. The plotted figures can be saved in various formats such as PNG, PDF, EPS, and SVG using the savefig() command. Similar to labeling the axes, we can also set and customize the font size of the tick labels using *set_xticklabels* and *set_yticklabels*. Further, the limit of the *x* and *y* axes can be specified using *set_xlim* and *set_ylim*. Moreover, all these customizations can also be implemented in a functional plot.

```
#CUSTOMIZED OBJECT ORIENTED PLOT
import matplotlib.pyplot as plt
import numpy as np
x2 = [1, 2, 3, 4, 5, 6, 7, 8, 9, 10]
x3 = [2, 4, 6, 8, 10, 12, 14, 16, 18, 20]
fig = plt.figure(figsize=(5,4),dpi=100)
#add_axes contains a list [x0, y0, width, height]
ax = fig.add_axes([0,0,1,1])
#plots function with different properties
ax.plot(x2,label = '$x2,color='r',marker='o',
        markerfacecolor='green',markersize=16,linestyle='solid',linewidth=
                                 2)
ax.plot(x3,label = '$x3,color='b',marker='*',
        markerfacecolor='yellow',markersize=12,linestyle='dashed',
                                 linewidth=4)
csfont = {'fontname':'serif'} #define the font family
ax.set_xticklabels(x2,fontsize=12,**csfont) #Sets the xticklabels and its
                                 font size.
ax.set_yticklabels(x3,fontsize=12,**csfont) #Sets the yticklabels and its
                                 font size.
ax.set_xlabel("X Label",fontsize=12,**csfont) #Sets the x-axis label with
                                 font size=12
ax.set_ylabel("Y Label",fontsize=12,**csfont) #Sets the y-axis label with
                                 font size=12
ax.set_xlim(-1,10) #Sets the x limit
ax.set_ylim(0,25) #Sets the y limit
ax.grid(color='k', ls = '-.', lw = 0.5) #Add color, linestyle and
                                 linewidth to the grid function
ax.legend(loc =2) #Sets the location of the legend to upper left
ax.set_title("Custom Object Oriented Plot",fontsize=12,**csfont) #Set the
                                 title with font size=12
ax.figure.savefig('linear.pdf') #Save the figure
```

Example 3.3.1 *(Matplotlib subplot)*

In this example, we demonstrate how to create multiple plots in a single figure. In order to compare and analyze different plots together, Matplotlib uses the subplots function to create multiple smaller axes within a single figure. The *subplots()* method has three parameters 'nrows', 'ncols', and 'index' to describe the layout of the figure. Here in Fig. 3.2 we create 4 plots that are stacked together in one figure. The nrows and ncols are 2, whereas the index ranges from 1 to 4.

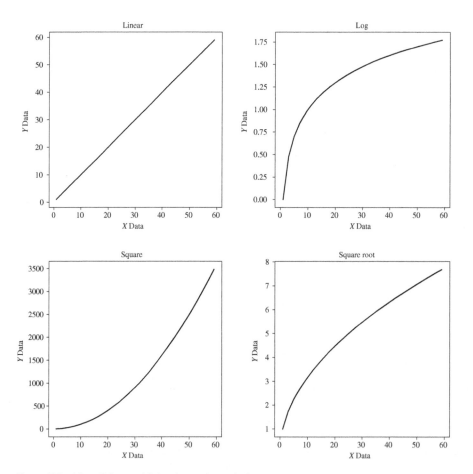

Figure 3.2   Visualizing multiple plots using subplots.

3.3.3   Two-dimensional Plotting

The Pyplot package is not only used for plotting simple graphs and curves but it can also be used to develop various other kinds of plots such as bar plots, scatter plots, and so on. This section covers the various kinds of such plots that can be generated using the pyplot package and also we will see the different commands and arguments that can be changed to customize these plots.

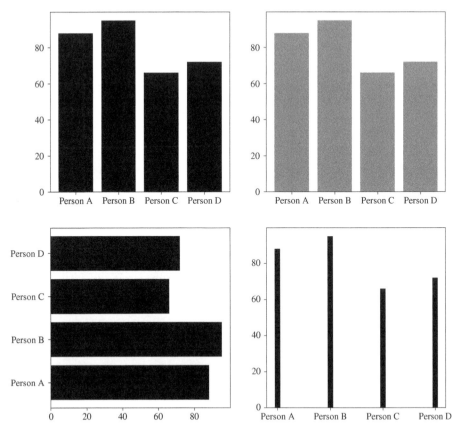

Figure 3.3   Different ways to generate a bar plot.

3.3.3.1   Bar Plot

The function used for plotting bar graph is *plt.bar*. This command generates vertical bars. Horizontal bar graphs can be created using *plt.barh* command. The *color* argument of the graph can be changed to show the bars in different colors. Additionally, the width of the bars can be modified by changing the *width* argument of the bar function. Similarly, you can also modify the height of the bars. In addition to direct plotting, you can change the positions, colors, and thickness of the bar to give more information about different categories of data. Stacked bars can also be plotted using this function by plotting one set of bar graphs over another. Figure 3.3 showcases commonly employed bar plot types.

```
import matplotlib.pyplot as plt
import numpy as np

x = np.array(["PersonA", "PersonB", "PersonC", "PersonD"])
y = np.array([88, 95, 66, 72])
plt.style.use('grayscale')
plt.figure(figsize=(10,10),dpi=90)
csfont = {'fontname':'serif'} #define the font family
plt.subplot(2, 2, 1)
plt.bar(x,y) #plot the bar graph
```

```
plt.xticks(fontsize=12,**csfont)
plt.yticks(fontsize=12,**csfont)
plt.subplot(2, 2, 2)
plt.bar(x, y, color = "grey") #plot the bar graph with a specific color

plt.xticks(fontsize=12,**csfont)
plt.yticks(fontsize=12,**csfont)
plt.subplot(2, 2, 3)
plt.barh(x, y) #plot the bar graph horizontally
plt.xticks(fontsize=12,**csfont)
plt.yticks(fontsize=12,**csfont)
plt.subplot(2, 2, 4)
plt.bar(x, y, width = 0.1) #plot the bar graph with a specific width

plt.xticks(fontsize=12,**csfont)
plt.yticks(fontsize=12,**csfont)
plt.show()
```

3.3.3.2 Histogram

Histogram plots are used to represent the distribution of the data. The command that is used for plotting histogram is *plt.hist*. Similar to bar plots, histogram plots can also be customized by changing the color of the bar, the number of bins and also the transparency of the plots by changing the *alpha* value. Figure 3.4 illustrates a histogram plot with 10 bins.

```
import numpy as np
import matplotlib.pyplot as plt
#draw random samples from a normal distribution with mean,standard
                                   deviation and size of the output
                                   array
x = np.random.normal(0,0.1,1000)
num_bins = 10
#histogram with specific bin size, face color and alpha
n, bins, patches = plt.hist(x, num_bins, facecolor='black', alpha=0.5)
csfont = {'fontname':'serif'} #define the font family
plt.xlabel('X data',fontsize=12,**csfont)
plt.ylabel('Frequency',fontsize=12,**csfont)
plt.xticks(fontsize=12,**csfont)
plt.yticks(fontsize=12,**csfont)
plt.show()
```

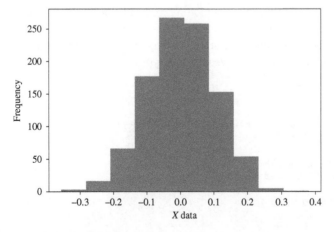

Figure 3.4 Histogram plot.

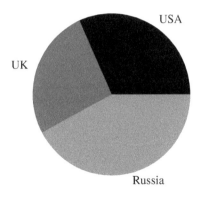 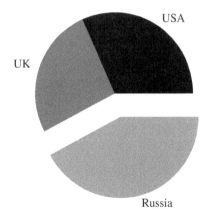

Figure 3.5 Types of pie plot.

3.3.3.3 Pie Plot

A pie plot is used to display a pie chart of one series of data. The plot consists of wedges that show the size of items and represent a portion of the whole pie. Pie charts are plotted using the command *plt.pie*. You can specify the labels of the pie plot using *labels* argument. Further, another method would be making a specified wedge stand out by using the *explode* argument. Similar to other plots, you can also specify different colors for different wedges of the pie plot. Figure 3.5 displays two commonly used pie charts. [

```
import matplotlib.pyplot as plt
import numpy as np
a = np.array([900, 742, 1200])
b = ["USA", "UK", "Russia"]
ep = [0, 0, 0.3]
plt.figure(figsize=(8,8),dpi=90)
plt.subplot(1, 2, 1)
plt.pie(a, labels = b, textprops={"fontsize":12,"family":"serif"}) #pie
                                  plot with label parameter
plt.subplot(1, 2, 2)
#pie plot with explode parameter that makes the specified wedge to stand
                                  out
plt.pie(a, labels = b, explode = ep, textprops={"fontsize":12,"family":"
                                  serif"})
plt.show()
```

3.3.3.4 Scatter Plot

Scatter plots can be used to show the variation in the data by allowing each data point to have individual points to represent them in the plot. The color of the scatter plot can be defined using the argument *color*. Different colors can be used to do a comparison between two different kinds of data. You can also add different colors to different points by adding the number of colors in the color parameter and doing the scatterplot. The customization technique can also be applied here to change the size of the markers using size parameter *s*. Just like the histograms, the *alpha* argument can be used to change the transparency of the points. Figure 3.6 provides a visual representation of a scatter plot.

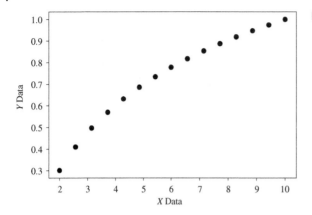

Figure 3.6 Scatter plot.

```
import matplotlib.pyplot as plt
import numpy as np
p = np.linspace(2,10,15)
q = np.log10(p)
plt.scatter(p,q, color='k') #Scatter plot with a defined color
csfont = {'fontname':'serif'} #define the font family
plt.xlabel("X Data",fontsize=12,**csfont) #define the x label
plt.ylabel("Y Data",fontsize=12,**csfont) #define the y label
plt.show()
```

3.3.3.5 Quiver Plot

Quiver plots are a form of 2D plots that represent the vectors associated with a point in the form of arrows. Quiver plots can be useful in visualizing flow or wave propagation such as in electric potential fields or gradients, where the direction and magnitude information are very important. Four parameters are used for quiver plots. X, Y are the x and y positions of the data points. U, V is the directional component of these points. In the code shown below, we create a grid out of two 1D arrays. The points in the grid correspond to the X, Y parameter, which corresponds to the location of the arrows. The x and y components of the arrow vectors are given by U and V parameters. The quiver plots can also be used to assign different colors to arrows using a c argument. Figure 3.7 provides a visual representation of a quiver plot.

```
import matplotlib.pyplot as plt
import numpy as np
x = np.arange(-1, 1.6, 0.2)
y = np.arange(-1, 1.6, 0.2)
#Define a rectangular grid out of two given one-dimensional arrays
X, Y = np.meshgrid(x, y)
U, V = X/5, -Y/5
#Quiver plot with X and Y as the starting positions of the arrows
#U and V are the directions of the arrow
plt.quiver(X, Y, U, V)
csfont = {'fontname':'serif'} #define the font family
plt.xlabel("X Data",fontsize=12,**csfont) #define the x label
plt.ylabel("Y Data",fontsize=12,**csfont) #define the y label
plt.xticks(fontsize=12,**csfont)
plt.yticks(fontsize=12,**csfont)
plt.show()
```

Figure 3.7   Quiver plot.

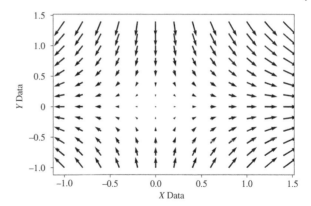

3.3.3.6   Contour Plot

Contour plots are used for representing three-dimensional surface data on a two-dimensional plot. The X, Y are the positional parameters, and the response function is given by a Z parameter. X and Y are two independent variables. In general, we initialize the X, Y parameter as a mesh grid spanning the space of two input arrays corresponding to x and y positions. Then, $Z = f(X, Y)$ is the third dimension that is represented using a contour plot. The contour plots using Matplotlib can be done using two commands: *contour()* and *contourf()*. Command *contour()* generates contour lines, whereas *contourf()* gives filled contour plots. Additionally, we can also add the desired color bar to show different contour regions. Figure 3.8 provides a visual representation of a contour plot.

```
import numpy as np
import matplotlib.pyplot as plt
x = np.linspace(-100, 100, 2000)
y = np.linspace(-100, 100, 2000)
#Define a rectangular grid out of two given one-dimensional arrays
X, Y = np.meshgrid(x,y)
Z = X**2+Y**2
plt.contourf(X, Y, Z) #Creates a filled contour plot
plt.colorbar() #Add a colorbar to the plot
csfont = {'fontname':'serif'} #define the font family
plt.xlabel("X Data",fontsize=12,**csfont) #define the x label
plt.ylabel("Y Data",fontsize=12,**csfont) #define the y label
plt.xticks(fontsize=12,**csfont)
plt.yticks(fontsize=12,**csfont)
plt.show()
```

3.3.3.7   Box Plot

Box or whisker plots can be used to obtain five details about the data: the minimum score, lower quartile (first), median, upper (second) quartile, and maximum score. Each box plot has a box going from the first quartile to the second quartile of the data, and a vertical line within the box that represents the median value and the lines begin from the minimum value and go to the maximum value. The main information that can be read from the box plot is the range of the data points and their median value. Figure 3.9 provides a visual representation of a box plot.

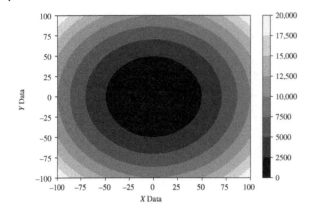

Figure 3.8 Contour plot.

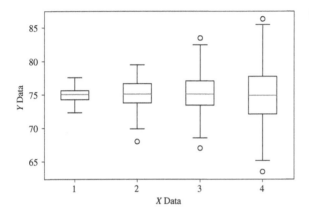

Figure 3.9 Box plot.

```
import matplotlib.pyplot as plt
import numpy as np
#create a list of normal distributions with varying standard deviation
x1 = [np.random.normal(75, std, 200) for std in range(1,5)]
#displays the minimum, median and maximum using the box plot
plt.boxplot(x1)
csfont = {'fontname':'serif'} #define the font family
plt.xlabel("X Data",fontsize=12,**csfont) #define the x label
plt.ylabel("Y Data",fontsize=12,**csfont) #define the y label
plt.xticks(fontsize=12,**csfont)
plt.yticks(fontsize=12,**csfont)
plt.show()
```

3.3.3.8 Violin Plot

Violin plots are similar to box plots and are used to check for variation in the distribution of data from different classes or categories. The violin plots also have added information related to the probability density of the data in addition to the mean, median, and interquartile range details. Hence, they can provide more information than simple box plots. *plt.violinplot* is used for obtaining violin plots. Figure 3.10 provides a visual representation of a violin plot.

Figure 3.10   Violin plot.

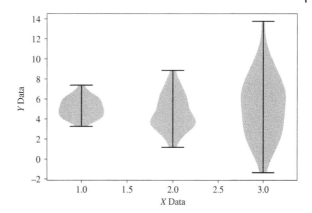

```
import matplotlib.pyplot as plt
import numpy as np
#create a list of normal distributions with varying standard deviation
xx = [np.random.normal(5, std, 100) for std in range(1,4)]
#displays the distribution of the data using the violin plot
plt.violinplot(xx)
csfont = {'fontname':'serif'} #define the font family
plt.xlabel("X Data",fontsize=12,**csfont) #define the x label
plt.ylabel("Y Data",fontsize=12,**csfont) #define the y label
plt.xticks(fontsize=12,**csfont)
plt.yticks(fontsize=12,**csfont)
plt.show()
```

3.3.4   Three-dimensional Plotting

3.3.4.1   3D Contour

Similar to the 2D contour plots discussed in Section 3.3.3.6, Pyplot can also be used to create three-dimensional contour plots. We use the command *plt.contour3D*. This function requires the X data and Y data to be in the form of a grid, and Z data is a function of X and Y. The plots can be created using various colormaps. You can also define the maximum number of samples in each direction. The code snippet shown below can be used to do a 3D contour plot. For doing a 3D plot, it is required to import *mplot3d* which enables 3D plotting. Figure 3.11 provides a visual representation of a 3D Contour plot.

```
import matplotlib.pyplot as plt
import nump as np
from mpl_toolkits import mplot3d #Importing the mplot3d toolkit to enable
                                 3d plots.
x_a = np.linspace(-1, 1, 10)
y_b = np.linspace(-1, 1, 10)
#Define a rectangular grid out of two given one-dimensional arrays.
X, Y = np.meshgrid(x_a, y_b)
Z = np.sqrt(X ** 2 + Y ** 2)
fig = plt.figure(figsize=(10,8))
csfont = {'fontname':'serif'} #define the font family
ax = plt.axes(projection='3d') #Creates a 3D axis.
#Creates the 3D contour plot with colormap greys.
```

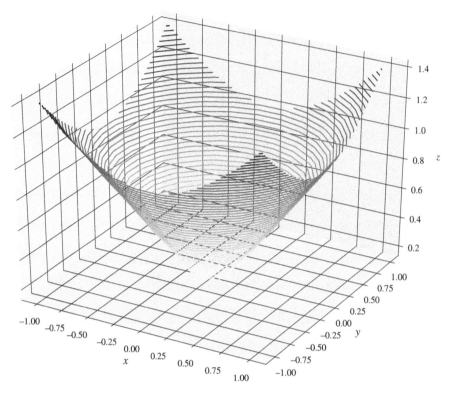

Figure 3.11   3D contour plot.

```
# Here 50 denotes the maximum number of samples used in each direction.
ax.contour3D(X, Y, Z, 50, cmap='Greys')
ax.set_xlabel('x',fontsize=12,**csfont) #labels the x-axis.
ax.set_ylabel('y',fontsize=12,**csfont) #labels the y-axis.
ax.set_zlabel('z',fontsize=12,**csfont) #labels the z-axis.
ax.xaxis.label.set_size(12) ## setting label size
ax.yaxis.label.set_size(12)
ax.zaxis.label.set_size(12)
ax.figure.savefig('3dcontour.pdf')
```

3.3.4.2   3D Surface

The surface plots are similar to 3D contour plots. The main difference is surface plots give us additional information about the functional dependencies between dependent and independent variables of three-dimensional data. The pyplot command used for plotting 3D surface plots is *plt_surface*. Similar to other 3D plots, we can specify the desired colormap for plotting. Figure 3.12 provides a visual representation of a 3D surface plot.

```
import matplotlib.pyplot as plt
import nump as np
from mpl_toolkits import mplot3d #Importing the mplot3d toolkit to enable
                                  3d plots.
x_a = np.linspace(-1, 1, 10)
y_b = np.linspace(-1, 1, 10)
```

```
#Define a rectangular grid out of two given one-dimensional arrays.
X, Y = np.meshgrid(x_a, y_b)
Z = np.exp(X ** 2 + Y ** 2)
fig = plt.figure(figsize=(10,8))
csfont = {'fontname':'serif'} #define the font family
ax = plt.axes(projection='3d') #Creates a 3D axis.
#Creates the 3D surface plot with colormap binary.
ax.plot_surface(X, Y, Z, cmap='binary')
ax.set_xlabel('x',fontsize=12,**csfont) #labels the x-axis.
ax.set_ylabel('y',fontsize=12,**csfont) #labels the y-axis.
ax.set_zlabel('z',fontsize=12,**csfont) #labels the z-axis.
ax.xaxis.label.set_size(12) ## setting label size
ax.yaxis.label.set_size(12)
ax.zaxis.label.set_size(12)
```

3.3.4.3 3D Wireframe

Wireframes are great tools for visualizing a three-dimensional plot of a function. The 3D wireframe takes the grid values as input and does a projection of this grid to a 3D surface. The wireframe plots have the advantage of better visualization of such 3D surfaces. The command used for such plots is *plot_wireframe*. You can specify the color of the wireframe using the *color* argument in the function. Figure 3.13 provides a visual representation of a 3D Wireframe plot.

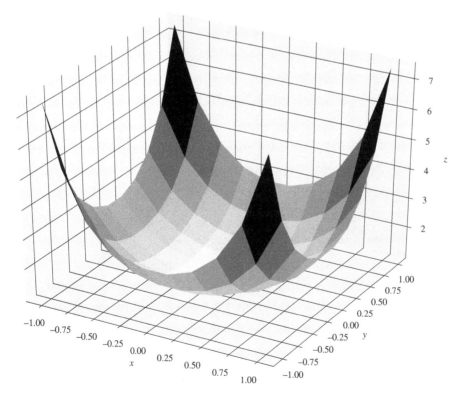

Figure 3.12   3D surface plot.

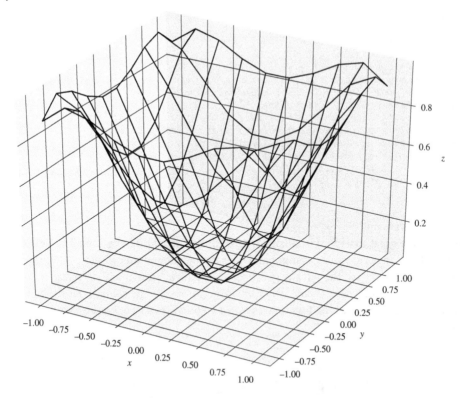

Figure 3.13 3D wireframe plot.

```
import matplotlib.pyplot as plt
import nump as np
from mpl_toolkits import mplot3d #Importing the mplot3d toolkit to enable
                                 3d plots.
x_a = np.linspace(-1, 1, 10)
y_b = np.linspace(-1, 1, 10)
#Define a rectangular grid out of two given one-dimensional arrays.
X, Y = np.meshgrid(x_a, y_b)
Z = np.sin(X ** 2 + Y ** 2)
fig = plt.figure(figsize=(10,8))
csfont = {'fontname':'serif'} #define the font family
ax = plt.axes(projection='3d') #Creates a 3D axis.
#Creates the 3D wireframe plot with color black.
ax.plot_wireframe(X, Y, Z, color='black')
ax.set_xlabel('x',fontsize=12,**csfont) #labels the x-axis.
ax.set_ylabel('y',fontsize=12,**csfont) #labels the y-axis.
ax.set_zlabel('z',fontsize=12,**csfont) #labels the z-axis.
ax.xaxis.label.set_size(12) ## setting label size
ax.yaxis.label.set_size(12)
ax.zaxis.label.set_size(12)
```

3.4 Scipy

Scipy is a data science library built on top of NumPy. Scipy has functions that are more optimized compared to NumPy. Therefore, Scipy allows you to process the multidimensional arrays in a faster and more efficient way compared to NumPy. The package can be used for performing different kinds of mathematical operations on multidimensional arrays. The different operations include algebraic and integration routines, statistical operations, and other special functions. Scipy is a great tool to work with N-dimensional images and can also be used for signal processing. The package is able to do different types of complex operations on large data which makes it quite useful as a data analysis tool.

The Scipy package can be installed in the Anaconda prompt using either of the following commands:

pip install scipy
conda install -c anaconda scipy

After installation, Scipy can be imported as follows:

```
import scipy            # importing scipy package
scipy._ _version_ _     # displaying the version of the scipy package
```

Output:

```
1.7.3
```

Scipy supports many multidimensional array operations, which are discussed below:

3.4.1 Data Input–Output Using Scipy

The *Scipy.io* library can be used to work around various types of file formats such as Matlab, IDL, and WAV sound files. The most commonly used files include *.mat* files. The *Scipy.io* provides functions to load, save, and work around with these *.mat* files. Similarly, the package allows reading, writing, and processing of other file formats. For each of the file formats, commands vary and these specific sets of commands can be used for reading and writing to those formats. For data created in Matlab the *Scipy.io* package supports only the.mat files created in versions above MATLAB 7.3.

```
import scipy.io as sio
import numpy as np

arr = np.array([1,2,3,4])   # create an array
sio.savemat('sample_data.mat', {'arr_samp': arr}) #saving the array by the
                                  name 'arr_samp' using sio.savemat

sample_arr = sio.loadmat('sample_data.mat') # loading the array into the
                                  variable from mat file using sio.
                                  loadmat
print(sample_arr['arr_samp'])
```

Output:

```
[[1 2 3 4]]
[('arr_samp', (1, 4), 'int64')]
```

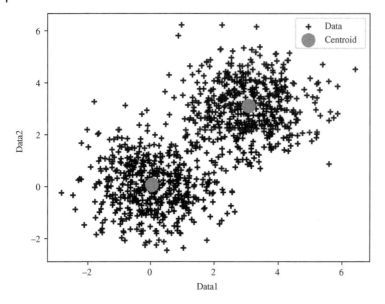

Figure 3.14 Scatterplot of the data with centroids.

3.4.2 Clustering Methods

Scipy.cluster is used to perform clustering operations on the input data points. A clustering operation is used to divide the data into different groups. During this operation, the data points that are similar to each other cluster together, and the data points that are dissimilar fall into separate groups. The most popular clustering approach used is K-means clustering. This is an unsupervised approach meaning the data points are not labeled. The K-means approach iterates through the training points such that the data points closer to the center are identified at each run. Further, the next step involves computing the mean of each cluster which becomes the new center. These two steps are iterated through till the centers do not move. Scipy.cluster has the implementation of the K-means algorithm.

The following code snippet shows the implementation of K-Means clustering on randomly generated data points. For this, first, we create two different random datasets of normal distribution using *np.random.randn* command. The second dataset (*data2*) is created by adding distance to the normal data to shift its center. Now, using the KMeans package, the centers are identified. Following this, we plot both the data and the centroids obtained using k-Means clustering (see Fig. 3.14). Note that, here we also use vector quantization(*vq*) to assign codes to the observations. These codes identify the cluster each point belongs.

```
from scipy.cluster.vq import kmeans, vq, whiten #importing the packages
                              required
#for Kmeans clustering
import numpy as np
import matplotlib.pyplot as plt
data1 = np.random.randn(500,2) # generating a random 2D data of normal
                              distribution
data2 = np.random.randn(500,2) + np.array([3,3]) # adding distance to the
                              previously generated data
# to create two clusters
```

```
data = np.vstack((data1,data2)) # stacking the two data together
[center,_] = kmeans(data, 2) # Apply Kmeans clustering to cluster the data

plt.scatter(data[:,0], data[:,1]) # plotting the scatterplots
plt.scatter(center[:,0], center[:,1]) # plotting the two centroids
plt.show()

# into two groups
out = vq(data, center)
print(out)
```

3.4.3   Constants

The package *scipy.constants* gives access to many constants. It includes different categories of constants such as mathematical constants (pi, golden), physical constants (Planck constant (h), Boltzmann constant (k), etc.), SI units (milli, micro, kilo), and other units (gram, degree, minute, etc.). These constants can be used in mathematical expressions to make calculations easier. They can be imported into the code in a similar way as other packages.

```
import scipy.constants
from scipy.constants import find

print(find('light')) # find all the possible constants with the keyword '
                                 light'
print(find('Planck')) #find all the possible constants with the keyword '
                                 Planck'

print(scipy.constants.physical_constants['Planck constant']) #printing
                                 Planck's constant
print(scipy.constants.golden_ratio) # printing the golden ratio
```

Output:

```
['speed of light in vacuum']

['Planck constant', 'Planck constant in eV/Hz', 'Planck length',
                                 'Planck mass', 'Planck mass energy
                                 equivalent in GeV', 'Planck
                                 temperature', 'Planck time', 'molar
                                 Planck constant', 'reduced Planck
                                 constant', 'reduced Planck
                                 constant in eV s', 'reduced Planck
                                 constant times c in MeV fm']
(6.62607015e-34, 'J Hz^-1', 0.0)

1.618033988749895
```

3.4.4   Linear Algebra and Integration Routines

The package *scipy.linalg* can be used for performing linear algebra operations in Python. The package is an implementation of basic linear algebra subprograms (BLAS) and linear algebra package (LAPACK) libraries, which are standard software used for linear algebra implementation. The *scipy.linalg* is faster compared to these libraries.

```
from scipy import linalg
import numpy as np

a = np.array([[1,2],[3,2]]) # create a square matrix
print('deteminant of matrix a=')
print(a, linalg.det(a))      # compute the determinant of the matrix
print('Inverse of the matrix a = ')
print(linalg.inv(a))         # compute the inverse of the matrix
val, vect = linalg.eig(a)    # calculate the eigenvalue and eigenvector of a
print('\neigenvalue =')
print(val)
print('\neigenvector =')
print(vect)
b = np.array([2,4])          # create another 2D vector which is the right-
                                         hand side of the algebra equation
print('Solution to equation using matrix a and b gives:')
print(linalg.solve(a,b))     # print the solution to the equation using a and
                                                    b
```

Output:

```
deteminant of matrix a=
[[1 2]
 [3 2]] -4.0

Inverse of the matrix a =
[[-0.5    0.5]
 [ 0.75 -0.25]]

eigenvalue =
[-1.+0.j   4.+0.j]

eigenvector =
[[-0.70710678 -0.5547002]
 [ 0.70710678 -0.83205029]]

Solution to equation using matrix a and b gives:
[1.   0.5]
```

The package *scipy.integrate* is used for doing single, double, and multiple integrations. Additionally, you can use this package for applying numerical analysis rules such as Simpson's rule and trapezoidal rule. This type of numerical integration becomes essential when we cannot do the integration analytically.

Look at the following example:

$$\int_{y=0}^{\frac{1}{2}} \int_{x=0}^{1-2y} xy \, dx \, dy = \frac{1}{96} \approx 0.0104167$$

```
from scipy import integrate
def f(x, y):
    return x*y
def bounds_y():
    return [0, 0.5]
def bounds_x(y):
    return [0, 1-2*y]
```

```
integ = integrate.nquad(f, [bounds_x, bounds_y])
print('\nafter integration')
print(integ)
```

Output:

```
after integration
(0.010416666666666668, 4.101620128472366e-16)
```

3.4.5 Optimization

The optimization module can be used in the case of minimizing or maximizing a function, especially in the case of curve fitting, or root fitting, that can be scalar or multidimensional. The package can deal with both constrained and unconstrained minimization problems. The package used is *scipy.optimize* and for minimization *minimize()* function is used. We can define any function and use this module to optimize a parameter by the minimum value of the function. For solving multivariate systems, the roots of these systems can be found using the *root()* command. The package also has most commonly used optimization approaches such as least squares (*least_squares()*) and curve-fitting techniques (*curve_fit()*).

Let us look into the following code snippet where we first create a function to optimize and find the minimum of the function using *scipy.optimize*.

Let us define the following function $f(x)$. $f'(x)$ is the derivative of this function.

$$f(x) = x^3 - 2x^2 + x$$
$$f'(x) = 3x^2 - 4x + 1$$
$$x_0 = \frac{1}{3}, 1$$

```
import matplotlib.pyplot as plt
from scipy import optimize
import numpy as np

def func(x):
        return   x**2 + 2*x + 1    # create the function to be optimized

x = np.linspace(-1,1,num=10)      # plot the data to visualize the function
plt.plot(x, func(x))
plt.show()
```

Figure 3.15 illustrates a graphical representation of the function $x^2 + 2x + 1$ that is the subject of optimization. In this case, optimization involves finding the best possible input values or parameters for this function to achieve a specific goal, such as maximizing or minimizing its output.

Next, using *minimize_scaler()* we can find the minimum of the function as shown below:

```
out = optimize.minimize_scalar(func)  #Find the minimum of the function
                                        using minimum_scalar
print(out)
```

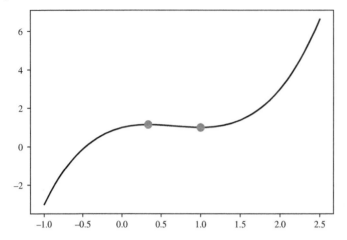

Figure 3.15 Plot of the function to be optimized.

Output:

```
success: True
fun: 1.0
x: 1.0
nit: 8
nfev: 11
```

3.4.6 Interpolation

Interpolation is a useful technique for estimating the missing values in a function using the known values. Scipy package *scipy.interpolate* is used to perform this operation. If we have a function and few points to describe the sequence of the data, the interpolate function can be used to predict values that fall into the existing set of data. This can be done in 1D data.

First, create an input signal consisting of 10 points, as displayed in Fig. 3.16, using the following code snippet:

```
import numpy as np
from scipy import interpolate
import matplotlib.pyplot as plt

#1D interpolation

x = np.linspace(0, 10, 10)
y = np.cos(2*x) + 1 # creating the input signal with 10 points

plt.plot(x, y,'o')
plt.legend(['input signal']) # plotting the input signal points
plt.title('input signal')
plt.show()
```

There are different kinds of interpolation: *'linear'*, *'cubic'*, *'quadratic'* etc. This kind of interpolation can be specified as an attribute to the *interpolate.interp1d()* function.

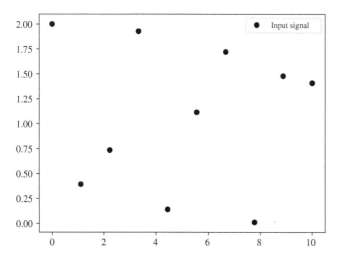

Figure 3.16 Plot of input signal.

Figure 3.17, provides a graphical representation that illustrates the results of the various kinds of interpolation, including 'linear', 'cubic', and 'quadratic'.

```
f1 = interpolate.interp1d(x, y,kind = 'linear') # performing 1D linear
                                    interpolation
f2 = interpolate.interp1d(x, y, kind = 'cubic') # performing 1D cubic
                                    interpolation
f3 = interpolate.interp1d(x, y, kind = 'quadratic') # performing 1D
                                    quadratic interpolation

x_new = np.linspace(0, 10, 30)

plt.plot(x, y, 'o', x_new, f1(x_new), '-', x_new, f2(x_new), '--', x_new,
                                    f3(x_new), '-*')
# plotting all the interpolated data points along with the original data
plt.legend(['data', 'linear', 'cubic','quadratic'])
plt.title('1D interpolation')
plt.show()
```

Smooth curves can be plotted through a limited number of points using the Splines command. We can specify the degree of the smoothing data. Let us define a different input data:

$$y = x^2 + sin(x) \tag{3.1}$$

After creating this input signal, random noise is added to this data making the signal distorted. Figure 3.18 illustrates the plot of this distorted data.

```
# using spline

x = np.linspace(0, 6, 50) # creating the input signal
y = x**2 + np.sin(x)
n = np.random.randn(50) # adding random noise to the data to
data = y + n             # make the signal distorted

plt.plot(x, data, 'o') # plotting the generated data
plt.title('input signal')
plt.show()
```

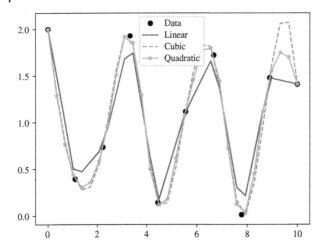

Figure 3.17 Interpolation comparison – 1-D linear, cubic, and quadratic.

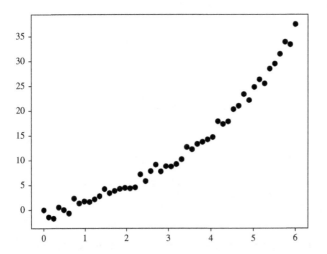

Figure 3.18 Plot of the distorted input signal.

Now using spline we can perform interpolation on this distorted data and also we can smoothen the data as shown in Fig. 3.19:

```
smth = interpolate.UnivariateSpline(x, data) # performing interpolation
                                    and smoothing using spline
x_new = np.linspace(0, 6, 1000)
plt.plot(x, data, 'o', x_new, smth(x_new), 'r*')
plt.legend(['data', 'smooth curve'])
plt.title('smoothing and curve fitting using spline package')
plt.show()
```

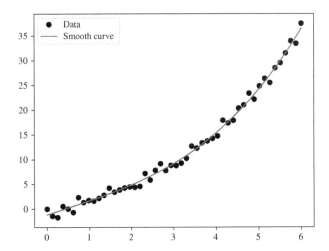

Figure 3.19 Smoothing and curve fitting using spline interpolation.

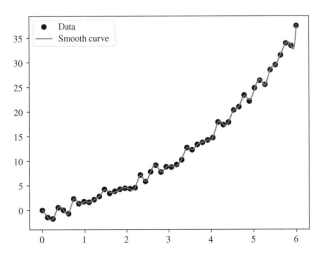

Figure 3.20 Smoothing and curve fitting using spline interpolation after adjusting the smoothing factor.

Additionally, we can also change the smoothing factor of the interpolated data as shown in Fig. 3.20:

```
smth.set_smoothing_factor(0.5)     # adjusting the smoothing factor
plt.plot(x, data, 'o', x_new, smth(x_new), 'g')
plt.legend(['data', 'smooth curve'])
plt.title('after setting the smooth factor as 0.5')
plt.show()
```

3.4.7 Image Processing

The package *scipy.ndimage* can be used to perform image processing operations in Python. The package can be used to display an image, perform geometric transformations such as rotation and flipping, filtering, and edge detection and can be used for segmentation, classification, etc. The Scipy package also has access to images through a library called miscellaneous routines (MISC) that can be used as a sample to perform the operations.

Example 3.4.1 *(Image processing operations using Scipy package)*
In this example, we are going to learn how to display an image imported from MISC package and apply image processing techniques to this image. Import the face image using the misc library in Scipy. Display the image and now let us perform some geometric transformations to the image. The ndimage library allows us to do several operations such as rotation, flipping, and cropping. Let us perform a downward flip using NumPy package followed by a rotation by an angle of 60° using ndimage library. In addition to geometric transformation, we can also do several filtering operations on the images. Begin with blurring the image using a standard Gaussian filter. Different kinds of filters can be accessed using the ndimage. Further, the sigma value can be tuned to see the difference between the intensity of blurring. Another important image processing that can be performed using this package is edge detection. Several methods are available. Let us apply the Prewitt algorithm to one of the channels of the original image and the cropped image. Display all the output images.

3.4.8 Special Functions

Apart from all the above-mentioned libraries, Scipy also provides us with special functions. *scipy.special* package gives us access to certain universal functions such as cubic root, exponential, permutation, combinations, and gamma functions. The syntax for each of these functions is slightly different. In the case of mathematical functions, i.e. exponential, gamma, cubic root, and element-wise operations are performed.

```python
import numpy as np
from scipy import special

a = np.array([1, 3, 5, 2])

print(special.cbrt(a)) # computing the cube root of a
print(special.exp10(a))# computing the 10^a
print(special.gamma(a))# computing the gamma to s

out_comb = special.comb(5, 2, exact = False,repetition=True)
                    # Combination(5,2)
print(out_comb)
out_perm = special.perm(5, 2, exact = True)
print(out_perm)      #permutation(5,2)
```

Output:

```
[1.         1.44224957 1.70997595 1.25992105]
[1.e+01 1.e+03 1.e+05 1.e+02]
[ 1.  2. 24.  1.]
15.0
20
```

3.5   Scikit-Learn

Scikit-learn is a free machine learning library in Python developed by David Cournapeau as a Google summer of code project in 2007. It has various features for preprocessing, model selection, classification, clustering, regression, and dimensionality reduction that are built on top of NumPy, SciPy, and Matplotlib.

The scikit-learn package can be installed in the Anaconda prompt using either of the following commands:

pip install scikit-learn
conda install scikit-learn

After installation, scikit-learn is imported as sklearn.

```
import sklearn
print(sklearn.__version__) #outputs the version of scikit-learn.
```

Output:

```
1.0.2
```

3.5.1   Scikit-Learn API

The scikit-learn application programming interface (API) consists of three basic interfaces namely estimator, predictor, and transformer that allow it to do most of the machine learning tasks. It also provides a wide variety of prebuilt algorithms to model the data with just a few lines of code.

3.5.1.1   Estimator Interface
It denotes the fundamental interface applied in scikit-learn. It uses the fit() method to train the machine learning model on the given dataset. All learning algorithms, regardless of regression or classification problem; supervised or unsupervised tasks use the estimator interface to fit the model on the training data. For example, in the case of supervised learning, the fit method takes in as input a feature vector as well as target labels so that the estimator learns and infers some properties on unseen data.

3.5.1.2   Predictor Interface
This is an extension of the estimator interface that uses the *predict()* method to make useful predictions given the test features. After training, the model for a given input feature vector, the predictor returns predicted labels in the form of probabilities as well as prediction scores. Moreover, in a machine learning pipeline in alternative to calling *fit()* and *predict()* separately, a single *fit_predict()* method can be used to first train a model and then obtain the prediction results.

3.5.1.3   Transformer Interface
It helps to perform various transformations on the data by enabling the *transform()* method. Scikit-learn provides a library of transformers for data preprocessing, dimensionality reduction, feature extraction, and feature selection. Commonly, the *transform()*

method is used after the *fit()* method since the operations that are used to convert the data are also treated as estimators. But for convenience, one can also use the *fit_transform()* method for efficiently modeling and transforming the training data simultaneously.

Example 3.5.1 *(A machine learning pipeline for classification.)*
In this example, we discuss how to use the scikit-learn instances to construct a basic machine learning pipeline. At first, we load the necessary modules and use the xor dataset defined in the previous codes. This dataset contains two labels corresponding to '0' and '1'. Before constructing the pipeline, the dataset is loaded and split into training and test data. A very basic pipeline that consists of a scaler, feature extractor, and classifier. As the preprocessing step, the *StandardScaler()* function is used to remove the mean and scale the data to unit variance. Next, the feature extraction is done using principal component analysis which uses the *PCA()* function to extract the most significant feature vectors. After implementing both transformers, the *MLPClassifier()* function is used to implement the multilayer perceptron (MLP) classifier that acts as the estimator. The classifier function inputs the size of the hidden layers and a maximum number of iterations. After adding these parameters the final model is fitted and the performance is evaluated by calculating the confusion matrix (see Fig. 3.21).

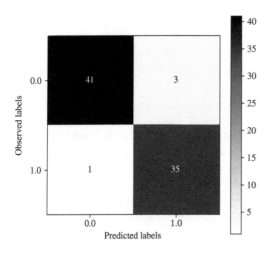

Figure 3.21 Confusion matrix for the classification of xor problem. The confusion matrix gives a summary of the overall performance of the classifier. It shows the number of true negatives (TN), false negatives (FN), false positives (FP), and true positives (TP) corresponding to each class. A higher value for TN and TP shows that the classifier performs well.

3.5.2 Loading Datasets

This module comes with a few small built-in datasets that can be used to illustrate the performance of various machine learning algorithms. These are known as toy datasets and they can be easily loaded with a few lines of code. In order to load these datasets, a simple format is followed as *load_DATASET()*, where DATASET refers to the name of the dataset. The main disadvantage of these datasets is that they are too small to be depictive of real-world problems in machine learning. Hence, this module comes with a dataset fetcher that can be

Figure 3.22 Creating blobs of points with a Gaussian distribution for clustering.

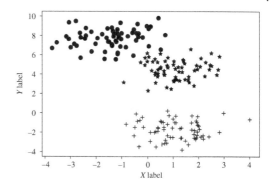

used to download and load larger real-world datasets. Additionally, the dataset generator functions can be used for developing controlled artificial datasets. Figure 3.22 illustrates a dataset comprising Gaussian blobs of points, which serves as the input data for a clustering analysis.

```
#LOADING THE TOY DATSET
from sklearn import datasets
data = datasets.load_wine() #Load and returns the wine dataset.

#LOADING REAL-WORLD DATASET
from sklearn.datasets import fetch_california_housing
house_data = fetch_california_housing() #Load the California housing
                                                dataset.
```

```
#LOADING GENERATED DATASET
from sklearn.datasets import make_blobs
import numpy as np
import matplotlib.pyplot as plt
#Develop isotropic Gaussian blobs for clustering.
X, y = make_blobs(n_samples=200, centers=3, n_features=3, random_state=0)
string=['*k','+k','ok']
for j in range(3):
  ind = np.where(y==j)
  plt.plot(X[ind,0],X[ind,1],string[j])
csfont = {'fontname':'serif'}
plt.xlabel("X label",fontsize=12,**csfont)
plt.ylabel("Y label",fontsize=12,**csfont)
plt.xticks(fontsize=12,**csfont)
plt.yticks(fontsize=12,**csfont)
plt.show()
```

3.5.3 Data Preprocessing

This is an extremely important step in machine learning since we need to process the raw data to boost the performance of the models. The commonly used preprocessing methods are shown in Table 3.1.

Table 3.1 Data preprocessing methods and functions.

Preprocessing methods	Functions
Standardization	StandardScaler()- Rescales data to have zero mean and unit variance.
	MinMaxScaler()- Scaling data to lie between the minimum and maximum value.
Normalization	Normalizer()- Scaling each data sample to have unit norm.
Imputing values	SimpleImputer()- Filling up missing values using four main strategies such as mean, most frequent, median, or a constant.
Polynomial features	PolynomialFeatures()- Adds complexity to the dataset by generating polynomial features.
Categorical features	OneHotEncoder()- Encodes each categorical value into a new categorical column and allocates a binary value to each column.
	OrdinalEncoding()- Encodes each unique category
	with a numerical value
Numerical features	KBinsDiscretizer()- Transforms the continuous numerical values into discrete bins.
	Binarizer()- Assigning a boolean value to each sample by thresholding the numerical features.
Custom transformers	FunctionTransformers()- Accepts an existing function and uses it to transform the data.

```
#STANDARDIZATION
import numpy as np
from sklearn.preprocessing import StandardScaler
from sklearn.preprocessing import MinMaxScaler
arr1 = np.array([[1,2,3],[4,5,6],[7,8,9]]) #define an array.
print("Original array:",arr1)
scale1 = StandardScaler() #define the preprocessing module.
scale2 = MinMaxScaler(feature_range=(0,1)) #define the preprocessing
                                  module.
arr_scale1 = scale1.fit_transform(arr1) #fit the transformer to the data.
arr_scale2 = scale2.fit_transform(arr1) #fit the transformer to the data.
org_arr1 = scale1.inverse_transform(arr_scale1) #transform back to
                                  original data.
org_arr2 = scale2.inverse_transform(arr_scale2) #transform back to
                                  original data.
print("Standardized array:",arr_scale1)
print("Minmax scaled array:",arr_scale2)
print("Transformed the standardized array:",org_arr1)
print("Transformed the minmax scaled array:",org_arr2)
```

Output:

```
Original array: [[1 2 3]
 [4 5 6]
 [7 8 9]]
Standardized array: [[-1.22474487 -1.22474487 -1.22474487]
 [ 0.          0.          0.        ]
 [ 1.22474487  1.22474487  1.22474487]]
```

```
Minmax scaled array: [[0.  0.  0.]
 [0.5 0.5 0.5]
 [1.  1.  1.]]
Transformed the standardized array: [[1. 2. 3.]
 [4. 5. 6.]
 [7. 8. 9.]]
Transformed the minmax scaled array: [[1. 2. 3.]
 [4. 5. 6.]
 [7. 8. 9.]]
[]
```

```
#NORMALIZATION
from sklearn.preprocessing import Normalizer
arr2 = np.array([[100,20,550],[43,620,111],[248,15,89]]) #define an array.
print("Original array:",arr2)
normal = Normalizer() #define the preprocessing module.
arr_normal = normal.fit_transform(arr2) #fit the transformer to the data.
print("Normalized array:",arr_normal)
```

Output:

```
Original array: [[100  20 550]
 [ 43 620 111]
 [248  15  89]]
Normalized array: [[0.17877106 0.03575421 0.98324084]
 [0.06811083 0.98206308 0.17582097]
 [0.9397041  0.05683694 0.33723252]]
```

```
#IMPUTING VALUES
import numpy as np
from sklearn.impute import SimpleImputer
arr3 = np.array([[np.nan, 2, 8, np.nan], [6, np.nan, np.nan, 12],
                                [7, 6, 4, np.nan]]) #define an array.
print("Original array:",arr3)
im = SimpleImputer(missing_values=np.nan, strategy='median') #define the
                                preprocessing module.
arr_im = im.fit_transform(arr3) #fit the transformer to the data.
print("Array after imputing values:",arr_im)
```

Output:

```
Original array: [[nan  2.  8. nan]
 [ 6. nan nan 12.]
 [ 7.  6.  4. nan]]
Array after imputing values: [[ 6.5 2.   8.  12. ]
 [ 6.   4.   6.  12. ]
 [ 7.   6.   4.  12. ]]
```

```
#POLYNOMIAL FEATURES
import numpy as np
from sklearn.preprocessing import PolynomialFeatures
arr4 = np.array([[5,8],[4,3],[7,9]]) #define an array.
print("Original array:",arr4)
poly = PolynomialFeatures(2) #define the preprocessing module.
poly_feat = poly.fit_transform(arr4) #fit the transformer to the data.
print("Polynomial features of array:",poly_feat)
```

Output:

```
Original array: [[5 8]
 [4 3]
 [7 9]]
Polynomial features of array: [[ 1.  5.  8. 25. 40. 64.]
 [ 1.  4.  3. 16. 12.  9.]
 [ 1.  7.  9. 49. 63. 81.]]
```

```
#CATEGORICAL FEATURES
import numpy as np
from sklearn.preprocessing import OneHotEncoder
from sklearn.preprocessing import OrdinalEncoder
arr5 = np.array([[1,'one'],[2,'two'],[3,'three']]) #define an array.
print("Original arry:",arr5)
enc1 = OneHotEncoder() #define the preprocessing module.
enc2 = OrdinalEncoder() #define the preprocessing module.
cat_feat1 = enc1.fit_transform(arr5).toarray() #fit the transformer to the
                                    data.
cat_feat2 = enc2.fit_transform(arr5) #fit the transformer to the data.
print("One hot encoded array:",cat_feat1)
print("Ordinal array:",cat_feat2)
```

Output:

```
Original array: [['1' 'one']
 ['2' 'two']
 ['3' 'three']]
One hot encoded array: [[1. 0. 0. 1. 0. 0.]
 [0. 1. 0. 0. 0. 1.]
 [0. 0. 1. 0. 1. 0.]]
Ordinal array: [[0. 0.]
 [1. 2.]
 [2. 1.]]
```

```
#NUMERICAL FEATURES
import numpy as np
from sklearn.preprocessing import KBinsDiscretizer
from sklearn.preprocessing import Binarizer
arr6 = np.array([[5, 8, 14], [17, 2, 12], [21, 6, 4]]) #define an array.
print("Original array:",arr6)
dis = KBinsDiscretizer(n_bins=[2, 3, 2], encode='ordinal') #define the
                                    preprocessing module.
bina = Binarizer(threshold=10, copy=True) #define the preprocessing module.

num_feat1 = dis.fit_transform(arr6) #fit the transformer to the data.
num_feat2 = bina.fit_transform(arr6) #fit the transformer to the data.
print("Array with bins:",num_feat1)
print("Binarized array:",num_feat2)
```

Output:

```
Original array: [[ 5  8 14]
 [17  2 12]
 [21  6  4]]
Array with bins: [[0. 2. 1.]
 [1. 0. 1.]
 [1. 1. 0.]]
Binarized array: [[0 0 1]
 [1 0 1]
 [1 0 0]]
```

```
#CUSTOM TRANSFORMERS
import numpy as np
from sklearn.preprocessing import FunctionTransformer
arr7 = np.array([[3, 9], [18, 27], [39, 63]]) #define an array.
print("Original array:",arr7)
trans = FunctionTransformer(np.expm1, validate=True) #define the
                                      preprocessing module.
cust_feat = trans.transform(arr7) #fit the transformer (exp(x)-1) to the
                                      data.
print("Transformed array:",cust_feat)
```

Output:

```
 Original array: [[ 3   9]
 [18 27]
 [39 63]]
Transformed array: [[1.90855369e+01 8.10208393e+03]
 [6.56599681e+07 5.32048241e+11]
 [8.65934004e+16 2.29378316e+27]]
```

3.5.4 Feature Selection

This process helps in the selection of the most relevant features from the data that contribute most to the prediction and hence plays a crucial role in building accurate machine learning models. Although scikit-learn provides several feature selection algorithms, two of the widely used methods are recursive feature elimination (RFE) and *SelectKBest*. RFE feature selector essentially is a backward selection process, that allows eliminating the least significant features after recursive training. On the other hand, *SelectKBest* is one of the univariate feature selection methods that can be used to select a number K of features based on statistical test results.

```
#Feature elimination using RFE
import pandas as pd
import seaborn as sns
from sklearn.feature_selection import RFE
from sklearn.ensemble import GradientBoostingClassifier
dat1 = sns.load_dataset('anagrams') #Load the dataset.
X1 = dat1.drop('attnr', axis = 1) #Create the independent variable.
y1 = dat1['attnr'] #Create the dependent variable.
#Select the significant features using Gradient boosting classifier
rfe = RFE(estimator=GradientBoostingClassifier(),n_features_to_select =2)
rfe.fit(X1, y1) #Fit the model.
print(X1.columns[rfe.get_support()]) #Display the best 2 features.
```

Output:

```
Index(['subidr', 'num3'], dtype='object')
```

Example 3.5.2 *(Feature selection using SelectKBest)*
In this example, we create a SelectKbest instance that selects the three best features of a predictor $\mathbf{x}_i$ based on their mutual information with a regressor y_i. The implementation is done on the 'diamonds' dataset from Seaborn. After loading the dataset, the script drops the features that are not numerical and extracts the regressor or scalar to be predicted (the number of carats) from the provided table of data. Then, it computes the mutual information of

each column of the data **X** with the column **y** of regressors. Please notice that **y** is the name of the y dimension, but later we use y to store the regressor, which is called carat in the database. Also, **x** is the name of the x dimension, and later we use **X** to store all inputs or predictors. As a result, the best features, which are the dimensions, are selected. Indeed, the carat measure is related to the volume of the diamond, and therefore the dimensions are the inputs that carry this information.

3.5.5 Supervised and Unsupervised Learning Models

In general, machine learning algorithms can be either supervised or unsupervised. In supervised learning, the models are trained using labeled data while the latter uses unlabeled data to identify the patterns in the dataset. The most commonly used supervised learning method includes linear models such as linear regression, logistic regression, ridge regression, and Lasso regression. A regression model is mainly used to predict continuous output variables by analyzing the correlation between them. In the case of classification tasks where discrete values are predicted, the main supervised algorithms include Decision trees, Naive Bayes classifiers, support vector machines, Random Forests, etc. But when labeled data is not available, unsupervised learning tasks such as manifold learning and clustering analysis are done for dimensionality reduction and for inferring the hidden structure of the data. A few examples of manifold learning algorithms are Isomap and t-SNE, whereas K-Means and Gaussian mixture models include the main clustering methods.

```
#Regression
import numpy as np
import matplotlib.pyplot as plt
from sklearn.linear_model import LinearRegression
# Create a NumPy array of data:
X = np.array([5, 10, 15, 20, 25, 30]).reshape((-1, 1))
y = np.array([12, 20, 25, 32, 35, 40])
model = LinearRegression() #Create a linear regression model.
model_fit = model.fit(X, y) #Fit the model.
y_pred = model_fit.predict(X) #Make predictions using the model.
print('Prediction:', y_pred) #Display the predictions.
```

Output:

```
Prediction: [13.61904762 19.1047619  24.59047619 30.07619048 35.56190476
             41.04761905]
```

```
#Classification
from sklearn.datasets import load_breast_cancer
from sklearn.model_selection import train_test_split
from sklearn import svm
from sklearn import metrics
ds = load_breast_cancer() #Load the dataset.
#Display the size of the feature and the label.
print('Dataset Size: ', ds.data.shape, ds.target.shape)
# Split dataset into training set and test set
X_train, X_test, y_train, y_test = train_test_split(ds.data, ds.target,
                                   test_size=0.2)
clf = svm.SVC(kernel='rbf') #Use the non linear kernel of SVM for
                            classification.
```

```
clf.fit(X_train, y_train) #Fit the model.
y_pred = clf.predict(X_test) #Make predictions using the model.
#Display the accuracy score.
print("Accuracy:",metrics.accuracy_score(y_test, y_pred))
```

Output:

```
Dataset Size:   (569, 30) (569,)
Accuracy: 0.9035087719298246
```

```
#Dimensionality Reduction
from sklearn.datasets import load_digits
from sklearn import manifold
digits = load_digits(n_class=6) #Load the dataset.
#Assign the feature and labels to variables.
X_digits, Y_digits  = digits.data, digits. target
#Display the size of the features.
print('Dataset Size: ', X_digits.shape)
#Define the Isomap model for dimensionality reduction.
isomap = manifold.Isomap(n_neighbors=10)
# Fit the model
X_iso= isomap.fit_transform(X_digits)
#Display the size of the reduced feature set.
print('Reduced Feature Size: ', X_iso.shape)
```

Output:

```
Dataset Size:   (1083, 64)
Reduced Feature Size:   (1083, 2)
```

```
#Clustering
import matplotlib.pyplot as plt
from sklearn.datasets import make_blobs
from sklearn.mixture import GaussianMixture
# Create dataset
X, y = make_blobs(n_samples=200, n_features=2,centers=4,
                  cluster_std=0.5, shuffle=True, random_state=0)
#Define the Gaussian Mixture Model with 4 clusters.
gmm = GaussianMixture(n_components=4).fit(X)
#Predicts the labels for the features.
labels = gmm.predict(X)
```

3.5.6 Model Selection and Evaluation

Model selection is an iterative process of finding the best model by evaluating its performance and tuning the hyperparameters of this model. Scikit-learn offers us many cross-validation techniques such as KFold, stratified k-fold, and Leave One Out to compare and select the most suitable model for the problem. Following this, various performance measures such as accuracy, precision, recall, and mean squared error are used to assess the model's quality. These are the metric functions of scikit-learn that are used to evaluate the prediction error for various classification or regression tasks.

```
from sklearn.datasets import load_iris
from sklearn.linear_model import LogisticRegression
from sklearn.model_selection import KFold
from sklearn.metrics import accuracy_score

dataset = load_iris() #Load the dataset
X, y = dataset.data, dataset.target #Assign the feature and labels to
                                     variables.
#Display the size of the features and labels.
print('Dataset Size: ', X.shape, y.shape)
scores = list()
# Initialize k-fold cross validation
k_fo = KFold(n_splits=5, shuffle=True)
# enumerate splits
count = 0
for train_i, test_i in k_fo.split(X):
    count = count+1
    train_X, test_X = X[train_i], X[test_i] #Extract the train and test
                                             data.
    train_y, test_y = y[train_i], y[test_i] #Extract the train and test
                                             data.
    model = LogisticRegression(solver= 'liblinear') #Assign the logistic
                                             regression model.
    model.fit(train_X, train_y) #Fit the model.
    yhat = model.predict(test_X) #Make predictions.
    acc = accuracy_score(test_y, yhat) #Evaluate the predictions using
                                             accuracy score.
    scores.append(acc)
    print('Accuracy for Fold {}: '.format(count), acc) #Print the accuracy
                                             for each fold.
```

Output:

```
Dataset Size:  (150, 4) (150,)
Accuracy for Fold 1:   0.9666666666666667
Accuracy for Fold 2:   0.9333333333333333
Accuracy for Fold 3:   0.9666666666666667
Accuracy for Fold 4:   0.9333333333333333
Accuracy for Fold 5:   0.9333333333333333
```

3.6 Pandas

Pandas is an open-source Python library built on NumPy. It provides various data structures and data analysis tools for flexible and high-performance data processing. The term pandas is coined from the word "panel data," which is an econometrics term for multivariate datasets. In general, Pandas are used for loading, cleaning, arranging, modeling, and investigating the data. The application of Pandas can be found in economics, statistics, stock prediction, analytics, and advertising.

The Pandas package can be installed in the Anaconda prompt using either of the following commands:

pip install pandas
conda install pandas

After installation, Pandas is imported using the alternate name pd.

```
import pandas as pd
print(pd.__version__) #outputs the version of Pandas.
```

Output:

```
1.3.5
```

3.6.1 Pandas Data Structures

3.6.1.1 Series

It is a one-dimensional labeled array, generally a column that contains similar data types. If the labels are not defined, the values are given their corresponding index number as their labels.

```
s = pd.Series([10,20,30,40], index = ['a','b','c','d'])
#defining a series with specified labels.
s1 = pd.Series([10,20,30,40]) #defining a series with no labels specified.
print(s1[0]) #outputs 10 by accessing the zeroth value of the series.
```

Output:

```
10
```

3.6.1.2 Dataframe

It is made up of multiple rows and columns, forming a table consisting of a collection of series. When we use a dictionary to construct a data frame, each key and value corresponds to a column of the data frame.

```
import pandas as pd
data = {'Day':['Monday','Thursday','Saturday'], 'Year':[2001,2010,2020]}
#defining a dataframe object to load the data from a dictionary of lists.
df = pd.DataFrame(data)
print(df)
```

Output:

```
        Day  Year
0     Monday  2001
1   Thursday  2010
2   Saturday  2020
```

Example 3.6.1 *(Different inputs for series and dataframe)*
In this example, we discuss the different ways to create a series and data frame from different inputs. In the previous code snippet, a series was defined using a list. The three other ways to define the input of a series are by using a dictionary, a scalar, or an array. Let us define a dictionary diction = {'apple':45, 'melon':20, 'avocado':32}. When it is passed as an input to the series without any index, the keys are used as the indices. Here the output column will contain the numbers 45, 20, and 30 with their indices as apple, melon, and

avocado. When a scalar is used as the input to the series, it is necessary to provide indices. The scalar repeats itself to match the length of the index. Finally, in order to create a series from an array, we import a NumPy module to use the array() function to define an array arr = np.array(['p',' a', 'n',' d', 'a','s']). This array is later given as input to the series. A data frame on the other hand can also have multiple inputs such as a list of lists, a list of dictionaries, a dictionary of NumPy array, and a dictionary of pandas series. When the input is a list of lists defined as list1=[['Japan',' Tokyo'],['Chile',' Santiago'],['Qatar', 'Doha']], each inner list corresponds to each row of the data frame. In the case of a list of dictionaries, we define list_dict = [{'Student': 'Robert', 'Subject': 'Physics', 'Marks': 90}, {'Student': 'Nick', 'Subject': 'Chemistry', 'Marks': 85}, {'Student': 'Audrey', 'Subject': 'Biology', 'Marks': 72}]. Here each key of the dictionary corresponds to the column names and each of the values represents each row. Next, to create a data frame from a dictionary of arrays, we first import a NumPy module to use the array() function. Let us define the array as arr = np.array([['Norton', 'Steve', 'Liam'], [5, 2, 7], ['Dancer', 'Singer', 'Producer']]). Next a dictionary of arrays is created as dict_arr = {'Name': arr[0],'Experience': arr[1],'Profession': arr[2]}. The dictionary keys denote the column names and each array element corresponds to a column. Finally, to create a dictionary we first define different series and then pass it to a dictionary as dict_series = {'Fruit': series1, 'Count': series2, 'Color':series3}. Here each series denotes a column whereas the dictionary keys represent the column names.

3.6.2 Data Selection

Pandas use data selection to choose specific rows and columns from the data frame. The data is identified using specific indicators such as axis labels, and this is further used in multiaxis indexing. Primarily, pandas use the *loc[]* operator to select specific rows by using the labels of the data frame. In order to select the data by position, integer-based indexing is implemented using the *iloc[]* operator.

```
import pandas as pd
data = {'Month':['December','March','October'],
'Season':['Winter','Spring','Fall']} #create a dictionary of lists.
df = pd.DataFrame(data) #define a dataframe.
df.loc[1] #loc function is used to return row 1.
df.loc[[1,2]] #returns rows 1 and 2.
df1 = pd.DataFrame(data, index = ["Climate1", "Climate2", "Climate3"])
#naming the indices of the dataframe
df1.loc["Climate1"] # returns the row corresponding to index Climate1.
df1.iloc[:2] #returns the row corresponding to index 1 and 2
```

3.6.3 Data Manipulation

3.6.3.1 Sorting
It can be done in two ways, which include sorting by label and by value. While sorting by label, the *sort_index()* method is used to sort row labels of the data frame and the default sorting is done in ascending order. Further, the order of sorting can be changed by setting the ascending parameter in the *sort_index()* function to false. In order to sort by column labels, the axis argument of the *sort_index()* function is set to 1. Next, the *sort_values()* method

of pandas is used to sort the values of the data frame along either axis by defining a 'by' argument.

```
#SORT BY LABEL
import pandas as pd
import numpy as np
#define a list of lists.
list_list = [['Canada','Ottawa'],['Italy','Rome'],['Peru','Lima']]
#create the dataframe.
df_nosort = pd.DataFrame(list_list,index=[3,1,2],columns=['Country', '
                              Capital'])
df_sorta = df_nosort.sort_index() #sorting by label in ascending order.
df_sortd = df_nosort.sort_index(ascending=False) #sorting by label in
                              descending order.
df_sortc = df_nosort.sort_index(axis=1) #sorting by column label.
```

```
#SORT BY VALUE
import pandas as pd
datax = {'A': [10,40,30,25],'B': [2016,2007,2020,2001]} #define a
                              dictionary of lists.
dfx_unsort = pd.DataFrame(datax, columns=['A','B']) #create a dataframe.
print(dfx_unsort) #outputs unsorted dataframe.
dfx_sort = dfx_unsort.sort_values(by = 'B') #sort by values along an axis.
dfx_sortm = dfx_unsort.sort_values(by = ['A','B']) #sort by multiple
                              columns.
print(dfx_sortm) #outputs sorted dataframe.
print(dfx_sortm.rank()) #assign rank to the values of the dataframe and
                              outputs the result.
```

Output:

```
    A    B
0   10   2016
1   40   2007
2   30   2020
3   25   2001
    A    B
0   10   2016
3   25   2001
2   30   2020
1   40   2007
    A    B
0  1.0  3.0
3  2.0  1.0
2  3.0  4.0
1  4.0  2.0
```

3.6.3.2 Grouping
This operation is used to split the data into groups and apply a function to these subsets. The most common functions are aggregation, transformation, and filtration. The main functionality of data aggregation is that it can be used to provide a statistical summary by computing the mean, sum, minimum, maximum, etc. In transformation, a group-specific computation is performed so that the output and input data frames are able to maintain the same size. Finally, filtration is used to eliminate unwanted data using a condition.

The two main functions for grouping include *groupby* and *get_group*. The *groupby* function is used to split the data frame by column name, and *get_group* function is used to select a group from a pandas *groupby* object.

```
#GROUPING THE DATAFRAME
import pandas as pd
data1 = {'Date':['1-1-2021', '1-2-2021', '1-3-2021', '1-4-2021',
                 '1-5-2021', '1-6-2021', '1-7-2021', '1-8-2021'],
         'High':[270, 214, 522, 632,
                 343, 836, 427, 132],
         'Low':[16, 24, 22, 32,
                33, 36, 27, 32],
         'Open':[45,183,261,382,
                 90,534,60,55],
         'Close':[103,89,333, 384,
                  200,136,68,118]} #define a dictionary. of lists.
df = pd.DataFrame(data1) #create a dataframe.
group1 = df.groupby('Date')
df.groupby('Date').groups #grouping data with one key.
group1.get_group('1-6-2021') #selects a single group.
```

```
#APPLYING A FUNCTION
import pandas as pd
import numpy as np
dataw = {'Name':['Fred', 'George', 'Fred', 'Harry',
'Ron', 'Percy', 'Harry', 'Fred'], #define a dictionary of lists.
         'Marks':[80, 95, 75, 70,
         98, 60, 75, 62]}
df = pd.DataFrame(dataw) #create a dataframe.
groupw = df.groupby('Name') #grouping data with one key.
groupw.aggregate(np.sum) #performing aggregation using aggregate method.
tf = lambda x: x - x.mean() #subtracting the mean.
groupw.transform(tf)   #applying the transform function.
groupw.filter(lambda x: len(x) >= 2) #filtering the data.
```

3.6.4 Handling Missing Data

This is a common problem prevalent in most real-time databases. The tabulated data might have multiple missing values leading to reduced performance for many data science problems. Henceforth, data cleaning is highly essential, and one of the most powerful tools employed is pandas. It uses various functions to detect the missing values and manages them efficiently as per the problem statement. The standard missing values in pandas are NaN(Not a number), NA(Not available), and None. In order to detect the missing values, pandas use the *isnull()* and *nonnull()* functions. They output the boolean values to denote the missing values in the data frame.

```
import pandas as pd
import numpy as np
datag = {'A':[None, 90, np.nan, 95],
         'B': [30, 45, 56, np.nan],
         'C':[np.nan, 40, 80, None],
         'D':[70, 40, 24, None]} #define a dictionary of lists.
df = pd.DataFrame(datag) #create a dataframe.
df.isnull() #check the missing values using isnull().
df.notnull() #check the missing values using notnull().
```

After finding the missing values, it is possible to either drop or replace these values in the data frame. The *dropna()* function is used to drop a row or column with null values. It has three parameters axis, how, and thresh. The default value of the axis is 0 representing the rows, whereas the how parameter takes either of the two string values 'any' or 'all'. The third parameter thresh inputs an integer that corresponds to a threshold for missing values in order for a row or column to be dropped. The *fillna()* function on the other hand is used to replace the missing values.

```
import pandas as pd
listq = [[200,np.nan,800],[np.nan,np.nan,600],
        [900,None,None],[500,np.nan,None]] #define a list of lists.
df = pd.DataFrame(listq,columns=['Column1','Column2','Column3']) #create
                                        the dataframe.
df.dropna(axis=1,how='any',thresh=3)
df1=df.dropna(axis=1,how='all') #drops a column when all of its values are
                                        missing.
df2=df.dropna(axis=1,thresh=2) #drops a column with atleast 2 missing
                                        values.
df3=df.fillna(0) #replaces the missing values with zeros.
```

3.6.5   Input–Output Tools

In practical problems, we usually work with data that already exists. Specifically, this data is saved in multiple formats, and it is most commonly stored as comma-separated values also known as CSV files. It is a table of values that are separated by commas and pandas use the read_csv() function to read this as a data frame and *to_csv()* function to save the data frame as a CSV file. Since CSVs do not have indexes like data frames, while reading the CSV file we add the index by setting the index_col parameter as zero. This forces pandas to use the first column of the data frame as the index. In the below code, we convert the xor dataset implemented in Example 3.1.3 to a data frame to illustrate how the users can read and write from custom datasets.

```
#WRITING TO A CSV FILE
import pandas as pd
#create a dictionary and define the dataframe.
df = pd.DataFrame({'Feature1':X[0,:],'Feature2':X[1,:],'Label': y[0,:]},
                                columns=['Feature1','Feature2','Label
                                '])
df.to_csv('pandas_write.csv',index=False) #write to a csv file and drop
                                        the index.
#READING FROM A CSV FILE
import pandas as pd
xor = pd.read_csv("pandas_write.csv") #read csv file as a dataframe.
print(xor.shape)
```

Output:

```
(400, 3)
```

The other common formats used for reading and writing data are Excel, JSON, and SQL. Pandas use functions such as read_excel, read_json, and read_sql to import the data from different sources. On the other hand, the to_excel, to_json, and to_excel commands are used in order to write a data frame to xlsx, JSON, and SQL formats.

3.6.6 Data Information Retrieval

The information present in the data can be inspected for data analysis using various pandas functions. The *info()* function provides the necessary details about the data frame. It summarizes the number of rows and columns, the number of non-null values, the data type in each column, and the memory usage of the data frame. Moreover, a detailed description of the statistical parameters such as mean and standard deviation can be retrieved using the *describe()* function. When there are a large number of values in a data frame, the contents can be examined by using two commands. The *head()* command outputs only the first five rows, whereas the *tail()* command outputs the last five rows of the data frame. Finally, the *value_counts()* function can be used in order to display the count of the unique rows of the data frame.

```
import pandas as pd
df = pd.read_csv("pandas_write.csv") #read csv file as a dataframe
df.info() #outputs details about the dataframe
df.head() #outputs the first five rows of the dataframe
df.tail() #outputs the last five rows of the dataframe
df.describe(include='all') #outputs some basic statistical details of a
                                 data frame of numeric values
df.Feature1.value_counts() #outputs a series with counts of distinct rows
                                 in the dataframe
```

3.6.7 Data Operations

Data analysis in pandas is further facilitated using functions that perform the merge, join, append, and concatenate operations. Both *merge()* and *join()* functions support horizontal combination, whereas *append()* and *concat()* are used for vertical combination. The main role of *merge()* function is to combine the data frame with common columns or indices. The different types of merge operations performed are left, right, inner, and outer. As the name suggests, the left and right operations use only keys from the left and right dataframe while preserving the key order. In the case of outer operation, the keys are sorted lexicographically, and it uses the union of keys from both left and right dataframe. The intersection of keys from both data frames is used in the inner operation, which further preserves the order of only the left keys.

```
import pandas as pd
df_left=pd.DataFrame({"keyx": ["A", "B", "C", "D"],
        "keyy": ["A", "A", "D", "B"],
        "Name": ["Alex", "Daniella", "Fiona", "Kiara"],
        "Age": ["23", "31", "26", "29"]}) #define a dataframe.
df_right = pd.DataFrame({"keyx": ["A", "B", "C", "D"],
        "keyy": ["A", "A", "A", "A"],
        "Job": ["Writer", "Painter", "Doctor", "Engineer"],
        "Country": ["Russia", "France", "Italy", "Greece"]}) #define
                                 another dataframe.
out = pd.merge(df_left, df_right, on=["keyx", "keyy"]) #merge two
                                 dataframes using the keys.
out1 = pd.merge(df_left, df_right, how='outer') #merges the union of keys
                                 from both dataframes.
```

The *join()* function is used to combine the columns of two data frames with different indexes. Here only one data frame can be specified and later by using the *join()* function it can be combined with the other data frame. This function uses the *lsuffix* and *rsuffix* parameters to define a suffix to add to any overlapping column.

```
import pandas as pd
#create a dataframe.
left_df = pd.DataFrame({"X": ["X1", "X2", "X3", "X4"],
"Y": ["Y1", "Y2", "Y3", "Y4"]},
index=[1,2,3,4])
#create another dataframe.
right_df = pd.DataFrame({"X": ["X11", "X12", "X13"],
"Q": ["Q1", "Q2", "Q3"]}, index=[1,3,4])
#join the dataframe with overlapping columns.
out = left_df.join(right_df,lsuffix='_left', rsuffix='_right')
```

The *concat()* function links the two data frames along an axis, either rows or columns. Unlike the merging techniques, concatenation does not allow the resultant dataset to have the rows of the input data frames shuffled together based on any commonality. Additionally, the *append()* function is used as a simple yet efficient shortcut for concatenation.

```
import pandas as pd
dfx = pd.DataFrame({'Name': ['A', 'B', 'C', 'D'],
    'Marks': [50,99,72,60]}) #define a dataframe.
dfy = pd.DataFrame({'Name': ['E', 'F', 'G', 'H'],
    'Marks': [76,85,93,96]}) #define another dataframe.
out = pd.concat([dfx, dfy]) #concatenate along the rows.
out1 = pd.concat([dfx, dfy], axis=1) #concatenate along the columns.
out2 = pd.concat([dfx, dfy], ignore_index=True) #concatenate to ignore
                                    existing indices.
out3 = dfy.append(dfx) #append along the rows.
```

3.6.8 Data Visualization

Pandas provide an easy-to-use interface built over matplotlib for data visualization by using less code. Unlike matplotlib, it uses less code to create a meaningful visual representation of the data. Pandas visualization tool uses the *plot()* function to produce line plots, scatter plots, bar graphs, histograms, pie plots, area plots, box plots, and kernel density estimation plots. It essentially provides a graphical representation of all the columns along with their labels. Figure 3.23 presents three distinct bar plots, and Fig. 3.24 shows the kernel density estimation plots created using the pandas library for data visualization.

```
import numpy as np
import pandas as pd
#define a dataframe.
df = pd.DataFrame(np.random.rand(8,5),columns=('Data1', 'Data2', 'Data3'))
print(df) #outputs the dataframe.

#LINE PLOT
df.plot() #line plot
df.plot(subplots=True, figsize=(10,10)) #create subplots for each columns.

#SCATTER PLOT
#scatter plot to check correlation.
df.plot(x="Data1", y="Data2", kind="scatter",color="red", marker="*", s=
                                    100)
```

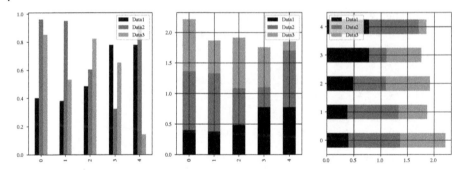

Figure 3.23 Different bar plots using pandas.

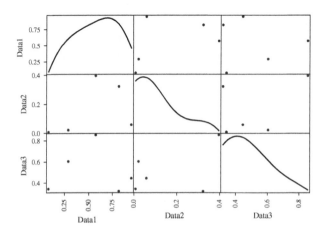

Figure 3.24 Kernel density estimation plot using pandas.

```
#BAR PLOT
fig, axes = plt.subplots(nrows=1, ncols=3,figsize=(15, 5))
df.plot(kind="bar",ax=axes[0]) #bar plot of the dataframe from the above
                               example.
#stacked bar plot to highlight the comparison between different
                               categories.
df.plot(kind="bar", stacked=True,grid = True, legend = True,ax=axes[1])
df.plot(kind="barh", stacked=True,grid = True, legend = True,ax=axes[2])
                               #horizontally stacked bar plot.
plt.show()
```

```
#HISTOGRAM PLOT
df.plot.hist(bins=20) #histogram plot.
#plot the histograms separately.
df[['Data1','Data2']].hist(bins=20,figsize=(10, 10))

#PIE PLOT
#specifying color to pie plot.
colors = ['lightgreen', 'lightpink', 'coral', 'magenta', 'yellow']
#subplots for the pie plot.
df.plot(kind='pie',colors=colors,subplots=True, figsize=(15, 4),title = "
                               Data points")

#AREA PLOT
```

```
#specifying colors to area plot.
color1=['coral', 'skyblue', 'yellow']
#The alpha parameter adds some translucent look to the area plot.
df.plot(kind='area', alpha=0.4, color=color1,figsize=(8, 6), title='Area
                            Plot', fontsize=12)
#Unstacked area plot.
df.plot(kind='area',stacked=False, figsize=(8, 6), fontsize=12)

#BOX PLOT
df.plot(kind='box',figsize=(8, 6)) #box plot.
df.plot.box(vert=False, positions=[1, 2, 3],figsize=(8, 6)) #horizontal
                            box plot.
```

```
#KERNEL DENSITY ESTIMATION PLOT
from pandas.plotting import scatter_matrix
#kernel density estimation plot
scatter_matrix(df[['Data1', 'Data2', 'Data3']], alpha = 0.9, diagonal = '
                            kde')
```

3.7 Seaborn

Seaborn is a data visualization library in Python that provides a high-level interface to Matplotlib. It is also a tool of choice for statistical data exploration in Python. The high-level commands in Seaborn are used to add esthetically pleasing default themes and custom color palettes to the statistical plots. Further, it is also used to extract visual information from data frames. The main dependencies of Seaborn are Python, NumPy, Scipy, pandas, and Matplotlib.

The Seaborn package can be installed in the Anaconda prompt using either of the following commands:

pip install seaborn
conda install seaborn

After installation, Seaborn is imported as follows.

```
import seaborn as sns
print(sns.__version__) #outputs the version of Seaborn.
```

Output:

```
0.11.2
```

3.7.1 Seaborn Datasets

The current version of seaborn provides a total of 18 built-in datasets. These datasets can be used to demonstrate the ability of seaborn and its powerful plotting functions. They are stored in designated GitHub repositories so that when seaborn is installed, the datasets are downloaded automatically. A list of the available datasets can be obtained using the function *get_dataset_names()*. Finally from the available datasets, we use the *sns.load_dataset* method to load them into a pandas dataframe.

```
import seaborn as sns
import pandas as pd
print(sns.get_dataset_names()) #list the available datasets in seaborn.
df = sns.load_dataset('iris') #loading dataset.
df.head() #viewing the first 5 rows of the dataframe.
```

3.7.2 Plotting with Seaborn

3.7.2.1 Univariate Plots

These plots are used to describe the nature of a single variable, and they represent the rate of occurrence of each unique value of a given variable. These visualizations are done using barplots and histograms, and the commonly used functions are the *histplot()* and *countplot()*. A *histplot()* outputs a histogram by plotting the distribution of the given variable. Figure 3.25 showcases a histogram plot focusing on a single variable, created using Seaborn. In the case of the *countplot()* function, it is used to display the distribution of categorical variables.

```
#HISTPLOT
import seaborn as sns
import matplotlib.pyplot as plt
df = sns.load_dataset('iris') #loading dataset.
#set figure
f, ax = plt.subplots(1,1)
csfont = {'fontname':'serif'} #define the font family
#graph histogram
sns.histplot(df['sepal_length'], bins=10, alpha=0.5, color='black', label=
                              'sepal length')
sns.histplot(df['sepal_width'], bins=10, alpha = 0.5, color='grey', label=
                              'sepal width')
#set legend
plt.legend(loc='upper right')
#set title & axis titles
plt.xlabel('Frequency',fontsize=12,**csfont) #labels the x-axis.
plt.ylabel('Values',fontsize=12,**csfont) #labels the y-axis.
plt.xticks(fontsize=12,**csfont)
plt.yticks(fontsize=12,**csfont)
#set x & y ranges
plt.xlim(0,10)
plt.ylim(0,40)
plt.savefig('uni.pdf')
plt.show()
```

```
#COUNTPLOT
sns.countplot(x="species", data=df)
plt.title("Count of Species")
plt.show()
```

3.7.2.2 Bivariate Plots

These plots are mainly used to demonstrate the relationship between two variables. Depending upon the type of variables, different types of functions such as *scatterplot()* and *jointplot()* are used for plotting. *Scatterplot()* method provides a joint representation of two or more variables by using a set of points and hence it is available in both 2D as well

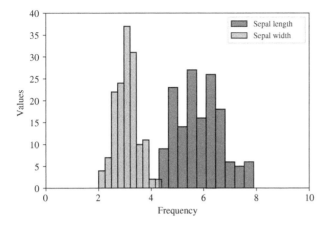

Figure 3.25 Univariate plot using the histplot() function.

as 3D. *Lineplot()* is a version of *scatterplot()* where the data is represented using a line. On the other hand, the *jointplots()* function is used in both univariate and bivariate plotting. Figure 3.26 showcases a joint plot between two variables. The central plot will correspond to a bivariate analysis, whereas the univariate plots of the variables are displayed on the top and right sides of the graph.

```
import seaborn as sns
import matplotlib.pyplot as plt
plt.style.use('grayscale')
df1 = sns.load_dataset('tips') #loading dataset.

######################################
#SCATTERPLOT
sns.scatterplot(x='total_bill', y='tip', data=df1, hue='time')
plt.title("Scatterplot of total_bill vs. tip") #displays the title.
plt.show()

######################################
#LINEPLOT
sns.lineplot(x="total_bill", y="tip", data=df1)
plt.title("Lineplot of total_bill vs. tip") #displays the title.
plt.show()
```

```
#JOINTPLOT
h=sns.jointplot(x='total_bill', y='tip', data=df1)
csfont = {'fontname':'serif'} #define the font family
h.ax_joint.set_xlabel('total_bill',fontsize=12,**csfont) #custom axis
                           label for x axis
h.ax_joint.set_ylabel('tip',fontsize=12,**csfont) #custom axis label for y
                           axis
plt.show()
```

3.7.2.3 Multivariate Plots
These plots can show the relationship between three or more different variables. In order to separate features in multiple dimensions, seaborn uses the hue parameter. The different

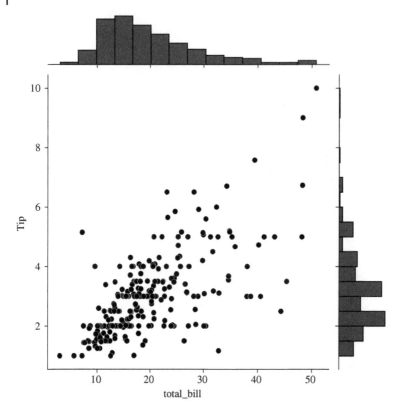

Figure 3.26 Joint plot of total_bill vs tip.

plot functions used for multivariate analysis are *scatterplot()*, *barplot()*, and *pairplot()*. While plotting three variables in *scatterplot()*, two variables can be numerical variables, while the third variable can be categorical and can be used to differentiate the groups within the data. Figure 3.27 showcases a scatterplot using three variables. In order to aggregate categorical

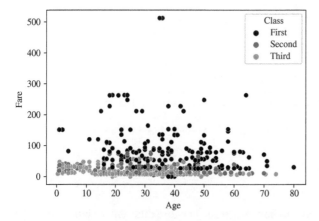

Figure 3.27 Multivariate plot using scatterplot() function.

data, we use *barplot()* to illustrate the relationship between the variables. Here two variables can be categorical, whereas the third can be a numerical variable. Finally, the *pairplot()* function shows the pairwise relationships in a dataset.

```
import seaborn as sns
import matplotlib.pyplot as plt
plt.style.use('grayscale')
df2 = sns.load_dataset('titanic') #loading dataset.
#BARPLOT
sns.barplot(x='who', y='age', data=df2, hue='class')
plt.show()
#####################################
#PAIRPLOT
sns.pairplot(df2[['survived', 'pclass', 'age', 'sibsp', 'parch']], hue='
                                survived')
plt.show()
```

```
#SCATTERPLOT
sns.scatterplot(x='age', y='fare', data=df2, hue='class')
csfont = {'fontname':'serif'} #define the font family
plt.xlabel('age',fontsize=12,**csfont)
plt.ylabel('fare',fontsize=12,**csfont)
plt.show()
```

Example 3.7.1   *(Plotting numerical and categorical variables)*
In this example, we discuss the different ways to visualize numerical and categorical variables. Numerical features are features with continuous data points. We can use two popular plots to observe the distribution and variability of these features. In the case of numerical features where the measurable quantity is features with continuous data points, we use boxplots and violinplots to facilitate the comparison between these variables. Boxplots are used to depict the distribution of the data through their quartiles, whereas violin plots are a combination of box plots and kernel density estimation plots. In order to visualize these plots, let us first load an inbuilt dataset 'flights' from Seaborn into a data frame named df3. Later the numerical variables 'year' and 'passengers' are passed on to the *boxplot()* and *violinplot()* methods for visualization. Meanwhile, to plot categorical features, seaborn uses plots such as *stripplot()* and *swarmplot()*. Here we load the inbuilt dataset named 'mpg' and compare its categorical features 'origin' and 'cylinders' against the numerical feature 'weight'. The stripplot is a single-axis scatterplot that is used to differentiate different categories by specifying the hue parameter. Whereas, swarm plots are similar to strip plots, but here the data points are arranged in such a manner that it does not overlap each other.

3.7.3   Additional Plotting Functions

3.7.3.1   Correlation Plots
In regression models, it is essential to check the correlation between the variables. Seaborn uses two main functions, *regplot()* and *lmplot()*, to visualize this linear relationship. Both these functions create a scatterplot of two variables, fit the regression model, and plot the resulting regression line. In each case, the resulting plots are identical, except that the shapes of the figures are different. Figure 3.28 displays a visual representation of the linear correlation between two variables, achieved through the use of the *lmplot()* function.

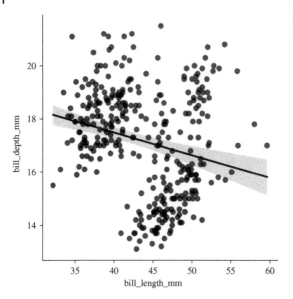

Figure 3.28 Correlation plot using lmplot() function.

3.7.3.2 Point Plots

These plots help to visualize the show point estimates and confidence intervals of values at each level of the categorical variable. They are mainly used to find the change in a variable as it shows the mean values and error rate surrounding those mean values.

3.7.3.3 Cat Plots

Cat plots show the frequencies of the classes of one or more categorical variables. The *catplot()* function provides a new framework to visualize and compare different features of the data by giving access to several types of plots. Currently, catplot encompasses eight different categorical plots available in Seaborn. We are able to specify the type of plot using the kind parameter and the default value for it is "strip", denoting *stripplot()*. Figure 3.29 presents a cat plot visualizing relationships between distinct categorical variables.

```
import seaborn as sns
import matplotlib.pyplot as plt
df5 = sns.load_dataset('penguins') #loading dataset.
#REGPLOT
sns.regplot(x="bill_length_mm", y="bill_depth_mm", data=df5)
plt.show()
```

```
#LMPLOT
sns.lmplot(x="bill_length_mm", y="bill_depth_mm", data=df5, order=1)
csfont = {'fontname':'serif'} #define the font family
plt.xlabel('bill_length_mm',fontsize=12,**csfont)
plt.ylabel('bill_depth_mm',fontsize=12,**csfont)
plt.show()
```

```
#POINTPLOT
sns.pointplot(x="sex", y="body_mass_g", hue="species", data=df5)
plt.show()
```

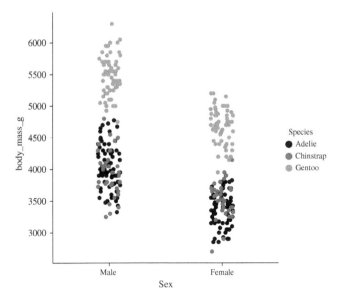

Figure 3.29 Categorical plot using catplot() function.

```
#CATPLOT
sns.catplot(x="sex", y="body_mass_g", hue="species", data=df5)
csfont = {'fontname':'serif'} #define the font family
plt.xlabel('sex',fontsize=12,**csfont)
plt.ylabel('body_mass_g',fontsize=12,**csfont)
plt.show()
```

Output:

3.8 Python Libraries for NLP

Natural language processing (NLP) is the subfield of artificial intelligence, linguistics, and computer science that provides computers the ability to understand and process human language. Through this technology, the machines are able to understand the context of documents/texts and can use them to automate certain repetitive tasks using languages. Some examples of natural language processing (NLP) include machine translation, text generation, summarization, spell checking, etc. The most popular NLP tools available in Python are NLTK and spaCy. Both these libraries can be installed and used for building chatbots, extracting entities, summarizing texts, etc.

3.8.1 Natural Language Toolkit (NLTK)

natural language toolkit (NLTK) is one of the most commonly used NLP libraries in python. It was developed by Steven Bird and Edward Loper from the University of Pennsylvania (Bird et al. 2009). NLTK comprises libraries that can be used to develop statistical and symbolic NLP programs using Python. It supports different functionalities such as tokenization, classification, stemming, semantic reasoning, tagging, and parsing. More details on NLTK API can be found here: https://www.nltk.org/.

The NLTK library can be installed in the Anaconda prompt using either of the following commands:

pip install nltk
conda install -c anaconda nltk

After installation, NLTK can be imported as follows:

```
import nltk
print(nltk.__version__)
```

Output:

```
3.8.1
```

3.8.2 SpaCy

SpaCy is an open-source library that is used for much more advanced NLP techniques (https://spacy.io). It was developed by Matthew Honnibal and Ines Montani and was first released on October 19, 2016 (github link). SpaCy has a lot of in-built functionalities and is known for its efficiency in analyzing data associated with NLP. SpaCy is more focused on production usage as it supports machine learning as well as deep learning workflows. This allows easy integration of SpaCy with Tensorflow and PyTorch. This package is mainly written in Python and Cython Choi et al. (2015). SpaCy has the ability to provide support in NLP-related tasks in various languages. The languages that are supported by SpaCy can be found here: Spacy|model-languages.

SpaCy can be installed in Anaconda prompt using the following commands

pip install -U spacy
conda install -c conda-forge spacy

The next step would be to download the English language pipeline *en_core_web_sm*, which is trained on web text data which includes entities, vocabulary, and syntax associated with the language.

python -m spacy download en_core_web_sm

After installation, the spaCy library can be imported as follows:

```
import spacy
print(spacy.__version__)
```

Output:

```
3.5.2
```

3.8.3 NLP Techniques

The NLP tools can be used for various kinds of functionalities or techniques that can be used to easily interpret the human language. These techniques can be further supplemented with statistical or machine-learning methods to automate the process. The basic idea behind these techniques includes breaking down the language into shorter, more interpretable elemental pieces. This can help understand the relationship between these pieces as well as interpret their meanings when put together.

Let us now look into the specific operations/techniques with the terminologies used for them in NLP. The NLP techniques discussed below are most commonly used for data preprocessing and cleaning, which helps in making the text data easy to analyze. Following this, we can implement algorithms or machine learning/deep learning techniques to process these features to perform the neccssary task.

3.8.3.1 Tokenization

This is the first preprocessing step in most of the NLP pipeline. Here, the unstructured data (natural language text) is divided into small discrete elements of information. In the process, an unstructured string is immediately converted to a numerical data structure. These discrete elements or components are called *tokens*. There are different ways to perform tokenization such as based on white space, punctuation, words, and sentences. An example of white space tokenization is shown in Fig. 3.30.

Let us analyze an example of tokenizing a sentence into words using NLTK. Note that for tokenizing using NLTK, we need to download *Punkt Sentence Tokenizer*, which uses an unsupervised algorithm to divide the text into sentences.

```
import nltk
nltk.download('punkt')
from nltk.tokenize import word_tokenize
# Let us use a simple sentence here
doc = """How are you doing?"""
word_tokenize(doc) # Tokenizing the sentence into words
```

Output:

```
['How', 'are', 'you', 'doing', '?']
```

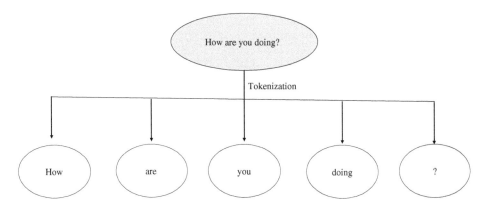

Figure 3.30 Example of a white space tokenization of a sentence.

Similar to word tokenization, we can also do sentence tokenization as follows:

```
import nltk
nltk.download('punkt')
from nltk.tokenize import sent_tokenize

# Let us use a quote by Benjamin Franklin as an example
doc = """Tell me and I forget. Teach me and I remember. Involve me and I
                                  learn."""

#Splitting the text into sentences
sent_tokenize(doc)
```

Output:

```
['Tell me and I forget.',
 'Teach me and I remember.',
 'Involve me and I learn.']
```

Similarly, tokenization can be done using SpaCy library as follows:

```
import spacy
nlp = spacy.load('en_core_web_sm')
# Create a Doc object
doc = nlp(u'How are you doing?')
# Print each token separately
for token in doc:
    print(token.text)
```

Output:

```
How
are
you
doing
?
```

To split the text into sentences using Spacy, the *sents* attribute can be used as follows:

```
import spacy
nlp = spacy.load('en_core_web_sm')

# Create a Doc object
doc = nlp(u'Tell me and I forget. Teach me and I remember. Involve me and
                                  I learn.')

# Print each token separately
for sent in doc.sents:
    print(sent.text)
```

Output:

```
Tell me and I forget.
Teach me and I remember.
Involve me and I learn.
```

Figure 3.31 Example of stemming.

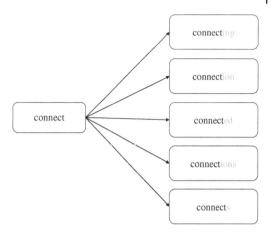

3.8.3.2 Stemming

Stemming is the process of getting the stem of a word by removing affixes from a specific word. The stem of the word corresponds to its basic form. In the English language, we come across several variants of a single term. This might result in redundancy during processing. Most of such words are associated with the same root word even though they are used to communicate in different grammatical contexts such as tense, case, person, and mood. An example of Stemming is shown in Fig. 3.31. In the example, *"connect"* is the stem word. The rest of the words i.e. *"connecting"*, *"connection"*, *"connected"*, *"connections"*, *"connects"* are associated with this root word *connect* and they share similar meaning as that of the root. In many NLP applications, this process can help in feature reduction by avoiding data redundancy associated with the language. This helps in avoiding repetition, hence helping to build a robust model.

```python
from nltk.stem import PorterStemmer
porter = PorterStemmer() # PorterStemmer
print(porter.stem("connecting"))
```

Output:

```
connect
```

Similar to NLTK, we can use SpaCy to perform stemming as follows:

```python
import spacy

# Load the English language model in Spacy
nlp = spacy.load("en_core_web_sm")
# Word for stemming and lemmatization
word = "connecting"
# Create a single-token document
doc = nlp(word)
# Stemming using Spacy
stemmed_word = doc[0].lemma_
print("Stemmed Word:", stemmed_word)
```

Output:

```
Stemmed Word: connect
```

3.8.3.3 Lemmatization

Lemmatization works similarly to stemming but has the added advantage of understanding the structure of the language to better interpret the context of the word and then associate it with a root word. Stemming can sometimes lead to root/stem words with meaningless base forms. However, lemmatization not only looks into word reduction but also considers the context of the word being used, hence giving it a meaningful base form. Let us take the example of the word *"caring"*. Stemming this word gives us *"car"*, whereas lemmatizing this word gives us the word *"care"* which is the right meaningful root word associated with *"caring"*. The only drawback of lemmatization is that it is computationally expensive. The process of lemmatization involves looking into the language's full vocabulary, which might require look-up tables etc. Therefore, for large datasets, stemming can be a good alternative option.

```
from nltk.stem import PorterStemmer
from nltk.stem import LancasterStemmer
porter = PorterStemmer() # PorterStemmer
lancaster = LancasterStemmer() # LancasterStemmer
print(porter.stem("caring"))
print(lancaster.stem("caring"))
```

Output:

```
care
car
```

Using the SpaCy library, we can perform stemming and lemmatization using the following code snippet:

```
import spacy

# Load the English language model in Spacy
nlp = spacy.load("en_core_web_sm")
# Word for stemming and lemmatization
word = "caring"
# Create a single-token document
doc = nlp(word)
# Stemming using Spacy
stemmed_word = doc[0].lemma_
# Lemmatization using Spacy
lemmatized_word = doc[0].lemma_ if doc[0].lemma_ != '-PRON-' else doc[0].
                                   text

# Print the results
print("Original Word:", word)
print("Stemmed Word:", stemmed_word)
print("Lemmatized Word:", lemmatized_word)
```

Output:

```
Original Word: caring
Stemmed Word: care
Lemmatized Word: care
```

3.8.3.4 Stop Words

Stop words correspond to a set of most commonly used words in a language. This can help a lot in processing speeds as well as in applications such as search query pages where it is important to bring up results by searching the relevant words instead of searching for the widely used words. For example, if we search for *"What is NLP?"*, we would like to learn more about *"NLP"* rather than talking about *"what is"*. Such common words need to be avoided in these kinds of applications. Generally, these stop words are stored in the form of a list, and this list can be used to avoid such words from being analyzed. Similarly, the stop words can also help in understanding the context of the search query better. For example, there can different types of search queries on the same topic, such as *"What is NLP?"* or *"Where is NLP used?"*. The stop words here, *"What is* and *"Where is"* can be quite useful in refining the search results.

```python
import nltk
from nltk.corpus import stopwords
from nltk.tokenize import word_tokenize
nltk.download('stopwords')
nltk.download('punkt')
sentence = "What is NLP?" # Example sentence
words = word_tokenize(sentence) # Tokenize the sentence into words
stop_words = set(stopwords.words('english')) # Get the English stopwords
                                from NLTK
filtered_words = [word for word in words if word.lower() not in stop_words
                        ] # Remove stopwords from the
                        sentence
print("Stopwords in the sentence are:", filtered_words) # Print the
                        filtered words
```

Output:

```
Stopwords in the sentence are: ['NLP', '?']
```

The removal of stopwords using the SpaCy library is shown in the below code snippet:

```python
import spacy
nlp = spacy.load('en_core_web_sm') # Load the English language model in
                                spaCy
sentence = "What is NLP?" # Example sentence
doc = nlp(sentence) # Tokenize the sentence using spaCy
filtered_words = [token.text for token in doc if not token.is_stop] #
                        Remove stopwords from the sentence
print("Stopwords in the sentence are:", filtered_words) # Print the
                        filtered words
```

Output:

```
Stopwords in the sentence are: ['NLP', '?']
```

Example 3.8.1 *(Sentiment analysis using NLTK)*
This example introduces one of the major applications of NLP, i.e. sentiment analysis. It focuses on identifying and extracting attitudes, sentiments, evaluations, and emotions

within textual data. It helps to determine whether the sentiment expressed in the text is positive, negative, or neutral. This analytical technique finds extensive applications in various industries such as healthcare, customer service, and banking. In Python, this can be implemented using the VADER (Valence Aware Dictionary for Sentiment Reasoning) function which is available in the NLTK package. It is a simple rule-based model for sentiment analysis that can efficiently handle vocabulary, abbreviations, capitalizations, repeated punctuations, emoticons, etc. VADER has the advantage of assessing the sentiment of any given text without the need for prior training.

In this example, we perform sentiment analysis on two sentences. The first sentence, "The hotel stay was horrible and uncomfortable," conveys a negative sentiment. The second sentence, "Always :) and be: D !" expresses a positive sentiment with the use of smiley faces. By analyzing the sentiment in these sentences by using VADER, we gain insights into the underlying emotions and evaluations conveyed within the text. The result generated by VADER is a dictionary of 4 keys neg, neu, pos, and compound. The neg, neu, and pos values represent the respective proportions of negative, neutral, and positive sentiments and their sum should equal 1. The compound score is a single value that represents the overall sentiment intensity of a given text and it ranges, between (most extreme negative) and +1 (most extreme positive).

Output:

```
The hotel stay was horrible and uncomfortable. {'neg': 0.55, 'neu': 0.45,
                                    'pos': 0.0, 'compound': -0.7269}
Always:) and be:D !------------------ {'neg': 0.0, 'neu': 0.291, 'pos': 0
                                    .709, 'compound': 0.8087}
```

3.9 TensorFlow

3.9.1 Introduction

TensorFlow is an open-source machine learning library developed by the Google Brain team in 2012. It comprises various sets of tools and libraries that can be imported into the Python environment for developing various deep-learning applications. It makes use of multidimensional arrays called tensors as the basic building blocks for implementing and optimizing mathematical operations. Tensorflow also supports the efficient use of large-scale datasets. The feature scalability and performance of TensorFlow are improved by the reuse of the same memory with the help of graphical processing unit (GPU) computations.

The TensorFlow package can be installed in the Anaconda prompt using either of the following commands:

pip install tensorflow
conda install -c conda-forge tensorflow

For getting GPU support for TensorFlow, we need to install *tensorflow-gpu* version which can be done in anaconda prompt using the following two methods:

pip install tensorflow-gpu
conda install -c anaconda tensorflow-gpu

After installation, TensorFlow is imported using the alternate name tf.

```
import tensorflow as tf
print(tf.__version__) #outputs the version of tensorflow.
```

Output:

```
2.11.0
```

3.9.2   Elements of Tensorflow

Tensors are the fundamental building blocks of TensorFlow, and they can have various shapes, denoting their dimensions, such as scalars (0-D), vectors (1-D), matrices (2-D), and higher-dimensional arrays. TensorFlow places strict constraints on the data types associated with tensors, ensuring both numerical accuracy and computational efficiency. Furthermore, TensorFlow operates within the framework of a computational graph, where mathematical operations are defined as nodes and tensors flow through these nodes to carry out computations. To execute this graph and effectively assess or modify the tensor values within it, TensorFlow employs a session. This combination of tensors, their shapes, data types, computational graphs, and sessions form the foundational components that empower TensorFlow for deep learning and machine learning tasks. Table 3.2 provides a detailed description of the main elements of TensorFlow.

3.9.3   TensorFlow Pipeline

In this section, we describe the basic steps involved in creating a TensorFlow code. The various steps involved in the process are illustrated using the below example (Example 3.9.1).

Example 3.9.1   (*Ridge regression using TensorFlow*)
In this example, we discuss how to implement a basic ridge regression model using TensorFlow. Ridge regression is a special case of linear regression with an added penalty term. While performing linear regression, a known independent variable 'X' is used to predict an unknown dependent variable 'y'. In case of a high correlation between the independent variables, we introduce a penalty term β to the linear regression equation. The overall expression for the cost function is given by

$$Cost = \underset{\beta}{\operatorname{argmin}} \|y - X\beta\|_2^2 + \lambda \|\beta\|_2^2 \tag{3.2}$$

At first, we import all the required libraries from Tensorflow and Python. Following this, we create a computational graph, load a predefined dataset from Scikit-Learn, and initialize

Table 3.2 Elements of tensorFlow.

Terminology	Definition	Example
Tensor	Multidimensional vectors or matrices representing data in higher dimensions.	Scalar: Zero-dimensional tensor Vector: One-dimensional tensor Matrix: Two-dimensional tensor
Shape	Number of elements in each dimension of a tensor.	Scalar = 25, shape = [] Vector = [1,2], shape = [2] Matrix = [[3, 4], [5, 5]], shape = [2,2] Tensor = [[[1,2], [2,5], [3,2]] [[4,5], [7,8], [4,1]]], shape = [2, 3, 2]
Type	Data structure that is used to represent tensor. Commonly used tensor types: 1. Constant: Fixed value data type (can be an integer, float, etc.) 2. Variables: Tensors whose value can be kept as well as updated over its run time. 3. Placeholder: These are basic level variables that act as holders for future data. Unlike variables, initialization is not required.	tf.constant(value) eg: tf.constant(5) tf.Variable(<initial-value>, name = <optional-name>) eg: tf.Variable([[1,1], [5,5]], name = 'matrix') tf.placeholder(<data_type>, shape = <shape>) eg: tf.placeholder(tf.float64, shape = [None,5])
Graph	Data structures that consists of nodes that allows the flow of computational operations.	a = 10 b = 6 out = tf.subtract(a,b)
Session	It is used to evaluate the computational operations in a graph.	s = tf.Session() s.run(out) s.close()

the variables using NumPy. Next, the placeholders are defined for the independent variable 'X' and the dependent variable 'y'. The model parameters 'A' and 'b', corresponding to slope and bias are initialized as TensorFlow variables. Further, we define the model operation on the node and the ridge regression cost function using Eq. (3.2). Later, various optimizers from the TensorFlow library are imported in order to compute the cost function. Finally, the session is run during training, and the ridge regression model is evaluated to obtain the desired output (see Fig. 3.32).

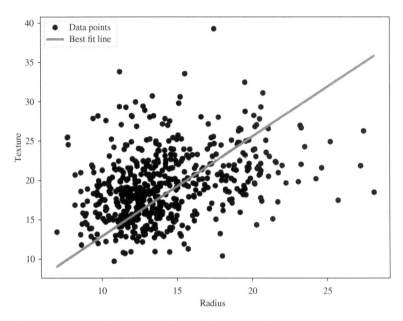

Figure 3.32 Plot of the best-fit line for ridge regression.

3.10 Keras

3.10.1 Introduction

TensorFlow is a low-level language with high complexity. Another deep-learning library named Keras can be used to simplify these complexities. It was developed at Google by an artificial intelligence researcher named Francois Chollet. Keras is an open-source high-level deep learning library, written in Python. It can run on top of various deep learning libraries such as Tensorflow, Cognitive Toolkit (CNTK), and Theano. Keras has a minimalistic structure that allows faster execution and implementation of complex neural networks in fewer lines of code. The key feature of Keras is the highly modular interface that makes it easier for the users to execute the code without having in-depth knowledge about the libraries. These existing modules can also be redesigned to create custom modules for the desired application. Keras supports both CPU and GPU, and it has been used widely in machine learning, computer vision, and time series-related applications.

The Keras package can be installed in the Anaconda prompt using either of the following commands:

pip install keras
conda install -c conda-forge keras

3.10.2 Elements of Keras

Keras is an easy-to-learn platform that incorporates a complete framework to implement any kind of neural network. The core components of Keras include the following: Model, Layer, and Core Modules.

3.10.2.1 Models

Keras models are composed of layers. The different layers constituting the Neural network are arranged to form the Keras model. Keras models contain the basic structural elements of neural networks. The simple linear composition models are called sequential models. Sequential models are the most commonly used model structure where we add each of the layers to the predefined sequential block using *model.add* command. The steps involved include importing the sequential model, followed by adding dense layers or other layers to the model. The subclassing technique can be used to develop further complex models. Function API models are used to develop complex models. The models developed using this method are more flexible compared to the sequential ones. It basically uses the approach of building using graphs of layers.

3.10.2.2 Layers

Layers are next in the hierarchy when looking at the structure of Keras implementation. In general, there are input, hidden, and output layers in the neural network model. The main advantage of Keras is the already available predefined layers. The most commonly used Keras layers are convolutional layers, pooling layers, recurrent layers, and core layers. In between the layers, the dropout layer can be added. Dropout layers are useful to avoid overfitting. Additionally, to complete the layers, the activation modules are also important. The layers are added one by one to create a sequential model setup.

3.10.2.3 Core Modules

Modules are the basic building blocks of any keras model architecture. These modules are built-in functions that support the Keras model ensuring its proper functioning. The modules used include *Activation functions* such as softmax and ReLU, *loss function module* (mean square error, Poisson, mean absolute error, etc.), *optimizer module* that uses optimizers such as adam and stochastic gradient descent (SGD), and *regularizers* (L1 and L2 regularizers). These predefined modules are important concepts that support the training of the Neural network models.

3.10.3 Keras Workflow

The first step of a basic Keras workflow is loading and preprocessing the training data. Keras has a few in-built datasets such as MNIST, CIFAR10, CIFAR100, IMDB, Fashion MNIST, Reuters newswire, and Boston housing price datasets that help you to build simple deep learning models. These predefined datasets can be accessed using the keras.datasets module. Generally, these data are stored as NumPy arrays, TensorFlow Dataset objects, or Python generators. These data are further preprocessed before feeding into the model. For example, for image data, the common preprocessing methods include center cropping, rescaling, assigning random rotation, and generating multiple versions of the images. Next, we define the desired model architecture using either the sequential API or the functional API. The sequential API allows you to create models by stacking them sequentially. Its main limitation is that it does not allow the sharing or branching of layers as well as to have multiple inputs or outputs. But these constraints are overcome by using the functional API, which provides more flexibility in creating complex networks. After building the model, it is compiled using the loss function, optimizer, and validation metrics (accuracy, mean square error). Further, the network is trained using the fit method for the desired number of epochs. The principal goal during training is the minimization of error and loss function. The three main loss functions available in Keras are binary cross-entropy (two-class classification), categorical cross-entropy (multiclass classification), and mean square error (regression). Based on the loss function, the network parameters are updated using the optimizers. Finally, the test data is introduced in order to evaluate the overall performance of the model.

Example 3.10.1 *(Creating a sequential model using Keras)*
In this tutorial, we will be implementing a simple sequential model in order to improve our understanding of the workflow in KERAS.

The first step is to load the data. Let us load the xor dataset defined in the previous codes. After loading the data, we split the data so that it has 320 training and 80 test samples. Following this, we construct the sequential model with two dense layers. The first dense layer has the number of output units as 2 with ReLU activation function and the second dense layer has 1 output unit corresponding to the labels. Finally, the SoftMax activation function is used to provide the probabilistic output corresponding to each class.

Once the sequential model is created, the next step is to compile the model. In this case, any optimizer can be used and so here we use the Adam optimizer with a default learning rate of 0.001. The type of loss function used for optimization is the binary cross-entropy loss that compares each of the predicted probabilities to the actual class output which can be either 0 or 1.

After compiling the model, we fit it with the training data and labels. The training batch size is initialized to 32, with the number epochs = 100 and the test data is used as the validation set to check the accuracy of the training.

When the training is completed, we can plot the loss function as shown in Fig. 3.33a to analyze the behavior of the model. Similarly, we can look at the training and validation accuracy as shown in Fig. 3.33b. Further, you can also plot the confusion matrix to compute the model performance as shown in Fig. 3.34.

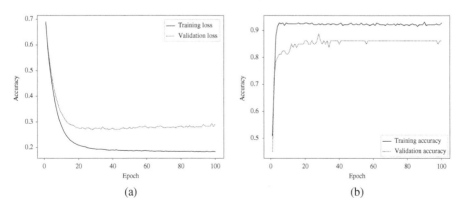

(a)   (b)

Figure 3.33 Loss and accuracy curves for training and validation. (a) Loss curve and (b) accuracy curve.

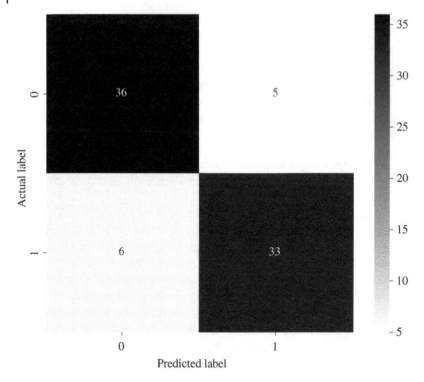

Figure 3.34 Confusion matrix for the XOR problem using the sequential model.

3.11 Pytorch

3.11.1 Introduction

PyTorch is one of the rapidly growing deep learning frameworks used by researchers to create new models. It was developed by Facebook's AI Research Lab in 2016. It is a Python-based package that offers a substitution for NumPy by using GPU optimized tensors for various computations. Another highlight of Pytorch is automatic differentiation that allows to training of neural networks by automatically computing the gradients. Pytorch also ensures that the graphs are built dynamically so that the users can make necessary changes even during run time. Moreover, the strong GPU support of Pytorch makes it a fast and powerful tool for running complex deep-learning programs.

The PyTorch can be imported using the following command:

```
import torch
print(torch.__version__) #displays the version of PyTorch
```

Output:

```
1.13.1+cu116
```

3.11.2 Elements of PyTorch

3.11.2.1 PyTorch Tensors

These are PyTorch objects that are used to represent multidimensional data. Tensors are considered similar to NumPy arrays, although NumPy arrays run only on CPU while tensors use both CPU and GPU. PyTorch is optimized for handling these tensors and accelerates computing by utilizing the GPU. While using a GPU, the tensors are initially assigned to the GPU memory with the help of a specific API named CUDA. It is a platform developed for parallel computing by NVIDIA for enhanced computations on the GPU. Any tensor can be assigned automatically to the device (CPU or GPU) you are using with the help of CUDA. Further operations and results using these tensors will also be computed and stored on this allocated device. But currently, the CUDA API is limited to being used only on NVIDIA GPUs.

The different types of tensors such as scalars, vectors, and matrices can be created using PyTorch using the following commands.

```
#SCALAR
s=torch.tensor(8) #read a scalar
print(s)
print(s.ndim) #displays the dimension of the scalar
print(s.item()) #extract the number from the scalar
```

Output:

```
tensor(8)
0
8
```

```
v=torch.tensor([3,5,7]) #read a vector
print(v)
print(v.ndim) #displays the dimension of the vector
print(v.shape)# displays how the elements are arranged in the vector
```

Output:

```
tensor([3, 5, 7])
1
torch.Size([3])
```

```
m=torch.tensor([[2,5],[8,9]]) #read a matrix
print(m)
print(m.ndim) #displays the dimension of the vector
print(m.shape) #displays how the elements are arranged in the vector
```

Output:

```
tensor([[2, 5],
        [8, 9]])
2
torch.Size([2, 2])
```

3.11.2.2 PyTorch Variables

These represent the wrapper around a PyTorch tensor. All the operations carried out using a tensor can be also done using variables since they both use the same API. But unlike tensors, PyTorch has an autograd package for the variables that allow it to compute the gradients automatically. For example, in a computational graph, if p is a variable, the tensor value and the gradient of p can be accessed by using *p.data* and *p.grad* commands, respectively. While performing backpropagation using a neural network, the parameters need to be optimized in order to minimize the error. In this case, the variables are at first imported from the torch.autograd package. Next, they are used to execute the operations in a directed acyclic graph (DAG) with function objects. After this calculation, the *.backward()* command is used for the computation of all the gradients during the backpropagation. A trainable variable can be initialized by passing the parameter *requires_grad* and setting it to boolean value True.

3.11.2.3 Dynamic Computational Graphs

These are directed acyclic graphs in which the nodes denote the variables, whereas the mathematical operations on these variables are represented using the edges. Unlike static graphs, they are efficient in handling variable-sized data. Dynamic graphs have the benefit of being more flexible and allow us to alter and evaluate the graph at any time. These graphs also allow line-by-line execution of the code thereby making the code debugging process much easier. The main drawback is the limited graph optimization time as it may take longer to rebuild the graph after each iteration of training.

3.11.2.4 Modules

It corresponds to the base class of PyTorch for constructing neural networks. All the elements of a network including the learnable parameters should inherit from *nn.Module*. Additionally, the commonly used loss functions for training neural networks are also included in the nn package. In PyTorch, the *nn* package provides higher-level abstractions over the graphs that are used for creating the neural networks. The module can contain other modules as well as submodules allowing it to have a nested tree form. The set of modules defined by the nn package is comparable to the neural network layers. Hence, while building a network, the main functionality of a module is to receive input tensors, hold the internal state of a tensor, and compute output tensors.

The below code snippet describes the implementation of a PyTorch module. Here the fully connected layer is constructed using the nn.Linear() module.

```
import torch
torch.manual_seed(20) #set a seed for reproducibility
linear_func=torch.nn.Linear(in_features=4,out_features=5) #create a fully
                                 connected layer using the module
x=torch.rand(size=(3,4)) #create the input for the fully connected layer
y=linear_func(x)
print("Input to the layer:",x)
print("Output of the layer:",y)
```

Output:

```
Input to the layer: tensor([[0.2113, 0.6839, 0.7478, 0.4627],
        [0.7742, 0.3861, 0.0727, 0.8736],
        [0.3510, 0.3279, 0.3254, 0.2399]])
Output of the layer: tensor([[ 0.1618,   0.0404,   0.3000,  -0.1494,  -0.2235]
                                   ,
        [ 0.0100, -0.5980,   0.1969,   0.0284,  -0.5175],
        [ 0.1903, -0.1587,   0.3172,  -0.1097,  -0.1623]],
        grad_fn=<AddmmBackward0>)
```

3.11.3   Workflow of Pytorch

The most basic step here is to import the necessary libraries and load the dataset that can be used for training the model. The preparation of the data includes preprocessing the data, splitting the data into train and test sets, and splitting the data into batches for the model to process. Similar to Keras, Pytorch also gives access to several datasets such as CIFAR10, CIFAR100, MNIST, Imagenet, and COCO. Pytorch provides access to dataloaders, which can be used to do data preparation efficiently. Dataloader can be used for complete setup of the data, which includes splitting the data into train and test sets, initializing batch size, preprocessing the data, and normalizing it. The next step is to build a network. The module used for that is *torch.nn* module. This works similarly to *Model* in Keras where we can initialize the number of layers, units, activation function, dropout layers, etc. The functional module (*torch.nn.functional*) helps in defining the path from the input to the output layer. The optimizers can be defined using *torch.optim* module. The training of the network is done using autograd package. The gradient with respect to all parameters is computed using the *.backward()* module. The loss function required for minimization of error criterion can be obtained from *torch.nn* module. Several loss functions are available in the package. Some examples are L1 loss, MSE loss, cross-entropy loss, etc.

Example 3.11.1   *(Building a neural network using Pytorch)*
This example implements the training and testing of a neural network model using the PyTorch deep learning framework. The primary objective is to classify handwritten digits from the MNIST dataset. Initially, download and load the MNIST dataset using PyTorch's 'DataLoader' function. It applies essential data transformations, including converting the images to tensors and normalizing the pixel values to a range between −1 and 1. This pre-processing step is crucial for ensuring that the data is suitable for training deep learning models.

Next, construct a feedforward neural network consisting of an input layer with 784 units (corresponding to flattened 28 × 28 pixel images), followed by two hidden layers with 128 and 64 units, respectively. ReLU activation functions are applied after each hidden layer to introduce nonlinearity. Finally, there is an output layer with 10 units, representing the 10 possible digit classes (0 to 9). The output layer utilizes a LogSoftmax activation function, which is common for classification tasks.

For training the neural network, the choice of the loss function is cross-entropy loss, a suitable option for addressing multiclass classification tasks such as digit recognition.

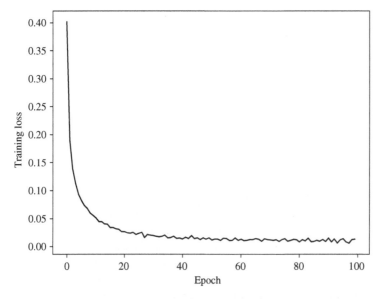

Figure 3.35 Plot illustrating the relationship between the training loss and the number of epochs.

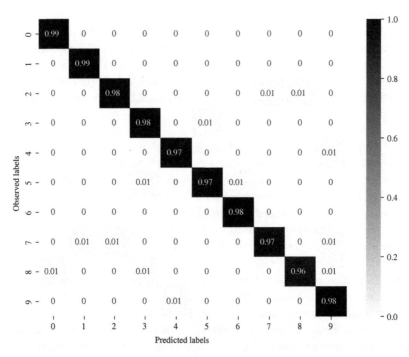

Figure 3.36 Confusion matrix is generated to obtain the summary of the performance of the classification model.

Moreover, the code employs the Adam optimizer, configured with a learning rate of 0.001, to facilitate the optimization process. The optimizer is responsible for updating the model's parameters during training, using gradients computed through backpropagation. The training loop runs for a total of 100 epochs. During each epoch, it processes the training data in mini-batches of 64 samples, performing forward and backward passes to compute gradients and update the model's parameters. The training loss for each epoch is subsequently computed and displayed, as depicted in Fig. 3.35.

After completing the training process, the code evaluates the trained model on the test dataset. It calculates and prints the overall accuracy of the test dataset, indicating how well the model generalizes to unseen data. Additionally, the confusion matrix is also computed to understand the model's performance on each digit class (see Fig. 3.36).

3.12   Conclusion

Python as a platform supports several programs or packages to implement deep learning-based approaches. The basic understanding of Python tools used for deep learning allows us to slowly learn the concepts of Deep learning in a much better way. Being a popular programming language, Python can be used as an interface to create web applications, can be connected to database systems to read and write files, handle big data, for prototyping, and product-based software development.

There are several packages that can support the implementation of deep learning applications in Python. The numerical package NumPy comes to use anywhere in our code as it helps us work around arrays and do numerical, algebraic, transforms, and multidimensional array computations. The visualization tools like Matplotlib, Seaborn, and Pandas are of great use for understanding the nature of the data. This feature can be useful for data analysis and visualization. Pandas can also be used for processing various kinds of data, which is useful for statistical, analytical, and mathematical modeling of the data. Other packages such as Scipy and Scikit-Learn can be used to do machine learning, signal processing, and image processing-related tasks. Additionally, they give access to a large number of datasets, which can aid us in testing and learning on them for developing machine learning applications. The three main packages: Tensorflow, Keras, and Pytorch can be used individually or in combination to develop structures and functions associated with any deep learning applications. TensorFlow is an open-source framework that can be considered as a math tool for neural networks. The networks can be built from scratch, and it also supports multiple levels of abstraction to build and train them. Keras, on the other hand, is a user-friendly, high-level application programming interface (API) that can be used for experimenting with different kinds of deep learning structures in a fast and efficient way. It can run on Tensorflow or Theano. Pytorch was developed recently by Facebook and is relatively simple to use and also has the advantage of efficient memory usage and processing speed along with a manageable coding experience.

Problems

3.1 List the different methods to assign value to variables and find the type of these variables.

3.2 In the given tuple $tp = (37,89,10,33,72,10,10,12,90,10,46)$
1. Find the sum of all elements.
2. Find the number of times the number 10 gets repeated.
3. Find the minimum and maximum value.
Print the results.

3.3 Define a 2-D empty NumPy array. Develop a Python code to fill this array with consecutive integer values. Also, calculate the memory size in bytes occupied by all the elements in this NumPy array.

3.4 Generate 15,000 random numbers from a Gaussian distribution with a mean of 16 and a variance of 3. Plot the histogram and a curved distribution line that best fits the data displayed by the histogram.

3.5 Singular value decomposition is a method for factorizing a $m \times n$ matrix $\mathbf{A}$ into 3 matrices such as $\mathbf{U}$ (orthonormal eigenvectors of $\mathbf{AA}^\mathsf{T}$), Σ (diagonal matrix containing square roots of eigenvalues) and $\mathbf{V}^\mathsf{T}$ (orthonormal eigenvectors of $\mathbf{A}^\mathsf{T}\mathbf{A}$). Use Scipy to perform singular value decomposition on the following matrix

$$\mathbf{A} = \begin{pmatrix} 10 & 12, & 33 \\ 64 & 35 & 46 \\ 70 & 18 & 39 \end{pmatrix}$$

3.6 GridSearchCV is a scikit_learn library that is used to select the optimal values for a model by performing hyperparameter tuning. Import this library from the model_selection package of scikit_learn and modify Example 3.5.1 to output the best model parameters.

3.7 Define a Pandas data frame with missing values. Apply linear interpolation on the data frame to fill these values and iterate over the rows of the interpolated data frame.

3.8 Data visualization using Seaborn.
- Load the taxis dataset from Seaborn.
- Use the Seaborn relplot() function to visualize the statistical relationship between any two numerical features of the dataset.
- Use the Seaborn scatterplot() function and repeat the above plot by adding color, label, and style to the graph.
- Split the graph into multiple graphs based on the categorical variables present in the dataset.

3.9 Given the following dataset D = [4,16,7,12,32,10,2,9,14,24,30,20,8,15], Make a Tensor-Flow data pipeline that:

   1. Gets the elements that are divisible by 2 from this dataset.
   2. Finds the square of this data.
   3. Shuffles the data with buffer_size = 3.

3.10 Define a custom relu activation function and add it to the Keras model defined in Example 3.10.1.

3.11 Create a class in PyTorch to load a custom dataset.

3.12 Using the classes defined in Examples 3.1.3 and 3.2.3, construct a training criterion for a multilayer perceptron using only classes and NumPy arrays. Reproduce the training results in Figs. 1.25 and 1.26 by creating separate functions for each of them.

4

Convolutional Neural Networks

4.1 Introduction

David Huben and Torsten Wiesel described two cell types in the visual cortex of cats (Hubel and Wiesel 1962). They suggested that these cells were in stages in the construction of the receptive field of the cat. In 1980, Fukushima (1980) developed an artificial model, called the neocognitron, based on Hubel and Wiesel's discoveries (Lindsay 2021). This model is considered the first CNN, and it consists of two layers of neurons. The first ones named the simple cells (s-cells) as the biological counterparts described by Hubel and Wiesel use a matrix of weights to apply a linear transformation to nonoverlapping locations of an input image to generate the s-cell response. The output of the s-cells is applied to an array of complex cells (c-cells), which perform a nonlinear operation on these outputs. This sequence is applied several times in order to mimic the behavior of the visual cortex.

During the 1990s, several hierarchical models similar to the one presented by Fukushima were introduced in Riesenhuber and Poggio (2000), but the most successful one, devised from the field of computer vision, was the CNN, first published in Y. LeCun (1989), but its structure seems to be inspired in the model by Huben and Wiesel. A CNN is a type of neural network for image processing that has been extremely successful in many applications. The model can be justified as a structure able to extract, in its successive elements of the hierarchy, features of increasing level of abstraction that are local in the first stages of the structure, but that become global as the information is processed in deeper stages of the neural network.

In this chapter, we describe the CNN in several stages. First, the overall structure is presented and commented on. Then, the basic idea of convolution is reviewed, and then the elements of the structure are detailed. The training of the neural network is then developed and compared to the backpropagation of a dense NN, and then the most successful developments based on the CNN are summarized.

4.2 Elements of a Convolutional Neural Network

The basic NN developed in Chapter 1 can be thought of as a structure designed to extract features of a pattern, represented as a vector, through a nonlinear representation in a higher

Deep Learning: A Practical Introduction, First Edition.
Manel Martínez-Ramón, Meenu Ajith, and Aswathy Rajendra Kurup.
© 2024 John Wiley & Sons Ltd. Published 2024 by John Wiley & Sons Ltd.
Companion website: https://github.com/DeepLearning-book

dimensional space, expanded by the nodes of a neuron layer. In the next layer, the features are represented in a higher level of abstraction, and, in the last layer, the features produce representations of the input pattern that can be linearly classified.

The trick used in an NN to produce such representations is to compute affine transformation of all the input features of vector $\mathbf{x}$ with the form $\mathbf{w}_j^{(l)\top}\mathbf{x} + b_j^{(l)}$, which are then passed through a nonlinear activation in node j of layer l. In some applications, like in ML applied to images, each input feature is related to only a few neighbor input features, and it may be nearly independent of other features. Indeed, where two pixels that are side by side may be highly dependent (almost the same color, almost the same intensity, similar behavior from frame to frame), but two pixels of the image that are far away will probably share low information in common. NNs are not directly able to treat differently the local and global relationships in this case. An image can be introduced into an NN without loss of generality by flattening it or transforming it into a vector with an arbitrary organization. Then, this vector is transformed into a different space by an affine transformation with a matrix $\mathbf{W}$ and a bias $\mathbf{b}$ so every single element of the output vector is a function of all pixels, so the spatial dependencies are not explicitly captured.

The CNN is an approach that can extract the spatial dependencies (and also the temporal dependencies in sequential data) through the application of a set of small spatial filters (more usually called convolutional kernels) that scan the image. Each one of these filters can extract different local features of the image if they are designed properly to do so.

Therefore, one can think of a layer of a CNN as a set of filters that automatically extract features from the input. These features are extracted automatically because the user does not need to design these filters. Instead, the CNN can be trained to do it automatically. These features and the filters can be often represented to extract some interpretations too. The overall description of a CNN was first published by Yan LeCun (1989), but probably the most cited article where the structure of the CNN is displayed is his 1998 paper (Y. LeCun et al. 1998), where the NN was used for handwritten digit recognition.

4.2.1 Overall Structure of a CNN

The basic block diagram structure of a CNN is depicted in Fig. 4.1. The structure consists of several layers that perform three different operations, which will be detailed and interpreted further. The input can be in general a multidimensional array but, for illustrative purposes, assume that this input is an image organized as a two-dimensional array or matrix.

In each of the so-called convolutional layers, the first block consists of what is known as a convolution block. This block is the one that filters the input pattern with a set of small

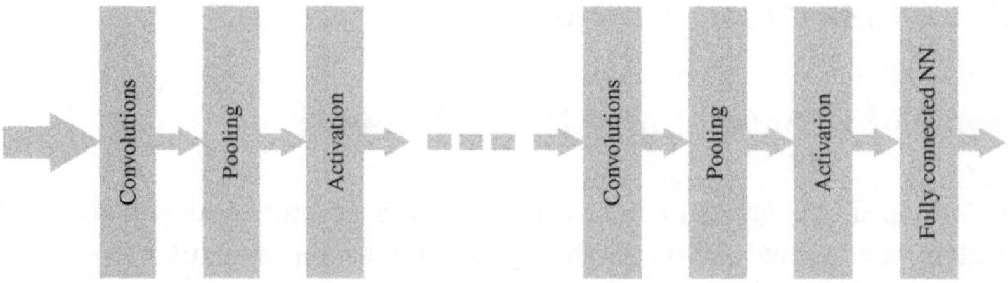

Figure 4.1 Basic block diagram of a CNN.

two-dimensional arrays called receptive fields or kernels. The filter operations are modeled as convolutions of the input with the receptive fields. Each receptive field outputs, then, a filtered image. The second block, called pooling block, simply subsamples the output of the convolution to reduce the number of pixels of the filtered images. There are several options for this block that will be explained below. The last element of each block consists of the nonlinear activation function applied to each one of the pixels of the filtered image. Again, there are several options for the activations, among them the sigmoid or the ReLU activations are introduced in Section 1.1. The output of the first layer with the three operations is a set of filtered and reduced images. The same three operations are then applied to each one of these smaller images several times and then the outputs of the last convolutional layer are flattened and introduced in a fully connected (FC) NN, which is a block with an MLP structure as the one introduced in Chapter 1. This section of the CNN is often called a dense network. Each one of the operations is detailed and interpreted in Subsections 4.2.2 to 4.2.6.

4.2.2 Convolutions

The convolution is the fundamental operation of the CNN and the one that gives this NN most of its unique properties. The convolution operation is, as explained above, the way to compute the filtering of an image with a kernel. But let us briefly describe the one-dimensional discrete time convolution of two signals first. Assume two discrete time signals $f[n]$ and $g[n]$. The convolution between two signals is defined as

$$(f * g)[n] = \sum_{m=-\infty}^{\infty} f[m]g[n-m] \tag{4.1}$$

At point n, the convolution is the sum of products of one signal times the other one shifted n positions and reversed. The output signal is the result of the modification of one signal with the other one. One of the signals is then a sliding waveform that is passed through the other one.

Figure 4.2 shows two examples of the convolution of two different signals. The left pane shows the operation over a Gaussian pulse (a square exponential function with variance equal to five and centered around the origin) and a rectangular pulse of width 10. The result of the convolution is in the lower left graph. As can be seen, the effect of the convolution

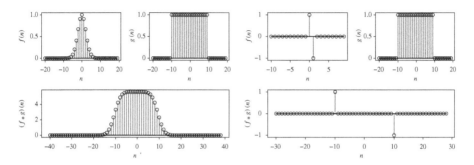

Figure 4.2 Examples of convolutions.

of the pulse with the Gaussian produces a smoothing of the pulse. This is an example of lowpass filtering since the edges of the second signal have been removed. The left pane shows a different situation where the Gaussian has been replaced by a function that can be called a *finite difference* operator. Indeed, at every instant n in Eq. (4.1), this operator multiplies all elements of the other function a by zero, except for elements n and $n-1$, so that the convolution, in this case, can be written as

$$(f * g)[n] = (\delta[n] - \delta[n-1]) * g[n] = g[n] - g[n-1] \tag{4.2}$$

which is a finite difference operation. Since function $g[n]$ is flat except in the edges, the operation results in a function that is zero except in these edges of positions $n = -1$ and $n = 10$ where it shows, respectively, the values 1 and -1. This is an interesting operation when applied to images because it can detect their edges, as we will see in example 4.2.1.

4.2.3 Convolutions in Two Dimensions

The extension of the convolution to two dimensions is immediate, and it keeps the idea of a function sliding over the other one. Assume that an image $\mathbf{I}$ of dimension $M_I \times N_I$ is available, and we define a *convolution kernel* $\mathbf{W}$ as an array of $M_W \times N_W$ dimensions, smaller than the image dimensions. Figure 4.3 shows an example of a convolutional operation where an image (represented by an array of bricks, each one is a pixel of the image) is convolved with two different convolution kernels $\mathbf{W}_1$ and $\mathbf{W}_2$, giving, as a result, two images that are the convolution of the two kernels with the image. The convolution operation can be defined as

$$(\mathbf{I} * \mathbf{W})[m, n] = \sum_{i=0}^{M_W-1} \sum_{j=0}^{N_W-1} \mathbf{W}[i,j]\mathbf{I}[m+i, n+j] \tag{4.3}$$

where $0 \leq m \leq M_I - M_W$ and $0 \leq N_I - N_W$. This is, the dimensions of the resulting array are $M_I - M_W + 1 \times N_I - N_W + 1$.

An example of a convolution can be seen in Fig. 4.4, where $\mathbf{I}$ is an array of dimensions 5×4 and the kernel $\mathbf{W}$ is a 2×2 array. The result of the convolution $\mathbf{W} * \mathbf{I}$ is depicted in the figure, and it has dimensions 4×3.

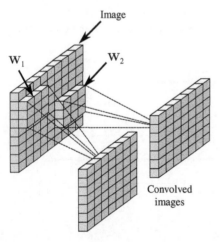

Image

$\mathbf{W}_1$

$\mathbf{W}_2$

Convolved images

Figure 4.3 Representation of convolutions of an image with two different convolution kernels.

Figure 4.4 Example of a 2D convolution.

I				
1	2	1	3	1
2	1	2	1	3
1	2	1	3	1
2	1	2	1	3

$*$

W	
0	1
1	0

$=$

W $*$ I			
4	2	5	2
2	4	2	6
4	2	5	2

The convolution is computed as in Eq. (4.3). The first value is achieved by multiplying the submatrix $\begin{bmatrix} 1 & 2 \\ 2 & 1 \end{bmatrix}$ marked with a square in the figure, elementwise with kernel $\begin{bmatrix} 0 & 1 \\ 1 & 0 \end{bmatrix}$ which gives the result $\begin{bmatrix} 0 & 2 \\ 2 & 0 \end{bmatrix}$. The elements of the product are added together, which gives the first element of the convolution. Then, the square is shifted to the next position to get the sub-matrix $\begin{bmatrix} 2 & 1 \\ 1 & 2 \end{bmatrix}$. This is again multiplied elementwise with the kernel, and the result is added together. The result is 2, which is the second element of the convolution. The operation is repeated for all possible shifts to obtain the convolution result.

Example 4.2.1 *(Finding the edges of an image)*

As an example of the convolution applied to a real image, we use the one in Fig. 4.5. The objective is to detect the edges of the figure. To that purpose, we use the following kernel

$$\mathbf{W} = \begin{pmatrix} -1 & -1 & -1 \\ -1 & 8 & -1 \\ -1 & -1 & -1 \end{pmatrix} \tag{4.4}$$

Figure 4.5 Example of the convolution of an image with a convolution kernel designed to enhance the edges of the image.

Notice that the sum of the array is zero, so if during the convolution, this array is multiplied by pixels of the image that have the same value, the result of the convolution at that position will be zero. If for a given position the pixel in the center is higher than the surrounding ones, the result will be positive. This kernel is used to find abrupt changes in the image, as edges.

The kernel is convolved with the image, and then the absolute value of the result of the convolution is computed for illustration purposes. The result of the operation can be seen in the right pane of Fig. 4.5. It can be seen that the most abrupt changes are enhanced in this image, for example, the edges of the cup or the ones of the pen, and in general, the shape of the objects is obtained in the convolution regardless of the pixel intensity of each object. This is an example of feature extraction on an image that could be used to classify or detect objects in an image. Convolutional NNs use convolutions as feature extractors, but the convolutions applied to a are not predesigned by the user. Instead, the parameters or weights of each one of the convolution kernels are trained using a gradient descent method to optimize a given cost function. Thus, the design of the convolution kernels is automatic.

4.2.4 Padding

There is a little problem with the convolution, and it is the fact that the array at the output of the convolution operator has decreased dimensions. In particular, if the input image has dimensions $M_I \times N_I$ and the convolution kernel $\mathbf{W}$ has dimensions $M_W \times N_W$, then the output image will be $M_I - M_W + 1 \times N_I - N_W + 1$ as stated before. Also, it must be noted that due to the nature of the convolution, the pixels at the edge of the image are seen only when the convolution kernel touches the edge of the image, while the rest of the pixels are seen a higher number of times. Therefore, in the convolution, the information on the edges is not used in the same way as the rest of the pixels. To mitigate or solve these two problems, the padding operation is used. This operation consists of adding columns and rows of zeros to the edges of the image. Assuming that we add p rows and p columns of zeros to the image, the dimensions of the convolution output will be

$$(M_I - M_W + p + 1) \times (N_I - N_W + p + 1) \tag{4.5}$$

An example of padding is in Fig. 4.6, where $p = 2$ rows and columns of zeros have been added to the input array.

Assume that $p/2$ rows are added to each side of the input image so the number of rows of the convolved image is equal to the number of rows of the input image. Then, the output dimensions are

$$M_O = M_I + p - M_W + 1 = M_I$$

Then

$$\frac{p}{2} = \frac{M_W - 1}{2}$$

hence M_W must be odd.

$$
\begin{array}{ccc}
\mathbf{I} & \mathbf{W} & \mathbf{W} * \mathbf{I}
\end{array}
$$

0	0	0	0	0	0	0
0	1	2	1	3	1	0
0	2	1	2	1	3	0
0	1	2	1	3	1	0
0	2	1	2	1	3	0
0	0	0	0	0	0	0

0	1
1	0

0	1	2	1	3	1
1	4	2	5	2	3
2	2	4	2	6	1
1	4	2	5	2	3
2	1	2	1	3	0

Figure 4.6 Example of zero padding in a convolution. The input, which has dimensions 5 × 4, has been padded with 2 zeros in each dimension. The output has dimensions 6 × 5 since the dimensions of the kernel are even. For a convolution kernel of dimensions 3 × 3, the output will have dimensions 5 × 4.

	I					
0	0	0	0	0	0	0
0	1	2	1	3	1	0
0	2	1	2	1	3	0
0	1	2	1	3	1	0
0	2	1	2	1	3	0
0	0	0	0	0	0	0

$*$

W	
0	1
1	0

$=$

W $*$ I		
0	2	3
2	4	6
2	2	3

Figure 4.7 Example of padding and stride, where $p = 1$ and $s = 2$. The resulting dimensions are 3×3.

4.2.5 Stride

The stride defines the amount of overlap between areas covered by the convolution kernel across the image. A stride of 1 means that two adjacent values of the convolution have been obtained by shifting one position of the convolution kernel in either direction. This is what the standard convolution defined in Eq. (4.3) does: for a given pair of indexes i, j, the product $\mathbf{W}[i,j]\mathbf{I}[m + i, n + j]$ is computed and then either i or j are incremented in one unit. Then, the overlap between the elements of the image that produces the first value of the convolution and the second one is a section of dimensions $M_w - 1 \times N_w$ or $M_w \times N_w - 1$.

A stride of s means that index i or index j is incremented in s positions, thus decreasing the fraction of overlapping between convolution values. As a consequence of the stride, the output has lower dimensions than the input. It is straightforward to see that for a convolution with padding p and stride s, the output dimensions will be

$$\left\lfloor \frac{M_I + p - M_w + s}{s} \right\rfloor \times \left\lfloor \frac{N_I + p - N_w + s}{s} \right\rfloor \tag{4.6}$$

Figure 4.7 shows an example of padding and stride, where $p = 1$ and $s = 2$, in whose case the overlap between convolution areas is zero. The resulting dimensions are $\left\lfloor \frac{5+2-2+2}{2} \right\rfloor \times \left\lfloor \frac{4+2-2+2}{2} \right\rfloor = 3 \times 3$.

Example 4.2.2 *(Adding stride to Example 4.2.1)*
In this example, a 2D convolution class included in Pytorch has been used to perform the same task as in the previous example, but padding and stride are added to observe the effect. The script of the example is coded and fully commented on in the corresponding Jupyter Notebook. The convolution kernel used in this example is the same as before, so the operation looks for edges in the image. Nevertheless, now a stride of 4 is applied, which means that every convolution is 4 pixels apart from each other either in the horizontal or vertical direction. The original image has dimensions 587×1024, so the final one, according to Eq. (4.6), has dimensions 147×256. The result can be seen in Fig. 4.8.

Figure 4.8   Results of Example 4.2.2.

4.2.6 Pooling

A pooling operation is a function applied to the output of a convolution that reduces the size of the convolution in a controlled way, which reduces the complexity of the structure. This is desired to limit the computational cost and the overfitting risk. The operation selects a window of the image, usually square, with $q \times q$ pixels, and it applies an operation to the pixels of each area to map them into a scalar. Next, the window is shifted to one or more positions (usually q) and the operation is repeated. Usually, max-pooling and average pooling are used in CNN. Max-pooling consists of selecting the maximum value among the pixels of the window, and average pooling computes the average of the pixels inside the window.

4.3 Training a CNN

The full derivation of the training of a CNN is developed in this section. While the final expression of the CNN backpropagation uses the convolution operator, this optimization is formally almost identical to the one of the MLP. The derivation of the operation is done through the identification of the 2D convolution as a sparse product of two matrices, which is useful to utilize the expression of the MLP backpropagation in order to obtain the CNN backpropagation.

4.3.1 Formulation of the Convolution Layer in a CNN

The convolution layers of the CNN need to be conveniently formulated to be implemented in a program, and their functionalities need to be extended in several ways. There are several facts to take into account when designing a convolutional layer. First, let us take a look at the data structure. The CNN was first introduced to process images that were monochromatic, but later the CNN was extended to process color images. Color images are usually constructed with three channels that represent the red, green, and blue colors (RGB) or affine transformations of them, as the YUV standard (see, e.g. Podpora et al. (2014)). Thus, every input sample to the CNN is then an array with three dimensions, say $[C_I, M_I, N_I]$ where the first dimension corresponds to the different colors in the case of an image. In general, we must think of an input sample as an array composed of different planes, each one called a channel.

Finally, to train a CNN, a collection of N images must be processed one at a time, but they are stored in the same array, thus having dimension $[N, C_I, M_I, N_I]$. This is the usual array (often called tensor) notation used in Python.

Every channel of every image is then convolved with several different convolution kernels. Assume that image I with dimensions $[C_I, M_I, N_I]$ is to be convolved with a convolution layer that has C_Z channels.

We define $\mathbf{W}_{j,k}$ as a convolution kernel that convolved with input channel I_j with dimensions $[M_I, N_I]$ and sends it to output channel $\mathbf{Z}_k$.

The general convolution operation is formulated as

$$\mathbf{Z}_k = \sum_{j=0}^{C_I-1} \mathbf{W}_{j,k} * I_j + \mathbf{B}_k \qquad (4.7)$$
$$0 \leq k \leq C_Z - 1$$

This operation computes the output channel $\mathbf{Z}_k$, with dimensions $[M_Z, N_Z]$, which is composed of the sum of the convolutions of all input channels with different kernels. After the convolution, a bias $\mathbf{B}_k$ is added to the operation.

As summarized in Section 4.2.1, convolutions are followed by a pooling function and then possibly a nonlinear activation. These blocks are stacked in layers, so more than one convolution operation is applied to the input data. To make the derivation of the BP algorithm for these layers, it is desirable to change the notation to make it closer to the one of the NN whose BP procedure is introduced in Chapter 1. In a convolution, the linear operation is a sparse version of the general linear operation of feature vector $\mathbf{h}^{(l-1)}$ in layer l of a NN, which is denoted as $\mathbf{z}^{(l)}$ in these networks. The application of a nonlinear activation to this vector gives feature vector $\mathbf{h}^{(l)}$. In a CNN, the input of a given convolution at layer l is then array $\mathbf{H}^{(l-1)}$, and the result of the convolution can be called $\mathbf{Z}^{(l)}$, and the application of a pooling and possibly a nonlinear activation gives the feature array $\mathbf{H}^{(k)}$. Therefore, the whole operation that includes convolution, pooling, and activation can be written as

$$\mathbf{Z}_k^{(l)} = \sum_{j=0}^{C^{(l-1)}-1} \mathbf{W}_{j,k}^{(l)} * \mathbf{H}_j^{(l-1)} + \mathbf{B}_k^{(l)}$$
$$\mathbf{H}_k^{(l)} = \varphi\left(\mathbf{Z}_k^{(l)}\right) \qquad (4.8)$$
$$0 \leq k \leq C^{(l)} - 1$$

where $\varphi(\cdot)$ here represents the combination of the pooling and activation functions. By defining the above operation, we have defined the following arrays (or tensors, if we use the standard deep learning notation):

- $\mathbf{H}^{(l)}$, with dimensions $[C^{(l)}, M^{(l)}, N^{(l)}]$, is an array containing the nonlinear output of layer l, each one with $C^{(l)}$ channels and size $M_H^{(l)} \times N_H^{(l)}$.
- $\mathbf{W}^{(l)}$ is an array of dimensions $[C^{(l-1)}, C^{(l)}, M_W^{(l)}, N_W^{(l)}]$ containing the convolution kernels, where $C^{(l-1)}$ determines the number of input channels and $C^{(l)}$ the number of output channels.

- **B** is an array of dimensions $[C^{(l)}, M^{(l)}, N^{(l)}]$ representing the bias term added to every pixel of each output channel.
- $\mathbf{Z}^{(l)}$ is the output of the convolution, with dimensions $[C^{(l)}, M_z^{(l)}, N_z^{(l)}]$, where $M_z^{(l)}, N_z^{(l)}$ are determined by Eq. (4.6).

4.3.2 Backpropagation of a Convolution Layer

The BP when using convolutional layers is analogous to the BP presented in Chapter 1. Indeed, a convolution layer operation is identical to the operation of a dense layer except for the fact that the connectivity is sparse. This can be easily illustrated with a figure. Assume a simple convolution layer where the input data has dimensions $M_I = 8$ and $N_I = 1$, so the input is a vector. There is only an input and an output channel, and the kernel is a vector of dimension $M_W = 2$. The stride applied to the convolution is $s = 2$ and then a pooling with $q = 2$. Graphically, the operation can be drawn as the one in Fig. 4.9.

The first layer of the figure represents the input, and the connections from the first one to the second one represent the convolutions between the input and the kernel. Note that the connection weights are repeated since they represent the elements of the convolution kernel. A convolution would generate an output of $N_I - N_W + 1 + 7$ elements, but since a stride of 2 is applied, then the output of the convolution has $\left\lfloor \frac{M_I + p - M_w + s}{s} \right\rfloor = 4$ elements, and only 8 out of the 32 possible connections are present. The convolution operation can be computed as operation $\mathcal{W}^{(l)^\top} \mathbf{h}^{(l-1)}$ where in this case $\mathcal{W}^{(l)}$ would be a matrix with the form

$$
\mathcal{W}^{(l)} = \begin{pmatrix}
w_0 & 0 & 0 & 0 \\
w_1 & 0 & 0 & 0 \\
0 & w_0 & 0 & 0 \\
0 & w_1 & 0 & 0 \\
0 & 0 & w_0 & 0 \\
0 & 0 & w_1 & 0 \\
0 & 0 & 0 & w_0 \\
0 & 0 & 0 & w_1
\end{pmatrix}
\tag{4.9}
$$

which is a sparse matrix.

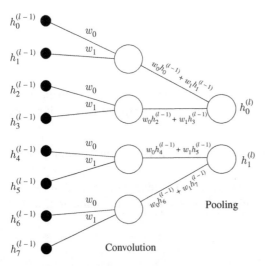

Figure 4.9 Convolution represented as sparse connectivity. The figure shows an input $\mathbf{h}^{(l-1)} = (h_0^{(l-1)}, \ldots, h_7^{(l-1)})^\top$ of 8 pixels organized in a vector, with a convolution kernel $\mathbf{w}^{(l)} = (w_0, w_1)^\top$ of two elements. The convolution is applied with a stride $s = 2$, and then a pooling of two pixels ($q = 2$) is added.

The next layer represents the pooling, which takes two adjacent pixels and outputs one. The resulting output has two pixels. This connection is also sparse since only 4 out of 8 possible connections exist.

During the BP process, the objective is to approximate solutions that satisfy

$$\frac{\partial J(\theta)}{\partial w^{(l)}_{j,k,m,n}} = 0$$

$$\frac{\partial J(\theta)}{\partial b^{(l)}_{k,m,n}} = 0$$

(4.10)

where superindex l is the index for layer k, and the subindexes are the indexes of the elements of arrays $\mathbf{W}$ and $\mathbf{B}$ by applying a gradient descent procedure as explained in Section 1.5.3. The computation of the gradients in a convolutional layer is analogous. Let us consider convolutional layer l where the input is array $\mathbf{H}^{(l-1)}_j$ and the output is $\mathbf{Z}^{(l)}_k$ corresponding to input channel j and output channel k.

We can compute derivatives (4.10) for this particular case in a very straightforward way by taking into account that the convolution layer is a sparse version of a standard layer, so we can compute the convolution as a normal layer linear operation.

Assuming that a CNN has L_C convolutional layers and L_D dense layers, and by using the same reasonings as in Section 1.5.3 we can arrive at an algorithm for the CNN BP. The CNN output can be written as a chain of embedded functions up to layer L_C as

$$\mathbf{o} = \mathbf{o}\left(\mathbf{W}^{(L_D+L_C)\top}\left(\cdots\mathbf{W}^{(L_C+1)\top}\boldsymbol{\varphi}_f\left(\mathbf{Z}^{(L_C)}\right) + \mathbf{b}^{(L_C+1)}\right)\right)$$

$$\mathbf{Z}^{(L_C)}_k = \sum_j \mathbf{W}^{(L_C)}_{j,k} * \mathbf{H}^{(L_C-1)}_j + \mathbf{B}^{(L_C)}_k$$

(4.11)

where in $\boldsymbol{\varphi}_f(\cdot)$ the subindex stands for *flattening*. This is the activation of the last convolutional layer, and therefore, this activation includes, besides the nonlinear function and the pooling, a flattening operation that maps all the pixels of the results of the convolutions into a vector, that is, then processed by the first dense layer. In other words, operation $\boldsymbol{\varphi}_f\left(\mathbf{Z}^{(L_C)}\right)$ produces output vector $\mathbf{h}^{(L_C)}$.

In this expression, we see the output, which is generated after the activation of the linear operation performed by array $\mathbf{W}^{(L_C+L_D)}$, which is the set of parameters of the last dense layers and the activation output of the previous layer. The first dense layer is the one with an index $L_C + 1$. Before that, the machine has convolutional layers with the arrays of kernels $\mathbf{W}^l, l \leq L_C$. But we have seen that these kernels can be changed by sparse matrices $\mathcal{W}^{(l)}_{j,k}$ that turn the convolutions into array products, so the function can be written as

$$\mathbf{o} = \mathbf{o}\left(\mathbf{W}^{(L_C+L_D)\top}\boldsymbol{\phi}\left(\cdots\mathbf{W}^{(L_C+1)\top}\boldsymbol{\varphi}_f\left(\left(\cdots\sum_j \mathcal{W}^{(L_C)}_{j,k}\mathbf{H}^{(L_C-1)}_j + \mathbf{B}^{(L_C)}_k\cdots\right)\right)\right)\right)$$

(4.12)

(where only output channel k of layer L_C is shown in the equation) and after that the BP can be derived exactly as in Subsection 1.5.3.

4.3.3   Forward Step in a CNN

Assume, for example, that a given batch of input samples $\mathbf{X}_i \in \mathbb{R}^{C^{(0)} \times D^{(0)}_1 \times D^{(0)}_2}$, $1 \leq i \leq N$ and their corresponding labels $\mathbf{y}_i$ are available for training purposes. Then, the forward step must be applied to the CNN for each one of these samples. In particular, all outputs of all layers for each one of the samples must be computed, i.e. we need to store outputs $\mathbf{Z}_i^{(l)}$ and $\mathbf{H}_i^{(l)}$ for all convolutional layers, and $\mathbf{z}_i^{(l)}$, $\mathbf{h}_i^{(l)}$, and $\mathbf{o}_i$ for the dense layers and the output. Besides, all output errors $\delta_i^{(L_C+L_D)} = \mathbf{o}_i - \mathbf{y}_i$, which must be computed and stored.

The backward procedure is the same as in a standard NN, and it is described in Subsections 4.3.4 and 4.3.5.

4.3.4 Backpropagation in the Dense Section of a CNN

The BP in the dense layer section of a CNN is identical to one of the MLP in Chapter 1, expressed in Eq. (1.110), that we reproduce here.

$$\delta_i^{(l-1)} = \mathbf{W}^{(l)}\delta_i^{(l)} \odot \phi'\left(\mathbf{z}_i^{(l-1)}\right)$$

$$\mathbf{W}^{(l-1)} \leftarrow \mathbf{W}^{(l-2)} - \mu\sum_{i=1}^{N}\mathbf{h}_i^{(l-2)}\delta_i^{(l-1)^\top}$$

$$\mathbf{b}^{(l-1)} \leftarrow \mathbf{b}^{(l-1)} - \mu\sum_{i=1}^{N}\delta_i^{(l-1)}$$

where $L_C + 1 \leq l \leq L_C + L_D$. This is, first, the errors $\delta_i^{(l)}$ are backpropagated to the previous layer, starting with the last layer, for which $\delta_i^{(L_C+L_D)}$ has been previously computed.

4.3.5 Backpropagation of the Convolutional Section of a CNN

By the notation of Eq. (4.12) that transforms the convolution into a product with a sparse matrix, the update can be expressed as follows:

$$\mathcal{W}_{j,k}^{(l-1)} \leftarrow \mathcal{W}_{j,k}^{(l-1)} - \mu\mathbf{H}_j^{(l-2)}\mathbf{\Delta}_k^{(l-1)^\top} \tag{4.13}$$

with the definition

$$\mathbf{\Delta}_k^{(l-1)} = \sum_m \mathcal{W}_{k,m}^{(l)}\mathbf{\Delta}_m^{(l)} \odot \varphi'\left(\mathbf{z}_k^{(l-1)}\right) \tag{4.14}$$

where array $\mathbf{\Delta}^{(l)}$ is the backpropagated error term, which is the counterpart of the error BP vector $\delta^{(l)}$ in an MLP. Here we express it in a capital symbol to denote that this term is an array with the same dimension as the corresponding convolution output $\mathbf{H}^{(l)}$.

Besides, we know that the product with $\mathcal{W}_{j,k}^{(l)}$ is equivalent to a convolution with $\mathbf{W}_{j,k}^{(l)}$, therefore we can write

$$\mathbf{W}_{j,k}^{(l-1)} \leftarrow \mathbf{W}_{j,k}^{(l-1)} - \mu\mathbf{H}_j^{(l-1)}\mathbf{\Delta}_k^{(l-1)^\top}$$
$$\mathbf{B}_k^{(l-1)} \leftarrow \mathbf{B}_k^{(l-1)} - \mu\mathbf{\Delta}_k^{(l-1)} \tag{4.15}$$

with the definition

$$\mathbf{\Delta}_k^{(l-1)} = \sum_m \mathbf{W}_{k,m}^{(l)} * \mathbf{\Delta}_m^{(l)} \odot \varphi'\left(\mathbf{Z}_k^{(l-1)}\right) \tag{4.16}$$

To formulate the algorithm, it is necessary to backpropagate error $\delta^{(L_C+1)}$ to $\mathbf{\Delta}^{(L_C)}$. This is straightforward if we remember that the last convolutional layer performs a pooling and then a flattening. Therefore, to backpropagate the error, it is necessary to undo the flattening and then undo the pooling (by filling with zeros the positions not selected by the pooling), to find an error $\mathbf{\Delta}^{(L_C+1)}$ with the same dimensions as $\mathbf{H}^{(L_C+1)}$. The pooling cannot be reversed, and therefore, to increase the dimensions to the same values as they were before the pooling, we just need to change the positions of $\mathbf{\Delta}^{(L_C+1)}$ corresponding to the positions discarded by max-pooling or to repeat the error values in the case that average pooling was applied. Then, the convolutional section BP applied over a batch of N samples is for all convolutional layers $L_C \geq l \geq 1$ as follows:

$$\mathbf{\Delta}_{i,k}^{(l-1)} = \sum_m \mathbf{W}_{k,m}^{(l)} * \mathbf{\Delta}_{i,m}^{(l)} \odot \phi' \left(\mathbf{Z}_{i,k}^{(l-1)} \right)$$

$$\mathbf{W}^{(l-1)} \leftarrow \mathbf{W}^{(l-1)} - \mu \sum_{i=1}^{N} \mathbf{H}_i^{(l-2)} \mathbf{\Delta}_i^{(l-1)\mathsf{T}} \qquad (4.17)$$

$$\mathbf{B}^{(l-1)} \leftarrow \mathbf{B}^{(l-1)} - \mu \sum_{i=1}^{N} \mathbf{\Delta}_i^{(l-1)}$$

Here, the subindex i refers to each one of the training input images. This set of equations is identic to Eq. (1.110), with the only difference that the outputs are matrices and the product inside the update for the convolution kernels is changed by a convolution product.

Example 4.3.1 *(Training and testing a CNN)*

In this example, the Canadian Institute for Advanced Research (CIFAR)10 database from the CIFAR is used to train and test a CNN. They are divided into 50,000 images for training and another 10,000 for test. A CNN has been constructed with three convolutional layers and three dense layers. The first convolutional layer has three input channels and 32 output channels. The second layer has 32 input channels and 64 output channels, and the third one has 64 input channels and 128 output channels. All kernels are 3×3. All convolutions are followed by ReLU activations and 2×2 max-pooling and no padding and stride is applied to the convolutions.

The first convolution, then, produces an output of 32 channels with dimension 32×30. After the max pooling, the output is reduced to 15×15. The second convolution outputs 64 channels with dimension 13×13, and after the max pool, the output is reduced to 6×6. Finally, the third convolution outputs 128 channels with dimension 4×4, reduced to 2×2 after the max pool. The channels are then placed in a vector (flattened). Since there are 12 channels with 4 pixels each, the vector has a dimension of 512. This vector is the input to a dense layer that connects to a second layer of 128 nodes, and this one to a third layer of 10 nodes. The first and second layers have ReLU activation and the third one has linear activation. Figure 4.10 illustrates the architecture of the CNN model used in this experiment.

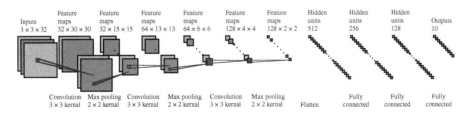

Figure 4.10 Architectural framework of the CNN model outlined in Example 4.3.1.

The CNN is trained with the 50,000 images of the training set with mini-batches of 50 images each, during 100 epochs. The training is performed using the Adam optimizer with $\gamma = 0.01, \beta_1 = 0.9, \beta_2 = 0.999, \epsilon = 10^{-8}$, and no weight decay.

The test was done with the 10,000 test images provided in the dataset. The overall accuracy was 75%. The confusion matrix of the experiment is shown in Fig. 4.11. The left pane shows the training convergence, and the right pane shows the confusion matrix of the CNN.

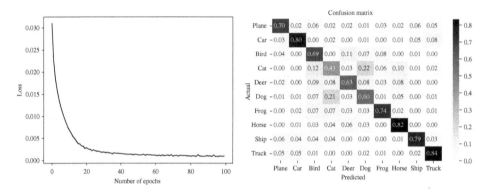

Figure 4.11 Loss as a function of the number of epochs and confusion matrix of Example 4.3.1.

4.4 Extensions of the CNN

CNNs have revolutionized the field of computer vision, especially in the field of object recognition and other visual-related applications. The ability of CNNs to extract hierarchical features from input data has made them quite popular, mainly in processing images. Researchers have explored different approaches to extend and enhance the traditional CNN architecture to tackle new challenges (M. Ajith and Calhoun 2023), each time improving the model performance in specific domains.

We will be going over a spectrum of such extensions and will explore more about the advantages and disadvantages of these architectures. Throughout the section, we will provide an overview of the different kinds of CNNs that were inspired by traditional architecture for solving complex challenges associated with image classification problems. The ability of these structures to efficiently process information at multiscale levels, especially in extracting meaningful features also helped with improved the interpretability of the model results and the features extracted. This indeed proved to be useful in various domains/applications. These extensions continue to be popular in different domains such as medical imaging (A. R. Kurup et al. 2023; Maqsood et al. 2019; Marcus et al. 2010; Byra et al. 2020), object detection (Zhiqiang and Jun 2017; M. Ajith and A. R. Kurup 2018; Duan et al. 2012), natural language processing (Wróbel et al. 2020; Moriya and Shibata 2018), or solar energy applications (M. Ajith and Manel Martínez-Ramón 2023).

4.4.1 AlexNet

AlexNet takes its name from Alex Krizhevsky, who introduced it in 2012 in collaboration with Ilya Sutskever and Geoffrey Hinton (Alex Krizhevsky et al. 2012). It was able to solve

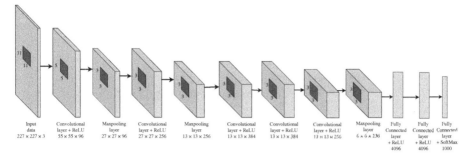

Figure 4.12 Alexnet architecture.

the problem of image classification on the ImageNet database consisting of 1000 different classes. Hence, this network was able to win the ImageNet ImageNet large scale visual recognition challenge (ILSVRC)-2012 competition with the highest accuracy. Its structure is shown in Fig. 4.12.

The red–green–blue (RGB) images with dimensions $224 \times 224 \times 3$ are passed through a set of 96 convolution kernels with dimensions $11 \times 11 \times 3$ to produce 96 outputs. The convolutions include a stride of 4 pixels. Each element of the outputs is passed through a ReLU function. The dimensions of each one of the convolution outputs are $\lfloor (224 - 11 + 4)/4 \rfloor = 54$, but authors report dimensions of 55×55, which may be produced by padding of 3 pixels.

In the overall architecture, initially, an input image of size $224 \times 224 \times 3$ is given to the first convolutional layer. This input is convolved using 96 kernels of size $11 \times 11 \times 3$ and stride 4. The second convolutional layer on the other hand used 256 kernels of size $5 \times 5 \times 48$. The following three convolutional layers are linked together without any pooling layers. The third and fourth convolutional layers have 384 kernels of size $3 \times 3 \times 256$ and $3 \times 3 \times 192$, respectively. Finally, the fifth convolutional layer contains 256 kernels of size $3 \times 3 \times 192$, and each of the FC layers has 4096 neurons.

The AlexNet paper introduced several novelties such as data augmentation, dropout, ReLU, overlapping pooling, and multi-GPU training. Both data augmentation and dropout were developed to eliminate the overfitting problem. While performing data augmentation, the network was given different variations of the same image. This strategy is used while training the models to increase the heterogeneity of the available data without gathering new data. Specifically, they increased the size of the data by a factor of 2048 by extracting random patches from the images and altering the intensities of the RGB channels.

Dropout was another technique introduced by Geoffrey E. Hinton in 2012 for preventing overfitting (Geoffrey E. Hinton et al. 2012b). In dropout, a neuron is dropped from the network with a predetermined probability (see Subsection 2.3.2). Every iteration uses a different network architecture, which forces each neuron to have more robust features. However, the number of iterations needed for the model's convergence is increased during dropout.

Previously, sigmoidal activation functions were the standard way of introducing nonlinearity to the CNN. But in AlexNet, the ReLU activation (see Section 1.4) was used for this purpose. The training time of ReLU-based CNNs was faster than compared to tanh or logistic activation functions. Since they are saturating nonlinear functions, they have a compact range between -1 or 0 and 1, whereas ReLU does not exhibit any restraints at its boundaries, thereby resulting in faster training.

Another unique feature of AlexNet is overlapping pooling so that the adjacent kernels over which the max is computed overlap each other. The traditional CNN used pooling layers without overlapping for downsampling the features. In AlexNet, the overlapping max-pooling layers helped to reduce the error rates of the classifier and avoided overfitting. Moreover, AlexNet used the ImageNet dataset that had roughly 1.2 million training images. To avoid the memory issue and increase the training time, multiple GPUs were used for training this network.

4.4.2 VGG

The visual geometric group (VGG) is another classic CNN network named after the research group from Oxford University that developed the architecture for the network. This network was developed in the year 2014 by Karen Simonyan and Andrew Zisserman (2015). This network was the second place holder in the ILSVRC 2014 competition.

The main idea of the VGG nets was to see the effect of the depth of the convolutional network on the accuracy in large-scale image recognition settings. Smaller convolutional filters were used in this network, which allowed the increased depth of the network by adding more weight layers.

The VGG architecture consists of a stack of convolutional layers through which the images are passed. The network uses convolutional filters of relatively smaller size and is significantly deeper in structure compared to previously developed structures using smaller convolutions (Ciresan et al. 2011). The framework has five max-pooling layers with a window size of 2×2 and a stride of 2. The max-pooling layers follow only a few convolutional layers and not all convolutional layers. The VGG architecture has three FC layers. The first two FC layers have 4096 nodes, the last one has 1000 nodes for each class, and the final layer uses a softmax activation.

The VGG framework was the first network to use a *preprocessing block* where the input size of the RGB images is cropped to 224×224 during training. The mean RGB value computed on the training set is subtracted from each pixel. Second, they use *smaller receptive fields* or kernels of 3×3 in the convolutional layers compared to the ones of ALexNets and their derivatives. The idea is that instead of using large receptive fields such as 11×11 (Alex Krizhevsky et al. 2012) and 7×7 (Matthew D. Zeiler and Fergus 2014; Sermanet et al. 2013), the same operation can be achieved by stacking the smaller 3×3 convolutional layers. The 3×3 layer stacked twice can be equally effective as that of a 5×5 receptive field. Similarly, the 7×7 receptive field can be replaced using 3 stacked 3×3 convolutional layers. In addition, the structure also incorporates 1×1 convolutions, which act as a linear transformation of the inputs. These units are then followed by ReLU activations (Alex Krizhevsky et al. 2012) for introducing nonlinearity. The stride for convolutions is set to 1.

The spatial resolution is preserved while performing padding of inputs. This is done by padding using just 1 pixel for 3×3 convolutional layers. The depth of the network is another key feature. The depth of the structure is varied by adding more weight layers. There are six different versions based on the number of weight layers in the network. The initial version had 11 weight layers which were increased to 16 layers (VGG-16) (Fig. 4.13) and lastly 19 layers (VGG-19). VGG-16 and VGG-19 were the most popular ones. The configurations were varied mainly by adding the convolutional layers. The FC layer remained the same for all the different versions.

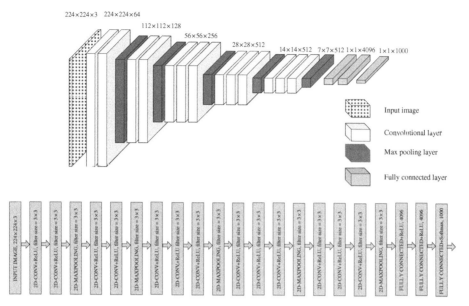

Figure 4.13 VGG-16 architecture.

4.4.3 Inception

The Inception-v1/GoogLeNet is a CNN architecture with 22 layers and 5M parameters (Szegedy et al. 2015). It was the winner of the ImageNet Large Scale Visual Recognition Competition in 2014. The previous CNN models were focused on going deeper to improve accuracy, but this compromised the computational cost of these networks. The Inception-v1 network consists of recurring blocks of convolutional designs called Inception modules that make it wider. A naive inception module performs max-pooling and 1×1, 3×3 and 5×5 convolutions on the input. The final outputs are generated after passing them through the concatenation layer. But the 3×3 and 5×5 convolutions were computationally expensive. Hence, dimensionality reduction was necessary, and it was achieved by incorporating 1×1 convolutions. The total number of layers utilized in the network's design is around 100, and a ReLU activation is used in all convolutions, including those inside the Inception modules. Toward the end of the architecture, the global average pooling layer replaced the FC layers, which further reduced the number of parameters and increased the top-1 accuracy by 0.6%. Thus, the complexity of the model was reduced to a great extent without decreasing the speed and accuracy.

The Inception-v1 contains the 1×1 convolutions that were first introduced in the Network In Network paper by Min Lin in 2013 (M. Lin et al. 2014a). The 1×1 convolutional layer was used to decrease the number of parameters by reducing the number of channels. Its activation function also added nonlinearity to the model. For example, consider the following operations in which we convolve $28 \times 28 \times 64$ input feature maps with $5 \times 5 \times 32$ filters. Here the total no. of parameters = $(28 \times 28 \times 32) \times (5 \times 5 \times 64) = 40$ million operations. Repeat the operations with the same input feature maps but with a 1×1 layer before the 5×5 convolutional layer. The total no. of parameters = $(28 \times 28 \times 16) \times (1 \times 1 \times 32) +$

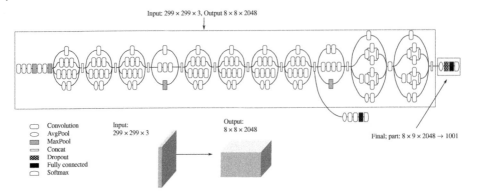

Figure 4.14 Inception-v3 architecture.

$(28 \times 28 \times 32) \times (5 \times 5 \times 16) = 10$ million operations. Hence, the use of 1×1 convolutions has reduced the number of operations by a factor of 4.

Additionally, the Inception-v1 network introduced two auxiliary classifiers to prevent the vanishing gradient problem. An auxiliary loss was computed by applying a softmax activation at the output of the inception module, and this loss was added to the main network loss. Other variations of inception such as Inception-v2 (Ioffe and Szegedy 2015), Inception-v3 (Fig. 4.14) (Szegedy et al. 2016), and Inception-v4 (Szegedy et al. 2017) were introduced in the later years to curb the limitations of the initial version.

4.4.4 ResNet

The residual neural network (ResNet) was a CNN architecture introduced in the year 2015 (He et al. 2016). These structures were the winner of localization, ImageNet detection, segmentation, and detection in the 2015 common objects in context (COCO) and ILSVRC competitions. These structures were successful in providing great generalization performance on image recognition tasks. The idea of ResNet was to develop an efficient way to curb the huge problem of vanishing gradients (Yoshua Bengio et al. 1994; Glorot and Yoshua Bengio 2010) associated with training deeper networks which indeed affects the convergence. Previously, this problem was addressed using normalized initialization (Y. A. LeCun et al. 2012; Glorot and Yoshua Bengio 2010; He et al. 2015) and intermediate normalization layers (Ioffe and Szegedy 2015). These techniques were able to make the networks with a significant number of layers converge using SGD and BP (Y. LeCun et al. 1989). The convergence was achieved, but there was another problem called the *degradation* problem whereas the network depth increases, the accuracy starts getting saturated and degrades rapidly later on (He et al. 2016). This resulted in higher training error after adding more layers to a deeper model compared to their shallower counterparts (He and J. Sun 2015).

ResNet was the first network to introduce residual learning and skip connections skipping one or more weight layers to solve the degradation problem. The idea was that instead of jumping through the stacked layers try to fit a residual mapping. For example, if the original mapping before adding the skip connection was $F_l(x_{l-i})$, then after skipping connection it will fit $G_l(x_{l-i})$, i.e. the stacked nonlinear layers will fit another mapping

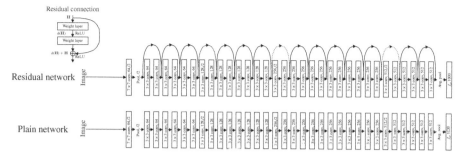

Figure 4.15 Resnet-34 architecture. Adapted from He, X. Zhang, et al., 2016 / IEEE.

$F_l(x_{l-i}) = G_l(x_{l-i}) - x_{l-i}$, where l is the layer index and i is the total number of layers skipped. The original mapping is hence transformed to $F_l(x_{l-i}) + x_{l-i}$. This is shown in Fig. 4.15 Using this technique, the optimization became simpler as it was easier to learn the residual mapping than the original underlying mapping. The connections are *identity mapping*, which is then added to the output of the stacked layers. These identity mappings do not add to the computational complexities, hence the number of parameters before and after remains the same. Through this concept, the structures were able to be successfully trained for 100s and 1000s of layers.

Other networks also used the shorter skip connections, in particular, gated shortcut connections such as highway network (R. K. Srivastava et al. 2015) and long short term memory (LSTM) (Schmidhuber and Hochreiter 1997). ResNets were very popular among them due to their capability of training very deep networks going up to 1001 layers, outperforming their shallower counterparts.

4.4.5 Xception

Xception was inspired by the concept of the Inception network introduced in 4.4.3. The Xception network was introduced by a Google researcher, Francois Chollet in 2017 (Chollet 2017), and it used the idea of depthwise separable convolutions by taking the concept of Inception to the extreme.

The Inception module introduced in Inception-V3 made use of 1×1 convolutions to capture cross-channel correlations, and the spatial correlations were learned using the regular 3×3 or 5×5 operations as shown in Fig. 4.16. This idea of the Inception module can be reformed to have the input passed through 1×1 convolution followed by just one particular size convolution for example: of 3×3 as shown in Fig. 4.17.

This version can be considered the "extreme version" of Inception. This version of the Inception module is close to the depthwise separable convolution operation. The concept of depthwise separable convolutions was introduced in Sifre and Mallat (2014) in 2014. These operations were also incorporated into programming frameworks such as Tensor-Flow in 2016 (Abadi et al. 2016). Depthwise separable convolution has two parts: depthwise convolution followed by pointwise convolution. Depthwise convolution performs spatial convolutions independently on each of the channels of the input. Pointwise convolution performs a 1×1 convolutional operation. This operation helps with projecting the output to a new channel space.

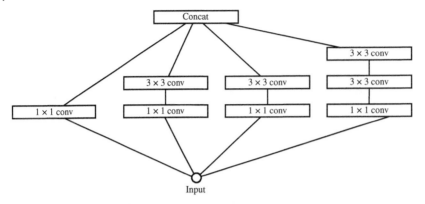

Figure 4.16 Inception module as in Inception-V3.

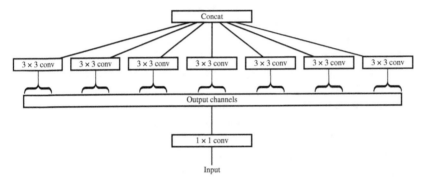

Figure 4.17 "Extreme" version of the Inception Module as described in [?].

The Xception architecture shown in Fig. 4.18 consists of 36 convolutional layers organized into 14 different modules. The stacked linear layers make use of depthwise separable convolutions. These modules include residual connections around them which are linear. The convolutional base is followed by a layer dedicated to logistic regression. The experiments were also evaluated for a configuration where a FC layer was also introduced ahead of a logistic regression layer. The number of parameters was nearly the same for both Inception V3 and Xception. The comparison between the models was done using two image classification setups: the famous single-labeled 1000-class classification on the ImageNet dataset and the 17000-class test for performing multilabel classification on the JFT dataset. The JFT dataset was an internal Google dataset first introduced in (Geoffrey E. Hinton et al. 2015). The dataset contains 350 million images with labels corresponding to 17000 classes. For both datasets, different optimization configuration was set. In both cases, the Xception architecture showed significant improvement in performance with a higher margin for the JFT dataset.

4.4.6 MobileNet

MobileNets (Howard et al. 2017) represent a class of efficient CNN models specifically designed for mobile and embedded vision applications. The first version of MobileNets was

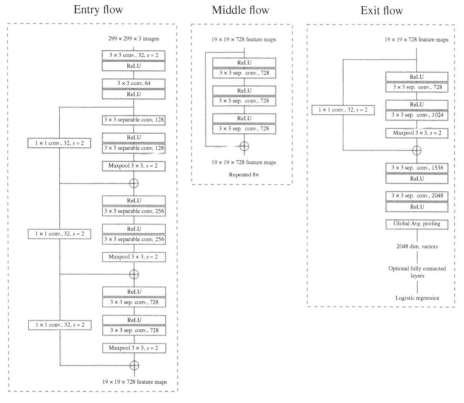

Figure 4.18 Xception architecture.

introduced by Google in 2017. These models leverage a novel convolutional layer called depthwise separable convolution, which was later adopted in advanced Inception models. This approach significantly reduces computational demands and model size compared to other well-known CNN architectures. MobileNets are characterized by their compactness, speed, and efficiency, and they find utility across a diverse range of applications, including object detection, fine-grain classification, face attribute analysis, and large-scale geolocalization. The key features of MobileNets are

4.4.6.1 Depthwise Separable Convolutions

The MobileNet model utilizes a convolution technique known as depth-wise separable convolutions. This method breaks down a standard convolution operation into two distinct steps: a depthwise convolution and a pointwise convolution with a 1×1 kernel. The depthwise convolution applies a single filter to each input channel, and then the pointwise convolution employs a 1×1 convolution to combine the results of the depthwise convolution (refer to Fig. 4.19). In contrast, a standard convolution carries out filtering and combining inputs in a single step. Depthwise separable convolutions effectively divide this process into two separate layers: one for filtering and another for merging inputs. This factorization technique brings about significant advantages, notably reducing computational demands and the overall size of the model.

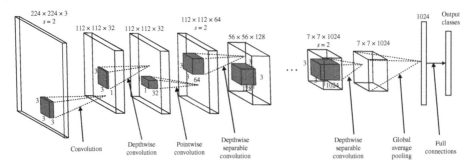

Figure 4.19 MobileNet architecture.

4.4.6.2 Width Multiplier

The width multiplier parameter which is represented as α was introduced to achieve an even smaller and faster MobileNet model. The purpose of this width multiplier α was to uniformly reduce the network's width at each layer. For any given layer and width multiplier α, the number of input channels M becomes αM, and the number of output channels N becomes αN. The width multiplier takes values in the range (0, 1], with typical settings being 1, 0.75, 0.5, and 0.25. When α equals 1, it represents the baseline MobileNet, and for $\alpha < 1$, it corresponds to reduced MobileNets. The width multiplier has the effect of quadratically reducing computational cost and the number of parameters by approximately α^2.

4.4.6.3 Resolution Multiplier

The resolution multiplier γ serves as an additional parameter used to reduce the computational demands of MobileNets. It is applied uniformly to shrink both the input image and the internal representation of each layer. In practical terms, γ is initially set according to the desired input resolution, allowing for flexible adjustments based on the level of computational efficiency you aim to achieve. The resolution multiplier γ falls within the range of (0, 1], which results in the input resolution of the network being set to values such as 224, 192, 160, or 128. When γ is equal to 1, it corresponds to the standard MobileNet, while γ values less than 1 represent MobileNets with reduced computational requirements. The resolution multiplier has the effect of reducing computational cost by a factor of γ^2.

MobileNets represent a computationally efficient CNN architecture, making them suitable for resource-constrained devices. These models are known for their compact size, making them easy to deploy on devices with limited memory and storage capacity. Users can fine-tune width multiplier, and resolution multiplier parameters to balance computational cost and model performance, making MobileNets adaptable to various scenarios. However, their compactness may limit their capacity for complex tasks, and aggressive parameter reductions can lead to trade-offs in model size versus performance. Nonetheless, MobileNet remains a compelling choice for achieving efficient deep learning inference on mobile platforms.

4.4.7 DenseNet

DenseNet was developed by Cornell Uni, Tsinghua Uni, and Facebook Research in 2017 for visual object recognition (G. Huang et al. 2017). In most CNN architectures, due to the depth

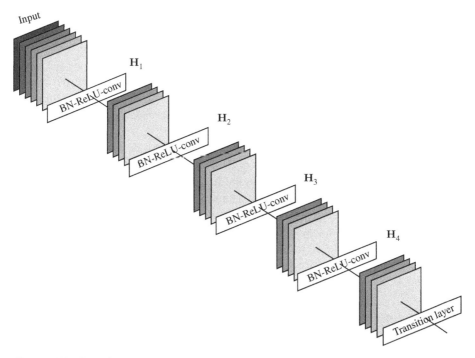

Figure 4.20 DenseNet architecture.

of the network, the information flow from input to output is disrupted and the model experiences the vanishing gradient problem. DenseNets were created to exploit the full potential of deep CNNs by applying feature reuse. Despite being similar to ResNets, the DenseNets improve accuracy by concatenating the feature maps from various layers. The mathematical formulation is shown in the below equation:

$$f^l = F^l([f^0, f^1, f^2, ... f^{l-1}]) \tag{4.18}$$

where F_l corresponds to the function that concatenates the output feature maps of the previous layers. This function can be a combination of operations such as batch normalization, ReLU, pooling, or convolution. The feature maps of all preceding layers, i.e. $f^0, f^1, f^2, ... f^{l-1}$ are sent into the lth layer f^l.

The key features of DenseNet are (see Fig. 4.20):

Dense blocks: DenseNets are composed of several dense blocks with n dense layers. Each dense layer is made up of 1×1 and 3×3 convolutions. The dense layer receives input from the preceding feature maps, which are then passed on to the subsequent layers. The number of filters in the convolutional layers changes with each dense block, while the size of the feature maps stays constant. Transition layers are the layers that exist between dense blocks. If a dense block comprises m feature maps, the transition layer creates θm output feature maps, where $0 < \theta \leq 1$. As a result, it aids in reducing the number of feature maps and improving the model's compactness.

Growth rate: The number of parameters and model complexity are determined by the initial number of feature maps. If each function F^l generates k feature maps, the lth layer must have $k^0 + k \times (l-1)$ input feature maps, where k^0 is the number of channels in the input layer. Here k is the hyperparameter which denotes the growth rate. This means that for each layer added, we add k additional feature maps to the overall number of feature maps and hence the total number of parameters. The feature maps may be viewed as the network's overall state. The authors have used a k value of 32 for all the experiments. These 32 feature maps are concatenated and fed as input to the next layer. Consequently, the growth rate governs how much new information each layer contributes to the overall system.

The main advantages of DenseNets include the requirement of fewer parameters for creating compact models that deliver state-of-the-art performances. Additionally, the network is also parameter efficient; a 250-layer model has just 15.3M parameters; and it outperforms models with more than 30M parameters, such as FractalNet and Wide ResNets. DenseNets can also extend to hundreds of layers while posing no optimization challenges. This structure produces constant improvements in accuracy as the number of parameters increases, with no indications of performance deterioration or overfitting. Furthermore, DenseNets require significantly fewer parameters and less computation to achieve state-of-the-art performance.

4.4.8 EfficientNet

EfficientNet was the latest model introduced by Tan and Q. Le (2019) in this series of image classification CNN architectures. EfficientNets were able to efficiently scale up ResNet and MobileNets using a compound coefficient scaling model as shown in Fig. 4.21. The results were evaluated on different state-of-the-art datasets. The common practice of model scaling was focused on increasing the number of layers depthwise or width-wise. Another approach was to introduce only high-resolution images as inputs for improved performance. But, in both these cases the requirement of manual tuning becomes huge. The idea of Efficient-Net was to scale up the CNNs using a more structured approach without compromising efficiency and performance.

The models analyzed the effect of scaling each of the dimensions in the network with respect to a fixed resource constraint. The baseline network was evaluated under the same condition for different scaling options which gave the scaling coefficient. The scaling coefficient is further used to scale up the model size and also to keep the computational cost minimal.

The base model plays a key role in determining the effectiveness of the model scaling approach. Additionally, using the neural architecture search approach (Wistuba et al. 2019) using the AutoML mobile neural architecture search (MNAS) (Tan et al. 2019) framework,

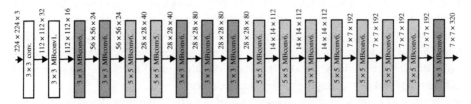

Figure 4.21 EfficientNet architecture.

a new base network was developed. The resulting model was similar to MNasNET and MobileNetV2 in structure but was larger in terms of higher FLOPs. The baseline model was scaled up using the compound coefficient scaling approach to obtain the family of EfficientNet models. The scaling approach was able to give an improvement in performance with respect to ResNet, DenseNet, Inception, etc. Hence, the EfficientNet family of models gave a good performance and model efficiency.

4.4.9 Transfer Learning for CNN Extensions

Most of the above-mentioned CNN extensions are heavy models and hence training them from scratch can be computationally expensive. Therefore, these models are trained commonly in a computationally simpler way using *Transfer Learning.* Transfer learning is an approach that uses the principle idea of helping machine learning algorithms to improve the performance in the domain of interest by borrowing labeled data or extracting knowledge from related domains (Pan 2014). Transfer learning can be defined as a machine learning technique that incorporates additional information apart from the knowledge gained from the training data which may be from one or more related domains. The approach focuses on the idea of reusing previously learned knowledge (Pan and Q. Yang 2009) and transferring the knowledge across domains (Zhuang et al. 2020).

In real-world scenarios, we can find many examples of transfer learning. For example, knowledge gained from playing the ukelele might help you with learning other instruments such as guitar and piano. A person having some musical background can learn musical instruments faster compared to someone who is not familiar with the background. In such a case, a person learning knowledge from a particular background is extending it or transferring it to learn a related task. Similarly, in machine learning, we can leverage the knowledge gained in one domain to be shared and applied in a related domain of interest. Now, in machine learning, this can be viewed as the train data and target data being in two different subdomains, with them being linked by a common higher-level domain which gives a foundation on how the subdomains are related (K. Weiss et al. 2016).

This kind of knowledge engineering using transfer learning is beneficial when it comes to fields where the data gets outdated frequently or fields where the data availability is low. The lack of sufficient training data poses difficulty in training such models efficiently. In such cases, the reuse of training data or extracted knowledge in related domains can be of great use for improving the performance of the system. The transfer learning idea has been implemented across different domains such as for object detection problems (M. Ajith and A. R. Kurup 2018), in image classification (M. Ajith and Manel Martínez-Ramón 2021, 2023), text classification (Harel and Mannor 2010), in medical fields (A. Kurup et al. 2020), image segmentation, and sentiment classification (C. Wang and Mahadevan 2011).

There are two different types of transfer learning: Homogeneous and heterogeneous (Pan 2014). Homogenous transfer learning directly correlates to a big data environment. The idea is to avoid the collection of more data samples and use the available resources from a domain to build predictive models for other target domains. Homogeneous transfer learning has overlapping feature space across both the source domain and target domain, and even the label spaces between the categories/tasks will be identical. Further, the homogeneous approaches can be subcategorized as instance-based, feature-based, relational-based, and parameter-based. These subcategories are based on the type of transfer of the model. As for heterogeneous transfer learning, the feature spaces are also heterogeneous, and they come from different domains with the labels being nonidentical.

The heterogeneous transfer learning problems are solved using two main approaches: symmetric transformations and asymmetric transformations. In the case of symmetric transformation, both the source and target domains are separately transformed into a common latent feature space. The asymmetrical transformation aims at transforming the source and target instances of the same class without having context feature bias (K. Weiss et al. 2016). In most of the heterogeneous scenarios, an initial assumption is made that the source and target instances are coming from the same domain and do not have any difference in distributions.

Now let us look into an example of transfer learning using the CNN extension. The example here depicts a homogeneous transfer learning approach where we are using a pretrained model learned on a larger dataset (ImageNet dataset) sharing a similar feature space as that of the training inputs to adapt to a new dataset. For using the CNN architecture for transfer learning, we remove the top layers of the model and freeze the rest of the layers which constitute the base model. The base model uses the pretrained weights obtained from the model trained on the large ImageNet database which has previously learned knowledge. This knowledge is transferred using a transfer learning approach to learn features that could help classification in the new dataset.

Example 4.4.1 *(Transfer Learning using CNN extensions)*
In this example, we dig deep into how to train these huge models. Here, we are implementing the transfer learning approach for training EfficientNet. For this example, the implementation is done using the same CIFAR10 database as in Example 4.4.1.

Dataset: As mentioned in Example 4.4.1, the CIFAR10 dataset consists of 50000 train images and 10,000 test images. First, we load the dataset as train and test sets. Further, the train images are split into train and validation sets. Following this, one-hot encoding is performed on the labels of the 10 possible categories (see Section 1.5.2.2). Once the data is configured, the next step is to perform image data augmentation (see Section 2.3.4). Data augmentation is helpful in artificially increasing the size of the dataset, which helps in improving the model performance.

Transfer learning model: The example uses EfficientNet models (introduced in Section 4.4.8) for demonstrating the transfer learning approach. This family of models is known for its balance in both efficiency and accuracy. The EfficientNet family consists of eight different versions (named B0 to B7). The model being used for this example is EfficientNet-B0. First, the base model is defined by removing the top layers and using pretrained weights. This freezes the top layers. Next, the trainable layers are added to the model. In this case, five dense layers are added on top of the base model. Note that the last layer has 10 outputs corresponding to the number of classes being classified (CIFAR10 has 10 classes on data to be classified).

Training: Following this, we can define the parameters and optimizer for compiling and then training the model. The model is trained with batches of 100 images during 50 epochs. The training is done using Adam Optimizer with $\mu = 0.001, \beta_1 = 0.9, \beta_2 = 0.999, \epsilon = 10^{-7}$ and no weight decay. Here, we also reduce the learning rate when the monitored metric (accuracy) has stopped improving.

Training loss
Validation loss
Loss
Number of epochs
Accuracy
Train accuracy
Validation accuracy
Number of epochs

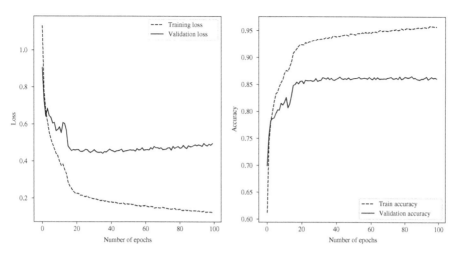

Figure 4.22 Loss and accuracy as a function of the number of epochs of Example 4.4.1.

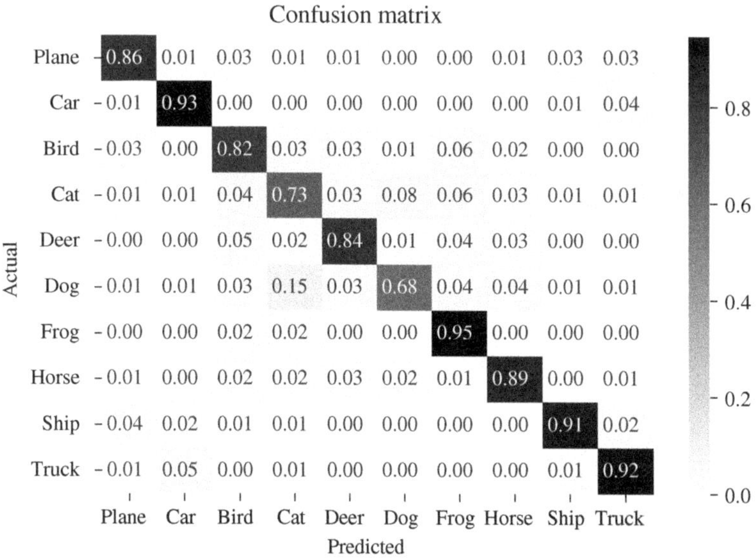

Confusion matrix
Plane 0.86 0.01 0.03 0.01 0.01 0.00 0.00 0.01 0.03 0.03
Car 0.01 0.93 0.00 0.00 0.00 0.00 0.00 0.00 0.01 0.04
Bird 0.03 0.00 0.82 0.03 0.03 0.01 0.06 0.02 0.00 0.00
Cat 0.01 0.01 0.04 0.73 0.03 0.08 0.06 0.03 0.01 0.01
Deer 0.00 0.00 0.05 0.02 0.84 0.01 0.04 0.03 0.00 0.00
Dog 0.01 0.01 0.03 0.15 0.03 0.68 0.04 0.04 0.01 0.01
Frog 0.00 0.00 0.02 0.02 0.00 0.00 0.95 0.00 0.00 0.00
Horse 0.01 0.00 0.02 0.02 0.03 0.02 0.01 0.89 0.00 0.01
Ship 0.04 0.02 0.01 0.01 0.00 0.00 0.00 0.00 0.91 0.02
Truck 0.01 0.05 0.00 0.01 0.00 0.00 0.00 0.00 0.01 0.92
Plane Car Bird Cat Deer Dog Frog Horse Ship Truck
Predicted
Actual
0.8
0.6
0.4
0.2
0.0

Figure 4.23 Confusion matrix of Example 4.4.1.

Testing and results: The test was done on the 10,000 images provided in the dataset. The overall accuracy was 85.4%. The convergence in terms of Loss and accuracy can be seen in Fig. 4.22. The confusion matrix is shown in Fig. 4.23. The convergence in terms of loss and accuracy can be seen in Fig. 4.22.

We can also train the EfficientNet-B0 from scratch to evaluate its result and compare it with that of architecture trained using transfer learning. For training the architecture from scratch the main change that we implement is to not have pretrained weights loaded to the base model. This lets the model train from scratch without any pretrained weights.

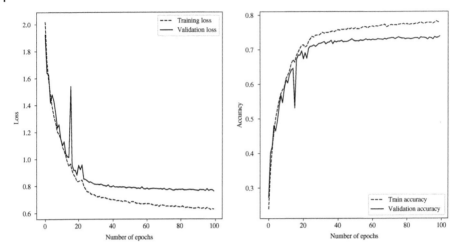

Figure 4.24 Loss and accuracy as a function of the number of epochs in case of training EfficientNet-B0 from scratch.

Confusion matrix

	Plane	Car	Bird	Cat	Deer	Dog	Frog	Horse	Ship	Truck
Plane	0.80	0.04	0.03	0.01	0.02	0.00	0.01	0.01	0.04	0.05
Car	0.01	0.88	0.00	0.00	0.00	0.00	0.02	0.00	0.01	0.06
Bird	0.08	0.01	0.61	0.05	0.07	0.04	0.10	0.03	0.00	0.01
Cat	0.01	0.02	0.07	0.52	0.06	0.12	0.12	0.04	0.01	0.03
Deer	0.02	0.00	0.06	0.04	0.68	0.02	0.11	0.06	0.01	0.00
Dog	0.01	0.00	0.03	0.23	0.05	0.54	0.06	0.06	0.01	0.02
Frog	0.00	0.01	0.02	0.03	0.02	0.01	0.90	0.00	0.00	0.01
Horse	0.01	0.01	0.03	0.02	0.05	0.04	0.02	0.80	0.00	0.02
Ship	0.08	0.04	0.01	0.01	0.01	0.00	0.01	0.00	0.81	0.03
Truck	0.03	0.09	0.00	0.01	0.01	0.00	0.01	0.01	0.01	0.83

Actual (vertical axis label), Predicted (horizontal axis label)

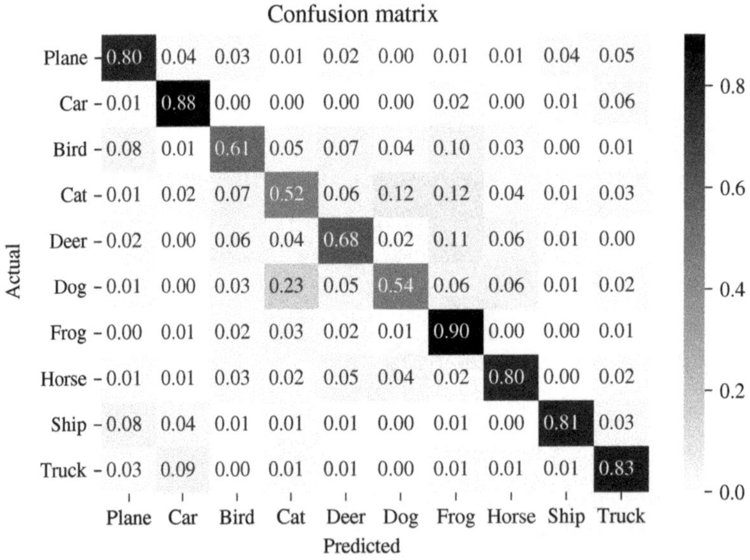

Figure 4.25 Confusion matrix in case of training EfficientNet-B0 from scratch.

The overall accuracy while training from scratch was obtained to be 73% and the loss and accuracy curves can be seen in Fig: 4.24. The convergence in terms of loss and accuracy for the case can be seen in Fig. 4.25.

We can see here that using transfer learning gives a balanced solution in terms of computational expense as well as performance. The approach has a better performance in terms of accuracy compared to CNN implementation and also training the architecture from scratch. In Example 4.4.1, we see the accuracy on the same dataset is 75%, and with the transfer learning method using EfficientNet-B0, the accuracy improved to 85.4%.

Additionally, under similar training conditions (same number of epochs, trainable layers, hyperparameters, and batch size) and training the architecture from scratch gave a much lesser accuracy of 73%. The performance could have been improved if the EfficientNet-B0 structure had been trained from scratch for a longer duration. Hence, for a more computationally effective solution transfer learning approach can be used instead. Using the transfer learning approach, training time can be reduced to a great extent compared to that of training the architecture from scratch.

The script corresponding to this example for training the architecture using transfer learning and from scratch has been implemented in TensorFlow Keras and can be seen in the corresponding Jupyter Notebook.

4.4.10   Comparisons Among CNN Extensions

The advent of AlexNet, which included the ReLU activation layer, started the emergence of deep learning in image classification in 2012. The use of a CNN in image classification improved the accuracy while minimizing the need to manually feature engineer each image. Following AlexNet, various CNN architectures were developed with more characteristics to efficiently categorize images. The accuracy of an algorithm for a classification task is the measure of the number of accurate predictions divided by the total number of data points. Now, in the case of the top-1 accuracy, you check if the predicted class with the highest probability is the same as the actual label. In the case of the top-5 accuracy, you check if the target label is one of your top 5 predictions, i.e. the ones with the highest probabilities. For example, consider a sentiment analysis machine learning classification task with seven classes such as anger, surprise, sadness, happiness, neutral, fear, and disgust. Let the image containing fear emotion be present during the test, and the output predictions of the classification model have the probabilities such as anger – 0.4, sadness – 0.2, fear – 0.3, happiness – 0.04, disgust – 0.03, neutral – 0.01, and surprise – 0.02. Here it can be seen while using top-1 accuracy, the output is counted as incorrect since it predicted anger. While using top-5 accuracy, the output is correct, as fear is among the top-5 predictions. Hence, in a classification problem with k possible labels, every classifier has 100% top-k accuracy. In the ImageNet classification problem, top-1, and top-5 accuracies are important units for evaluating the performance of the various models (see Fig. 4.26 and Fig. 4.27). In 2012, AlexNet competed in the ImageNet challenge and easily outperformed all prior nondeep learning-based models. It was trained on a GTX580 GPU with 3GB of RAM. In the ImageNet large scale visual recognition challenge (ILSRVC), it achieved a top-5 accuracy of 84.6%. In 2014, the VGG network was introduced that used a deeper structure with much smaller filters. The Visual Geometry Group at Oxford University proposed two new designs, VGG-16 and VGG-19, with the key distinction being that VGG-16 utilized 16 convolutions while VGG-19 used 19. The authors believed that the extra layers enhanced the robustness of the model and allowed it to learn more complex features. As a result of the new layers, the number of parameters increases from 138 to 143M. So these structures are computationally expensive with 138M total parameters and each image having a memory of 96MB, which is significantly larger than a normal image. Furthermore, in the 2014 ILSVRC competition, VGG-16 was the runner-up with a top 5 accuracy rate of 91.90%. The Google researchers proposed a novel architecture called the

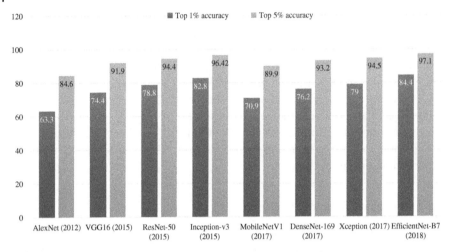

Figure 4.26 Comparison of top 1% and top 5% accuracy of different CNN architectures for image classification.

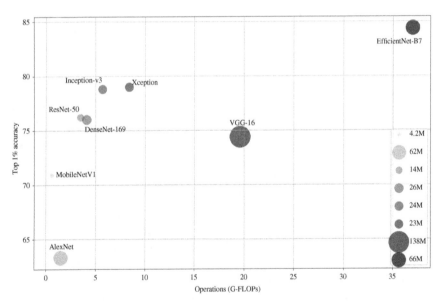

Figure 4.27 Comparison of top 1% accuracy, number of parameters and operations (G-Flops) different CNN architectures for image classification.

GoogLeNet network, also known as the Inception-v1 architecture, in 2014. With a top 5 accuracy rate of 93.3%, the authors won the ImageNet competition. The basic idea behind the GoogLeNet architecture was to employ several convolution layers in the same block to go not only deeper but also wider; these blocks are known as Inception blocks. The existence of an inception module allows the network to gather several aspect ratios of the same image by employing the convolution layers in parallel. The biggest disadvantage of this network is the computational power required to train it with a large number of deep and wide layers. Following the popularity of Inception-v1, the authors released subsequent versions such as Inception-v2 and Inception-v3 in the subsequent years. Among these networks, Inception-v1 and Inception-v3 are the most popular architectures. Six convolution layers are utilized in the Inception-v1 inception blocks, whereas seven convolution layers are used in the Inception-v3 inception blocks. The computational cost of Inception-v3 which is 42 layers deep is just roughly 2.5 times that of Inception-v1. Finally, the Inception-v3 has also achieved a top 5 error rate of 3.58% and finished first runner up at the ILSVRC 2015.

The ResNet, which stands for residual network, was also developed in 2015, and its key advantage is the use of residual connections, which allows for the usage of a large number of layers. Moreover, increasing the network's depth rather than its width results in fewer parameters. Hence, to be fully trained, this network requires huge datasets, resulting in a computationally expensive training process. There are several ResNet architectural versions, which have the same principle but with a variable number of layers. Also, ResNet won the 2015 ILSVRC and COCO competitions with a top five accuracy rate of 94.4%.

In 2017, DenseNet was developed after being inspired by ResNet. However, instead of residual connections, the authors proposed using dense blocks. The DenseNet architecture maximizes the residual mechanism by densely connecting each layer to its succeeding layers. As a result, feature and gradient transmission is more effective, and the network is easier to train. DenseNet utilized fewer parameters and achieved a top 5 accuracy rate of 93.2% on the ILSVRC competition. The information loss is minimized between the deep layers due to the presence of connections between all layers. It also minimizes vanishing gradients and helps in feature reuse. However, this structure requires a very large dataset to achieve a good performance. Later in 2017, the Inception-v3 architecture inspired the Xception network, and the fundamental concept was to replace the inception module with depthwise separable convolutions. The Xception model outperformed the VGG-16, ResNet-152, and Inception-v3 architectures, with a top 5 accuracy rate of 94.50% on the ILSVRC challenge. In comparison with Inception, Xception has fewer parameters and is faster. As a result, the main advantage of this network is that even though it has a deep structure it utilizes a minimum number of parameters. This makes it computationally efficient in comparison to other deep networks.

In 2017, a group of Google researchers introduced MobileNetV1. MobileNets, and Xception share similar concepts but have different advantages. Xception has high precision, whereas MobileNets is a lightweight model that strikes the balance between model compression and accuracy. Later in 2018, MobileNetV2 was presented as an improvement to V1 followed by other versions in upcoming years. The key differences between the MobileNetV2 architecture and the V1 design are that the former uses residual connections and the expand/projection layers. The MobileNetV2 has fewer parameters than the v1 and scored slightly higher on the classification test. The top-5 accuracy for MobileNetV1 on ImageNet is 89.9%, compared to 91.9% for VGG-16. Hence, the MobileNets can be used to replace the VGGNet-16 that is widely used as a feature extractor for otherNNs for an instant 10 speedup. Furthermore, MobileNets also offers a huge speed boost as it uses only 4.2M learned parameters in comparison to VGG-16 which uses 138M parameters.

In 2019, Google released a research paper on EfficientNet, a new family of CNNs. Instead of laborious manual tweaking, these CNNs provide a more principled way for scaling up a CNN to improve accuracy and efficiency. To enhance accuracy, typical techniques strive to increase the depth and scale the width of the networks. However, the majority of deeper networks suffer from vanishing gradients and are difficult to train. Although strategies such as batch normalization and skip connections are useful in tackling this problem, empirical investigations show that accuracy decreases as network depth increases. Increasing width, on the other hand, hinders the network from learning complicated characteristics, resulting in diminishing accuracy. Unlike traditional techniques, EfficientNets evenly scales each dimension with a given set of scaling coefficients, exceeding the state-of-the-art accuracy. The initial architecture was EfficientNet-B0, which achieved 93.5% top-5 accuracy with only 5.3M parameters, while the most recent version, EfficientNet-B7, achieves state-of-the-art 97.1% top-5 accuracy on ImageNet while being significantly smaller and quicker. Efficient-Nets were evaluated on eight commonly used transfer learning datasets to further evaluate their performance, and they obtained state-of-the-art accuracy in 5 out of the 8 datasets.

4.5 Conclusion

This chapter provides an overview of the CNN. This structure, which has been proven to be very successful in image processing, is inspired in what is believed to be the structure of the visual cortex of mammals, and the successive layers of the network extract features that are at the initial states local ones, but that become also global in deeper stages.

The nature of the CNN is sparse, this is, the convolutions can be seen as sparse matrix multiplications between the inputs and the convolution kernels. This fact, among other properties, makes the CNN less computationally complex than a fully connected neural network with similar depth.

The training process consisting of forward and BP is explained in detail, and the derivation is done by using the basic equation of the MLP BP together with the representation of the convolution as sparse matrix multiplication, to prove that this backpropagation is formally very similar to the one of the MLP.

Finally, popular models derived from CNN are presented, and the chapter is concluded by summarizing the advantages and trade-offs of CNN.

Problems

4.1 *Modify the code of Example 4.5.1 in order to use the VGG16 model for classification of CIFAR10 dataset using transfer learning. Similar to Example 4.5.1 Keras has built-in libraries to load the VGG16 model. The example in the Keras documentation on VGG16 (https://keras.io/api/applications/vgg/) can be used to load the VGG16 model.*
- *Compare the confusion matrix with EfficientNetB0.*
- *Remove the data augmentation step and analyze the performance difference.*

4.2 *List the advantages and disadvantages of deep and wide architectures in CNNs.*

4.3 *Select a pretrained CNN model and visualize the filters in one of its convolutional layers. Explain how these filters change during training and what kind of features they detect.*

4.4 *Download the COCO dataset, which includes labeled images and annotations (bounding box coordinates and class labels). You can find the dataset at the official COCO website:* http://cocodataset.org/. *Implement an object detection task utilizing a CNN architecture like Faster R-CNN, with ResNet serving as the backbone network. Evaluate the trained model on the test dataset using common metrics like average precision (AP), intersection-over-union (IoU), and mean average precision (mAP).*

4.5 *Explain the concept of dilated convolutions in CNN architectures. How do dilated convolutions differ from regular convolutions in terms of receptive field and feature extraction? Provide examples of applications where dilated convolutions are advantageous.*

4.6 *Explore methods for making CNN models more interpretable. How can techniques like gradient-based visualization (Selvaraju et al. 2017), occlusion analysis (Matthew D. Zeiler and Fergus 2014), and class activation maps (CAM) (Zhou et al. 2016) be used to understand what features a CNN has learned and how it makes predictions?*

4.7 *Build an age estimation model using transfer learning with a pretrained CNN architecture. Given a dataset of facial images labeled with individuals' ages, design and train a model to estimate the age of individuals from facial features. Utilize a pretrained ResNet50 to leverage knowledge from a large-scale image dataset. Evaluate the model's performance on a validation set using regression evaluation metrics and compare it to a baseline model trained from scratch. Finally, deploy the model to estimate ages in new facial images and analyze its accuracy and potential sources of error.*

4.8 *Develop a CNN-based semantic segmentation model for autonomous vehicles to segment input images into distinct classes of objects and road-related entities such as cars, pedestrians, lanes, traffic signs, and obstacles. Utilize the Cityscapes dataset, which provides urban street scenes with pixel-level annotations, for training and validation. The dataset can be downloaded from the official Cityscapes website:* https://www.cityscapes-dataset.com/. *Design and train the model, incorporate data preprocessing techniques, specify the loss function, and set up the criteria for evaluation.*

4.9 *Explain the importance of hyperparameters in CNN training. Discuss key hyperparameters like learning rate, batch size, and the number of layers. How can a grid search or random search approach be used to find optimal hyperparameter values for a CNN architecture?*

4.10 *Select a pretrained CNN model and fine-tune it on a custom dataset for a specific task. Evaluate the model's performance using different optimizers, including SGD, Adam, and RMSprop. Analyze how the choice of optimizer affects training speed, convergence, and final accuracy.*

5

Recurrent Neural Networks

5.1 Introduction

The NNs, including CNNs, use predetermined input and output sizes and a feedforward mechanism for the information flow. However, sequential data requires a mechanism to retain past information to predict future values due to the dependencies between the data points. For these problems, a class of networks known as recurrent neural network (RNN) is frequently utilized.

The RNN was introduced in the decade of 1980 by various scholars. The work by Rumelhart et al. (1986) introduces the backpropagation algorithm for both FFNNs and RNNs, where the RNNs are introduced with an application to learn sequences of alphanumeric characters. The first applications of RNN were in head tracking for virtual reality (Saad et al. 1999), financial time-series prediction (Giles et al. 1997), music synthesis (Liang et al. 1999) and electric load forecast (Costa et al. 1999), among others (Medsker and L. Jain 2001).

While they are inspired in the FFNN, they can deal with variable-length sequential data. In as way, one can think of the comparison between a CNN and an RNN by noticing that a CNN has a finite time (or space) response, while an RNN has an infinite time response as a consequence of its recurrent nature.

They have a high-dimensional hidden state with nonlinearities that give them the ability to recall and process previous information. The RNN takes an input, modifies its hidden state, and produces a prediction at every timestep. The high-dimensional hidden state of the RNN allows it to integrate data over several timesteps and utilize it to generate precise predictions. RNNs take advantage of current prediction to provide the future one, and this mechanism is commonly known as a recurrence. Let us assume that we have an input word "apple," and it is first fed into an FFNN. The network processes the word by considering a single character at a time and predictions are made for the character that comes after "l." This task becomes impossible for the model since it does not have any memory about the previous characters "a," "p," "p," and "l." RNNs on the other hand memorize the previous inputs due to their internal memory. Hence, they are commonly used for sequential data like speech (Lim et al. 2016), text (Sutskever et al. 2011), audio (Feng et al. 2017), video (Güera and Delp 2018), weather (Alemany et al. 2019), and financial data (Tino et al. 2001).

Deep Learning: A Practical Introduction, First Edition.
Manel Martínez-Ramón, Meenu Ajith, and Aswathy Rajendra Kurup.
© 2024 John Wiley & Sons Ltd. Published 2024 by John Wiley & Sons Ltd.
Companion website: https://github.com/DeepLearning-book

There are several variants of RNN, including long short-term memory (LSTM) networks and gated recurrent unit (GRU). These variants introduce additional gates and memory cells that help the network to better propagate information over longer periods of time. Overall, the architecture of an RNN is defined by the number of units in the network, the type of units used, and the connections between the units.

5.2 RNN Architecture

Probably the earliest RNN to be incepted, before the works of Rumelhart, Hinton, and Williams, is the Hopfield Network, introduced in 1982 by John Hopfield (1982), but in this paper, the author acknowledges that his structure was first introduced in 1974 by W. A. Little (1974) in order to model the existence of persistent states in the brain. Hopfield's work is the first one that incorporates the idea of recurrence in artificial neural networks. This network has a set of neurons with binary threshold outputs that are bidirectionally connected to each other (Fig. 5.1). The Hopfield network was used in system optimization problems as the classic traveling salesman problem (Hopfield and Tank 1985). Continuous state Hopfield networks were used to model the human memory (Amit and Amit 1989). See Section 7.2 for more details about the Hopfield network.

5.2.1 Structure of the Basic RNN

The first RNN of interest for sequence modeling that can be trained using the backpropagation algorithm as described in Rumelhart et al. (1986) is the so-called Elman network, introduced by J. L. Elman in 1990 (Elman 1990), which follows a similar structure introduced by M. Jordan (1986).

An Elman RNN block consists of a single unit in the network, along with the input and output connections for that unit. The structure is represented in Fig. 5.2. At time instant t, the unit receives an input $\mathbf{x}_t$ as well as a feedback consisting of the hidden state $\mathbf{h}_{t-1}$ computed from the previous time step. The unit processes this input and produces a new hidden state $\mathbf{h}_t$ whose nonlinear activation is a hyperbolic tangent. The RNN then computes linear transformation $\mathbf{z}_t$ of the hidden state $\mathbf{h}_t$. This is followed by a nonlinear activation that produces output $\mathbf{o}_t = \left[o_{0,t}, \ldots, o_{K-1,t}\right]^{\top}$, which is usually a softmax activation when the

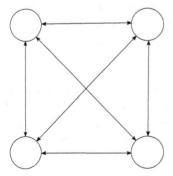

Figure 5.1 A Hopfield network is a type of RNN where all nodes are interconnected. The states described by each node are binary. Continuous state Hopfield networks were used to model the human memory.

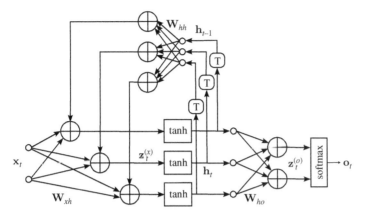

Figure 5.2 RNN. The input sample $\mathbf{x}_t$ is linearly transformed and then added to a linear transformation of the previous hidden state $\mathbf{h}_{t-1}$. There, the blocks marked with labels T represent one sample delay or, equivalently, one sample memory registers where when sample $\mathbf{h}_t$ is introduced, value $\mathbf{h}_{t-1}$ is at the output. The combination is applied to a hyperbolic tangent activation to produce a hidden state $\mathbf{h}_t$. This state is then processed to produce output $\mathbf{o}_t$. Biases $\mathbf{b}_h$ and $\mathbf{b}_o$ are not shown for simplicity. The compact version of the RNN is shown in Fig. 5.3.

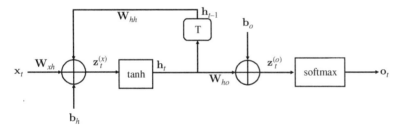

Figure 5.3 Compact representation of an RNN. The input vector $\mathbf{x}_t$ is transformed through matrix $\mathbf{W}_{xh}$ and then bias vector $\mathbf{b}_h$ is added. After this, the resulting vector is passed through the nonlinear activation (hyperbolic tangent) to produce state vector $\mathbf{h}_t$. This vector is then delayed with delay T, which can be thought of as a first in first out (FIFO) memory of one element, where when $\mathbf{h}_t$ is introduced, the previous value $\mathbf{h}_{t-1}$ is extracted. The state $\mathbf{h}_{t-1}$ is then transformed with $\mathbf{W}_{hh}$ and added to the transformed input. State $\mathbf{h}_t$ is also transformed with matrix $\mathbf{W}_{ho}$ and bias vector $\mathbf{b}_0$ and then passed through the softmax activation to produce the output.

RNN is used for multiclass classification among K classes. This process is repeated at each time step in the sequence, allowing the RNN to process sequential data.

Thus, a standard RNN predicts the output sequence $\mathbf{o}_1, \ldots, \mathbf{o}_T$ from a given a sequential input $\mathbf{x}_1, \ldots, \mathbf{x}_T$ by passing it through multiple hidden states $\mathbf{h}_1, \ldots, \mathbf{h}_T$. The expressions for the output and hidden states are

$$
\begin{aligned}
\mathbf{z}_t^{(x)} &= \mathbf{W}_{xh}^\top \mathbf{x}_t + \mathbf{W}_{hh}^\top \mathbf{h}_{t-1} + \mathbf{b}_h \\
\mathbf{h}_t &= \tanh(\mathbf{z}_t^{(x)}) \\
\mathbf{z}_t^{(o)} &= \mathbf{W}_{ho}^\top \mathbf{h}_t + \mathbf{b}_o \\
\mathbf{o}_t &= \mathbf{o}(\mathbf{z}_t^{(o)}) = \mathrm{softmax}(\mathbf{z}_t^{(o)})
\end{aligned}
\tag{5.1}
$$

where operation softmax($\mathbf{z}_t^{(o)}$) produces a vector with elements softmax($z_{k,t}^{(o)}$). The computation of the hidden states and output states in the forward pass of the RNN is done by repeating these operations.

The three matrices $\mathbf{W}_{xh}$, $\mathbf{W}_{hh}$, and $\mathbf{W}_{ho}$ together with the bias vectors $\mathbf{b}_h$ and $\mathbf{b}_0$ perform respectively the affine transformation from the input to the hidden state, the transformation from the hidden state $\mathbf{h}_{t-1}$ to $\mathbf{h}_t$ and from the hidden state to the output.

The recurrent nature of the network is shown in Eq. (5.1), where one can see that the hidden state $\mathbf{h}_t$ contains information for input $\mathbf{x}_t$, but it also retains information coming from the previous inputs, carried by previous state $\mathbf{h}_{t-1}$. It is straightforward to see that for any set of non-null parameters, this structure has an infinite-time impulse response, this is, assuming a nonzero input $\mathbf{x}_1$ followed by an infinite sequence of null vectors $\mathbf{x}_t = \mathbf{0}$, recursive Eq. (5.1) produces an varying input $\mathbf{h}_t$ for an indefinite time. In a feedforward array, such a sequence will produce a constant response for $t > 1$.

The interpretation of the function of the three weight matrices is straightforward. Input matrix $\mathbf{W}_{xh}$ is in charge of the extraction of features from the input at instant t, while output matrix $\mathbf{W}_{ho}$ is used to interpret the hidden state $\mathbf{h}_t$ in terms of the task at hand, this is, to infer a classification or regression from the hidden state. Therefore, the only recurrent matrix is $\mathbf{W}_{hh}$, which is the one designated to store the information of the sequence that relates past instants of time to the classification or regression at hand.

5.2.2 Input–Output Configurations

The RNN learn from sequences of inputs, which can be configured in several ways, depending on the particular task to solve. These structures are used in many sequence learning problems such as in NLP and speech recognition. RNNs can be categorized input different types based on the number of inputs and outputs being processed it. It is to be noted that these types can both be extended to univariate and multivariate models based on the application at hand.

An RNN is said to be *Single Input–Single Output* when the structure is constructed so the input is a single pattern or element of a sequence, and the output is also an element corresponding to the response of the input. These structures represent the traditional Vanilla Neural network architecture. These models are also known as *One-to-One* RNN.

Single input–multiple output architectures are commonly known as *One-to-many* RNN. They receive one input and generate multiple outputs. An example of a One-to-many RNN would be an Image captioning model where the input is a single image and the output is a sequence of words or sentences describing the image.

The *Multiple inputs–Single Output* configuration learns from multiple input nodes and gives only one output. They are more commonly known as *Many-to-One* RNN. An example of this category of RNN would be an architecture that takes a sequence of words as input to detect the sentiment of the text in the form of a label such as positive or negative. Another example would be predicting a nth sample using a sequence of past $n - 1$ samples. These models can be used to provide an overall label or summary of a sequence of inputs.

Last, the *Multiple input–multiple outputs* RNN use multiple inputs to produce multiple outputs. They are more commonly known as *Many-to-Many* RNN. Many-to-many RNNs are often used where both the input and output sequences are in the form of a sequence. For example, this approach can be used in forecasting problems to predict n future samples from past m samples. In this scenario, both the input and output data are sequence data. Similarly, another example would be translating a sequence of words from one language to another word by word which also uses sequence data as input and output. The number of input samples can be the same as that of the output samples $m = n$, There can also be cases where the input and output samples are not equal. This often happens in translation problems where the translation of a sentence in one language can be shorter or longer compared to that of the output language.

5.3 Training an RNN

Dynamic visualization of the RNN is shown in Fig. 5.4 where the structure is unrolled over the input sequence. The corresponding compact representation is in Figs. 5.5 and 5.6. Here every neuron in the hidden layer receives input from both the most recent hidden states and the current input vector at each time step. This representation is useful to illustrate the training process, where each time instant here can be seen as a layer of a neural network, similar to the FFNN, with two main differences with respect to these structures. First, the RNN produces an output at each layer. Namely, in the layer corresponding to instant t, the structure produces output $\mathbf{o}_t$. Also, weights $\mathbf{W}_{xh}$, $\mathbf{W}_{hh}$, $\mathbf{W}_{ho}$, $\mathbf{b}_h$ and $\mathbf{b}_0$ are the same in each layer, while in an FFNN the weights are different and they have different dimensions.

By observing these fundamental differences, a backpropagation algorithm based on the same principles as the ones applied for FFNN in Chapter 1 and CNN in Chapter 4 can be applied to this type of neural network. Here, the backpropagation through the layers of Fig. 5.4 is actually performed from the last time instant to the first one, and for this reason, this algorithm is known as backpropagation through time (BPTT) (R. J. Williams and Zipser 1995).

Assume that the RNN is designed to classify among K classes of data and a training sequence $\mathbf{x}_t \in \mathbb{R}^D, \mathbf{y}_t \in \mathbb{R}^K, 1 \leq t \leq T$ is available. We must then maximize the cross entropy between the labels and the outputs or, equivalently, the output likelihood. This is, the cost function to optimize is

$$J_{ML}(\theta, \mathbf{X}, \mathbf{Y}) = \sum_{t=1}^{T} \ell(\mathbf{x}_t) = -\sum_{t=1}^{T} \sum_{k=0}^{K-1} y_{k,t} \log \text{softmax}\left(z_{k,t}^{(o)}\right) \tag{5.2}$$

where $l(\mathbf{x}_t)$ is the cross entropy loss of Eq. (1.75) expressed as a function of the input pattern $\mathbf{x}_t$. Here the matrices are defined as $\mathbf{X} = [\mathbf{x}_1 \ldots \mathbf{x}_T]$ and $\mathbf{Y} = [\mathbf{y}_1 \ldots \mathbf{y}_T]$.

Parameter $\theta = \{\mathbf{W}_{xh}, \mathbf{W}_{hh}, \mathbf{W}_{ho}\}$ symbolizes the set of all trainable parameters of the RNN.

The BPTT algorithm is now derived by computing the derivative of the cost function with respect to each parameter at each time instant.

It should be noticed that there is a peculiarity in the training of these structures that comes from their recurrent nature. We must consider that the hidden state $\mathbf{h}_t$ at every instant

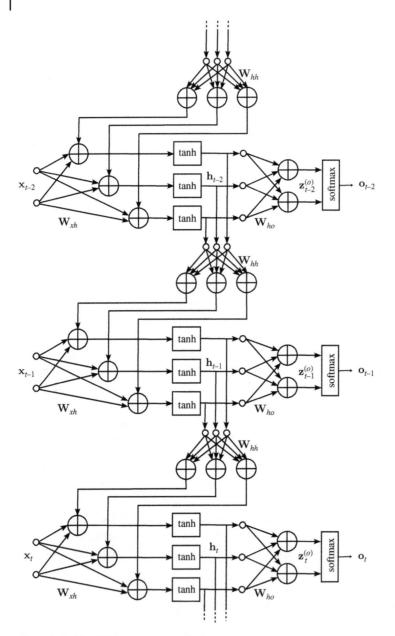

Figure 5.4 The RNN structure unrolled.

depends on the states $\mathbf{h}_{t'}$, $t' < t$. During the application of the backpropagation through the chain rule $\nabla_{\mathbf{h}_t} J_{ML}$ appears. For the case of $t = T$,

$$\nabla_{\mathbf{h}_T} J_{ML} = \frac{\delta \mathbf{z}_T^{(o)}}{\delta \mathbf{h}_T} \nabla_{\mathbf{z}_T^{(o)}} J_{ML} \tag{5.3}$$

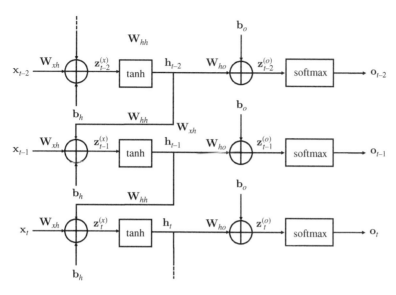

Figure 5.5 Compact representation of the RNN structure unrolled.

Figure 5.6 Even more compact representation
of the RNN structure unrolled.

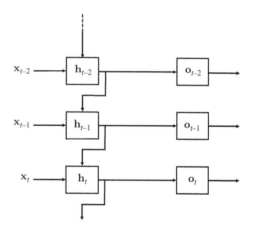

where the gradient of the cost function with respect to $\mathbf{z}_T^{(o)}$ is the error at the output, as it can be seen by computing the derivatives of the cost function with respect to $z_{k,T}^{(o)}$

$$\frac{dJ_{ML}}{dz_{k,T}^{(o)}} = \frac{dJ_{ML}}{do_{k,T}} \frac{o_{k,t}}{dz_{k,T}^{(o)}} = \frac{dJ_{ML}}{do_{k,T}} o'_{k,T} = \delta_{k,T} \tag{5.4}$$

where $\frac{\delta \mathbf{z}_T^{(o)}}{\delta \mathbf{h}_T}$ is the Jacobian matrix whose components are $\frac{dz_{i,T}^{(o)}}{dh_{j,t}} = w_{ho,i,j}$. With this, we can write gradient (5.3) as

$$\nabla_{\mathbf{h}_T} J_{ML} = \mathbf{W}_{hh} \delta_T \tag{5.5}$$

and since the output of the RNN is a softmax, $\delta_t = \text{softmax}(\mathbf{z}_t^{(o)}) - \mathbf{y}_t$ a shown in Eq. (1.78).

A more general case is seen where we compute the gradient with respect to a time instant $t < T$. In this case, the cost function in Eq. (5.2) contains $\mathbf{h}_t$ in element $\ell(\mathbf{x}_t)$ and in the next one, $\ell(\mathbf{x}_{t+1})$, since, from Eq. (5.1)

$$\mathbf{h}_{t+1} = \tanh\left(\mathbf{z}_{t+1}^{(x)}\right) = \tanh\left(\mathbf{W}_{xh}^{\top}\mathbf{x}_{t+1} + \mathbf{W}_{hh}^{\top}\mathbf{h}_t + \mathbf{b}_h\right) \tag{5.6}$$

and then, Jacobian $\frac{\delta \mathbf{h}_{t+1}}{\delta \mathbf{h}_t}$ appears in the chain rule, with elements $\frac{\delta h_{i,t+1}}{\delta h_{i,t}}$, and that must be developed carefully. By applying the chain rule of calculus to these elements, it can be found that

$$\frac{\delta h_{j,t+1}}{\delta h_{i,t}} = \frac{\delta h_{j,t+1}}{\delta z_{j,t+1}^{(x)}}\frac{\delta z_{j,t+1}^{(x)}}{\delta h_{i,t}} = \frac{\delta h_{j,t+1}}{\delta z_{j,t+1}^{(x)}}\frac{\delta \mathbf{w}_{hh,j}^{\top}\mathbf{h}_t}{\delta h_{i,t}} \tag{5.7}$$

The first one of the derivatives of the right side of expression (5.7) is the derivative of the hyperbolic tangent in Eq. (5.1) evaluated with $z_{j,t+1}^{(x)}$. The second of the derivatives simply results in the parameter $w_{hh,i,j}$, which is inside matrix $\mathbf{W}_{hh}$. Therefore, derivative (5.7) is written as

$$\frac{\delta h_{j,t+1}}{\delta h_{i,t}} = w_{hh,i,j}\tanh'\left(z_{j,t+1}^{(x)}\right) \tag{5.8}$$

and therefore, Jacobian $\frac{\delta \mathbf{h}_{t+1}}{\delta \mathbf{h}_t}$ is the matrix resulting of multiplying each column j of matrix $\mathbf{W}_{hh}$ by derivative $\tanh'\left(z_{j,t+1}^{(x)}\right)$, which can be expressed as (Salehinejad et al. 2017)

$$\frac{\delta \mathbf{h}_{t+1}}{\delta \mathbf{h}_t} = \mathbf{W}_{hh}\text{diag}\left(\tanh'\left(\mathbf{z}_{t+1}^{(x)}\right)\right) \tag{5.9}$$

where $\text{diag}\left(\tanh'\left(\mathbf{z}_{t+1}^{(x)}\right)\right)$ constructs a diagonal matrix with the derivatives of the tangent, and it post multiplies matrix $\mathbf{W}_{hh}$ so column k of the matrix is multiplied by $\tanh\left(z_{k,t+1}^{(x)}\right)$. With all these elements, the gradient of the cost function with respect to hidden state $\mathbf{h}_t$ is

$$\nabla_{\mathbf{h}_t}J_{ML} = \frac{\delta \mathbf{z}_t^{(o)}}{\delta \mathbf{h}_t}\nabla_{\mathbf{z}_t^o}J_{ML} + \frac{\delta \mathbf{h}_{t+1}}{\delta \mathbf{h}_t}\nabla_{\mathbf{h}_{t+1}}J_{ML}$$

$$= \mathbf{W}_{ho}\delta_t + \mathbf{W}_{hh}\text{diag}\left(\tanh'\left(\mathbf{z}_{t+1}^{(x)}\right)\right)\left(\nabla_{\mathbf{h}_{t+1}}J_{ML}\right) \tag{5.10}$$

The first term of the right side of Eq. (5.10) is the expression of the error backpropagated from the output at instant t through the output weights $\mathbf{W}_{ho}$. The error backpropagated from the next time instant is the second term, which contains the output error at instant $t+1$ backpropagated to the network at instant t through the hidden weights $\mathbf{W}_{hh}$.

This is a recursive gradient, where $\mathbf{W}_{hh}$ appears again inside the gradient with respect to $\mathbf{h}_{t+1}$ and, as a result when the full recursion is computed, this matrix appears raised to the power $T - t$. This can produce difficulties in learning long-term dependencies, as we will see in Section 5.4.

5.3.1 Gradient with Respect to the Output Weights

We start with the derivation of the gradient with respect to parameters $\mathbf{W}_{ho}$ by just noticing that the output of the RNN can be expressed as

$$\mathbf{f}(\mathbf{x}_t) = \text{softmax}\left(\mathbf{z}_t^{(o)}\right) = \text{softmax}\left(\mathbf{W}_{ho}^{\top}\mathbf{h}_t + \mathbf{b}_o\right) \tag{5.11}$$

For this set of parameters, we do not need to go deeper into the function because this parameter matrix is not found anymore in the recursion, as it is just an output matrix. Indeed, if we take a look into Fig. 5.5 and we follow the path from output $\mathbf{o}_t$ backward in time, we see that the matrix is never revisited. Therefore, the derivative of the cost function at instant t with respect to parameter $w_{ho,i,j}$ is

$$\frac{dJ_{ML}}{dw_{ho,i,j}} = \sum_{t=1}^{T} \frac{dJ_{ML}}{do_{j,t}} \frac{do_{j,t}}{dz_{j,t}^{(0)}} \frac{dz_{j,t}^{(0)}}{dw_{ho,i,j}}$$

$$= \sum_{t=1}^{T} \frac{dJ_{ML}}{do_{j,t}} o'_{j,t} h_{i,t}$$

$$= \sum_{t=1}^{T} \delta_{j,t} h_{i,t} \tag{5.12}$$

In vector notation, the gradient with respect matrix $\mathbf{W}_{ho}$ is then

$$\nabla_{\mathbf{W}_{ho}} J_{ML} \left(\mathbf{o}_t \right) = \sum_{t=1}^{T} \mathbf{h}_t \delta_t^{\top} \tag{5.13}$$

where δ_t has components $\delta_{j,t}$. When the output of the RNN is a softmax, $\delta_{j,t} = \text{softmax}(z_{j,t}^{(0)}) - y_{j,t}$ (see Eq. (1.78)), therefore

$$\delta_t = \text{softmax}(\mathbf{z}_t^{(0)}) - \mathbf{y}_t \tag{5.14}$$

The derivation can be repeated for biases $\mathbf{b}_o$, with the result

$$\nabla_{\mathbf{b}_o} J_{ML} \left(\mathbf{o}_t \right) = \sum_{t=1}^{T} \delta_t \tag{5.15}$$

5.3.2 Gradient with Respect to the Input Weights

By inspection of Fig. 5.5, if we undo the path from $\mathbf{o}_t$, the error term δ_t at this point must be first backpropagated through $\mathbf{W}_{ho}$ in order to reach $\mathbf{W}_{xh}$ at input $\mathbf{x}_t$, but then, it has to be repeatedly backpropagated through $\mathbf{W}_{hh}$ in order to reach the input matrix at each one of the inputs $\mathbf{x}_{t-t'}$.

If we compute directly the gradient with respect to the weights, the chain rule must be used as follows. First, the gradient $\nabla_{\mathbf{h}_t} J_{ML}$ of the cost function is computed with respect to $\mathbf{h}_t$, which is done in Eq. (5.10). After, we need to compute the derivatives of the components of $\mathbf{h}_t$ with respect to each component of $\mathbf{z}_t^{(x)}$, which will give the derivative of the hyperbolic tangent activation. The final element of the chain is the gradient of $\mathbf{z}_t^{(x)}$ with respect to $\mathbf{W}_{xh}$, which gives vector $\mathbf{x}_t$. The product of these elements has to be written in the right order so the gradient has the same dimensions as matrix $\mathbf{W}_{xh}$. The result is

$$\nabla_{\mathbf{W}_{xh}} J_{ML} = \sum_{t=1}^{T} \nabla_{\mathbf{W}_{xh}} \mathbf{z}_t^{(x)} \left(\nabla_{\mathbf{h}_t} J_{ML} \right)^{\top} \frac{\delta \mathbf{h}_t}{\delta \mathbf{z}_t^{(x)}}$$

$$= \sum_{t=1}^{T} \mathbf{x}_t \left(\nabla_{\mathbf{h}_t} J_{ML} \right)^{\top} \text{diag} \left(\tanh' \left(\mathbf{z}_t^{(x)} \right) \right) \tag{5.16}$$

In this expression, we find Jacobian $\frac{\delta \mathbf{h}_t}{\delta \mathbf{z}_t^{(x)}}$ with elements $\frac{dh_{i,t}}{dz_{j,t}^{(x)}}$. Since the state $\mathbf{h}_t$ is an elementwise hyperbolic tangent operation, these elements are zero if $i \neq j$ and otherwise, $\frac{dh_{i,t}}{dz_{i,t}^{(x)}} = \tanh'(z_{i,t}^{(x)})$. Therefore, this Jacobian is a diagonal matrix containing these elements.

A similar result can be found for the biases

$$\nabla_{\mathbf{b}_h} J_{ML} = \sum_{t=1}^{T} \mathrm{diag}\left(\tanh'\left(\mathbf{z}_t^{(x)}\right)\right)\left(\nabla_{\mathbf{h}_t} J_{ML}\right) \tag{5.17}$$

The above equations have the same form as any previously computed gradient, this is it is the product of the input sample $\mathbf{x}_t$ as a column vector times a vector representing the backpropagated error, which, in this case, it is embedded in the (recursive) gradient with respect to the hidden state. This is, the error backpropagated to the input can be written as $\mathrm{diag}\left(\tanh'\left(\mathbf{z}_t^{(x)}\right)\right)\left(\nabla_{\mathbf{h}_t} J_{ML}\right)$.

5.3.3 Gradient with Respect to the Hidden State Weights

For this set of weights, the backpropagation of the error at instant t goes from the output $\mathbf{o}_t$ in Fig. 5.5, it is transformed with output weights $\mathbf{W}_{ho}$, and this error is used to update $\mathbf{W}_{hh}$ with the input to these weights, which is $\mathbf{h}_{t-1}$. The backpropagation in time then goes to the previous time instant, which requires another transformation of the error with the hidden state matrix.

In order to see this, we can just compute the gradient of the cost function as in Section 5.3.2.

$$\nabla_{\mathbf{W}_{hh}} J_{ML} = \sum_{t=1}^{T} \nabla_{\mathbf{W}_{hh}} \mathbf{z}_t^{(x)} \left(\nabla_{\mathbf{h}_t} J_{ML}\right)^{\top} \frac{\delta \mathbf{h}_t}{\delta \mathbf{z}_t^{(x)}}$$

$$= \sum_{t=1}^{T} \mathbf{h}_{t-1} \left(\nabla_{\mathbf{h}_t} J_{ML}\right)^{\top} \mathrm{diag}\left(\tanh'\left(\mathbf{z}_t^{(x)}\right)\right) \tag{5.18}$$

Algebraically, the only difference is that the gradient of $\mathbf{z}_t^{(x)}$ is computed now with respect to the hidden weights, and the result is the input to these weights, i.e. $\mathbf{h}_{t-1}$, This, inside the summation along time, is the BPTT.

Finally, one may assume that weights $\mathbf{b}_h$ belong to the hidden layers. For these biases, the backpropagated error (without multiplying it times an input) is applied as an update. If we remove $\mathbf{h}_{t-1}$ from (5.18), we obtain the same result as in Eq. (5.17).

5.3.4 Summary of the Backpropagation Through Time in an RNN

All the above elements of the training can be summarized as follows in order to describe the backpropagation procedure in an RNN. Assuming a labeled training batch consisting of a sequence with T samples, the first step is to compute the output errors δ_t, $1 \leq t \leq T$. These errors are then used to update the output weights with Eqs. (5.13) and (5.15).

$$\mathbf{W}_{ho} \leftarrow \mathbf{W}_{ho} - \mu \sum_{t=1}^{T} \mathbf{h}_t \delta_t^{\top}$$

$$\mathbf{b}_o \leftarrow \mathbf{b}_o - \mu \sum_{t=1}^{T} \delta_t \tag{5.19}$$

With the output errors, the gradient of the cost function with respect to the hidden states is computed recursively through time as

$$\nabla_{\mathbf{h}_T} J_{ML} = \mathbf{W}_{ho} \delta_T \tag{5.20}$$

for the last time instant, and

$$\nabla_{\mathbf{h}_t} J_{ML} = \mathbf{W}_{ho} \delta_t + \mathbf{W}_{hh} \text{diag}\left(\text{tanh}'\left(\mathbf{z}_{t+1}^{(x)}\right)\right)\left(\nabla_{\mathbf{h}_{t+1}} J_{ML}\right) \tag{5.21}$$

for the previous instants. Then, these gradients are used to update the rest of the weights. For the input weights, with Eqs. (5.16) and (5.17) we obtain the updates

$$\mathbf{W}_{xh} \leftarrow \mathbf{W}_{xh} - \mu \sum_{t=1}^{T} \mathbf{x}_t \left(\nabla_{\mathbf{h}_t} J_{ML}\right)^{\mathsf{T}} \text{diag}\left(\text{tanh}'\left(\mathbf{z}_t^{(x)}\right)\right)$$

$$\mathbf{b}_h \leftarrow \mathbf{b}_h - \mu \sum_{t=1}^{T} \text{diag}\left(\text{tanh}'\left(\mathbf{z}_t^{(x)}\right)\right)\left(\nabla_{\mathbf{h}_t} J_{ML}\right) \tag{5.22}$$

The hidden weights are then updated with Eq. (5.18).

$$\mathbf{W}_{hh} \leftarrow \mathbf{W}_{hh} - \mu \sum_{t=1}^{T} \mathbf{h}_{t-1} \left(\nabla_{\mathbf{h}_t} J_{ML}\right)^{\mathsf{T}} \text{diag}\left(\text{tanh}'\left(\mathbf{z}_t^{(x)}\right)\right) \tag{5.23}$$

Example 5.3.1   *(Time-series prediction using RNN)*
This example illustrates the implementation of RNN using PyTorch. The RNN in the example is built to perform one step-ahead prediction of a time series that consists of a harmonic signal with the expression

$$x[t] = \cos\left[\frac{\pi}{6}t\right] + \frac{1}{2}\cos\left[\frac{\pi}{3}t\right] + \frac{1}{2}\cos\left[\frac{2\pi}{3}t\right] + g[t] \tag{5.24}$$

for $0 \leq t \leq 200$, and where $g[n]$ is an additive Gaussian noise of independent and identically distributed samples with standard deviation $\sigma = 0.1$. The data shown in Fig. 5.7 is divided into 150 samples for training and 50 for testing. The data is scaled between 0 and 1. As part of the data preprocessing, we must construct a data structure to train and test the RNN. A total of N_T samples are used to train an RNN whose input is a sliding window of W samples. The desired output corresponds to the first sample after the last one of the sliding window.

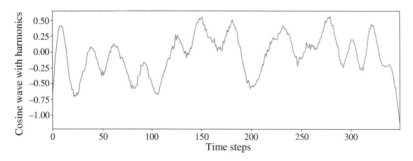

Figure 5.7   Plot of the cosine function with harmonics against the time points.

In other words, if the input pattern at instant n is vector $\mathbf{x}[t]$ then the corresponding output is $y = x[t+1]$ where

$$\mathbf{x}[t] = (x[t-W+1], \ldots, x[t])^{\mathsf{T}} \tag{5.25}$$

The input time series is arranged in an array representing each one of the elements of the sliding window at each time instant as:

$$\mathbf{X} = \begin{pmatrix} x[0] & x[1] & \cdots & x[N_T - W - 1] \\ x[1] & x[2] & \cdots & x[N_T - W] \\ \vdots & \vdots & \cdots & \vdots \\ x[W-1] & x[W] & \cdots & x[N_T - 2] \end{pmatrix} \tag{5.26}$$

which is an array of dimensions $W \times N_T - W$. The corresponding regressors or desired output array contains the samples to be predicted. If one looks at the first column of the matrix (5.26), it can be seen that the one step ahead sample to be predicted is $x[W]$, and the last column of this matrix is the predictor for sample $x[N_T - 1]$, which is the last sample of the training sequence. Therefore, the array of $N_T - W$ regressors at the output of the RNN is

$$\mathbf{y} = \left(x[W], \ldots, x[N_T - 1] \right)^{\mathsf{T}} \tag{5.27}$$

In this approach, the RNN model is trained to make single-step predictions. To train the model, we iterate over the training data and update the model parameters by minimizing the loss function. In this case, we use the Adam optimizer and MSE loss for optimization. The Adam optimizer is used to update the model parameters based on the gradients of the loss with respect to the model parameters. The number of hidden units, this is, the dimension of the hidden state $\mathbf{h}_t$, is set to 100. Figure 5.8 shows the loss curve of the training samples for 500 epochs. After the convergence of the loss function, the trained model is used for prediction in the test data. A plot highlighting the actual and the predicted test output is shown in Fig. 5.9 to visualize the performance of the model.

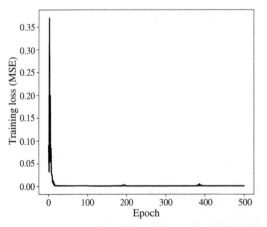

Figure 5.8 Plot of the loss function vs the number of epochs.

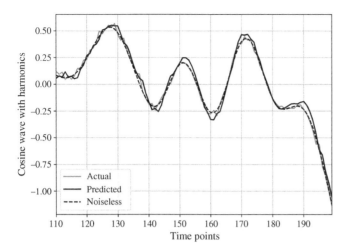

Figure 5.9   Visualization of the predicted and the actual output.

5.4   Long-Term Dependencies: Vanishing and Exploding Gradients

The RNN structure is intended to infer an output sequence from input sequences by learning about the input sequences across time. This property follows from the structure of the RNN, which is of an infinite impulse response nature. As a comparison, an FFNN has a finite response, this is, if a test pattern is presented at the input, it will produce a given output and, when another pattern is presented at the input, the output will be produced in a way that is independent of the previous input. Therefore, the FFNN does not keep any information on past inputs. The RNN, contrary to the FFNN, keeps information on past inputs, and therefore the output is a function that depends on the history of the input sequence. The structure extracts the information from the input sequence through time to perform a task as recognition or prediction. Nevertheless, when the information needed to perform the task at hand spans a long time, the RNN has difficulties capturing this information (Yoshua Bengio et al. 1994; Allen-Zhu et al. 2019; Pascanu et al. 2013; A. H. Ribeiro et al. 2020). The problem is rooted both in the internal structure of the RNN and in the gradient-based training that has been presented in Section 5.3.

The phenomena that make the preservation of long-term dependencies difficult in an RNN are called the exploding and vanishing problems. The explanation of these phenomena is relatively simple if we take into account the equations of the training recursion or BPTT. Particularly, it has been stated that this procedure implies the recursive computation of the Jacobian in Eq. (5.9). By using it in the recursion in Eq. (5.21), it is straightforward to see that this recursion simplicity includes the product of Jacobians (Salehinejad et al. 2017):

$$\prod_{t=t'}^{T-1} \frac{\delta \mathbf{h}_{t+1}}{\mathbf{h}_t} = \prod_{t=t'}^{T-1} \mathbf{W}_{hh} \mathrm{diag}\left(\tanh'\left(\mathbf{z}_{t+1}^{(x)}\right)\right) \tag{5.28}$$

In the best-case scenario, the derivatives of the hyperbolic tangent are all unitary and then in this case, in stage t of the BPTT we find matrix $\left(\mathbf{W}_{hh}\right)^{T-t}$. This matrix is square, so it admits an eigendecomposition

$$\left(\mathbf{W}_{hh}\right)^{T-t} = \left(\mathbf{Q}_{hh}\boldsymbol{\Lambda}_{hh}\mathbf{Q}_{hh}^{\mathsf{T}}\right)^{T-t} = \mathbf{Q}_{hh}\boldsymbol{\Lambda}_{hh}^{T-t}\mathbf{Q}_{hh}^{\mathsf{T}} = \sum_d \lambda_{hh,d}^{T-t}\mathbf{q}_{hh,d}\mathbf{q}_{hh,d} \tag{5.29}$$

where $\mathbf{Q}_{hh}$ and $\boldsymbol{\Lambda}_{hh}$ are respectively the eigenvector matrix and the diagonal matrix containing the eigenvalues of the decomposition. When $t \ll T$ two possible problems arise. The first one appears when one eigenvalue is less than 1. In this case, $\lambda_{hh,d}^{T-t}$ tends to zero. This is known as the vanishing gradient phenomenon. The opposite problem appears when one eigenvalue is higher than 1, and in this case, its power diverges. This is the so-called exploding gradient problem. Notice that this product of Jacobians multiplies the error backpropagated to the instant $T - t$. If the vanishing gradient phenomenon dominates, that translates into the RNN neglecting or excluding the information carried in sample $\mathbf{x}_{T-t}$ and hidden state $\mathbf{h}_{T-t-1}$ from the training. Therefore, if there is a dependency on this or previous samples for the classification of the sequence at instant T, this will not be stored in the hidden state weights or the input weights. If the exploding gradient phenomenon dominates, then the backpropagation will simply diverge.

Yosua Bengio and co-workers proposed in 1994 in his paper (Yoshua Bengio et al. 1994) solutions to thevanishing and exploding gradient phenomena for the RNNs to be able to learn long-term dependencies. Rather than changing the structure of the RNN, they considered the fact that this problem originated from the gradient descent procedure inside the BPTT. The first alternative presented consisted of using simulated annealing (S. Kirkpatrick et al. 1983; Corana et al. 1987). Roughly speaking, the algorithm performs a random search by assigning a random value to the parameters and then accepting or rejecting them based on a criterion consisting of computing the output error with respect to these parameters. The process is repeated for a set of random values. After that, new random values are generated around the chosen ones, they are accepted or rejected, and the process starts over. The generation of random points has a variance that decreases with time, simulating an annealing process that cools down with time. While the process can show good results, it is naturally very slow compared to other methods. Multi-grid random search is also proposed, which is a process similar to the simulated annealing but generating points around the best point only.

Another proposed algorithm is based on pseudo-Newton approximations of the cost function (Becker and Cun 1988). Essentially, for a given value of the weights, a second-order approximation of the surface of the cost function can be constructed with the gradient and the Hessian (or an approximation of it). Then, it is easy to find analytically the optimum value of this approximation, which is taken as a new point to start over the algorithm until convergence.

While these solutions and others also proposed may solve the problem, other structures have been proposed further that tackle directly solutions to capture long-term dependencies such as the long short-term memory network, that will be introduced in Section 5.7.

5.5 Deep RNN

The deep recursive neural network (DRNN) is a natural extension of the RNN to endow it with higher expressive capacity. While there are several ways to extend an RNN, the easiest one is to stack multiple recurrent hidden layers (Pascanu et al. 2019) as in Figs. 5.10 and 5.11, This structure is called a stacked RNN. A different structure that is also a deep RNN is the so-called deep-transition RNN, which, instead of using a linear layer to compute the transition between hidden states, uses a fully connected (FC) neural network. These networks have been used in music prediction and language modeling among others.

Example 5.5.1 *(Digit classification using DRNN)*
This example illustrates the implementation of DRNN for digit classification using PyTorch. A commonly used dataset in machine learning for digit recognition applications is the MNIST dataset (Y. LeCun et al. 1998). It is an inbuilt dataset in PyTorch and it consists

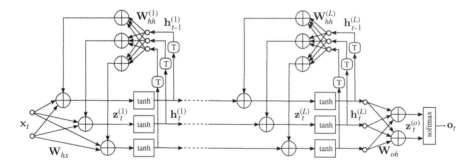

Figure 5.10 Deep recursive neural network.

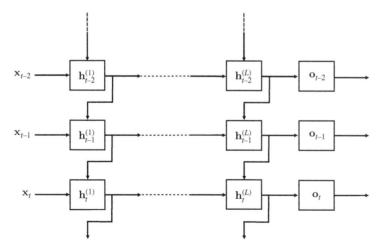

Figure 5.11 Compact representation of an unrolled DRNN.

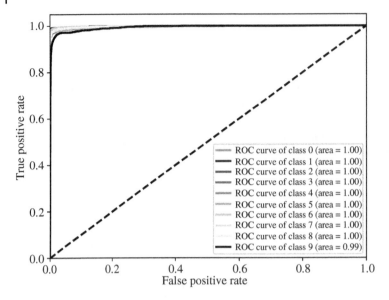

Figure 5.12 ROC curve for MNIST digit classification.

of 70,000 grayscale images of hand-written digits (0–9), with 60,000 images in the training set and 10,000 in the test set. The DeepRNN architecture used in this example has more than 1 recurrent layer and it uses the default activation function, which is the hyperbolic tangent function. The RNN is followed by a FC layer which takes the last hidden state of the RNN and maps it to the number of output classes. Here we use 3 recurrent layers, 1 dense layer, and 10 output classes. The DeepRNN is trained on a set of image-label pairs using the cross-entropy loss criterion and the Adam optimizer. Next, the forward pass of the model is performed on the input images to obtain the predicted outputs and the cross-entropy loss function calculates the loss between the predicted and actual labels. Following this, the backward pass is performed to compute the gradients of the loss with respect to the parameters of the model. Later the optimizer is updated to adjust the parameters of the model based on the computed gradients. The model is trained for five epochs, and its performance is evaluated on the test data using metrics such as accuracy, precision, recall, and f1 score. Additionally, the receiver operation characteristic (ROC) curve is used to analyze the DeepRNN model by plotting the true positive rate against the false positive rate. The area under the ROC curve in Fig. 5.12 represents the overall performance of the model. This ranges from 0 to 1, where 0 indicates that the classifier makes all incorrect predictions and 1 indicates a perfect classifier. The zoomed-in ROC curve in Fig. 5.13 provides a detailed view of the curve, highlighting the model's performance in a specific region. The plot focuses on the trade-off between the false positive rate and the true positive rate, revealing finer details of the model's discrimination capability.

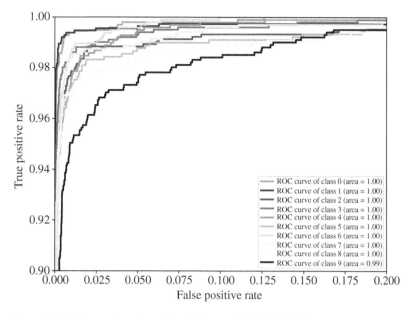

Figure 5.13 Zoomed version of the ROC curve for MNIST digit classification.

5.6 Bidirectional RNN

The RNN presented so far is intended to infer some latent variable $\mathbf{y}_t$ from input samples $1 \leq t \leq t$ of a given sequence and the present sample, this is, from the past and the present. In signal processing, this approach is often called causal, since the present and the future are modeled with dependencies on the past. Nevertheless, when the whole sequence is available, the inference of the latent variable at instant t can be modeled as dependent on samples of the next instants. This is sometimes called anti-causal modeling.

The bidirectinal recursive neural network (BRNN) (Schuster and Paliwal 1997) was introduced to make causal and anti-causal inferences in sequences. The BRNN has been used in handwritten recognition (Liwicki et al. 2007), translation (Sundermeyer et al. 2014), and part-of-speech detection, among others.

The BRNN (Fig. 5.14) has the following forward and backward state equations:

$$\mathbf{h}_t = \tanh\left(\mathbf{W}_{xh}^\top \mathbf{x}_t + \mathbf{W}_{hh}^\top \mathbf{h}_{t-1} + \mathbf{b}_h\right)$$
$$\mathbf{h}_t' = \tanh\left(\mathbf{W}_{xh'}^\top \mathbf{x}_t + \mathbf{W}_{h'h'}^\top \mathbf{h}_{t+1}' + \mathbf{b}_{h'}\right) \tag{5.30}$$

and the output is computed as in the standard RNN with the following equations

$$\mathbf{o}_t = \text{softmax}\left(\mathbf{W}_{ho}^\top \mathbf{h}_t + \mathbf{W}_{h'o}^\top \mathbf{h}_t' + \mathbf{b}_o\right) \tag{5.31}$$

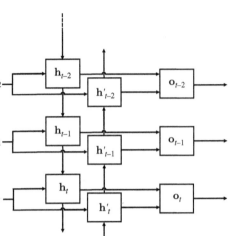

Figure 5.14 Bidirectional RNN.

The DRNN has also training that is similar to one of the standard RNN. The derivation is left as an exercise for the student.

5.7 Long Short-Term Memory Networks

The long short-term memory network (LSTM) is a variation of RNNs that can handle long-term connections and that was first introduced by Sepp Hochreiter and Jürgen Schmidhuber in 1997 (Schmidhuber and Hochreiter 1997). Ideally, RNNs are capable of handling any kind of long-term as well as short-term dependencies present in the input sequences. For instance, in the case of short-term connections, only the most recent information needs to be examined to perform the current task. In this situation, RNNs can store activation representations of current inputs utilizing their feedback connections. However learning to store information over long time intervals by recurrent backpropagation, on the other hand, consumes time, owing to decreasing error backflow. The gradients in time tend to explode or vanish in traditional BPTT (R. J. Williams and Zipser 1995; Paul J. Werbos 1988) or Real-Time Recurrent Learning (Robinson and Fallside 1987). As the gradients grow smaller and approach zero, the weights stay constant and cause vanishing gradients. But when gradients explode, the weights fluctuate and result in the divergence of the gradient descent algorithm. Hence, Hochreiter and Schmidhuber designed LSTM to tackle the problems posed by standard RNNs.

First, it is worth noticing that these phenomena of vanishing and exploding gradients can be avoided if Eq. (5.28) remains constant. The LSTM passes an internal state from one time instant to the next one, with unit gain and without using any nonlinear function. This ensures that the gradient can be propagated without exploding or vanishing. In the original LSTM paper by Hochreiter and Schmidhuber this mechanism is called constant error carousel (CEC). Later, in equivalent depictions of the LSTM structure, this mechanism has been called internal state c_t (see, e.g. (A. Zhang et al. 2021)).

5.7.1 LSTM Gates

The LSTM unit is a cell whose inputs are the internal state $\mathbf{c}_{t-1}$, the hidden state $\mathbf{h}_{t-1}$, and the present input pattern $\mathbf{x}_t$. The LSTM unit computes the values of three gates, usually called forgetting gate $\mathbf{f}_t$, input gate $\mathbf{i}_t$, and output gate $\mathbf{o}_t$. The expressions of these three activations are

$$\mathbf{f}_t = \sigma\left(\mathbf{W}_{xf}^{\mathsf{T}}\mathbf{x}_i + \mathbf{W}_{hf}\mathbf{h}_{t-1} + \mathbf{b}_f\right)$$
$$\mathbf{i}_t = \sigma\left(\mathbf{W}_{xi}^{\mathsf{T}}\mathbf{x}_i + \mathbf{W}_{hi}\mathbf{h}_{t-1} + \mathbf{b}_i\right)$$
$$\mathbf{o}_t = \sigma\left(\mathbf{W}_{xo}^{\mathsf{T}}\mathbf{x}_i + \mathbf{W}_{ho}\mathbf{h}_{t-1} + \mathbf{b}_o\right) \tag{5.32}$$

From the above expressions, it is clear that these gates can be seen as three neural network layers in a parallel configuration (Fig. 5.15), but usually it is more convenient, for the sake of simplicity, to represent them in a compact fashion as in Fig. 5.16.

The input node $\tilde{\mathbf{c}}_t$ is also computed as a function of the previous hidden state $\mathbf{h}_{t-1}$ and the input pattern $\mathbf{x}_t$, but its corresponding activation is a hyperbolic tangent (Fig. 5.17), i.e.

$$\tilde{\mathbf{c}}_t = \tanh\left(\mathbf{W}_{xc}^{\mathsf{T}}\mathbf{x}_i + \mathbf{W}_{hc}\mathbf{h}_{t-1} + \mathbf{b}_c\right) \tag{5.33}$$

5.7.2 LSTM Internal State

The above gates and the input node are used in the LSTM unit to compute the so-called internal state $\mathbf{c}_t$. This state is first multiplied elementwise by the forgetting gate $\mathbf{f}_t$. This operation is intended to attenuate or erase components of the previous internal state $\mathbf{c}_{t-1}$ when it is necessary. Therefore, the forgetting gate is trained so it can forget the internal state as a function of the previous hidden state and the current input. After this operation, the previous internal state is used to compute the present one. The operation is done in

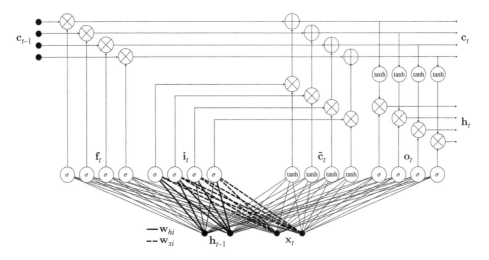

Figure 5.15 The full structure of the LSTM gates. They are four NN layers placed in parallel, where, in the figure, the weights $\mathbf{W}_{hf}$ and $\mathbf{W}_{xf}$ that map the previous hidden state $\mathbf{h}_{t-1}$ and the input pattern $\mathbf{x}_t$ into the forgetting gate $\mathbf{f}_t$ are shown. This representation is never used in the LSTM. Instead, the more compact representation in Fig. 5.19 is commonly used.

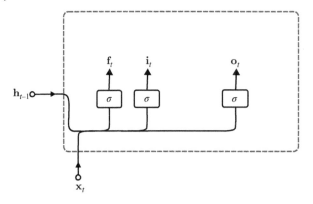

Figure 5.16 Compact representation of the three LSTM gates. The first one ($\mathbf{f}_t$) is trained to partially or totally forget the previous internal state if forgetting is necessary. The second one ($\mathbf{i}_t$) determines how much of the input must be taken into account in order to modify the internal state. The third one ($\mathbf{o}_t$) constitutes the output, and it will modulate the internal state $\mathbf{c}_t$ to compute state $\mathbf{h}_t$.

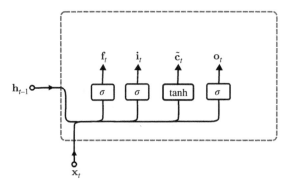

Figure 5.17 The LSTM gates and input node $\tilde{\mathbf{c}}_t$.

two steps. First, an update of the previous current state is computed by elementwise multiplication of the input node $\tilde{\mathbf{c}}_t$ and the input gate $\mathbf{i}_t$. Essentially, $\tilde{\mathbf{c}}_t$ is used to update the previous internal state to obtain the new one. The input gate is therefore trained to determine what fraction of each component of the input node is necessary for the update. The full expression of the forgetting and update operations shown in Fig. 5.18 is

$$\mathbf{c}_t = \mathbf{c}_{t-1} \odot \mathbf{f}_t + \tilde{\mathbf{c}}_i \odot \mathbf{i}_t \tag{5.34}$$

Here it is worth noticing the equivalence of the structure in Fig. 5.18 with the unit gain self-feedback described as constant error carousel (CEC) in the original paper by Schmidhuber and Hochreiter (1997). Indeed, the backpropagation of the error through the internal state line is done without transformation through any nonlinear function derivative or weight matrix, therefore avoiding the phenomena of vanishing or exploding gradients.

5.7.3 Hidden State and Output of the LSTM

The full structure of the LSTM cell is depicted in Fig. 5.19. The output of the LSTM is the gate $\mathbf{o}_t$. This output must be normalized in order to produce a softmax output, which will be

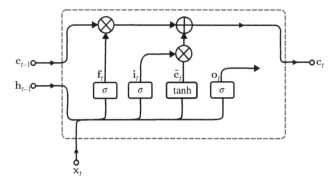

Figure 5.18 The forgetting gate $\mathbf{f}_t$ is elementwise multiplied with the internal state at the previous instant $\mathbf{c}_{t-1}$. If the outputs of the forgetting gate are low, this means that this gate is applying a forgetting factor to the internal state. At the same time, input gate $\mathbf{i}_t$ elementwise multiplies input node $\tilde{\mathbf{c}}_t$, and the product is added to the previous internal state to produce the new internal state $\mathbf{c}_t$.

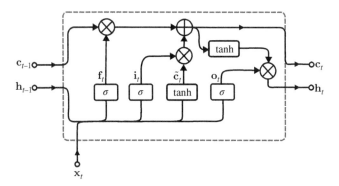

Figure 5.19 The hidden state $\mathbf{h}_t$ is constructed with the internal state $\mathbf{c}_t$ modulated by the output state. This figure represents the full structure of the LSTM.

used for the classification and to compute the error for the backpropagation, but this gate is also used to modulate the hidden state, and this is why the activations are sigmoids, which ensures that each element of the output gate ranges from 0 to 1. The computation of the hidden state is done as

$$\mathbf{h}_t = \tanh\left(\mathbf{c}_t\right) \odot \mathbf{o}_t \qquad (5.35)$$

Notice that the internal state is not bounded by a nonlinear operation in order to avoid vanishing effects. Therefore, the hidden state $\mathbf{h}_t$ is constructed by simply bounding the values of the internal state between −1 and +1 with a hyperbolic tangent activation. Then, the output of this activation is elementwise multiplied by the output gate. If an element of the output gate is close to 1, then the corresponding element of the hidden state is kept and transmitted to the next stage. But if an element of the output gate is close to zero, the corresponding element of the hidden state is inhibited. To interpret this, we must notice that when element k of the output gate is low, that means that the class of input $\mathbf{x}_t$ is probably not k, i.e. $p\left(y_t = k|\mathbf{x}_t\right) \approx 0$. Therefore, we drop the corresponding component of the hidden state so it does not influence the next cells with respect to the current time instant.

5.7.4 LSTM Backpropagation

The backpropagation in an LSTM is similar to the one that was derived for the Elman RNN in Section 5.3. Here we assume that the output of the LSTM is its hidden state, but it is common to use this state in an FC structure in order to perform a given task, in which case the backpropagation can be extended straightforwardly. The cost function in our case is to be expressed as a function of the hidden states, and therefore δ_t is

$$\delta_t = f(\mathbf{h}_t) - \mathbf{y}_t \tag{5.36}$$

The hidden state depends on the elementwise product of the output state $\mathbf{o}_t$ and the internal state passed through the hyperbolic tangent activation, as defined in Eq. (5.35). By applying the chain rule, the gradient of the cost function with respect to the output gate is

$$\nabla_{\mathbf{o}_t} J_{ML} = \nabla_{\mathbf{h}_t} J_{ML} \frac{\delta \mathbf{h}_t}{\delta \mathbf{o}_t} = \delta_t \odot \tanh(\mathbf{c}_t) \tag{5.37}$$

where in this expression we find Jacobian $\frac{\delta \mathbf{h}_t}{\delta \mathbf{o}_t}$ with elements $\frac{d h_{i,t}}{\delta o_{j,t}}$. The elements of this Jacobian out of the diagonal are zero since the product is elementwise. Since the error component δ_t is a vector, it is convenient to express the product of this vector times the Jacobian as an elementwise product.

Next, we compute, by using the chain rule, the gradient with respect to the internal state $\mathbf{c}_t$ by using the same procedure, with the result

$$\nabla_{\mathbf{c}_t} J_{ML} = \delta_t \odot \mathbf{o}_t \odot \tanh'(\mathbf{c}_t) \tag{5.38}$$

By visual inspection of Fig. 5.19, it can be seen that this internal state is a function of the previous state $\mathbf{c}_{t-1}$, the forgetting gate bbf_t, the input node $\tilde{\mathbf{c}}_t$, and the input gate $\mathbf{i}_t$, as defined in Eq. (5.34), so progression with the chain rule needs to compute the gradient with respect to these variables. The results are the following. For the internal state, the gradient is

$$\nabla_{\mathbf{c}_{t-1}} J_{ML} = \nabla_{\mathbf{c}_t} J_{ML} \frac{\delta \mathbf{c}_t}{\delta \mathbf{c}_{t-1}} = \delta_t \odot \mathbf{o}_t \odot \tanh'(\mathbf{c}_t) \odot \mathbf{f}_t \tag{5.39}$$

By following the same procedure, we obtain the gradients for the input gate, the input state, and the forgetting gate as

$$\nabla_{\mathbf{i}_t} J_{ML} = \delta_t \odot \mathbf{o}_t \odot \tanh'(\mathbf{c}_t) \odot \tilde{\mathbf{c}}_t \tag{5.40}$$

$$\nabla_{\tilde{\mathbf{c}}_t} J_{ML} = \delta_t \odot \mathbf{o}_t \odot \tanh'(\mathbf{c}_t) \odot \mathbf{i}_t \tag{5.41}$$

$$\nabla_{\mathbf{f}_t} J_{ML} = \delta_t \odot \mathbf{o}_t \odot \tanh'(\mathbf{c}_{t-1}) \tag{5.42}$$

The above gradients are necessary to compute the updates of the weights in Eqs. (5.32) and (5.33). We start with the output gate weights $\mathbf{W}_{xo}$, $\mathbf{W}_{ho}$, and $\mathbf{b}_o$. They are inside of the sigmoid activation corresponding to the output gate. Therefore, the gradient with respect to these weights is the result of the chain rule applied over the gradient with respect to $\mathbf{o}_t$. From Eq. (5.32), the gradients of the output gate with respect to these weights are $\nabla_{\mathbf{W}_{xo}}\mathbf{o}_t = \sigma'(\mathbf{z}_o) \odot \mathbf{x}_i$, $\nabla_{\mathbf{W}_{xo}}\mathbf{o}_t = \sigma'(\mathbf{z}_o) \odot \mathbf{h}_{t-1}$, and $\nabla_{\mathbf{b}_{xo}}\mathbf{o}_t = \sigma'(\mathbf{z}_o)\odot$. With this, and making use of expression (5.36), the results are

$$\nabla_{\mathbf{W}_{xo}}J_{ML} = \nabla_{\mathbf{o}_t}J_{ML} \cdot \nabla_{\mathbf{W}_{xo}}\mathbf{o}_t = \delta_t \odot \tanh(\mathbf{c}_t) \odot \sigma'(\mathbf{z}_o) \odot \mathbf{x}_t$$

$$\nabla_{\mathbf{W}_{ho}}J_{ML} = \nabla_{\mathbf{o}_t}J_{ML} \cdot \nabla_{\mathbf{W}_{ho}}\mathbf{o}_t = \delta_t \odot \tanh(\mathbf{c}_t) \odot \sigma'(\mathbf{z}_o) \odot \mathbf{h}_{t-1}$$

$$\nabla_{\mathbf{b}_o}J_{ML} = \nabla_{\mathbf{o}_t}J_{ML} = \delta_t \odot \tanh(\mathbf{c}_t) \odot \sigma'(\mathbf{z}_o) \tag{5.43}$$

Similarly, the gradient with respect to forgetting gate weights is

$$\nabla_{\mathbf{W}_{xf}}J_{ML} = \delta_t \odot \mathbf{o}_t \odot \tanh'(\mathbf{c}_t) \odot \mathbf{c}_t \odot \sigma'(\mathbf{z}_f) \odot \mathbf{x}_t$$

$$\nabla_{\mathbf{W}_{hf}}J_{ML} = \delta_t \odot \mathbf{o}_t \odot \tanh'(\mathbf{c}_t) \odot \mathbf{c}_t \odot \sigma'(\mathbf{z}_f) \odot \mathbf{h}_{t-1}$$

$$\nabla_{\mathbf{b}_f}J_{ML} = \delta_t \odot \mathbf{o}_t \odot \tanh'(\mathbf{c}_t) \odot \mathbf{c}_t \odot \sigma'(\mathbf{z}_f) \tag{5.44}$$

The gradient with respect to the input gate weights follows the expression

$$\nabla_{\mathbf{W}_{xi}}J_{ML} = \delta_t \odot \mathbf{o}_t \odot \tanh'(\mathbf{c}_t) \odot \tilde{\mathbf{c}}_t \odot \sigma'(\mathbf{z}_g) \odot \mathbf{x}_t$$

$$\nabla_{\mathbf{W}_{hi}}J_{ML} = \delta_t \odot \mathbf{o}_t \odot \tanh'(\mathbf{c}_t) \odot \tilde{\mathbf{c}}_t \odot \sigma'(\mathbf{z}_g) \odot \mathbf{h}_{t-1}$$

$$\nabla_{\mathbf{b}_i}J_{ML} = \delta_t \odot \mathbf{o}_t \odot \tanh'(\mathbf{c}_t) \odot \tilde{\mathbf{c}}_t \odot \sigma'(\mathbf{z}_g) \tag{5.45}$$

Finally, the gradient with respect to the input state weights is

$$\nabla_{\mathbf{W}_{xc}}J_{ML} = \delta_t \odot \mathbf{o}_t \odot \tanh'(\mathbf{c}_t) \odot \mathbf{c}_t \odot \sigma'(\mathbf{z}_f) \odot \mathbf{x}_t$$

$$\nabla_{\mathbf{W}_{hc}}J_{ML} = \delta_t \odot \mathbf{o}_t \odot \tanh'(\mathbf{c}_t) \odot \mathbf{c}_t \odot \sigma'(\mathbf{z}_f) \odot \mathbf{h}_{t-1}$$

$$\nabla_{\mathbf{b}_c}J_{ML} = \delta_t \odot \mathbf{o}_t \odot \tanh'(\mathbf{c}_t) \odot \mathbf{c}_t \odot \sigma'(\mathbf{z}_f) \tag{5.46}$$

Example 5.7.1 *(Time-series prediction using LSTM)*
This example illustrates the implementation and use of an LSTM using Keras. The LSTM in the example is built to perform one step-ahead prediction of a time series. The used sequence is a dataset called flight data available in the Seaborn package. This dataset records the number of flight passengers that flew on a given route every month from 1949 to 1960. The months are labeled from 0 to 143.

The time-series data obtained from the dataset is shown in Fig. 5.20. The plot shows a clear seasonal pattern and growing trend. Seasonality is a property of a time series in which the data goes through predictable and recurring changes on a yearly basis.

Once the data is loaded and visualized, the passenger data is extracted and divided into train and test sets. The training dataset consists of the first 126 samples, and the test set is constructed with the remaining samples from months 127 to 144. Feature normalization is performed using the MinMaxScaler function. Note that, we fit only the training data to the MinMaxScaler function and transform both train and test data using the same scaling operation. This is the most efficient way of analyzing the model performance ensuring that the test data is completely new to the model.

Once, we have the train and test sets, the data needs to be modified into a sequence. Since we are predicting one time-step ahead, we divide the data in the following format similar

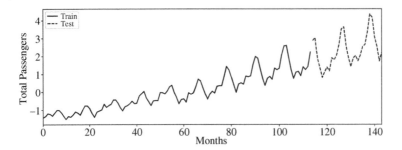

Figure 5.20 Flights time-series data.

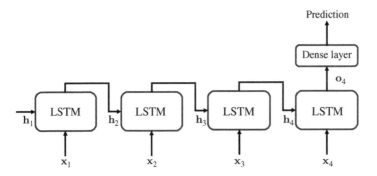

Figure 5.21 Architectural framework of the LSTM model used for time-series prediction.

to the arrangement in Eq. (5.26) shown in Example 5.7.1. Once we have the data in the desired format, we move on to building the LSTM model for training.

In Keras, similar to Example 3.10.1, we can build a sequential model having an LSTM layer followed by a dense layer both with a tanh activation. Here, the loss function is set as MSE, and the optimizer is initialized to Adam. The number of hidden units, this is, the dimension of the hidden state $\mathbf{h}_t$, is set to 4. An illustration of the model is shown in Fig. 5.21.

Once the model setup is ready, we can fit the training data to the LSTM model. The training is performed for 1000 epochs to obtain the final model.

Figure 5.22a shows the loss curve of the training samples for 1000 epochs. After the convergence of the loss function, the trained model is used for prediction in the test data. A plot highlighting the actual and the predicted test output is shown in Fig. 5.22b.

5.7.5 Machine Translation with LSTM

A translation machine consists of a structure where the inputs are sequences of different lengths in a given *input language* (e.g. English):

> *Spring begins today.*

and whose outputs are sentences of a different length in a *target language* (e.g. French):

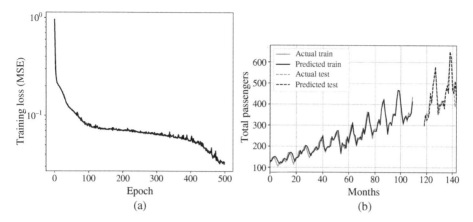

Figure 5.22 (a) shows the training loss curve for LSTM model over 1000 epochs. (b) shows the comparison between the actual time series and the prediction performed by the LSTM.

Le printemps commence aujourd'hui.

At first sight, large feedforward structures like CNN may seem like a good idea since they can have a great number of parameters, necessary to store the complexities of both the source and the target language. It is noteworthy that for each language, a translator must have available more than 10^5 words of each language. To this first complexity, we must add the language structure complexities. As a result, actual translation machines may need many millions of parameters. But to these difficulties, another one must be added, and it is the fact that the sequences to be translated have arbitrary lengths, and the same sentence can have two different lengths in two different languages, as is the case of the example above. While deep feedforward structures have been successfully used in language, in particular for speech processing (see e.g. the works by Geoffrey E. Hinton et al. (2012c) in acoustic modeling or (George E. Dahl et al. 2011) in speech recognition), these structures are tremendously limited in their use for translation due to the fact that the input and output dimensions are fixed.

Coding a sentence with arbitrary length into a vector of fixed dimensionality, neverthe-less, is possible with the use of RNN, through the use of its hidden state. One of the first suc-cessful variable length machine translation schemes is given by Sutskever et al. (2014) while working at Google, Inc. The main idea of the translation strategy is depicted in Fig. 5.23. The structure consists of two sections. In the figure, the upper section is the so-called encoder, and it is in charge of encoding or compressing a sequence of words into a hidden state. The lower section is another RNN, and it uses the hidden state as an input in order to translate the sentence.

The first step for sequence-to-sequence translation consists of creating a word embedding, this is, a dictionary of tokens, this is, a corpus of words for each language, where each word is associated with a token. A token is a vector of integers representing each one of the words. The corpus may also contain signs such as stops, commas, and the beginning of sequence (_BOS) and end of sequence (_EOS) tokens.

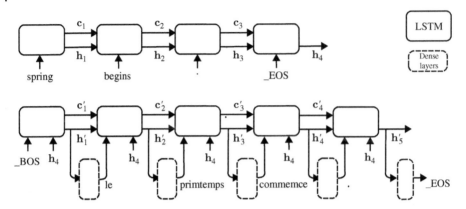

Figure 5.23 Sequence to sequence translation with LSTM. The upper sequence codes the English sentence "spring begins." into state $\mathbf{h}_4$. The lower sequence uses this state to sequentially translate the sentence into the French sentence "le primtemps commence."

Assuming that word embeddings are available for both languages, the methodology works as follows. An RNN (for example the Elman RNN or an LSTM) is initialized with the token corresponding to the first word of the sequence (spring). The recurrent block is then fed back with the current state and the next word (begins). The process is iterated until the _EOS is found, indicating that the recursion can be finished. The final state $\mathbf{h}_T$ of the encoding machine is then used in the decoder RNN for the translation. This state is concatenated with the _BOS token. The hidden state $\mathbf{h}_1'$ of the decoder RNN is then used as the input of an FC structure with as many softmax outputs as words in the target dictionary to predict the token of the first word of the translated sequence. The hidden state, together with the internal state $\mathbf{c}_1'$, and the predicted token are fed back into the RNN to predict the next token. When the recursion predicts the _EOS token, the translation is finished. In the paper by Sutskever et al. (2014), a deep LSTM is used. Such a structure simply stacks several LSTM blocks, so the state of each one is fed back into itself and at the same time, it is used as an input to the next one. These structures have been successful in speech recognition tasks (Graves et al. 2013; Sak et al. 2014).

The FC output estimates the probability of each word in the dictionary, and this output is used to optimize the structure according to a ML criterion. In particular, the criterion is intended to maximize the translation log-likelihood

$$J_{ML} = \frac{1}{|S|} \sum_{T,S} \log p\left(T|S\right) \tag{5.47}$$

where $|\cdot|$ denotes the cardinality of the source sequence s and T is the target sequence. Equivalently, one can minimize the NLL of the sequence, which is equal to the previous expression with a minus sign. Accounting for the length of the sequence is important here, as it will be discussed in Section 5.7.6.

5.7.6 Beam Search in Sequence to Sequence Translation

In the sequence-to-sequence translation method described above, each token of the target sequence is decided through the observation of the probability of each token in the dictionary estimated by a FC layer whose output has thousands of elements, corresponding to the number of words in the target dictionary.

This practically guarantees that at each iteration, a subset of words will have a high probability, thus adding uncertainty to the prediction. In order to reduce the uncertainty, each iteration is repeated with a subset (or beam) of k tokens with the highest probability. The procedure creates a tree of decisions whose paths have associated probabilities that can be computed and then the decision is taken according to them.

The procedure is illustrated as follows. Assume a dictionary with only three tokens $\mathbf{y}_1$, $\mathbf{y}_2$, $\mathbf{y}_3$, and _EOS. In the *greedy search* illustrated in Fig. 5.24, at each iteration a token is chosen according to the maximum probability criterion, which is then introduced in the next iteration to compute a new set of probabilities. According to all estimated probabilities, the obtained sequence is $\mathbf{y}_1, \mathbf{y}_2, \mathbf{y}_3$, _EOS. But notice that in the first iteration, token $\mathbf{y}_3$ has a significant probability and, therefore, it is worth trying the evolution of the tree starting with this. This is the principle of the beam search.

In a beam search, at each iteration, the k tokens with the highest probability are chosen and then sequentially used as input for the next iteration. This produces k possible outcomes of the FC output, which creates k possible paths. In the example of Fig. 5.25, a beam search

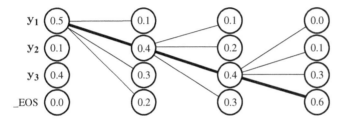

Figure 5.24 Greedy search in sequence-to-sequence translation. The dictionary has tokens $\mathbf{y}_1$, $\mathbf{y}_2$, $\mathbf{y}_3$, and _EOS. After the first iteration of the decoder, the FC layer outputs the probabilities 0.5, 0.3, 0.2, and 0.0, and therefore token $\mathbf{y}_1$ is used in the next iteration, where $\mathbf{y}_2$ obtains the highest probability. The procedure is repeated until token _EOS is chosen, as it has the maximum probability.

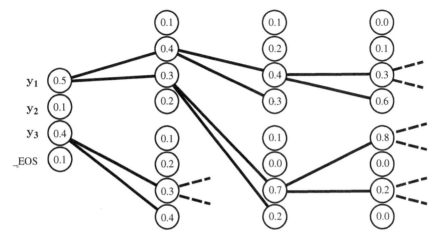

Figure 5.25 Beam search with $k = 2$ in a dictionary with four tokens.

with $k = 2$ is applied. During the first recursion of the decoder, the FC layer outputs four probabilities, of which $\mathbf{y}_1$ and $\mathbf{y}_3$ have the highest probabilities. Them, both tokens are tested as inputs for the next recursion, which creates two sets of probabilities. If $\mathbf{y}_1$ is used, then $\mathbf{y}_2$ and $\mathbf{y}_3$ have the highest probability. If $\mathbf{y}_3$ are used, $\mathbf{y}_3$ and _EOS are the most probable. This creates more possible paths in the next iteration, where 4 tokens are tested. Each time that _EOS is found among the k most probable tokens, the corresponding path is finished. After all paths are finished, the log-likelihoods or the NLL of the paths is computed, and the path with the lowest NLL is chosen.

Table 5.1 summarizes the (unfinished) process of Fig. 5.25. Among all the finished paths, all except the one with the lowest NLL are discarded. The search must be continued for all the remaining paths. Notice that since the sequences have different lengths, here it is very important to divide the log probabilities in Eq. (5.47) by the sequence length. Of course, this translation example is not realistic, because two of the non-discarded sequences have a word repeated two and three times, which, in natural languages is very very very unlikely.

Once all paths are finished, the final translation will be the sequence with the lowest NLL or, in other words, the translation with the highest probability.

Sutskever et al. (2014) describe the experimental setup as follows. They used the WMT 2014 English–French translation dataset (Bojar et al. 2014), with 12 million sentences, 284 million French words, and 304 million English words, with a dictionary containing 160.000 English words and 80.000 French words. The source language was English. The out-of-dictionary words were changed by a UNK (unknown) token, and the translations were produced by beam search. The authors noticed that the results improved slightly when the source sentences were reversed.

The tested structures were single and deep LSTMs with hidden states of 1000 cells. The word embeddings had dimension 1000 (this is, the tokens were coded in vectors of length 1000), and the output of the FC structure was a softmax of dimension 80.0000. The parameters of the LSTM were initialized at random with a uniform distribution between -0.08 and 0.08, and the optimization algorithm was a momentum gradient descent with $\mu = 0.7$. The gradient descent was applied in batches of 128 sequences. Also, in order to avoid any

Table 5.1 Probabilities of the tokens across finished and unfinished paths in Fig. 5.25 and NLL of each one of the paths.

T	1	2	3	4	$NLL(T\|S)$
$\mathbf{y}_1, \mathbf{y}_2, \mathbf{y}_3, \mathbf{y}_3$	0.5	0.4	0.4	0.3	0.93
$\mathbf{y}_1, \mathbf{y}_2, \mathbf{y}_3,$ _EOS	0.5	0.4	0.4	0.6	0.76
$\mathbf{y}_1, \mathbf{y}_2,$ _EOS	0.5	0.4	0.3		~~0.94~~
$\mathbf{y}_1, \mathbf{y}_3, \mathbf{y}_3, \mathbf{y}_1$	0.5	0.3	0.7	0.8	0.62
$\mathbf{y}_1, \mathbf{y}_3, \mathbf{y}_3, \mathbf{y}_3$	0.5	0.7	0.7	0.2	0.75
$\mathbf{y}_1, \mathbf{y}_3,$ _EOS	0.5	0.3	0.2		~~1.17~~
$\mathbf{y}_3, \mathbf{y}_3$	0.4	0.3			1.06
$\mathbf{y}_3,$ _EOS	0.4	0.4			~~0.92~~

All finished paths except the one with lowest NLL can be discarded.

Table 5.2 Bilingual Evaluation Understudy (BLEU).

BLEU score	Interpretation
<10	Almost useless
10–19	Hard to get the gist
20–29	Clear gist, significant grammatical errors
30–40	Understandable to good translations
40–50	High-quality translations
50–60	Very high quality, adequate, fluent translations
>60	Quality often better than human

Source: Data from Google Cloud.

Table 5.3 Comparisons among different sequence to sequence translation mechanisms.

Method	BLEU score
Bahdanau et al. (2014)	28.45
Baseline system	33.30
Single forward LSTM, beam size 12	26.17
Single reversed LSTM, beam size 12	30.59
Ensemble of 5 reversed LSTMs, beam size 1	33.00
Ensemble of 2 reversed LSTMs, beam size 12	33.27
Ensemble of 5 reversed LSTMs, beam size 2	34.50
Ensemble of 5 reversed LSTMs, beam size 12	34.81

Source: Sutskever et al. (2014)/NeurIPS.

possible exploding gradients, the training included a hard limit constraint in the norm of the weights. The evaluation metrics were the bilingual evaluation understudy (BLEU) (see Table 5.2).

Table 5.3 shows the main results of the experiments, where the best performance was shown by an ensemble of 5 LSTM with reversed input sequence and a beam size of 12.

Example 5.7.2 *(Text generation using Bidirectional LSTM)*
The bidirectional long short-term memory network (B-LSTM) follows the same structure as the BRNN in Fig. 5.14 where the hidden state blocks are simply changed by LSTM blocks. This example uses B-LSTM to generate a story given an input text of a fixed length.

For this example, we can use the **The Sleeping Beauty** book by C.S. Evans. The Project Gutenberg Ebook of Sleeping Beauty is used here which can be found at https://www .gutenberg.org/files/25451/25451-8.txt. The entire book is used here as the training data. Before using the entire book as text input, the irrelevant sections or symbols are removed so that only the actual text containing the story is fed to the model. This ensures efficient learning of the model from the input data.

Once we have the cleaned-up version of the text, we can load it into the notebook. Following this, we need to perform certain preprocessing steps to convert the data into the desired format for the model to learn from. It is important to note that the model understands small chunks of information compared to big sentences. So we need to first tokenize the text to obtain the words in the text. The preprocessing steps include converting all the text to lower case followed by splitting them into smaller chunks based on the next line. Once we split the data into chunks, we fit it into the tokenizer to map each of the words to a number. Therefore, the sentence shown below would be converted to a set of numbers:

once upon a time there were a king and a queen
[346, 41, 4, 68, 25, 19, 4, 32, 2, 4, 45]

Following this, we need to convert the sentence to a sequence so that it can be fed to the model. The sequence is built by appending the adjacent token every time so that the model can learn the usage of the tokens consecutively in a sentence. This problem is similar to a time-series problem as also we construct the input in a sequential manner so that the model can learn what comes next. Below (Table 5.4) is an illustration of how the tokens look like after converting them into a sequence:

Since the model can accept only a fixed length of input, each of these sequence is prepadded with zeros as follows (in Table 5.5):

Now, since we have the sequence, we can convert the input into predictors and labels by splitting the last column of the sequence as the label and keeping the rest as the input to the model.

Table 5.4 After converting the sentence to sequence.

[346, 41]
[346, 41, 4]
[346, 41, 4, 68]
[346, 41, 4, 68, 25]
[346, 41, 4, 68, 25, 19]
[346, 41, 4, 68, 25, 19, 4]
[346, 41, 4, 68, 25, 19, 4, 32]
[346, 41, 4, 68, 25, 19, 4, 32, 2]
[346, 41, 4, 68, 25, 19, 4, 32, 2, 4]
[346, 41, 4, 68, 25, 19, 4, 32, 2, 4, 45]

Table 5.5 Prepadding the sequence with zeros.

[0, 0, 0, 0, 0, 0, 0, 0, 0, 0, 0, 0, 0, 0, 0, 346, 41]
[0, 0, 0, 0, 0, 0, 0, 0, 0, 0, 0, 0, 0, 0, 346, 41, 4]
[0, 0, 0, 0, 0, 0, 0, 0, 0, 0, 0, 0, 0, 346, 41, 4, 68]

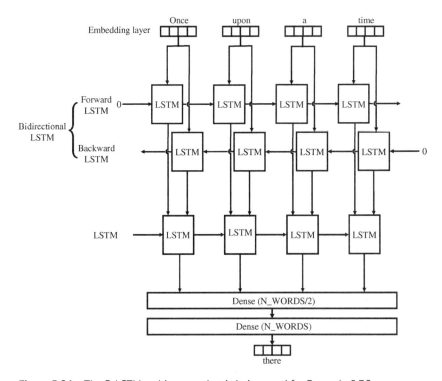

Figure 5.26   The B-LSTM architecture that is being used for Example 5.7.2.

As for the model, it consists of an embedding layer, which receives the tokens. This is then followed by a B-LSTM with 150 hidden units. Next, we add the dropout layer with dropout probability 20%. To this model, we can add LSTM with 100 units followed by two dense layers. The final dense layers have the same number of outputs as the total words. The overall architecture is shown in Fig. 5.26. The loss function used here is the categorical cross entropy and we use the Adam optimizer. The metric in this case is the accuracy as we are trying to see how well the model predicts the label token.

The model is trained for 100 epochs. But we can train the model for a longer duration as well as this will benefit the performance a lot. For the sake of this experiment with 100 epochs of training, the model was able to predict the following:

Input text:
"There was once a sweet prince"
Model output:
"There was once a sweet prince guarded there
was a hundred years passed away at the end of
that time"

For better performance, the model can be trained even further for more number of epochs.

5.8 Gated Recurrent Units

The traditional RNNs suffer from the vanishing gradient problem, which can make it difficult to propagate important information from the past to the present, leading to a loss of context and meaning. The GRU (Cho et al. 2014a) is a new type of RNN that uses a gating mechanism to update or forget information from the past selectively was proposed to address these issues. The GRU is intended to find a compromise between the ease of use and interpretability of classic RNNs and the complexity of more sophisticated designs such as LSTMs. It was found to be more effective on several benchmark datasets for machine translation. The performance comparison of GRU to that of LSTMs showed that it is faster to train, and it uses less memory. GRU outperformed traditional RNNs and is competitive with LSTMs while processing datasets with longer sequences.

GRUs solve the vanishing gradient problem using two gates namely the update gate and reset gate. These gates decide what information to retain or discard through to the output. The update gate determines both how much information to retain from the previous hidden state and how much information to use in the current hidden state. The reset gate functions much like the forgetting gate of an LSTM. This gate determines how much of the previous hidden state to discard and how much information to consider when updating the current hidden state.

In a GRU, the hidden state of instant $t - 1$ is concatenated with current input $\mathbf{x}_t$ and passed through two dense layers with sigmoid activation (Fig. 5.27) that constitute the reset $\mathbf{r}_t$ and update $\mathbf{u}_t$ gates, with expressions

$$\mathbf{r}_t = \sigma \left(\mathbf{W}_{xr}^\top \mathbf{x}_t + \mathbf{W}_{hr}^\top \mathbf{h}_{t-1} + \mathbf{b}_r \right)$$
$$\mathbf{u}_t = \sigma \left(\mathbf{W}_{ur}^\top \mathbf{x}_t + \mathbf{W}_{ur}^\top \mathbf{h}_{t-1} + \mathbf{b}_u \right) \tag{5.48}$$

After this, a candidate state $\tilde{\mathbf{h}}_t$ is computed by passing the elementwise product of the reset gate $\mathbf{r}_t$ with the previous state $\mathbf{h}_t$ through a dense layer with tanh activation (Fig. 5.28), this is,

$$\tilde{\mathbf{h}}_t = \tanh \left(\mathbf{W}_{xh}^\top \mathbf{x}_t + \mathbf{W}_{hh}^\top \left(\mathbf{r}_t \odot \mathbf{h}_{t-1} \right) + \mathbf{b}_h \right) \tag{5.49}$$

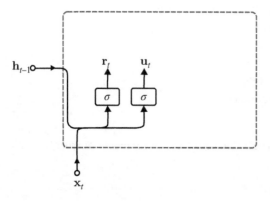

Figure 5.27 Reset and update gates in the GRU.

Figure 5.28 Candidate hidden state in the GRU.

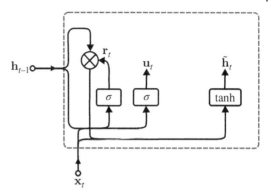

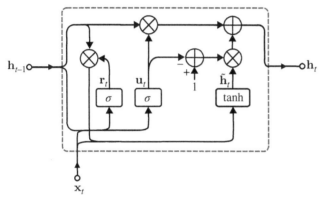

Figure 5.29 Computation of the new hidden state.

Finally, a convex combination of the previous state $\mathbf{h}_{t-1}$ and the candidate state $\tilde{\mathbf{h}}_t$ is constructed through the update gate $\mathbf{u}_t$ (Fig. 5.29) as

$$\mathbf{h}_t = \mathbf{u}_t \odot \mathbf{h}_{t-1} + \left(\mathbf{1} - \mathbf{u}_t\right) \odot \tilde{\mathbf{h}}_t \qquad (5.50)$$

which computes the new state.

Example 5.8.1 *(Sentiment analysis using GRU)*

Sentiment analysis is a technique used in NLP to determine the polarity of a given text. There are several types of sentiment analysis, but one of the most generally used ways categorize data as positive or negative. This aids in the study of various text elements, such as comments, tweets, and customer reviews, in order to understand the insights and feedback from the audience. In this example, we use the NLTK, which is an open-source framework for developing applications that handle human language data. It includes robust text-processing libraries for common NLP operations. For instance, in the nltk.tokenize package, the word tokenize method is used to split a text into smaller pieces known as tokens. These tokens may include sentences or individual words.

The implementation of this example for sentiment analysis is done using the IMDB movie dataset (A. Maas et al. 2011). This dataset has 50,000 movie reviews for binary sentiment classification. Both training and testing have 25,000 movie reviews each that are labeled by sentiment (positive/negative). The dataset is used to estimate the amount of favorable and unfavorable reviews by applying GRU for classification. The next step involves data preprocessing and this process entails eliminating any unnecessary information, addressing formatting problems, managing missing value, and fixing any mistakes in grammar or spelling errors. For the IMDB dataset, this process has the following steps:

Removal of stopwords: Common terms like "the," "a," and "an" that appear often in a speech are known as stopwords. They are often eliminated from the text because they do not contribute any information to the analysis.

HTML tag removal: Unstructured text often has a significant amount of background noise. HTML tags are usually one of these elements that do not significantly contribute to studying and interpreting the text, thus it should be avoided.

Lowercasing: Change all characters to lowercase to reduce the total quantity of distinct words.

Stemming: Stemming is a method for eliminating affixes from words to reveal their basic structure. For instance, the term bloat is the stem of the phrases bloating, bloats, and bloated. Porter's method (Porter 1980) for stemming is one of the popular stemming algorithms. The Porter Stemmer class in NLTK allows us to apply Porter Stemmer algorithms for the words we need to stem.

Tokenization: The text is divided into tokens or individual words during the tokenization process.

In the next step, the reviews are encoded as integers so that they can be used as input to the GRU model. Then, a dictionary is created that counts the number of times each word appears in IMDb reviews. Each word in the review serves as a key in this dictionary, and its matching count acts as the value. The words are arranged in decreasing order by the number of occurrences so that these words appear at the start of the dictionary. For example, consider two reviews for a movie:

"This movie was thrilling. It was good!"
"I hated the ending of the movie. It was horrible."

The resultant dictionary will be as follows:

{"this": 1, "movie": 2, "was": 3, "thrilling": 1, "it": 2, "good": 1, "I": 1, "hated": 1, "the": 2, "ending": 1, "of": 1, "horrible": 1}

Following that, an index mapping dictionary is created to assign a unique index to each word in the IMDb review. This is accomplished by iterating over the reviews and assigning lower indices to frequently occurring words. The resultant index mapping dictionary will be as follows:

{"was": 1, "movie": 2, "it": 3, "the": 4, "this": 5, "thrilling": 6, "good": 7, "I": 8, "hated": 9, "ending": 10, "of": 11, "horrible": 12} After completing the encoding of the reviews, the labels are encoded. Since there are two output labels, we shall designate the "positive" label as 1 and the "negative" as 0. Next, the outliers present in the reviews are identified by measuring various statistical parameters such as mean, minimum, maximum, and standard deviation. As a result, outliers are eliminated by removing reviews that are considerably longer or shorter than the average review length. Moreover, as the length of each review varies, padding must be added or words must be truncated to maintain the same size.

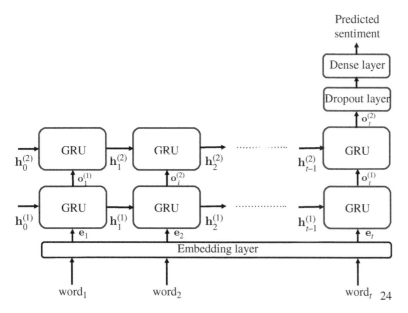

Figure 5.30 Architectural framework of the GRU model used for sentiment analysis.

Lastly, the preprocessed and feature-extracted reviews and labels are divided into 80% for training, 10% for validation, and 10% for testing. The dataset is trained using the GRU, and the overall model architecture consists of an embedding layer, a GRU layer, a FC layer, and an activation function layer. An embedding layer transforms input in the form of words represented as integers into continuous vectors of a predetermined length. The main objective of the embedding layer is to represent the input in a way that accurately conveys its semantics/meaning. Hence, words with similar meanings, such as "joy" and "cheerful," will have similar embeddings, whereas nonidentical words will have different embeddings. See Section 6.4 for additional details.

During the forward pass in training, the input is first passed through the embedding layer to obtain an embedded tensor, which is then fed into the GRU layer. To prevent overfitting, a dropout with a probability of 0.5 is applied to the output of the GRU layer. Finally, the resulting tensor is passed through a FC layer with a sigmoid activation function. The network is trained for 10 epochs with a batch size of 50 using the binary cross-entropy loss function and Adam optimizer. The embedding dimension is the number of dimensions used to represent each word in the input data, and in this case, it is set to 400. Additionally, the model employs a GRU with two recurrent layers, where each layer has 256 hidden units. The resultant sentiment analysis model is illustrated in Fig. 5.30.

5.9 Conclusion

The RNN models, originally inspired in the Hopfield network, are the first structures able to process sequential models with arbitrary length. Indeed, the previously introduced deep structures are designed to process inputs with fixed dimensions, and, hence, their use for sequences is limited.

The Elman RNN is the first recursive structure, introduced to make predictions based on the information stored in the hidden layer conveyed by the past elements of the sequence. The training of the RNN is carried out by the backpropagation of the error. The particularity of the RNN is that the error is backpropagated from the current output at each time instant to the present input and to all the past inputs, and this is why this optimization is called backpropagation through time. The RNN has many variants, among them the bidirectional RNN is used in those cases where at a time instant, elements of posterior time instants in the sequence are available. This is particularly interesting in translation or text prediction. Deep structures consisting of stacking several RNN or others, as RNN with hidden states based on FC neural networks exist.

A main drawback of the RNN consists of the vanishing and exploding gradients phenomena, that in particular preclude the retention of information from remote samples, or long-term information. This is due to the fact that the backpropagation contains a term that is a function of the *t*th power of the hidden matrix weight. The LSTM is a recursive neural network introduced to solve this problem by the propagation of an internal state that is not processed by the matrix. The GRU was introduced later to produce similar results with a lower computational complexity.

The RNN has played a prominent role in tasks related to signal processing and language modeling, such as translation, part of speech detection, financial time series, energy load forecast, and others.

Problems

5.1 *Modify the code of Example 5.3.1 in order to implement multistep prediction for 10 timesteps ahead. Determine the model performance by plotting MSE as a function of the horizon.*

5.2 *Implement an LSTM model from scratch in the programming language of your preference and replicate the Example 5.7.1 using the same seaborn flights dataset to predict single time step ahead. Further, modify the code to perform multistep prediction and evaluate the model performance.*

5.3 *Implement a deep LSTM with 3 layers of basic LSTM cells, each with 256 hidden units. Use this network to classify the MNIST dataset of handwritten digits into corresponding numeric values. Evaluate the performance by plotting the ROC curve for this multiclass classification.*

5.4 *In the sentiment analysis problem presented in Example 5.8.1, remove the preprocessing step and implement the model using Keras. Evaluate the impact of the preprocessing step on the model's performance by comparing the resulting confusion matrices with and without the preprocessing step.*

5.5 *Implement a bidirectional LSTM model for sentiment classification in Example 5.8.1 and check if it outperforms the GRU model.*

5.6 *Describe the importance of data preprocessing when working with sequential data in RNNs. What are some common preprocessing steps and why are they necessary for effective model training?*

5.7 *The Stanford Sentiment Treebank (SST) dataset (Socher et al. 2013) consists of movie reviews labeled with sentiment scores ranging from 0 (highly negative) to 4 (highly positive). In this problem, a pretrained word embedding named Global Vectors for Word Representation (GloVe) embedding (Pennington et al. 2014) is used to train an LSTM. These embeddings are pretrained on a large collection of text and hence capture the semantic relationships between words, allowing for better generalization when retrained to newer datasets.*

Implement a multiclass sentiment classification model on the SST dataset using the pretrained GloVe word embeddings. Assess the model on the test sets and report the accuracy, precision, recall, and F1 score.

5.8 *Use the historical stock price data to build a GRU-based model for stock price prediction. Yahoo Finance provides historical stock price data for a wide range of publicly traded companies. You can access this data through their website: https://finance .yahoo.com/. Predict future stock prices based on historical price and volume data and evaluate the model's performance using appropriate evaluation metrics.*

5.9 *Explain why regularization techniques are important in training RNNs, particularly LSTMs and GRUs. Discuss common regularization methods used in RNN architectures and their impact on model generalization.*

5.10 *Use a time-series electrocardiogram data for anomaly detection using LSTM. The dataset can be downloaded from the website: http://www.timeseriesclassification .com/description.php?Dataset=ECG5000. This dataset contains 5000 time series samples of electrocardiogram data, with both normal and anomalous ECG patterns. Train an LSTM-based model to detect anomalies in this dataset and evaluate the model's performance using metrics like precision, recall, and F1-score.*

6

Attention Networks and Transformers

6.1   Introduction

Attention mechanisms are a natural step in the evolution of the way in which AI is under-stood and designed, in an attempt to imitate the function of the biological neural tissue (see e.g. (Lotter et al. 2020)). The first versions of deep learning (DL) mechanisms were inspired by the structure of the brain tissue, and later, researchers tried to reproduce the function of the memory. Starting in the first years of the 21st century, major investigations focused on human behavior, which produced an explosion of advanced and very complex AI structures.

The inception of the first neural network mechanisms can be seen as an attempt to mimic the structure of a biological neuron, through the introduction of the perceptron by Warren McCulloch and Walter Pitts in 1948 and first implemented by Frank Rosenblatt (1958).

Yan LeCun, in the 1980s, featured a quantum leap in the development of machine learning-based AI for image processing. In order to find the inspiration for that work, we need to go back to 1959, when David Hubel and Torsten Wiesel first described the visual cortex in cats. A neural network structure that imitated the cortex model, constructed with artificial neurons, the first functional image recognition machine, was the CNN, first introduced by LeCun in 1989. CNN structures, which somehow modeled biological vision (Kriegeskorte 2015). These approaches roughly simulated the structure of the brain tissue in a simplified fashion (Kuzovkin et al. 2018; De Cesarei et al. 2021). This neural network was successful in character recognition to handwritten digits with unprecedented accuracy. This was the first one of a series of models with increasing complexity that ended with some very successful image recognition structures around 2012. Several CNNs were published that had outstanding accuracy in classifying images among 1000 different classes, and they were trained which huge image databases.

The previous approaches roughly simulated the structure of the brain tissue in a sim-plified fashion and worked for visual recognition. But what about language model (LM)s? At practically the same time, recurrent neural networks (RNNs) were first introduced as a model that went away from such a merely structural conceptualization to take an approach based on the function of the brain, in particular, to reproduce the persistence of the mem-ory (Bitzer and Kiebel 2012; Güçlü and Van Gerven 2017; Hallez et al. 2023), and they were

Deep Learning: A Practical Introduction, First Edition.
Manel Martínez-Ramón, Meenu Ajith, and Aswathy Rajendra Kurup.
© 2024 John Wiley & Sons Ltd. Published 2024 by John Wiley & Sons Ltd.
Companion website: https://github.com/DeepLearning-book

first applied by John Hopfield in 1982 to solve optimization problems. In 1997, alternative recurrent models, already introduced by Jeff Elman in 1972 and later improved.

An even more sophisticated path toward the evolution of AI was opened when researchers started to devise mechanisms to emulate human behavior through attention mechanisms. Interestingly, the use of these mechanisms gave rise to the first machines that could likely pass the Turing test (Pinar Saygin et al. 2000). The first released attention-based chatbot released by Google Inc., developed in 2017 and named language model for dialogue applications (LaMDA) (Thoppilan et al. 2020) created a significant amount of controversy when Blake Lemoine, one of the engineers of the team that developed the chatbot, suggested that the machine may present signs that imitate consciousness (Tiku 2022), something that was widely misinterpreted as him claiming that the machine was actually sentient. He was doing a study related to gender, ethnicity, and religious biases. In the course of his experiments, he asked what religion the machine would be if it was an officiant in Israel. The machine responded "The only true one: the Jedi religion." That triggered in him a feeling that the machine was perceiving that the question was tricky, and deflected with irony. Lemoine concluded that if the machine was not able to pass the Turing test, we can say that it is not sentient, but if it passed, then we cannot discard it.

Blaise Agüera y Arcas, an AI research leader at Google denied that claim. But this opened a debate that escalated later. In March 2023, MLRI researcher Eliezer Yudkowsky wrote in Time Magazine "Progress in AI capabilities is running vastly, vastly ahead of progress in AI alignment or even progress in understanding what the hell is going on inside those systems. If we actually do this, we are all going to die."

In May of this year, Geoffrey Hinton, the godfather of AI resigned from Google in order to "freely speak out about the risks of AI." He claimed that a part of him now regrets his life's work (C. Metz 2023). He thinks that the computer models that we have now may be better than the human brain for certain tasks, and the idea of artificial superintelligence may come very soon.

Yoshua Bengio, a second father of AI, is more specific: AI can pass the Turing test, and they can fool us into thinking that they are human beings: which can destabilize democracy through disinformation since AI is basically in the hands of anyone. An AI can achieve levels of complexity similar to those of the human brain without the limitations of the human brain, so one of these machines can be smarter than we are. A machine could act in a way that we could not, and it could, for example, misuse legislation by finding loopholes more efficiently that the smartest lawyer. Bengio claims a regulatory body for these and many more, maybe unknown, issues of AI. He signed, with Hinton and many other scientists, a letter claiming a pause in the AI experiments.[1] See also Bilefsky (2023).

Max Tegmark, another of the authors of the letter, an MIT researcher in AI wrote an article in Time Magazine (Tegmark 2023) that warns of the risk of extinction due to the AI. He wrote "Before superintelligence and its human extinction threat, AI can have many other side effects worthy of concern, ranging from bias and discrimination to privacy loss, mass surveillance, job displacement, growing inequality, cyberattacks, lethal autonomous weapon proliferation, humans getting 'hacked', human enfeeblement and loss of meaning,

---

1 https://futureoflife.org/open-letter/pause-giant-ai-experiments.

non-transparency, mental health problems (from harassment, social media addiction, social isolation, dehumanization of social interactions) and threats to democracy[...]."

The debate is open and, beyond educated apocalyptic claims, it is a natural consequence of the great and previously unseen power of AI nowadays in general and, in particular, of attention mechanisms.

6.2 Attention Mechanisms

Attention is a core human brain functioning mechanism and is a complex cognitive function (Rensink 2000; Corbetta and Shulman 2002). One important property of the human learning mechanism is the ability to concentrate on information in parts and not as an entirety. This capability of human learning is called attention. For example, while perceiving things visually humans tend to focus on certain parts or aspects of the scene, and this part is identified by them to find similarities with other scenes having the same component. Humans tend to learn to focus on an individual aspect rather than the scene as a whole (Niu et al. 2021). Therefore, humans process information by selecting high-value features from a huge information source with the help of limited resources for processing information. With this kind of approach, humans learn more accurately and efficiently over time. This type of learning in humans is referred to as an attention mechanism as they focus or attend to certain specific information out of massive information.

Attention in machine learning refers to giving importance and priority to certain pieces of input data while disregarding the rest to replicate the cognitive attention mechanism. It enabled researchers to develop algorithms that can distinguish between input components that are crucial for solving an issue and those that are not. According to research, adding an attention layer to several types of deep learning neural networks increases their performance (Bahdanau et al. 2014). The attention model has been utilized successfully in practice to address a variety of real-world issues in the fields of natural language processing (NLP) and computer vision, including language translation (Z. Lin et al. 2017), document classification (Z. Yang et al. 2016), image captioning (K. Xu et al. 2015), and image synthesis (S. E. Reed et al. 2016a). For instance, in tasks involving machine translation, only selected words may be useful for predicting the subsequent word. While in an image-captioning problem, certain areas of the input image are more useful for generating the caption. Attention models integrate the idea of relevance by assisting the model to constantly focus on only those portions of the input that aid in effectively finishing the task.

6.2.1 The Nadaraya–Watson Attention Mechanism

In 1964, Nadaraya and Watson proposed a regression model (Nadaraya 1964; Watson 1964) that may be considered an initial foundation of attention mechanisms in deep learning. It is a non-parametric regression approach that computes the conditional probability of a target variable given a set of features or predictor variables, with no assumptions about the actual data distribution. Given n training data with features and their associated target values $(\mathbf{x}_1, \mathbf{y}_1), (\mathbf{x}_2, \mathbf{y}_2), \ldots, (\mathbf{x}_n, \mathbf{y}_n)$, for a new instance $\mathbf{x}_j$ (this instance is usually called a *query* in this context), we want to estimate the target value $\hat{y}_j$. A naive regression model may simply estimate the median or average value of the target variable for all observations without taking into account the relationship with the features. The expression for this model can be defined as:

$$\hat{y}_j = \sum_{i=1}^{n} y_i \tag{6.1}$$

On the other hand, the Nadaraya–Watson model assigns weights for every observation and aggregates the weighted responses to determine the regression function at a specific point. The weights represent the significance of each of the training feature samples to the query **x**. Thus the Nadaraya–Watson model is able to capture more complicated and non-linear interactions between features and target variables than the naive approach. The target variable $\hat{y}$ may be estimated in this case as

$$\hat{y}_j = \sum_{i=1}^{n} \alpha_{i,j} y_i \tag{6.2}$$

Coefficients $\alpha_{i,j}$ are referred to as the *attention coefficients*, and they are computed as

$$\alpha_{i,j} = \frac{K\left(\frac{x_j - x_i}{h}\right)}{\sum_{k=1}^{n} K\left(\frac{x_j - x_k}{h}\right)} \tag{6.3}$$

where $K(\cdot)$ is a kernel function, or a positive definite function that is used to measure the similarity between samples x_i and **x**. By virtue of the Mercer's Theorem (Aizerman 1964), positive definite functions are equivalent to dot products of mappings of vectors x_i, x_j into a higher dimension Hilbert space. The kernels used in the Nadaraya and Watson regression papers were radial basis functions as the square exponential kernel, (sometimes called Gaussian kernel) the Epanechnikov Epanechnikov (1969) kernel, the triangular kernel, and others, this is, functions that are circularly symmetric around the origin and monotonically decreasing when the distance $|x_i - x|$ increases. Therefore, parameter h establishes the width of the kernel that controls the bias-variance tradeoff of the regression (Geman et al. 1992).

Essentially, the weighting function in the Nadaraya–Watson regression model and the attention mechanism in the current deep learning models have a conceptual similarity. These models aim to give more priority to specific regions of the input while making a prediction. Nevertheless, there exist some significant differences between the two models. For instance, in the Nadaraya–Watson model, the weights are determined based on the distance between the test point and the training samples. However, the weights in the attention mechanism are learned by the model during training and frequently rely on the content of the input sequence.

Example 6.2.1 *(Nadaraya–Watson regression model)*
This example implements the Nadaraya–Watson model for non-parametric regression. To perform the estimation, it takes four inputs, which are two sequences representing the independent variable x_i, the dependent variables y_i, a query point **x**, which is the point for which we want to estimate the function value y, and a kernel parameter that determines the influence of nearby points on the estimation.

In this example, a set of random data with $x_i \in \mathbb{R}$ is generated containing 100 random values ranging from 0 to 10. The dependent variable is generated by computing a sinusoid of the independent variable plus some noise as

$$y_i = \sin(\omega x_i) + g_i \tag{6.4}$$

where sequence g_i is a set of Gaussian random values with zero mean and variance 1.

Next, a set of query points is defined as $x_j = j$, $0 \le j \le 10$. These query points will serve the purpose of estimating the function values in the regression model. The width parameter h in Eq. (6.3) is set to 0.5, which determines the width of a square exponential kernel $K(x_j - x_i) = \exp\left(\|x_i - x_j\|/h\right)$ and affects the smoothness of the estimated function. Finally, the Nadaraya–Watson model is applied to each query point, utilizing the defined function. As a result, a list of estimated function values is obtained by evaluating the model at each query point. Figure 6.1 plots the data points and the Nadaraya–Watson regression line. The resulting plot helps visualize the relationship between the independent and dependent variables, showcasing the effectiveness of the Nadaraya–Watson model in capturing the underlying pattern in the data.

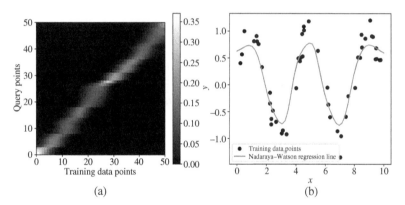

(a) (b)

Figure 6.1 (a) Attention matrix represents the attention weights between the training data and the queries. (b) Nadaraya–Watson regression model.

6.2.2 The Bahdanau Attention Mechanism

The sequence-to-sequence translation machine presented in Section 5.7.5 based on an encoder–decoder architecture constructed with recurrent networks may have a major limitation due to the fact that the source sequence is entirely coded in a single hidden state **h**. The encoder–decoder architecture is efficient for tasks where the source sequence is small. However, when the sequence is long, it becomes challenging for the encoder–decoder to store all the contextual information as a single fixed-length vector. By coupling the attention mechanism with the traditional encoder–decoder framework, the decoder can selectively focus on relevant parts of the input sequence when generating each output token. This enables the model to overcome the limitation of the fixed-length context vector and improves its performance in tasks with longer input sequences.

Consider the given source and target sentences in a machine translation task from English to German:

- **Source (English)**: "How does the bird fly?"
- **Target (German)**: "Wie fliegt der Vogel?"

The word "How" in the source sequence is linked to the word "Wie" in the target sequence. Moreover, "bird" corresponds to "Vogel," and "fly" translates to "fliegt" in German. Instead of analyzing the entire sequence, the focus shifts to specific sections that influence the prediction in the target sentence. The word "does" is given less importance, resulting in its hidden states in the context vector computation containing less information compared to terms like "bird" and "flight."

This limitation can be overcome with the use of attention mechanisms. The power of attention mechanisms relies on the fact that these mechanisms only attend to the parts of the input sequence that are important for the prediction of the next word. These are the parts of the sentence that are then used to modify the state before producing the next prediction. This is essentially the idea that gave rise to the transformers.

The attention mechanisms were developed by Bahdanau and his team for sequence-to-sequence modeling tasks (Bahdanau et al. 2014). It is a type of neural network architecture that is commonly used for applications that involve processing sequences of data, not only for machine translation (Neubig 2017) but also for speech recognition (Prabhavalkar et al. 2017), and text summarization (Shi et al. 2021).

In the Bahdanau attention model shown in Fig. 6.2, the source sequence x_i, $1 \leq I \leq T$ is first passed through an encoder consisting of a bidirectional RNN which creates a collection of hidden states h_i, capturing the contextual information of the input. At each time step

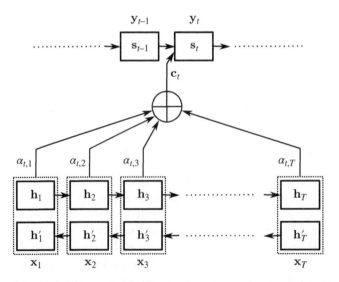

Figure 6.2 The Bahdanau attention mechanism. Source: Adapted from Bahdanau et al. (2014). At instant t, the decoder is fed with a linear combination c_t of the forward section of the encoder recurrent network. The elements of the linear combination are attention coefficients that use the present decoder state and the forward states of the encoder.

i of the encoder, it produces a hidden state $\mathbf{h}_i$ and at each time step t of the decoder, it produces a hidden state $\mathbf{s}_t$ as a function of the previous state $\mathbf{s}_{t-1}$, the previously decoded word $\mathbf{y}_{i-1}$ and a context vector $\mathbf{c}_i$ as

$$\mathbf{s}_t = \tanh(\mathbf{s}_{t-1}, \mathbf{y}_{t-1}, \mathbf{c}_t) \tag{6.5}$$

Alignment scores are calculated as a measure of similarity between the current decoder time step and each encoder hidden state. The alignment score may be determined in several ways; however, Bahdanau utilized the additive alignment score, which can be represented as:

$$\mathbf{f}(\mathbf{s}_{t-1}, \mathbf{h}_i) = \mathbf{v}_a^T \tanh\left(\mathbf{W}_a \begin{bmatrix} \mathbf{s}_{t-1} \\ \mathbf{h}_i \end{bmatrix}\right) \tag{6.6}$$

where $\mathbf{v}_a$ and $\mathbf{W}_a$ are, respectively, a learnable vector and matrix of the alignment score. The alignment scores are normalized using a softmax function to generate the attention weights $\alpha_{t,i}$. The softmax procedure ensures that the weights are between 0 and 1 and the sum of the total weights is equal to 1. The attention weights determine how much of each source's hidden state should be taken into account when calculating the output. For the ith encoder hidden state, the attention weight can be determined as follows:

$$\alpha_{t,i} = \frac{\exp(\mathbf{f}(\mathbf{s}_{t-1}, \mathbf{h}_i))}{\sum_{i'=1}^{T} \exp(\mathbf{f}(\mathbf{s}_{t-1}, \mathbf{h}_{i'}))} \tag{6.7}$$

where T is the length of the source sequence. Finally, the context vector $\mathbf{c}_t$ is generated by calculating the weighted sum of the encoder hidden states and their respective context vectors.

$$\mathbf{c}_t = \sum_{i=1}^{T} \alpha_{t,i} \mathbf{h}_i \tag{6.8}$$

The new state $\mathbf{s}_t$ of the decoder RNN is then used as the input of a dense structure in order to predict the token corresponding to the next word. A compact representation of the process is represented in Fig. 6.3.

The experiments presented in Bahdanau et al. (2014) were applied to English to French translation, with the bilingual corpora provided with ACL WMT'14,[2] and a subset of the

Figure 6.3 A compact representation of the Bahdanau attention mechanism. The input source of *T* elements is fed into a bidirectional RNN (encoder) that outputs a sequence of *T* states. The attention mechanism computes attention scores between the present state of the target RNN (decoder) and then a linear combination of the states, together with the previous decoder state is used to generate a new state that is fed into a dense layer to produce the next predicted word.

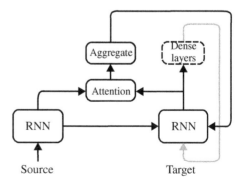

2 http://www.statmt.org/wmt14/translation-task.html.

most used words in both languages were tokenized with the use of the open-source machine translation package Moses.[3,4] The model is compared to the RNN encoder–decoder proposed in Cho et al. (2014b), both systems constructed with RNNs with 1000 hidden units. The output of the decoder consisted of a multilayer network (labeled as *dense layers* in Fig. 6.3) with a single MaxOut activation (see Section 1.4) in the hidden layer and a softmax output in order to compute the probability of the predicted word. A beam search (see Section 5.7.6) is used for the translation. When the method is trained with sentences of up to 50 words, its BLEU score was 31.44, while the same experiment performed on an RNN encoder–decoder showed a BLEU of 24.19.

6.2.3 Attention Pooling

In Sections 6.2.1 and 6.2.2 we have seen different examples. In this section, a more formal definition of attention is derived, and all the concepts previously introduced are redefined for clarity.

Assume that a database is available where each entry i has two fields, namely a key $\mathbf{k}_i$ and a value $\mathbf{v}_i$. In order to retrieve values of interest, a query $\mathbf{q}$ is constructed and compared to all the keys in the database. A classic query would be, for example, a sentence written in SQL (a language used to construct queries in databases) that establishes a set of conditions. For example, in a people database, get all entries whose name is "Óscar García." The result will retrieve the data (value) corresponding exclusively to the people with this name (used as a key). An approximate search will extend the results to those people whose name is "Oscar Garcia" (without the tildes) or "Óscar Garci," people with longer names ("Óscar Gómez García"), or people with typos or alphabet code errors in their names ("óscar Garcíia"). The approximate search can establish a score that denotes the degree of similarity between the query and the key. This is the idea of an attention mechanism, applied to any type of data.

Now assume a set of queries, keys, and values that have a representation as vectors constructed with real numbers, and that the result of the query is to be reconstructed as a linear combination of the retrieved values in a way formally equal to the Nadaraya–Watson regression in Eq. (6.2). The result of the query can be written as

$$\mathbf{z} = \sum_{i=1}^{N} \alpha(\mathbf{q}, \mathbf{k}_i)\mathbf{v}_i \tag{6.9}$$

where $\alpha(\mathbf{q}, \mathbf{k}_i)$ is the so-called *attention score* between query $\mathbf{q}$ and key $\mathbf{k}_i$, and its value is high if the similarity between both is high. Equation (6.9) is called an *attention pooling*. Representation $\mathbf{z}$ is a result of the attention of the query toward all keys. The attention scores must satisfy a couple of properties, namely

$$0 \leq \alpha(\mathbf{q}, \mathbf{k}_i) \leq 1$$
$$\sum_{i=1}^{N} \alpha(\mathbf{q}, \mathbf{k}_i) = 1 \tag{6.10}$$

---

3 https://www2.statmt.org/moses/index.php?n=Main.HomePage.
4 https://pypi.org/project/mosestokenizer.

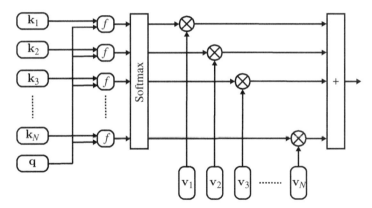

Figure 6.4 Attention mechanism.

This is, the linear combination in Eq. (6.9) must be convex. The scores must satisfy the properties of a probability mass function, something that is satisfied with the use of a softmax function. Therefore, in order to construct an attention pooling, an appropriate non-negative function $f(\mathbf{q}, \mathbf{k}_i)$ that measures similarity between the query and the keys must be found and then all the similarity outputs must be processed with a softmax function to construct the set of scores as depicted in Fig. 6.4.

The dot product between vectors is an adequate similarity function. For a collection of vectors over a hypersphere of radius r, the dot product between two vectors is minimal $(-r^2)$ if both vectors have opposite directions and it is maximal (r^2) if both vectors are equal. But since the function must be not nonnegative, one can use the exponential of the negative dot product, which is then a nonnegative function. If the query $\mathbf{q}$ and the keys $\mathbf{k}_i$ have a Euclidian norm that is approximately constant, then the softmax operation applied to these exponentials is

$$\alpha\left(\mathbf{k}_i, \mathbf{q}\right) = \frac{\exp\left(D^{1/2}\mathbf{q}^\mathsf{T}\mathbf{M}\mathbf{k}_i\right)}{\sum\limits_{j=1}^{N} \exp\left(D^{1/2}\mathbf{q}^\mathsf{T}\mathbf{M}\mathbf{k}_j\right)} \tag{6.11}$$

where the dot product is normalized with the length D of the query and key vectors and matrix $\mathbf{M}$ is needed when the query and the key do not have the same dimension in order to map them into a common space. In this case, the operation is called a scaled dot product.

6.2.4 Representation by Self-Attention

The idea of attention pooling can be implemented for machine learning. Assuming a sequence of N elements $\mathbf{x}_1, \ldots, \mathbf{x}_N$, a representation of the entire sequence can be constructed as a function of the attention $\alpha_{i,j} = \alpha\left(\mathbf{k}_i, \mathbf{q}_j\right)$ of each one of the patterns over all the sequence. Representation

$$\mathbf{z}_j = \sum_{i=1}^{N} \alpha_{i,j}\mathbf{v}_i \tag{6.12}$$

will then contain information on local and global relationships between elements of the sequence according to a similarity criterion, to be used for a given task.

In self-attention, the queries, keys, and values are all represented by the elements of the sequence. Assuming that the dot product-based attention in Eq. (6.11) is used to compute the attention coefficient between elements $\mathbf{x}_i$ and $\mathbf{x}_j$, one of the elements will be playing the role of the query and the other will be the key. But this attention mechanism is very simple, and it is essentially a function of the angle between both vectors. If we want to make this comparison more powerful, we can transform the query and the key with a parameter matrix with arbitrary coefficients. The similarity criterion is then driven by the values of these two matrices, which need to have the same dimensions for the dot product to work. The value can also be mapped in a given space by a matrix. The queries, keys, and values are then transformed as $\mathbf{q}_i = \mathbf{W}^{(q)\top}\mathbf{x}_i$, $\mathbf{k}_i = \mathbf{W}^{(k)\top}\mathbf{x}_i$, and $\mathbf{v}_i = \mathbf{W}^{(v)\top}\mathbf{x}_i$. Matrices $\mathbf{W}^{(q)}$ and $\mathbf{W}^{(k)}$ must have the same size, while matrix $\mathbf{W}^{(v)}$ has arbitrary size. This structure is built this way for the parameters in the matrices to be easily trainable.

If matrix $\mathbf{A}$ is constructed with entries $\alpha_{i,j}$ corresponding to the attention coefficients, and matrix $\mathbf{X}$ contains column vectors $\mathbf{x}_i$ then the representation of all input data through the attention mechanism can be written as

$$\mathbf{Z} = (\mathbf{W}^{(v)\top}\mathbf{X})\mathbf{A} \tag{6.13}$$

6.2.5 Training the Self-Attention Parameters

The parameter matrices that transform the data into queries, keys, and values are trainable by using the standard backpropagation method, according to, for example, to the ML criterion and a given task. For example, if a sequence $\mathbf{x}_i$, $1 \leq i \leq N$ is available, the attention mechanism will produce a representation $\mathbf{z}_i$. This representation can be passed through a FC layer to perform a given pattern recognition task. In this simple structure, we only have three layers (see Fig. 6.5).

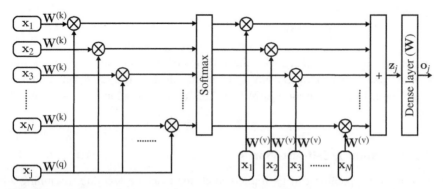

Figure 6.5 Representation $\mathbf{z}_j$ of a single element $\mathbf{x}_j$ through dot product attention over a sequence of N elements processed through a dense layer with weights $\mathbf{W}$ to illustrate the backpropagation procedure. The output error is backpropagated to the output $\mathbf{z}_j$ to update parameters $\mathbf{W}^{(v)}$ and then to the output of the softmax function in order to update $\mathbf{W}^{(k)}$ and $\mathbf{W}^{(q)}$. The process must be repeated for all elements of the sequence.

The output of the fully connected layer will give an error δ_j, one error vector per element of the sequence. For each one of the elements of this sequence, this error will be backpropagated to the output of the self-attention mechanism with the backpropagation equations introduced in Chapter 1, in particular with Eq. (1.110). Let us call $\delta_j^{(v)}$ to the error backpropagated to the self-attention layer output. Here, we find representation $\mathbf{z}_j$, which can be expressed as a combination of the values corresponding to each one of the elements of the sequence as

$$\mathbf{z}_j = \sum_{i=1}^{N} \alpha_{i,j} \mathbf{W}^{(v)\mathsf{T}} \mathbf{x}_i = \mathbf{W}^{(v)\mathsf{T}} \sum_{i=1}^{N} \alpha_{i,j} \mathbf{x}_i \tag{6.14}$$

Following Eq. (1.104), and taking into account that here there are no nonlinear activations, the error backpropagated to this point is $\delta_j^{(v)} = \mathbf{W}\delta_j$ where $\mathbf{W}$ are the weights of the dense layer. Then we apply Eq. (1.103), which says that the update for $\mathbf{W}^{(v)}$ and element $\mathbf{x}_j$ is constructed with the product of the input times the error, where the input is the linear combination of the sequence, as seen in Eq. (6.14), this is

$$\mathbf{W}^{(v)} \leftarrow \mathbf{W}^{(v)} - \mu \left(\sum_{i=1}^{N} \alpha_{i,j} \mathbf{x}_i \right) \delta_j^{(v)\mathsf{T}} \tag{6.15}$$

Therefore, similarly as in (1.110), the update taking into account all elements of the input sequence are

$$\mathbf{W}^{(v)} \leftarrow \mathbf{W}^{(v)} - \mu \sum_{i=1}^{N} \sum_{j=1}^{N} \alpha_{i,j} \mathbf{x}_i \delta_j^{(v)\mathsf{T}} \tag{6.16}$$

Here it is worth introducing a matrix notation for this update. We define $\mathbf{\Delta}^{(v)}$ as the matrix containing all the backpropagated errors $\delta_j^{(v)}$, and using the already defined matrices containing elements $\mathbf{x}_i$ and $\alpha_{i,j}$, the previous update can be written as

$$\mathbf{W}^{(v)} \leftarrow \mathbf{W}^{(v)} - \mu \mathbf{X} \mathbf{A} \mathbf{\Delta}^{(v)\mathsf{T}} \tag{6.17}$$

The updates for $\mathbf{W}^{(q)}$ and $\mathbf{W}^{(k)}$ are also derived by backpropagating error $\delta_j^{(v)}$ to the output of these matrices, but it is left as Problem 6.2 for the reader.

6.2.6 Multi-head Attention

The actual power of attention mechanisms consists of constructing representations that are a function of a diversity of attention modules. Each one of these modules is called an attention head, and a representation that combines different attention mechanisms is called a multi-head attention mechanism.

The mechanism is illustrated in Fig. 6.6, where a single query $\mathbf{q}_j$ is represented with the keys and values corresponding to element i of the sequence, to produce the scalar component $z_{i,j}$ of the representation. In a self-attention mechanism, the query is represented by element $\mathbf{x}_j$ of the sequence itself, and the key and value are represented by element $\mathbf{x}_i$. These values are linearly transformed S times by arrays $\mathbf{W}_S^{(q)}, \mathbf{W}_S^{(k)}, \mathbf{W}_S^{(v)}$. produces a vector $\mathbf{h}_{i,j,s}$ which is a nonlinear operation of query j with key and value i, to produce the

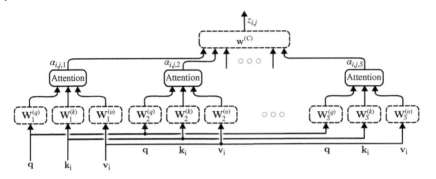

Figure 6.6 Multi-head attention.

attention element s, with the form

$$\mathbf{h}_{i,j,s} = \mathbf{f}\left(\mathbf{W}_s^{(q)\top}\mathbf{q}_j, \mathbf{W}_s^{(k)\top}\mathbf{k}_i, \mathbf{W}_s^{(v)\top}\mathbf{v}_i\right) \tag{6.18}$$

Function $\mathbf{f}(\cdot)$ can be a dot product score function as in (6.11) or an additive attention score, in which case, the output is expressed as

$$\mathbf{h}_{i,j,s} = \tanh\left(\mathbf{W}_s^{(q)\top}\mathbf{q}_j + \mathbf{W}_s^{(k)\top}\mathbf{k}_i + \mathbf{W}_s^{(v)\top}\mathbf{v}_i\right) \tag{6.19}$$

with an arbitrary dimension. The sequence of outputs is concatenated in a vector and then mapped through an output matrix $\mathbf{W}^{(C)}$ as

$$\mathbf{z}_{i,j} = \mathbf{W}^{(C)}\begin{bmatrix}\mathbf{h}_{i,j,1}\\ \vdots \\ \mathbf{h}_{i,j,N}\end{bmatrix} \tag{6.20}$$

which can be interpreted as the representation of the query j through multiple attention criteria applied to sample i. Then, assuming that vector $\mathbf{z}_{i,j}$ has dimension D_z, and a sequence of N elements is to be represented through S multi-head attention heads, then the sequence will be represented by $N \times N$ vectors of dimension D_z, which can be stored in a three-dimensional array.

6.2.7 Positional Encoding

In machine-to-machine translation and other NLP applications, the position of each word relative to the sequence that is to be processed is fundamental for the meaning of the sentence. The same has to be said of the possible applications of attention mechanisms to other types of data, namely images or sequences of images, where the images are chinked into patches and introduced in an attention machine. The position of each patch inside the image is fundamental to interpreting the image and extracting knowledge from it.

Therefore, the elements of the sequences used as inputs must contain information about their position that can be used by these attention mechanisms. The concept of positional encoding was introduced with this purpose in Vaswani et al. (2017) for sequence translation. The authors point out that their model does not contain any recurrence or any convolutional operation that can take advantage of the positions from a structural point of view. In other words, if we introduce a sequence into a recurrent structure or a convolutional structure, it will produce an output. If we change the order of the elements, the output will be different. In an attention mechanism, the output will be the same, but with a different order. This is, the attention mechanism does not inherently capture the particularities of a different position of the sequences.

This inconvenience can be overcome by *injecting* positional information to each one of the elements by simply adding a positional vector to each element. This vector has to have the same length as the elements of the sequence. This idea was originally introduced by Gehring et al. (2017). Given a sequence of elements $\tilde{\mathbf{x}}_i \in \mathbb{R}^D$, with components $\tilde{x}_{i,j}$, subindex i represents the position of the element inside the sequence and j the position of each scalar inside each vector. Then, a positional encoding is applied as

$$\mathbf{x}_i = \tilde{\mathbf{x}}_i + \mathbf{p}_i \tag{6.21}$$

where $\mathbf{p}_i$ is a positional vector whose components with even and odd indexes are

$$
\begin{aligned}
p_{i,2j} &= \sin\left(\frac{i}{T^{\frac{2j}{D}}}\right) \\[2ex]
p_{i,2j+1} &= \cos\left(\frac{i}{T^{\frac{2j}{D}}}\right)
\end{aligned}
\tag{6.22}
$$

for $1 \leq 2i, 2i + 1 \leq D$. In Vaswani et al. (2017) parameter T is set to 10^4, while the dimension of the sequence elements is 512.

Example 6.2.2 (*Visualization of positional encoding*)

This example illustrates the generation and visualization of positional encoding, which are commonly employed in sequence models like transformers. When dealing with tasks that rely on the order of elements in a sequence, such as NLP or time series analysis, it becomes crucial for the model to grasp the relative positions of those elements. Positional encoding plays a vital role in enabling the model to distinguish between elements based on their positions within the sequence. In this example, position encodings are generated for a given sequence length denoted as s and dimensionality denoted as D. The positional encoding matrix, denoted as $\mathbf{P} \in \mathbb{R}^{s \times D}$, is created with all initial values set to zero.

The position encodings are computed using sine and cosine functions. The even-indexed columns (starting from 0) of matrix $\mathbf{P}$ are assigned the values obtained by applying the sine function to the sequence index divided by a denominator based on the dimensionality. The denominator is obtained by evaluating the equation $T^{\frac{2j}{D}}$, where T is equal to 10,000 and j represents the indexes. Similarly, the odd-indexed columns are assigned cosine values using the same calculation. In this specific example, position encodings are generated for a sequence length of 100 and a dimensionality of 512. The resulting position encodings are visualized in Fig. 6.7, where the x-axis represents the dimension of the position encodings, while the y-axis represents the position in the sequence. Furthermore, a 3D plot is also generated to visualize the position encodings. This 3D plot in Fig. 6.8 provides an additional perspective, where the x-axis represents the dimension, the y-axis represents the position in the sequence, and the z-axis represents the value of the position encoding.

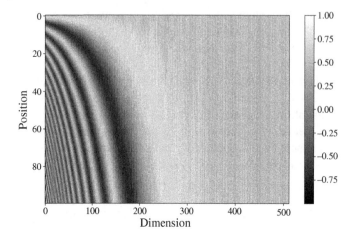

Figure 6.7   Visualization of positional encoding in 2D.

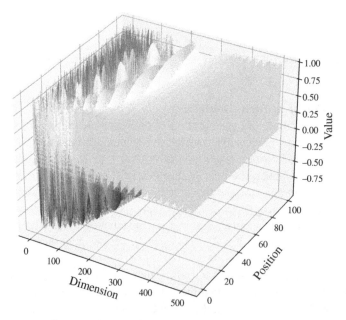

Figure 6.8   Visualization of positional encoding in 3D.

Example 6.2.3   *(Multi-head attention implementation)*

In this toy example, we use an attention mechanism to predict text, where the training data is a poem with 18,696 words in English. The mechanism has an input consisting of eight characters of the poem, and the target is the next character of the sequence. During the training, the error between the actual input and the desired one is computed and then a backpropagation is used to optimize the structure. The sequence of characters at the input is embedded with a dictionary that contains 30 embeddings corresponding to the characters present in the text, which are all lowercase letters in the English alphabet plus 4 punctuation characters. The length of each embedding is 32, this is, each character is coded in a token of length 32. This is coded as a simple example of how multi-head attention can be constructed.

The structure contains one attention layer where each character of the input sequence is transformed in a token through the embedding, and then introduced into two different dense layers, to produce a query and a key. Assuming a matrix $\mathbf{X}$ containing a sequence, the queries and keys are

$$\begin{aligned} \mathbf{Q} &= \mathbf{W}^{(q)\top}\mathbf{X} \\ \mathbf{K} &= \mathbf{W}^{(k)\top}\mathbf{X} \end{aligned} \tag{6.23}$$

The size of these vectors has been chosen as 16. The dot product between all queries and keys are computed to obtain the attention matrix $\mathbf{A}$ and the upper diagonal of the dot product matrix is discarded by multiplying it by a triangular matrix of ones. This is done so the attention between a character and a future one is not used, so the prediction is based only on past characters. The query is computed with a third linear dense layer as $\mathbf{v}_i = \mathbf{W}^{(v)\top}\mathbf{x}_i$. This vector is then transformed by the attention coefficients to get the attention representation. The representation for the whole sequence is

$$\mathbf{Z} = \text{softmax}(\mathbf{VA}) \tag{6.24}$$

Sixteen of such attention mechanisms are implemented to create a multi-head attention with 16 heads, so 16 attention matrices $\mathbf{A}_1, \ldots, \mathbf{A}_{16}$ are computed, and then 16 attention representations $\mathbf{z}_{i,1}, \ldots, \mathbf{z}_{i,16}$ are obtained. These vectors are then concatenated and used as input of a dense layer with 32 logistic outputs (as many as elements in the input embeddings). The output of this dense layer is used as input of a dense layer with softmax output and length 30, corresponding to the 30 characters.

The whole structure is trained with a cross-entropy or ML criterion and a backpropagation (see Chapter 1). The data is split into a training and a validation set, the first one containing 90% of the data. At every 1000 epochs of the training, the training and validation losses are computed. The evolution of these errors is illustrated in Fig. 6.9. It can be seen that this optimization decreases the error with the number of iterations.

Figure 6.9 Test and validation errors in the text prediction Example 6.2.3.

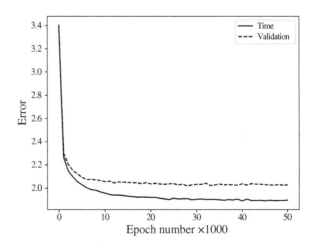

During the test, the structure generates text in a recursive way. When a character is predicted, it is used as input to predict the next one. Nevertheless, this machine still does not work in practice, due to the low complexity of the parameters. For example, the first predicted sentence is *"of theanr the meat,"* which is pure gibberish. The same data is used in Example 6.3.1 below, where an attention mechanism with the same structure that this one is used in a transformer structure, with a more successful result.

Example 6.2.4 **(*Machine translation with encoder–decoder attention*)**
An LSTM network-based encoder–decoder model with attention is utilized to translate text from German to the English language. The encoder interprets the German-language input sequence and stores the relevant data as a context vector. On the other hand, the decoder uses this context vector as input to create the output sequence in English. The network uses the data downloaded from the website: https://tatoeba.org. Tatoeba is an open and free machine translation dataset comprising sentences and translations that are collaboratively contributed by volunteers worldwide. The training set comprises approximately 199,378 sentence pairs in German and English, while the test set encompasses approximately 22,154.

The input text undergoes preprocessing, which involves converting it into lowercase, removing leading and trailing spaces, as well as eliminating punctuation and newline characters using regular expressions. Following preprocessing, the text is tokenized, resulting in a list of tokens that are returned for further processing. Also, special tokens such as <sos> (start of sentence) and <eos> (end of sentence) are included to identify the beginning and conclusion of each sentence. Next, vocabularies are constructed for both the German and English fields using the training data. The vocabulary size is limited to a maximum of 10,000 words, and any word occurring less than twice in the training data is considered an unknown token. As a result, only the 10,000 most frequent words are retained in the vocabulary for each language.

The structure introduced is a sequence-to-sequence model equipped with attention, specifically utilizing a B-LSTM network architecture, as shown in Fig. 6.10. It is composed of three key elements: an encoder, a decoder, and an attention layer. The sequence-to-sequence model takes a source sequence (German) and a target sequence (English) as inputs and generates the translated output sequence. The encoder processes the source sequence, and the decoder generates the target sequence using attention mechanisms to focus on relevant parts of the source during decoding.

The encoder block is configured with the following hyperparameters: It takes the German language's specific vocabulary size as input, utilizes an embedding size of 256, consists of a single layer with 512 hidden units, and incorporates a dropout probability of 0.5 to aid in regularization during the training process. The encoder consists of an embedding layer, an LSTM layer with bidirectional processing, and linear layers for transforming the hidden and cell states. During the forward pass, the input sequence is embedded, passed through the LSTM, and the final hidden and cell states are updated and returned.

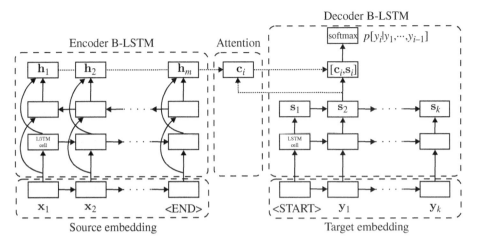

Figure 6.10 The encoder–decoder B-LSTM architecture for German to English translation.

In the same manner, the decoder is composed of an embedding layer of size 256, an LSTM layer, an attention layer, a linear layer responsible for generating the output, and a dropout layer of probability 0.5. During the forward pass, the decoder takes three main inputs: the current target token, the encoder states, and the decoder's previous hidden and cell states. It then calculates attention scores between the encoder states and the previous hidden state of the decoder. These attention scores are combined to form a context vector, which is then concatenated with the current target token's embedding. The combined input is passed through the LSTM layer, and the output from the LSTM is used to predict the next target token in the sequence. Figure 6.10 denotes the architecture of the encoder–decoder model used for translating German to English.

The training procedure is executed for a total of 100 epochs. At each epoch, the model processes batches containing pairs of source and target sequences from the training dataset. The model takes the source sequence and the corresponding target sequence as inputs to generate predictions. The cross-entropy loss is then utilized to compute the loss between the model's predictions and the actual target values. To prevent potential issues with exploding gradients during training, the gradients are computed and clipped. Subsequently, the Adam optimizer is updated with the calculated gradients, and the loss is recorded for the purpose of visualization and monitoring the training progress.

The assessment of the machine translation model involves an evaluation of its performance using the test dataset. Additionally, an attention map is generated to visually evaluate the translation quality of the model. The attention map is displayed as an image, where the x-axis represents the words in the German sentence and the y-axis represents the words in the translated English sentence (see Fig. 6.11). This visualization helps understand which parts of the German sentence the model paid attention to while generating the English translation.

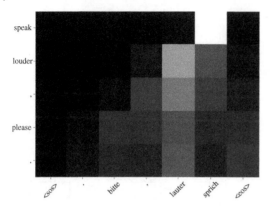

Figure 6.11 Visualization of the attention mechanism of a neural machine translation model, specifically for translating German sentences to English. The attention map is then displayed as a heatmap, with brighter areas indicating higher attention.

Output:

```
ACTUAL GERMAN: . tisch einem an sitzt tom
ACTUAL ENGLISH: tom is sitting at a table .
PREDICTED ENGLISH: tom is sitting on a table .
=====================================================================
ACTUAL GERMAN: . bitte, lauter sprich
ACTUAL ENGLISH: please speak more loudly .
PREDICTED ENGLISH: speak louder, please .
=====================================================================
ACTUAL GERMAN: . aufzupassen kinder toms auf, helfen mir musst du
ACTUAL ENGLISH: i need you to help me take care of tom <unk> kids .
PREDICTED ENGLISH: you need to help me look at tom <unk> children .
=====================================================================
ACTUAL GERMAN: ? das du brauchst <unk>
ACTUAL ENGLISH: what do you need that for ?
PREDICTED ENGLISH: what do you need for for ?
=====================================================================
ACTUAL GERMAN: . sich langweile er, sagte tom
ACTUAL ENGLISH: tom said that he <unk> bored .
PREDICTED ENGLISH: tom said he <unk> bored .
=====================================================================
```

6.3 Transformers

Attention-based models were mainly introduced to perform sequence-to-sequence tasks mainly in language processing, for example, machine translation. Later, they were also extended to accept other types of inputs such as images or videos, an example would be image captioning. The models were initially built with RNN encoder–decoder architecture without attention. Such models were taking input sequences one word at a time and providing the output the same way. Later on, attention was introduced which connected the encoder and decoder parts of the models using the attention mechanism. This helped the models to understand the relationship between the encoder outputs and the hidden states of the decoder.

The encoder–decoder architecture was upscaled in Transformer architecture as it did not use any type of time-series models such as RNNs or LSTMs. Later on, several other variants of transformers were introduced. Most of these models were application-specific. These modified transformer-based architectures mainly constituted the family of large language model (LLM)s. These variants were only either encoder-only models, decoder-only models, or encoder–decoder hybrid models. The encoder-only architectures are autoencoding models that were developed using only the encoder part of the transformer architecture and can be used mainly for classification tasks such as sentiment analysis, named entity recognition (NER), word classification, etc. These models are particularly focused on reconstructing sentences and, therefore, have the denoising objective. The decoder models tend to understand the unidirectional context of the sentence and are autoregressive models. Such models use only the decoder part of the transformer. Additionally, there have been more advanced encoder–decoder architectures that make use of both the components of transformer architecture. These models can be very useful in tasks with varying lengths for input and output sequences as well as in scenarios where there exists a complex mapping between input and output sequences. An example of the tasks would be text summarization and text translation.

In the following, we summarize the most popular architectures that are being used in applications of different domains. We will also explore more about the encoder-only, decoder-only, and encoder-decoder models in detail later.

Transformers are one of the most popular networks that made use of attention mechanism (Vaswani et al. 2017). This architecture was a great advancement in the models using attention mechanisms. In fact, transformer models inspired several advanced NLP-associated architectures such as GPT-2, GPT-3, bidirectional encoder representations from transformer (BERT), etc.

The encoder–decoder architectures that were introduced before made use of RNNs or LSTMs to process sequential data using the attention mechanism. The attention mechanism was incorporated by taking a weighted sum of all the previous encoder states. Therefore, the decoder assigns more importance or greater weight to a particular element of the input. The main disadvantage of this approach was that each input sequence had to be treated as a single element at a time. This results in increased sequential computation, i.e. if we take the input to the encoder as $(\mathbf{x}_1, \mathbf{x}_2, \ldots, \mathbf{x}_n)$ which is converted to a continuous sequence representation of context vector given by $(\mathbf{z}_1, \mathbf{z}_2, \ldots, \mathbf{z}_n)$. Given $\mathbf{c}$, the decoder generates the output sequence $(\mathbf{o}_1, \mathbf{o}_2, \ldots, \mathbf{o}_n)$ one element at a time. Therefore, due to its recurrent nature, the model has to wait for the entire sequence again as the additional input for generating the next. This results in increased time consumption and computational burden. To solve this problem, the transformer model incorporates both stacked self-attention and point-wise, fully connected layers in the encoder–decoder architecture. The features are obtained without using any recurrent units. The efficiency of the structure is improved further by using only weighed sum and activations. This makes the architecture computationally efficient and parallelizable. The complete architecture is shown in Fig. 6.12.

From Fig. 6.12, it is clear that the transformer structure has an encoder part on the left half and a decoder part on the right half. Both the encoder and decoder combine the self-attention mechanism with a position-wise feed-forward network.

The encoder part of the architecture consists of S layers. Each of the layers consists of two sub-layers: one with a multi-head self-attention mechanism introduced in Section 6.2.6,

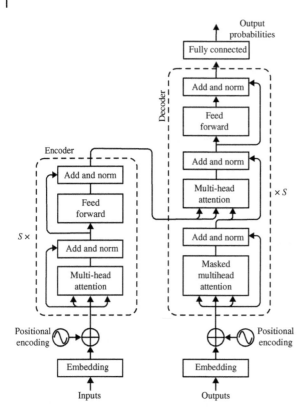

Figure 6.12 The transformer structure. Source: Adapted from Vaswani et al. (2017).

and the second layer is a position-wise fully connected feed-forward network. The structure also uses residual connections for each of the sub-layers. This is then followed by layer normalization (J. L. Ba et al. 2016). The output of each sub-layer is given by

$$\text{LayerNorm}(\mathbf{x} + F_{sl}(\mathbf{x})) \qquad (6.25)$$

where $F_{sl}(\mathbf{x})$ is the function implemented by the given sub-layer. The output dimensions are kept constant. In the original work (Vaswani et al. 2017), the embedding layers as well as all the sub-layers used the same output dimension of $D_{model} = 512$.

The decoder architecture is composed of the same S layers. The decoder architecture has the same sub-layers as the encoder with an added third sub-layer. This third sub-layer performs multi-head attention on the encoder output. The residual connections across each sub-layer are implemented the same way as the encoder layer. Further, layer normalization is also applied toward the end. The self-attention sub-layer is modified in the decoder to prevent the positions from attending consecutive positions.

The multi-head attention layer shared between the encoder and decoder attention layer uses queries from the previous decoder layer and the keys and values are the encoder outputs. This setup is very similar to the encoder–decoder attention technique used in sequence-to-sequence models such that the decoder attends to all the positions in the input sequence. The self-attention layers in both the encoder and decoder are set up such that each position in the encoder/decoder attends to all the positions in the previous layer of the encoder/decoder. However, in the decoder layer to avoid the leftward flow of information masking is performed where the output embeddings are shifted by one position to make sure the predictions of the position t are only dependent on the outputs of positions at instants prior to t. This helps in masking out (setting to $-\infty$) all the input values of the softmax with the illegal connection. This is done using a padding mask and look-ahead mask. The masking operation helps in performing causal attention mainly to discard the outputs occurring in the future.

The transformer architecture uses the scaled dot product introduced in Eq. (6.11), with the normalization or scaling factor $(1/\sqrt{D})$ as the dimension of the keys, i.e. $D = D_k$.

The fully connected feed-forward network is present in both the encoder and decoder. This fully connected network is applied to each of the positions separately. This layer performs two linear transformations with ReLU activations between these transformations, as shown in Eq. (6.26). These linear transformations that are implemented are the same across different positions, however, the parameters stay different from layer to layer.

$$FCN(\mathbf{x}) = \mathbf{W}_2^\top \max(0, \mathbf{W}_2^\top \mathbf{x} + \mathbf{b}_1) + \mathbf{b}_2 \qquad (6.26)$$

As for the sequence input to the models, transformers also make use of embeddings. The embeddings are used to convert the input and output tokens to vectors. These vectors have the dimension D_{model}. Another feature of these networks is the use of the softmax function and learned linear transformation of the decoder output to convert them to probabilities of the next token. Further, the same weight is shared between the pre-softmax layer and two of the embedding layers. However, in the embedding layer, the weights are scaled by a factor of $\sqrt{D_{model}}$.

Example 6.3.1 *(Text generation using a decoder-only transformer architecture)*
In this example, a model to predict text is constructed with the same purpose as in Example 6.2.3, this is, given a sequence of characters, the structure is trained to predict a character given the previous ones. The text used during the training is the same as the one used in Example 6.2.3, but here, the decoder part of the transformer in Fig. 6.12 is used. In the figure, the decoder uses a cross-attention mechanism that takes the key and the query from the encoder. In the present example, the key, query, and value are taken from the previous multi-head attention. The structure is presented in Fig. 6.13.

The description of the blocks is as follows. The output is a vector of probabilities with the same length as the total number of characters in the training set. After a prediction, the predicted character is decided based upon the maximum probability element in the output vector. The input is fed with a sequence of previous predicted characters (during the training, instead of the predicted outputs, the target or desired ones are used). The maximum length of the sequence is set to 256. Each character is passed through an embedding block that produces, for each character, a vector of length 384 (note that in the previous example, the length was 32). Each vector is added a positional encoding.

The first block called the masked multi-head attention, is implemented in a way similar to the one in Example 6.2.3. For each of the six attention heads implemented in this block, a matrix of attention coefficients is computed, and then they are masked with a lower triangular matrix. This way, only the representation of each character is constructed with attention coefficients corresponding to the previous characters. The value is transformed with the six attention coefficient matrices to obtain six attention representations, which

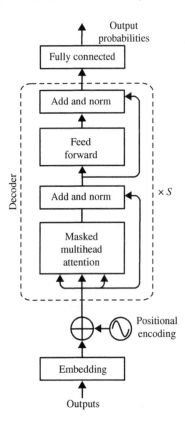

Figure 6.13 Decoder-only transformer structure used in Example 6.3.1.

are concatenated. In this example, the concatenated representations are passed through another linear layer with the same dimensions at the input and output. After this, each attention head is applied a 20% dropoff, and the result is the output of the multi-head attention, which is the attention representation of the input sequence.

This output is passed through an Add and normalization block. If the multi-head attention representation of an element of a sequence is z_i, then the mean and the variance of this vector are computed as

$$\mu_i = \frac{1}{D}\sum_j z_{i,j}$$

$$\sigma_i = \frac{1}{D}\sum_j (z_{i,j} - \mu_i)^2$$

(6.27)

where D is the length of the vector. Then, the vector is normalized with these values. This process is known as (J. L. Ba et al. 2016). The result is added to the input of the previous multi-head attention.

The result of the previous operation is fed into a feed-forward network, which consists of a linear layer, followed by a ReLU activation, another linear layer, and a dropout of 20%. The result is then passed again through an add and normalization block.

This process is repeated $S = 6$ times. The result of this operation is then passed into the fully connected block. In this block, the input is again normalized using the same layer normalization process explained above and then passed through a linear layer with as many inputs as characters in the embedding dictionary.

The structure is trained with an Adam optimizer, a total of 5000 epochs, and a learning rate $\mu = 5 \times 10^{-5}$. The structure is tested to generate several sentences with the result below:

Generated text:

her the jakes wolle the own,
And left long blooked fram with your lack
The gold will behind flaJohbin Maureen.
Where lily wedding, they she lay were girl my now
Where she and Im dweet forget you fall.
The paled shows houses quijewely hence.
Heet ver unery will be hows
There though longs were a gave they bow
Twas down the runky row
Till how the arts now
Twy thy hey same loves easing bright
The mainlys where, here nor plays of wnine
They she eyes protest the for over
My broad friends to rave a see well

While in the previous Example 6.2.3, the generated works did not have any meaning, most of the words generated in this example do have a meaning in English. Nevertheless, the sentences are meaningless, due to the relative simplicity of this model. In a more sophisticated language model, the predictions would be words instead of characters, and the context used to predict (i.e. the sequence used as input to predict the next word) would consist of sentences. This way, the sentences, and not only the words, can constitute meaningful units.

Example 6.3.2 *(Time-series forecast using encoder only transformer architecture)*
Now let us understand the working of transformer architecture from a time-series perspective. In Chapter 5, we used LSTMs and RNNs for performing time-series forecasting. Transformers are mostly used in NLP-related applications. However, we can also use them for time-series classification and forecasting. We will be replicating the Example 5.3.1 using transformer architecture. Note that, here we will be using only the encoder part of the transformer architecture to perform the time-series prediction. In Example 5.3.1, a one-step ahead prediction of a time series data was introduced that consisted of harmonic signal given by Eq. (5.24). The generation of the data and pre-processing part follows the same procedure as in Example 5.3.1. Due to the higher number of parameters of the model, a larger dataset size is used here. Therefore, the training dataset set size is increased to 25,000 samples and the test dataset contains 2500 samples.

The transformer architecture used here consists of only the encoder part. As you can see in Fig. 6.12, the encoder part consists of multi-head attention block, layer normalization and feed-forward part. In this case, for the feed-forward network we can also add additional layers such as convolutional layers to extract more information from the data.

Similar to the encoder block of transformer architecture Fig. 6.12, we have the layer normalization followed by Multi-head attention block. This portion of the encoder block performs normalization followed by attention. The residual connections are also made similar to the original architecture by skipping from input layer to the output of the multi-head attention block.

As for the feed-forward part, again the Layer normalization is performed at the beginning followed by the feed-forward section. So since the main aim was to extract complex features from the data, 1d CNN layers were substituted instead of the usual feed-forward neural network. The skip connections are again made similar to the original architecture. The number of heads is set to 2 and the number of transformer blocks used is 4. After stacking all the transformer blocks, the output is flattened and then finally passed through an LSTM layer with the number of hidden units equal to the number of time steps that is being predicted. The overall architecture used in this experiment is shown in Fig. 6.14.

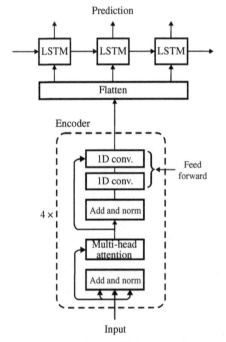

Figure 6.14 Architecture of the transformer model used in Example 6.3.2.

While compiling the model, Adam optimizer is used for optimization and Mean squared error is used as the loss function to track the performance. The training loss is shown in Fig. 6.15. Further, the testing part shows the result of actual vs predicted in Fig. 6.16.

We can improve the model performance even further by modifying and experimenting with the final layers. We can add more LSTM layers which would further help in capturing more time-dependent information.

Figure 6.15 Training loss MSE over 100 epochs in Example 6.3.2.

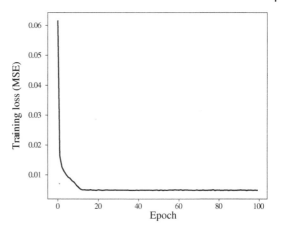

Figure 6.16 Actual vs predicted sequences in Example 6.3.2.

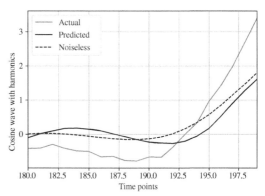

6.4 BERT

The type of structures named Bidirectional Encoder Representations from Transformers (BERT) is a model coming under the family of LMs which was introduced by researchers at Google in 2018 (Devlin et al. 2018). It was originally introduced for English Language and became one of the most famous baseline models for NLP. In particular, this model incorporated the idea of efficient transfer learning in NLP-related tasks.

The main motivation behind such a model was the lack of sufficient training data for specific NLP tasks. Though we have huge amounts of text data to train a model, it is difficult to partition them into datasets dedicated to specific NLP tasks. Even if we split the data into task-specific datasets, it would result in just a few labeled training examples for each of the specific tasks. Most of the deep learning-based NLP methods require a large amount of labeled training samples to perform well. Hence, to tackle this issue with task-specific datasets, the researchers developed generic language representation models trained on huge amount of unlabeled text available on the web. This part of the training is called pre-training. The models are then further fine-tuned to specific NLP task datasets similar to transfer learning. For example, let us say we have a model that can predict the next word in a sentence, and this model was pre-trained on a huge dataset.

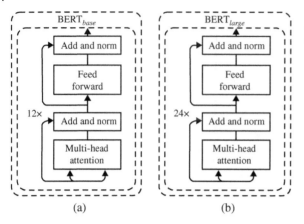

Figure 6.17 BERT architecture with two different sizes. (a) BERT$_{base}$ with 12 layers of transformer blocks. (b) BERT$_{large}$ with 24 layers of transformer blocks.

This model can be used for question–answer tasks by just fine-tuning this model with a small amount of this task-specific labeled dataset constituting question answering (QA) sequences.

6.4.1 BERT Architecture

BERT architecture is based on the transformer architecture introduced in Section 6.3 and consists of the encoder layers from the transformer architecture. The architecture makes use of bidirectional training of the transformer architecture, and it has proven to perform better in the context of LMs. The basic transformer has an encoder and decoder part. The encoder part receives the input text, and the decoder predicts the output for the task. BERT being a language representation model, only the encoder part of the transformer is used.

As for the architecture of BERT, there were two versions introduced in Devlin et al. (2018) shown in Fig. 6.17. BERT$_{base}$ consisted of 12 layers of transformer blocks, 768 hidden units, and 12 self-attention heads in the encoder stack. It has a total of 110M parameters. BERT$_{large}$ is the larger model with 24 layers, 1024 hidden units, and 16 self-attention heads with 340M parameters on the encoder side. Both these models basically had the encoder portion of the transformer architecture. Another notable difference of BERT from other architectures is the use of a different input data representation. The input sentence is not just a sequence of tokens, but it also has the possibility of packing two sentences together.

6.4.2 BERT Pre-training

Prior to BERT, most of the LMs focused on looking at a text in one particular direction from left to right. Most of these models were introduced for completing the sentence by predicting the next word of the sequence. BERT, on the other hand, introduced the idea of bidirectional training which is one of the most important innovations of this model and allowed it to work better to understand the context of the language better than the previous one-directional LMs.

BERT achieves this using two techniques during training. The first one is the use of a method called masked LM (MLM). In this approach, in a sentence, 15% of the words are masked randomly and the model tries to predict these words. The main goal of this approach is to predict the masked words in the sentence, and to perform this, the model needs to understand the full context behind the sentence in any direction. This allows the model to consider both left and right surroundings simultaneously to predict the missing words. This is a very powerful approach as the model now tries to fit in the words based on the context of the sentence. This kind of approach identifies the word based on other words in the sentence. For example, the use of the word "*close*" in both these sentences: *Our home is close to the factory.* and *The shop was closed when I visited.* It can be better understood based on the context of the sentence. The one-directional models might look at the word "*close*" based on only the previous words in the sentence. However, context-based models like that of BERT complete the word using a representation of the other words in the sentence irrespective of the direction.

As for the MLM approach, there can be the problem that the model might get biased to predict the masked token only when it is present in the input. The main goal of this approach is to make sure that the Masked token is predicted regardless. In order to achieve this, some randomizations were introduced in this approach. Out of the 15% of masked tokens, 10% of the time these tokens were replaced with random tokens, 10% of the time the tokens were kept as such, and for the rest of the 80% of the time tokens were actually masked. While training BERT loss function takes only the prediction for the masked tokens into account and ignores predictions related to the normal tokens.

The other unsupervised task introduced during the pre-training of BERT model is the next sentence prediction (NSP). This allows the model to have the ability to understand the relationship between two different sentences. This particular understanding is not captured well across other LMs. This can be very important in NLP tasks such as natural language inference (NLI) and QA. BERT model achieves this by adding additional metadata as a preprocessing step before passing the input to the encoder part. The following embeddings are added to the input embeddings as a preprocessing step (Fig. 6.18):

Token embeddings: This a *[CLS]* token that is added to the input word at the beginning of the first sentence. The *[SEP]* token is included at the end of each sentence.
Segment embeddings: This is introduced for differentiating between the sentences. A marker indicating sentence *A* or *B* is added to each token.
Positional embeddings: The position of each token in the sentence is indicated using this embedding.

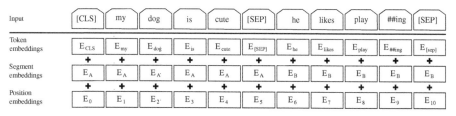

Figure 6.18 Input data representation in BERT. The input embeddings are constructed by adding the token embeddings together with the segmentation and the position embeddings. Source: Reproduced from Devlin et al. (2018).

To facilitate the task of NSP, during the training phase, BERT model receives the input in the form of a pair of sentences, i.e. sentences *A* and *B* per sample. While choosing these sentences as input pairs, it is made sure that 50% of the time the sentence *B* is actually the subsequent sentence of *A* and is labeled as *IsNext*. For the rest of the 50% cases, *B* is a random sentence and is labeled as *NotNext*. Using this approach, the model has to predict whether sentence *B* is random or not based on the pattern of whether there is a disconnection between the sentence pair. Further, several steps are performed to understand if sentence *B* is connected to sentence *A*. Firstly, the whole input sequence is passed through the transformer model. Then, the output having *[CLS]* token is converted into a vector of length 2. This is done using a classification layer. Following this, the sequence is determined to be as *IsNext* sequence using the softmax output of the classifier. The training of the BERT model involves training of both MLM and NSP together to minimize the combined loss function corresponding to both strategies.

6.4.3 BERT Fine-Tuning

Fine-tuning of BERT is performed based on the tasks it is used for. This model can be used for various language tasks with an addition of a small layer. For all of these tasks, the input data was in the form of sentence pairs or text pairs. During fine-tuning the model for individual tasks, the task-specific input sentences are passed into the BERT model and the parameters are fine-tuned end-to-end. The input sentence pair can be the question–answering pair, paraphrasing sentence pair, hypothesis-premise pair, or paragraph summary pair. In the case of classification tasks, such as sentiment analysis or entailment, the *[CLS]* representation is passed to the output layer. As for the token-level tasks, the token representations are passed into the output layer which helps in performing token-level tasks.

6.4.4 BERT for Different NLP Tasks

BERT model was used to train on 11 different tasks.

Sentence classification tasks: One of the main applications that BERT is used for includes classification tasks such as sentiment analysis or Intent classification. In this case, a classification layer with layer weights $\mathbf{W} \in \mathbb{R}^{n \times H}$ (n = number of labels) is added at the top of the transformer output. Also, a final hidden vector $\mathbf{h} \in \mathbb{R}^{H}$ is also added corresponding to the *[CLS]* token. The standard classification loss is computed using

$$l = \log(\mathrm{softmax}(\mathbf{W}^{T}\mathbf{h})) \tag{6.28}$$

In Devlin et al. (2018), the dataset used for testing the classification tasks was the general language understanding evaluation (GLUE) datasets (A. Wang et al. 2018). The fine-tuning was done on these datasets for 3 epochs and the batch size was set to 32. For the most widely used task, MNLI, BERT achieves 4.6% accuracy improvement. It was also observed that BERT_{LARGE} outperforms BERT_{BASE} in all the tasks, mainly for the tasks with limited training data. As for the classification task, a single sentence (Fig. 6.19b) classification or sentence pair (Fig. 6.19a) both are possible. The only difference is that in case of the sentence pair classification tasks, the two sentences are concatenated together for achieving classification.

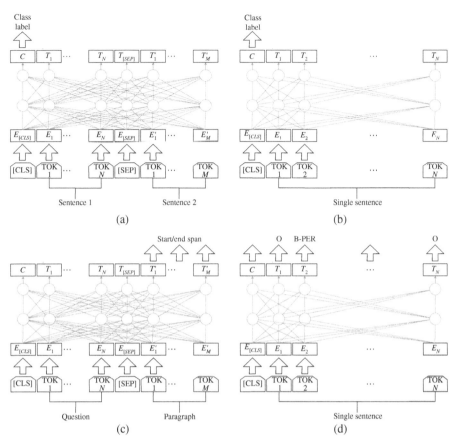

Figure 6.19 Fine-tuning BERT architecture for various NLP tasks. (a) Sentence pair classification tasks. (b) Single sentence classification tasks. (c) Question answering tasks. (d) Single sentence tagging tasks.

Sentence completion: The other task was performed using the situations with adversarial generations (SWAG) dataset. The SWAG dataset included 113,000 sentence-completion examples in the form of sentence pairs (Zellers et al. 2018). This was to evaluate the most plausible continuing sentence or grounded commonsense inference. The main task was to identify the best continuation sentence out of the four choices that were provided. The input representation for this task had four sentence pairs where the given sentence (A) was concatenated with the possible continuation (B), i.e. one of four choices. The only additional parameter that was introduced during fine-tuning is a vector whose dot-product with [CLS] token gives a score for each of the four choices that were normalized using the Softmax layer. For this task, the fine-tuning was done with a batch size of 16, the learning rate of $2e^{-5}$, and the number of epochs for fine-tuning was set to 3.

Question answering: QA task was experimented with using Stanford question answering dataset (SQuAD). SQuAD is a dataset that contains 100,000 question–answer pairs (Rajpurkar et al. 2016). The main task was to identify the text span of the answer in a passage given a question. For this task, the input was represented as the input question

(*A* embedding), and the entire paragraph (*B* embedding) packed together as shown in Fig. 6.19c. The main idea is to identify the start vector and end vector during fine-tuning. The training objective is initialized on the sum of log-likelihoods to identify the exact start and end positions. Again, for this task, the model was fine-tuned for 3 epochs and the batch size was set to 32. A similar approach can be followed for NER task as well.

Single sentence tagging: This task is similar to NER, where the model needs to predict a particular tag for every word in the input. For this task, each of the sentence is tokenized into sub-words which are then passed through the embedding layer. In Fig. 6.19d, we can see that the final hidden states of each of the input token is passed on to a classification layer. Therefore, the model provides predictions for each of these tokens. The labels in this case would be derived from the type of tagging task the model is intended to perform. Each of the sentence in the training data will also have the labels associated with the tagging task.

Overall, The BERT architecture has proved to be an innovative transformer-based architecture for NLP-related tasks with the added advantage of understanding the context of the text, especially in terms of capturing the relationships between words in the sentence. We will now look into an example of Intent classification using BERT.

Example 6.4.1   *(Intent classification using pre-trained BERT model)*
Intent classification refers to the task of determining the intention or purpose behind a given text or user query. It involves categorizing a piece of text into predefined classes or categories based on its intended meaning. It is a fundamental task in natural language understanding (NLU) and plays a crucial role in various applications, including chatbots, virtual assistants, customer support systems, and more. The airline travel information systems (ATIS) dataset is a widely used benchmark dataset for intent classification and slot filling in the field of NLU. It was collected from the travel domain and contains queries and their corresponding intents and slots.

Here are some examples of intents and queries from the ATIS dataset:

- Intent: flight_time, Query: "What time does the flight from Boston to New York depart?"
- Intent: flight_booking, Query: "I want to book a flight from San Francisco to Los Angeles."
- Intent: flight_status, Query: "Is my flight from Chicago to Denver delayed?"
- Intent: flight_cost, Query: "How much does a ticket from Seattle to Houston cost?"
- Intent: airport_information, Query: "What is the phone number for O'Hare International Airport?"

In the ATIS dataset, the intent represents the intention or purpose of the user query. The queries are user-generated sentences or questions related to airline travel information. The dataset also includes slot annotations, where each slot corresponds to a specific piece of information extracted from the query (e.g. source airport, destination airport, departure time, etc.). However, in this example, we are focusing on intent classification. It provides a realistic representation of the types of queries users might ask in the context of airline travel.

The ATIS dataset is composed of user queries and the corresponding intent labels. The intent classification task in this scenario utilizes the BERT model, a state-of-the-art language representation model. The first step involves loading the pre-trained BERT tokenizer, which will be instrumental in processing the text data and converting it into a format suitable for BERT's input. The tokenizer can be applied to a list of sentences, and it will split each sentence into subwords or tokens. The tokenizer replaces each subword in the sentence with its numerical ID, effectively converting the sentence into a sequence of numerical tokens that represent the original text. The BERT model has a fixed vocabulary, containing a predefined set of subwords and special tokens such as "[CLS]" (classification) and "[SEP]" (separator).

For instance, the "[CLS]" token is inserted at the beginning of each input sequence. This token is essential for classification tasks, as it helps BERT understand that the input is meant for classification purposes. On the other hand, the "[SEP]" token is inserted at the end of each input sequence. It is a separator between sentences when dealing with multiple sentences in tasks like sentence pair classification. During tokenization, the tokenizer automatically inserts these special tokens at the appropriate positions in the input sequence to adhere to BERT's input format requirements.

For example, consider the sentence: "What is the flight duration to Los Angeles?" The tokenization process might look like the following:

- **Tokenized sentence**: ["[CLS]," "what," "is," "the," "flight," "duration," "to," "los," "angeles," "?," "[SEP]"]
- **Token IDs**: [101, 2054, 2003, 1996, 3463, 5265, 2000, 7622, 3817, 1029, 102]

Here, "101" corresponds to the ID for the "[CLS]" token, and "102" corresponds to the ID for the "[SEP]" token. The other token IDs represent the numerical IDs for the subwords "what," "is," "the," "flight," "duration," "to," "los," "angeles," and "?" respectively. Thus, the provided train and test sentences are tokenized and encoded using the BERT tokenizer, with truncation and padding applied for consistent input lengths. After this tokenization process, the numerical representation of the sentence is ready to be fed into the BERT model for classification.

The "BertForSequenceClassification" is a pre-trained BERT model fine-tuned specifically for sequence classification tasks. In this instance, the model is loaded from the "bert-base-uncased" variant, which uses the BERT architecture with a pre-trained model on a large corpus of uncased text. Here, the number of labels is set as 8, and it indicates that the model is customized for a sequence classification task with eight different intent classes. This model can input tokenized and encoded sequences and produce classification scores for each intent class as output. The output can be further processed to predict the most probable intent class for a given sentence.

The training parameters are as follows: the batch size is set to 16, the number of epochs is 5, and the learning rate is 0.00001. The optimizer is defined as AdamW, which is a variant of the Adam optimizer specifically designed for Transformer-based models like BERT. The loss function is cross-entropy loss, appropriate for multi-class classification tasks.

Therefore, the mini-batch training efficiently processes the data, calculates loss and accuracy metrics, and prints the results for each epoch, allowing for model performance monitoring and analysis. After the training, the model is put into evaluation mode which calculates the test loss and the number of correctly predicted samples for the test dataset. At the end of the evaluation, the test accuracy is calculated by dividing the number of correctly predicted test samples by the total number of samples in the test dataset.

Output:

```
Epoch 1/5
Train Loss: 199.2293 | Train Accuracy: 0.8244
Test Loss: 11.4113 | Test Accuracy: 0.9425

Epoch 2/5
Train Loss: 52.4783 | Train Accuracy: 0.9617
Test Loss: 2.9591 | Test Accuracy: 0.9900

Epoch 3/5
Train Loss: 23.1584 | Train Accuracy: 0.9857
Test Loss: 1.8841 | Test Accuracy: 0.9950

Epoch 4/5
Train Loss: 12.4296 | Train Accuracy: 0.9948
Test Loss: 1.8042 | Test Accuracy: 0.9938

Epoch 5/5
Train Loss: 6.9761 | Train Accuracy: 0.9979
Test Loss: 1.8635 | Test Accuracy: 0.9925
```

6.5 GPT-2

In the field of NLP, LMs were traditionally applied to tasks like question answering, machine translation, reading comprehension, and summarization. These tasks utilized supervised learning with task-specific datasets. Although these models excelled at their individual tasks due to their training on specific datasets, they often struggled to generalize effectively when encountering new inputs (Recht et al. 2018). Additionally, they were susceptible to even minor changes in data distribution and task requirements (J. Kirkpatrick et al. 2017).

To address this challenge, a shift was proposed toward more general systems capable of performing various tasks without relying on manually created and labeled training datasets for each task. The dominant approach in machine learning involves collecting task-specific training examples, training models to replicate these behaviors, and evaluating their performance on independent and identically distributed held-out examples. While this methodology has successfully advanced narrow expert systems, it reveals its shortcomings when faced with diverse and varied inputs.

The limited generalization observed in current NLP systems can be attributed to their heavy reliance on single-task training with single-domain datasets. To address this challenge and enhance system robustness, researchers have adopted multitask learning (Caruana 1997). This approach involves training models on diverse domains and tasks, ultimately improving overall performance (Yogatama et al. 2019). The current best-performing systems utilize a combination of pre-training and supervised fine-tuning, where models are initially pre-trained on extensive text corpora and then fine-tuned on specific tasks using smaller supervised datasets. This approach has a rich history, following a more flexible transfer methods trajectory. Initially, word vectors were learned and utilized as inputs to task-specific architectures (Mikolov et al. 2013; Collobert et al. 2011). Subsequently, the focus shifted to transferring contextual representations of recurrent networks (Dai and Q. V. Le 2015). More recently, cutting-edge research suggests that task-specific architectures are no longer essential, and the transfer of multiple self-attention blocks alone suffices (Radford et al. 2018; Devlin et al. 2018).

The introduction of zero-shot task transfer (Pal and Balasubramanian 2019) using LMs marks a significant advancement in the field. LMs were found to adeptly handle downstream tasks in a zero-shot setting, without the need for any parameter or architecture modifications. This type of approach demonstrated remarkable potential, showcasing the LMs' versatility in effectively tackling various tasks without explicitly training data for each task.

Learning to perform a single task can be represented as estimating a conditional distribution $p(\text{output} \mid \text{input})$. However, to achieve a more general system that can handle diverse tasks, the model should be conditioned not only on the input but also on the task to be performed, denoted as $p(\text{output} \mid \text{input}, \text{task})$. This formalization is commonly employed in multitasking and meta-learning settings. Such settings can be implemented at the architectural level using task-specific encoders and decoders or at the algorithmic level (Finn et al. 2017).

6.5.1 Language Modeling

Language modeling involves constructing and training a statistical model capable of predicting the probability of word or symbol sequences in a given language. This process entails analyzing extensive textual data and learning the patterns, relationships, and probabilities of different word sequences within the language. By employing LMs, tasks can be defined flexibly, allowing inputs and outputs to be represented as sequences of symbols (McCann et al. 2018).

A highly proficient LM has the potential to deduce and execute diverse tasks presented through natural language sequences, thereby enhancing its predictive abilities, independent of the data's source. In this scenario, the model can effectively engage in unsupervised multitask learning. To explore this notion, LMs' performance is assessed in a zero-shot setting, encompassing a broad spectrum of tasks, to evaluate their capacity to generalize without explicit task-specific training.

Datasets: In most prior studies, LMs were trained on single-domain text sources, such as news articles (Jozefowicz et al. 2016), Wikipedia (Merity et al. 2016), or fiction books (R. Kiros et al. 2015). However, the approach focuses on building a more extensive and diverse dataset, involving the collection of natural language demonstrations of tasks from various domains and contexts. To achieve this, a new web scraping process was developed, prioritizing high-quality documents curated and filtered by human reviewers. The resulting dataset, known as WebText, consists of the textual subset extracted from 45 million links. A combination of content extractors, including Dragnet (Peters and Lecocq 2013) and Newspaper1, was used to extract text from HTML responses.

The following analysis utilized a preliminary version of WebText, which excluded links created after December 2017. After applying de-duplication and heuristic-based cleaning, this preliminary version contains slightly over 8 million documents, with a total text size of approximately 40 GB. To ensure distinct training and evaluation datasets, all Wikipedia documents were removed from WebText, as Wikipedia is a common data source for other datasets and could introduce overlapping training data with the test evaluation tasks.

Input representation: A comprehensive LM should be capable of computing the probability and generating any possible string. However, current large-scale LMs have limitations due to preprocessing steps like lowercasing, tokenization, and out-of-vocabulary tokens, which restrict the range of modellable strings. Although processing Unicode strings as UTF-8-byte sequences addresses this issue, existing byte-level LMs are not as competitive as word-level LMs on vast datasets like the One Billion Word Benchmark (Al-Rfou et al. 2019).

Byte pair encoding (BPE) (Sennrich et al. 2015) is an intermediate solution between character and word-level language modeling, effectively balancing frequent symbol sequences with word-level inputs and infrequent symbol sequences with character-level inputs. While standard BPE implementations use Unicode code points, leading to a large base vocabulary, a byte-level version requires only a smaller vocabulary of size 256. However, directly applying BPE to byte sequences can result in suboptimal merges, leading to the inclusion of multiple variations of common words like "cat" (e.g. "cat," "cat!," and "cat?"). As a consequence, this inefficiently utilizes vocabulary slots and model capacity. To mitigate this, the proposed approach prevents BPE from merging across character categories, except for spaces, optimizing compression efficiency and minimizing word fragmentation. This input representation combines the benefits of word-level language models and the flexibility of byte-level approaches. It enables the evaluation of any Unicode string on various datasets, regardless of preprocessing, tokenization, or vocabulary size.

Model and training: The language model used is built upon the Transformer architecture and bears resemblances to the OpenAI GPT model but with several modifications (see Fig. 6.20). Layer normalization was shifted to the input of each sub-block, resembling a pre-activation residual network. Moreover, an extra layer of normalization was included after the final self-attention block. The model utilizes a modified initialization method that addresses the accumulation on the residual path as the model depth increases. The weights of residual layers were scaled by a factor of $\frac{1}{\sqrt{N}}$, where N corresponds to the number of residual layers. The vocabulary was expanded to 50,257, enabling the model to handle a wider variety of tokens and words. Moreover, the context size was extended from 512 to 1024 tokens, making it easier for the model to understand longer connections between words. Additionally, a larger batch size of 512 was used to improve training efficiency.

Four LMs were trained and evaluated, covering a range of sizes spaced approximately in a log-uniform manner. The smallest model in this setup consists of 12 layers and 117M parameters, making it equivalent to the original GPT. The next size-up comprises 24 layers, matching the largest model in BERT. In contrast, the largest model, known as GPT-2, is composed of 48 layers and 1542M parameters, significantly surpassing the parameter

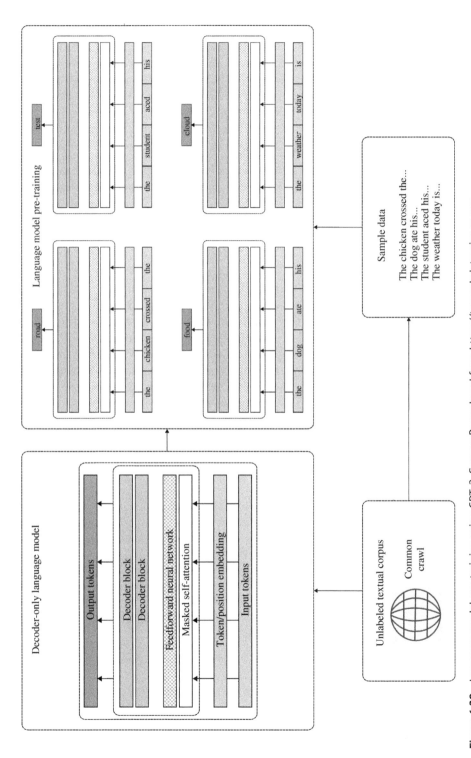

Figure 6.20 Language model pre-training using GPT-2. Source: Reproduced from https://towardsdatascience.com.

count of the original GPT. To optimize the models, the learning rate for each one was manually adjusted to achieve the best perplexity on a 5% held-out sample of WebText.

Zero-shot results: For exploring zero-shot domain transfer, the study aimed to assess the performance of WebText LMs in their primary task of language modeling. The evaluation was conducted by computing the log probability of datasets using a WebText LM and dividing it by the number of canonical units, such as characters, bytes, or words. The WebText LMs were tested on diverse datasets, presenting out-of-distribution challenges, including standardized text, tokenization artifacts, shuffled sentences, and even rare strings like "<UNK>" occurring only 26 times in 40 billion bytes.

As depicted in Table 6.1, WebText LMs exhibited strong domain transfer capabilities across various datasets, surpassing state-of-the-art approaches on 7 out of 8 datasets in a zero-shot setting. Significant improvements were evident on smaller datasets, such as Penn treebank (PTB) and WikiText-2, which contained only 1 to 2 million training tokens (Gong et al. 2018). The model also demonstrated substantial progress on datasets specifically designed to assess long-term dependencies, such as LAMBADA (Paperno et al. 2016) and the children's book test (CBT) (Hill et al. 2015). However, when compared to prior work on the one billion word (1BW) Benchmark (Chelba et al. 2013), this model's performance was notably lower, attributed to the dataset's size and highly disruptive pre-processing, including sentence-level shuffling that removed all long-range structures.

GPT-2's performance was assessed in various tasks, including question answering, reading comprehension, summarization, and translation. The Winograd Schema Challenge was designed to assess a system's capacity for commonsense reasoning by evaluating its ability to resolve ambiguities in the text. In this challenge, GPT-2 achieved a 7% improvement in accuracy, surpassing the previous state-of-the-art in the Winograd Schema Challenge. For reading comprehension, GPT-2 either matched or surpassed three out of four baseline systems. In the summarization task, it was only marginally better than randomly selecting three sentences from the article, and it dropped when the task hint was removed. Meanwhile, in translation tasks, GPT-2 demonstrated lower performance

Table 6.1 Zero-shot results of GPT-2 on different datasets.

Dataset	Evaluation metric	Value
LAMBADA	Accuracy	63.24
	Perplexity	8.63
CBT-Common Nouns	Accuracy	93.30
CBT-Named Entities	Accuracy	89.05
WikiText2	Perplexity	18.34
PTB	Perplexity	35.76
enwik8	Bits per character	0.93
text8	Bits per character	0.98
WikiText103	Perplexity	17.48
1BW	Perplexity	42.16

compared to a bilingual lexicon-based method for French-to-English translation. However, for English-to-French translation, it surpassed many unsupervised baselines, although still falling short of the current best-unsupervised translation approach. In question answering, GPT-2 provided a reasonable probability estimate of giving an accurate answer and demonstrated good performance in the 30 most confident questions, achieving an accuracy of 63.1%. However, it was noticeably less effective than the state-of-the-art approach.

Example 6.5.1 *(Text generation using pre-trained GPT-2)*
Text generation is an NLP task that involves producing coherent and contextually relevant textual content. It has a wide range of applications, including chatbots, creative writing, content generation, code generation, translation, summarization, and more. The goal of text generation is to create human-like text that follows grammatical rules, maintains context, and conveys meaningful information.

The given example showcases the utilization of the Hugging Face Transformers library for generating text through a pre-trained GPT-2 language model. The code utilizes the GPT2LMHeadModel and GPT2Tokenizer classes from the Transformers library, which simplifies the process of working with language models. The "GPT2LMHeadModel" class represents the GPT-2 language model, while the "GPT2Tokenizer" class handles the tokenization of input text. Next, a prompt is established for initiating the text generation. The prompt is a short introductory sentence: "On a distant planet, a curious explorer stumbles upon an ancient temple guarded by." This will serve as the starting point for the generated text.

Subsequently, the GPT2Tokenizer is employed to perform tokenization on the provided prompt. Tokenization involves the division of the input text into smaller entities referred to as tokens. These tokens are the fundamental building blocks that the GPT-2 model comprehends. This tokenization procedure yields two important outputs: "input_ids" and "attention_mask." The "input_ids" represents the tokenized form of the prompt, and the "attention_mask" is used to specify which tokens the model should pay attention to during text generation. To initiate text generation, the pre-trained model is provided with inputs including the tokenized input, attention mask, maximum generated text length, end-of-sequence token ID, and the desired count of generated sequences. The generated text is then decoded so that it converts the token IDs back into human-readable text. Various decoding techniques can be configured based on the desired output style, such as controlling the level of randomness, temperature settings, and other relevant parameters. Temperature setting refers to a parameter that influences the randomness and creativity of the generated text. It is a value that controls the likelihood of selecting less probable words during the generation process. The different decoding methods available are as follows:

Greedy search: It is a technique that involves selecting the word with the highest probability from the set of all possible words at each step of the generation process. This method is employed when no specific parameters are provided for the generation process. The resulting text generated using Greedy Search remains consistent for a given prompt, meaning that if the same starting point is used, the generated text will be identical. However, there are notable issues associated with greedy search. Firstly, its deterministic nature can lead to repetitive and predictable output, resulting in a lack of diversity in the generated content. Additionally, greedy search tends to disregard words with lower probabilities that could lead to more coherent and contextually relevant sentences in the longer term.

Beam search: It is an enhanced text generation technique that maintains a collection of the top B sequences with the highest probabilities at each generation step, ultimately selecting the sequence with the highest cumulative probability as the final output. The parameter B, determines the number of sequences retained and considered during each step of generation. However, beam search introduces certain challenges. One significant issue is its tendency to generate repetitive sequences, making it difficult to control the diversity and creativity of the generated content. Unlike human language, which embraces variety and spontaneity, beam search can produce predictable and monotonous language patterns.

Sampling: It is a text generation approach that injects randomness into the process by selecting the next word according to a probability distribution derived from preceding words. Here the concept of temperature adjustment is used to modulate the likelihood of word selection. Top K sampling is a variant of sampling that adds an element of control. In this method, the top K words with the highest probabilities are identified based on the given distribution. Subsequently, the next word is selected randomly from this reduced set of K words. On the other hand, Top-P sampling takes a different approach. It involves choosing the next word from words that cumulatively account for a probability greater than or equal to p. Both these approaches strike a balance between randomness and control, allowing for creative and varied text generation while ensuring that the chosen words are still among the most probable options.

In this instance, we utilize the beam search method for decoding. Below, you will find the prompt and the resulting generated text.

Output:

```
Prompt: On a distant planet, a curious explorer stumbles upon an ancient
                      temple guarded by

Generated Text 1: On a distant planet, a curious explorer stumbles upon an
                      ancient temple guarded by a
                      mysterious creature. The creature is
                      a giant, with a long, dark, and
                      twisted body.
```

6.6 Vision Transformers

The emergence of the ViT (Dosovitskiy et al. 2020) represents a significant advancement in integrating language and vision within a single model architecture. In 2021, this transformer model showcased superior performance and efficiency compared to CNNs for image classification tasks. Subsequently, a study conducted in June 2021 incorporated a transformer backend into ResNet, resulting in a substantial reduction in costs and improved accuracy (B. Wu et al. 2020; Xiao et al. 2021). ViT has recently emerged as a compelling alternative to CNNs, which currently serve as the state-of-the-art for various computer vision tasks related to image recognition. ViTs find wide-ranging applications in various popular image recognition tasks, encompassing object detection, image segmentation, image classification, and action recognition (Khan et al. 2022).

Transformer models are typically designed to process inputs in the form of words or tokens. However, when considering the application of transformers to image recognition, there arises a need to establish an analogous concept to words in the context of images. One approach includes treating each pixel as an individual word. Nevertheless, it should be acknowledged that the computational complexity associated with calculating the attention matrix is $O(N^2)$, where N denotes the sequence length. If we were to treat each pixel as a distinct word, an example being a relatively modest image size of 64×64, the resulting attention matrix would assume dimensions of 4096×4096. Clearly, this presents an intractable computational burden, even for the most powerful GPUs.

Hence, ViT models employ a strategy that involves treating patches of pixels of the input. Within this framework, the RGB image I with dimensions $M_I \times N_I \times C_I$ is divided into fixed-sized patches of $P_I \times P_I \times C_I$. Each patch is then flattened and passed through a trainable linear layer called an embedding layer. The primary purpose of the embedding layer is to convert the flattened patch, which is initially a high-dimensional input, into a lower-dimensional representation called an embedding. This conversion is accomplished using a set of adjustable weights. By applying the same weights to all image patches, the embedding layer ensures that patches with similar visual characteristics have similar embedded representations. These resulting vectors with dimension D serve as patch embeddings, representing the information within each small image patch. Subsequently, the patch embeddings are flattened and used as a sequence of tokens, which are fed into the transformer model. Position embeddings are added to the patch embeddings to preserve positional information. Standard learnable 1D position embeddings are used, as no significant performance gains have been observed from the utilization of more advanced 2D-aware position embeddings. Overall, during the first step, the ViT model encodes an image by arranging it into a sequence of fixed-size patches that do not overlap. These patches are then subjected to linear embedding, transforming them into 1D vectors, considered input tokens within the transformer architecture, as depicted in Fig. 6.21.

The tokens are then fed into a transformer encoder, which includes multiheaded self-attention (MSA), MLP blocks, and Layernorm. In the ViT, MSA involves performing parallel self-attention operations, with each attention head focusing on different input patches of the input image. MLP blocks in the ViT process the information extracted by the self-attention mechanism. These blocks consist of two fully connected layers, followed by the application of a Gaussian error linear unit (GELU) activation function (Hendrycks and Gimpel 2016). Following this, Layernorm is employed to normalize the activations within each layer of the transformer encoder. It contributes to training stability and enhances the overall model performance. Hence, these components work together to capture complex relationships and dependencies between the input tokens and generate meaningful output predictions for image recognition tasks.

In the context of image classification, CNNs have an inductive bias for spatial locality and translation equivariance. This bias assumes that local patterns and features are important

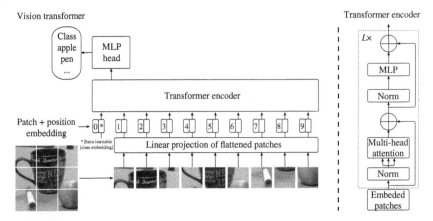

Figure 6.21 Structure of the Vision Transformer. The image is split into a set of patches with fixed size, and they are then linearly embedded. The embeddings are used as input for a standard transformer encoder. The classification is performed through the technique of adding an extra learnable classification token. Source: Dosovitskiy et al. 2020/Cornell University.

for image understanding and that the spatial arrangement of features is preserved across the image. The ViT exhibits a significantly lower image-specific inductive bias compared to CNNs. In contrast, the ViT's MLP layers are the only components that possess a local receptive field, while the self-attention layers operate globally, allowing each token to attend to all other tokens. This global perspective enables the model to understand the contextual information and long-range dependencies within the input. The ViT makes limited use of the two-dimensional neighborhood structure. It is mainly employed at the initial stages of the model, where the image is divided into patches. Additionally, during fine-tuning, the position embeddings are adjusted to accommodate images with different resolutions. However, apart from these cases, the position embeddings at the start do not encode any information about the 2D positions of the patches. Consequently, all spatial relationships between the patches need to be learned from the beginning.

6.6.1 Comparison between ViTs and CNNs

The original research on ViTs investigates the ability of three models, namely ResNet, ViT, and a hybrid model, to learn representations. The hybrid model presents an alternative approach where the input sequence is constructed from feature maps obtained through a CNN, rather than using raw image patches. In this model, the patch embedding projection is applied to patches extracted from a CNN feature map. To understand the data requirements of each model, pre-training is conducted on datasets of varying sizes, and their performance is evaluated on numerous benchmark tasks. When considering the computational cost of pre-training, ViT demonstrates highly favorable performance, achieving state-of-the-art results on most recognition benchmarks at a lower pre-training cost.

The experiment involved the utilization of a few pre-training datasets. These include the ILSVRC-2012 ImageNet dataset with 1000 classes and 1.3 million images, its superset ImageNet-21k (Jia Deng et al. 2009) with 21,000 classes and 14 million images, and

Table 6.2 Exploring ViT model alternatives.

Models	ViT-Base	ViT-Large	ViT-Huge
Layers	12	24	32
Hidden size	768	1024	1280
MLP size	3072	4096	5120
Heads	12	16	16
Params	86M	307M	632M

JFT (C. Sun et al. 2017) with 18,000 classes and 303 million high-resolution images. The pre-trained models were tested on several benchmark datasets: ImageNet using both the original validation labels and the cleaned-up ReaL labels (Beyer et al. 2020), CIFAR-10/100 (A. Krizhevsky 2009), Oxford-IIIT Pets (Parkhi et al. 2012), and Oxford Flowers-102 (Nilsback and Zisserman 2008). Additionally, the Visual Task Adaptation Benchmark (VTAB) classification suite (Zhai et al. 2019), comprising 19 diverse tasks was also evaluated. VTAB measures transfer learning performance across various tasks using 1000 training examples per task. The tasks are categorized into natural, specialized (medical and satellite imagery), and structured tasks (requiring geometric understanding).

ViT configurations are based on those employed for BERT (Devlin et al. 2018), as summarized in Table 6.2. The "Base" and "Large" models are directly adapted from BERT, and a larger "Huge" model is added to this work. In the subsequent discussion, a concise notation is used to denote the model size and input patch size. For instance, ViT-L/16 represents the "Large" variant with a 16×16 input patch size. The sequence length of the Transformer is inversely proportional to the square of the patch size, resulting in smaller patch sizes requiring more computational resources. In the case of the baseline CNNs, ResNet is utilized, with the replacement of batch normalization layers by group normalization and the adoption of standardized convolutions (Qiao et al. 2019). These adjustments result in enhanced transfer capabilities (Kolesnikov et al. 2020), and the modified model is denoted as ResNet (BiT). In the case of the hybrid model, the intermediate feature maps are fed into ViT with a patch size of one pixel.

All models, including ResNets, are trained using Adam with $\beta_1 = 0.9, \beta_2 = 0.999$, a batch size of 4096, and a high weight decay of 0.1. For fine-tuning, SGD with momentum and a batch size of 512 is employed for all models. In the ImageNet results presented in Fig. 6.22, fine-tuning is conducted at higher resolutions: 512 for ViT-L/16 and 518 for ViT-H/14. Additionally, Polyak & Juditsky (1992) averaging with a factor of 0.9999 is applied (Ramachandran et al. 2019). Figure 6.22 shows the comparison made between two large models, ViT-H/14 and ViT-L/16, and state-of-the-art CNNs from the literature. The first point of comparison was with BigTransfer (BiT), which utilizes supervised transfer learning with large ResNets. The second comparison involved NoisyStudent, a large EfficientNet trained using semi-supervised learning on ImageNet and JFT300M with removed labels. NoisyStudent currently holds the state-of-the-art position on ImageNet, while BiT-L performs well on the other datasets considered in this research.

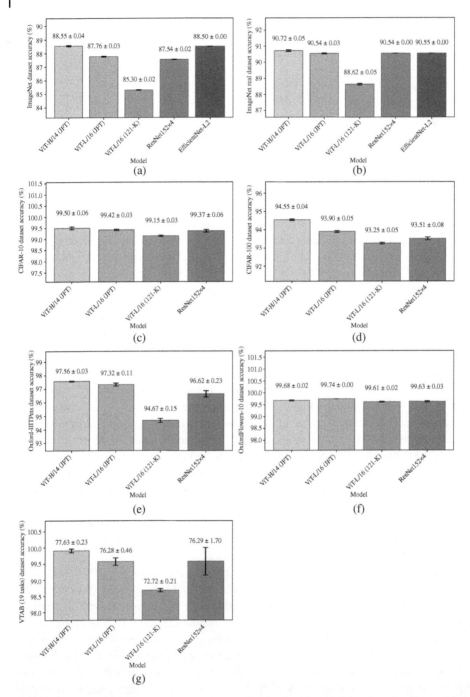

Figure 6.22 Assessment of popular image classification benchmarks by comparing them with the ViTs. The different databases used are: (a) ImageNet, (b) ImageNet Real (c) CIFAR-10, (d) CIFAR-100 (e) Oxford-IIIT Pets (f) Oxford Flowers-102 (g) and the VTAB (19 tasks).

The models were trained on TPUv3 hardware, and the pre-training process took 2.5 k, 0.68 k, 0.23 k, 9.9 k, and 12.3 k TPUv3-core-days for ViT-H/14 (JFT), ViT-L/16 (JFT), ViT-L/16 (I21-K), ResNet152x4, and EfficientNet-L2, respectively. TPUv3-core-days is a metric obtained by multiplying the number of TPUv3 cores (2 per chip) used for training by the training duration in days. The results indicate that the smaller ViT-L/16 model, pre-trained on JFT-300M, outperforms ResNet152x4 pre-trained on the same dataset on all tasks while demanding significantly fewer computational resources for training. The larger model, ViT-H/14, further enhances performance, particularly on more challenging datasets like ImageNet, CIFAR-100, and the VTAB suite. Notably, even the larger model required considerably less computation to complete pre-training compared to prior state-of-the-art methods.

Finally, the ViT-L/16 model pre-trained on the public ImageNet-21k (I21-K) dataset also demonstrated strong performance across most datasets while necessitating fewer resources for pre-training. Specifically, this model could be trained using a standard cloud TPUv3 with 8 cores in approximately 30 days.

Example 6.6.1 *(Image captioning using pre-trained ViT)*
Image captioning constitutes an end-to-end sequence-to-sequence embedding task, where the input sequences are image pixels, and the desired output is a caption that describes the image. This example uses a pre-trained image captioning model to generate captions for images. The model employed for image captioning is the vit-gpt2-image-captioning model, made accessible through the Hugging Face library. Hugging Face is an open-source platform for data science and machine learning, empowering users to create, train, and deploy machine learning models. A standout feature of the platform is its transformer library, which is specifically designed for NLP applications.

Three pre-trained models from the Transformers library have been introduced. Let's now provide a brief overview of their functions.

VisionEncoderDecoderModel: This model is a combination of two powerful architectures: ViT and GPT-2 (Radford et al. 2019). ViT was originally designed for image classification tasks. It applies the Transformer architecture, initially developed for NLP, to process image data. The core concept of ViT involves treating the input image as a sequence of patches, which are then fed into a standard Transformer encoder. By dividing the image into smaller patches and applying linear projections, spatial information is embedded into the patch embeddings. These embeddings, along with positional embeddings, undergo multiple Transformer layers to capture both global and local dependencies within the image.

GPT-2 is a LM based on the Transformer architecture. It is trained on a large corpus of text data, allowing it to generate coherent and contextually relevant text. The model follows a decoder-only architecture, utilizing multiple stacked Transformer decoder layers to generate text while attending to previously generated tokens and their context. By combining the strengths of ViT and GPT-2, the ViT-GPT2 architecture enhances ViT with the powerful language generation capabilities of GPT-2. Thus, the ViT-GPT2 model combines a vision encoder and a language decoder, leveraging both visual and textual information for image captioning.

GPT2TokenizerFast: This tokenizer is specifically designed for the GPT-2 LM. It has been developed using the Hugging Face tokenizers library, which has been integrated into the transformer's framework. This tokenizer comes pre-trained and is fully equipped to handle all the essential features necessary for the captioning task. With its pre-training, the GPT2TokenizerFast efficiently tokenizes input text, breaking it down into individual tokens, subwords, or special tokens that the GPT-2 model can understand and process. Additionally, the tokenizer handles tasks like padding, truncation, and special token embeddings required to facilitate the captioning process effectively.

Moreover, this tokenizer has been trained to treat spaces as integral parts of the tokens. This means that how a word is encoded will depend on its position in the sentence, especially concerning spaces before or after the word.

For instance, consider the word "example" in the following two sentences:

- This is an example.
- Example is given here.

In the first sentence, the word "example" is at the end of the sentence and follows a space after "an." In the second sentence, "example" is at the beginning of the sentence and does not have a space before it. Due to the tokenizer's training, these two instances of the word "example" will be encoded differently, reflecting their unique positions in their respective sentences. This behavior helps the model understand sentence structures and relationships between words, contributing to more accurate and context-aware language generation and processing. Hence by utilizing the GPT2TokenizerFast, we can efficiently prepare textual data to be fed into the GPT-2 model for generating high-quality and contextually appropriate captions.

ViTImageProcessor: It is responsible for processing the image before training, such as normalizing and resizing the image into the appropriate dimensions. Additionally, it performs data augmentation to improve model generalization and performance.

In this example, a pre-trained ViT-GPT2 model is employed to perform image captioning on a sample test image. The initial step involves loading essential components such as the pre-trained model, tokenizer, and image processor. In this case, since the image is loaded from a web URL. Once the image is loaded, it needs to be preprocessed to prepare it for input to the pre-trained model. The image is passed through the ViT Image Processor which applies transformations such as resizing, normalization, and converting the image to a tensor.

After the image is preprocessed, it is passed as input to the pre-trained model and generates captions based on the visual features extracted from the image by the vision encoder. The captions are generated using the language decoder component of the ViT-GPT2 architecture. The generated captions are in the form of sequences of tokens. The GPT2TokenizerFast is used to convert these tokenized sequences back into human-readable text strings. It helps to reconstruct the original sentences by removing any special tokens or special formatting added during tokenization. Figure 6.23 displays the sample image and its generated caption.

A woman walking down a path with a backpack Diana Piklaps / Pexels

Figure 6.23   Image captioning using pre-trained ViT.

6.7   Conclusion

Transformers are an important breakthrough in DL because they achieved previously unseen results in language processing, including machine translation, text summarization, text generation, and many others, but the use of these techniques also produced important advances in image processing, including synthetic image generation, image captioning or image classification, just to cite some.

Attention mechanisms are at the core of transformers, and they are an efficient way of representing input features as a combination of other features given by attention scores. These scores determine which parts of the input sequence (for example a sentence of arbitrary length or a sequence of patches of an image) are relevant for the representation. This methodology to code an input differs from the traditional methods that are intended to extract the information present in the data in order to compress it. Attention mechanisms are closer to the behavior of the brain by taking these elements of a sequence that are relevant and discarding the rest. Self-attention criteria are constructed by linear transformation of the sequences tokens that are learned by backpropagation according to the task at hand, which can be supervised or unsupervised, and multiple attention heads are used simultaneously in order to provide the machine with an unprecedented expressive capability.

The original transformer structure used for machine translation has been presented in this chapter, which is an encoder–decoder structure where the encoding is based on self-attention mechanisms and the decoder is based on a cross-attention mechanism between the source sequence and the elements of the target sequence previously decoded. After this, particular attention has been given to the BERT structure, which is based on an encoder architecture only, and to the GPT model, based on this structure. Examples of application of this structure have been presented.

Finally, the main vision transformers have been described and examples have been presented for image classification and image captioning.

Problems

6.1 *Reproduce Example 6.2.1 for different values of the width parameter h. What is the effect of using a very small or very high value for this parameter in the estimation and in the attention matrix?*

6.2 *Complete the derivation of the backpropagation equations for the self-attention weights that are presented in Section 6.2.5.*

6.3 *Adapt the Example 6.2.4 to develop a transformer model to perform German-to-English text translation. Compute the BLEU scores and compare the results with the B-LSTM encoder–decoder in Example 6.2.4.*

6.4 *Investigate the application of transformers in the domain of protein structure prediction by using the critical assessment of structure prediction (CASP) dataset (Kryshtafovych et al. 2021). The dataset contains a collection of amino acid sequences along with their corresponding experimentally determined 3D structures, and it can be downloaded from the website https://www.predictioncenter.org/download_area.*

1. *Design a transformer-based model to predict the 3D structure of proteins from their amino acid sequences.*
2. *Explain how the self-attention mechanism can be utilized to capture long-range dependencies between amino acids and aid in accurately predicting the protein's structure.*
3. *Compare the performance of your transformer-based model with traditional methods used for protein structure prediction, discussing both accuracy and computational efficiency.*
4. *Highlight the potential advantages and challenges of using transformers for this critical bioinformatics task.*

6.5 *Modify the Example 6.5.1 and implement decoding methods such as beam search and sampling and compare the outcomes. Analyze how each decoding method influences the quality and style of the generated text.*

6.6 *Reproduce the image classification experiment conducted in the ViT paper (Dosovitskiy et al. 2020) for different patch sizes and analyze their impact on classification accuracy. Explain how changing the patch size affects the model's ability to capture local and global image features.*

6.7 *Implement a fine-tuning pipeline for the BERT model on a sentiment analysis task using a dataset of your choice. Train the model and evaluate its performance on a test set. Discuss the challenges of choosing an appropriate learning rate and batch size during fine-tuning and how they can impact the model's convergence and final accuracy.*

6.8 *Develop a custom multi-head attention module in PyTorch or Keras. Use it to process an input sequence and visualize the attention weights for different heads.*

6.9 *Design an experiment to evaluate the impact of different positional encoding schemes in transformer models. Compare the results with and without positional encodings.*

6.10 *Explain the concept of transfer learning with pre-trained models like BERT and GPT-2.*

    1. *Discuss the advantages of transfer learning, such as improved performance, reduced training data requirements, and faster convergence in downstream tasks.*

    2. *Explore the limitations of pre-trained models, including computational resources, model size, and domain-specific adaptability.*

7

Deep Unsupervised Learning I

7.1 Introduction

In the field of artificial intelligence and machine learning, there exists a fascinating subfield known as unsupervised deep learning. Unsupervised learning techniques play an important role in revealing hidden patterns and representations within large and complex datasets, without the need for explicit labels. In contrast to supervised learning, which depends on having labeled examples to make predictions, unsupervised learning operates in a self-guided manner. It seeks to capture complex relationships, dependencies, and latent features that exist within data, making it invaluable in scenarios where labeled data is scarce or expensive to obtain. In this case, three models have become essential components of deep unsupervised learning: restricted Boltzmann machine (RBM), autoencoder (AE), and deep belief networks (DBNs).

RBMs are a type of probabilistic graphical model that excels at learning intricate patterns in high-dimensional data. They are composed of visible and hidden layers of binary units, connected by weighted edges. Through a process called *Gibbs sampling*, RBMs iteratively adjust their parameters to approximate the data distribution. Gibbs sampling effectively explores the joint probability distribution of the visible and hidden units in the RBM. By iteratively updating the states of these units, it allows the RBM to learn and adapt its weights and biases to better match the data distribution. Over time, as more Gibbs sampling steps are performed, the RBM converges to a state that approximates the data distribution more accurately. RBMs have found applications in diverse domains, including recommendation systems (R. Salakhutdinov et al. 2007), dimensionality reduction (Van Der Maaten et al. 2009), and feature learning (Längkvist et al. 2014), as they can efficiently capture complex data representations.

AE, on the other hand, are NN architectures designed for unsupervised feature learning and data compression. They were initially explored in the 1990s for non-linear data compression, extending the concept of principal component analysis (PCA). An AE consists of an encoder and a decoder, where the encoder maps the input data into a lower-dimensional bottleneck layer (latent space), and the decoder reconstructs the original input from this representation. The output vector from the bottleneck layer in AEs can be employed for non-linear data compression. The goal of training an AE is to minimize the

Deep Learning: A Practical Introduction, First Edition.
Manel Martínez-Ramón, Meenu Ajith, and Aswathy Rajendra Kurup.
© 2024 John Wiley & Sons Ltd. Published 2024 by John Wiley & Sons Ltd.
Companion website: https://github.com/DeepLearning-book

reconstruction error, effectively forcing it to capture the most salient features of the data. AEs have become instrumental in various domains, such as image denoising (Gondara 2016), anomaly detection (Sakurada and Yairi 2014), and generative modeling (Yoshua Bengio et al. 2013).

DBNs were initially introduced as probabilistic generative models to provide an alternative to the discriminative nature of traditional neural nets. It is a specific type of deep neural network (DNN) that consists of layers stacked with RBMs. They leverage the strengths of both RBMs and NNs to create hierarchical representations of data. The RBM layers capture low-level features, while the neural network layers learn increasingly abstract and complex representations. Moreover, DBNs are versatile in their applications, as they can address unsupervised learning challenges by reducing feature dimensionality and also handle supervised learning tasks for constructing classification or regression models.

These unsupervised learning methods have found applications in a wide range of domains, addressing challenges where obtaining labeled data is difficult or costly. By letting algorithms uncover meaningful insights on their own, unsupervised learning can unlock the full potential of data, paving the way for improved decision-making, data-driven discoveries, and enhanced model performance across a wide range of applications.

7.2 Restricted Boltzmann Machines

A RBM is a neural structure introduced by Geoffrey E. Hinton and Sejnowski (1983) and Ackley et al. (1985), used to represent a domain from examples of that domain. This way, the machine constructs a generative model that can produce examples with the same probability distribution as the distribution of the examples presented.

7.2.1 Boltzmann Machines

The RBM is constructed from the concept of the Boltzmann machine (BM), which is a structure of nodes s_i (see Fig. 7.1) fully connected through bidirectional edges. Each connection between node i and node j has a bidirectional weight $w_{ij} \in \mathbb{R}$. Each node has a binary state 1 or 0, that are computed probabilistically as a function of the states of its connected nodes and their corresponding weights. If two connected nodes have a positive weight, this means that both nodes positively support their state, and when a weight is negative, that means that each node negates the state of the other. The structure is equal to the Hopfield Network (Hopfield 1982), mentioned in Section 5.2.

The global state of the network can be described by a function called the *energy* of the system, which is defined as

$$E = -\sum_{i<j} w_{ij} s_i s_j - \sum_i b_i s_i \tag{7.1}$$

The energy of the system can be interpreted as to what extent the combination of states violates the constraints implicit in the problem domain. The minimization of the energy produces an interpretation of the input that satisfies increasingly the constraints of the problem domain. A simple algorithm to find the values of the free states that find a local

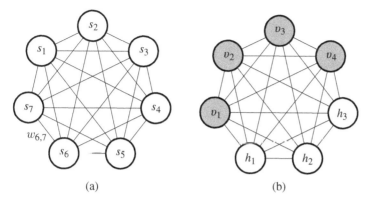

Figure 7.1 (a) A fully connected Boltzmann machine. Each node has a binary state $s_i \in \{0,1\}$. Each pair s_i, s_j of nodes are connected by weight $w_{i,j}$. (b) A Boltzmann machine with hidden nodes h_i and visible nodes v_i. Visible nodes can be clamped or given particular states during training.

minimum in the energy is simply to switch each hypothesis into the state that gives the minimum energy. Indeed, the energy gap between states of node j, or the energy contribution related to the choice of state 1 for node j is

$$\Delta E_j = \sum_i w_{ij} s_i + b_j \tag{7.2}$$

If the contribution of forcing state $s_j = 1$ decreases the energy, the state is chosen. Otherwise, the state is rejected. To escape the local minima, noise can be added to the decision by choosing states in a stochastic way. The method adopted in Geoffrey E. Hinton and Sejnowski (1983) consists of choosing state 1 with probability

$$p_j = \frac{1}{1 + e^{\frac{-\Delta E_j}{T}}} = \sigma\left(\frac{\Delta E_j}{T}\right) \tag{7.3}$$

where T is a parameter that can be interpreted as a temperature. This function is a logit where if the temperature is $T = 0$, the derivative at the origin is infinite, and when the temperature increases, the derivative decreases. If the temperature is zero, then the decision is hard (we choose $h_k = 1$ if $\Delta E_k > -b_j$ and zero otherwise). If the temperature is positive, the probability of $s_k = 1$ increases with the energy gap. The ratio between the probabilities of the two states obeys the *Boltzmann distribution*

$$\frac{p_0}{p_1} = e^{\frac{E_1 - E_0}{T}} \tag{7.4}$$

The model in Eq. (7.3) is very important for the solvability of the problem, as it uses a probabilistic representation that describes the behavior of the nodes rather than their states, and it is based on a differentiable function that makes the problem mathematically tractable.

7.2.2 Training a Boltzmann Machine

Assume that a subset of the nodes are *clamped* or forced to be in a certain state for training purposes. These are the *visible* nodes v_i, while the nodes that are not clamped are the *hidden* nodes h_i. To train the parameters, at each step of the training, two phases are defined.

In the positive phase, the visible units are clamped according to the given inputs, and the probabilities of the hidden units are modeled using these inputs. We define distribution over the training set as $p(\mathbf{v})$. In the negative phase, the clamping is removed and the probabilities of the visible nodes are computed from the hidden nodes as $p(\mathbf{v'})$. Then, the Kullback–Leibler (KL) divergence between both probabilities is computed as

$$KL(p(v)\|p(v')) = \sum_k p(v_k) \log \frac{p(v_k)}{p(v'_k)} \tag{7.5}$$

and the gradient of this divergence with respect to a weight $w + i, j$ can be computed, taking into account Eq. (7.3), with the result

$$\frac{\delta G}{\delta w_{i,j}} = \frac{1}{T}\left(p_{ij} - p'_{ij}\right) \tag{7.6}$$

where p_{ij} is the probability that nodes i and j have state 1 in the positive phase and $p'_{i,j}$ is the probability that they have state 1 in the negative phase.

7.2.3 The Restricted Boltzmann Machine

The RBM was introduced in Smolensky (1986) as a Boltzmann machine where the connections are *restricted* to be between visible and hidden nodes, but where there are no connections between any two visible nodes or any two hidden nodes. In their works Geoffrey E. Hinton et al. (2006) and Geoffrey E. Hinton and R. R. Salakhutdinov (2006), these structures are used to construct generative machines. A representation of an RBM is depicted in Fig. 7.2, where it can be seen that it can be arranged into a two-layer model where the input is connected to a feature layer.

The energy function corresponding to this structure is written as

$$E(\mathbf{v}, \mathbf{h}) = -\sum_{i,j} w_{ij} v_i h_j - \sum_{i,j} b_i v_i - \sum_i c_i h_i \tag{7.7}$$

where b_i, c_i are the biases of the visible and hidden units. The probability $p(h_i)$ of that state of hidden unit i is one is expressed as in Eq. (7.3). The training of the RBM follows the same strategy as in the BM. More specifically, assume a set of binary input data $\{\mathbf{x}_1, \dots, \mathbf{x}_N\}$, $\mathbf{x}_i \in \mathbb{R}^{D_0}$ and an RBM with D_0 visible nodes and $D_1 < D_0$ hidden nodes. For each input sample, visible state probabilities are clamped with the values of that sample. Then, the probabilities of the hidden nodes are computed as

$$p(h_j|\mathbf{v}) = \sigma\left(\sum_i w_{ij} v_i + c_j\right) \tag{7.8}$$

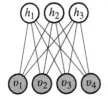

Figure 7.2 A restricted Boltzmann machine.

where $\mathbf{v}$ represents the vector containing all visible states. States h_i of the hidden nodes are set to 1 with these probabilities. This is what constitutes the positive phase of the training. In the negative phase, the visible units are unclamped, and their probabilities are chosen as a function of hidden states as

$$p(v_j'|\mathbf{h}) = \sigma\left(\sum_i w_{ij}h_i + b_j\right) \tag{7.9}$$

where $\mathbf{h}$ is a vector containing all hidden states. Finally, hidden states are updated again with generated inputs v_i' to obtain states h_i'. This is repeated for all samples, and then a sample estimation of Eq. (7.6) is computed, with the restriction that the connections or weights between hidden nodes and the ones between visible nodes are zero. Taking into account that probabilities p_{ij} and $p_{i,j}'$ are defined as Bernoulli mass functions, we can redefine and estimate them as

$$p_{ij} = p\left(v_i = 1, h_j = 1\right) = \mathbb{E}\left[v_i h_j\right] \approx \frac{1}{N}\sum_{k=1}^N v_{i,n} h_{j,n}$$

$$p_{ij}' = p\left(v_i' = 1, h_j' = 1\right) = \mathbb{E}\left[v_i' h_j'\right] \approx \frac{1}{N}\sum_{k=1}^N v_{i,n}' h_{j,n}' \tag{7.10}$$

and then, an update rule can be constructed as

$$w_{ij} \leftarrow w_{ij} + \mu\sum_{k=1}^N \left(v_{i,n}h_{i,n} - v_{i,n}'h_{i,n}'\right) \tag{7.11}$$

The criterion that gives this training procedure is known as *contrastive divergence* (Geoffrey E. Hinton 2002). Weights w_{ij} can be expressed as matrix $\mathbf{W} \in \mathbb{R}^{D_0 \times D_1}$ and therefore the above expression can be written as (K. P. Murphy 2012)

$$\mathbf{W} \leftarrow \mathbf{W} + \mu\left(\mathbf{V}\mathbf{H}^\mathsf{T} - \mathbf{V}'\mathbf{H}'^\mathsf{T}\right) \tag{7.12}$$

where matrices $\mathbf{H} \in \mathbb{R}^{D_1 \times N}$ and $\mathbf{V}, \mathbf{V}' \in \mathbb{D}_0 \times \mathbb{N}$ contain states $v_{i,n}$, $v_{i,n}'$, and $h_{i,n}$, respectively. The biases are updated similarly. We simply need to assume that a bias is a connection between all nodes in the layer and a single state with a value equal to 1, and, as a result

$$\mathbf{b} \leftarrow \mathbf{b} + \mu\left(\mathbf{V} - \mathbf{V}'\right) \cdot \mathbf{1}$$
$$\mathbf{c} \leftarrow \mathbf{c} + \mu\left(\mathbf{H} - \mathbf{H}'\right) \cdot \mathbf{1} \tag{7.13}$$

where vector $\mathbf{1}$ multiplying the state matrices is a column vector of N ones.

An immediate way of extending the RBM to the DL area is to construct a machine that stacks a series of RBM structures. Such models are known as a deep Boltzmann machine (DBM) (R. Salakhutdinov and G. Hinton 2009). The advantage of this structure is that the training can be done layer-wise since all layers are conditionally independent of each other given the previous and following layers. A DBN has the same structure, except that it is partially directed, which can be trained using a form of greedy layer-wise algorithm.

7.3 Deep Belief Networks

The DBN (Geoffrey E. Hinton et al. 2006; Geoffrey E. Hinton 2007) were the first noncon-volutional model that could be successfully trained when constructed as deep structures. Indeed, the existing deep models before the DBN were very hard to train since they posed many practical difficulties, and therefore, Kernel machines and the support vector machine (SVM) (see, e.g. Schölkopf and Sung (1997) and Smola et al. (1998) or Gaussian process (GP) (Rasmussen and C. K. I. Williams 2005)) were the most popular learning machines at that time (I. Goodfellow et al. 2016).

In a DBN, the structure is constructed as a stack of RBM. This is because the struc-ture has several layers of hidden units with no connections between nodes of the same layer. The hidden units are binary, but the input and output layers can have a continuous representation.

7.3.1 Training a DBN

The training of a DBM proposed by Hinton is simply to apply the contrastive divergence sequentially to each one of the layers starting from the input one (see e.g. (Yoshua Bengio et al. 2006)). It is proven that using this procedure, when a new layer is added, a bound on the training likelihood is increased (Geoffrey E. Hinton et al. 2006). When it is necessary to fine-tune it with labeled training data. For example, in Geoffrey E. Hinton et al. (1995), the wake-sleep algorithm is proposed. After the fine-tuning of the structure, a gradient descent can be applied with respect some criterion to continue training the model. For example, if the structure is to be used in supervised learning, the likelihood with respect to a set of desired outputs y_k corresponding to training samples $\mathbf{x}_k$ can be used Kurup et al. (2019).

Example 7.3.1 *Using a DBN for feature extractions in the MNIST classification.*
Here we illustrate the use of a DBN to extract nonlinear features from images that can be used as the input of a simple classification model in order to improve its performance. The input data is the MNIST handwritten digit database, whose pixel values are normalized between 0 and 1, and therefore these values can be interpreted as the probability of each pixel being 1. The DBM uses a Bernoulli distribution for its nodes.

In this experiment, a stack of two RBMs are used. The first one has 64 inputs, corre-sponding to the 64 pixels of the images, and 100 hidden units. The second one has 100 visible units and 100 hidden units. They are trained by contrastive divergence during 10 iter-ations each, and then a simple classifier of one layer with 10 outputs, corresponding to the 10 classes and softmax output is trained using ML. For the sequential training of both structures, 80% of the data has been used as training data, and the rest for test.

Figure 7.3 shows the differences in the classification performance between both classi-fiers. It can be seen that with the use of extracted features, the classification is improved. For example, class "1" goes from 107 correct classifications to 160. In average, the classifi-cation accuracy increases from 78% to 87%. If the first layer is constructed with 256 nodes, the accuracy increases to 89%.

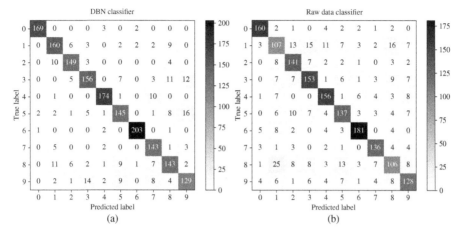

Figure 7.3 (a) Shows the confusion matrix of the combination of the DBM and the classifier for the MNIST dataset. (b) Shows the confusion matrix for a raw data classifier.

7.4 Autoencoders

An AE is an NN designed to compress input data into a meaningful representation and reconstruct it as closely as possible to the original data. Geoffrey Hinton and the parallel distributed processing (PDP) research group first introduced AEs in (Rumelhart 1986). They aimed to solve the challenge of *backpropagation without a teacher* by utilizing the input data as a guide to the learning process. In a traditional supervised learning scenario, the labels provide the correct answers for training. AEs use unsupervised learning, where the model learns from the input data without explicit labels.

Over the past decade, starting around 2006, AEs have regained prominence within the framework of the deep architecture paradigm (Geoffrey E. Hinton et al. 2006; Geoffrey E. Hinton and R. R. Salakhutdinov 2006; Yoshua Bengio et al. 2007; Erhan et al. 2010). During this time AEs, notably in the form of RBMs, were arranged hierarchically and trained in an unsupervised manner from the bottom up. Afterward, the process involved a supervised learning phase to train the top layer and refine the architecture. These architectures demonstrated exceptional performance on various classification and regression challenges.

AEs are *generative* models that can be used in many applications due to their ability to learn representations. These learned representations can be assumed to have useful properties which was translated to its many variants. A few of the common applications using AE architecture or its variants include facial recognition (Geoffrey E. Hinton et al. 2011; A. R. Kurup et al. 2019), compression, denoising, feature reduction, clustering, anomaly detection and image processing (Ye et al. 2018; Bando et al. 2018; Bevilacqua et al. 2008).

7.4.1 Autoencoder Framework

An AE neural network represents an unsupervised learning algorithm that employs back-propagation, with the target values set to replicate the input data. The basic configuration of

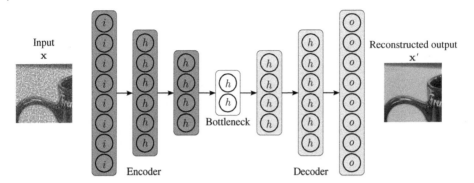

Input x

Encoder

Bottleneck

Decoder

Reconstructed output x′

Figure 7.4 A fundamental view of the AE architecture, illustrating its encoder-decoder structure.

an AE is shown in Fig. 7.4. It consists of three layers: the input layer, the hidden layer, and the output layer. The input layer, together with the hidden layers, serves as the encoder, while the hidden layer in conjunction with the output layers functions as the decoder. The AE operates by taking an input vector, $\mathbf{x} \in R_d$, and initially transforming it into a hidden representation, $\mathbf{h} \in R_d$, through a mapping function defined as:

$$\mathbf{h} = \sigma(\mathbf{W}^T\mathbf{x} + \mathbf{b}) \tag{7.14}$$

Here $\mathbf{x}$ represents input data and $\mathbf{h}$ signifies latent variables within the information bottleneck (IB). The concept of IB (Tishby et al. 2000), posits that it can extract essential information by compressing the data flow in the network. These compressed pieces of information are known as latent variables or representations. *Latent variables* are unobservable random variables extracted from the distribution, offering abstract insights into data topology and distribution. The equation $f(\mathbf{x}) = \mathbf{h}$ forms the encoder part of the network. Conversely, to reconstruct the input, the decoder takes latent variables from the bottleneck and constructs a reverse mapping function, denoted as $f'(\mathbf{h}) = \mathbf{x}'$ which is defined as:

$$\mathbf{x}' = \sigma(\mathbf{W}'\mathbf{h} + \mathbf{b}') \tag{7.15}$$

For example, consider an input image sized at 28 × 28. This image needs to be flattened before it can be fed into a neural network. When flattened, the representation becomes a vector of 784 elements, which is then inputted into the *encoder*. The output of the encoder is directed toward the bottleneck's latent space to create a compact representation. For instance, having 8, 16, or any other chosen number of nodes in the latent space indicates the effective reduction of a 784-sized image into a more compact dimension. Subsequently, the *decoder* network endeavors to reconstruct the original 28 × 28 input image from this compressed state within the bottleneck. After the image is reconstructed, a comparison is made between the reconstructed image and the original image. This involves calculating the difference and determining the loss.

The training process of an AE involves optimizing the model parameters ($\mathbf{W}, \mathbf{W}', \mathbf{b}$, and $\mathbf{b}'$) to minimize the reconstruction error between the input data $\mathbf{x}$ and the reconstructed output $\mathbf{x}'$. This optimization is performed using an optimizer such as SGD and involves employing loss functions such as MSE or binary *cross-entropy*, especially in binary scenarios. Consequently, this type of network is trained in an unsupervised manner with the objective of reproducing its input at the output layer.

The MSE is computed as the sum of squared differences between the individual data points:

$$E[e(\mathbf{x}, \mathbf{x}')] = \frac{1}{2N} \sum_{i=1}^{N} \|\mathbf{x}_i - \mathbf{x}'_i\|_2^2 \tag{7.16}$$

The cross-entropy error, represented as $J_{CE}(\mathbf{x}, \mathbf{x}')$, is computed as a measure of dissimilarity between the input data $\mathbf{x}$ and the reconstructed output $\mathbf{x}'$. This error is quantified by evaluating the negative sum over all data points from 1 to N of a logarithmic expression. Specifically, it calculates the negative log-likelihood of the reconstruction.

$$J_{CE}(\mathbf{x}, \mathbf{x}') = -\sum_{i=1}^{N} (\mathbf{x}_i \log \mathbf{x}'_i + (1 - \mathbf{x}_i) \log(1 - \mathbf{x}'_i)) \tag{7.17}$$

In recent years, the deep learning literature has witnessed the emergence of various AE architectures, each particularly designed to tackle specific challenges and tasks. Among the notable variants of AEs, the undercomplete AE stands out for its focus on acquiring compact and informative representations through constraints on the hidden layer's size, which encourages feature selection and compression. The denoising AE has been engineered to robustly learn meaningful features, even in the presence of noisy or corrupted input data, making it invaluable for noise reduction and data denoising tasks.

Meanwhile, convolutional AEs are proficient in handling structured data like images, utilizing convolutional layers to capture spatial hierarchies. This enables their use in applications such as image reconstruction, generation, and feature learning. Sparse AEs, another noteworthy variant, emphasizes the importance of sparsity in the learned representations. By promoting sparse activations in the hidden layer, these AEs encourage the selection of only the most essential features, enhancing interpretability and reducing redundancy. Lastly, variational autoencoders (VAEs) introduce probabilistic encoding, enabling AEs to effectively model data distributions and generate diverse samples.

Example 7.4.1 *(Anomaly detection using AEs)*
Anomaly detection is a vital data analysis technique that identifies infrequent items, occurrences, or observations showing significant deviations from the dataset. Anomalies, also called outliers or novelties, can be of interest due to their uniqueness and importance. They might signal errors, fraud, rare events, or unusual phenomena needing attention. This technique applies to domains like finance, cybersecurity, manufacturing, and healthcare, where detecting unusual behavior holds substantial significance.

AEs are particularly well-suited for effective anomaly detection due to several reasons. First, anomaly detection often encounters situations where labeled anomalous instances are either scarce or absent. In such unsupervised scenarios AEs, gain insights from the distribution of normal data without using labeled anomalies for training. Second, through training on normal data, AEs adeptly grasp the underlying patterns and inherent structures within the dataset. Consequently, they become proficient at generating precise reconstructions of regular data instances. Lastly, anomalies tend to yield heightened reconstruction errors as they pass through the AE. This discrepancy arises because anomalies deviate from the established patterns, leading to more substantial disparities between their original and reconstructed representations.

Here we are trying to detect anomalies in Amazon (AMZN) stock prices from 1997 to 2023. The data is obtained through Yahoo Finance which is a popular and widely used online platform that offers a comprehensive suite of tools, data, and resources related to stocks, investments, market trends, financial news, and more. It provides historical stock price data that you can access by searching for the stock symbol "AMZN" on its website. You can then navigate to the "Historical Data" section to download or view the data. Here we have downloaded this data from the URL https://finance.yahoo.com/ and saved it as a CSV file. The CSV file has seven columns, namely Date, Open, High, Low, Close, Adj Close, and Volume. Here we only use the "Date" and "Close" columns for the detection. The trend of AMZN's stock price is shown in Fig. 7.5 by plotting the closing prices over time.

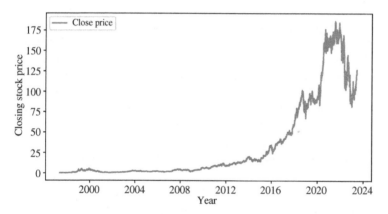

Figure 7.5 AMZN stock price over the years.

Following that, the initial stages of data preprocessing involve establishing the sizes of the training and test datasets, and subsequently partitioning the data accordingly. The "Close" prices are transformed into standardized features, whereby their mean is subtracted and they are scaled to attain unit variance. Subsequently, input–output pairs are crafted for both the training and test datasets. In this context, each input is formed from a sequence of data points spanning the designated number of time steps, with the corresponding output being the data point right after the sequence. For this purpose, a sequence length of 30 time steps has been specified.

The model architecture for this application is an LSTM AE. It consists of several layers that collectively enable the model to learn temporal patterns and generate reconstructed sequences. The first layer in the architecture is an LSTM layer with 64 hidden units that function as the encoder. Following the encoder, a dropout layer is added to mitigate over-fitting. This dropout layer randomly deactivates 20% of the units during each training iteration, thereby enhancing the model's generalization capability. A RepeatVector layer is then introduced, which repeats the encoded representation of the input sequence. This repetition ensures that the same encoded representation is available for every time step in the decoding process, facilitating accurate sequence reconstruction.

Subsequently, another LSTM layer comes into play, serving as the decoder. This decoder LSTM layer mirrors the encoder's configuration, with 64 hidden units. To counter overfitting on the decoding side, a second dropout layer, with the same 20% deactivation rate, is incorporated. The final layer in the architecture is a TimeDistributed layer coupled with a dense layer. The number of units in this dense layer corresponds to the number of features in the output data, which ensures the proper reconstruction of the sequence.

In the training stage, the model is configured with mean absolute error (MAE) loss function and optimized using the Adam optimizer. Training takes place across 100 epochs, with each epoch processing a batch size of 32 data points. The trained model is used to predict reconstructed data for both the training and test sets. A threshold for anomaly detection is set as the maximum training MAE loss. Anomalies are shown as points above the threshold, helping to visualize the time points where the stock prices deviate significantly from the expected pattern. The test data's loss values are compared against the threshold to label anomalies.

The loss values and the anomaly threshold are plotted over time in Fig. 7.6 to visually identify anomalies. Additionally, the visualization extends to Fig. 7.7, wherein the anomalies are depicted alongside their respective dates and the original closing prices.

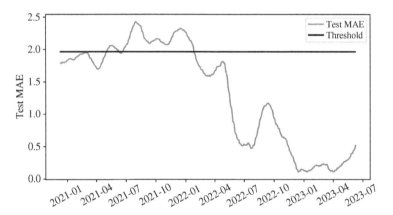

Figure 7.6 Thresholding the test MAE loss to identify the anomalies.

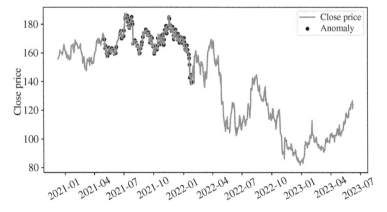

Figure 7.7 Visualization of anomalies in the original closing prices of AMZN.

7.5   Undercomplete Autoencoder

Undercomplete AE is the simplest architecture in the family of AEs. In general, AEs are unsupervised learning approaches where the neural network is trained to generate the copy of input at the output end (Buongiorno et al. 2019). In AE, the hidden layer **h** generates a latent representation of the input data **x**. This latent representation is used to reconstruct the copy of the data. The encoder part generates the codes which gives a higher-level representation of the data that needs to be reconstructed by the decoder layer. The number of layers in the encoder defines how well the input data is coded. In other words, the encoder layers need to approximate the data well so that it can reconstructed properly by the decoder.

An important factor in the level of compression that is achieved includes the input size and the size of the latent code. The AEs can be constructed in such a manner that either the size of the code is greater, smaller, or equal to that of the size of the input. When the size of the code is greater than the size of the input, such networks are called overcomplete AE. When the size of code and input are equal, they are complete AE. In undercomplete AEs, the latent code generated is a compressed representation of input, i.e. the size of code is lesser compared to that of the size of the input (see Fig. 7.8) (Thies and Alimohammad 2019). The idea behind undercomplete AE is to train a network that reconstructs the data using a smaller representation. This type of network focuses on learning the most significant features of the training data. Applications that commonly rely on these models include *compression* (Thies and Alimohammad 2019), image denoising (Dodda et al. 2022), and anomaly detection (Sreenatha and Mallikarjuna 2023).

The training criterion of undercomplete autoencoders is the same as that of the AE in general, i.e. using the train data to minimize the MSE which corresponds to the difference between actual input **x** and reconstructed output **x′**. In general, the loss function corresponds to the following:

$$\min_{\mathbf{W}} \mathbb{E}\left[e_i^2\right] = \min\left(\mathbb{E}\left[(\mathbf{x}_i - \mathbf{x}_i')^2\right] + c_1 r(\mathbf{W}) + c_2 r(\mathbf{x}, \hat{\mathbf{x}})\right) \tag{7.18}$$

Figure 7.8   An example of undercomplete AE architecture.

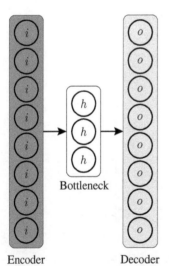

Encoder   Decoder

where the first term corresponds to the standard MSE, the second term is the weight regularization and the third term is for sparsity regularization. c_1 and c_2 are the scaling factors to adjust the weight of each of the terms in the function. These regularization functions can be as simple as that of L_1, and L_0 norms. These regularization techniques help with the generalization capabilities of the model.

7.6 Sparse Autoencoder

The basic architecture of autoencoders tries to approximate identity function since the ultimate aim of such models is to reconstruct the input. This might seem like a trivial solution. However, if we implement certain constraints to the network, i.e. by limiting a certain number of hidden units, we can learn interesting details as well as structures of the data (A. Ng et al. 2011; H. Lee et al. 2007).

Consider we have an input size of $n = 100$ and we are trying to reconstruct this input using 50 hidden units. In this scenario, if the input features are Gaussian independently and identically distributed (i.i.d.), meaning there is no correlation between the input samples, the task of reconstruction might be difficult. However, if we have an input with some features that are correlated to each other, then we can assume that the neural network might be able to identify a few of those correlations in the data. This means the network can learn those correlations to reconstruct the input.

The above example points to a scenario where we have a lesser number of hidden units compared to the input. What if the number of hidden units is large? In such a case, the argument would be to impose certain constraints on the network. We can introduce **sparsity** constraint over the hidden units. This would enable the AE to learn the structure of data even with a large number of hidden units. Sparse autoencoder (SAE) shown in Fig. 7.9 limits the constraints by penalizing activations within the layers using a sparsity parameter. This means that the network will be limited to certain specific attributes or features associated with the input. Given an observation, the model will try to encode and decode using only a smaller number of neurons at a time. The idea of sparse penalty term was inspired by sparse coding introduced in Olshausen and Field (1996).

Within the network, assuming sigmoid activation, a neuron can either be in an "active" state (outputs value close to 1) or an "inactive" state (outputs value close to 0). If we call the activation of ith hidden unit as $\mathbf{h}_i(\mathbf{x})$ for a given input $\mathbf{x}$. The average activation of the hidden unit i (over the entire training set) which corresponds to the sparse penalty term (Jun Deng et al. 2013) is given by

$$\hat{\rho}_i = \frac{1}{N}\sum_{j=1}^{N}\mathbf{h}_i(\mathbf{x}_j) \tag{7.19}$$

where N corresponds to the number of input examples. Now this average activation of the hidden unit i can be approximately enforced to a parameter called *sparsity parameter* or sparsity level, ρ.

$$\hat{\rho}_i = \rho \tag{7.20}$$

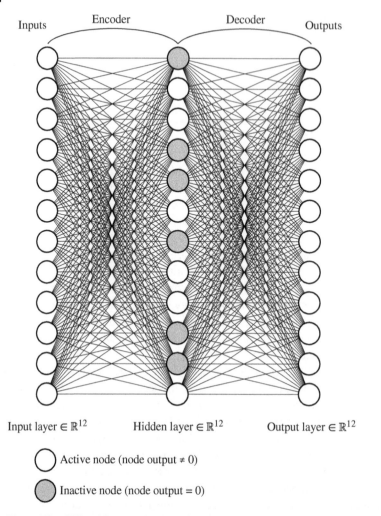

Figure 7.9 SAE architecture. Node activations vary depending on the inputs. Therefore, not always the same nodes become inactive. Source: https://towardsdatascience.com/Medium.

The sparsity parameter value is generally close to 0, for example, $\rho = 0.05$. This would push the hidden state activation to a near 0 value, making the hidden layer mostly "inactive" (W. Sun et al. 2016). This sparsity parameter is now added to the objective function to penalize ρ_i in case it deviates significantly from ρ. This can be expressed using the penalty term:

$$P_{penalty} = \sum_{i=1}^{D_l} \boldsymbol{KL}(\rho||\rho_i) \tag{7.21}$$

where D_l is the number of neurons present in the hidden layer l. $\boldsymbol{KL}(\rho||\rho_i)$ corresponds to the KL divergence (Kullback and Leibler 1951) given by:

$$\boldsymbol{KL}(\rho||\rho_i) = \rho \log \frac{\rho}{\rho_i} + (1-\rho)\log \frac{1-\rho}{1-\rho_i} \tag{7.22}$$

The above approach makes sure that when $\rho = \rho_i$, then the $\mathbf{KL}(\rho || \rho_i) = 0$. Otherwise, when ρ_j diverges from ρ, the $\mathbf{KL}(\rho || \rho_i)$ increases monotonically. Hence, this acts like a sparsity constraint. Now, the overall cost function can be written as:

$$J_{sp}(\mathbf{W}, \mathbf{b}) = J(\mathbf{W}, \mathbf{b}) + \lambda \sum_{i=1}^{D_l} KL(\rho || \rho_i) \tag{7.23}$$

where λ is the weight of the sparsity penalty term. Note that the $J_{sp}(\mathbf{W}, \mathbf{b})$ is directly related to parameters $\mathbf{W}$ and $\mathbf{b}$ and we need to minimize the cost function to obtain the two parameters. Again, the SGD approach is used to train this type of architecture, and the $\mathbf{W}$ and $\mathbf{b}$ get updated at each iteration. The forward pass computes the average activation ρ_i to obtain the sparse error. The BP helps with updating the weight and bias parameters. Using this approach the (SAE) learns the feature representations relevant for the reconstruction of input data.

7.7 Denoising Autoencoders

So far we have looked into AE models that have identical input and output as the main goal was to reconstruct the input and learn representations of it that would be relevant for reconstruction. Also, we looked into models that can perform this reconstruction using different strategies by modifying the number of layers or by putting a constraint on the hidden units. There can be applications where we need the AE model that learns generalizable coding to recreate the original data even if we pass corrupted data. *Denoising* is such an application where the input is noisy or corrupted data, while the expectation from the model is to provide a noiseless output.

Denoising autoencoder (DAE) (Vincent et al. 2008) changes the reconstruction criterion for a more interesting and challenging objective of cleaning partially corrupted data, i.e. *denoising*. The assumption made for implementing this criteria is that: firstly, the higher-level representation is expected to be robust and stable even under corruptions of input. Secondly, the denoising task helps with extracting useful features associated with the structure of input data and is a type of constraint that helps the model learn better. This would help the model to capture a better high-level representation of the data (Vincent et al. 2010).

7.7.1 Denoising Autoencoder Algorithm

Denoising autoencoder (DAE) is a variation of the traditional AE. As described before, the idea behind DAE is to retrieve the original clean input using the corrupted version of it (Ferles et al. 2018). The first step in this approach is to corrupt the input data using a stochastic mapping given by:

$$\hat{\mathbf{x}} \sim \mathbf{Q}^{(d)}(\hat{\mathbf{x}}|\mathbf{x}) \tag{7.24}$$

where $\hat{\mathbf{x}}$ is the corrupted version of input $\mathbf{x}$. Similar to Eq. (7.14), the input $\hat{\mathbf{x}}$ is encoded to a hidden representation given by:

$$\mathbf{h} = \sigma(\mathbf{W}^{\mathsf{T}}\hat{\mathbf{x}} + \mathbf{b}) \tag{7.25}$$

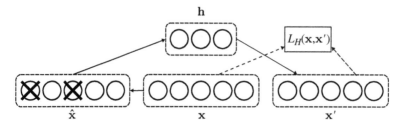

Figure 7.10 The DAE architecture. Source: Adapted from Vincent et al. (2010).

where instead of the original input we pass the noisy input $\hat{\mathbf{x}}$. Note that the parameters in the encoder part are the $\mathbf{W}^{\mathsf{T}}$ and $\mathbf{b}$. Further, the reconstruction is obtained similar to Eq. (7.15) given by:

$$\mathbf{x}' = \sigma(\mathbf{Wh} + \mathbf{b}') \tag{7.26}$$

and the parameters associated with the decoder portion include $\mathbf{W}$ and $\mathbf{b}'$. Both sets of encoder and decoder parameters are trained to minimize the average reconstruction error on the training dataset. This means the idea is to have the $\mathbf{x}'$ to be as close to the uncorrupted $\mathbf{x}$ as possible. Now, the main difference in the case of denoising is that the $\mathbf{x}'$ is a deterministic function of $\hat{\mathbf{x}}$ rather than $\mathbf{x}$ as in AE. The loss function is either the cross-entropy loss $(e_{ce}(\mathbf{x}, \mathbf{x}'))$ when using sigmoid combined with affine transformation in the decoder or the MSE loss $(e_{mse}(\mathbf{x}, \mathbf{x}'))$ in case of just affine decoder. The parameters are initialized randomly, followed by optimization using stochastic gradient descent.

It is to be noted that the same reconstruction error is being minimized between the clean $\mathbf{x}$ and reconstructed $\mathbf{x}'$ which corresponds to maximization of the lower bound on mutual information between the reconstruction $\mathbf{x}'$ and the clean noiseless version $\mathbf{x}$. The main difference now is that $\mathbf{x}'$ is obtained using the deterministic mapping to the corrupted input $\mathbf{x}$ shown in Fig. 7.10. This allows the model to learn the hidden representation through far more clever mapping than just identity mapping. This indeed aids with extracting useful features to aid the denoising application.

7.8 Convolutional Autoencoder

Convolutional autoencoder (CAE) combines the concept of CNNs introduced in Chapter 4 and Autoencoder framework. Since CNNs are best known for their ability to model image data, (CAE) can be used for applications such as image compression (Akyazi and Ebrahimi 2019; Cheng et al. 2018), image denoising (Gondara 2016), anomaly detection (M. Ribeiro et al. 2018; Chow et al. 2020; Shen Yan et al. 2023), etc.

Autoencoders pose the main limitation of not being able to capture the two-dimensional details in an image or video frame sequences (Masci et al. 2011). This can introduce redundancy in the network parameters which may de-emphasize the local information associated with the images. Most of the successful object recognition models (Lowe 1999; Serre et al. 2005) had the ability to extract localized scale-invariant features that occurred repeatedly across the input. The concept of CAE was first introduced in Masci et al. (2011). Unlike the conventional AE, in CAE, the weights are shared across all the locations in input. This helps in preserving the spatial locality which is similar to CNN. In CAE, the latent representation is in the form of image patches. Hence, the linear combination of these image patches is used for reconstruction.

As for the CAE architecture, the concept is similar to the one described in Section 7.4.1. Consider a single channel input $\mathbf{x}$. Similar to Eq. (7.14), the latent representation of the kth feature map corresponding to input $\mathbf{x}$ is given by the following equation:

$$\mathbf{h}^{(k)} = \sigma(\mathbf{W}^{(k)} * \mathbf{x} + \mathbf{b}^{(k)}) \tag{7.27}$$

where the bias is broadcast across the whole map, σ is the activation function and $*$ stands for the two-dimensional convolutional operation between the weights of kth feature map $(\mathbf{W}^{(k)})$ and the input. For each latent map, only a single bias is used. This is done to make sure that each filter specializes in features of the entire input as having different bias values per pixel might introduce many degrees of freedom. The reconstruction part is performed using the following equation:

$$\mathbf{x}' = \sigma\left(\sum_{k \in H} \tilde{\mathbf{W}}^{(k)} * \mathbf{h}^{(k)} + \mathbf{c}\right) \tag{7.28}$$

where the flip operation across the two dimensions is indicated using $\tilde{\mathbf{W}}$. H corresponds to the group of latent feature maps and again, we are using just a single bias $\mathbf{c}$ across the entire input per channel. The cost function used for training purposes is the minimization of MSE given by the following equation:

$$\min_{\mathbf{W}} \mathbb{E}\left[e_i^2\right] = \min\left(\mathbb{E}\left[(\mathbf{x}_i - \mathbf{x}_i')^2\right]\right) \tag{7.29}$$

Similar to the standard neural networks, the backpropagation algorithm is used to compute the gradient of the error function with respect to the parameters, i.e. $\mathbf{W}^{(k)}$. These weights are then further updated using the stochastic gradient descent approach.

The translation-invariance can be achieved in the case of CAE using a Maxpooling layer similar to CNNs. This layer helps with downsampling the latent representation using a constant factor. This factor is usually taken as the maximum value of the overlapping sub-regions. The advantage of this approach is that it improves the selectivity of the filter as this approach considers the match that occurs between the feature and the input data over the region of interest. The max-pooling operation used in the case of CAE erases the non-maximal values in the nonoverlapping sub-regions, introducing sparsity over hidden representations. This allows the feature detection process to be more broadly applicable, hence the common/trivial solutions are avoided. Further, during the reconstruction part, the sparse latent code formed using this approach decreases the number of filters required for decoding each pixel. Hence, the filters tend to be more general in nature. Subsequently, the max pool layers pose an advantage of not needing L1/L2 regularization overweights or hidden units.

Example 7.8.1 (Building a CAE for Image denoising using MNIST)

The MNIST dataset is used here to demonstrate the Image denoising using CAE. Here, we will use the digits data to map the noisy images to clean digits images. The first step is to load the MNIST data. After loading the dataset, we preprocess it to normalize and reshape the images to a standard size of 28 × 28.

Following this, we need to add noise to each of the images. We can do that using the following equation:

$$\hat{I} = I + \epsilon \tag{7.30}$$

where I is the original image, ϵ is the noise vector. $\hat{I}$ is the noisy image that will be used to experiment with the CAE architecture for performing Image denoising. Now, we need to split the data into train and test splits. We have 60,000 images in the training and 10,000 images in the test dataset. Also, we will be duplicating this data with and without noise. A few examples of training samples with and without the noise are shown in Fig. 7.11.

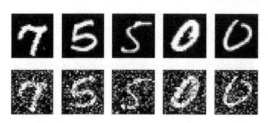

Figure 7.11 Example of train data and noisy data.

The next step is to construct the CAE architecture. We have the encoder part and the decoder part. The encoder part consists of two 2D convolutional layers with "ReLU" activation, filter size of (3, 3) with number of filters = 32. Each of these convolutional layers is followed by a 2D max-pooling layer with pooling size = (2, 2) which helps in spatial downsampling. The decoder part consists of stacked transposed 2D Convolutions with the same filter size with a stride of 2 and the same number of filters. This output is then further passed through 2D convolutional layers with 1 filter of size (3, 3) with a sigmoid activation.

Once we have the encoder and the decoder part ready, we can stack them and train the model. The optimizer used for this example is Adam and the loss function used here is the binary cross-entropy.

When we proceed to train the model, first we pass the train data as both the input as well as the label or target. This is because the main aim of the model is to reconstruct the image at the decoder end, which makes sure that the right latent representations are learned at the bottleneck part of the CAE. We train the model for 50 epochs with a batch size = 128. Once the model is trained we can use the noiseless test data as the input to the encoder and see the predicted output. This should look the same (see Fig. 7.12) showing that the model is able to learn the representations properly.

Figure 7.12 Input and predictions for clean test data.

Now let us fit the model on the noisy data as the input and clean data as the target. Using this approach, we are trying to make the CAE denoise the images. In this case, we are training the model for 100 epochs with the same batch size. Once the training is done, the

Figure 7.13 Input and predictions for noisy test data.

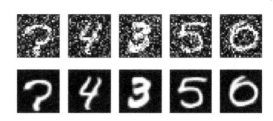

predictions are made on the noisy test data and you can see the CAE does a wonderful job in denoising the images, as shown in Fig. 7.13

7.9   Variational Autoencoders

There arise several challenges to performing inference and learning in directed probabilistic models with continuous latent variables that have intractable posterior distributions. In many cases, these posterior distributions cannot be computed analytically, making traditional approaches like exact Bayesian inference or Markov chain Monte Carlo (MCMC) (Gilks et al. 1995) computationally expensive. The variational Bayesian (VB) methodology is based on the notion of approximating intractable posterior distributions with more manageable alternatives. Rather than directly engaging with the intricacies of the complex posterior distribution, a selection is made from a family of distributions, referred to as the variational distribution. The optimization challenge consequently transforms into determining the member within this chosen family that best approximates the true posterior distribution. The closeness of approximation is measured by assessing the KL divergence, a mathematical metric used to quantify the dissimilarity between the variational distribution and the true posterior.

A common strategy in *probabilistic modeling* is the adoption of the mean-field approximation (Honkela and Valpola 2004), wherein the variational distribution is assumed to exhibit factorization properties, thereby helping the optimization process. This factorization implies that the complex problem can be deconstructed into simpler, independent components. However, despite this simplification, the calculation of expectations associated with this variational distribution may still pose computational challenges and remain intractable. To mitigate the challenges presented, one may employ the reparameterization trick (Kingma and Welling 2013). This technique enables the representation of a random variable in terms of a deterministic function of another variable, coupled with a controlled source of randomness. This transformation facilitates differentiation through the previously random sampling process. Thus this method makes the process of optimizing a mathematical model suitable for use with SGD.

The stochastic gradient variational Bayes (SGVB) estimator is an estimator for the variational lower bound, a critical metric in probabilistic modeling and variational inference (VI). It is derived through the application of the reparameterization trick combined with Monte Carlo sampling to provide approximations for the expectations involved in the optimization process. This methodology facilitates the utilization of standard stochastic gradient ascent techniques in optimizing the variational lower bound. Meanwhile, the auto-encoding variational Bayes (AEVB) algorithm is introduced while dealing with i.i.d. datasets and continuous latent variables. This algorithm leverages the SGVB estimator for the optimization of a recognition model. The role of this recognition model is to facilitate efficient approximate posterior inference through a process known as ancestral sampling. Ancestral sampling entails the incremental generation of samples layer by layer within the generative model. When this recognition model is implemented as a neural network, it gives rise to the concept of a VAE (Kingma and Welling 2019) (see Fig. 7.15). A VAE encompasses both an encoder network (the recognition model) and a decoder network (the generative model), thus enabling the acquisition of a probabilistic mapping between the data space and a lower-dimensional latent space. Specifically, the encoder approximates the true posterior distribution of latent variables given the observed data, while the decoder generates data samples based on these latent variables.

The utility of the learned approximate posterior inference model, represented by the encoder network, extends beyond the training of the generative model. It finds application in various domains, including data point recognition, denoising by reconstructing clean data from noisy inputs, representation learning for extracting meaningful latent features, and data visualization techniques.

7.9.1 Latent Variable Inference: Lower Bound Estimation Approach

A *lower bound* estimator, characterized as a stochastic objective function, is derived for a range of directed graphical models featuring continuous latent variables. This analysis assumes an i.i.d. dataset with latent variables linked to each data point. The primary objectives encompass two phases: firstly, the calculation of ML or maximum A posteriori (MAP) inference concerning global parameters, and secondly, the VI of the latent variables.

Consider a dataset denoted as $\mathbf{X}$ comprising N i.i.d. samples, where each sample corresponds to either a continuous or discrete variable. These data are generated through a stochastic process involving an unobserved continuous random variable z_i. This generative process encompasses two sequential steps. The initial step involves producing a value z_i drawn from a prior distribution $p_{\theta^*}(\mathbf{z})$, followed by the subsequent step of generating a value $\mathbf{x}_i$ from a conditional distribution $p_{\theta^*}(\mathbf{x}|\mathbf{z})$. Both the prior distribution $p_{\theta^*}(\mathbf{z})$ and the conditional likelihood $p_{\theta^*}(\mathbf{x}|\mathbf{z})$ are assumed to originate from parametric distribution families identified as $p_{\theta}(\mathbf{z})$ and $p_{\theta}(\mathbf{x}|\mathbf{z})$, respectively. Additionally, the probability density functions (PDF) associated with these distributions demonstrate differentiability at nearly all points w.r.t both model parameters θ and latent variables $\mathbf{z}$. Throughout this generative procedure, the true values of the parameters θ^* and the latent variables z_i remain unknown. Here, the integral of the marginal likelihood $p_{\theta}(\mathbf{x}) = \int p_{\theta}(\mathbf{z})p_{\theta}(\mathbf{x}|\mathbf{z})d\mathbf{z}$ poses significant computational challenges, making it intractable to calculate its derivative. Consequently, determining the true posterior density $p_{\theta}(\mathbf{z}|\mathbf{x}) = \frac{p_{\theta}(\mathbf{x}|\mathbf{z})p_{\theta}(\mathbf{z})}{p_{\theta}(\mathbf{x})}$ becomes an infeasible task. These intractable computations are commonly encountered in scenarios involving moderately complex likelihood functions, as observed in neural networks with non-linear hidden layers. Figure 7.14 shows the *intractable posterior* distribution of the generative model.

To address the aforementioned challenges effectively, a recognition model denoted as $q_{\phi}(\mathbf{z}|\mathbf{x})$ is introduced, serving as an approximation to the true posterior $p_{\theta}(\mathbf{z}|\mathbf{x})$. In contrast

Figure 7.14 Intractable posterior. The continuous lines represent the generative model $p_\theta(\mathbf{z})p_\theta(\mathbf{x}|\mathbf{z})$. The dashed lines represent the variational approximation $q_\phi(\mathbf{z}|\mathbf{x})$ to the intractable posterior distribution $p_\theta(\mathbf{z}|\mathbf{x})$. The generative parameters θ and the variational parameters ϕ are inferred simultaneously. Source: Adapted from Kingma and Welling 2013.

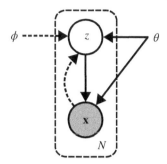

to typical factorized approximate posteriors in mean-field VI, $q_\phi(\mathbf{z}|\mathbf{x})$ doesn't necessarily adhere to a factorial structure, and its parameters ϕ are not derived from closed-form expectations. Instead, a methodology is proposed for jointly learning the recognition model parameters ϕ alongside the generative model parameters θ. Here the latent variables $\mathbf{z}$ can be interpreted as latent representations. Therefore, $q_\phi(\mathbf{z}|\mathbf{x})$ is also referred to as a probabilistic encoder because, given an input data point $\mathbf{x}$, it generates a distribution encompassing the potential values of the latent representation $\mathbf{z}$. Similarly, $p_\theta(\mathbf{x}|\mathbf{z})$ is termed a probabilistic decoder since, given a latent code latent representation $\mathbf{z}$, it produces a distribution covering the possible corresponding values of $\mathbf{x}$. This encoder–decoder framework plays a pivotal role in unraveling the hidden structures within the data.

Let us first define the marginal likelihood for the entire dataset, by summing the individual marginal likelihoods for each data point.

$$\log p_\theta(\mathbf{x}_1, \mathbf{x}_2 \cdots \mathbf{x}_N) = \sum_{i=1}^{N} \log p_\theta(\mathbf{x}_i) \tag{7.31}$$

Next, consider approximating $p_\theta(\mathbf{z}|\mathbf{x})$ with an alternative distribution, denoted as $q_\phi(\mathbf{z}|\mathbf{x})$. Define this distribution in a way that it possesses a tractable form (Odaibo 2019). If the parameters of $q_\phi(\mathbf{z}|\mathbf{x})$ can be chosen such that it closely resembles $p_\theta(\mathbf{z}|\mathbf{x})$, it can be used for approximate inference of the intractable distribution. In this task, KL divergence serves as a metric for measuring the differences between two probability distributions. The KL divergence calculated between the approximate and true posterior distributions is expressed as follows:

$$KL(q_\phi(\mathbf{z}|\mathbf{x}_i)\|p_\theta(\mathbf{z}|\mathbf{x}_i)) = -\int q_\phi(\mathbf{z}|\mathbf{x}_i) \log\left(\frac{p_\theta(\mathbf{z}|\mathbf{x}_i)}{q_\phi(\mathbf{z}|\mathbf{x}_i)}\right) d\mathbf{z} \geq 0 \tag{7.32}$$

Utilizing Bayes' theorem on the equation above results in:

$$KL(q_\phi(\mathbf{z}|\mathbf{x}_i)\|p_\theta(\mathbf{z}|\mathbf{x}_i)) = -\int q_\phi(\mathbf{z}|\mathbf{x}_i) \log\left(\frac{p_\theta(\mathbf{x}_i|\mathbf{z})p_\theta(\mathbf{z})}{q_\phi(\mathbf{z}|\mathbf{x}_i)p(\mathbf{x}_i)}\right) d\mathbf{z} \geq 0 \tag{7.33}$$

The above equation can be deconstructed using logarithmic laws, resulting in:

$$KL(q_\phi(\mathbf{z}|\mathbf{x}_i)\|p_\theta(\mathbf{z}|\mathbf{x}_i)) = -\int q_\phi(\mathbf{z}|\mathbf{x}_i)\left[\log\left(\frac{p_\theta(\mathbf{x}_i|\mathbf{z})p_\theta(\mathbf{z})}{q_\phi(\mathbf{z}|\mathbf{x}_i)}\right) - \log p(\mathbf{x}_i)\right] d\mathbf{z} \geq 0$$

$$\tag{7.34}$$

Expanding the integrand in the RHS results in:

$$- \int q_\phi(z|x_i) \log \left(\frac{p_\theta(x_i|z)p_\theta(z)}{q_\phi(z|x_i)} \right) dz + \int q_\phi(z|x_i) \log p(x_i) dz \geq 0 \qquad (7.35)$$

In the equation provided above, it is important to observe that $\log p(x_i)$ is a constant and can, therefore, be factored out of the second integral, leading to:

$$- \int q_\phi(z|x_i) \log \left(\frac{p_\theta(x_i|z)p_\theta(z)}{q_\phi(z|x_i)} \right) dz + \log p(x_i) \int q_\phi(z|x_i) dz \geq 0 \qquad (7.36)$$

As $q_\phi(z|x_i)$ is a probability distribution, its integration in the equation above equals 1. Then, by moving the integral to the opposite side of the inequality, we obtain the following:

$$\log p(x_i) \geq \int q_\phi(z|x_i) \log \left(\frac{p_\theta(x_i|z)p_\theta(z)}{q_\phi(z|x_i)} \right) dz \qquad (7.37)$$

Reformulating the equations by utilizing logarithmic rules.

$$\log p(x_i) \geq \int q_\phi(z|x_i) \left[\log p_\theta(x_i|z) + \log p_\theta(z) - \log q_\phi(z|x_i) \right] dz \qquad (7.38)$$

Identifying the right-hand side of the inequality above as an expectation, we express it as follows:

$$\log p(x_i) \geq \mathbb{E}_{\sim q_\phi(z|x_i)} \left[\log p_\theta(x_i, z) - \log q_\phi(z|x_i) \right] \qquad (7.39)$$

Furthermore, employing Eq. (7.37), we deduce the following:

$$\log p(x_i) \geq \int q_\phi(z|x_i) \log \left(\frac{p_\theta(z)}{q_\phi(z|x_i)} \right) dz + \int q_\phi(z|x_i) \log p_\theta(x_i|z) dz \qquad (7.40)$$

$$\log p(x_i) \geq -KL(q_\phi(z|x_i)||p_\theta(z)) + \mathbb{E}_{\sim q_\phi(z|x_i)}[\log p_\theta(x_i|z)] \qquad (7.41)$$

The right-hand side of the preceding equation corresponds to the evidence lower bound (ELBO), also referred to as the variational lower bound $J_{ELBO}(\theta, \phi)$.

$$J_{ELBO}(\theta, \phi) = -KL(q_\phi(z|x_i)||p_\theta(z)) + \mathbb{E}_{\sim q_\phi(z|x_i)}[\log p_\theta(x_i|z)] \qquad (7.42)$$

Within the ELBO, the KL term acts as a regularizer, imposing constraints on the form of the approximate posterior. Meanwhile, the second term is termed a reconstruction term as it quantifies the likelihood of the data's reconstruction by the decoder. The objective is to differentiate and optimize the lower bound with regard to both the variational parameters ϕ and the generative parameters θ. However, the gradient concerning the variational parameters ϕ poses challenges. The conventional method, the Monte Carlo gradient estimator, exhibits significant variance, rendering it impractical for the intended purposes.

7.9.2 Reparameterization Trick

The challenges associated with estimating the lower bound and its parameter derivatives prompted the introduction of a pragmatic estimation method. This approach relies on an approximate posterior distribution, denoted as $q_\phi(z|x)$ tailored to capture the latent variables given the observed data x. Within this framework, a *reparameterization* technique is employed, wherein the continuous random variable $z \sim q_\phi(z|x)$ is expressed as a deterministic variable $z = g_\phi(\epsilon, x)$. Here ϵ is an auxiliary noise variable characterized by an independent marginal distribution $p(\epsilon)$, and $g_\phi(.)$ represents a vector-valued function parameterized by ϕ. This transformation enables us to efficiently compute gradients and derivatives, facilitating parameter optimization.

The reparameterization proves advantageous as it allows to reformulate the expectation w.r.t $q_\phi(z|x)$. This transformation yields a Monte Carlo estimate of the expectation that can be easily differentiated w.r.t ϕ. Given the deterministic mapping of z

$$q_\phi(z|x)\prod_i dz_i = p(\epsilon)\prod_i d\epsilon_i \tag{7.43}$$

where $dz = \prod_i dz_i$.

$$\int q_\phi(z|x)f(z)dz = \int p(\epsilon)f(z)d\epsilon = \int p(\epsilon)f(g_\phi(\epsilon, x))d\epsilon \tag{7.44}$$

Using the above equation a differentiable estimator can be constructed as follows:

$$\int q_\phi(z|x)f(z)dz \simeq \frac{1}{N}\sum_{n=1}^{N}f(g_\phi(x, \epsilon_n)) \tag{7.45}$$

where $\epsilon_n \sim p(\epsilon)$. Therefore, this reparameterization technique can be employed to derive a differentiable estimator for the variational lower bound. Consequently, we can create Monte Carlo approximations of expectations involving a function $f(z)$ with respect to $q_\phi(z|x)$ in the following manner:

$$\mathbb{E}_{q_\phi(z|x_i)}[f(z)] = \mathbb{E}_{p(\epsilon)}\left[f(g_\phi(\epsilon, x_i))\right] \simeq \frac{1}{N}\sum_{n=1}^{N}f(g_\phi(\epsilon_n, x_i)) \tag{7.46}$$

This method is applied to the variational lower bound Eq. (7.39), resulting in the creation of a generic SGVB estimator $\tilde{J}^A_{ELBO}(\theta, \phi) \simeq J_{ELBO}(\theta, \phi)$.

$$\tilde{J}^A_{ELBO}(\theta, \phi) = \frac{1}{N}\sum_{n=1}^{N}\log p_\theta(x_i, z_{(i,n)}) - \log q_\phi(z_{(i,n)}|x_i) \tag{7.47}$$

where $z_{(i,n)} = g_\phi(\epsilon_{(i,n)}, x_i)$.

A second version of the SGVB estimator $\tilde{J}^B_{ELBO}(\theta, \phi) \simeq J_{ELBO}(\theta, \phi)$, can be constructed using Eq. (7.42). Commonly, it is possible to analytically compute the KL divergence term in Eq. (7.42). As a result, the estimation process only involves sampling to determine the expected reconstruction error $\mathbb{E}_{\sim q_\phi(z|x_i)}[\log p_\theta(x_i|z)]$. This estimator can be represented as follows:

$$\tilde{J}^B_{ELBO}(\theta, \phi) = -KL(q_\phi(z|x_i)||p_\theta(z)) + \frac{1}{N}\sum_{n=1}^{N}(\log p_\theta(x_i|z_{(i,n)})) \tag{7.48}$$

7.9.3 Illustration: Variational Autoencoder Implementation

In this section, the focus is on an illustrative example involving the application of a neural network as the probabilistic encoder, represented as $q_\phi(z|x)$. This encoder plays a crucial

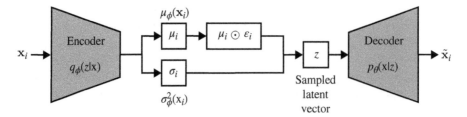

Figure 7.15 VAE architecture. Source: Addo et al. (2022)/MDPI/CC by 4.0.

role in approximating the posterior distribution within the generative model, $p_\theta(\mathbf{x}, \mathbf{z})$. Furthermore, the AEVB algorithm is employed to jointly optimize two parameter sets denoted as θ and ϕ.

Assume that the prior distribution governing the latent variables adopts a specific form, characterized as the centered isotropic multivariate Gaussian, and denoted as $p_\theta(\mathbf{z}) = \mathcal{N}(\mathbf{z}; 0, \mathbf{I})$. In the case of the data distribution, $p_\theta(\mathbf{x}|\mathbf{z})$, two scenarios are considered: a multivariate Gaussian for continuous data and a Bernoulli for binary data. In both cases, the distribution parameters are derived from z using a neural network referred to as an MLP. It is important to note that the true posterior distribution, $p_\theta(\mathbf{z}|\mathbf{x})$, remains intractable. In these scenarios, it can be assumed that the true posterior distribution has an approximate Gaussian shape with an almost diagonal spread. Thus, it is feasible to employ a variational approximate posterior $q_\phi(\mathbf{z}|\mathbf{x})$ that resembles a multivariate Gaussian with a diagonal spread pattern.

$$\log_{q_{q_\phi}}(\mathbf{z}|\mathbf{x}_i) = \log \mathcal{N}(\mathbf{z}; \mu_i, \sigma_i^2 \mathbf{I}) \tag{7.49}$$

The mean μ_i and standard deviation σ_i of the approximated posterior, are outputs generated by the encoding MLP.

$$\log p(\mathbf{x}|\mathbf{z}) = \log \mathcal{N}(\mathbf{z}; 0, \sigma^2 \mathbf{I}) \tag{7.50}$$

where $\mathbf{h} = \tanh(\mathbf{W}_1^{(l)}\mathbf{h} + \mathbf{b}_1^{(l)})$, $\mu = \mathbf{W}_2^{(l)}\mathbf{h} + \mathbf{b}_2^{(l)}$, and $\log \sigma^2 = \mathbf{W}_3^{(l)}\mathbf{h} + \mathbf{b}_3^{(l)}$. The terms $\mathbf{W}_1^{(l)}$, $\mathbf{W}_2^{(l)}, \mathbf{W}_3^{(l)}, \mathbf{b}_1^{(l)}, \mathbf{b}_2^{(l)}$, and $\mathbf{b}_3^{(l)}$ represent the weights and biases associated with the MLP and θ, which functions as part of the decoder in the model. However, when this network serves as an encoder, denoted as $q_\phi(\mathbf{z}|\mathbf{x})$, the roles of z and x are reversed, and the weights and biases are associated with variational parameters ϕ.

Following that, samples from the posterior distribution $\mathbf{z}_{(i,n)} \sim q_\phi(\mathbf{z}|\mathbf{x}_i)$ are drawn using the equation $\mathbf{z}_{(i,n)} = g_\phi(\mathbf{x}_i, \epsilon_n) = \mu_i + \sigma_i \odot \epsilon_n$, where $\epsilon_n \sim \mathcal{N}(0, \mathbf{I})$. It is important to note that both $p_\theta(\mathbf{z})$ and $q_\phi(\mathbf{z}|\mathbf{x})$ in this model follow Gaussian distributions. In this specific scenario, the estimator described in Eq. (7.48) is employed (Fig. 7.15). The resulting estimation for this model can be expressed as follows:

$$J(\theta, \phi) \simeq \frac{1}{2}\sum_{m=1}^{M}(1 + \log((\sigma_{(i,m)})^2) - (\mu_{(i,m)})^2 - (\sigma_{(i,m)})^2) + \frac{1}{N}\sum_{n=1}^{N}(\log p_\theta(\mathbf{x}_i|\mathbf{z}_{(i,n)})) \tag{7.51}$$

Example 7.9.1 *(Data imputation using variational autoencoders)*
Data imputation is a method employed in data analysis and preprocessing to deal with missing or incomplete data points in a dataset. Missing data can occur for various reasons, such

as data collection errors, sensor failures, non-responses in surveys, or other data acquisition issues. Data imputation aims to address these missing values by estimating their values based on the available information in the dataset.

Here we illustrate the use of a VAE for data imputation. A synthetic data set is created, comprising 100 data points sampled from a standard normal distribution. It then generates a binary mask, and this mask assigns a 20% probability of being 0 (indicating a missing value) and an 80% probability of being 1 (indicating an observed value) to each entry. Subsequently, the dataset is formed by element-wise multiplication of original data and the binary mask.

The VAE model is composed of two primary components: an encoder and a decoder. The encoder accepts the observed data as input and encompasses several layers. It starts with a dense layer consisting of 32 units and a ReLU activation function. Two additional dense layers are employed to compute the mean and log-variance of the latent space. The latent variable is sampled from a Gaussian distribution based on these mean and log-variance values, using the reparameterization trick. On the contrary, the decoder takes the latent variable as input. It contains a dense layer with 32 units and ReLU activation, followed by an output layer with 1 unit. This output layer aims to reconstruct the missing values in the dataset. The VAE model establishes a connection between the encoder and decoder. It accepts the encoder's output and passes it through the decoder to generate the imputed data.

The VAE's loss function is composed of two essential terms: the reconstruction loss and the KL divergence Loss. The reconstruction loss measures the dissimilarity between the input data and the reconstructed data using mean squared error. The KL divergence loss penalizes the discrepancy between the learned latent distribution and a standard Gaussian distribution, promoting a normally distributed latent space. The total VAE loss is a combination of these two terms, with the KL divergence term weighted by a factor of 0.1. This weight can be adjusted to suit specific application requirements. This VAE model is compiled using the Adam optimizer, and it undergoes training for 100 epochs, employing a batch size of 32. Following training, the VAE is utilized to impute missing values within the dataset.

Output:

```
Original Data     Data with Missing Values     Imputed Data
[1.76405235]      [1.76405235]                 [1.6616584]
[0.40015721]      [0.40015721]                 [0.48738545]
[0.97873798]      [0.]                         [-0.08713832]
[2.2408932]       [2.2408932]                  [1.5226918]
[1.86755799]      [1.86755799]                 [1.9301624]
[-0.97727788]     [-0.97727788]                [-0.99653774]
[0.95008842]      [0.95008842]                 [1.0577495]
[-0.15135721]     [-0.15135721]                [-0.19752263]
[-0.10321885]     [-0.]                        [0.01812577]
[0.4105985]       [0.4105985]                  [0.10737716]
```

7.10 Conclusion

This chapter gives a comprehensive outline of deep unsupervised learning. Here we discuss two main categories of deep unsupervised learning: probabilistic and non-probabilistic models. Here, we focus on two powerful structures used in unsupervised learning: DBNs and AE. Both these architectures are crucial pillars in the field of neural networks as they facilitate the extraction of meaningful features from complex high-dimensional data. We talk about RBMs and its training criterion. Following this, we introduce DBNs where the basic elements of the DBN architecture are discussed in detail along with the contrastive divergence training. DBNs come under the category of probabilistic models and it is known for its ability to learn complex features in an unsupervised manner. The strength of DBN lies in its ability to undergo unsupervised training and subsequent fine-tuning using methods such as backpropagation. The training of the DBN as well as its extensions are discussed in detail. the higher-level abstractions learned by DBN is used for various application such as speech recognition, image processing, computer vision, etc.

Autoencoders, on the other hand, learn representations of the data that are compact and efficient. Their ability to summarize the data representation is instrumental in applications such as dimensionality reduction, denoising, compression, etc. The learning of AE happens through the encoder and decoder framework. It is through this encoder–decoder setup that the AE learn meaningful information from the raw input data. We further discuss the complete architecture of the AE. We defined the training methodology of these structures in general. Later on, we cover the extensions of AEs such as DAE, CAE, and VAE being a few of them. The applications of AE span various domains of data analysis and pattern recognition. As we move forward exploring more Deep learning architectures, these concepts will continue to evolve and get extended to develop more complex architectures and models.

Problems

7.1 *Experiment with Example 7.3.1 in the following aspects:*
  - *Cross-validate the number of contrastive divergence iterations with a validation set constructed with 20% of the training data.*
  - *Validate the number of layers and the number of nodes between 10 and 256.*
  - *Train a structure with a single RBM with 100 hidden nodes. Represent each connection from all of the 64 input nodes to each one of the hidden nodes in an 8 × 8 grid. Interpret the result.*

7.2 *Generate a set of 400 data where each 100 samples are drawn from one of four circularly symmetric Gaussian distributions with means equal to the canonical vectors of a base of 10 dimensions and variance 1.*

  Construct a DBN with several layers and a number of nodes decreasing from 10 dimensions to two dimensions. The input layer must be defined with Gaussian input distribution, and the output layer needs a Gaussian distribution as well. The hidden nodes must have Bernoulli distributions.

  Train the DBN using contrastive divergence and plot the outputs corresponding to the training samples. Use a different color for the outputs corresponding to each one of the Gaussians. Interpret the results for different number of layers from 2 to 5.

7.3 *Build a simple autoencoder using a deep learning framework of your choice (e.g. Keras or PyTorch) to compress grayscale images. Utilize the Labeled Faces in the Wild dataset (G. B. Huang et al. 2008), which comprises grayscale facial images, available for download at the following website*: http://vis-www.cs.umass.edu/lfw/. *Train the model to learn efficient representations of the images and evaluate its compression performance by measuring the compression ratio and the quality of the reconstructed images.*

7.4 *Implement a VAE to generate novel images from a given dataset, such as the CelebA dataset. The dataset comprises diverse color images of celebrity faces, featuring individuals from entertainment, sports, and politics, and it can be downloaded from the website*: https://mmlab.ie.cuhk.edu.hk/projects/CelebA.html. *Experiment with the latent space of the VAE and analyze how changing specific latent variables can control the generation of unique facial features, expressions, or artistic styles in the generated images. Additionally, evaluate the quality of the generated images using MSE, structural similarity index (SSIM), and visual inspection.*

7.5 *Apply a sparse autoencoder to the Iris dataset, which is a simplified dataset comprising measurements of four features (sepal length, sepal width, petal length, and petal width) for three species of iris flowers (setosa, versicolor, and virginica). The goal is to demonstrate how a sparse autoencoder can be utilized for feature selection by identifying the most significant features in this low-dimensional dataset.*

7.6 *Design a convolutional autoencoder for semantic segmentation of images. Use the Cityscapes dataset, a comprehensive collection of urban street scenes captured in various cities, which includes images and corresponding pixel-wise labels. The dataset can be downloaded from the website*: https://www.cityscapes-dataset.com/. *Train the model to segment objects or regions of interest within the images. Calculate metrics such as IoU and pixel-wise accuracy to quantitatively assess segmentation accuracy.*

7.7 *Implement an undercomplete autoencoder for text data. Use a small dataset and train the autoencoder to learn a reduced-dimensional representation of the input text and evaluate its performance by comparing the original and reconstructed text. Provide the code and discuss the results.*

7.8 *Define sequence-to-sequence autoencoders and their applications in language modeling. Explain the architecture of such autoencoders, including the encoder, bottleneck layer, and decoder. How are sequence-to-sequence autoencoders different from traditional sequence-to-sequence models like RNNs or LSTMs?*

7.9 *Extend a basic VAE to a semi-supervised VAE by incorporating labeled data. Use a partially labeled dataset such as MNIST with some labeled digits. Modify the VAE to perform both unsupervised and semi-supervised tasks. In the unsupervised task, the main aim is to generate and reconstruct data samples, while in the semi-supervised* task, design a mechanism for utilizing the labeled data to improve the model's performance in tasks like classification or attribute prediction. Evaluate its performance based on metrics such as classification accuracy, generative quality, and the model's ability to leverage both labeled and unlabeled data effectively.

7.10 Compare and contrast VAEs with MCMC methods for approximate Bayesian inference. List the advantages and disadvantages of each approach.

7.11 Design and implement a DBN or image classification using a deep learning framework.
- Train the DBN on the MNIST dataset and evaluate its performance in terms of accuracy. Include a discussion of the architecture choices made.
- Extend the evaluation by fine-tuning the pre-trained DBN using a supervised learning approach for image classification. Compare the performance of the fine-tuned DBN with the initial DBN.
- Discuss the advantages of fine-tuning and any challenges encountered.

7.12 Implement a simple RBM on a small binary image dataset. Use Scikit-learn to generate synthetic image data. Ensure that each image is flattened into a 1D array as input for the RBM. Demonstrate its capability to reconstruct data. Provide code and a report detailing the architecture, training procedure, and results.

8

Deep Unsupervised Learning II

8.1 Introduction

The underlying aspiration of deep learning resides in the endeavor to construct intricate, hierarchical models capable of representing probability distributions. These models aim to encapsulate diverse forms of data frequently encountered in artificial intelligence domains (Yoshua Bengio 2009). Such data encompasses a spectrum ranging from natural images and audio waveforms containing speech to symbolic representations present in natural languages. The predominant achievements in the field of deep learning have been primarily centered around *discriminative models*. These models are chiefly tasked with the classification of high-dimensional and intricate sensory inputs into discrete categories (Alex Krizhevsky et al. 2012; Geoffrey E. Hinton et al. 2012c). The success of these models relied on the adept application of computational algorithms, such as backpropagation and dropout, in conjunction with the utilization of piecewise linear activation functions (Glorot et al. 2011; Jarrett et al. 2009). These activation functions offer favorable attributes in terms of gradient computations, contributing significantly to the efficacy of discriminative model training.

In contrast, the arena of *deep generative models* has encountered comparatively reduced impact. This can be attributed to the inherent complexities associated with approximating numerous intractable probabilistic computations that manifest in the context of ML estimation and related methodologies. Consequently, researchers have explored alternative approaches, such as undirected graphical models incorporating latent variables, notably RBMs (Geoffrey E. Hinton et al. 2006), and their assorted derivatives. In these models, conducting inference can be computationally expensive and often intractable, especially as the model becomes deeper and more complex. However, we can estimate these calculations using MCMC methods, but they may not guarantee convergence to the true posterior distribution (Yoshua Bengio et al. 2014). Another common approach involves using deep belief networks (DBNs), which are hybrid models featuring a single undirected layer alongside multiple directed layers. Although DBNs offer a quick and approximate

Deep Learning: A Practical Introduction, First Edition.
Manel Martínez-Ramón, Meenu Ajith, and Aswathy Rajendra Kurup.
© 2024 John Wiley & Sons Ltd. Published 2024 by John Wiley & Sons Ltd.
Companion website: https://github.com/DeepLearning-book

layer-by-layer training method, they still face computational challenges due to their combination of both undirected and directed graphical model elements.

Some approaches in the field of generative modeling do not require a defined probability distribution. Instead, they focus on training a generative machine to produce samples consistent with the desired distribution. A recent development in this domain is the generative stochastic network (GSN) framework (Yoshua Bengio et al. 2014), an extension of generalized denoising autoencoders (Yoshua Bengio et al. 2013). Both GSNs and generalized DAE learn how to create new data points that resemble the data they were trained on. They achieve this by modeling the transitions between different data states, like how a Markov chain models transition between states, but with parameters that they learn during training. In contrast, the *Adversarial Nets* framework does not necessitate a Markov chain for the purpose of sampling. This framework eliminates the need for feedback loops during the generation process. In the context of neural networks, feedback loops can make training and generation more complex. Instead, adversarial nets use piecewise linear units (a type of activation function in neural networks) to enhance the performance of the backpropagation algorithm. However, when these piecewise linear units are used within feedback loops repeatedly, they can face issues related to activations that grow without bounds, which can be problematic for stable training. Recent advancements in training generative models like VAE (Kingma and Welling 2013) and Stochastic Backpropagation (Rezende et al. 2014), have shed light on the need for stable training methods.

Furthermore, in the wider context of generative modeling, effectively using piecewise linear activation functions presents a significant challenge. Hence, the latest approach for estimating generative models not only addresses these difficulties but also holds the potential to improve data generation, thus contributing to the ongoing evolution of stable training strategies for generative machines. In this framework of adversarial nets, the generative model participates in a competitive scenario with a discriminative model. The discriminative model is tailored to develop the ability to distinguish whether a given sample originates from the model's distribution or the actual data distribution. Conceptually, one can compare the generative model to a team of counterfeiters striving to create fake currency discreetly, while the discriminative model functions in a manner resembling law enforcement, working diligently to detect counterfeit currency. This competitive dynamic drives both teams to improve their methods until counterfeit items are indistinguishable from genuine ones.

Importantly, this framework offers the potential to develop customized training algorithms suitable for a wide range of models and optimization techniques. In this research endeavor, a unique scenario is specifically explored in which the generative model generates samples by passing random noise through a MLP, and the discriminative model also takes the form of a MLP. This case is referred to as *Adversarial Nets* (Ian Goodfellow et al. 2020). In this scenario, both models can be trained using the backpropagation method, and sample generation from the generative model can be accomplished through forward propagation, removing the need for approximate inference or Markov chains.

8.2   Elements of GAN

Generative adversarial networks (GANs) (Ian Goodfellow et al. 2020) were mainly introduced to decipher the generative modeling problem by learning and modeling the probability distribution that generated the samples. From the estimated probabilities GANs are able to generate more examples of the same distribution. There are various generative models out there; however, GANs have proven to be the most effective generative model, especially in terms of constructing or generating high-resolution images. GANs are now being used for both semi-supervised as well as unsupervised learning approaches.

The simplest way to understand the concept behind GANs is through the analogy of an art forger and an art expert (Creswell et al. 2018). The *generator G* models the data in the same way as the forger creates forgeries. The idea of the forger *G* is to make realistic images. The *discriminator D* is the expert and the main objective of *D* is to differentiate between the real and the forged images. It is important that both Generator *G* and discriminator *D* are trained simultaneously as they compete with each other making the generator learn the distribution of the data properly. The generator *G* doesn't have any access to real images and the learning criterion of *G* is determined by its interaction with discriminator *D*. Discriminator, however, has access to both synthetic images and a stack of real images. The error signal for the discriminator is computed in a simplistic manner by determining whether the image came from the stack of real images or from the generator. This error signal is also propagated to the Generator and is used for its training making it produce forgeries that are close to the real image with better quality.

To summarize, the GANs consists of a Generative and discriminative model. The main goal of the generative model is to synthesize the data resembling the real data. Discriminator on the other hand differentiates the real data from the synthesized ones (Aggarwal et al. 2021; M.-Y. Liu and Tuzel 2016). The higher level illustration of the training process of the Generator and discriminator is shown in Fig. 8.1.

Unsupervised learning aims at learning useful information about the data by examining the dataset consisting of unlabeled input samples (Ian Goodfellow et al. 2020). So far, we have looked into a few of the unsupervised learning methods in Chapter 7, which can be used for many applications such as clustering, dimensionality reduction, compression, etc. Most of the discussed methods perform unsupervised model training by minimizing the reconstruction error.

Generative modeling is a type of unsupervised learning where training samples, $\mathbf{x}$ are obtained from an unknown distribution $p_{data}(\mathbf{x})$. The main objective of the generative modeling algorithm is to approximate $p_{data}(\mathbf{x})$ as closely as possible by training a model $p_{model}(\mathbf{x})$. This approximation is learned using a function $p_{model}(\mathbf{x}|\theta)$. Here, θ corresponds to a set of parameters used to control the function $p_{model}(\mathbf{x}|\theta)$. The final goal is to search for the optimum parameter values that make p_{data} as similar as possible to p_{model}. Let us look into how generative modeling is implemented in the two elements of GAN architecture, i.e. generator and discriminator. It is to be noted that both the generator and discriminator are implemented using a multilayer Neural network and generally consist of convolutional layers and/or fully connected layers.

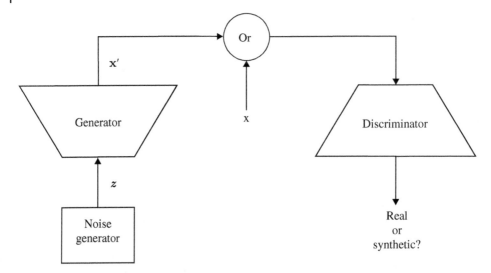

Figure 8.1 A higher level illustration of the training process for GAN using Generator G and discriminator D. The Generator is trained to map a noise sample z to a synthetic data sample x'. The discriminator is optimized to classify the real (x) and the synthetic or fake (x') data. Source: Adapted from Creswell et al. 2018.

8.2.1 Generator

The *Generator* network in GANs defines $p_{model}(x)$ implicitly. This means that the generator network does not necessarily evaluate the density function p_{model}. This is different from the explicit density modeling networks. The explicit density model networks first try to represent the density function, from which it can also generate the samples. The main problem with such explicit generative modeling techniques was its expensive nature to generate samples. Implicit generative models like GANs avoid this issue altogether. The generator draws samples from the distribution p_{model}. The generator function is defined here as $G(z; \theta^{(G)})$, with $\theta^{(G)}$ being the set of trainable parameters for the generator. The generator is defined using a prior distribution $p(z)$ defined over vector z. This vector z is of random nature in a deterministic setting and serves as the input to the generator. We can think of z to be analogous to the seed of a pseudo-random number generator. It is to be noted that the prior distribution, $p(z)$ tends to have an unstructured distribution which makes the samples z from this distribution noise. The main objective of the generator now is to transform this unstructured noise z to the realistic samples, i.e. as close to x.

8.2.2 Discriminator

The *Discriminator* is the second learning model in GANs. This network performs the task of differentiating between the real and fake which helps in perfecting the output of the generator. The discriminator now looks into samples x first. It then provides an estimate $D(x; \theta^{(D)})$ identifying whether the x is real, that is belonging to the training samples or fake (that is belonging to the p_{model} running by generator). Intuitively, the discriminator tries to predict whether the input it receives is real or fake. This part is formulated in different manners in different works. However, the original GAN formulation estimated the probability of the input being real or fake with the assumption that the real and fake distributions are samples frequently. Let us consider an example of images. For a fixed Generator, the Discriminator is trained to classify whether the image is being obtained from the training examples (real) or if it is being drawn from the fixed Generator (fake) (Creswell et al. 2018).

8.3 Training a GAN

Now that we have an understanding of the generator and discriminator part of GANs, the next step is to learn how these structures are trained to obtain the optimal parameters. Before that, let us dive into the overall structure of GANs.

The GANs can be imagined as a two-participant zero-sum game where the loss or gain of one person is actually equal to the gain or loss of the other (Salehi et al. 2020). The two architectures, i.e. the generator and the discriminator train together. The generator learns the statistical distribution of the input data and tries to construct fake data. The goal of the generator is to create counterfeit data indistinguishable from the real data such that the discriminator is misled into thinking they are real. Discriminator on the other hand is a classifier that differentiates the given input of whether it looks like real data or if it is artificially generated data. Both these structures continuously train together and optimize themselves to improve their capabilities. Both the networks are trained in such a manner that they become experts in their respective tasks, hence making the results look very close to real.

Let us first define the cost incurred by each participant. For the generator, this cost is given by: $J^{(G)}(\theta^{(G)}, \theta^{(D)})$. For the discriminator, the cost is $J^{(D)}(\theta^{(G)}, \theta^{(D)})$. Both participants will train to minimize their own cost functions. For example, the discriminator will have a cost that will encourage it to classify the data correctly as whether it is real or fake. The generator's cost function, on the other hand, will generate samples corresponding to those that we incorrectly classified by the discriminator as real. This way each of the participants will understand their weakness as well the opponent's weakness to take advantage of it and improve the generation and classification task.

There are various methods by which these costs can be specifically formulated. In the original GAN architecture (Ian Goodfellow et al. 2020), the discriminator acts just like a regular binary classifier where the cost $J^{(D)}$ is defined as the negative log-likelihood that the network assigns to the real vs fake labels given the input. For the generator, as per the original work, two different versions of cost $J^{(G)}$ were used: minimax GAN (M-GAN) and non-saturating GAN (NS-GAN). The M-GAN made use of the cost given as follows:

$$J^{(G)} = -J^{(D)} \tag{8.1}$$

This cost would correspond to a *minimax* game by flipping the sign of the cost function of the discriminator.

The NS-GAN is another approach where the labels of the discriminator are flipped instead of its cost. This would correspond to the minimization of the negative likelihood of the *wrong* labels that were assigned by the discriminator. The advantage of the latter method is that it prevents the gradient saturation problem that arises while training the model.

This would ensure both the models are competing with each other such that the generator works to produce the most realistic fake data very close to the real ones. The discriminator also simultaneously works on improving its classification skills by identifying even the close-to-real fake data from the generator.

The major problem with this approach is due to a complication that one participant's cost is in fact a function of the other participant's parameter, in addition to the fact that each of the participants controls its own parameters. This situation can be reduced to optimization by minimizing the function as shown by L. Metz et al. (2016):

$$J^{(G)}\left(\theta^{(G)}, \arg\min_{\theta^{(D)}} J^{(D)}\left(\theta^{(G)}, \theta^{(D)}\right)\right) \tag{8.2}$$

However, minimization of the above function would be difficult using the *argmin* operation. Another approach to this would be to use the game theory literature to resolve this complication. Hence, the ultimate aim of optimization is to establish a *Nash equilibrium* (Ratliff et al. 2013) between the two participants. The Nash equilibrium point would correspond to the point that is equal to the local minimum of each participant's cost with respect to its parameters. The assumption is that the other participant's parameters do not change and with local moves, once the point is reached the cost cannot be reduced any further. The most common training approach would be to use a gradient-based optimizer which would repeatedly take steps on both participants simultaneously and then incrementally minimize the cost incurred by each participant with respect to its own parameters.

While training GANs, the parameter of one network is updated while the other stays fixed. In Ian Goodfellow et al. (2020), it is shown that for a fixed generator, there exists a unique optimal discriminator given by:

$$D^*(\mathbf{x}) = \frac{p_{data}(\mathbf{x})}{p_{data}(\mathbf{x}) + p_{model}(\mathbf{x})} \tag{8.3}$$

Further, the generator G is optimal when $p_{model}(\mathbf{x}) = p_{data}(\mathbf{x})$. This would mean that for every sample drawn from $\mathbf{x}$ the optimal discriminator would predict 0.5 for all these samples. Therefore, an optimal generator G will successfully be able to confuse the discriminator D's decision to such an extent that it won't be able to distinguish between real and synthesized samples.

Let us try to understand this using an example as shown in Fig. 8.2. Using this illustration, we can understand how the generator learns the scaling of the inverse cumulative distribution function (CDF) for the data-generating distribution. In Fig. 8.2, the discriminator function D is represented using a dotted line, and the data generating distribution p_{data} is represented by lines with bold black dots, and the generative distribution p_{model} is represented using the solid black line. The GANs are trained by continuously updating the discriminator function D. This allows the discriminator to distinguish between the samples from data generating distribution p_{data} from that of the generative distribution p_{model}. The upper horizontal line indicates a part of the domain of $\mathbf{x}$. the horizontal line below corresponds to the domain from which z is sampled. It is to be noted that, in this case, sampling is performed uniformly. The arrows that are pointing upwards indicate the mapping of z to $\mathbf{x}$ given by $\mathbf{x} = G(z)$. This mapping imposes the non-uniform generative distribution p_{model} on transformed samples.

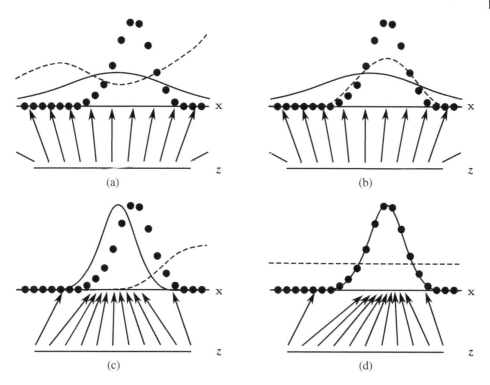

Figure 8.2 An illustration showing the basic intuition behind the GAN training process using 1D Gaussian distribution. Source: Adapted from Ian Goodfellow, Pouget-Abadie, et al. 2020.

In Fig. 8.2a, we are considering the network at the initialization phase where the p_{model} is first initialized as a 1D unit gaussian and D is a randomly set DNN as you can see from the plot. For Fig. 8.2b, we have the G held fixed and the discriminator D is trained to convergence. In this scenario, from the previous discussion, we can see that D converges into Eq. (8.3) which is the optimal discriminator. In Fig. 8.2c, both G and D are gradually trained for some time. In this case, we can note that the samples $\mathbf{x}$ that were generated by G arrive at regions where the data is more likely to be classified well. This corresponds to the direction of increasing D and the estimate of D is updated based on the update in G. Fig. 8.2d shows the *Nash equilibrium* scenario, where neither of the participants shows any improvement in their performance since $p_{model}(\mathbf{x}) = p_{data}(\mathbf{x})$ and the generator G is optimal. This indeed means that the discriminator is unable to classify the real vs fake, i.e. $D(\mathbf{x}) = \frac{1}{2}$. This is represented by a constant line showing that all the points are equally likely to be predicted as real or fake.

In reality, the G and D are trained in simultaneous gradient steps, which means it is not necessary that D will be optimal at every step of training. Therefore, the training would mainly solve the function:

$$\min_G \max_D J(D, G) = \mathbb{E}_{\mathbf{x} \sim p_{data}(\mathbf{x})}[\log D(\mathbf{x})] + \mathbb{E}_{\mathbf{z} \sim p_z(\mathbf{z})}[\log(1 - D(G(\mathbf{z})))] \qquad (8.4)$$

In the above equation, we have real data $\mathbf{x}$ drawn from the dataset and the fake data synthesized by the generator continuously. The discriminator is trained on the real data and tries to identify the real class of input. The fake data is constructed by randomly sampling a vector z from the prior distribution over the model's latent variables. Therefore, the generator basically produces sample $G(z)$. So the generator tries to provide structure to unstructured data z by making it indistinguishable from the training samples. The discriminator then tries to classify this fake data. It is to be noted that the backpropagation algorithm can be implemented to utilize the derivatives of the discriminator's output with respect to its input for training the generator network. The generator is not given any specific targets. However, the discriminator training process is similar to that of a binary classifier except that the *fake* class comes from a varying distribution as the generator learns.

Example 8.3.1 *(GANs for generating 1D Gaussian data)*
GANs are utilized to generate 1D Gaussian data, simulating univariate datasets with characteristics similar to the bell-shaped, continuous probability distribution that defines the Gaussian distribution. The input dataset consists of 1000 samples, each drawn from a normal distribution with a mean of 0 and a standard deviation of 1. The GAN architecture includes a generator network, which is responsible for creating synthetic samples. It comprises several fully connected layers with activation functions. The input to this network is a 10-dimensional vector, and it progressively transforms this input into a single-dimensional output. Leaky ReLU activations are used as activation functions, and batch normalization layers enhance training stability.

The discriminator is a separate neural network designed to distinguish between real and synthetic data. Like the generator, it consists of fully connected layers with Leaky ReLU activation functions. It takes one-dimensional input and produces a binary classification output, indicating whether the input data is real or fake. The activation function used here is the sigmoid function. The discriminator is compiled with a binary cross-entropy loss function, which measures the difference between the predicted labels and the actual labels (real or fake). The Adam optimizer is employed with a learning rate of 0.0002 and a momentum parameter of 0.5. The GAN model combines the generator and discriminator. It takes a 10-dimensional input, processes it through the generator to produce synthetic data, and then passes this generated data to the discriminator. The GAN aims to generate data that is convincing enough to deceive the discriminator. The GAN model is compiled with the same binary cross-entropy loss function as the discriminator, but with distinct optimizer settings. Here, the Adam optimizer employs a lower learning rate of 0.0001 and a momentum parameter of 0.5. The GAN undergoes a total of 1000 training epochs to refine its generative and discriminative abilities.

During each epoch, the discriminator is trained with two batches of data: one containing real data with corresponding real labels (set to 1), and the other containing fake data generated by the generator with fake labels (set to 0). This dual training process enables the discriminator to become adept at distinguishing genuine data from synthetic data. Simultaneously, the GAN is trained with batches of random noise (the generator's input) and target labels set to 1. The GAN seeks to generate data that is realistic enough to fool the discriminator into classifying it as genuine.

After training, the generator creates synthetic data samples and displays them alongside real data using histograms. Figure 8.3 shows the real data's histogram in light gray, and the generated data's histogram is in gray.

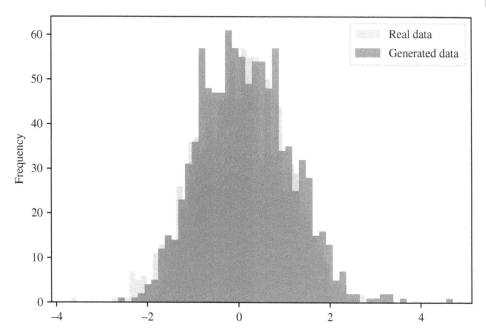

Figure 8.3 Comparison of real and generated data distributions: a histogram plot illustrating the similarity between the 1D Gaussian real data (light gray) and synthetic data generated by a GAN model (gray). The GAN successfully mimics the bell-shaped Gaussian distribution, showcasing its ability to produce data with characteristics resembling the original dataset.

8.4 Wasserstein GAN

Wasserstein GAN (WGAN) is a variation of GAN framework introduced in 2017 by Arjovsky et al. Arjovsky et al. (2017). The variant was focused on improving the stability of learning GANs. Though GANs have gained popularity in various applications such as image synthesis (M.-Y. Liu and Tuzel 2016; Shu et al. 2017), semantic segmentation (Isola et al. 2017; V. Nguyen et al. 2017), etc., due to their successful modeling of probability distributions, these architectures are known for their training complexity (H. Liu et al. 2019).

We know that GAN framework has two sub-models: Generator G and discriminator D that are trained together on a set of training samples. The generator tries to generate samples of data that are indistinguishable compared to the real data. Discriminator, on the other hand, tries to distinguish between the real samples and the ones generated by the generator. Considering that the models are fully differentiable, we can train both these models using backpropagation. Since the architecture is based on a two-player game, there is no guarantee of convergence to equilibrium in terms of training. The competition that occurs between these two participants makes it difficult to train the complete architecture such that they produce meaningful images. The stabilization of GAN training has itself been a field of interest among researchers (Berthelot et al. 2017; Roth et al. 2017; Gulrajani et al. 2017; Hjelm et al. 2017). Further, the generator and the discriminator do not correlate with the quality of samples which makes it difficult to understand whether there is improvement in terms of convergence of the generator or whether it has collapsed

(Engelmann and Lessmann 2021). This problem is called mode collapse, where the generator tries to map all the values of z to the same output. This result corresponds to the maximin-game rather than the minimax game, meaning the generator just identifies a single sample that the discriminator is unable to distinguish from the real examples and sticks to it. This is not the ideal purpose of the training of GANs.

WGAN aims at tackling this issue by performing the optimization of the framework using a different type of distance known as the *Wasserstein 1 distance*. There are different types of distances that can be used as a metric to measure the divergences between two distributions $p_1, p_2 \in p(\mathcal{X})$ where $\mathcal{X}$ is a compact metric set and $p(\mathcal{X})$ corresponds to the space of probability measures that are defined on $\mathcal{X}$ (Arjovsky et al. 2017):

Total variation (TV) distance:

$$TV(p_1, p_2) = \sup_{A \in \Omega} |p_1(A) - p_2(A)| \tag{8.5}$$

This metric is the standard statistical distance metric and provides the maximum difference in the probabilities assigned by p_1 and p_2. Note that Ω is the collection of subsets of a sample space and $\sup_{A \in \Omega}$ is the supremum (least upper bound) taken over all sets A in the set Ω. The value of this ranges from 0 to 1 and is 0 when the two distributions are identical and 1 when both of them are completely disjoint.

KL divergence (Kullback and Leibler 1951) is given by equation:

$$KL(p_1 \| p_2) = \int \log\left(\frac{p_1(x)}{p_2(x)}\right) p_1(x) dv(x) \tag{8.6}$$

In the above equation, the assumption is that both p_1 and p_2 are continuous and they admit probability densities with respect to the measure v that is defined on $\mathcal{X}^2$. The divergence in this case is asymmetric and does not satisfy *triangular inequality*.

Jenson–Shanon (JS) divergence:

$$JS(p_1, p_2) = KL(p_1 \| p_3) + KL(p_2 \| p_3) \tag{8.7}$$

where, p_3 is the mixture of $\frac{(p_1+p_2)}{2}$. The divergence in this case is symmetrical and it is always defined as we are able to always choose $v = p_3$.

Wasserstein 1 distance: This is also called the earth-mover (EM) distance and is given by the following equation:

$$W(p_1, p_2) = \inf_{J \in \Pi(p_1, p_2)} \mathbb{E}_{(x_1, x_2) \in J}\left[\|x_1 - x_2\|\right] \tag{8.8}$$

where, the set of all joint distributions $J(x_1, x_2)$ is denoted as $\Pi(p_1, p_2)$. The marginals of $J(x_1, x_2)$ are p_1 and p_2. The operation $\inf_{J \in \Pi(p_1, p_2)}$ is the infimum (the greatest lower bound) taken over all possible joint distributions J. The naming of EM came from the intuition that $J(x_1, x_2)$ can be considered as the "mass" that needs to be transported from x_1 to x_2 for transforming the distribution p_1 into p_2. The EM distance is the "cost" for the optimum transportation plan until one probability distribution equalizes to the other.

If we look at GANs, even if p_{model} and p_{data} have disjoint supports, the Wasserstein 1 distance can be meaningful to be used for optimization. For example, say if we have two candidates say p^1_{model} and p^2_{model}, then using Wasserstein 1 distance we can compute which distribution is the closest to p_{data} even if there is no overlap between them. On the other hand, for JS distance metric, it might return infinite for non-overlapping distributions (Engelmann and Lessmann 2021).

The Wasserstein 1 distance can be approximated to modify the GAN objective Eq. (8.4) as follows:

$$\min_{G} \max_{D} J_W(D, G) = \mathbb{E}_{\mathbf{x} \sim p_{data}(\mathbf{x})}[D(\mathbf{x})] - \mathbb{E}_{\mathbf{z} \sim p_z(\mathbf{z})}[D(G(\mathbf{z}))] \qquad (8.9)$$

This holds as long as D is a k-Lipschitz function which will control the rate at which the function corresponding to D can change. *Lipschitz constraint* ensures the smoothness and differentiability of the function almost anywhere. This constraint can be implemented using *weight clipping* of D such that it lies in a specific space or fixed box like $[-b, b]$. Hence, GANs can be converted to WGANs with weight clipping using two modifications: (1) removing the log in the loss function and (2) clipping the weight of the discriminator. Removal of the logarithm in the loss function helps with the gradient stability during training. Weight clipping helps with the weight parameter to lie in a compact space after each gradient update. The main drawback of weight clipping would be if we set the parameter b to be large. In such a scenario, the duration can be longer for the weight to reach a certain limit, which can cause the training of the discriminator to be difficult. As for smaller values for the parameter, b can easily lead to vanishing gradients when there are a large number of layers as well as when batch normalization is not incorporated.

The continuous and differentiable nature of EM distance helps in training the WGAN discriminator to optimality. Hence, the more we train the WGAN discriminator, the better or more reliable the *Wasserstein gradient* as it is differentiable everywhere. this is illustrated in Fig. 8.4. When both GAN and WGAN discriminator are trained until optimality, it can

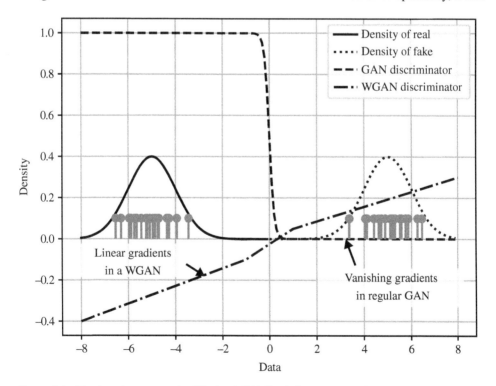

Figure 8.4 The learning approach of Optimal GAN discriminator and optimal WGAN discriminator for differentiating two Gaussian distributions. The minimax GAN discriminator is seen to saturate and results in vanishing gradients. WGAN discriminator successfully provides clean gradients across all the parts of the space. Source: Adapted from Arjovsky et al. (2017).

be seen that the GAN discriminator trains learn faster to classify between the real and fake samples but does not provide relevant gradient information. On the other hand, WGAN discriminator seems to converge to a linear function which provides cleaner gradients across the space and it never saturates.

Therefore, WGAN provides an alternative model that ensures stability in training compared to the traditional GANs. It helps with getting rid of problems such as mode collapse, helps to deal with vanishing gradient issues, and captures meaningful distances between different probability distributions.

8.5 DCGAN

In recent years, there has been significant activity in the domain of learning reusable feature representations from large, unlabeled datasets. In the field of computer vision, one can harness the vast reservoir of unlabeled images and videos to acquire valuable intermediate representations that can subsequently enhance various supervised learning tasks, such as image classification. One well-established approach to unsupervised representation learning involves clustering data and using these clusters to improve classification accuracy. In the context of images, a common method is to perform hierarchical clustering of image patches (Coates and A. Y. Ng 2012). This allows for the creation of robust image representations. Another popular technique is training autoencoders (Vincent et al. 2010) or ladder structures (Rasmus et al. 2015). These models encode images into compact codes and then decode them to recreate the original images with great precision.

An effective approach for creating resilient image representations involves the utilization of GANs during training, allowing the generator and discriminator networks' components to serve as feature extractors for supervised tasks. Nonetheless, early GAN implementations yielded images that exhibited issues with noise and clarity. A notable enhancement emerged with the introduction of the Laplacian pyramid extension, leading to superior image quality. This advancement brought its own challenge, as these images still suffered distortions when multiple models were sequentially connected, primarily due to the introduction of noise. Consequently, these methods have yet to fully exploit the potential of the generators in supervised tasks.

Previous efforts to upscale GANs using convolutional neural networks (CNNs) for image modeling yielded unsuccessful results. Through extensive model exploration, a family of architectures named deep convolutional generative adversarial networks (DCGANs) (Radford et al. 2015) was identified that achieved stable training across various datasets and facilitated the training of higher-resolution and deeper generative models. The key idea in this approach is to incorporate and adapt three innovations that have been popularly used in CNN architectures. The first modification involves the usage of the all convolutional net (Springenberg et al. 2014), which substitutes conventional spatial pooling functions, such as max pooling, with *strided convolutions*. This change allows the network to essentially teach itself how to down-sample spatial information. This approach is applied to both the generator and the discriminator, allowing them to learn how to enhance spatial details on their own.

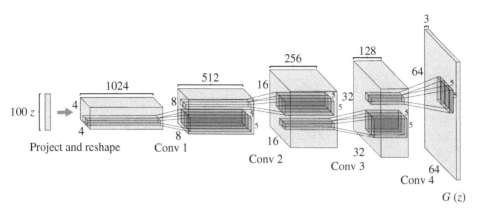

Figure 8.5 DCGAN generator architecture used for LSUN scene modeling. Source: Adapted from Radford et al. (2015).

The second modification involves the elimination of fully connected layers that appear following the convolutional layers. Instead, an intermediary approach has proven to be more effective, which utilizes the features extracted from the deepest convolutional layers and connects them directly to the input and output components of the generator and discriminator. The initial GAN layer, which receives a uniform noise distribution as input, may be considered fully connected because it essentially performs a matrix multiplication. However, the outcome of this operation is subsequently transformed into a four-dimensional tensor and serves as the foundational input for the convolutional stack. Conversely, for the discriminator, the feature map of the last convolution layer is flattened into a one-dimensional array, which is then utilized to generate a singular output via a sigmoid function. This single output quantifies the authenticity of the input data, providing a value within the range of 0 to 1, representing the likelihood of the data being real or fake. Figure 8.5 provides a visual depiction of the model architecture employed in the DCGAN.

Next, batch normalization is applied, a technique that enhances learning stability by standardizing the input for each unit to have a mean of zero and a variance of one. However, the direct application of batch normalization to all layers resulted in sample oscillations and model instability. To address this, batch normalization is intentionally omitted from the generator's output layer and the discriminator's input layer. Additionally, the generator employs the ReLU activation function, except for the output layer, which utilizes the tanh function. In contrast, the discriminator benefits from the leaky rectified activation function (A. L. Maas et al. 2013), particularly for higher-resolution modeling. This differs from the original GAN paper, which utilized the (MaxOut) activation.

8.5.1 DCGAN Training and Outcomes Highlights

DCGANs were trained on three datasets: large-scale scene understanding (LSUN) (F. Yu et al. 2015), Imagenet-1k, and a newly curated Faces dataset. To illustrate the model's scalability with larger datasets and higher-resolution image generation, a model was trained on the LSUN bedrooms dataset, which contains just over 3 million training examples.

The Faces dataset was created by scraping images containing human faces from random web image queries using individuals' names obtained from dbpedia, with the criteria that these individuals were born in the modern era. This dataset comprises 3 million images from 10,000 individuals. An OpenCV face detector was applied to these images to retain sufficiently high-resolution detections, resulting in approximately 350,000 face boxes used for training. Additionally, Imagenet-1k served as a source of natural images for unsupervised training.

The training images did not undergo any preprocessing steps, except for scaling to ensure they fell within the range of the tanh activation function, which is $[-1, 1]$. Training was carried out using mini-batch SGD with a batch size of 128. Weight initialization was performed by sampling from a normal distribution with a mean of zero and a standard deviation of 0.02. All models employed a LeakyReLU activation function with a consistent slope of 0.2. The optimization was done using the Adam optimizer with carefully tuned hyperparameters. Initially, the recommended learning rate of 0.001 was found to be too high, and it was subsequently reduced to 0.0002. Furthermore, maintaining the momentum term at the suggested value of 0.9 led to training oscillations and instability, so it was adjusted to 0.5 to enhance training stability.

A common approach to assessing the quality of unsupervised representation-learning algorithms involves employing them as feature extractors on supervised datasets and evaluating the performance of linear models applied to these features. For instance, on the CIFAR-10 dataset, a highly effective baseline performance of 80.6% accuracy has been demonstrated using K-means as the feature learning algorithm (Coates and A. Ng 2011). An extension of this base algorithm, incorporating multiple layers in an unsupervised manner, reaches an accuracy of 82.0%. To assess the representations learned by DCGANs for supervised tasks, training was conducted on the Imagenet-1k dataset. Subsequently, the discriminator's convolutional features were used from all layers and max pooling was applied to each layer's representation to generate a 4×4 spatial grid. These features are then flattened and concatenated to create a 28,672-dimensional vector. A regularized linear L2-SVM classifier is trained on top of this vector, achieving an accuracy of 82.8%, surpassing the performance of all K-means-based approaches. Nevertheless, DCGANs slightly underperform compared to Exemplar CNNs (Dosovitskiy et al. 2014), which achieve 84.3% accuracy. *Exemplar CNNs* train conventional discriminative CNNs in an unsupervised manner to distinguish specifically chosen, heavily augmented exemplar samples from the source dataset.

In another experiment, DCGANs were employed as feature extractors for the purpose of classifying StreetView house numbers (SVHN) digits (Netzer et al. 2011). In the SVHN dataset, the features extracted by the discriminator in a DCGAN are utilized for supervised tasks, particularly in scenarios where there is limited labeled data available. For the supervised training phase, 1000 training examples are randomly selected, with a focus on ensuring that they are evenly distributed across different classes. These examples are then used to train a regularized linear L2-SVM classifier which resulted in a test error rate of 22.48%. This achievement is particularly noteworthy considering the limited availability of only 1000 labeled examples. This result also surpasses an alternative CNN modification that was specifically designed to leverage unlabeled data (Zhao et al. 2015). A comparative analysis was made to evaluate whether the DCGAN's CNN architecture was the key factor behind the model's performance. To do so, a purely supervised CNN with the same architecture was trained on the same dataset. The optimization process involved exploring 64 different hyperparameter combinations (Bergstra and Yoshua Bengio 2012). However, this purely supervised CNN surprisingly exhibited a significantly higher validation error rate of 28.87%.

Example 8.5.1 *(DCGANs for generating synthetic images)*

DCGANs are utilized to generate synthetic digit images resembling the digits 0 to 9 as they appear in the MNIST dataset. The MNIST dataset is a well-known collection of handwritten digit images, consisting of 28×28 pixel grayscale images of digits from 0 to 9. These images are commonly used for tasks such as digit recognition. However, in this problem, the aim is to generate new, realistic digit images that resemble those in the MNIST dataset.

The DCGAN architecture includes a generator network, which is responsible for creating synthetic images. It starts with a dense layer taking a 100-dimensional random noise vector as input and reshaping it into a 3D tensor. Batch normalization standardizes activations, while LeakyReLU introduces non-linearity, and two transposed convolutional layers upsample the tensor. The first upsampling layer has 64 filters, a kernel size of 5, and a stride of 2, maintaining spatial dimensions. Batch normalization and LeakyReLU activation are applied again. The final layer has one filter, a kernel size of 5, and a stride of 2, using the hyperbolic tangent activation function to generate images.

The discriminator network is a binary classifier that distinguishes real from fake images. It begins with a convolutional layer with 64 filters, a kernel size of 5, and a stride of 2 with LeakyReLU activation. Another convolutional layer follows with 128 filters, a kernel size of 5, and a stride of 2, also using LeakyReLU activation. The Flatten layer converts the 2D output into a 1D vector. Lastly, a dense layer with one neuron and a sigmoid activation function produces a probability score. Values close to 0 indicate fake images, while values close to 1 indicate real images.

The DCGAN is trained through a process of adversarial training. The generator's goal is to generate images that can fool the discriminator, while the discriminator aims to correctly distinguish between real and fake images. Consequently, several essential hyperparameters are specified to govern the training process of the DCGANs. The dimension of the random noise vector is set to 100, influencing the diversity of generated images. A batch size of 32 is employed to determine the number of samples used in each training iteration. The DCGAN undergoes a total of 10,000 training epochs to refine its generative and discriminative abilities. The learning rate for the Adam optimizer is set to 0.0002, controlling the step size during weight updates, while the beta parameter for the Adam optimizer is configured as 0.5 to influence the optimizer's behavior during training. These hyperparameters collectively shape the DCGAN's learning process and ultimately impact the quality of the generated digit images.

Images produced during training are periodically stored at predefined intervals. Whenever the ongoing training epoch is a multiple of 1000, a set of 16 synthetic images is generated from random noise. Figure 8.6 illustrates these generated images that are presented in a 4×4 grid for easy visualization.

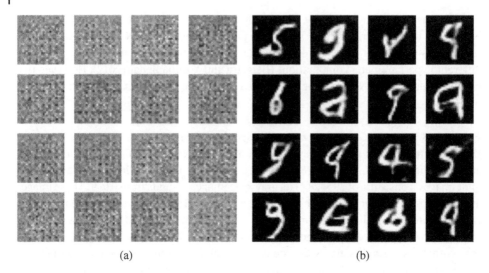

(a) (b)

Figure 8.6 (a) Generated images at Epoch 0: the initial output of the GAN model, where random noise is transformed into synthetic images. (b) Generated images at Epoch 9000: the progress of the GAN as it evolves over time, producing increasingly refined and realistic synthetic images.

8.6 cGAN

In recent years, supervised neural networks, particularly convolutional networks (Szegedy et al. 2015), have achieved significant success in various tasks. However, they face two primary challenges. First, when dealing with an extensive range of output categories, scaling these models becomes a computationally expensive task. For instance, in the case of an image labeling problem, there can be numerous potential labels for a single image. Second, much of the existing research has focused on establishing one-to-one mappings from inputs to outputs, overlooking the more natural probabilistic one-to-many mapping that is often encountered in real-world problems. For example, during image labeling, annotators might use varying but closely related terms to describe the same image.

To address these challenges, researchers propose innovative approaches. One strategy involves leveraging additional information from different sources, such as natural language data, to create meaningful label representations that improve prediction accuracy and allow for generalization to unseen labels. Additionally, a solution for the one-to-many mapping problem is to adopt conditional probabilistic generative models (Mirza and Osindero 2014). In this framework, inputs such as images condition the prediction process, resulting in the generation of a distribution encompassing multiple potential outcomes, as opposed to providing a single deterministic response. In the case of unconditioned generative models, the process of generating data lacks precise control or guidance regarding the characteristics of the produced data. However, through the act of conditioning the generative model with additional information, it becomes possible to exercise intentional influence over the data generation process. Such conditioning can take various forms, including the use of class labels to make the model generate specific kinds of data, the utilization of partial data to complete missing portions (Ian Goodfellow et al. 2013b), or the incorporation of information from different data modalities to direct the generative process toward the desired outcomes.

GANs can become more versatile by incorporating extra information, denoted as **y**, into their models. This additional information, **y**, can take various forms, such as class labels or data from different sources. The way this is achieved is by including **y** as an input for both the generator and discriminator. In the generator, **y** is combined with the initial noise input, typically denoted as $p_z(\mathbf{z})$, to form a joint hidden representation. The GAN framework provides flexibility in how this hidden representation is constructed, allowing for various ways to incorporate the additional information. Conversely, in the discriminator, the primary input data, **x**, and the supplementary information, **y**, are simultaneously presented as inputs to a discriminative function, typically represented by a MLP. This approach equips GANs with the capacity to generate data conditioned on specific attributes or contextual information, broadening their applicability across various domains and tasks. Figure 8.7 provides an overview of the configuration of a basic conditional adversarial network.

The following expression illustrates the objective function of a two-player minimax game, with a generator denoted as G and a discriminator referred to as D in a cGAN:

$$\min_{G} \max_{D} J_c(D, G) = \mathbb{E}_{\mathbf{x} \sim p_{data}(\mathbf{x})}[\log D(\mathbf{x}|\mathbf{y})] + \mathbb{E}_{\mathbf{z} \sim p_z(\mathbf{z})}[\log(1 - D(G(\mathbf{z}|\mathbf{y})))] \quad (8.10)$$

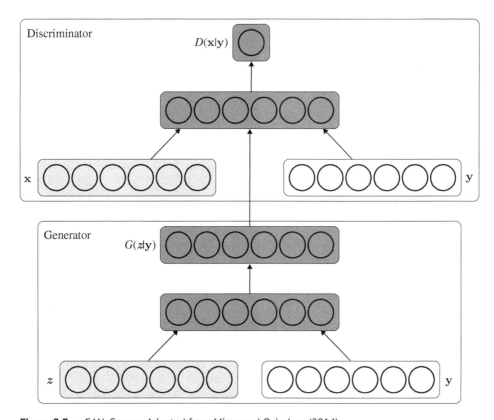

Figure 8.7 cGAN. Source: Adapted from Mirza and Osindero (2014).

8.6.1 cGAN Training and Outcomes Highlights

The *conditional adversarial neural network* was trained on MNIST images, where each image was conditioned on a class label represented as a one-hot vector. In the generator network, a random noise vector z of length 100 was sampled from a uniform distribution within a unit hypercube. Both the noise vector z and the class label vector y were processed through hidden layers with ReLU activation. These hidden layers had sizes of 200 and 1000 units, respectively, and the outputs of these two sets of hidden layers were combined into a single hidden layer with 1200 units. Finally, there was a final output layer with a sigmoid activation function responsible for generating 784-dimensional MNIST samples.

The discriminator network processed the input image x through a MaxOut layer with 240 units and 5 pieces or groups. In this setup, each of these five groups within the Max-Out layer operated as a distinct set of neurons, with the output being determined by the neuron within each group that exhibited the highest activation for the given input. On the other hand, the class label y was processed through a MaxOut layer with 50 units and 5 pieces. Both hidden layers were then combined into a joint MaxOut layer with 240 units and 4 pieces before being passed through a sigmoid layer.

The training process for the model employed SGD with mini-batches of 100 samples. Initially, a learning rate of 0.1 was used, and this learning rate was gradually reduced exponentially to reach 0.000001, with a decay factor of 1.00004. Additionally, momentum was incorporated into the training process, starting with an initial value of 0.5 and gradually increasing to 0.7. To prevent overfitting, a dropout with a probability of 0.5 was applied to both the generator and discriminator networks. The stopping point during training was determined by relying on the log-likelihood estimate obtained from the validation set.

Furthermore, conditional adversarial networks were employed for the automated tagging of images with multilabel predictions. In this approach, image characteristics are extracted using a pre-trained convolutional model trained on the ImageNet dataset, while textual representations are generated from a collection of user-generated tags, titles, and descriptions sourced from the YFCC100M dataset (Thomee et al. 2016). The training process encompasses the utilization of fixed convolutional and language models during adversarial network training. Experiments were conducted on the MIR Flickr 25,000 dataset, with the exclusion of images that lacked any tags. The model's training process closely resembled that of the MNIST dataset training. The hyperparameters and architectural decisions were determined through a combination of cross-validation and a blend of random grid search and manual selection.

8.7 CycleGAN

CycleGAN (Zhu et al. 2017) is a novel method presented to tackle the problem of image-to-image translation without the need for paired training data. Image-to-image translation (Isola et al. 2017) involves transforming an image from one representation to another, such as converting grayscale images to color or mapping edge-maps (simplified sketches outlining the shapes and contours of objects in an image) to photographic images. Extensive research efforts spanning the domains of computer vision, image processing, computational photography, and graphics have yielded robust translation systems in supervised settings (Eigen and Fergus 2015; Hertzmann et al. 2023; Johnson et al. 2016). These systems operate effectively when provided with pairs of example images. However, acquiring such paired data can be challenging and resource-intensive for various applications. For instance, datasets suitable for tasks like semantic segmentation (Cordts et al. 2016) are relatively scarce and typically of limited scale. Acquiring input–output pairs for graphics-related tasks, such as artistic stylization, can be even more demanding, given the intricacy of the desired output, often necessitating the involvement of artistic expertise. In numerous cases, such as object transfiguration, where, for instance, a zebra needs to be transformed into a horse, defining the precise desired output becomes a complex process.

Numerous methods were designed to overcome the need for paired training examples. For instance, Rosales et al. Resales et al. (2003) propose a Bayesian framework that combines a prior derived from a patch-based Markov random field computed from a source image and a likelihood term obtained from multiple style images. More recently, approaches like CoGAN (M.-Y. Liu and Tuzel 2016) and cross-modal scene networks (Aytar et al. 2017) utilize a weight-sharing strategy to learn a shared representation across domains. Concurrently, Liu and collaborators (M.-Y. Liu et al. 2017) extend the above framework by incorporating a combination of VAE and GAN. Another parallel line of research (Shrivastava et al. 2017; Taigman et al. 2016; Bousmalis et al. 2017) promotes the sharing of specific content features between input and output, even in the presence of style differences. These methods also leverage adversarial networks and introduce additional terms to ensure the output's proximity to the input within predefined metric spaces, such as class label space, image pixel space, and image feature space.

In contrast to the methods mentioned earlier, CycleGAN does not depend on a task-specific, pre-defined similarity measure between the input and output, nor does it make an assumption that the input and output must exist within the same low-dimensional embedding space. This characteristic renders CycleGAN to be a versatile solution applicable to a wide range of vision and graphics tasks. The fundamental assumption here is that an underlying connection exists between these domains, implying that they represent different portrayals of the same underlying scene. The primary goal is to uncover this hidden relationship through the training of a mapping function represented as $G : X \rightarrow Y$. This entails utilizing one set of images in the domain X and another set in the domain Y. The objective is to ensure that the resulting output, denoted as $\hat{y} = G(\mathbf{x})$ for any x in X, closely resembles the images in Y. This is achieved by training an adversary to differentiate between $\hat{y}$ and $\mathbf{y}$. Thus, the optimal G consequently transforms domain X into a domain $\hat{Y}$ that follows the same distribution as Y. It is important to note that this approach does not ensure a one-to-one correspondence between individual input and output images, as there exist infinitely many mappings G that can induce the same distribution over $\hat{y}$. Additionally, in practice, optimizing the adversarial objective on its own often leads to a phenomenon referred to as *mode collapse*, where all input images map to the same output image, hindering the optimization process.

To address these challenges, a structured approach is introduced that relies on the concept of cycle consistency. This implies that when a sentence undergoes translation, such as from English to French and subsequently from French to English, it should be possible to restore the original sentence. In mathematical terms, if there's a translator $G : X \rightarrow Y$ and another translator $F : Y \rightarrow X$, both G and F should function as inverses of each other, establishing

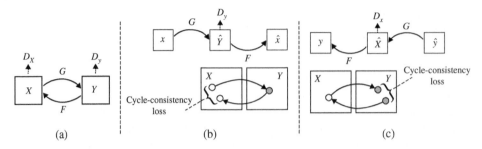

Figure 8.8 CycleGAN model formulation. Source: Reproduced from the original paper (Zhu et al. 2017).

one-to-one mappings between the two domains. To ensure this property, both G and F are trained simultaneously, and a *cycle consistency loss* (Zhou et al. 2016) is introduced. This loss function encourages the condition $F(G(\mathbf{x})) \approx \mathbf{x}$ and $G(F(\mathbf{y})) \approx \mathbf{y}$. By combining this loss with adversarial losses applied to domains X and Y, a comprehensive objective for unpaired image-to-image translation is formulated. Here the two domains X and Y has training samples $\{x_i\}_{i=1}^N$ where $x_i \in X$ and $\{y_i\}_{i=1}^N$ where $y_i \in Y$. The data distribution is denoted as $\mathbf{x} \sim p_{data}(\mathbf{x})$ and $\mathbf{y} \sim p_{data}(\mathbf{y})$. As depicted in Fig. 8.8, this model presents two mapping functions: $G : X \to Y$ and $F : Y \to X$, along with corresponding adversarial discriminators, D_Y and D_X. Here D_Y's role is to encourage G to translate X into outputs that are indistinguishable from those in domain Y, while D_X performs a similar task in the reverse direction with F. The objective includes two types of terms: adversarial losses, which aim to align the distribution of generated images with the data distribution in the target domain, and cycle consistency losses, which serve to ensure that the learned mappings G and F do not contradict each other.

Adversarial losses are applied to both mapping functions. The objective for the mapping function $G : X \to Y$ and its discriminator D_Y is expressed as:

$$J(G, D_Y, X, Y) = \mathbb{E}_{\mathbf{y} \sim p_{data}(\mathbf{y})}[\log D_Y(\mathbf{y})] + \mathbb{E}_{\mathbf{x} \sim p_{data}(\mathbf{x})}[\log(1 - D_Y(G(\mathbf{x})))] \tag{8.11}$$

where G is tasked with generating images $G(\mathbf{x})$ that closely resemble samples from domain Y, while D_Y's role is to differentiate between generated samples $G(\mathbf{x})$ and authentic samples $\mathbf{y}$. The objective here is for G to minimize this function, while its adversary D aims to maximize it. This can be mathematically represented as $\min_G \max_{D_Y} J(G; D_Y; X; Y)$.

Nonetheless, if a network possesses sufficient capacity and complex function-processing capabilities, it has the potential to transform the same input images into multiple random permutations within the target domain. Therefore, relying solely on adversarial losses cannot ensure that the learned function can accurately map an individual input, represented as x_i to a desired output, denoted as y_i. *Cycle consistency* is used to address this challenge and narrow down the space of possible mapping functions. Hence for every image $\mathbf{x}$ from domain X, the image translation cycle should have the ability to bring $\mathbf{x}$ back to its original form: $\mathbf{x} \to G(\mathbf{x}) \to F(G(\mathbf{x})) \approx \mathbf{x}$. This property is referred to as *forward cycle consistency*. Similarly, for each image y from domain Y, the functions G and F should also exhibit backward cycle consistency: $y \to F(\mathbf{y}) \to G(F(\mathbf{y})) \approx \mathbf{y}$. The overall cycle consistency loss

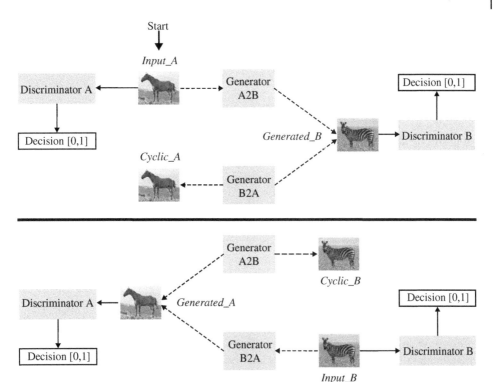

Figure 8.9 CycleGAN model formulation. (a) Mapping functions and associated adversarial discriminators (b) Forward cycle-consistency loss and (c) Backward cycle-consistency loss. Source: Reproduced from the blog https://hardikbansal.github.io/CycleGANBlog/ last accessed November 30, 2023."

function can be expressed as follows:

$$J_{cyc}(G, F) = \mathbb{E}_{\mathbf{x} \sim p_{data}(\mathbf{x})}[\|F(G(\mathbf{x})) - \mathbf{x}\|_1] + \mathbb{E}_{\mathbf{y} \sim p_{data}(\mathbf{y})}[\|G(F(\mathbf{y})) - \mathbf{y}\|_1] \tag{8.12}$$

The complete objective at hand is as follows:

$$J_{CYC}(G, F, D_X, D_Y) = J(G, D_Y, X, Y) + J(F, D_X, Y, X) + \lambda J_{cyc}(G, F) \tag{8.13}$$

Here, the parameter λ denotes the weight given to the cycle consistency loss term. The CycleGAN framework is shown in Fig. 8.9.

8.7.1 CycleGAN Training and Outcomes Highlights

The architectural framework for the generative networks is drawn from the work of Johnson and their colleagues Johnson et al. (2016), who demonstrated impressive results in neural style transfer and super-resolution. This network structure comprises three convolutional layers, along with several residual blocks (He et al. 2016), two *fractionally strided convolutions* with a stride of $\frac{1}{2}$, and a final convolutional layer responsible for mapping features to

RGB values. For images of size 128×128, six blocks are used, while for images of 256×256 resolution and higher, nine blocks are employed. In the case of the discriminator networks, the architecture employed consists of a 70×70 PatchGANs (Ledig et al. 2017). These discriminator networks are designed to classify whether 70×70 overlapping image patches are genuine or generated.

In the model training procedure of cost function J, the *negative log-likelihood* objective has been replaced with a least-squares loss. This change in the loss function is known to be more stable during training and results in higher-quality outcomes. Specifically, for $J(G; D; X; Y)$, the approach is to train the generator G to minimize $\mathbb{E}_{\mathbf{x} \sim p_{data}(\mathbf{x})}[(D(G(\mathbf{x})) - 1)^2]$. The discriminator D is also trained to minimize $\mathbb{E}_{\mathbf{y} \sim p_{data}(\mathbf{y})}[(D(\mathbf{y}) - 1)^2] + \mathbb{E}_{\mathbf{x} \sim p_{data}(\mathbf{x})}[(D(G(\mathbf{x}))^2]$. Meanwhile, when the model's performance fluctuates during training, instead of updating the discriminators solely based on images generated by the latest generators, an image buffer storage mechanism is employed to retain the 50 most recent images generated by the generator. This buffer likely maintains a history of generated images over training iterations. This provides a more stable and consistent set of training examples for the discriminator, facilitating better convergence of the GAN. Further, the networks start training with a constant learning rate of 0.0002 for 100 epochs, followed by linear decay to zero over the next 100 epochs. In all the experiments the parameter λ is set to be 10 and the Adam solver has a batch size of 1.

The CycleGAN model is assessed in comparison to several baseline methods through a combination of qualitative and quantitative metrics. This evaluation encompasses two main objectives: first, the translation of semantic labels into images, a task conducted using the Cityscapes dataset (Cordts et al. 2016), and second, the transformation of maps into aerial photographs using data sourced from Google Maps. Furthermore, perceptual studies are conducted on Amazon Mechanical Turk to gauge the realism of the model's generated outputs. In these perceptual studies, participants are presented with pairs of images, one being authentic and the other generated either by the CycleGAN or alternative methods. Participants are then instructed to determine which image they believe to be real.

While perceptual studies are the established benchmark for evaluating graphical realism, the evaluation of the Cityscapes labels-to-photo task employs an automated quantitative metric like the FCN score, as depicted in Table 8.1. The FCN metric assesses the interpretability of the generated photos using an off-the-shelf semantic segmentation algorithm known as the FCN. The FCN generates a label map for a given generated photo, which can then be compared to the input ground truth labels using standard semantic segmentation metrics such as per-pixel accuracy, per-class accuracy, and mean class IoU. The underlying

Table 8.1 Comparison of FCN scores of CycleGAN with various baseline models using the Cityscapes dataset.

Methods	CoGAN	BiGAN	SimGAN	Feature loss + GAN	pix2pix	CycleGAN
Per-pixel acc	0.40	0.19	0.20	0.06	0.71	0.52
Per-class acc	0.10	0.06	0.10	0.04	0.25	0.17
Class IoU	0.06	0.02	0.04	0.01	0.18	0.11

concept is that if a photo is generated from a label map specifying "car on the road," it is considered successful if the FCN applied to the generated photo correctly identifies "car on the road."

8.7.2 Applications of CycleGAN

CycleGAN demonstrates its versatility in various tasks, even when paired training data is limited or unavailable. The major applications of CycleGAN are as follows:

Collection style transfer: This application involves training the model on landscape photographs from sources like Flickr and WikiArt. Unlike traditional *neural style transfer*, this method aims to mimic the style of entire collections of artworks, allowing for the generation of photos in the style of specific artists like Cezanne, Monet, Van Gogh, or Ukiyo-e. The dataset includes a substantial number of images for each artist.

Object transfiguration: In this application, the model is trained to translate one object class from the ImageNet dataset to another. Each object class contains around 1000 training images. Unlike some approaches that focus on translating objects within the same category, this method aims to transform objects between visually similar categories.

Season transfer: This application involves training the model on a dataset of winter and summer photos of Yosemite, downloaded from Flickr. The goal is to translate images between these two seasonal contexts, allowing for transformations from winter scenes to summer scenes and vice versa.

Photo generation from paintings: For this task, the model translates paintings into photographs. To improve the quality of translations, an additional loss is introduced to encourage color composition preservation between input and output. This helps in ensuring that the generated photos maintain the color integrity of the original paintings.

Photo enhancement: In this application, the model is trained on flower photos from Flickr. The source domain comprises smartphone photos with deep depth of field (DoF) due to a small aperture, while the target domain consists of DSLR photos with shallower DoF due to a larger aperture. The model successfully generates photos with shallower DoF, enhancing the aesthetic quality of smartphone photos.

8.8 StyleGAN

Computer vision applications demand higher resolution and quality of images. It has been observed through various applications that networks inspired from GANs have been able to produce high-resolution and good-quality images over the years. The style transfer technique in computer vision is an application that is explored a lot using different architectures inspired from GANs. The *StyleGAN* architecture was introduced to control the image synthesis process and this architecture was motivated by the style transfer literature (X. Huang and Belongie 2017). StyleGAN was first introduced by NVIDIA researchers in late 2018 (Karras et al. 2019). Following the main version, other subsequent versions such as StyleGAN2 (Karras et al. 2020a) and StyleGAN2-ADA (Karras et al. 2020b) were also released which refined the architecture as well as training methodology. The

StyleGAN architecture makes use of the intermediate latent space to perform controlled image modifications, i.e. the architecture will be able to modify a given image rather than the randomly generated one by GANs (Abdal et al. 2019).

The GAN inspired architectures have seen their rapid utilization in the field of computer vision with fast-paced improvements in image quality and resolution generated by such networks. DCGAN introduced in Section 8.5 was the first milestone to use the fully CNN in GANs. Following this various other architectures came up in different computer vision applications with improvements in different training aspects such as loss functions (Mao et al. 2017; Arjovsky et al. 2017), normalization or regularization (Miyato et al. 2018; Gulrajani et al. 2017), as well as based on the architecture (Gulrajani et al. 2017). The computational power was always a question for achieving high-quality training and most of the testing was performed on poor-quality and low-resolution image datasets due to the high computational demand. This computation issue was addressed in the work of Karras *et al.* Karras et al. (2017) where they collected and created a high-quality human face dataset CelebA-HQ and introduced a progressive methodology for training GANs over higher-resolution input for image generation tasks. The architecture was called ProGAN and it was the first GAN model to generate realistic 1024×1024 high-resolution human face images. However, the training and generation using complex datasets such as ImageNet was still a challenge. Later on, in Brock et al. (2018), using the BigGAN model, it was argued that the training of GANs can be improved by using a larger batch size. Following this Karras et al., came up with another much more diverse and high-quality human face dataset called Flickr-Faces-HQ (FFHQ). Using this dataset StyleGAN was introduced which improved the performance of GANs especially on the human face image generation tasks.

StyleGAN architecture re-designs the generator architecture to expose novel approaches that would accommodate the controlling of the image synthesis process. The generator, in this case, adjusts to the "style" of the image at each convolutional layer. It starts with a learned constant input and the modification to adjust the "style" is learned based on the latent code. This would allow the architecture to directly control the strength of the features of the image even at different scales. Additionally, noise is also injected into the network which enables it to perform scale-specific interpolation operations and mixing. This architecture does not change or modify the discriminator network or the loss function and focuses on only improving the generator part of the GAN network.

Unlike the traditional generator, in StyleGAN the input latent code is embedded into an intermediate latent space which captures the variation represented in the network. Also, the input latent space must be aligned with the probability density of the training data which might lead to some entanglement. It is claimed that the latent space is unrestrictive, the degree of entanglement is explained using two automated metrics: perceptual path and linear separability. Using these metrics, later it is shown that StyleGAN generator architecture allows more linear as well as less entangled representations with different variation factors compared to that of the traditional generator architecture.

In a traditional generator, the input latent code is provided using an input layer which is the first layer of the feedforward network, as shown in Fig. 8.10a. For StyleGAN, the input layer is removed completely, instead starting part is basically learning from a constant. Let us consider the latent space being represented as $\mathcal{Z}$ and the latent code as $\mathbf{z}$.

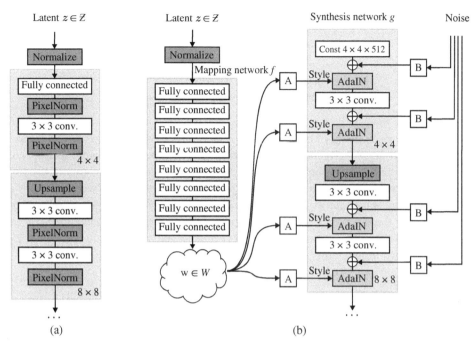

Figure 8.10 (a) Traditional vs (b) style-based generator. Source: Karras, Laine, and Aila 2019 / IEEE / Public Domain.

Now, a *non-linear mapping network* given by $f : \mathcal{Z} \rightarrow \mathcal{W}$ produces $\mathbf{w} \in \mathcal{W}$, as shown in Fig. 8.10b. For the sake of simplicity, the dimensions of both these spaces are set to 512. the mapping f is created using MLP of 8 layers, as shown in Fig. 8.10. This mapping basically is an affine transformation that learned and specialized $\mathbf{w}$ to various styles $\mathbf{y}$. The styles $\mathbf{y} = (\mathbf{y}_s, \mathbf{y}_b)$ basically control the adaptive instance normalization (AdaIN) (X. Huang and Belongie 2017; Ghiasi et al. 2017; Dumoulin et al. 2016; Dumoulin et al. 2018) operation which comes after each convolution layer in the synthesis network. The synthesis network consists of 18 layers. The AdaIN operation can be represented as the following:

$$AdaI\,N(\mathbf{x}_i, \mathbf{y}) = \mathbf{y}_{s,i}\frac{\mathbf{x}_i - \mu(\mathbf{x}_i)}{\sigma(\mathbf{x}_i)} + \mathbf{y}_{b,i} \tag{8.14}$$

where each of the feature maps given by $\mathbf{x}_i$ is normalized individually and then the scaling is performed followed by adding bias using some scalar component of style $\mathbf{y}$. The dimension of $\mathbf{y}$ is two times the number of feature maps for each layer. In Fig. 8.10, we can see that the first step is to do a mapping from the input to the intermediate latent space $\mathcal{W}$. This mapping is then used to control the AdaIN for each convolutional layer. The AdaIN operation is particularly suitable for this purpose due to its efficiency and ability to provide compact representation. Following this, Gaussian noise is added before evaluating the non-linearity. The noise input helps in introducing stochastic detail to the generation process. This noise image is passed onto each of the feature maps with the help of the learned scale factors. This is then finally added to the output of the corresponding convolution as shown in the figure. "A" in Fig. 8.10b corresponds to the learned affine transformation and "B" is the addition of learned per-channel scaling factors with the noise input. Compared to other style transfer approaches, StyleGAN performs a spatially invariant style **y** from vector **w** instead of using a fixed image.

8.8.1 StyleGAN Properties and Outcome Highlights

The redesign of the generator not only helps with the controlled image synthesis but also improves the image quality considerably. For evaluation purposes, the metric that is used for StyleGANs is the FID (Heusel et al. 2017). It is claimed to be a much better metric than the inception score in capturing the similarity of generated images compared to the real image. This score also helps with capturing the level of disturbance as well. Since, it's a distance measure, for similarity the lower the value the better the result. FID is the distance d between two Gaussians with one having mean μ_1 and covariance Σ_1 obtained from a particular probability distribution p_1. The other Gaussian has mean μ_2 and covariance, Σ_2 which is obtained from another distribution p_2. The FID distance is given by:

$$d^2((\mu_1, \Sigma_1), (\mu_2, \Sigma_2)) = \|\mu_1 - \mu_2\|_2^2 + Tr(\Sigma_1 + \Sigma_2 - 2(\Sigma_1 \Sigma_2)^{1/2}) \tag{8.15}$$

The evaluation of StyleGAN was performed on two different datasets n CELEBA-HQ (Karras et al. 2017) and FFHQ (Karras et al. 2019). Table 8.2 shows the results related to the quality of images generated using the FID metric with best scores indicated in bold for each dataset. The starting baseline model was that of ProGAN (Karras et al. 2017) which was then improved using bilinear upsampling/downsampling operations (R. Zhang 2019). Further, the comparison of performance is done for (c) adding the mapping network along with AdaIN operation (d) removing the traditional input layer and learning from the constant tensor instead, as shown in Fig. 8.10. In column (e), the noise input is introduced, and then finally, (f) the mixing regularization is added. The results keep improving as we progress along the table which shows that modifying the network to (e) from the base architecture (b) has improved the FIDs significantly.

The main objective of StyleGAN generator was to make controlled image synthesis possible and this was achieved using scale-specific modifications to different styles. There is a mapping network and affine transformations which allows the network to draw samples corresponding to each of the styles from the distribution that is learned by the generator. The synthesis network then generates a novel image based on these style collections.

Table 8.2 The FID scores for different generator designs.

Dataset	(a) Progressive GAN (Karras et al. 2017)	(b) + Tuning (incl. bilinear up/down	(c) + Mapping and styles	(d) Remove traditional input layer	(e) + Noise inputs	(f) + Mixing regularization
CelebA-HQ	7.70	6.11	5.34	5.07	**5.06**	5.17
FFHQ	8.04	5.25	4.85	4.88	4.42	**4.40**

The FID here was calculated using 50,000 images randomly drawn from the training set (Karras et al. 2019).

Additionally, the modification of a certain subset of styles affects only some specific aspects of the image, meaning, the styles are localized within the network.

Next, let us understand the localization aspect of the network. Considering the AdaIN operation shown in Eq. (8.14) each of the channels is first normalized to zero mean and unit variance. Following this, to the normalized channels, the scales and biases are applied based on the style.

Style mixing: The localization of styles in the network is further facilitated by using *mixing regularization*. In this process, two random latent codes are used to produce a given percentage of images during training instead of just using the usual one latent code approach. Let's say we pass two latent codes z_1 and z_2 through the mapping network to obtain $\mathbf{w}_1$ and $\mathbf{w}_2$ which help in controlling the styles such that $\mathbf{w}_1$ comes before the crossover point followed by $\mathbf{w}_2$. This type of regularization approach prevents the network from getting confused about the correlation between adjacent styles. Using this technique, the localization improves during the training. It also improves the tolerance of the model to adverse operations along with retaining high-level, meaningful attributes of the image.

Stochastic variation: The aspects that introduce randomness in human faces can be many, such as hairs, freckles, pores, etc. These aspects can be indeed randomized without any impact on the perception of the image. To achieve this *stochastic variation* in the image, the StyleGAN generator adds *per-pixel noise* after each convolution. This makes sure that the generator can produce different noise realizations of the same image. It can be noted that these noise realizations affect only the stochastic aspect of the image. The effect of the noise is localized in the network. At any point in the generator, the network is always pushed toward introducing some novelty content as possible. The localized effect for the stochastic variation is ensured by adding a fresh set of noise to each layer. This makes sure that there are no side effects from the earlier activations.

Disentanglement: The main goal of *disentanglement* is that the latent space consists of linear subspaces, where each of these subspaces controls an individual factor of variation. Additionally, the sampling probability of each of these variation factors in $\mathcal{Z}$ should match the corresponding density of the training set. In the case of StyleGAN, the sampling from $\mathcal{W}$ is basically induced from the mapping $f(\mathbf{z})$. The mapping can be manipulated so that the factors of variation are more linear. Therefore, realistic images can be easily generated based on disentangled representation compared to entangled representation. The metric introduced for quantifying this disentanglement includes *Perceptual path length* and *linear separability*. Both these disentanglement methods can be used as regularizers during training.

Perceptual path length quantifies the drastic variations that the image undergoes as interpolation is performed in the latent space. For example, the perceptually smoother transition is observed in a less curved latent space compared to a highly curved latent space. The basis for this metric is from the perceptual pairwise image distance (R. Zhang et al. 2018) which stands for the weighted difference between two VGG16 embeddings (Simonyan and Zisserman 2015). here the weights are fit in such a way that they agree with human perceptual similarity judgments. If we subdivide an interpolation path in the latent space into linear segments, the total perceptual length of this path can be defined as the sum of perceptual differences over each of these segments, using the image distance metric. The other metric that can be used to quantify the disentanglement of the latent space is linear separability. Using this metric, we can quantify how well the points in latent space can be separated into two distinct portions using a linear hyperplane. This approach would provide us with sets that correspond to a specific binary characteristic of the image.

Overall, the architecture is capable of performing better *interpolation*, along with adding better disentangling of latent variation factors. Also, the added features in the generator helped the model to perform unsupervised separation of higher-level characteristics and stochastic variation in the synthesized images.

8.9 StackGAN

Creating photo-realistic images from textual descriptions is a significant challenge with wide-ranging applications, such as enhancing photos through editing and facilitating computer-aided design tasks. In recent times, GANs, have exhibited promising capabilities in the synthesis of real-world images. Specifically, when conditioned on provided text descriptions, cGANs (S. E. Reed et al. 2016a, 2016b) have demonstrated the ability to produce images closely aligned with the intended textual meaning. However, augmenting existing state-of-the-art GAN models with additional upsampling layers for the purpose of generating high-resolution images typically leads to training instability and the generation of nonsensical outputs. The primary challenge in generating high-resolution images with GANs lies in the fact that the distributions representing natural images and the implied model distributions may not effectively overlap within the expansive, high-dimensional pixel space (Sønderby et al. 2016; Arjovsky and Bottou 2017). This issue becomes more pronounced as the resolution of the images in question increases. Even though prior works indicate the successful generation of credible 64×64 images conditioned on textual descriptions, however, these images often lacked intricate details and vivid object components.

Therefore, to tackle the problem of text-to-photo-realistic image synthesis more effectively, the approach with stacked generative adversarial networks (StackGAN) decomposes it into two more manageable sub-problems. To create high-resolution images with realistic details, a simple yet efficient StackGAN method was introduced (see Fig. 8.11). This method breaks down the text-to-image generation process into two stages:

Stage I GAN: This stage sketches the fundamental shape and primary colors of the object based on the provided text description. It also generates the background layout from a random noise vector, resulting in a low-resolution image.

Stage II GAN: In the second stage, the low-resolution image from Stage I is refined to correct any defects and enhance the object's details. It achieves this by re-evaluating the text description, ultimately producing a high-resolution, photo-realistic image.

The improved likelihood of the model distribution, derived from a somewhat aligned, lower-resolution image, overlapping with the distribution of the actual image, serves as the fundamental reason why Stage II GAN can produce superior high-resolution images. This capability allowed StackGAN to generate the first photorealistic 256×256 resolution images based on textual descriptions.

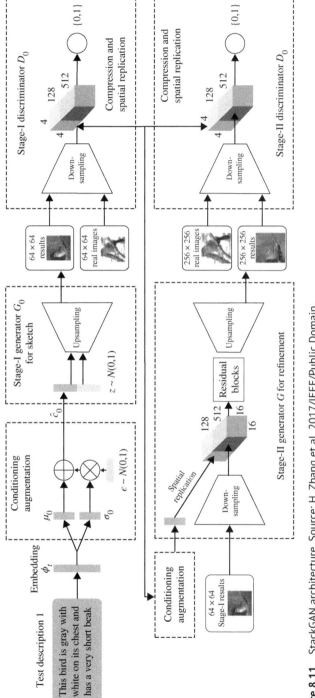

Figure 8.11 StackGAN architecture. Source: H. Zhang et al. 2017/IEEE/Public Domain.

During the implementation of StackGAN, the initial process involves the encoding of a textual description denoted as **t**, using an encoder, resulting in the generation of a text embedding ψ_t. However, the latent space associated with the text embedding typically possesses high dimensionality, often exceeding 100 dimensions. When confronted with limited data, this high dimensionality can lead to non-smoothness within the latent data manifold. Hence, a novel approach called *conditioning augmentation* was introduced to produce additional conditioning variables $\hat{c}$. Contrary to the fixed conditioning text variable **c** described in prior studies, a distinct approach involves the random sampling of latent variables $\hat{c}$. These variables are drawn from an independent Gaussian distribution represented as $\mathcal{N}(\mu(\psi_t), \Sigma(\psi_t))$ where both the mean $\mu(\psi_t)$ and the diagonal covariance matrix $\Sigma(\psi_t)$ are determined as functions of the text embedding. Consequently, conditioning augmentation helps in augmenting the number of training pairs, which is particularly beneficial when working with a limited set of image-text pairs.

To further promote smoothness within the conditioning manifold and prevent overfitting (Larsen et al. 2016), an additional regularization term becomes part of the generator's training objective:

$$KL(\mathcal{N}(\mu(\psi_t), \Sigma(\psi_t)) \| \mathcal{N}(0, \mathbf{I})) \tag{8.16}$$

The above term measures the KL divergence between the conditioning Gaussian distribution, which is modeled by $\mathcal{N}(\mu(\psi_t), \Sigma(\psi_t))$, and a standard Gaussian distribution, represented as $\mathcal{N}(0, I)$. This technique promotes smoothness within the latent conditioning manifold by permitting minor, random adjustments within it, ultimately enhancing the variety of synthesized images.

Let ψ_t represent the text embedding obtained from the textual description using a pretrained encoder (S. E. Reed et al. 2016a). The *Gaussian conditioning variables* $\hat{c}_0$ linked to this text embedding are sampled from a Gaussian distribution $\mathcal{N}(\mu_0(\psi_t), \Sigma_0(\psi_t))$. This sampling procedure aims to capture the semantic essence of the textual description represented by ψ_t while introducing valuable variations. While conditioned on $\hat{c}_0$ and a stochastic variable ϵ, Stage I GAN undergoes a training process. This results in the maximization of J_{D_0}, which evaluates the authenticity of the generated images, and the simultaneous minimization of J_{G_0}. The latter focuses on aligning the generated images with the provided textual description, and this iterative training procedure progressively enhances the performance of both the discriminator D_0 and the generator G_0.

$$J_{D_0} = \mathbb{E}_{(I_0, t) \sim p_{data}}[\log D_0(I_0, \psi_t)] + \mathbb{E}_{\epsilon \sim p_\epsilon, t \sim p_{data}}[\log(1 - D_0(G_0(\epsilon, \hat{c}_0), \psi_t))] \tag{8.17}$$

$$J_{G_0} = \mathbb{E}_{\epsilon \sim p_\epsilon, t \sim p_{data}}[\log(1 - D_0(G_0(\epsilon, \hat{c}_0), \psi_t))]$$
$$+ \lambda KL(\mathcal{N}(\mu_0(\psi_t), \Sigma_0(\psi_t)) \| \mathcal{N}(0, \mathbf{I})) \tag{8.18}$$

Here, I_0 represents the real image, the text description **t** originates from the actual data distribution p_{data}, and ϵ constitutes a noise vector, drawn randomly from the distribution p_ϵ.

The initial output of Stage I GAN often results in low-resolution images that lack detailed object parts and may even exhibit shape distortions. To overcome these shortcomings, Stage II GAN uses low-resolution images and text embedding, aiming to correct imperfections in the Stage I results. This reintroduction of textual information previously overlooked enables Stage II GAN to generate more complex and photo-realistic details in the final images. To achieve this, Stage II GAN considers the *low-resolution output*, represented as $\mathbf{s}_0 = G_0(\epsilon; \hat{\mathbf{c}}_0)$, and incorporates Gaussian latent variables $\hat{\mathbf{c}}$ in the training process for both the discriminator D and the generator G. This training involves an optimization approach, where the objective is to maximize J_D while simultaneously minimizing J_G.

$$J_D = \mathbb{E}_{(\mathbf{I},\mathbf{t})\sim p_{data}}[\log D(\mathbf{I}, \boldsymbol{\psi}_t)] + \mathbb{E}_{\mathbf{s}_0\sim p_{G_0},\mathbf{t}\sim p_{data}}[\log(1 - D(G(s_0, \hat{\mathbf{c}}), \boldsymbol{\psi}_t))] \tag{8.19}$$

$$J_{G_0} = \mathbb{E}_{\mathbf{s}_0\sim p_{G_0},\mathbf{t}\sim p_{data}}[\log(1 - D(G(\mathbf{s}_0, \hat{\mathbf{c}}), \boldsymbol{\psi}_t))]$$
$$+ \lambda KL(\mathcal{N}(\mu(\boldsymbol{\psi}_t), \Sigma(\boldsymbol{\psi}_t))\|\mathcal{N}(0, \mathbf{I})) \tag{8.20}$$

In contrast to the original GAN framework, this stage does not use the random noise variable ϵ assuming that necessary randomness is already contained within $\mathbf{s}_0$. The Gaussian conditioning variables $\hat{\mathbf{c}}$ in this stage and the $\hat{\mathbf{c}}_0$ in Stage I GAN both derive from the same pre-trained text encoder, resulting in the generation of identical text embeddings, denoted as $\mathbf{t}$.

8.9.1 StackGAN Training and Outcomes Highlights

During the implementation of Stage I GAN generator, the process of obtaining the *text conditioning variable* $\hat{\mathbf{c}}_0$ is as follows: The text embedding $\boldsymbol{\psi}_t$ is initially fed into a fully connected layer, resulting in the generation of μ_0 and σ_0, for a Gaussian distribution defined as $\mathcal{N}(\mu_0(\boldsymbol{\psi}_t), \Sigma_0(\boldsymbol{\psi}_t))$. Subsequently, $\hat{\mathbf{c}}_0$ is sampled from this Gaussian distribution and concatenated with a noise vector to facilitate the generation of an image with dimensions $M_0 \times N_0$ through a series of upsampling blocks.

The text embeddings $\boldsymbol{\psi}_t$ are first reduced in dimensionality by the discriminator D_0 using a fully connected layer. Then, this condensed text information is spatially duplicated to create a multidimensional tensor with dimensions $B_d \times B_d \times C_d$. Simultaneously, the associated image data undergoes downsampling until it reaches a spatial dimension of $B_d \times B_d$. Next, the image's feature map is combined with the spatially duplicated text tensor along the channel dimension. A 1×1 convolutional layer is applied to this combined tensor to extract important features representing the relationship between the textual and visual elements. Finally, a single-node fully connected layer is used to determine a decision score, which indicates the discriminator's judgment.

The Stage II generator uses an encoder-decoder network architecture with residual blocks. It takes a *text embedding* $\boldsymbol{\psi}_t$ and transforms it into the text conditioning vector $\hat{\mathbf{c}}$, which is replicated spatially into a tensor with dimensions $B_g \times B_g \times C_g$. Concurrently, the Stage I GAN's output, denoted as s_0, undergoes several downsampling blocks in the form of an encoder until it reaches the spatial dimensions $B_g \times B_g$. The features extracted from both the image and text are concatenated along the channel dimension and are passed through a series of residual blocks. Ultimately, a sequence of upsampling layers in the decoder is employed to generate a high-resolution image with dimensions $M \times N$. This generator plays a crucial role in enhancing input images by rectifying imperfections and introducing realistic details.

The discriminator in this stage shares similarities with the Stage I discriminator but incorporates additional downsampling blocks due to the larger image size. To promote improved alignment learning between the image and conditioning text, the approach uses a matching-aware discriminator for both stages (S. Reed et al. 2016b). During training, the discriminator considers real images paired with their corresponding text descriptions as positive sample pairs. Meanwhile, negative sample pairs include two groups: one with real images and mismatched text embeddings, and the other with synthetic images and their corresponding text embeddings.

During the training phase, the process begins by training D_0 and G_0 of the Stage I GAN for 600 epochs while keeping Stage II GAN fixed. Then, the training shifts to iteratively train D and G of the Stage II GAN for another 600 epochs, with Stage I GAN fixed. All networks are trained using the Adam solver, with a batch size of 64 and an initial learning rate of 0.0002. The learning rate is reduced to half of its previous value every 100 epochs. The experiments used three different datasets: CUB (Wah et al. 2011), which includes 200 bird species with 11,788 images; Oxford-102 (Nilsback and Zisserman 2008), comprising 8189 flower images across 102 categories; and MS COCO (T.-Y. Lin et al. 2014b), a more challenging dataset with images featuring multiple objects and diverse backgrounds. MS COCO had 80 k training images and 40 k validation images, each with 5 descriptions, while the CUB and Oxford-102 datasets had 10 descriptions for each image.

A numerical evaluation technique called the *Inception score* (Salimans et al. 2016) is employed for quantitative assessment.

$$I = \exp(\mathbb{E}_\mathbf{x} KL(p(\mathbf{y}|\mathbf{x})\|p(\mathbf{y}))) \tag{8.21}$$

Here, $\mathbf{x}$ represents an individual-generated sample, and $\mathbf{y}$ corresponds to the label predicted by the Inception model. The underlying concept of this metric revolves around the idea that effective models should produce various meaningful images. Consequently, the KL divergence between the overall distribution of labels $p(\mathbf{y})$ and labels given a specific image $p(\mathbf{y}|\mathbf{x})$ will be large. Although the inception score has been shown to correlate with human perceptions of visual quality, it does not evaluate the alignment between the generated images and the provided text descriptions. To address this aspect, human evaluations are also conducted. The Inception scores and average human ranks for the proposed StackGAN and the compared methods such as GAN-INT-CLS (S. Reed et al. 2016b) and GAWWN (S. E. Reed et al. 2016a) are listed in Table 8.3.

Table 8.3 Evaluation of inception scores and average human ranks for different datasets using various methods.

	Metric					
	Inception score			Human rank		
Dataset	GAN-INT-CLS	GAWWN	StackGAN	GAN-INT-CLS	GAWWN	StackGAN
CUB	2.88 ± 0.04	3.62 ± 0.07	3.70 ± 0.07	2.81 ± 0.03	1.99 ± 0.04	1.37 ± 0.02
Oxford	2.66 ± 0.03	—	3.20 ± 0.01	1.87 ± 0.03	—	1.13 ± 0.03
COCO	7.88 ± 0.07	—	8.45 ± 0.03	1.89 ± 0.04	—	1.11 ± 0.03

8.10 Diffusion Models

In the past, probabilistic models have struggled with a challenging dilemma characterized by a balancing act between two opposing objectives: *tractability* and *flexibility*. Models that are tractable, such as Gaussian or Laplace distributions, are straightforward to study and apply to data. Nonetheless, they encounter difficulties when attempting to encompass the intricate patterns within complex datasets. Conversely, flexible models can mold themselves to the patterns within any given dataset by employing a non-negative function $\phi(\mathbf{x})$ to establish their distribution $p(\mathbf{x}) = \frac{\phi(\mathbf{x})}{Z}$, where Z represents a normalization constant. Nevertheless, calculating this normalization constant is a computationally expensive task. Dealing with these adaptable models frequently necessitates the use of resource-intensive *Monte Carlo* techniques for tasks like assessment, training, or generating samples.

Several analytical approximations are available that improve, yet do not completely eliminate, this tradeoff. Examples include mean field theory and its extensions (Tanaka 1998), variational Bayes (M. I. Jordan et al. 1999), contrastive divergence (Welling and Geoffrey E. Hinton 2002), minimum probability flow (Sohl-Dickstein et al. 2011), minimum KL contraction (Lyu 2011), proper scoring rules (Gneiting and Raftery 2007), score matching (Hyvärinen and Dayan 2005), pseudolikelihood (Besag 1975), loopy belief propagation (K. Murphy et al. 2013), and many others. Furthermore, non-parametric approaches can also demonstrate significant effectiveness.

In recent years, an innovative method emerged for building probabilistic models, offering multiple advantages. This methodology provides exceptional flexibility in model structure, ensures precise data sampling, enables seamless integration with other probability distributions, and facilitates cost-efficient evaluation of both the model's log-likelihood and the likelihood of individual states. This approach relies on the utilization of a Markov chain to systematically transition from one distribution to another, drawing inspiration from *nonequilibrium statistical physics* (Jarzynski 1997) and *Sequential Monte Carlo* (Neal 2001). Specifically, it involves the construction of a generative Markov chain, which helps in the transformation of a straightforward, well-defined distribution, such as a Gaussian, into the desired target data distribution through a diffusion process.

The fundamental concept underlying diffusion models is rather straightforward. They start with an initial input image and progressively introduce Gaussian noise to it through a sequence of steps, which we refer to as the forward process. Importantly, this is distinct from the forward pass of a neural network. It serves as a crucial step in generating the target data for our neural network. Subsequently, a neural network is trained to reconstruct the original data by reversing the noise application process. This ability to model the inverse process enables the generation of novel data, which is commonly referred to as the reverse diffusion process or the sampling process of a generative model.

In recent years, numerous generative models based on diffusion have been introduced, all sharing similar foundational concepts. These include diffusion probabilistic models (Sohl-Dickstein et al. 2015), noise-conditioned score networks (Y. Song and Ermon 2019), and denoising diffusion probabilistic models (Ho et al. 2020).

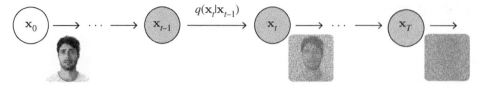

Figure 8.12 Forward diffusion process. Source: Reproduced from paper (Ho et al. 2020) / Neural Information Processing Systems Foundation.

8.10.1 Forward Diffusion Process

Consider a data point sampled from a real data distribution, denoted as $\mathbf{x}_0$ drawn from the distribution $q(\mathbf{x})$. Let's define a forward diffusion process where Gaussian noise with a variance of β_t is incrementally added to $\mathbf{x}_0$ over the course of T steps. This produces a sequence of noisy samples: $\mathbf{x}_1, \mathbf{x}_2, \ldots, \mathbf{x}_T$. More specifically, at each step of the *Markov chain*, Gaussian noise with variance β_t is introduced to $\mathbf{x}_{t-1}$, resulting in a new latent variable $\mathbf{x}_t$ with a distribution of $q(\mathbf{x}_t|\mathbf{x}_{t-1})$. This diffusion process can be formulated as follows:

$$q(\mathbf{x}_t|\mathbf{x}_{t-1}) = \mathcal{N}\left(\mathbf{x}_t; \mu_t = \sqrt{1 - \beta_t}\mathbf{x}_{t-1}, \Sigma_t = \beta_t\mathbf{I}\right) \tag{8.22}$$

In this case, the distribution $q(\mathbf{x}_t|\mathbf{x}_{t-1})$ shown in Fig. 8.12 is a normal distribution characterized by a mean, denoted as μ_t, which is equal to $\sqrt{1 - \beta_t}\mathbf{x}_{t-1}$, and a standard deviation, denoted as Σ_t, which is a diagonal matrix consisting of variances β_t.

The *forward trajectory*, starting from the initial data distribution and undergoing T diffusion steps, can be written in closed form as follows:

$$q(\mathbf{x}_{1:T}|\mathbf{x}_0) = \prod_{t=1}^{T} q(\mathbf{x}_t|\mathbf{x}_{t-1}) \tag{8.23}$$

As the step t increases, the distinctive characteristics of the data sample x_0 gradually diminish. Ultimately, as the parameter T approaches infinity, $\mathbf{x}_T$ converges to an isotropic Gaussian distribution.

In this case, the *reparameterization trick* is employed, enabling tractable closed-form sampling of x_t at any timestep t. Let us define $\alpha_t = 1 - \beta_t$, $\bar{\alpha}_t = \prod_{j=1}^{t} \alpha_j$ and $\epsilon_0 \ldots \epsilon_{t-2}, \epsilon_{t-1} \sim \mathcal{N}(0, \mathbf{I})$. The sampling of x_t can be expressed as follows:

$$\begin{aligned} \mathbf{x}_t &= \sqrt{1 - \beta_t}\mathbf{x}_{t-1} + \sqrt{\beta_t}\epsilon_{t-1} \\ &= \sqrt{\alpha_t}\mathbf{x}_{t-2} + \sqrt{1 - \alpha_t}\epsilon_{t-2} \\ &= \cdots\cdots\cdots\cdots \\ &= \sqrt{\bar{\alpha}_t}\mathbf{x}_0 + \sqrt{1 - \bar{\alpha}_t}\epsilon_0 \end{aligned} \tag{8.24}$$

Consequently, for the generation of a sample $\mathbf{x}_t$, the following distribution can be employed:

$$q(\mathbf{x}_t|\mathbf{x}_{t-1}) = \mathcal{N}(\mathbf{x}_t; \sqrt{\bar{\alpha}_t}\mathbf{x}_0, \sqrt{1 - \bar{\alpha}_t}\mathbf{I}) \tag{8.25}$$

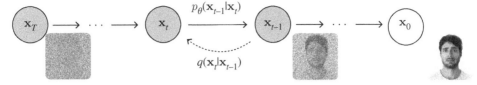

Figure 8.13 Reverse diffusion process. Source: Reproduced from paper (Ho et al. 2020) / Neural Information Processing Systems Foundation.

8.10.2 Reverse Diffusion Process

Reversing the above forward process and sampling from $q(\mathbf{x}_{t-1}|\mathbf{x}_t)$ enables us to reconstruct the true sample from a Gaussian noise input, $\mathbf{x}_T \sim \mathcal{N}(0, \mathbf{I})$. In practical terms, the knowledge of $q(\mathbf{x}_{t-1}|\mathbf{x}_t)$ is limited, and estimating it becomes intractable since it uses complex computations related to the data distribution. Consequently, one can opt for an approximation of $q(\mathbf{x}_{t-1}|\mathbf{x}_t)$ through the utilization of a parameterized model, denoted as p_θ (see Fig. 8.13). Given that $q(\mathbf{x}_{t-1}|\mathbf{x}_t)$ also exhibits Gaussian characteristics, particularly when β_t is sufficiently small, there is the flexibility to choose p_θ to be Gaussian and focus solely on parameterizing the mean and variance:

$$p_\theta(\mathbf{x}_{t-1}|\mathbf{x}_t) = \mathcal{N}(\mathbf{x}_{t-1}; \boldsymbol{\mu}_\theta(\mathbf{x}_t, t), \boldsymbol{\Sigma}_\theta(\mathbf{x}_t, t)) \tag{8.26}$$

The *reverse trajectory* for all timesteps can be written in closed form as follows:

$$p_\theta(\mathbf{x}_{0:T}) = p_\theta(\mathbf{x}_T)\prod_{t=1}^{T}p_\theta(\mathbf{x}_{t-1}|\mathbf{x}_t) \tag{8.27}$$

8.10.3 Diffusion Process Training

A diffusion-based generative model can be trained by maximizing the log-likelihood of the sample generated at the end of the reverse process to ensure that it closely matches the original data distribution. During training, the approach draws inspiration from VAEs and reformulates the training objective using a *variational lower bound*, referred to as ELBO, as demonstrated in Eq. (7.42). After various calculations, this final term for the variational lower bound loss, denoted as $\mathcal{L}_{vlb}$, is derived for individual timesteps:

$$J_{vlb} = J_0 + J_1 + \cdots + J_{T-1} + J_T \tag{8.28}$$

$$J_0 = -\log p_\theta(\mathbf{x}_0|\mathbf{x}_1) \tag{8.29}$$

$$J_{t-1} = KL(q(\mathbf{x}_{t-1}|\mathbf{x}_t, \mathbf{x}_0)\|p_\theta(\mathbf{x}_{t-1}|\mathbf{x}_t)) \tag{8.30}$$

$$J_T = KL(q(\mathbf{x}_T|\mathbf{x}_0)\|p_\theta(\mathbf{x}_t)) \tag{8.31}$$

The simplification of the loss function J_{vlb} involves omitting certain terms, leaving only J_{t-1}. This term represents the KL divergence between the posterior of the forward process (conditioned on $\mathbf{x}_t$ and the initial sample $\mathbf{x}_0$) and the parameterized reverse diffusion process. The term $q(\mathbf{x}_{t-1}|\mathbf{x}_t, \mathbf{x}_0)$ is referred to as *forward process posterior distribution*. The deep-learning model's task during training is to estimate the parameters of this Gaussian posterior in such a manner that it minimizes the KL divergence.

$$q(\mathbf{x}_{t-1}|\mathbf{x}_t, \mathbf{x}_0) = \mathcal{N}(\mathbf{x}_{t-1}; \tilde{\mu}_t(\mathbf{x}_t, \mathbf{x}_0), \tilde{\beta}_t \mathbf{I}) \tag{8.32}$$

where $\tilde{\mu}_t(\mathbf{x}_t, \mathbf{x}_0) = \frac{\sqrt{\bar{\alpha}_{t-1}}\beta_t}{1-\bar{\alpha}_t}\mathbf{x}_0 + \frac{\sqrt{\alpha_t}(1-\bar{\alpha}_{t-1})}{1-\bar{\alpha}_t}\mathbf{x}_t$ and $\tilde{\beta}_t = \frac{1-\bar{\alpha}_{t-1}}{1-\bar{\alpha}_t}\beta_t$. In this context, the expression of $\mathbf{x}_0$ within $\tilde{\mu}$ can be formulated in terms of $\mathbf{x}_t$ by employing the *reparameterization trick* outlined in Eq. (8.24). Furthermore, in the training phase, we establish that $\Sigma_\theta(\mathbf{x}_t, t)$ in Eq. (8.26) equals $\sigma^2 \mathbf{I}$.

$$\tilde{\mu}_t(\mathbf{x}_t) = \frac{1}{\sqrt{\alpha_t}}\left(\mathbf{x}_t - \frac{\beta_t}{\sqrt{1-\bar{\alpha}_t}}\epsilon\right) \tag{8.33}$$

Settings

$$\tilde{\mu}_\theta(\mathbf{x}_t, t) = \frac{1}{\sqrt{\alpha_t}}\left(\mathbf{x}_t - \frac{\beta_t}{\sqrt{1-\bar{\alpha}_t}}\epsilon_\theta(\mathbf{x}_t, t)\right) \tag{8.34}$$

The loss term was further simplified by omitting a weighting factor, and this simplified version demonstrated superior performance compared to the full objective:

$$J_{t-1} = \mathbb{E}_{\mathbf{x}_0, \epsilon}\left[\frac{\beta_t^2}{2\sigma_t^2 \alpha_t(1-\bar{\alpha}_t)}\|\epsilon - \epsilon_\theta(\sqrt{\bar{\alpha}_t}\mathbf{x}_0 + \sqrt{1-\bar{\alpha}_t}\epsilon, t)\|^2\right] \tag{8.35}$$

At training and inference times, the β's, α's and x_t are known. Consequently, the model's sole task is to predict the noise at each timestep. The final loss function is a result of reducing it to a mean squared error between the noise introduced in the forward process and the noise the model predicts.

Example 8.10.1 *(Text-to-image generation using stable diffusion)*

Let's try out the stable diffusion model. Here, we are using the text-to-image latent diffusion model which is trained on 512×512 image data from a subset of the LAION-5B dataset (https://laion.ai/blog/laion-5b/) database. The base model uses a frozen CLIP ViT-L/14 image and text model that maps text and images to a common shared vector space (model details). The CLIP model was developed by researchers at OpenAI to measure the robustness of computer vision-related tasks. This CLIP model assesses the ability of models to generalize image classification tasks. ViT-L/14 (Dosovitskiy et al. 2020; Dong et al. 2022) is being used as an image encoder. For the text encoder, the base model uses a masked self-attention transformer model.

Stable diffusion models are based on the concept of latent diffusion models. These models are capable of reducing memory and computational complexity by performing a diffusion process in a lower dimensional space called latent space. The three main components of latent diffusion are a text encoder, VAE and U-Net (Ronneberger et al. 2015).

Let us try to understand the full pipeline of the latent diffusion process. First, the text encoder is used to transform the input prompt: "DSLR image of an elderly woman in black and white" into a latent space that can be understood by U-Net. In this case, the model is a transformer-based encoder that can map the input tokens to text embeddings.

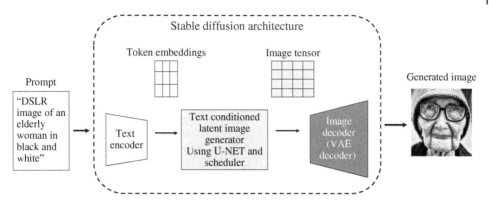

Figure 8.14 Stable diffusion model architecture used in the example.

The VAE has the encoder and the decoder part. The encoder part converts the image to lower-dimensional latent space and serves as an input to the U-Net model. The decoder, on the other hand, transforms the latent representation back to the image. For the forward diffusion process, the latent representations are obtained using the VAE encoder. Also, here more and more noise is added at each step.

U-Net also has an encoder and decoder part. The encoder part compresses the image representation to lower lower-resolution image representation. The decoder converts back the lower-resolution image to the original higher-resolution image representation which is comparatively less noisy. The stable diffusion U-Net conditions the output based on text embeddings using cross-attention layers.

The reverse diffusion process output corresponds to denoised latent representations. During inference, these are converted back to images using the VAE decoder. The overall architecture is shown in Fig. 8.14.

The model used here includes 860M UNet and 123M text encoder making it a lightweight version to try and experiment with.

Hugging face Diffusers library is used for obtaining the pre-trained model and performing inference using a prompt. For this, first, the pre-trained weights are loaded corresponding to all the components in the model. The model used here is the Stable Diffusion version 1.4 (CompVis/stable-diffusion-v1-4) which is one of the variants of the diffusion libraries. This variant provides a 512 × 512 image.

After loading all the pre-trained weights, this will be used for generating images based on the prompt that is provided. In this case, we have used the following prompt:

DSLR image of an elderly woman in black and white

Using the pre-trained weights, it can be seen that the images generated look like Fig. 8.15. The model performs really well in understanding the text prompt to specifically give the image quality and depth similar to how the pictures are captured using DSLR cameras. Further, the model can also be used to generate different images using the same prompt shown in Fig. 8.16.

Figure 8.15 The stable diffusion model-generated image for the prompt "DSLR image of an elderly woman in black and white."

Figure 8.16 A grid of model-generated images for the prompt "DSLR image of an elderly woman in black and white."

8.11 Conclusion

GANs represent a groundbreaking advancement in the field of computer vision for generative architectures. The results achieved by GANs have exceeded the performance of earlier methods in deep unsupervised learning, which were known for their remarkable capabilities. Over the years, different types of GANs have emerged, each with their own unique architecture and applications. From the original vanilla GAN to more specialized variants like DCGAN, CycleGAN, and cGAN, GANs have demonstrated their versatility in generating realistic data, transferring styles, and solving complex problems in domains ranging from image synthesis to text-to-image translation. The central concept of every GAN variant is based on a two-player minimax game. The adversarial training framework puts the generator against the discriminator in an ongoing feedback loop, facilitating the creation of realistic and high-quality synthetic data.

One key aspect of GANs' versatility is their ability to serve not only as data generators but also as tools for feature learning and representation learning. Beyond their primary objective of generating data, some GAN models incorporate secondary objectives, such as learning meaningful features or representations through related semantic tasks. These learned features can subsequently be employed for classification or recognition tasks in unsupervised settings, extending the utility of GANs beyond generative tasks. However, GANs also pose challenges, including issues related to training stability, mode collapse, and ethical concerns surrounding the generation of deepfake content and potential misuse. Despite these challenges, ongoing research and development in the GAN domain are actively addressing these issues.

Moreover, the development of GANs has given rise to the emergence of diffusion models as a significant advancement within this field. These models, which fall under the umbrella of generative models, have gained a lot of attention due to their unique approach to probabilistic generative modeling. Unlike traditional GANs, which rely on adversarial training, diffusion models work by gradually improving a data sample, making it more realistic through a series of diffusion steps. This distinctive approach has shown promise in generating high-quality samples and addressing some of the stability issues associated with GANs. Diffusion models provide an alternative viewpoint on generative modeling, and their incorporation into the field reflects an explorative for data generation and representation learning.

Problems

8.1 *Employ the GAN model to generate synthetic digit images that closely resemble the MNIST dataset's handwritten digits (0–9). Key hyperparameters include a 100-dimensional noise vector, a batch size of 64, 10,000 training epochs, and a learning rate of 0.0002 for the Adam optimizer. Evaluate the quality of these generated images by calculating the Inception Score.*

8.2 *Define "mode collapse" in the context of GANs. Explain why mode collapse occurs and discuss some strategies to mitigate or prevent it during GAN training. Provide examples or scenarios where mode collapse might be problematic in generating realistic data.*

8.3 *Use the CIFAR-10 dataset with labels and modify the cGAN architecture to conditionally generate samples based on a given label. Include code for both the generator and discriminator, and demonstrate how the conditional information improves the quality of generated images.*

8.4 *Design a GAN ensemble for improved image synthesis. Construct an ensemble of GANs, incorporating different GAN architectures such as DCGAN, cGAN, and StackGAN, all trained on the dataset of your choice.*

8.5 *Experiment with a variety of ensemble techniques, including averaging, voting, or blending, to synthesize superior images. The objective is to devise an ensemble strategy* that skillfully merges the outputs of these individual GANs to generate high-quality images. Evaluate the quality of the images produced by the ensemble against those generated by the standalone GANs, employing both visual inspection and quantitative metrics.

8.6 Assess the strengths and weaknesses of the ensemble method, considering scenarios where this approach proves more advantageous during its implementation.

8.7 StackGAN incorporates both a text-to-image and an image-to-text generation network. Describe five advantages and challenges of this dual network approach in StackGAN.

8.8 Explain the concept of latent space in StyleGAN. How does StyleGAN manipulate this latent space to control the appearance of generated images?

8.9 What are the advantages of using diffusion models in image synthesis compared to other generative models like VAEs or GANs?

8.10 Provide a detailed analysis of the trade-off between model quality and inference speed when using diffusion models for image generation.
1. Train a diffusion model on a custom dataset and optimize it for maximum image quality.
2. Evaluate the quality of generated images using relevant metrics like Inception Score, FID, and perceptual metrics.
3. Measure the inference speed of the trained diffusion model on a range of hardware configurations (e.g. CPU, GPU, or specialized hardware like TPUs). Report the inference time per image.

9

Deep Bayesian Networks

9.1 Introduction

Deep learning (DL) models can be seen as very powerful approximations, that are able to perform complex machine learning tasks. The power of these machines relies, roughly speaking, on the high (often tremendous) number of parameters for the models, that endow the structure with a high expressive capability in the space of the input pattern. This is the ultimate reason why these machines have been successfully used in complex pattern recognition tasks, such as image processing, speech recognition, and other natural language processing tasks, and in complex generative tasks, including realistic synthetic image generation, just to cite some well-known applications.

The drawback of the structural complexity of DL machines is overfitting (Szegedy et al. 2013). Overfitting is a universal phenomenon particularly important in DL that can be controlled by controlling the capacity of the machine in various ways, among them dropout (N. Srivastava et al. 2014), cost functions that force sparsity in the parameters, and controlling the Frobenius norm of the weights of the machine (often called weight decay), are strategies that have been addressed in this book. These strategies have an interpretation from the point of view of Bayesian learning (Gal and Ghahramani 2016; Q. Li and N. Lin 2010).

Bayesian learning is a way to address the overfitting phenomenon by modeling the uncertainty of the weights. This is done by imposing a prior probability distribution in the weights of the neural network, and this strategy has proven to be particularly advantageous in presence of small datasets. But beyond the potential improvement of the generalization properties in neural networks, the use of Bayesian techniques has another interesting property. Bayesian neural networks are able to estimate the model uncertainties. Not only the uncertainty on the model parameters, which can be obtained by the inference of a posterior probability distribution of these parameters, but it is also possible to estimate the uncertainty in the performance of the machine through the construction of predictive posterior distribution. This provides the user with additional knowledge, which can be used to determine whether the machine is producing a reliable prediction.

Deep Learning: A Practical Introduction, First Edition.
Manel Martínez-Ramón, Meenu Ajith, and Aswathy Rajendra Kurup.
© 2024 John Wiley & Sons Ltd. Published 2024 by John Wiley & Sons Ltd.
Companion website: https://github.com/DeepLearning-book

9.2 Bayesian Models

Throughout this book, we have presented the main deep learning architectures, ranging from the standard MLP to the transformers, and generative approaches. Most of these models are trained using the backpropagation algorithm that is constructed over the criterion of the maximization of the output likelihood conditional to the available training input patterns. This is, for a given set of parameters $\theta \in \mathbb{R}^D$ (containing, for example, all weights $w_{i,j}^{(l)}, b_j^{(l)}$ of a neural network), the criterion for its optimization can be written as

$$\theta_{opt} = \arg \max_{\theta} \log p(\mathbf{Y}|\mathbf{X}, \theta) \tag{9.1}$$

and since the probability in Eq. (9.1) is the likelihood of the desired outputs $\mathbf{y}_i$ given the corresponding inputs $\mathbf{x}_i$, this is a maximum likelihood (ML) criterion (see Eq. (1.57)). Assuming that the labels or regressors $\mathbf{y}_i$ are conditionally independent given the observation of the input pattern $\mathbf{x}_i$, then the log probability is estimated as the sample estimation of the negative log-likelihood (NLL) of the data (see Eq. (1.58)), which is equivalent to the data cross-entropy (see Eq. (1.63) for binary classification, Eq. (1.78) for the multiclass classification case or Eq. (1.82) for multitask regression, as examples). The NLL is also used in Bayesian inference, but it is applied in a different way.

9.2.1 The Bayes' Rule

Bayesian inference is rooted in the Bayes' theorem or Bayes' rule, which is summarized here. Assume two random variables u and v. Assume that the first variable u is observed, and a probabilistic model in relation with the latent or unobservable variable v can be established with the form $p(u|v)$, this is the probability of the observation u varies depending on the chosen hypothesis for v.

Now, assume that while variable v is unobservable, we have a specific probabilistic model $p(v)$ for this variable. This is what we call a prior probability, which is what we know about it before having any additional knowledge. Roughly speaking, the goal of the Bayesian inference is to guess the most probable value of v given the observation of u, which depends on v. This information is contained in the posterior probability distribution $p(v|u)$. The Bayes' rule establishes that this posterior probability is (Bertsekas and Tsitsiklis 2000)

$$p(v|u) = \frac{p(u|v)p(v)}{p(u)} \tag{9.2}$$

where

$$p(u) = \int_v p(u|u)p(v) \tag{9.3}$$

is called the marginal likelihood or sometimes the belief function. This function is often not available, and therefore the posterior is not available either, but a function that is proportional to it as

$$\tilde{p}(v|u) \propto p(u|v)p(v) \tag{9.4}$$

For the above function to have properties of a probability density function, its integral defined over the domain of v mist be unitary, so it has to be divided by the integral

$\int_v p(u|v)p(v)dv$, which proves Eq. (9.3). Expression (9.2) is proven from the definition of conditional probability, which says that if a variable u is dependent of a variable v, the probability of u conditional to the observation of v is

$$p(u|v) = \frac{p(u,v)}{p(v)} \qquad (9.5)$$

whose proof is left as an exercise for the reader.

9.2.2 Priors as Regularization Criteria

The criterion of minimization of the NLL is complemented with an additional term for regularization purposes as summarized in Section 2.3.1. In particular, the L_2 regularization criterion is widely used and, in this case the criterion can be written as

$$\theta_{opt} = \arg\min_{\theta} \left(-\log p(\mathbf{Y}|\mathbf{X}, \theta) + \frac{\lambda}{2}\|\theta\|^2 \right) \qquad (9.6)$$

The above criterion is sometimes called a maximum a posteriori (MAP) criterion (M. Ajith and Manel Martínez-Ramón 2019), as it can be seen from a Bayes perspective.

If we define, without loss of generality, the set of all parameters of a deep learning model as parameters $\theta = \{\mathbf{W}^{(1)}, \mathbf{b}^{(1)}, \ldots, \mathbf{W}^{(L)}, \mathbf{b}^{(L)}\}$, including all arrays and biases of the layers of the structure. In such a learning model, parameters θ can be taken as unobservable or latent variables, while the training data is the set of observables. Therefore, the Bayes' rule can be applied as

$$p(\theta|\mathbf{Y}, \mathbf{X}) = \frac{p(\mathbf{Y}|\mathbf{X}, \theta)p(\theta)}{p(\mathbf{Y}|\mathbf{X})} \qquad (9.7)$$

The derivation of this expression from the Bayes rule is not immediate and it is left as an exercise for the reader. Its logarithm can be written as

$$\log p(\theta|\mathbf{Y}, \mathbf{X}) = \log p(\mathbf{Y}|\mathbf{X}, \theta) + \log p(\theta) + \text{constant} \qquad (9.8)$$

where the constant term, that can be neglected, is the logarithm of the marginal likelihood, which does not depend on the parameters. If, for the set of parameters, the corresponding prior model is simply the multivariate Gaussian distribution $p(\theta) \propto \exp(-\frac{\lambda}{2}\|\theta\|^2)$, then the above expression can be written as $\log p(\mathbf{Y}|\mathbf{X}, \theta) - \frac{\lambda}{2}\|\theta\|^2$ and therefore, Eq. (9.6) can be called a MAP criterion.

The prior distribution plays the role of *prior* belief or knowledge about the problem. The no free lunch theorem (NFL) theorems (Wolpert 1996a, 1996b) express in the sentence "there is no such thing as a free lunch" that we cannot find a single optimization for all problems. The first theorem states that any two algorithms perform equally when their performance is averaged over all possible problems. The second theorem says that if an algorithm outperforms another one for a given cost function, then the reverse situation must be true for all other cost function dynamics (Wolpert and Macready 1997). If the algorithm does not contain prior information, the algorithm cannot learn from the data in a way that can generalize to test data. In Bayesian learning, this prior knowledge can be specified by the use of priors.

9.3   Bayesian Inference Methods for Deep Learning

A difference between a classical approach and a Bayesian approach is in how the posterior for the parameters is chosen. In a classical approach, the parameter of the prior is adjusted by a cross-validation of parameter λ. In a Bayesian approach, the way in which this parameter is adjusted is different, based on a probabilistic criterion, which can provide a better estimation of the posterior. Moreover, the Bayesian perspective allows to extract additional knowledge of the structure and the process. In particular, the Bayesian model encodes the uncertainties present in the learning model. The likelihood constructed with the training data contains the information related to the of the model, this is, the uncertainties due to the noise or error present in the process. The posterior expresses what is usually called the Epistemic Uncertainty, or the uncertainty in the model parameters due to the limited information carried by the data.

Therefore, a Bayesian model not only provides a probabilistic way to explain the regularization of the structure but also a way to quantify the uncertainties of the model (Hubin and Storvik 2023). Indeed, a posterior distribution of the test samples, usually called the can be constructed by marginalization through the posterior probability of the model parameters. In order to construct such posterior, we first need a posterior probability of the prediction $f(\mathbf{x})$ as $p(f(\mathbf{x})|\mathbf{x}, \theta)$, and then the marginal predictive posterior is found as

$$p(f(\mathbf{x})|\mathbf{x}, \mathbf{X}) = \int p(f(\mathbf{x})|\mathbf{x}, \theta) p(\theta|\mathbf{Y}, \mathbf{X}) d\theta \tag{9.9}$$

The difficulty with this inference is that the computation of the parameter posterior is intractable due to its high dimensionality and the fact that it is a nonconvex problem (MacKay 1992). In order to circumvent this difficulty, two different frameworks for inference have been developed. The first one falls in the family of the Markov chain Monte Carlo (MCMC) methods (Hastings 1970), and the second one is based on variational inference (VI) (Blei et al. 2017). In this section, these fundamental ideas used in Bayesian inference for DL are reviewed.

The literature in Bayesian inference for DL is very extensive. The interested reader can find a variety of tutorials (Lampinen and Vehtari 2001; Goan and Fookes 2020; H. Wang and Yeung 2020; Jospin et al. 2022) that introduce the basics and the different approaches to the problem of training a neural network from a Bayesian perspective.

9.3.1   Markov Chain Monte Carlo Methods

The original MCMC algorithm was introduced in Metropolis and Ulam (1949) and Hastings (1970), and the idea behind the algorithm consists of constructing a Markov chain of the parameters where at each time instant a parameter is sampled with a probability that depends on the previously visited samples, in order to construct a stationary distribution of these parameters (Hitchcock 2003; Chib and Greenberg 1995). In this chapter, we present the basic MCMC algorithm, which is the Metropolis–Hasting algorithm.

The Metropolis–Hasting algorithm starts with an initial arbitrary value $\theta(0)$ for the set of parameters. For a given sample $\theta(n)$, a proposal (prior) probability distribution $q(\theta|\theta(n))$ around this sample is used. Then, a new sample $\theta(n + 1)$ is drawn from this distribution.

The new sample is then tested by computing a posterior distribution $p(\mathbf{Y}|\mathbf{X}, \theta(n+1))$. This is, in a deep learning setup, the probabilistic output of the learning machine. The corresponding posterior probability for the sample is

$$p(\theta(n+1)|\theta(n), \mathbf{Y}, \mathbf{X}) = \frac{q(\theta(n+1)|\theta(n))p(\mathbf{Y}|\mathbf{X}, \theta(n+1))}{p(\mathbf{Y}|\mathbf{X})} \tag{9.10}$$

We can ignore the denominator in the Bayes' rule here because it is not available, and we simply state that the posterior is proportional to the prior times the likelihood. Then, an *acceptance probability* is stated as

$$r = \min\left(1, \frac{q(\theta(n+1)|\theta(n))p(\mathbf{Y}|\mathbf{X}, \theta(n+1))}{q(\theta(n)|\theta(n+1))p(\mathbf{Y}|\mathbf{X}, \theta(n))}\right) \tag{9.11}$$

The quotient of this expression has, in the numerator, the posterior of the new sampled parameters $\theta(n+1)$, which depends (through the prior), on the previous set of parameters, and also on the training data. If the new posterior is higher than the previous one, the quotient is higher than 1, and then $r = 1$, which means that the new sample has to be accepted. If the previous posterior was higher, then the result of r is the quotient, so the sample must be accepted with a probability that is high if both posteriors are similar, and with a low probability if the new posterior is low compared to the previous one. This allows the system to occasionally pick the new set of parameters even if the posterior is worse. Notice that the prior of the previous sample is simply computed as a distribution around the new sample. If the distribution is symmetric, this is $q(\theta|\theta') = q(\theta'|\theta)$, for example, when the prior is a simple circularly symmetrical Gaussian, the formula is simplified as

$$r = \min\left(1, \frac{p(\mathbf{Y}|\mathbf{X}, \theta(n+1))}{p(\mathbf{Y}|\mathbf{X}, \theta(n))}\right) \tag{9.12}$$

Usual proposal distributions q are Gaussian distributions, since it is sufficient for those proposals to produce samples that move from one sample to another one with a nonzero likelihood in the targets. Therefore, a reasonable option is

$$p(\theta|\theta(n)) \propto \exp\left((\theta|\theta(n))^\top s^2 \mathbf{M}^{-1}(\theta|\theta(n))\right) \tag{9.13}$$

where $\mathbf{M}$ is a given covariance matrix and s^2 is a scale factor. In some cases, it is possible to compute the Hessian of the cost function surface at point $\theta(n)$, and then the distribution will follow the curvature of this surface (Roberts and Rosenthal 2001). In many cases, however, the Hessian cannot be easily computed or it has an unreasonable computational burden, and then one can choose an identity matrix for the covariance. In this case, the distribution is symmetric, and the acceptance probability is the one in Eq. (9.13).

Example 9.3.1 *(Metropolis–Hasting over the Beale surface)*
Here we compare the standard gradient descent (GD) algorithm to the Metropolis–Hasting algorithm in a toy example. The cost function is simulated with the Beale function that was also used in Example 2.5.1.

The function is defined as

$$L(w_1, w_2) = (a - w_1 + w_1 w_2)^2 + (b - w_1 + w_1 w_2^2)^2 + (c - w_1 + w_1 w_2^3)^2 \tag{9.14}$$

with $a = 1.5, b = 2.25, c = 2.2625$.

In order to run the GD algorithm and the Metropolis–Hasting algorithm with a covariance matrix, we need to compute the gradient and the Hessian of the function. The components of the gradient are

$$
\begin{aligned}
\frac{dL}{dw_1} &= 2(a - w_1 + w_1 w_2)(-1 + w_2) \\
&\quad + 2(b - w_1 + w_1 w_2^2)(-1 + w_2^2) + 2(c - w_1 + w_1 w_2^3)(-1 + w_2^3) \\
\frac{dL}{dw_2} &= 2(a - w_1 + w_1 w_2)w_1 + 4(b - w_1 + w_1 w_2^2)w_1 w_2 \\
&\quad + 6(c - w_1 + w_1 w_2^3)(w_1 w_2^2)
\end{aligned}
\tag{9.15}
$$

and the components of the Hessian are

$$
\begin{aligned}
\frac{dL^2}{d^2 w_1} &= 2(-1 + w_2)^2 + 2(-1 + w_2^2)^2 + 2(-1 + w_2^3)^2 \\
\frac{dL^2}{d^2 w_2} &= 2w_1^2 + 2(a - w_1 + w_1 w_2) + 8w_1^2 w_2^2 + 4(b - w_1 + w_1 w_2^2)w_1 \\
&\quad + 18w_2^4 w_1^2 + 12(c - w_1 - w_1 w_2^3)w_1 w_2 \\
\frac{dL^2}{dw_1 dw_2} &= 2w_1(-1 + w_2) + 2(a - w_1 + w_1 w_2) + 4w_1 w_2(-1 + w_2^2) \\
&\quad + 4(b - w_1 + w_1 w_2^2)w_2 + 6w_1 w_2^2(-1 + w_2^3) \\
&\quad + 6(c - w_1 + w_1 w_2^3)w_2^2
\end{aligned}
\tag{9.16}
$$

where we use the property that $\frac{dL^2}{dw_1 dw_2} = \frac{dL^2}{dw_2 dw_1}$ in order to construct the Hessian matrix.

In the experiment, the initial value for the set of parameters is $\mathbf{w}^\top = (1.2, 2)$. The gradient descent algorithm is set with $\mu = 10^{-3}$. The Metropolis-Hasting (MH) algorithm uses a Gaussian distribution as a proposal for the parameter prior. Figure 9.1 shows the results of the experiment. The continuous line shows the behavior of the gradient descent. The dashed line shows the MH algorithm with $s = 0.3$ and $\mathbf{M} = \mathbf{I}$. The dashed-dotted line shows the MH

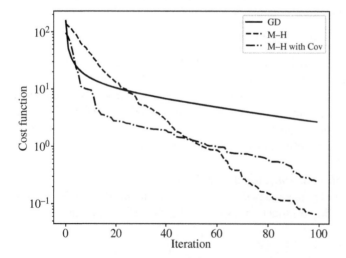

Figure 9.1 Comparison of the error behavior when using GD (solid line), the basic Metropolis–Hasting algorithm (dash), and the Metropolis–Hasting algorithm with a covariance function computed as the Hessian of the error surface (dash-dot).

algorithm with $s = 0.1$ and where $\mathbf{M}$ is chosen as the Hessian

$$
\mathbf{M} = \begin{pmatrix} \dfrac{dL^2}{d^2 w_1} & \dfrac{dL^2}{dw_1 dw_2} \\ \dfrac{dL^2}{dw_2 w_1} & \dfrac{dL^2}{d^2 w_2} \end{pmatrix}
\tag{9.17}
$$

constructed with Eq. (9.16). The MH with identity covariance is slower than the GD, but it can be seen that it achieves a lower value of the cost function by more than a magnitude order in about 80 iterations. The use of a covariance function significant of the shape of the surface (the Hessian) helps the MH algorithm to achieve faster convergence by favoring those directions with higher variation. It achieves a value of 10 about three times faster than the other two algorithms and after that, it behaves with a speed that is roughly the same as the one of the MH with an identity matrix. This is explained by the fact that in areas where the cost function is very small, the surface is very flat, and the Hessian tends to be an identity matrix.

9.3.2 Hamiltonian MCMC

The Hamiltonian MCMC variant (Neal et al. 2011) (see also Betancourt (2017)) is an improvement of the MH MCMC algorithm that uses a Hamiltonian function to guide the process so the chosen sample of the parameters has a reduced correlation with the previous sample while maintaining a high probability of acceptance. The Hamiltonian is defined as a function $H(\theta, \mathbf{p})$, where $\mathbf{p}$ is defined as the momentum of a particle at position θ. The Hamiltonian is constructed as

$$
H(\theta, \mathbf{p}) = u(\theta) + k(\mathbf{p})
\tag{9.18}
$$

where $u(\Theta)$ is called the potential energy and it is defined as the negative logarithm of a function proportional to the probability density of the distribution of the parameters, and $k(\mathbf{p})$ is defined as the kinetic energy, typically defined as $k(\mathbf{p}) = \frac{1}{2}\mathbf{p}^\mathsf{T}\mathbf{M}^{-1}\mathbf{p}$, where $\mathbf{M}$ is a positive definite matrix. This function represents the total energy of a particle, and it has the properties of a Hamiltonian function.

The distribution that is used to sample the parameters is then constructed with the potential function as

$$
p(\theta, \mathbf{p}) = \frac{1}{Z} \exp\left(\frac{-H(\theta, \mathbf{p})}{T} \right) = \frac{1}{Z} \exp\left(\frac{-u(\theta)}{T} \right) \exp\left(\frac{-k(\mathbf{p})}{T} \right)
\tag{9.19}
$$

where T is a positive constant that simulates the temperature of the system, and $Z = \int_{\theta,\mathbf{p}} \exp\left(\frac{-H(\theta,\mathbf{p})}{T} \right) d\theta d\mathbf{p}$ is the normalization factor needed for the distribution to have probability density properties. The function of interest in this equation is the posterior distribution for the parameters. Function $u(\theta)$ is then constructed as the negative logarithm of the product between the prior of the parameters and the likelihood of the observations (which is proportional to the posterior) as

$$
u(\theta) = -\log\left(p(\theta) p(\mathbf{Y}|\mathbf{X}, \theta) \right)
\tag{9.20}
$$

Also, kinetic energy $k(\mathbf{p})$ can be simply modeled as

$$k(\mathbf{p}) = \sum_{i=1}^{D} \frac{p_i^2}{2m_i} \tag{9.21}$$

in whose case $\mathbf{M}$ is defined as a diagonal matrix.

In the first step of the algorithm, the position $\theta(n+1)$ is updated with respect to the momentum $\mathbf{p}(n)$ in the following steps, known as the Leap Frog algorithm, that numerically solves the Hamilton equations. Assume that at a given instant, the system has position $\theta(n, 0)$ and a random momentum $\mathbf{p}(n, 0)$ is chosen given a Gaussian distribution. Then for $k = 1$ to L, the following iteration is repeated

$$
\begin{aligned}
\mathbf{p}\left(n, \tfrac{k}{2}\right) &= \mathbf{p}(n, k-1) - \tfrac{\mu}{2}\nabla_\theta u(\theta)|_{\theta = \theta(n,k-1)} \\
\theta(n, k) &= \theta(n, k-1) + \mu \mathbf{M}^{-1}\mathbf{p}\left(n, \tfrac{k}{2}\right) \\
\mathbf{p}(n, k) &= \mathbf{p}\left(n, \tfrac{k}{2}\right) - \tfrac{\mu}{2}\nabla_\theta u(\theta)|_{\theta(n,k)}
\end{aligned}
\tag{9.22}
$$

These equations solve the problem of finding the next position $\theta(n, L)$ and new momentum $\mathbf{p}(n, L)$ given an initial position $\theta(n, 0)$ and a random momentum $\mathbf{p}(n, 0)$. Then, the new position is chosen with a probability r by using the Metropolis–Hasting criterion

$$r = \min\left(1, \frac{p\left(\theta(n, L), \mathbf{p}(n, L)\right)}{p\left(\theta(n, 0), \mathbf{p}(n, 0)\right)}\right) \tag{9.23}$$

with the use of distribution (9.19). Then, the next position of the parameters is chosen as

$$\theta(n + 1, 0) = \begin{cases} \theta(n, L), & \text{with probability } r \\ \theta(n, 0), & \text{with probability } 1 - r \end{cases} \tag{9.24}$$

and the algorithm (9.22) is iterated until convergence.

The Hamiltonian MCMC is a powerful algorithm for Bayesian inference, but it has two main parameters, μ and L, that need to be chosen in advance or through some sort of cross-validation. This is not straightforward, provided that in general there are no clear criteria to select it, and the usual practice is to make use of heuristics (Neal et al. 2011). In order to avoid this inconvenience, the software packages for inference using MCMC usually implement the no-U-turn sampler (NUTS) (Hoffman et al. 2014).

Example 9.3.2 *(Neural network Regression with MCMC inference)*
This example, extracted from the University of Amsterdam Deep Leanning Course[1] is one-dimensional regression problem where generating function, from which a set of training samples is extracted, has the expression

$$f(x) = x + 0.3 \sin(2\pi x) + 0.3 \sin(4\pi x) \tag{9.25}$$

A set of 500 samples drawn from uniform distributions in each of the intervals $-0.2 \leq x \leq 0.2$ and $0.6 \leq x \leq 1$ is obtained and they are added a Gaussian noise of standard deviation $\sigma = 0.3$ and zero mean.

---

1 https://uvadlc.github.io/.

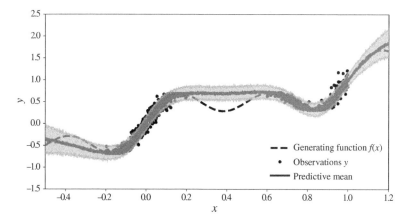

Figure 9.2 Example of neural network regression and confidence intervals with MCMC in a neural network with one hidden layer of five nodes.

The neural network used to perform the regression task is a fully connected structure with one hidden layer and five nodes with hyperbolic tangent activation, while the input and output consist of one node. The output has a linear activation. The neural network is trained with the Hamiltonian MCMC. The prior is chosen as a circularly symmetric Gaussian distribution $\mathcal{N}(\mathbf{0}, 10\mathbf{I})$ and the likelihood is also Gaussian distributions, and th. The result can be seen in Fig. 9.2. The inference has been done from the samples generated in the two intervals. A test has been done with 3000 uniform samples of x in the interval $-0.5 \leq x \leq 1.2$, The prediction confidence interval is obtained by sampling the posterior predictive distribution, from which the prediction variance is estimated. The depicted confidence is the 2σ (95%) interval. It can be seen from the figure that the confidence interval is a little optimistic, since the contained samples seem to be less than 95%. In the interval between 0.2 and 0.6 the prediction is poor, since there is no information about the function in this interval. Observe also how the confidence interval is wider in the segments between -0.4 and -0.2 and between 1 and 1.2.

Figure 9.3 contains the result of the regression with a different neural network, where the number of layers has been increased to five and where the number of nodes in each of the hidden layers is 10. The prior distribution is again a Gaussian, but the variance has been set to five. In this graph, the confidence interval is estimated in a better way. In particular, the segment $-0.2 \leq x \leq 0.6$ has a poor estimation due to a lack of information. Hence, the confidence interval is wide, indicating the estimation uncertainty.

9.3.3 Variational Inference

The MCMC algorithms are very efficient in sampling from an exact posterior (Bardenet et al. 2017), but their drawbacks are obvious from the analysis of the previously introduced algorithms. These methods may have poor scalability when the number of parameters is large, which is the case of DL. The methods based on VI, also used in Section 7.9 to train autoencoders, have a better scalability in DL, and this is why they have more popularity in this field.

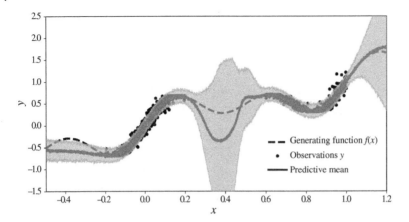

Figure 9.3 Example of neural network regression and confidence intervals with MCMC in a neural network with five hidden layers of 10 nodes each.

In VI, rather than using an exact posterior and sample from it, a parametric function $q_\phi(\theta)$ is used that depends on a set of parameters ϕ to approximate the actual posterior. This approximation is usually called variational. In order to approximate the actual posterior with the parametric one, the Kullback–Leibler (KL) divergence could be used, which is defined here as

$$KL(q_\phi|p) = \int_\theta q_\phi(\theta) \log\left(\frac{q_\phi(\theta)}{p(\theta|\mathbf{Y}, \mathbf{X})}\right) d\theta \qquad (9.26)$$

This criterion, however, cannot be directly applied, because the actual posterior is not available. Indeed, this is the function that must be approximated. But the posterior can be reformulated by following the Bayes' rule and the equation can be written as

$$KL(q_\phi|p) = \int_\theta q_\phi(\theta) \log\left(\frac{q_\phi(\theta)p(\mathbf{Y}|\mathbf{X})}{p_\varphi(\theta)p(\mathbf{Y}|\mathbf{X}, \theta)}\right) d\theta \qquad (9.27)$$

and the denominator in the logarithm contains term $p_\varphi(\theta)p(\mathbf{Y}|\mathbf{X}, \theta)$, corresponding to the parameter prior (which depends on its own parameters φ) times the data likelihood. By operating in the equation, the following expression can be obtained

$$\mathcal{F}(\theta, \mathbf{X}, \mathbf{Y}) = \int_\theta q_\phi(\theta) \log\left(\frac{p_\varphi(\theta)p(\mathbf{Y}|\mathbf{X}, \theta)}{q_\phi(\theta)}\right) d\theta \qquad (9.28)$$
$$= \log p(\mathbf{Y}|\mathbf{X}) - KL(q_\phi|p)$$

which means that maximizing the KL divergence between the posterior and the approximate posterior q_ϕ is equivalent to minimizing $\mathcal{F}(\theta, \mathbf{X}, \mathbf{Y})$, which is the evidence lower bound (ELBO), also called the negative variational free energy (Neal and Geoffrey E. Hinton 1998; Yedidia et al. 2000), also used in Section 7.9.1.

The most common choice for the variational distribution $q_\phi(\theta)$ is a Gaussian with a diagonal covariance matrix σ_i with elements σ_i^2 in its diagonal and with a mean μ, both vectors with the same length as the total number of parameters in set θ.

A common way to optimize the ELBO is the use of stochastic variational inference (SVI) (van de Schoot et al. 2021; Hubin and Storvik 2023). The methodology consists of applying stochastic gradient descent to the inference. This is useful when the datasets used for training are large, but the convergence is slow when compared to the standard gradient descent applied to a likelihood function. The usual functions for $q_\phi(\theta)$ are multivariate Gaussians (Graves 2011), Gamma functions and Dirichlet distributions (Jospin et al. 2022). The method presented in Ghahramani and Beal (2000) factorizes the elements of the ELBO to separately treat the data and the parameters, which simplifies the procedure and gives an optimization algorithm that is a generalization of the Expectation–Maximization algorithm. The algorithm also applies a Gaussian prior for the parameters with an identity matrix as a covariance matrix.

9.3.4 Bayes by Backpropagation

The Bayes by backpropagation algorithm (Blundell et al. 2015) uses an approximation to the ELBO function as

$$F(\theta, \mathbf{X}, \mathbf{Y}) \approx \sum_{n=1}^{M} \left(\log q_\phi(\theta(n)) - \log p_\varphi(\theta(n)) - \log p(\mathbf{Y}|\mathbf{X}, \theta(i)) \right) \tag{9.29}$$

where $\theta(1), \dots, \theta_M$ are M samples of the model parameters drawn from the variational posterior $q_\phi(\theta)$. The distribution is chosen as a Gaussian with mean μ and a diagonal covariance whose standard deviations (elements of the diagonal) are written as $\sigma = \log(1 + \exp(\rho))$, where it must be understood that ρ is a vector with components $\rho_j \in \mathbb{R}$ and σ is a vector with components $\sigma_j = \log(1 + \exp(\rho_j))$. This expression is convenient to make sure that standard deviations σ_j are always positive for any vector ρ. Therefore, the posterior parameters can be defined as $\phi = (\mu, \rho)$. Let us define function

$$f(\theta) = \log q_\phi(\theta) - \log p_\varphi(\theta) - \log p(\mathbf{Y}|\mathbf{X}, \theta) \tag{9.30}$$

and assume that the parameter set θ is arranged as a vector containing all parameters $w_{i,j}^{(l)}, b_j^{(l)}$ of a DL model.

The posterior parameters can be iteratively optimized with respect to the ELBO in the following steps, which have to be iterated until convergence:

1. Sample a vector $\varepsilon(n)$ from distribution $\mathcal{N}(\mathbf{0}, \mathbf{I})$.
2. Compute sample $\theta(n) = \mu + \log(1 + \exp(\rho)) \odot \varepsilon(n)$.
3. Compute the gradients of function $f(\theta)$ evaluated at $\theta(n)$, whose elements $1 \leq j \leq D$ are

$$\begin{aligned}
\Delta_{\mu_j(n)} &= \frac{df(\theta)}{d\theta_j}\Big|_{\theta(n)} + \frac{df(\theta)}{d\mu_j}\Big|_{\theta(n)} \\
\Delta_{\rho_j(n)} &= \frac{df(\theta)}{d\theta_j}\Big|_{\theta(n)} \frac{\epsilon_j}{1 + \exp(-\rho_j)} + \frac{df(\theta)}{d\rho_j}\Big|_{\theta(n)}
\end{aligned} \tag{9.31}$$

4. Update the variational parameters with the above gradients

$$\begin{aligned}
\mu_j &\leftarrow \mu_j - \alpha \Delta_{\mu_j(n)} \\
\rho_j &\leftarrow \mu_j - \alpha \Delta_{\rho_j(n)}
\end{aligned} \tag{9.32}$$

In the derivatives of Eq. (9.31) we find the derivatives $\frac{df(\theta)}{d\theta_j}\big|_{\theta(n)}$, which by visual inspection of the expression of Eq. (9.30), can be written as

$$\frac{df(\theta)}{d\theta_j} = -\frac{d}{d\theta_j}\log p(\mathbf{Y}|\mathbf{X}, \theta) \tag{9.33}$$

which is simply computed with the standard backpropagation algorithm presented in Section 1.5.3 for the MLp and in Chapters 4 and successive ones for CNN, RNN, and others.

Once the algorithm has converged, a MAP prediction of a test sample $\mathbf{x}^*$ can be done with the use of the MAP estimation of the parameters provided by the variational posterior $q_\phi(\theta)$. The confidence interval of the prediction can be estimated by sampling equation of (9.9), the predictive posterior in the usual case where the integral is not tractable. The procedure consists of simply drawing samples of the parameters from the parameter posterior, and obtaining predictions of $\mathbf{x}^*$ with these sampled parameters. Then, a statistical measure of the obtained outputs (for example, 2σ or 95% confidence intervals) can be computed for a regression application or the posterior Bernoulli or Multinoulli probability in a classification application.

Example 9.3.3 (*Regression with variational Bayesian neural networks*)
The regression in Fig. 9.4 shows the data model of Example 9.3.2 is used in a neural network of a single layer with five nodes and hyperbolic tangent activation, but the inference is variational, with results similar to the ones in Fig. 9.2.

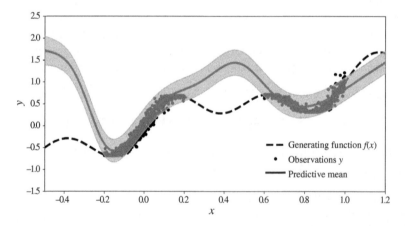

Figure 9.4 Neural network regression and confidence intervals with variational in a neural network with one hidden layers of five nodes.

9.4 Conclusion

Neural networks are particularly underspecified by the training data, given that the number of parameters is in many cases much higher than the number of training samples. The use of Bayesian approaches is a compelling way to regularize neural networks. Most importantly,

Bayesian methods offer a way to quantify the uncertainty of the model parameters by the inference of a parameter posterior with the possibility to compute a predictive posterior, from which to calculate (often numerically) confidence intervals in the prediction.

In this chapter, we covered the basic elements of Bayesian learning. We first stated the relationship between the regularization and the parameter priors, and then we summarized the two main methodologies for Bayesian inference, which are the MCMC and the VI frameworks.

Among the MCMC methods, the standard Metropolis–Hasting algorithm has been summarized, with a variant that includes the Hessian of the cost function surface, and the Hamiltonian Metropolis–Hasting algorithm, that uses a Hamiltonian function (modeling the trajectory of the parameter as a particle with kinetic and potential energy). While the MCMC methods. While the MCMC methods are able to produce inference sampling from the exact posterior, they may present scalability problems.

VI methods are more popular in Bayesian learning because they have better scalability properties through the use of an approximate parametric variational posterior. The Bayes by backpropagation has been presented as it is a standard methodology for Bayesian inference in DL. This method can be seen as an extension to the standard backpropagation algorithm that, instead of optimizing a likelihood function, can optimize a posterior distribution of the model weights.

Problems

9.1 *Prove the Bayes' theorem using the definition of conditional probability in Eq. (9.5)*

9.2 *provide a proof for Eq. (9.7). Start with the expression of the posterior as*

$$p(\theta | \mathbf{Y}, \mathbf{X}) = \frac{p(\mathbf{Y}, \mathbf{X} | \theta) p(\theta)}{p(\mathbf{Y}, \mathbf{X})} \tag{9.34}$$

and with the fact that since a conditional probability has to satisfy the properties of a probability function, then for three random variables u, v, w,

$$p(u | v, w) = \frac{p(u, v | w)}{p(v | w)} \tag{9.35}$$

9.3 *Particularize the predictive posterior of Eq. (9.9) to the univariate regression case. Assume that a Gaussian parameter posterior has been estimated using any Bayesian method and that it has a mean $\hat{\theta}$ and a covariance $\mathbf{M}$. The likelihood of the regression model is the one in Eq. (1.81) particularized to one dimension regression.*

1. *Prove that the predictive posterior is Gaussian.*
2. *Given a test sample $\mathbf{x}$, what is the mean of the predictive posterior?*
3. *Propose a method to compute the variance of the prediction.*

9.4 *Provide a proof for Eq. (9.28) that describes the ELBO.*

9.5 *Derive Equations (9.31).*

9.6 *Use the scripts of Example (1.5.4) to implement a toy example Bayes by backpropagation algorithm. In the exercise, you should use the function backward written in the Python script to implement the update in Equations (9.31).*

    Plot the training error as a function of the number of epochs and compare it with the original algorithm.

9.7 *Modify the experiment in Example 9.3.3 so the neural network has five layers with 10 nodes each. Compare your results with these of Fig. 9.3.*

List of Acronyms

1BW	one billion word
AdaGrad	adaptive gradient
AdaIN	adaptive instance normalization
Adam	adaptive moment estimation
AE	autoencoder
AEVB	auto-encoding variational Bayes
AI	artificial intelligence
AMZN	Amazon
ANN	artificial neural network
AP	average precision
ATIS	airline travel information systems
BERT	bidirectional encoder representations from transformer
BiT	BigTransfer
BLEU	bilingual evaluation understudy
B-LSTM	bidirectional long short-term memory network
BM	Boltzmann machine
BP	backpropagation
BPE	byte pair encoding
BPTT	backpropagation through time
BRNN	bidirectional recursive neural network
CAE	convolutional autoencoder
CAM	class activation maps
CASP	critical assessment of structure prediction
CBT	children's book test
CDF	cumulative distribution function
CIFAR	Canadian Institute for Advanced Research
CNN	convolutional neural network
COCO	common objects in context
DAE	denoising autoencoder
DBM	deep Boltzmann machine
DBN	deep belief network
DCGAN	deep convolutional generative adversarial network

Deep Learning: A Practical Introduction, First Edition.
Manel Martínez-Ramón, Meenu Ajith, and Aswathy Rajendra Kurup.
© 2024 John Wiley & Sons Ltd. Published 2024 by John Wiley & Sons Ltd.
Companion website: https://github.com/DeepLearning-book

DL	deep learning
DNN	deep neural network
DoF	deep depth of field
DRNN	deep recursive neural network
ELBO	evidence lower bound
EM	earth-mover
FC	fully connected
FCN	fully convolutional network
FFNN	feedforward neural network
FID	Fréchet inception distance
FIFO	first in first out
GAN	generative adversarial network
GD	gradient descent
GELU	Gaussian error linear unit
GLUE	general language understanding evaluation
GP	Gaussian process
GPT-2	generative pretrained transformer 2
GPU	graphical processing unit
GRU	gated recurrent unit
GSN	generative stochastic network
GUI	graphical user interface
i.i.d.	independent and identically distributed
IB	information bottleneck
ILSVRC	ImageNet large scale visual recognition challenge
IoU	intersection-over-union
JS	Jenson–Shanon
KL	Kullback–Leibler
LaMDA	language model for dialogue applications
Lasso	least absolute shrinkage and selector operator
LLM	large language model
LM	language model
LMS	least mean squares
LSTM	long short-term memory network
LSUN	large-scale scene understanding
MAE	mean absolute error
MAP	maximum a posteriori
mAP	mean average precision
MaxOut	maximum output
MCMC	Markov chain Monte Carlo
M-GAN	minimax GAN
MH	Metropolis-Hastings
ML	maximum likelihood
MLM	masked LM
MLP	multilayer perceptron
MMSE	minimum mean square error
MSA	multiheaded self-attention

MSE	mean square error
Nadam	Nesterov-accelerated adaptive momentum estimation
NER	named entity recognition
NFL	no free lunch theorem
NLI	natural language inference
NLL	negative log-likelihood
NLP	natural language processing
NLTK	natural language toolkit
NLU	natural language understanding
NN	neural network
NS-GAN	non-saturating GAN
NSP	next sentence prediction
NUTS	no-U-turn sampler
PCA	principal component analysis
PDF	probability density function
PDP	parallel distributed processing
PTB	Penn treebank
QA	question answering
RBM	restricted Boltzmann machine
ReLU	rectified linear unit
ResNet	residual neural network
RGB	red–green–blue
RMSProp	root mean square propagation
RNN	recurrent neural network
ROC	receiver operation characteristic
SAE	sparse autoencoder
seq2seq	sequence-to-sequence
SGD	stochastic gradient descent
SGVB	stochastic gradient variational Bayes
Squad	Stanford question answering dataset
SSIM	structural similarity index
StackGAN	stacked generative adversarial networks
SVHN	StreetView house numbers
SVI	stochastic variational inference
SVM	support vector machine
SWAG	situations with adversarial generations
TV	total variation
VAE	variational autoencoder
VB	variational Bayesian
VGG	visual geometric group
VI	variational inference
ViT	vision transformer
WGAN	Wasserstein GAN
WLLN	weak law of large numbers
XOR	exclusive OR

Notation

In the nomenclature of this book, scalar variables are represented with a lowercase normal letter, while the constants are represented with normal uppercase letters. The vectors are represented as bold lowercase letters (e.g. $\mathbf{w}$), and they are assumed to be column vectors. Matrices and multidimensional arrays are represented as bold uppercase letters (e.g. $\mathbf{W}$). When functions map to $\mathbb{R}$, they are also represented with normal face, and when they map to a vector space, they are represented in boldface.

Below is an exhaustive list of the notation used in the book. The list is simply grouped in functions, Greek symbols (including scalars, vectors, and arrays), matrices and vectors represented with Latin characters, other symbols, and scalars represented with Latin characters.

Functions

$\mathbf{f}(\mathbf{x})$	mathematical function of a neural network.
ℓ_i	loss function measured over a training sample $\mathbf{x}_i$.
$\mathbb{E}_u$	expectation operator computed with respect to the probability density of variable u.
$\mathcal{N}(\cdot)$	normal or Gaussian distribution.
$\sigma(\cdot)$	logistic function $\frac{d\sigma(z)}{dz} = \sigma(z)(1 - \sigma(z))$.
$\max(\cdot, \cdot)$	maximum operator.
$\min(\cdot, \cdot)$	minimum operator.
$\tanh(\cdot)$	hyperbolic tangent function $\tanh(z) = \frac{e^z - e^{-z}}{e^z + e^{-z}}$.
$\tilde{J}^A_{ELBO}(\boldsymbol{\theta}, \boldsymbol{\phi}), \tilde{J}^B_{ELBO}(\boldsymbol{\theta}, \boldsymbol{\phi})$	generic SGVB estimator, an approximation of $J_{ELBO}(\boldsymbol{\theta}, \boldsymbol{\phi})(.)$
D	discriminator in a GAN.
$D(\mathbf{x}; \theta)$	discriminator function in which $\mathbf{x}$ is the input to the function D and θ represents the parameters of the function.
$D^*(.)$	optimal discriminator in a GAN.
f	nonlinear mapping network in StyleGAN
$f[n], g[n]$	generic discrete time functions.
F_{sl}	function implemented by a give sub-layer in transformers
G	generator in a GAN.

Deep Learning: A Practical Introduction, First Edition.
Manel Martínez-Ramón, Meenu Ajith, and Aswathy Rajendra Kurup.
© 2024 John Wiley & Sons Ltd. Published 2024 by John Wiley & Sons Ltd.
Companion website: https://github.com/DeepLearning-book

G, F	generic image mapping function.
$G(\mathbf{z}; \theta)$	generator function in which $\mathbf{z}$ is the input to the function G and θ represents the parameters of the function.
$H(\cdot, \cdot)$	Hamiltonian function.
$J(\theta, \mathbf{X}, \mathbf{y})$	cost function or optimization criterion.
$J(D, G)$	cost function of GAN.
$J^{(D)}(\theta^{(G)}, \theta^{(D)})$	cost function of the discriminator.
$J^{(G)}(\theta^{(G)}, \theta^{(D)})$	cost function of the generator.
$J_{cyc}(G, F)$	cycle consistency loss function.
$J_{CYC}(G, F, D_X, D_Y)$	cost function of CycleGAN.
$J_c(D, G)$	cost function of cGAN.
$J_{ELBO}(\theta, \phi)$	variational lower bound in VAE.
$J_{ML}(\theta, \mathbf{X}, \mathbf{y})$	maximum likelihood cost function or optimization criterion, also known as cross-entropy cost function.
$J_{sp}(\mathbf{W}, \mathbf{b})$	cost function of SAE.
$J_W(D, G)$	cost function of WGAN.
$k(\cdot)$	kinetic energy function in Hamiltonian MCMC.
$p(\cdot)$	probability density function.
$p_\psi(\cdot)$	parametric distribution used as a prior in Variational Inference.
$q_\phi(\cdot)$	parametric distribution used as an approximate posterior in Variational Inference.
$r(\cdot)$	regularization with respect to a parameter.
$u(\cdot)$	potential energy function in Hamiltonian MCMC.
$Q^{(d)}$	stochastic mapping in Denoising AE.

Greek symbols

α	width multiplier in MobileNet.
$\alpha\,(\mathbf{k}, \mathbf{q})$	attention coefficient between key $\mathbf{k}$ and query $\mathbf{q}$.
α_t	complement of β_t in diffusion process
$\alpha_{t,i}$	attention weight between states in the Bahdanau attention mechanism.
$\bar{\alpha}_t$	cumulative product of α values up to time step t in diffusion process.
$\delta^{(L)}$	error vector computed at the output of a neural network when this output is multiclass (classification) or multitask (regression).
$\delta_i^{(l)}$	error vector backpropagated from the output to layer l of a neural network for training sample $\mathbf{x}_i$.
δ_t	error at the output of an RNN at instant t.
ϵ	a noise vector, drawn randomly from the distribution p_ϵ in StackGAN.
β	number used in exponentially decay windows of the elementwise squared gradient in Adam.
β	number used in exponentially decay windows of the elementwise squared gradient in RMSProp.
β_1	number used in exponentially decay windows of the gradient in Adam.

β_t	variance of Gaussian in diffusion process at time step t
ρ	sparsity level in Sparse Autoencoders.
ϕ	variational parameters in VAE.
Σ	covariance matrix.
$\sigma(\cdot)$	vector of logistic functions $\sigma(\cdot)$.
θ	generative parameters in VAE.
θ, θ^*	set of all parameters of a machine learning structure.
$\varphi(\cdot)$	function constructed as the combination of the pooling operation and nonlinear activation function in a CNN.
$\varphi_f(\cdot)$	function constructed as the combination of the flattening operation and nonlinear activation function in a CNN.
$\delta[n]$	kronecker's delta function.
$\Delta^{(l)}$	array of errors backpropagated to layer l.
$\delta_i^{(L)}$	prediction or classification error measured at the output of a single output neural network for training sample $\mathbf{x}_i$.
$\delta_{k,i}^{(l)}$	error measured at the output to layer l of a neural network for training sample $\mathbf{x}_i$ and for class k.
γ	resolution multiplier in MobileNet.
λ	weight given to the cycle consistency loss term in CycleGAN
λ	weight of the sparsity penalty term.
λ	weight regularization parameter in cost functions.
μ	learning rate.
ν	a measure, which assigns a non-negative real number to each measurable set.
Ω	collection of subsets of a sample space.
$\phi(\cdot$	non-negative function in diffusion models.
$\phi(\cdot)$	generic nonlinear activation.
ψ_t	text embedding of a textual description t.
σ	standard deviation in a univariate Gaussian distribution.

Matrices and vectors

$\mathbf{b}^{(l)}$	bias in layer l of a neural network.
$\mathbf{B}_k^{(l)}$	bias corresponding to the channel k of layer l in a CNN.
$\mathbf{f}_t$	forgetting gate of an LSTM.
$\mathbf{c}_t$	internal state of an LSTM.
$\mathbf{g}_k$	accumulated elementwise squared gradient.
$\mathbf{H}$	group of latent feature maps in CAE.
$\mathbf{H}^{(l)}$	multidimensional array containing the nonlinear outputs of layer l of a neural network, typically a convolutional neural network.
$\mathbf{h}^{(l)}$	nonlinear output of layer l of a neural network.
$\mathbf{h}_t$	hidden state at instant t in an RNN.
$\mathbf{I}$	identity matrix
$\mathbf{i}_t$	internal state modifier of an LSTM.

$\mathbf{k}_i$	query in an attention mechanism.
$\mathbf{o}$	output of a neural network.
$\mathbf{o}_t$	output gate of an LSTM.
I	input image in convolutional neural networks.
$\mathbf{p}$	momentum vector in Hamiltonian MCMC.
$\mathbf{p}_i$	positional encoding vector in an attention mechanism.
$\mathbf{q}_i$	key in an attention mechanism.
$\mathbf{s}_0$	low-resolution output in Stage-II GAN of StackGAN.
$\mathbf{w}$	Column vector containing the parameters of an estimator.
$\mathbf{w}(k)$	value of a set of parameters in instant k of an iterative optimization.
$\mathbf{W}^{(l)}$	array of parameters of layer l in a neural network. An array of convolution kernels in layer l of a convolutional neural network.
$\mathbf{W}^{(q)}, \mathbf{W}^{(k)}, \mathbf{W}^{(v)}$	matrices of the transformation to an input to the query, key and value vectors in a self-attention attention mechanism.
$\mathbf{W}_{hf}$	weight vector that connects the previous state with the forgetting gate in an LSTM.
$\mathbf{W}_{hf}$	weight vector that connects the previous state with the output gate in an LSTM.
$\mathbf{W}_{hi}$	weight vector that connects the previous state with the internal gate in an LSTM.
$\mathbf{W}_{xf}$	weight vector that connects the input with the forgetting gate in an LSTM.
$\mathbf{W}_{xf}$	weight vector that connects the input with the output gate in an LSTM.
$\mathbf{W}_{xh}$	weight matrix of the hidden layer in an RNN.
$\mathbf{W}_{xh}$	weight matrix of the input layer in an RNN.
$\mathbf{W}_{xh}$	weight matrix of the output layer in an RNN.
$\mathbf{W}_{xi}$	weight vector that connects the input with the internal gate in an LSTM.
$\mathbf{X}$	matrix containing column vectors $\mathbf{x}_i, 1 \le i \le N$.
$\mathbf{x}$	column vector containing the input features of a learning model.
$\mathbf{x}'$	reconstructed input.
$\mathbf{x}_i$	input feature in a learning model.
$\mathbf{Z}^{(l)}$	multidimensional array containing the linear outputs of layer l of a neural network, typically a convolutional neural network.
$\mathbf{z}^{(l)}$	linear output of layer l of a neural network.
$\mathbf{Z}_k^{(l)}$	linear output of channel k at layer l of a CNN.
$\mathbf{z}_t^{(o)}$	linear output of an RNN at instant t.
$\mathbf{z}_t^{(x)}$	linear output of the input layer in an RNN at instant t.
$\hat{I}$	noisy image in CAE.
$\hat{\mathbf{x}}$	corrupted or noisy input.
$\tilde{\mathbf{h}}$	output of a layer to which a dropout procedure has been applied.
$\tilde{\mathbf{W}}$	flip operation across the two dimensions of matrix $\mathbf{W}$
$g_\phi(\cdot)$	a vector-valued function parameterized by ϕ in VAE.
$K(\cdot)$	Kernel function
$\mathcal{W}^{(l)}$	convolution kernel expressed as a sparse matrix.
$\hat{\mathbf{g}}_k$	biased accumulated elementwise squared gradient in Adam.

$\hat{\mathbf{v}}_k$	biased accumulated gradient in Adam. Value in an attention mechanism.
$\tilde{\mathbf{c}}_t$	input node of an LSTM.

Other symbols

$\mathbb{R}$	the set of real numbers.
$\mathcal{W}$	intermediate latent space in StyleGAN
$\mathcal{X}$	compact metric set.
$\mathcal{Z}$	latent space representation in StyleGAN
$\nabla_{\mathbf{w}}$	gradient operator computed with respect to vector $\mathbf{w}$.
$\odot$	elementwise product between two equal dimension vectors or matrices.
$\inf\limits_{\mathcal{J} \in \Pi(p_1, p_2)}$	the infimum (the greatest lower bound) taken over all possible joint distributions $\mathcal{J}$.
$\sup\limits_{A \in \Omega}$	supremum (least upper bound) taken over all sets A in the set Ω.
$\top$	transpose operator.
X, Y	domains of functions

Scalars

z	latent variable
$\hat{c}$	conditioning variable generated using conditioning augmentation in StackGAN.
b	bias of a linear model.
b	weight clipping parameter of discriminator in WGAN.
B, C	dimensions of tensor.
c	fixed conditioning text variable.
D	dimension of a space. Number of elements of a vector.
D_l	number of nodes in layer l of a neural network.
$e(\cdot, \cdot)$	mean square error between two variables of a model.
e_k	estimation error of a model.
f^l	feature map of layer l in a DenseNet.
J_{CE}	cross-entropy error of a model.
L	number of layers in a neural network.
l	index for the lth layer of a neural network.
L_1	absolute value regularization.
L_2	quadratic norm regularization.
L_C	number of convolutional layers in a CNN.
L_D	number of dense layers in a CNN.
M, N	number of elements in a set of data.
M_I	horizontal dimension of an image.
M_W	horizontal dimension of a two-dimensional convolutional kernel.

N_I	vertical dimension of an image.
N_W	vertical dimension of a two-dimensional convolutional kernel.
p	number of rows and columns added in a padding operation.
s	number of positions shifted in a stride operation.
$w_{m,n,i,j}^{(l)}$	weight or parameter that connects node m, n of two-dimensional layer $l-1$ of a neural network with node i, j of two-dimensional layer l in a neural network.
w_i	element i of vector $\mathbf{w}$.
$w_{i,j}^{(l)}$	weight or parameter that connects node i of layer $l-1$ with node j in layer l. It is entry i, j of matrix $\mathbf{W}^{(l)}$.
y_i	scalar representing a label in classification or a regressor in a regression model.
Z	normalization constant in diffusion models.
Z	normalization factor in a probability density function.
z	linear output of a neuron.

Bibliography

Abadi, Martín et al. (2016). "TensorFlow: Large-scale machine learning on heterogeneous distributed systems". In: URL: https://arxiv.org/pdf/1603.04467.

Abdal, Rameen, Yipeng Qin, and Peter Wonka (2019). "Image2StyleGAN: How to embed images into the StyleGAN latent space?" In: *Proceedings of the IEEE/CVF international conference on computer vision*, pp. 4432–4441.

Ackley, David H., Geoffrey E. Hinton, and Terrence J. Sejnowski (1985). "A learning algorithm for Boltzmann machines". In: *Cognitive Science* 9.1, pp. 147–169.

Addo, Daniel et al. (2022). "EVAE-Net: An ensemble variational autoencoder deep learning network for COVID-19 classification based on chest X-ray images". In: *Diagnostics* 12.11, p. 2569.

Aggarwal, Alankrita, Mamta Mittal, and Gopi Battineni (2021). "Generative adversarial network: An overview of theory and applications". In: *International Journal of Information Management Data Insights* 1.1, p. 100004.

Aizerman, Mark A. (1964). "Theoretical foundations of the potential function method in pattern recognition learning". In: *Automation and Remote Control* 25, pp. 821–837.

Ajith, Meenu and Vince D. Calhoun (2023). "Functional network connectivity based mental health category prediction from Rest-fMRI data". In: *2023 IEEE 20th international symposium on biomedical imaging (ISBI)*, pp. 1–5. DOI: 10.1109/ISBI53787.2023.10230721.

Ajith, Meenu and Aswathy Rajendra Kurup (2018). "Pedestrian detection: Performance comparison using multiple convolutional neural networks". In: *International conference on machine learning and data mining in pattern recognition*. Springer, pp. 365–379.

Ajith, Meenu and Manel Martínez-Ramón (2019). "Unsupervised segmentation of fire and smoke from infra-red videos". In: *IEEE Access* 7, pp. 182381–182394. DOI: 10.1109/ACCESS.2019.2960209.

Ajith, Meenu and Manel Martínez-Ramón (2021). "Deep learning based solar radiation micro forecast by fusion of infrared cloud images and radiation data". In: *Applied Energy* 294, p. 117014.

Ajith, Meenu and Manel Martínez-Ramón (2023). "Deep learning algorithms for very short term solar irradiance forecasting: A survey". In: *Renewable and Sustainable Energy Reviews* 182, p. 113362.

Akyazi, Pinar and Touradj Ebrahimi (2019). "Learning-based image compression using convolutional autoencoder and wavelet decomposition". In: *IEEE conference on computer vision and pattern recognition workshops*. CONF.

Alemany, Sheila et al. (2019). "Predicting hurricane trajectories using a recurrent neural network". In: *Proceedings of the AAAI conference on artificial intelligence*. Vol. 33. 01, pp. 468–475.

Allen-Zhu, Zeyuan, Yuanzhi Li, and Zhao Song (2019). "On the convergence rate of training recurrent neural networks". In: *Advances in Neural Information Processing Systems 32 (NeurIPS 2019)*.

Al-Rfou, Rami et al. (2019). "Character-level language modeling with deeper self-attention". In: *Proceedings of the AAAI conference on artificial intelligence*. Vol. 33.01, pp. 3159–3166.

Amit, Daniel J. and Daniel J. Amit (1989). *Modeling Brain Function: The World of Attractor Neural Networks*. Cambridge University Press.

Arjovsky, Martin and Léon Bottou (2017). "Towards principled methods for training generative adversarial networks". In: URL: https://arxiv.org/pdf/1701.04862.

Arjovsky, Martin, Soumith Chintala, and Léon Bottou (2017). "Wasserstein generative adversarial networks". In: *International conference on machine learning*. PMLR, pp. 214–223.

Aytar, Yusuf et al. (2017). "Cross-modal scene networks". In: *IEEE Transactions on Pattern Analysis and Machine Intelligence* 40.10, pp. 2303–2314.

Ba, Jimmy Lei, Jamie Ryan Kiros, and Geoffrey E. Hinton (2016). "Layer normalization". In: URL: https://arxiv.org/pdf/1607.06450.

Bahdanau, Dzmitry, Kyunghyun Cho, and Yoshua Bengio (2014). "Neural machine translation by jointly learning to align and translate". In: url: https://arxiv.org/pdf/1409.0473.

Bando, Yoshiaki et al. (2018). "Statistical speech enhancement based on probabilistic integration of variational autoencoder and non-negative matrix factorization". In: *2018 IEEE international conference on acoustics, speech and signal processing (ICASSP)*. IEEE, pp. 716–720.

Bardenet, Rémi, Arnaud Doucet, and Chris Holmes (2017). "On Markov chain Monte Carlo methods for tall data". In: *Journal of Machine Learning Research* 18.47, pp. 1–43.

Beale, Evelyn M.L. (1955). "On minimizing a convex function subject to linear inequalities". In: *Journal of the Royal Statistical Society Series B: Statistical Methodology* 17.2, pp. 173–184.

Becker, S. and Yan Le Cun (1988). "Improving the convergence of back-propagation learning with second-order methods". In: *Proceedings of the 1988 connectionist models summer school*, pp. 29–37.

Bengio, Yoshua (2009). "Learning deep architectures for AI". In: *Foundations and Trends® in Machine Learning* 2.1, pp. 1–127.

Bengio, Yoshua, Patrice Simard, and Paolo Frasconi (1994). "Learning long-term dependencies with gradient descent is difficult". In: *IEEE Transactions on Neural Networks* 5.2, pp. 157–166.

Bengio, Yoshua et al. (2006). "Greedy layer-wise training of deep networks". In: *Advances in neural information processing systems 19 (NIPS 2006)*.

Bengio, Yoshua et al. (2007). "Scaling learning algorithms towards AI". In: *Large-Scale Kernel Machines* 34.5, pp. 1–41.

Bengio, Yoshua et al. (2013). "Generalized denoising auto-encoders as generative models". In: *Advances in neural information processing systems 26 (NIPS 2013)*.

Bengio, Yoshua et al. (2014). "Deep generative stochastic networks trainable by backprop". In: *International conference on machine learning*. PMLR, pp. 226–234.

Bergstra, James and Yoshua Bengio (2012). "Random search for hyper-parameter optimization". In: *Journal of Machine Learning Research* 13.2, pp. 281–305.

Berthelot, David, Thomas Schumm, and Luke Metz (2017). "Began: Boundary equilibrium generative adversarial networks". In: URL: https://arxiv.org/pdf/1703.10717.

Bertsekas, Dimitri P. and John N. Tsitsiklis (2000). *Introduction to Probability*. Athena Scientific.

Besag, Julian (1975). "Statistical analysis of non-lattice data". In: *Journal of the Royal Statistical Society Series D: The Statistician* 24.3, pp. 179–195.

Betancourt, Michael (2017). "A conceptual introduction to Hamiltonian Monte Carlo". In: URL: https://arxiv.org/pdf/1701.02434.

Bevilacqua, Vitoantonio et al. (2008). "Retinal fundus biometric analysis for personal identifications". In: *Advanced Intelligent Computing Theories and Applications. With Aspects of Artificial Intelligence: 4th International Conference on Intelligent Computing, ICIC 2008, Shanghai, China, September 15–18, 2008 Proceedings 4*. Springer, pp. 1229–1237.

Beyer, Lucas et al. (2020). "Are we done with ImageNet?" In: URL: https://arxiv.org/pdf/2006 .07159.

Bilefsky, Dan (2023). "He Helped Create A.I. Now, He Worries About 'Killer Robots'". In: *The New York Times*.

Bird, Steven, Ewan Klein, and Edward Loper (2009). *Natural Language Processing with Python: Analyzing Text with the Natural Language Toolkit*. O'Reilly Media, Inc.

Bishop, Christopher M. (2006). *Pattern Recognition and Machine Learning (Information Science and Statistics)*. Berlin, Heidelberg: Springer-Verlag. ISBN: 0387310738.

Bitzer, Sebastian and Stefan J. Kiebel (2012). "Recognizing recurrent neural networks (rRNN): Bayesian inference for recurrent neural networks". In: *Biological Cybernetics* 106, pp. 201–217.

Blei, David M., Alp Kucukelbir, and Jon D. McAuliffe (2017). "Variational inference: A review for statisticians". In: *Journal of the American Statistical Association* 112.518, pp. 859–877.

Blundell, Charles et al. (2015). "Weight uncertainty in neural network". In: *International conference on machine learning*. PMLR, pp. 1613–1622.

Bojar, Ondřej et al. (2014). "Findings of the 2014 workshop on statistical machine translation". In: *Proceedings of the 9th workshop on statistical machine translation*, pp. 12–58.

Bollapragada, Raghu et al. (2018). "A progressive batching L-BFGS method for machine learning". In: *International conference on machine learning*. PMLR, pp. 620–629.

Bousmalis, Konstantinos et al. (2017). "Unsupervised pixel-level domain adaptation with generative adversarial networks". In: *Proceedings of the IEEE conference on computer vision and pattern recognition*, pp. 3722–3731.

Brock, Andrew, Jeff Donahue, and Karen Simonyan (2018). "Large scale GAN training for high fidelity natural image synthesis". In: URL: https://arxiv.org/pdf/1809.11096.

Buongiorno, Domenico et al. (2019). "An undercomplete autoencoder to extract muscle synergies for motor intention detection". In: *2019 International joint conference on neural networks (IJCNN)*. IEEE, pp. 1–8.

Byra, Michal et al. (2020). "Knee menisci segmentation and relaxometry of 3D ultrashort echo time cones MR imaging using attention U-Net with transfer learning". In: *Magnetic Resonance in Medicine* 83.3, pp. 1109–1122.

Byrd, Richard H. et al. (2011). "On the use of stochastic hessian information in optimization methods for machine learning". In: *SIAM Journal on Optimization* 21.3, pp. 977–995.

Cao, Yuan and Quanquan Gu (2019). "Generalization bounds of stochastic gradient descent for wide and deep neural networks". In: *Advances in neural information processing systems 32 (NeurIPS 2019)*.

Caruana, Rich (1997). "Multitask learning". In: *Machine Learning* 28, pp. 41–75.

Chelba, Ciprian et al. (2013). "One billion word benchmark for measuring progress in statistical language modeling". In: URL: https://arxiv.org/pdf/1312.3005.

Cheng, Zhengxue et al. (2018). "Deep convolutional autoencoder-based lossy image compression". In: *2018 Picture coding symposium (PCS)*. IEEE, pp. 253–257.

Chib, Siddhartha and Edward Greenberg (1995). "Understanding the metropolis-hastings algorithm". In: *The American Statistician* 49.4, pp. 327–335.

Cho, Kyunghyun et al. (2014a). "Learning phrase representations using RNN encoder-decoder for statistical machine translation". In: *Proceedings of the 2014 Conference on Empirical Methods in Natural Language Processing, EMNLP 2014, October 25–29, 2014, Doha, Qatar, A meeting of SIGDAT, a Special Interest Group of the ACL*. Ed. by Alessandro Moschitti, Bo Pang, and Walter Daelemans. ACL, pp. 1724–1734.

Cho, Kyunghyun et al. (2014b). "On the properties of neural machine translation: Encoder-decoder approaches". In: URL: https://arxiv.org/pdf/1409.1259.

Choi, Jinho D., Joel Tetreault, and Amanda Stent (2015). "It depends: Dependency parser comparison using a web-based evaluation tool". In: *Proceedings of the 53rd annual meeting of the association for computational linguistics and the 7th International joint conference on natural language processing (Volume 1: Long Papers)*, pp. 387–396.

Chollet, François (2017). "Xception: Deep learning with depthwise separable convolutions". In: *Proceedings of the IEEE conference on computer vision and pattern recognition*, pp. 1251–1258.

Chow, Jun Kang et al. (2020). "Anomaly detection of defects on concrete structures with the convolutional autoencoder". In: *Advanced Engineering Informatics* 45, p. 101105.

Ciresan, Dan Claudiu et al. (2011). "Flexible, high performance convolutional neural networks for image classification". In: *22nd international joint conference on artificial intelligence*.

Coates, Adam and Andrew Ng (2011). "Selecting receptive fields in deep networks". In: *Advances in neural information processing systems 24 (NIPS 2011)*.

Coates, Adam and Andrew Y. Ng (2012). "Learning feature representations with k-means". In: *Neural Networks: Tricks of the Trade, 2nd Edition*. Springer, pp. 561–580.

Collobert, Ronan et al. (2011). "Natural language processing (almost) from scratch". In: *Journal of Machine Learning Research* 12.ARTICLE, pp. 2493–2537.

Corana, Angelo et al. (1987). "Minimizing multimodal functions of continuous variables with the "simulated annealing" algorithm—Corrigenda for this article is available here". In: *ACM Transactions on Mathematical Software (TOMS)* 13.3, pp. 262–280.

Corbetta, Maurizio and Gordon L. Shulman (2002). "Control of goal-directed and stimulus-driven attention in the brain". In: *Nature Reviews Neuroscience* 3.3, pp. 201–215.

Cordts, Marius et al. (2016). "The cityscapes dataset for semantic urban scene understanding". In: *Proceedings of the IEEE conference on computer vision and pattern recognition*, pp. 3213–3223.

Costa, Mario et al. (1999). "Short term load forecasting using a synchronously operated recurrent neural network". In: *IJCNN'99. International joint conference on neural networks. Proceedings (Cat. No. 99CH36339)*. Vol. 5. IEEE, pp. 3478–3482.

Cover, Thomas M. and Joy A. Thomas (2006). *Elements of Information Theory, 2nd Edition (Wiley Series in Telecommunications and Signal Processing)*. Wiley-Interscience.

Creswell, Antonia et al. (2018). "Generative adversarial networks: An overview". In: *IEEE Signal Processing Magazine* 35.1, pp. 53–65.

Dahl, George E. et al. (2011). "Context-dependent pre-trained deep neural networks for large-vocabulary speech recognition". In: *IEEE Transactions on Audio, Speech, and Language Processing* 20.1, pp. 30–42.

Dai, Andrew M. and Quoc V. Le (2015). "Semi-supervised sequence learning". In: *Advances in neural information processing systems 28 (NIPS 2015)*.

De Cesarei, Andrea et al. (2021). "Do humans and deep convolutional neural networks use visual information similarly for the categorization of natural scenes?" In: *Cognitive Science* 45.6, e13009.

Deng, Jia et al. (2009). "ImageNet: A large-scale image database". In: *2009 IEEE conference on computer vision and pattern recognition*. IEEE, pp. 248–255.

Deng, Jun et al. (2013). "Sparse autoencoder-based feature transfer learning for speech emotion recognition". In: *2013 Humaine association conference on affective computing and intelligent interaction*. IEEE, pp. 511–516.

Devlin, Jacob et al. (2018). "BERT: Pre-training of deep bidirectional transformers for language understanding". In: URL: https://arxiv.org/pdf/1810.04805.

Dodda, Vineela Chandra et al. (2022). "An undercomplete autoencoder for denoising computational 3D sectional images". In: *Adaptive Optics and Applications*. Optica Publishing Group, p. JW2A–19.

Dong, Xiaoyi et al. (2022). "Clip itself is a strong fine-tuner: Achieving 85.7% and 88.0% top-1 accuracy with vit-b and vit-l on ImageNet". In: *arXiv preprint arXiv:2212.06138*.

Dosovitskiy, Alexey et al. (2014). "Discriminative unsupervised feature learning with convolutional neural networks". In: *Advances in neural information processing systems 27 (NIPS 2014)*.

Dosovitskiy, Alexey et al. (2020). "An image is worth 16x16 words: Transformers for image recognition at scale". In: URL: https://arxiv.org/pdf/2010.11929.

Dozat, T. and Incorporating Nesterov momentum into Adam (2016). "ICLR 2016 workshop submission". In: URL: https://openreview.net/forum.

Duan, Lixin, Dong Xu, and Ivor Tsang (2012). "Learning with augmented features for heterogeneous domain adaptation". In: *arXiv preprint arXiv:1206.4660*.

Duchi, John, Elad Hazan, and Yoram Singer (2011). "Adaptive subgradient methods for online learning and stochastic optimization". In: *Journal of Machine Learning Research* 12.7, pp. 2121–2159.

Dumoulin, Vincent, Jonathon Shlens, and Manjunath Kudlur (2016). "A learned representation for artistic style". In: URL: https://arxiv.org/pdf/1610.07629.

Dumoulin, Vincent et al. (2018). "Feature-wise transformations". In: *Distill* 3.7, e11.

Eigen, David and Rob Fergus (2015). "Predicting depth, surface normals and semantic labels with a common multi-scale convolutional architecture". In: *Proceedings of the IEEE international conference on computer vision*, pp. 2650–2658.

Elman, Jeffrey L. (1990). "Fnding structure in time". In: *Cognitive Science* 14.2, pp. 179–211.

Engelmann, Justin and Stefan Lessmann (2021). "Conditional Wasserstein GAN-based oversampling of tabular data for imbalanced learning". In: *Expert Systems with Applications* 174, p. 114582.

Epanechnikov, Vassiliy A. (1969). "Non-parametric estimation of a multivariate probability density". In: *Theory of Probability & Its Applications* 14.1, pp. 153–158.

Erhan, Dumitru et al. (2010). "Why does unsupervised pre-training help deep learning?" In: *Proceedings of the 13th international conference on artificial intelligence and statistics.* JMLR Workshop and Conference Proceedings, pp. 201–208.

Feng, Weijiang et al. (2017). "Audio visual speech recognition with multimodal recurrent neural networks". In: *2017 International joint conference on neural networks (IJCNN).* IEEE, pp. 681–688.

Ferles, Christos, Yannis Papanikolaou, and Kevin J. Naidoo (2018). "Denoising autoencoder self-organizing map (DASOM)". In: *Neural Networks* 105, pp. 112–131.

Finn, Chelsea, Pieter Abbeel, and Sergey Levine (2017). "Model-agnostic meta-learning for fast adaptation of deep networks". In: *International conference on machine learning.* PMLR, pp. 1126–1135.

Fukushima, Kunihiko (1980). "Neocognitron: A self-organizing neural network model for a mechanism of pattern recognition unaffected by shift in position". In: *Biological Cybernetics* 36.4, pp. 193–202.

Gal, Yarin and Zoubin Ghahramani (2016). "Dropout as a Bayesian approximation: Representing model uncertainty in deep learning". In: *International conference on machine learning.* PMLR, pp. 1050–1059.

Gehring, Jonas et al. (2017). "Convolutional sequence to sequence learning". In: *International conference on machine learning.* PMLR, pp. 1243–1252.

Geman, Stuart, Elie Bienenstock, and René Doursat (1992). "Neural networks and the bias/variance dilemma". In: *Neural Computation* 4.1, pp. 1–58.

Ghahramani, Zoubin and Matthew Beal (2000). "Propagation algorithms for variational Bayesian learning". In: *Advances in neural information processing systems 13 (NIPS 2000).*

Ghiasi, Golnaz et al. (2017). "Exploring the structure of a real-time, arbitrary neural artistic stylization network". In: URL: https://arxiv.org/pdf/1705.06830.

Giles, C. Lee, Steve Lawrence, and Ah Chung Tsoi (1997). "Rule inference for financial prediction using recurrent neural networks". In: *Proceedings of the IEEE/IAFE 1997 computational intelligence for financial engineering (CIFEr).* IEEE, pp. 253–259.

Gilks, Walter R., Sylvia Richardson, and David Spiegelhalter (1995). *Markov Chain Monte Carlo in Practice.* CRC Press.

Glorot, Xavier and Yoshua Bengio (2010). "Understanding the difficulty of training deep feedforward neural networks". In: *Proceedings of the 13th international conference on artificial intelligence and statistics.* JMLR Workshop and Conference Proceedings, pp. 249–256.

Glorot, Xavier, Antoine Bordes, and Yoshua Bengio (2011). "Deep sparse rectifier neural networks". In: *Proceedings of the 14th international conference on artificial intelligence and statistics.* JMLR Workshop and Conference Proceedings, pp. 315–323.

Gneiting, Tilmann and Adrian E. Raftery (2007). "Strictly proper scoring rules, prediction, and estimation". In: *Journal of the American Statistical Association* 102.477, pp. 359–378.

Goan, Ethan and Clinton Fookes (2020). "Bayesian neural networks: An introduction and survey". In: *Case Studies in Applied Bayesian Data Science: CIRM Jean-Morlet Chair, Fall 2018*, pp. 45–87.

Gondara, Lovedeep (2016). "Medical image denoising using convolutional denoising autoencoders". In: *2016 IEEE 16th international conference on data mining workshops (ICDMW)*. IEEE, pp. 241–246.

Gong, Chengyue et al. (2018). "FRAGE: Frequency-agnostic word representation". In: *Advances in neural information processing systems 31 (NeurIPS 2018)*.

Goodfellow, Ian et al. (2013a). "Maxout networks". In: *Proceedings of the 30th International Conference on Machine Learning*. Ed. by Sanjoy Dasgupta and David McAllester. Vol. 28. Proceedings of Machine Learning Research 3. Atlanta, Georgia, USA: PMLR, pp. 1319–1327.

Goodfellow, Ian et al. (2013b). "Multi-prediction deep Boltzmann machines". In: *Advances in Neural Information Processing Systems 26 (NIPS 2013)*.

Goodfellow, I., Y. Bengio, and A. Courville (2016). *Deep Learning*. Cambridge, MA, USA: The MIT Press.

Goodfellow, Ian et al. (2020). "Generative adversarial networks". In: *Communications of the ACM* 63.11, pp. 139–144.

Graves, Alex (2011). "Practical variational inference for neural networks". In: *Advances in neural information processing systems 24 (NIPS 2011)*.

Graves, Alex, Abdel-rahman Mohamed, and Geoffrey E. Hinton (2013). "Speech recognition with deep recurrent neural networks". In: *2013 IEEE international conference on acoustics, speech and signal processing*. IEEE, pp. 6645–6649.

Güçlü, Umut and Marcel A.J. Van Gerven (2017). "Modeling the dynamics of human brain activity with recurrent neural networks". In: *Frontiers in Computational Neuroscience* 11, p. 7.

Güera, David and Edward J. Delp (2018). "Deepfake video detection using recurrent neural networks". In: *2018 15th IEEE international conference on advanced video and signal based surveillance (AVSS)*. IEEE, pp. 1–6.

Gulrajani, Ishaan et al. (2017). "Improved training of Wasserstein GANs". In: *Advances in neural information processing systems 30 (NIPS 2017)*.

Hallez, Quentin, Martial Mermillod, and Sylvie Droit-Volet (2023). "Cognitive and plastic recurrent neural network clock model for the judgment of time and its variations". In: *Scientific Reports* 13.1, p. 3852.

Harel, Maayan and Shie Mannor (2010). "Learning from multiple outlooks". In: URL: https://arxiv.org/pdf/1005.0027.

Hastie, Trevor (2020). "Ridge regularization: An essential concept in data science". In: *Technometrics* 62.4, pp. 426–433.

Hastings, W. Keith (1970). "Monte Carlo sampling methods using Markov chains and their applications". In: *Biometrika* 57.1, pp. 97–109.

Haykin, Simon (1996). *Adaptive Filter Theory, 3rd Edition*. USA: Prentice-Hall, Inc. ISBN: 013322760X.

Haykin, Simon S. (2005). *Adaptive Filter Theory*. Pearson Education India.

He, Kaiming and Jian Sun (2015). "Convolutional neural networks at constrained time cost". In: *Proceedings of the IEEE conference on computer vision and pattern recognition*, pp. 5353–5360.

He, Kaiming et al. (2015). "Delving deep into rectifiers: Surpassing human-level performance on ImageNet classification". In: *Proceedings of the IEEE international conference on computer vision*, pp. 1026–1034.

He, Kaiming et al. (2016). "Deep residual learning for image recognition". In: *Proceedings of the IEEE conference on computer vision and pattern recognition*, pp. 770–778.

Hendrycks, Dan and Kevin Gimpel (2016). "Gaussian error linear units (GELUs)". In: URL: https://arxiv.org/pdf/1606.08415.

Hertzmann, Aaron et al. (2023). "Image analogies". In: *Seminal Graphics Papers: Pushing the Boundaries 2*, pp. 557–570.

Heusel, Martin et al. (2017). "GANs trained by a two time-scale update rule converge to a local Nash equilibrium". In: *Advances in neural information processing systems 30 (NIPS 2017)*.

Hill, Felix et al. (2015). "The goldilocks principle: Reading children's books with explicit memory representations". In: URL: https://arxiv.org/pdf/1511.02301.

Hinton, Geoffrey E. (2002). "Training products of experts by minimizing contrastive divergence". In: *Neural Computation* 14.8, pp. 1771–1800.

Hinton, Geoffrey E. (2007). "Learning multiple layers of representation". In: *Trends in Cognitive Sciences* 11.10, pp. 428–434.

Hinton, Geoffrey E. and Ruslan R. Salakhutdinov (2006). "Reducing the dimensionality of data with neural networks". In: *Science* 313.5786, pp. 504–507.

Hinton, Geoffrey E. and Terrence J. Sejnowski (1983). "Optimal perceptual inference". In: *Proceedings of the IEEE conference on Computer Vision and Pattern Recognition*. Vol. 448. Citeseer, pp. 448–453.

Hinton, Geoffrey E. et al. (1995). "The "wake-sleep" algorithm for unsupervised neural networks". In: *Science* 268.5214, pp. 1158–1161.

Hinton, Geoffrey E., Simon Osindero, and Yee-Whye Teh (2006). "A fast learning algorithm for deep belief nets". In: *Neural Computation* 18.7, pp. 1527–1554.

Hinton, Geoffrey E., Alex Krizhevsky, and Sida D. Wang (2011). "Transforming auto-encoders". In: *Artificial Neural Networks and Machine Learning–ICANN 2011: 21st International Conference on Artificial Neural Networks, Espoo, Finland, June 14–17, 2011, Proceedings, Part I 21*. Springer, pp. 44–51.

Hinton, Geoffrey E., Nitish Srivastava, and Kevin Swersky (2012a). *Neural networks for machine learning. Lecture 6a: overview of mini-batch gradient descent.* URL: http://www.cs.toronto.edu/~hinton/coursera/lecture6/lec6.pdf.

Hinton, Geoffrey E. et al. (2012b). "Improving neural networks by preventing co-adaptation of feature detectors". In: *CoRR* abs/1207.0580.

Hinton, Geoffrey E. et al. (2012c). "Deep neural networks for acoustic modeling in speech recognition: The shared views of four research groups". In: *IEEE Signal Processing Magazine* 29.6, pp. 82–97.

Hinton, Geoffrey E., Oriol Vinyals, and Jeff Dean (2015). "Distilling the knowledge in a neural network". In: 2.7. URL: https://arxiv.org/pdf/1503.02531.

Hitchcock, David B. (2003). "A history of the Metropolis–Hastings algorithm". In: *The American Statistician* 57.4, pp. 254–257.

Hjelm, R. Devon et al. (2017). "Boundary-seeking generative adversarial networks". In: URL: https://arxiv.org/pdf/1702.08431.

Ho, Jonathan, Ajay Jain, and Pieter Abbeel (2020). "Denoising diffusion probabilistic models". In: *Advances in neural information processing systems 33 (NeurIPS 2020)*, pp. 6840–6851.

Hoerl, Arthur E. and Robert W. Kennard (1970). "Ridge regression: applications to nonorthogonal problems". In: *Technometrics* 12.1, pp. 69–82.

Hoffman, Matthew D., Andrew Gelman, et al. (2014). "The No-U-Turn sampler: adaptively setting path lengths in Hamiltonian Monte Carlo". In: *Journal of Machine Learning Research* 15.1, pp. 1593–1623.

Hole, Arne (1996). "Vapnik-Chervonenkis generalization bounds for real valued neural networks". In: *Neural Computation* 8.6, pp. 1277–1299.

Honkela, Antti and Harri Valpola (2004). "Variational learning and bits-back coding: an information-theoretic view to Bayesian learning". In: *IEEE Transactions on Neural Networks* 15.4, pp. 800–810.

Hopfield, John J. (1982). "Neural networks and physical systems with emergent collective computational abilities". In: *Proceedings of the National Academy of Sciences of the United States of America* 79.8, pp. 2554–2558.

Hopfield, John J. and David W. Tank (1985). ""Neural" computation of decisions in optimization problems". In: *Biological Cybernetics* 52.3, pp. 141–152.

Howard, Andrew G. et al. (2017). "MobileNets: Efficient convolutional neural networks for mobile vision applications". In: *CoRR* abs/1704.04861.

Huang, Xun and Serge Belongie (2017). "Arbitrary style transfer in real-time with adaptive instance normalization". In: *Proceedings of the IEEE international conference on computer vision*, pp. 1501–1510.

Huang, Gary B. et al. (2008). "Labeled faces in the wild: A database forstudying face recognition in unconstrained environments". In: *Workshop on faces in 'Real-Life' Images: detection, alignment, and recognition*.

Huang, Gao, Zhuang Liu, and Kilian Q. Weinberger (2017). "Densely connected convolutional networks". In: *2017 IEEE conference on computer vision and pattern recognition (CVPR)*, pp. 2261–2269.

Hubel, David H. and Torsten N. Wiesel (1962). "Receptive fields, binocular interaction and functional architecture in the cat's visual cortex". In: *The Journal of Physiology* 160.1, p. 106.

Hubin, Aliaksandr and Geir Storvik (2023). "Variational Inference for Bayesian Neural Networks under Model and Parameter Uncertainty". In: URL: https://arxiv.org/pdf/305.00934.

Hyvärinen, Aapo and Peter Dayan (2005). "Estimation of non-normalized statistical models by score matching". In: *Journal of Machine Learning Research* 6.4, pp. 695–709.

Ioffe, Sergey and Christian Szegedy (2015). "Batch normalization: Accelerating deep network training by reducing internal covariate shift". In: *International conference on machine learning*. PMLR, pp. 448–456.

Isola, Phillip et al. (2017). "Image-to-image translation with conditional adversarial networks". In: *Proceedings of the IEEE conference on computer vision and pattern recognition*, pp. 1125–1134.

Jarrett, Kevin et al. (2009). "What is the best multi-stage architecture for object recognition?" In: *2009 IEEE 12th international conference on computer vision*. IEEE, pp. 2146–2153.

Jarzynski, Christopher (1997). "Equilibrium free-energy differences from nonequilibrium measurements: A master-equation approach". In: *Physical Review E* 56.5, p. 5018.

Jing, Yongcheng et al. (2020). "Neural style transfer: A review". In: *IEEE Transactions on Visualization and Computer Graphics* 26.11, pp. 3365–3385.

Johnson, Justin, Alexandre Alahi, and Li Fei-Fei (2016). "Perceptual losses for real-time style transfer and super-resolution". In: *Computer Vision–ECCV 2016: 14th European Conference, Amsterdam, The Netherlands, October 11–14, 2016, Proceedings, Part II 14*. Springer, pp. 694–711.

Jordan, Michael I. (1986). *Serial Order: A Parallel Distributed Processing Approach*. Technical Report, June 1985-March 1986. Tech. rep. California Univ., San Diego, La Jolla (USA). Inst. for Cognitive Science.

Jordan, Michael I. et al. (1999). "An introduction to variational methods for graphical models". In: *Machine Learning* 37, pp. 183–233.

Jospin, Laurent Valentin et al. (2022). "Hands-on Bayesian neural networks—A tutorial for deep learning users". In: *IEEE Computational Intelligence Magazine* 17.2, pp. 29–48.

Jozefowicz, Rafal et al. (2016). "Exploring the limits of language modeling". In: URL: https://arxiv.org/pdf/1602.02410.

Karras, Tero et al. (2017). "Progressive growing of GANs for improved quality, stability, and variation". In: URL: https://arxiv.org/pdf/1710.10196.

Karras, Tero, Samuli Laine, and Timo Aila (2019). "A style-based generator architecture for generative adversarial networks". In: *Proceedings of the IEEE/CVF conference on computer vision and pattern recognition*, pp. 4401–4410.

Karras, Tero, Samuli Laine, Miika Aittala, et al. (2020a). "Analyzing and improving the image quality of stylegan". In: *Proceedings of the IEEE/CVF conference on computer vision and pattern recognition*, pp. 8110–8119.

Karras, Tero et al. (2020b). "Training generative adversarial networks with limited data". In: *Advances in neural information processing systems 33 (NeurIPS 2020)*, pp. 12104–12114.

Khan, Salman et al. (2022). "Transformers in vision: A survey". In: *ACM Computing Surveys (CSUR)* 54.10s, pp. 1–41.

Kingma, Diederik P. and Jimmy Ba (2014). "Adam: A method for stochastic optimization". In: URL: https://arxiv.org/pdf/1412.6980.

Kingma, Diederik P. and Max Welling (2013). "Auto-encoding variational Bayes". In: URL: https://arxiv.org/pdf/1312.6114.

Kingma, Diederik P. and Max Welling (2019). "An introduction to variational autoencoders". In: *Foundations and Trends® in Machine Learning* 12.4, pp. 307–392.

Kirkpatrick, Scott, C. Daniel Gelatt Jr., and Mario P. Vecchi (1983). "Optimization by simulated annealing". In: *Science* 220.4598, pp. 671–680.

Kirkpatrick, James et al. (2017). "Overcoming catastrophic forgetting in neural networks". In: *Proceedings of the National Academy of Sciences of the United States of America* 114.13, pp. 3521–3526.

Kiros, Ryan et al. (2015). "Skip-thought vectors". In: *Advances in neural information processing systems 28 (NIPS 2015)*.

Kolesnikov, Alexander et al. (2020). "Big transfer (bit): General visual representation learning". In: *Computer Vision–ECCV 2020: 16th European Conference, Glasgow, UK, August 23–28, 2020, Proceedings, Part V 16*. Springer, pp. 491–507.

Kriegeskorte, Nikolaus (2015). "Deep neural networks: A new framework for modeling biological vision and brain information processing". In: *Annual Review of Vision Science* 1, pp. 417–446.

Krizhevsky, Alex (2009). "Learning Multiple Layers of Features from Tiny Images". Master's Thesis, University of Toronto.

Krizhevsky, Alex, Ilya Sutskever, and Geoffrey E. Hinton (2012). "ImageNet classification with deep convolutional neural networks". In: *Advances in Neural Information Processing Systems*. Ed. by F. Pereira et al., Vol. 25. Curran Associates, Inc.

Kryshtafovych, Andriy et al. (2021). "Critical assessment of methods of protein structure prediction (CASP)—Round XIV". In: *Proteins: Structure, Function, and Bioinformatics* 89.12, pp. 1607–1617.

Kullback, Solomon and Richard A. Leibler (1951). "On information and sufficiency". In: *The Annals of Mathematical Statistics* 22.1, pp. 79–86.

Kumar, Siddharth Krishna (2017). "On weight initialization in deep neural networks". In: URL: https://arxiv.org/pdf/1704.08863.

Kurup, Aswathy Rajendra, Meenu Ajith, and Manel Martínez-Ramón (2019). "Semi-supervised facial expression recognition using reduced spatial features and deep belief networks". In: *Neurocomputing* 367, pp. 188–197.

Kurup, A. et al. (2020). "Automated detection of malarial retinopathy using transfer learning". In: *2020 IEEE Southwest symposium on image analysis and interpretation (SSIAI)*. IEEE, pp. 18–21.

Kurup, Aswathy Rajendra et al. (2023). "Automated malarial retinopathy detection using transfer learning and multi-camera retinal images". In: *Biocybernetics and Biomedical Engineering* 43.1, pp. 109–123.

Kuzovkin, I. et al. (2018). Activations of deep convolutional neural networks are aligned with gamma band activity of human visual cortex". *Communications Biology* 1, pp. 1–12.

Lampinen, Jouko and Aki Vehtari (2001). "Bayesian approach for neural networks—review and case studies". In: *Neural Networks* 14.3, pp. 257–274.

Längkvist, Martin, Lars Karlsson, and Amy Loutfi (2014). "A review of unsupervised feature learning and deep learning for time-series modeling". In: *Pattern Recognition Letters* 42, pp. 11–24.

Larsen, Anders Boesen Lindbo et al. (2016). "Autoencoding beyond pixels using a learned similarity metric". In: *International conference on machine learning*. PMLR, pp. 1558–1566.

LeCun, Yann (1989). "Generalization and network design strategies". In: *Connectionism in Perspective* 19.143–155, p. 18.

LeCun, Yann et al. (1989). "Backpropagation applied to handwritten zip code recognition". In: *Neural Computation* 1.4, pp. 541–551.

LeCun, Yann et al. (1998). "Gradient-based learning applied to document recognition". In: *Proceedings of the IEEE* 86.11, pp. 2278–2324.

LeCun, Yann A et al. (2012). "Efficient backprop". In: *Neural Networks: Tricks of the trade*. Springer, pp. 9–48.

Ledig, Christian et al. (2017). "Photo-realistic single image super-resolution using a generative adversarial network". In: *Proceedings of the IEEE conference on computer vision and pattern recognition*, pp. 4681–4690.

Lee, Honglak, Chaitanya Ekanadham, and Andrew Ng (2007). "Sparse deep belief net model for visual area V2". In: *Advances in neural information processing systems 20 (NIPS 2007).*

Li, Qing and Nan Lin (2010). "The Bayesian elastic net". In: *Bayesian Analysis* 5.1, pp. 151–170.

Liang, Sheng-Fu, Alvin W.Y. Su, and Cheng-Teng Lin (1999). "A new recurrent-network-based music synthesis method for Chinese plucked-string instruments-Pipa and Qin".
In: *IJCNN'99. International Joint Conference on Neural Networks. Proceedings (Cat. No. 99CH36339).* Vol. 4. IEEE, pp. 2564–2569.

Lim, Wootaek, Daeyoung Jang, and Taejin Lee (2016). "Speech emotion recognition using convolutional and recurrent neural networks". In: *2016 Asia-Pacific signal and information processing association annual summit and conference (APSIPA).* IEEE, pp. 1–4.

Lin, Min, Qiang Chen, and Shuicheng Yan (2014a). "Network in network". In: *2nd International Conference on Learning Representations, ICLR 2014, Banff, AB, Canada, April 14–16, 2014, Conference Track Proceedings.* Ed. by Yoshua Bengio and Yann LeCun.

Lin, Tsung-Yi et al. (2014b). "Microsoft COCO: Common objects in context". In: *Computer Vision–ECCV 2014: 13th European Conference, Zurich, Switzerland, September 6–12, 2014, Proceedings, Part V 13.* Springer, pp. 740–755.

Lin, Zhouhan et al. (2017). "A structured self-attentive sentence embedding". In: URL: https://arxiv.org/pdf/1703.03130.

Lindsay, Grace W. (2021). "Convolutional neural networks as a model of the visual system: Past, present, and future". In: *Journal of Cognitive Neuroscience* 33.10, pp. 2017–2031.

Little, William A. (1974). "The existence of persistent states in the brain". In: *Mathematical Biosciences* 19.1–2, pp. 101–120.

Liu, Dong C. and Jorge Nocedal (1989). "On the limited memory BFGS method for large scale optimization". In: *Mathematical Programming* 45.1, pp. 503–528.

Liu, Ming-Yu and Oncel Tuzel (2016). "Coupled generative adversarial networks". In: *Advances in neural information processing systems 29 (NIPS 2016).*

Liu, Ming-Yu, Thomas Breuel, and Jan Kautz (2017). "Unsupervised image-to-image translation networks". In: *Advances in neural information processing systems 30 (NIPS 2017).*

Liu, Huidong, Xianfeng Gu, and Dimitris Samaras (2019). "Wasserstein GAN with quadratic transport cost". In: *Proceedings of the IEEE/CVF international conference on computer vision,* pp. 4832–4841.

Liwicki, Marcus et al. (2007). "A novel approach to on-line handwriting recognition based on bidirectional long short-term memory networks". In: *Proceedings of the 9th international conference on document analysis and recognition, ICDAR 2007.*

Lotter, William, Gabriel Kreiman, and David Cox (2020). "A neural network trained for prediction mimics diverse features of biological neurons and perception". In: *Nature Machine Intelligence* 2.4, pp. 210–219.

Lowe, David G. (1999). "Object recognition from local scale-invariant features". In: *Proceedings of the 7th IEEE International Conference on Computer Vision.* Vol. 2. IEEE, pp. 1150–1157.

Lyu, Siwei (2011). "Unifying non-maximum likelihood learning objectives with minimum KL contraction". In: *Advances in Neural Information Processing Systems 24 (NIPS 2011).*

Maas, Andrew et al. (2011). "Learning word vectors for sentiment analysis". In: *Proceedings of the 49th annual meeting of the association for computational linguistics: Human language technologies,* pp. 142–150.

Maas, Andrew L., Awni Y. Hannun, Andrew Y. Ng (2013). "Rectifier nonlinearities improve neural network acoustic models". In: *Proceedings of ICML*. Vol. 30.1. Atlanta, GA, p. 3.

MacKay, David J.C. (1992). "A practical Bayesian framework for backpropagation networks". In: *Neural Computation* 4.3, pp. 448–472.

Mao, Xudong et al. (2017). "Least squares generative adversarial networks". In: *Proceedings of the IEEE international conference on computer vision*, pp. 2794–2802.

Maqsood, Muazzam et al. (2019). "Transfer learning assisted classification and detection of Alzheimer's disease stages using 3D MRI scans". In: *Sensors* 19.11, p. 2645.

Marcus, Daniel S. et al. (2010). "Open access series of imaging studies: Longitudinal MRI data in nondemented and demented older adults". In: *Journal of Cognitive Neuroscience* 22.12, pp. 2677–2684.

Masci, Jonathan et al. (2011). "Stacked convolutional auto-encoders for hierarchical feature extraction". In: *Artificial Neural Networks and Machine Learning–ICANN 2011: 21st International Conference on Artificial Neural Networks, Espoo, Finland, June 14–17, 2011, Proceedings, Part I 21*. Springer, pp. 52–59.

McCann, Bryan et al. (2018). "The natural language decathlon: Multitask learning as question answering". In: URL: https://arxiv.org/pdf/1806.08730.

McCulloch, Warren S. and Walter Pitts (1943). "A logical calculus of the ideas immanent in nervous activity". In: *The Bulletin of Mathematical Biophysics* 5.4, pp. 115–133.

Medsker, Larry R. and L.C. Jain (2001). "Recurrent neural networks". In: *Design and Applications* 5, pp. 64–67.

Merity, Stephen et al. (2016). "Pointer sentinel mixture models". In: URL: https://arxiv.org/pdf/1609.07843.

Metropolis, Nicholas and Stanislaw Ulam (1949). "The Monte Carlo method". In: *Journal of the American Statistical Association* 44.247, pp. 335–341.

Metz, Cade (2023). "The Godfather of AI Leaves Google and Warns of Danger Ahead". In: *The New York Times*.

Metz, Luke et al. (2016). "Unrolled generative adversarial networks". In: URL: https://arxiv.org/pdf/1611.02163.

Mikolov, Tomas et al. (2013). "Distributed representations of words and phrases and their compositionality". In: *Advances in neural information processing systems 26 (NIPS 2013)*.

Mirza, Mehdi and Simon Osindero (2014). "Conditional generative adversarial nets". In: URL: https://arxiv.org/pdf/1411.1784.

Mishkin, Dmytro and Jiri Matas (2015). "All you need is a good init". In: URL: https://arxiv.org/pdf/1511.06422.

Miyato, Takeru et al. (2018). "Spectral normalization for generative adversarial networks". In: URL: https://arxiv.org/pdf/1802.05957.

Møller, Martin (1993). "Supervised learning on large redundant training sets". In: *International Journal of Neural Systems* 4.01, pp. 15–25.

Moreno-Díaz, Roberto and Arminda Moreno-Díaz (2007). "On the legacy of W.S. McCulloch". In: *Biosystems* 88.3. BIOCOMP 2005: Selected papers presented at the International Conference - Diffusion Processes in Neurobiology and Subcellular Biology, pp. 185–190.

Moriya, Shun and Chihiro Shibata (2018). "Transfer learning method for very deep CNN for text classification and methods for its evaluation". In: *2018 IEEE 42nd annual computer software and applications conference (COMPSAC)*. Vol. 2. IEEE, pp. 153–158.

Murphy, Kevin P. (2012). *Machine Learning: A Probabilistic Perspective*. MIT Press.

Murphy, Kevin, Yair Weiss, and Michael I. Jordan (2013). "Loopy belief propagation for approximate inference: An empirical study". In: *arXiv preprint arXiv:1301.6725*.

Nadaraya, Elizbar A (1964). "On estimating regression". In: *Theory of Probability & Its Applications* 9.1, pp. 141–142.

Nair, Vinod and Geoffrey E. Hinton (2010). "Rectified linear units improve restricted Boltzmann machines". In: *ICML*.

Neal, Radford M. (2001). "Annealed importance sampling". In: *Statistics and Computing* 11, pp. 125–139.

Neal, Radford M. and Geoffrey E. Hinton (1998). "A view of the EM algorithm that justifies incremental, sparse, and other variants". In: *Learning in Graphical Models*. Springer, pp. 355–368.

Neal, Radford M. et al. (2011). "MCMC using Hamiltonian dynamics". In: *Handbook of Markov Chain Monte Carlo* 2.11, p. 2.

Nesterov, Yurii Evgen'evich (1983). "A method of solving a convex programming problem with convergence rate $O(k^2)$". In: *Doklady Akademii Nauk* 269.3, pp. 543–547.

Netzer, Yuval et al. (2011). "Reading digits in natural images with unsupervised feature learning". In: *NIPS Workshop on Deep Learning and Unsupervised Feature Learning 2011*.

Neubig, Graham (2017). "Neural machine translation and sequence-to-sequence models: A tutorial". In: URL: https://arxiv.org/pdf/1703.01619.

Ng, Andrew Y. (2004). "Feature selection, L 1 vs. L 2 regularization, and rotational invariance". In: *Proceedings of the 21st international conference on Machine learning*, p. 78.

Ng, Andrew et al. (2011). "Sparse autoencoder". In: *CS294A Lecture Notes* 72.2011, Stanford University, pp. 1–19.

Nguyen, Vu et al. (2017). "Shadow detection with conditional generative adversarial networks". In: *Proceedings of the IEEE international conference on computer vision*, pp. 4510–4518.

Nilsback, Maria-Elena and Andrew Zisserman (2008). "Automated flower classification over a large number of classes". In: *2008 6th Indian conference on computer vision, graphics & image processing*. IEEE, pp. 722–729.

Niu, Zhaoyang, Guoqiang Zhong, and Hui Yu (2021). "A review on the attention mechanism of deep learning". In: *Neurocomputing* 452, pp. 48–62.

Novikoff, Albert B. (1963). "On Convergence Proofs on Perceptrons". In: *Proceedings of the Symposium on the Mathematical Theory of Automata* 12.1, pp. 615–622.

Odaibo, Stephen (2019). "Tutorial: Deriving the standard variational autoencoder (VAE) loss function". In: URL: https://arxiv.org/pdf/1907.08956.

Olshausen, Bruno A. and David J. Field (1996). "Emergence of simple-cell receptive field properties by learning a sparse code for natural images". In: *Nature* 381.6583, pp. 607–609.

Orr, Genevieve (1996). "Removing noise in on-line search using adaptive batch sizes". In: *Advances in Neural Information Processing Systems 9 (NIPS 1996)*.

Pal, Arghya and Vineeth N. Balasubramanian (2019). "Zero-shot task transfer". In: *Proceedings of the IEEE/CVF conference on computer vision and pattern recognition*, pp. 2189–2198.

Pan, Sinno Jialin (2014). "Transfer learning". In: *Data Classification: Algorithms and Applications* 21.

Pan, Sinno Jialin and Qiang Yang (2009). "A survey on transfer learning". In: *IEEE Transactions on Knowledge and Data Engineering* 22.10, pp. 1345–1359.

Paperno, Denis et al. (2016). "The LAMBADA dataset: Word prediction requiring a broad discourse context". In: URL: https://arxiv.org/pdf/1606.06031.

Parkhi, Omkar M. et al. (2012). "Cats and dogs". In: *2012 IEEE conference on computer vision and pattern recognition*. IEEE, pp. 3498–3505.

Pascanu, Razvan, Tomas Mikolov, and Yoshua Bengio (2013). "On the difficulty of training recurrent neural networks". In: *International conference on machine learning*. PMLR, pp. 1310–1318.

Pascanu, Razvan et al. (2019). "How to construct deep recurrent neural networks. arXiv 2013". In: URL: https://arxiv.org/pdf/1312.6026.

Pennington, Jeffrey, Richard Socher, and Christopher D. Manning (2014). "Glove: Global vectors for word representation". In: *Proceedings of the 2014 conference on empirical methods in natural language processing (EMNLP)*, pp. 1532–1543.

Peters, Matthew E. and Dan Lecocq (2013). "Content extraction using diverse feature sets". In: *Proceedings of the 22nd international conference on world wide web*, pp. 89–90.

Pinar Saygin, Ayse, Ilyas Cicekli, and Varol Akman (2000). "Turing test: 50 years later". In: *Minds and Machines* 10.4, pp. 463–518.

Podpora, Michal, Grzegorz Pawel Korbas, and Aleksandra Kawala-Janik (2014). "YUV vs RGB-choosing a color space for human-machine interaction". In: *FedCSIS (Position Papers)*. Citeseer, pp. 29–34.

Polyak, Boris T. (1964). "Some methods of speeding up the convergence of iteration methods". In: *Ussr Computational Mathematics and Mathematical Physics* 4.5, pp. 1–17.

Porter, Martin F. (1980). "An algorithm for suffix stripping". In: *Program* 14.3, pp. 130–137.

Prabhavalkar, Rohit et al. (2017). "A Comparison of sequence-to-sequence models for speech recognition". In: *Interspeech*, pp. 939–943.

Prechelt, Lutz (1998). "Early stopping-but when?" In: *Neural Networks: Tricks of the trade*. Springer, pp. 55–69.

Qiao, Siyuan et al. (2019). "Micro-batch training with batch-channel normalization and weight standardization". In: URL: https://arxiv.org/pdf/1903.10520.

Radford, Alec, Luke Metz, and Soumith Chintala (2015). "Unsupervised representation learning with deep convolutional generative adversarial networks". In: URL: https://arxiv.org/pdf/1511.06434.

Radford, Alec et al. (2018). "Improving language understanding by generative pre-training". In: URL: https://deepsense.ai/wp-content/uploads/2023/03/language_understanding_paper.pdf.

Radford, Alec et al. (2019). "Language models are unsupervised multitask learners". In: *OpenAI Blog* 1.8, p. 9.

Rajpurkar, Pranav et al. (2016). "Squad: 100,000+ questions for machine comprehension of text". In: URL: https://arxiv.org/pdf/1606.05250.

Ramachandran, Prajit et al. (2019). "Stand-alone self-attention in vision models". In: *Advances in neural information processing systems 32 (NeurIPS 2019)*.

Rasmus, Antti et al. (2015). "Semi-supervised learning with ladder networks". In: *Advances in neural information processing systems 28 (NIPS 2015)*.

Rasmussen, Carl Edward and Christopher K.I. Williams (2005). *Gaussian Processes for Machine Learning (Adaptive Computation and Machine Learning)*. The MIT Press.

Ratliff, Lillian J., Samuel A. Burden, and S. Shankar Sastry (2013). "Characterization and computation of local Nash equilibria in continuous games". In: *2013 51st Annual allerton conference on communication, control, and computing (Allerton)*. IEEE, pp. 917–924.

Recht, Benjamin et al. (2018). "Do CIFAR-10 classifiers generalize to CIFAR-10?" In: URL: https://arxiv.org/pdf/1806.00451.

Reed, Scott E. et al. (2016a). "Learning what and where to draw". In: *Advances in neural information processing systems 29 (NIPS 2016)*.

Reed, Scott et al. (2016b). "Generative adversarial text to image synthesis". In: *International conference on machine learning*. PMLR, pp. 1060–1069.

Rensink, Ronald A. (2000). "The dynamic representation of scenes". In: *Visual Cognition* 7. 1-3, pp. 17–42.

Resales, R., K. Achan, and B. Frey (2003). "Unsupervised image translation". In: *Proceedings 9th IEEE international conference on computer vision*. IEEE, pp. 472–478.

Rezende, Danilo Jimenez, Shakir Mohamed, and Daan Wierstra (2014). "Stochastic backpropagation and approximate inference in deep generative models". In: *International conference on machine learning*. PMLR, pp. 1278–1286.

Ribeiro, Manassés, André Eugênio Lazzaretti, and Heitor Silvério Lopes (2018). "A study of deep convolutional auto-encoders for anomaly detection in videos". In: *Pattern Recognition Letters* 105, pp. 13–22.

Ribeiro, Antônio H et al. (2020). "Beyond exploding and vanishing gradients: analysing RNN training using attractors and smoothness". In: *International conference on artificial intelligence and statistics*. PMLR, pp. 2370–2380.

Riesenhuber, Maximilian and Tomaso Poggio (2000). *Computational Models of Object Recognition in Cortex: A Review*. Tech. rep. MIT, Artificial Intelligence Laboratory.

Robbins, Herbert and Sutton Monro (1951). "A stochastic approximation method". In: *The Annals of Mathematical Statistics*, 22.3, pp. 400–407.

Roberts, Gareth O. and Jeffrey S. Rosenthal (2001). "Optimal scaling for various Metropolis-Hastings algorithms". In: *Statistical Science* 16.4, pp. 351–367.

Robinson, A.J. and Frank Fallside (1987). *The Utility Driven Dynamic Error Propagation Network*. Vol. 1. University of Cambridge Department of Engineering Cambridge.

Ronneberger, Olaf, Philipp Fischer, and Thomas Brox (2015). "U-Net: Convolutional networks for biomedical image segmentation". In: *Medical Image Computing and Computer-Assisted Intervention–MICCAI 2015: 18th International Conference, Munich, Germany, October 5–9, 2015, Proceedings, Part III 18*. Springer, pp. 234–241.

Rosenblatt, Frank (1957). *The Perceptron, A Perceiving and Recognizing Automaton (Project Para)*. Cornell Aeronautical Laboratory.

Rosenblatt, Frank (1958). "The perceptron: a probabilistic model for information storage and organization in the brain". In: *Psychological Review* 65.6, p. 386.

Roth, Kevin et al. (2017). "Stabilizing training of generative adversarial networks through regularization". In: *Advances in neural information processing systems 30 (NIPS 2017)*.

Rumelhart, David E., Geoffrey E. Hinton, and Ronald J. Williams (1986). "Learning representations by back-propagating errors". In: *Nature* 323.6088, pp. 533–536.

Saad, E.W., T.P. Caudell, and D.C. Wunsch (1999). "Predictive head tracking for virtual reality". In: *IJCNN'99. International Joint Conference on Neural Networks. Proceedings (Cat. No.99CH36339)*. Vol. 6, pp. 3933–3936.

Sak, Hasim, Andrew W. Senior, and Françoise Beaufays (2014). "Long short-term memory recurrent neural network architectures for large scale acoustic modeling". In: *Interspeech*, pp. 338–342.

Sakurada, Mayu and Takehisa Yairi (2014). "Anomaly detection using autoencoders with nonlinear dimensionality reduction". In: *Proceedings of the MLSDA 2014 2nd workshop on machine learning for sensory data analysis*, pp. 4–11.

Salakhutdinov, Ruslan and Geoffrey Hinton (2009). "Deep Boltzmann machines". In: *Artificial intelligence and statistics*. PMLR, pp. 448–455.

Salakhutdinov, Ruslan, Andriy Mnih, and Geoffrey Hinton (2007). "Restricted Boltzmann machines for collaborative filtering". In: *Proceedings of the 24th international conference on Machine learning*, pp. 791–798.

Salehi, Pegah, Abdolah Chalechale, and Maryam Taghizadeh (2020). "Generative adversarial networks (GANs): An overview of theoretical model, evaluation metrics, and recent developments". In: URL: https://arxiv.org/pdf/2005.13178.

Salehinejad, Hojjat et al. (2017). "Recent advances in recurrent neural networks". In: URL: https://arxiv.org/pdf/1801.01078.

Salimans, Tim et al. (2016). "Improved techniques for training GANs". In: *Advances in neural information processing systems 29 (NIPS 2016)*.

Santurkar, Shibani et al. (2018). "How does batch normalization help optimization?" In: *Advances in neural information processing systems 31 (NeurIPS 2018)*.

Schmidhuber, Jürgen and Sepp Hochreiter (1997). "Long short-term memory". In: *Neural Computation* 9.8, pp. 1735–1780.

Schölkopf, Bernhard and Kah-Kay Sung (1997). "Comparing support vector machines with Gaussian Kernels to radial basis function classifiers". In: *IEEE Transactions on Signal Processing* 45.11, pp. 2758–65.

van de Schoot, Rens et al. (2021). "Bayesian statistics and modelling". In: *Nature Reviews Methods Primers* 1.1, p. 1.

Schuster, Mike and Kuldip K. Paliwal (1997). "Bidirectional recurrent neural networks". In: *IEEE Transactions on Signal Processing* 45.11, pp. 2673–2681.

Selvaraju, Ramprasaath R. et al. (2017). "Grad-CAM: Visual explanations from deep networks via gradient-based localization". In: *Proceedings of the IEEE international conference on computer vision*, pp. 618–626.

Sennrich, Rico, Barry Haddow, and Alexandra Birch (2015). "Neural machine translation of rare words with subword units". In: URL: https://arxiv.org/pdf/1508.07909.

Sermanet, Pierre et al. (2013). "OverFeat: Integrated recognition, localization and detection using convolutional networks". In: URL: https://arxiv.org/pdf/1312.6229.

Serre, Thomas, Lior Wolf, and Tomaso Poggio (2005). "Object recognition with features inspired by visual cortex". In: *2005 IEEE Computer Society Conference on Computer Vision and Pattern Recognition (CVPR'05)*. Vol. 2. IEEE, pp. 994–1000.

Shawe-Taylor, John and Nello Cristianini (2004). *Kernel Methods for Pattern Analysis*. Cambridge University Press.

Shewchuk, Jonathan Richard (1994). "An introduction to the conjugate gradient method without the agonizing pain".

Shi, Tian et al. (2021). "Neural abstractive text summarization with sequence-to-sequence models". In: *ACM Transactions on Data Science* 2.1, pp. 1–37.

Shimodaira, Hidetoshi (2000). "Improving predictive inference under covariate shift by weighting the log-likelihood function". In: *Journal of Statistical Planning and Inference* 90.2, pp. 227–244.

Shrivastava, Ashish et al. (2017). "Learning from simulated and unsupervised images through adversarial training". In: *Proceedings of the IEEE conference on computer vision and pattern recognition*, pp. 2107–2116.

Shu, Zhixin et al. (2017). "Neural face editing with intrinsic image disentangling". In: *Proceedings of the IEEE conference on computer vision and pattern recognition*, pp. 5541–5550.

Sifre, Laurent and Stéphane Mallat (2014). "Rigid-motion scattering for texture classification". In: URL: https://arxiv.org/pdf/1403.1687.

Simonyan, Karen and Andrew Zisserman (2015). "Very deep convolutional networks for large-scale image recognition". In: *3rd International Conference on Learning Representations, ICLR 2015, San Diego, CA, USA, May 7–9, 2015, Conference Track Proceedings*. Ed. by Yoshua Bengio and Yann LeCun.

Smola, Alex, Bernhard Schölkopf, and Klaus R. Müller (1998). "General cost functions for support vector regression". In: *Proceedings of the 9th Australian conference on neural networks*. Brisbane, Australia, pp. 79–83.

Smolensky, Paul (1986). "Information processing in dynamical systems: foundations of harmony theory". In: *Parallel Distributed Processing: Explorations in the Microstructure of Cognition*, vol. 1. MIT Press: Cambridge, MA, USA 15, p. 18.

Socher, Richard et al. (2013). "Recursive deep models for semantic compositionality over a sentiment treebank". In: *Proceedings of the 2013 conference on empirical methods in natural language processing*, pp. 1631–1642.

Sohl-Dickstein, Jascha, Peter B. Battaglino, and Michael R. DeWeese (2011). "New method for parameter estimation in probabilistic models: Minimum probability flow". In: *Physical Review Letters* 107.22, p. 220601.

Sohl-Dickstein, Jascha et al. (2015). "Deep unsupervised learning using nonequilibrium thermodynamics". In: *International conference on machine learning*. PMLR, pp. 2256–2265.

Sønderby, Casper Kaae et al. (2016). "Amortised map inference for image super-resolution". In: URL: https://arxiv.org/pdf/1610.04490.

Song, Yang and Stefano Ermon (2019). "Generative modeling by estimating gradients of the data distribution". In: *Advances in neural information processing systems 32 (NeurIPS 2019)*.

Springenberg, Jost Tobias et al. (2014). "Striving for simplicity: The all convolutional net". In: URL: https://arxiv.org/pdf/1412.6806.

Sreenatha, M. and P.B. Mallikarjuna (2023). "A fault diagnosis technique for wind turbine gearbox: An approach using optimized BLSTM neural network with undercomplete autoencoder". In: *Engineering, Technology & Applied Science Research* 13.1, pp. 10170–10174.

Srivastava, Nitish et al. (2014). "Dropout: A simple way to prevent neural networks from overfitting". In: *The Journal of Machine Learning Research* 15.1, pp. 1929–1958.

Srivastava, Rupesh K., Klaus Greff, and Jürgen Schmidhuber (2015). "Training very deep networks". In: *Advances in neural information processing systems 28 (NIPS 2015)*.

Sun, Wenjun et al. (2016). "A sparse auto-encoder-based deep neural network approach for induction motor faults classification". In: *Measurement* 89, pp. 171–178.

Sun, Chen et al. (2017). "Revisiting unreasonable effectiveness of data in deep learning era". In: *Proceedings of the IEEE international conference on computer vision*, pp. 843–852.

Sundermeyer, Martin et al. (2014). "Translation modeling with bidirectional recurrent neural networks". In: *Proceedings of the 2014 conference on empirical methods in natural language processing (EMNLP)*, pp. 14–25.

Sutskever, Ilya, James Martens, and Geoffrey E. Hinton (2011). "Generating text with recurrent neural networks". In: *ICML*.

Sutskever, Ilya, James Martens, George Dahl, et al. (2013). "On the importance of initialization and momentum in deep learning". In: *International conference on machine learning*. PMLR, pp. 1139–1147.

Sutskever, Ilya, Oriol Vinyals, and Quoc Le (2014). "Sequence to sequence learning with neural networks". In: *Advances in neural information processing systems 27 (NIPS 2014)*.

Szegedy, Christian et al. (2013). "Intriguing properties of neural networks". In: URL: https://arxiv.org/pdf/1312.6199.

Szegedy, Christian et al. (2015). "Going deeper with convolutions". In: *Proceedings of the IEEE conference on computer vision and pattern recognition*, pp. 1–9.

Szegedy, Christian et al. (2016). "Rethinking the inception architecture for computer vision". In: *2016 IEEE conference on computer vision and pattern recognition (CVPR)*. IEEE, pp. 2818–2826.

Szegedy, Christian et al. (2017). "Inception-v4, Inception-ResNet and the impact of residual connections on learning". In: *Proceedings of the 31st AAAI Conference on Artificial Intelligence*. AAAI'17. AAAI Press, pp. 4278–4284.

Taigman, Yaniv, Adam Polyak, and Lior Wolf (2016). "Unsupervised cross-domain image generation". In: URL: https://arxiv.org/pdf/1611.02200.

Tan, Mingxing and Quoc Le (2019). "EfficientNet: Rethinking model scaling for convolutional neural networks". In: *International conference on machine learning*. PMLR, pp. 6105–6114.

Tan, Mingxing et al. (2019). "MnasNet: Platform-aware neural architecture search for mobile". In: *Proceedings of the IEEE/CVF conference on computer vision and pattern recognition*, pp. 2820–2828.

Tanaka, Toshiyuki (1998). "Mean-field theory of Boltzmann machine learning". In: *Physical Review E* 58.2, p. 2302.

Taylor, Luke and Geoff Nitschke (2018). "Improving deep learning with generic data augmentation". In: *2018 IEEE symposium series on computational intelligence (SSCI)*. IEEE, pp. 1542–1547.

Tegmark, Max (2023). "The 'don't look up' thinking that could doom us with AI". In: *Time Magazine*.

Thies, Jameson and Amirhossein Alimohammad (2019). "Compact and low-power neural spike compression using undercomplete autoencoders". In: *IEEE Transactions on Neural Systems and Rehabilitation Engineering* 27.8, pp. 1529–1538.

Thomee, Bart et al. (2016). "YFCC100M: The new data in multimedia research". In: *Communications of the ACM* 59.2, pp. 64–73.

Thoppilan, Romal et al. (2020). "LaMDA: Language models for dialog applications". In: *International conference on artificial intelligence and statistics*. PMLR, pp. 2370–2380. arXiv: 2201.08239 [cs.CL].

Tibshirani, Robert J. (1996). "Regression shrinkage and selection via the Lasso". In: *Journal of the Royal Statistical Society: Series B (Methodological)* 58.1, pp. 267–288.

Tikhonov, Andrey N. and Vasilii Iakkovlevich Arsenin (1977). *Solutions of Ill-Posed Problems*. Vol. 14. Winston, Washington, DC.

Tiku, Nitasha (2022). "The Google engineer who thinks the company's AI has come to life". In: *The Washington Post* 11.

Tino, Peter, Christian Schittenkopf, and Georg Dorffner (2001). "Financial volatility trading using recurrent neural networks". In: *IEEE Transactions on Neural Networks* 12.4, pp. 865–874.

Tishby, Naftali, Fernando C. Pereira, and William Bialek (2000). "The information bottleneck method". In: URL: https://arxiv.org/abs/physics/0004057.

Ulyanov, Dmitry, Andrea Vedaldi, and Victor Lempitsky (2016). "Instance normalization: The missing ingredient for fast stylization". In: URL: https://arxiv.org/pdf/1607.08022.

Van Der Maaten, Laurens, Eric O. Postma, and H. Jaap van den Herik (2009). "Dimensionality reduction: A comparative review". In: *Journal of Machine Learning Research* 10.66–71, p. 13.

Vapnik, Vladimir N. (1998). *Statistical Learning Theory*. Wiley-Interscience.

Vaswani, Ashish et al. (2017). "Attention is all you need". In: URL: https://arxiv.org/pdf/1706.03762.

Vincent, Pascal et al. (2008). "Extracting and composing robust features with denoising autoencoders". In: *Proceedings of the 25th international conference on Machine learning*, pp. 1096–1103.

Vincent, Pascal, Hugo Larochelle, Isabelle Lajoie, et al. (2010). "Stacked denoising autoencoders: Learning useful representations in a deep network with a local denoising criterion". In: *Journal of Machine Learning Research* 11.12.

Wah, Catherine et al. (2011). "The Caltech-UCSD Birds-200-2011 dataset".

Wang, Chang and Sridhar Mahadevan (2011). "Heterogeneous domain adaptation using manifold alignment". In: *22nd International joint conference on artificial intelligence*.

Wang, Hao and Dit-Yan Yeung (2020). "A survey on Bayesian deep learning". In: *ACM Computing Surveys (CSUR)* 53.5, pp. 1–37.

Wang, Alex et al. (2018). "GLUE: A multi-task benchmark and analysis platform for natural language understanding". In: URL: https://arxiv.org/pdf/1804.07461.

Watson, Geoffrey S. (1964). "Smooth regression analysis". In: *Sankhyā: The Indian Journal of Statistics, Series A* 26.4, pp. 359–372.

Weiss, Karl, Taghi M. Khoshgoftaar, and DingDing Wang (2016). "A survey of transfer learning". In: *Journal of Big Data* 3.1, pp. 1–40.

Welling, Max and Geoffrey E. Hinton (2002). "A new learning algorithm for mean field Boltzmann machines". In: *International Conference on Artificial Neural Networks*. Springer, pp. 351–357.

Werbos, P.J. (1974). "Beyond Regression: New Tools for Prediction and Analysis in the Behavioral Sciences". PhD thesis. Harvard University.

Werbos, Paul J. (1988). "Generalization of backpropagation with application to a recurrent gas market model". In: *Neural Networks* 1.4, pp. 339–356.

Widrow, Bernard and Marcian E Hoff (1960). Adaptive Switching Circuits. Tech. rep. Stanford Universty, CA. Stanford Electronics Laboratories.

Williams, Ronald J. and David Zipser (1995). "Gradient-based learning algorithms for recurrent networks and their computational complexity". In: *Backpropagation: Theory, Architectures, and Applications* 433, p. 17.

Wistuba, Martin, Ambrish Rawat, and Tejaswini Pedapati (2019). "A survey on neural architecture search". In: URL: https://arxiv.org/pdf/1905.01392.

Wolpert, David H. (1996a). "The existence of a priori distinctions between learning algorithms". In: *Neural Computation* 8.7, pp. 1391–1420.

Wolpert, David H. (1996b). "The lack of a priori distinctions between learning algorithms". In: *Neural Computation* 8.7, pp. 1341–1390.

Wolpert, David H. and William G. Macready (1997). "No free lunch theorems for optimization". In: *IEEE Transactions on Evolutionary Computation* 1.1, pp. 67–82.

Wróbel, Krzysztof et al. (2020). "Compression of convolutional neural network for natural language processing". In: *Computer Science* 21.1. DOI: 10.7494/csci.2020.21.1.3375.

Wu, Yuxin and Kaiming He (2018). "Group normalization". In: *Proceedings of the European conference on computer vision (ECCV)*, pp. 3–19.

Wu, Bichen et al. (2020). "Visual transformers: Token-based image representation and processing for computer vision". In: URL: https://arxiv.org/pdf/2006.03677.

Xiao, Tete et al. (2021). "Early convolutions help transformers see better". In: *Advances in Neural Information Processing Systems* 34, pp. 30392–30400.

Xu, Kelvin et al. (2015). "Show, attend and tell: Neural image caption generation with visual attention". In: *International conference on machine learning*. PMLR, pp. 2048–2057.

Yan, Shen et al. (2023). "Hybrid robust convolutional autoencoder for unsupervised anomaly detection of machine tools under noises". In: *Robotics and Computer-Integrated Manufacturing* 79, p. 102441.

Yang, Zichao et al. (2016). "Hierarchical attention networks for document classification". In: *Proceedings of the 2016 conference of the North American chapter of the association for computational linguistics: Human language technologies*, pp. 1480–1489.

Ye, Fanghua, Chuan Chen, and Zibin Zheng (2018). "Deep autoencoder-like nonnegative matrix factorization for community detection". In: *Proceedings of the 27th ACM international conference on information and knowledge management*, pp. 1393–1402.

Yedidia, Jonathan S., William Freeman, and Yair Weiss (2000). "Generalized belief propagation". In: *Advances in neural information processing systems 13 (NIPS 2000)*.

Yogatama, Dani et al. (2019). "Learning and evaluating general linguistic intelligence". In: URL: https://arxiv.org/pdf/1901.11373.

Yu, Fisher et al. (2015). "LSUN: Construction of a large-scale image dataset using deep learning with humans in the loop". In: URL: https://arxiv.org/pdf/1506.03365.

Zeiler, Matthew D. (2012). "ADADELTA: An adaptive learning rate method". In: URL: https://arxiv.org/pdf/1212.5701.

Zeiler, Matthew D. and Rob Fergus (2014). "Visualizing and understanding convolutional networks". In: *European conference on computer vision*. Springer, pp. 818–833.

Zellers, Rowan et al. (2018). "SWAG: A large-scale adversarial dataset for grounded commonsense inference". In: URL: https://arxiv.org/pdf/1808.05326.

Zhai, Xiaohua et al. (2019). "A large-scale study of representation learning with the visual task adaptation benchmark". In: URL: https://arxiv.org/pdf/1910.04867.

Zhang, Richard (2019). "Making convolutional networks shift-invariant again". In: *International conference on machine learning*. PMLR, pp. 7324–7334.

Zhang, Han et al. (2017). "StackGan: Text to photo-realistic image synthesis with stacked generative adversarial networks". In: *Proceedings of the IEEE international conference on computer vision*, pp. 5907–5915.

Zhang, Richard et al. (2018). "The unreasonable effectiveness of deep features as a perceptual metric". In: *Proceedings of the IEEE conference on computer vision and pattern recognition*, pp. 586–595.

Zhang, Aston et al. (2021). "Dive into deep learning". In: URL: https://arxiv.org/pdf/2106.11342.

Zhao, Junbo et al. (2015). "Stacked what-where auto-encoders". In: URL: https://arxiv.org/pdf/1506.02351.

Zhiqiang, Wang and Liu Jun (2017). "A review of object detection based on convolutional neural network". In: *2017 36th Chinese control conference (CCC)*. IEEE, pp. 11104–11109.

Zhou, Tinghui et al. (2016). "Learning dense correspondence via 3D-guided cycle consistency". In: *Proceedings of the IEEE conference on computer vision and pattern recognition*, pp. 117–126.

Zhu, Jun-Yan et al. (2017). "Unpaired image-to-image translation using cycle-consistent adversarial networks". In: *Proceedings of the IEEE international conference on computer vision*, pp. 2223–2232.

Zhuang, Fuzhen et al. (2020). "A comprehensive survey on transfer learning". In: *Proceedings of the IEEE* 109.1, pp. 43–76.

Index

Deep Learning: A Practical Introduction, First Edition.
Manel Martínez-Ramón, Meenu Ajith, and Aswathy Rajendra Kurup.
© 2024 John Wiley & Sons Ltd. Published 2024 by John Wiley & Sons Ltd.
Companion website: https://github.com/DeepLearning-book